The Practice of
SOCIAL RESEARCH

Also by Earl Babbie
and available from
Wadsworth Publishing Company:

Social Research for Consumers
Survey Research Methods
Understanding Sociology: A Context for Action
Observing Ourselves: Essays in Social Research
Apple Logo for Teachers

The Practice of
SOCIAL RESEARCH

FOURTH EDITION

EARL BABBIE

Wadsworth Publishing Co.
Belmont, California
A Division of Wadsworth, Inc.

Practicing Social Research, 4th Edition by
Earl Babbie and Theodore C. Wagenaar, guided
activities to accompany this textbook, is
available from your bookstore.

Sociology Editor: Sheryl Fullerton
Production Editor: Gary Mcdonald
Editorial Assistant: Liz Clayton
Designer: Lisa Mirski
Print Buyer: Karen Hunt
Copy Editor: Mary Roach

Printed in the United States of America
2 3 4 5 6 7 8 9 10—89 88 87 86
ISBN 0-534-05658-X

Library of Congress Cataloging in Publication Data

Babbie, Earl R.
   The practice of social research.

   Bibliography: p.
   Includes index.
   1. Social sciences—Research.   2. Social sciences—
Methodology.   I. Title.
H62.B2 1986   300'.72   85-13865
ISBN 0-534-05658-X

DEDICATION

Georg von Bekesy
1899–1972

Werner Erhard

Contents in Brief

Contents in Detail

Preface

The purpose of this book is to introduce you to the *logic* and the *skills* of social scientific research. First, I want to give you all the fundamentals you need to *do* social research on your own. The acid test of the book in that regard will come when you set out to do an empirical research project, find that the situations facing you do not exactly match anything dealt with in the book, and discover that you are able to create compromises that represent the best bridge between your situation and the fundamental logic of scientific inquiry.

Second, I want to train you as a responsible *consumer* of social scientific research. You will be bombarded with the findings of this kind of research for the rest of your life. To evaluate it effectively, you must be familiar with the accepted techniques for research and know the logic that makes them acceptable. With this knowledge, you'll be able to assess the importance and implications of the research findings presented to you by others.

There is a big gap between the world of research in the abstract and the world of actually conducting a social scientific experiment. On one side, things are perfectly neat, logical, and "scientific." On the other side, chaos reigns. Subjects don't show up for experiments, interviewers make mistakes and lose questionnaires, people lie and misunderstand, and no findings are as clear and conclusive as we'd like.

It was my desire to bridge this gap—to create a teaching method that would deal effectively with both worlds—that led me to write my first textbook, *Survey Research Methods*. Published in 1973, *SRM* dealt with a specialized area of social research, but we soon found teachers asking for a similar approach in a more general research methods text. In response to this suggestion, I wrote the first edition of this book, *The Practice of Social Research*. The book was published in 1975, and we were delighted to find that both students and faculty found it useful. The book was revised in 1979 and 1983; what you have is the further revised fourth edition.

Acknowledgments

It would be impossible to acknowledge adequately all the people who have been influential in forming this book. My earlier methods text, *Survey Research Methods*, was dedicated to Samuel Stouffer, Paul Lazarsfeld, and Charles Glock. I would like to state again the acknowledgment of my debt to them.

Several colleagues were acknowledged for their comments during the writing of the first, second, and third editions of this book, and I would like to repeat my thanks to them here. Though revised, the present book still reflects their contributions. Many other colleagues were of assistance in the revision of the book. I particularly want to thank the instructors who reviewed the manuscript of this edition and made helpful suggestions:

Kristine L. Anderson, Florida Atlantic University

Gordon Bear, Ramapo College

Shirley Laska, University of New Orleans

Charles McClintock, Cornell University

Kathleen McKinney, Oklahoma State University

Howard Openshaw, Georgia State University

Sidney Stahl, Purdue University

Gayle T. Wykle, University of Alabama at Birmingham

The book, both in its present form and in its earlier editions, is also very much a product of my relationship with Steve Rutter, now Vice-President of Editorial Acquisitions at Wadsworth Publishing Company. Steve is truly a master at his craft, and working with him for more than a decade has been one of the special joys of my life as an author. The book's publication has also been greatly assisted by the efforts and skills of five other people at Wadsworth: Sheryl Fullerton, sociology editor; Debbie Fox and Liz Clayton, her assistants; Gary Mcdonald, production editor; and Lisa Mirsky, designer.

Ted Wagenaar has contributed extensively to this book. Ted and I co-author the accompanying workbook, *Practicing Social Research*, but that's only the tip of the iceberg. Ted is a cherished colleague, welcomed critic, good friend, and altogether decent human being. I am grateful also for the SPSS^x appendix prepared by Jeffrey M. Jacques, Florida A&M University.

I want to acknowledge a special debt to my friend and colleague Hanan Selvin. Hanan never fails to stimulate and inspire me both in research methods and in life. I particularly honor Hanan's commitment to the responsible use of language and have enjoyed the nits we've picked together.

My wife, Sheila, has contributed to this book in more ways than can be stated. Her insight and support take me always to the horizon of my purpose and allow me to look beyond it.

Finally, I would like to dedicate this book on social research to two people who are not regarded as social scientists. The first is Georg von Bekesy, a distinguished physiologist whom I met about four years before his death in 1972. Professor von Bekesy was that rare Renaissance man: a person interested in and insightful about everything, winner of the 1961 Nobel Prize in Medicine-Physiology, possessor of a dozen or so doctorates and fluent in as many languages, an expert in fine art, the gentlest of people, and the *compleat* scientist.

Despite our short acquaintance, Professor von Bekesy gave me a feeling for science that has affected my own research and the contents and spirit of this book. He provided a model of the scientist intent on using science to improve the quality of life on the planet and contribute to the lives of others.

The second dedication is to Werner Erhard, founder of the est training, the Hunger Project, the Breakthough Foundation, and other organizations dedicated to empowering individuals to improve the quality of life on the planet. While Werner is not a scientist in the customary meaning of that term, he has a profound grasp and appreciation of science that has greatly enhanced the clarity and enthusiasm that I have been able to bring to my writing. Like von Bekesy, Werner offers a model of service to others as a way of being more than just a passenger on Spaceship Earth. He has inspired me to view my teaching and textbook writing in the context of service to others and making a difference in the world.

In this same spirit, I offer this book to you: to support you in learning the skills and logic of social research, to share the challenge and the excitement of it with you, and to encourage you to use what you learn to make your own contribution to the quality of life on your planet.

Prologue

The Importance of Social Research

In many ways, the twentieth century hasn't been one of our better periods. Except for the relatively carefree twenties, we've moved from World War I to the Great Depression to World War II to the Cold War and its threat of thermonuclear holocaust to Vietnam and on to the current concerns over the environmental destruction of our planet. Many sage observers have written about the insecurity and malaise of people who grew up during portions of this century.

A case could be made that these are not the best of times. At the same time, this period in history has seen countless individual efforts and social movements aimed at making the world work. Much of the commitment to creating humane social affairs has arisen on college campuses, and perhaps you find that commitment in yourself.

As you look at the flow of events in the world around you, if you want to make a significant contribution to the lives of future generations, you have a broad range of choices available to you. Environmental problems are many and varied. Prejudice and discrimination are with us still, and there are several different targets for you to focus your attention on. Or consider the fact that some fifteen million people die each year as a consequence of starvation. There is, in short, no end of

the ways in which you could demonstrate to yourself that your life matters, that you make a difference.

Given all the things you could choose from—things that really *matter*—why should you spend your time learning social research methods? I want to address that question at the start, since I'm going to suggest that you devote some of your time and attention to learning about such things as social theory, sampling, interviewing, experiments, computers, and so forth—things that can seem pretty distant from solving the world's pressing problems. The point I'll make in the following few pages is that social science is not only relevant to the kinds of major problems I've just listed, but it holds *the* answers to them.

Many of the *big* problems we've faced and still face in this century have been the result of technology. The threat of nuclear war is an example. Not unreasonably, therefore, we have tended to look to technology and the technologists for solutions to those problems. Unfortunately, every technological solution so far has turned out to be a new problem. At the beginning of this century, for example, many people worried about the danger of horse manure piling up continually higher and higher in city streets. That problem was averted, through technology, with the invention of the automobile. Now, no one worries about manure in the streets; instead we worry about a new and deadlier kind of pollutant in the air we breathe.

Similarly, we have attempted to avoid nuclear attack by building better bombs and missiles of our own—so that no enemy would dare attack. But that hasn't worked either. Since our potential enemies operate on the same reasoning that we do, they too have built ever bigger and more powerful weapons. There is no technological end in sight for the escalating nuclear weapons race.

The simple fact is that technology alone will never save us. It will never make the world work. You and I are the only ones who can do that. The only real solutions lie in the ways we organize and run our social affairs. That becomes evident when you look at all the social problems that persist today despite the clear presence of viable, technological solutions.

Overpopulation, for example, is a pressing problem in the world today. The number of people currently living on earth is severely taxing our planet's life support systems, and this number is rapidly increasing year after year. If you study the matter, however, you'll find that we already possess all the technological developments we need to stem population growth. It is technologically possible and feasible for us to stop population growth on the planet at whatever limit we want. Yet, overpopulation worsens each year.

Clearly, the solution to overpopulation is a social one. The causes of population growth lie in the norms, values, and customs that make up organized social life, and that is where the solutions are hidden. Ultimately, only social science can save us from overpopulation.

Or consider the problem of starvation on the planet. Each year, some 15 million people die as a consequence of starvation. That amounts to 28 people a minute, every minute of every day, and 21 of them are children. Virtually everyone would agree that this situation is deplorable. All would prefer it otherwise. We tolerate this level of starvation on the planet in the belief that it is currently inevitable. Perhaps one day someone will invent a method of producing food that will defeat starvation once and for all.

When you study the issue of starvation in the world, however, you learn some astounding facts. First, you learn that the earth currently produces more than enough food to feed everyone without requiring sacrifices from those of us who are eating well. Moreover, this level of production does not even take account of farm programs that pay farmers *not* to plant and produce all the food they could.

Second, you learn that there are carefully worked out and tested methods for ending starvation. In fact, since World War II, more than thirty countries have actually taken on and ended their own problem of starvation. Some did it through food distribution programs. Others focused on land reform. Some collectivized; others developed agribusiness. Many applied the advances of the Green Revolution. Taken together, these many proven solutions make it possible to totally eliminate starvation on the planet. Still, 15 million die each year: 21 children every minute of every hour of every day.

Why haven't we ended starvation? The answer, again, lies in the organization and operation of our social life. New developments in food production will not end starvation any more than earlier ones have. People will continue starving on this planet until we are able to *master* our social affairs rather than being enslaved by them.

Possibly, the problems of overpopulation and starvation may seem distant to you, occurring somewhere "over there," on the other side of the globe. To save space, let me skip over the conclusion, increasingly reached, that there is no "over there" anymore: that there is only "over here" in today's world. Instead, I'll mention some social problems undeniably close to home.

In June 1978, California voters passed by a 2-to-1 margin a proposition setting a constitutional limit on property taxes in the state, effectively reducing municipal government revenues by almost two-thirds, even though official pronouncements prior to passage predicted chaos and disastrous reduction of government services, including fire and police protection. Despite such dire warnings, Proposition 13 passed on a wave of popular frustration with the uncontrollable growth of taxation, and other states have followed in California's footsteps.

The problems of contemporary American life are manifold. The tax revolt is not only financial but involves the feeling that tax revenues only buy red tape and corruption. It is also related to the general problem of inflation. Workers having trouble making ends meet win pay raises only to find that the cost of living has increased more than their pay, and the good life seems ever more distant.

In one sense, the workers who are losing the battle with inflation are the lucky ones. Millions of others are unable to get work at all, including a growing number of college graduates and even those with Ph.D.s. People who would prefer to support themselves and their families are forced to live on food stamps, welfare, and unemployment payments—at a cost to dignity as well as living standard. The welfare spinoff from unemployment, moreover, creates a heavier tax burden on those who are losing the battle with inflation already.

Crime thrives, and city streets are now considered hazardous to your health. Each day's crop of news carries stories of murder, robbery, and senior citizens being mugged and having their Social Security checks stolen. Most criminals who are apprehended never go to prison and those who do emerge more hardened than before.

Problems such as these—and hundreds more—cannot be dismissed as being "over there." They exist where you live. And problems like these are unlikely to be solved by technology. You and I are the only ones who can solve them. If we don't take on the challenge, no one will. The question is whether you and I will solve our social problems before they create a final solution for us. So, let's get on with it.

We can't solve our social problems until we understand how they come about and persist. Social science research offers a way of examining and understanding the operation of human social affairs. It provides points of view and technical procedures that uncover things that would otherwise escape our awareness. Often, as the cliché goes, things are not what they seem, and social science research can make that clear. One example ought to illustrate this fact.

For years, the general issue of race relations in America has often touched on the special problems facing the black American family. Most have agreed that the black family was matriarchal, that is, dominated by the wife/mother. The white family, by contrast, has been widely recognized as egalitarian with patriarchal traces. The matriarchal pattern of the black family has been seen as a special barrier to the achievement of equality by blacks in America. Indeed, the controversial Moynihan Report stressed the need for changes in the black family.

Several surveys have supported the conclusion that the black family was matriarchal. Asked who made the most important decisions in their families when they were growing up, black respondents in the survey were most likely to say their mothers did. The majority said their mothers exercised more power in the family than their fathers did. Similarly, most black adults surveyed have reported that the wives in their own families make most of the important decisions. The pattern of black matriarchy has seemed clear and consistent.

This documented pattern has produced considerable discussion and disagreement over the years. Political conservatives have often cited it as evidence of an inherent weakness in the character of black males. How, they have asked, can blacks expect to achieve equality when the men are so weak and submissive? Such apparent character flaws, then, have been used for years to explain and justify why blacks have fared so badly in American society.

From a liberal point of view, the facts have been explained quite differently. The pattern of matriarchy has been explained as a product of slavery—when families were forcibly separated—and of modern welfare laws that often force husbands/ fathers to desert their families as the only means of obtaining government assistance for them.

These two ideological points of view present the same facts quite differently, then, and the years of debate have not significantly altered either points of view or facts. In 1969, however, two sociologists took a look at the matter from a totally different point of view. What they did exemplifies the social scientific approach, and what they discovered demonstrates the value of that approach.

Herbert Hyman and John Shelton Reed began by confirming that the surveys did indeed suggest a matriarchal pattern in the black American family.* As expected, they found consistent reports from blacks that wives/mothers were more powerful in family life than husbands/fathers. Then they looked at something others had overlooked: the answers given by *white respondents* in the same surveys. What do you suppose they discovered? *The answers given by white men and women were the same as those given by blacks!* Thus, Hyman and Reed concluded that if the black family is a matriarchy, so is the white family in America. Women seem to dominate white families to the same degree that they seem to dominate black ones. Thus, if black men are weak and submissive through some sort of character defect, then the same must be said of white men.

Many of the things social scientists study—including all the social problems we intend to solve—are a source of deep emotion and firm conviction for people generally. The depth of feeling and firmness of position in such cases makes effective inquiry into the facts difficult at best. All too often, we only manage to confirm our initial prejudices. The special value of social science research methods is that they offer a way of addressing such issues with logical and observational rigor. They let us pierce through our personal viewpoints and get a look at the world that lies beyond our normal vision. And it is that "world beyond" that holds the solutions to the social problems we face today.

At a time of increased depression and disillusionment, we are tempted daily to retreat from confronting social problems into the concerns of an ever-narrowed

*"Black Matriarchy Reconsidered: Evidence from Secondary Analysis of Sample Surveys," *Public Opinion Quarterly,* Vol. 33 (1969), pp. 346–354.

self-interest, despite the cost of becoming insignificant specks of protoplasm on a dust ball whirling through space. Social science research offers an opportunity to take on those problems and discover the experience of making a difference after all. The choice is yours, and I invite you to take on the challenge. Your instructor and I would like to share the excitement of social science with you.

The Practice of
SOCIAL RESEARCH

PART 1
An Introduction to Inquiry

Science is a familiar word used by everyone. Yet images of science differ greatly. For some, science is mathematics; for others it is white coats and laboratories. It is often confused with technology or equated with difficult high school or college courses.

Science is, of course none of these things per se. It is difficult, however, to specify exactly what science is. Scientists would, in fact, disagree on the proper definition. For the purposes of this book, however, we shall look at science as a method of inquiry—a way of learning and knowing things about the world around us. Contrasted with other ways of learning and knowing about the world, science has some special characteristics, and we'll examine these traits in this opening set of chapters.

Dr. Benjamin Spock, the renowned author-pediatrician, begins his books on child care by assuring new mothers that they already know more about child care than they think they do. I want to begin this book on social scientific research methods on the same note. It will become clear to you before you've read very far that you *do* know a great deal about the practice of scientific social research already. In fact, you've been conducting scientific research all your life. From that perspective, the purpose of this book is to assist you in sharpening skills you already have and perhaps to show you some tricks that may not have occurred to you.

Part 1 of the book is intended to lay the groundwork for the discussions that follow in the rest of the book—to examine the fundamental characteristics and issues that make science different from other ways of knowing things. In Chapter 1, we'll begin with a look at native human inquiry, the sort of thing you've been doing all your life. In the course of that examination, we'll see some of the ways people go astray in trying to understand the world around them, and I'll summarize the primary characteristics of scientific inquiry that guard against those errors.

Chapter 2 deals specifically with social scientific inquiry, the structure and creation of social scientific theories, and the links between theory and research. The lessons of Chapter 1 are applied in the study of human social behavior. You will discover that, although special considerations arise in studying people, the basic logic of all science is the same.

In their attempt to develop generalized understanding, scientists seek to discover patterns of interrelationships among variables. Very often, these interrelationships take a cause-and-effect form. Chapter 3 is addressed to the nature and logic of causation as appropriate to social scientific research. This theoretical chapter lays the basis for the following ones on analytical techniques.

The overall purpose of Part 1 is to construct a backdrop against which to view more specific aspects of research design and execution. By the time you complete Part 1, you should be ready to look at some of the more concrete aspects of social research.

1

Human Inquiry and Science

What You'll Learn in This Chapter

We'll examine the way people learn about their world and the mistakes they make along the way. We'll also begin to see what makes science different from other ways of knowing things.

INTRODUCTION

This book is about knowing things. Although you will probably come away from the book knowing some things you don't know right now, my primary purpose is to assist you in looking at *how* you know things, not what you know. Let's start out by examining a few of the things you probably know already.

You probably know that you have to breathe to live. Obviously, if you stopped breathing, you'd die. You probably also know that it's cold on the dark side of the moon, and you know that people speak Chinese in China.

How do you know? If you reflect on it for a minute, you'll see that you know these things because somebody told them to you, and you believed what you were told. You may have read in *National Geographic* that people speak Chinese in China, and that made sense to you, so you didn't question it. Perhaps your physics or astronomy instructor told you that it was cold on the dark side of the moon, or maybe you read it in *Newsweek*. That's how you know.

Some of the things you know seem absolutely obvious to you. If I asked you how you knew that you have to breathe to live, you'd probably say, "Everybody knows that." There are a lot of things that everybody knows. Everybody knows that the world is round, for example. Of course, a few hundred years ago, everybody knew that the world was flat.

Much of what you know is a matter of agreement and belief. Little of it is based on personal experience and discovery. A big part of growing up in any society, in fact, is the process of learning to accept what everybody around you "knows" is so. If you don't know those same things, you can't really be a part of the group. If you were to seriously question whether you have to breathe to live, you'd quickly find yourself set apart from other people. You might be sent to live in a hospital with other people who ask questions like that.

Although it's important for you to see that most of what you know is a matter of believing what you've been told, I also want you to see that there's nothing wrong with you in that respect. That's simply the way we've structured human societies. The fundamental basis of knowledge is agreement. Since you couldn't learn all those things through personal experience and discovery alone, we've set things up so that you can simply believe what others tell you.

There are other ways of knowing things, however. In contrast to knowing things through agreement, it is also possible to know things through direct experience—through observation. If you dive into a glacial stream flowing down through the Canadian Rockies, you don't need anyone to tell you it's cold. You notice that all by yourself. The first time you stepped on a thorn, you knew that hurt even before anyone told you.

TWO REALITIES

Ultimately, you live in a world of two realities. Part of what you know could be called your *agreement reality:* the things you consider to be real because you've been told they are real. Another part is what could be called *experiential reality:* the things you know as a function of your direct experience. The first is a product of what people have told you, the second a product of your own experience. The problem is that both seem very real.

Let's take an example. Imagine that you've come to a party at my house. It's a high-class affair, and the drinks and food are excellent. In particular, you are taken by one of the appetizers I bring around on a tray. It's a breaded, deep-fried appetizer with an especially zesty taste. You have a couple and they are delicious! You have more. Soon you are subtly moving around the room so as to be wherever I arrive with a tray of these nibblies.

Finally, you can't contain yourself any more. "What are they?" you ask. "How can I get the recipe?" And I let you in on the secret: "You've been eating breaded, deep-fried *worms!*" Your response is dramatic: your stomach rebels and you promptly throw up all over the living room rug. Awful! What a terrible thing to serve guests!

The point of the story is that both feelings about the appetizer would be very real. Your initial liking for them was certainly real, but so was the feeling you had when you found out what you'd been eating. It should be evident, however, that the feeling of disgust you had when you discovered you were eating worms would be strictly a product of the agreements you have with those around you that worms aren't fit to eat. That's an agreement you began entering into the first time your parents found you sitting in a pile of dirt with half of a wriggling worm dangling from your lips. You learned worms were not kosher in our society when they pried your mouth open and reached down your throat in search of the other half of the worm.

Aside from the agreements we have, what's wrong with worms? They are probably high in protein and low in calories. Bite-sized and easily packaged, they are a distributor's dream. They are also a delicacy for some people who live in societies that lack our agreement that worms are disgusting. Some people might love the worms but would be turned off by the deep-fried bread-crumb crust.

Reality, then, is a tricky business. How can you really know what's real? People have grappled with that question for thousands of years. And science is one of the answers that has arisen out of that grappling.

Science offers an approach to both agreement reality and experiential reality. Scientists have certain criteria that must be met

before they will accept the reality of something they haven't personally experienced. In general, an assertion must have both logical and empirical support: it must make sense and it must align with observations in the world. Why do earth-bound scientists accept the assertion that it's cold on the dark side of the moon? First, it makes sense, since the surface heat of the moon comes from the sun's rays. Second, the scientific measurements made on the moon's dark side confirm the expectation. So, scientists accept the reality of things they don't personally experience—they accept an agreement reality—but they have special standards for doing so.

More to the point of this book, however, science offers a special approach to the discovery of reality through personal experience. It offers a special approach to the business of inquiry. Whereas *epistemology* is the science of knowing, *methodology* (a subfield of epistemology) might be called "the science of finding out." This book is an examination and presentation of social science methodology, and we're going to concern ourselves with how social scientists find out about human social life.

In the remainder of this chapter, we're going to look at inquiry as an activity. We'll begin by examining inquiry as a native, natural human activity. It is something you and I have engaged in every day of our lives. Next, we'll look at some kinds of errors we make in normal inquiry, and we'll conclude by examining what makes science different. We'll see some of the ways in which science guards against the common human errors in inquiry.

NATIVE HUMAN INQUIRY

Practically all people, and many lower animals as well, exhibit a desire to predict their future circumstances. We seem quite willing, moreover, to undertake this task using *causal* and *probabilistic reasoning*. First, we generally recognize that future circumstances are somehow *caused* or conditioned by present ones. We learn that getting an education will affect how much money we earn later in life, and that swimming beyond the reef may bring an unhappy encounter with a shark. Sharks, on the other hand, may learn that hanging around the reef may bring a happy encounter with unhappy swimmers. As students we learn that studying hard will result in better examination grades.

Second, people, and seemingly other animals, also learn that such patterns of cause and effect are *probabilistic* in nature: the effects occur more often when the causes occur than when the causes are absent—but not always. Thus, students learn that studying hard produces good grades in most instances, but not every time. We recognize the danger of swimming beyond the reef without believing that every such swim will be fatal.

We will return to these concepts of causality and probability throughout the book. As we'll see, science makes them more explicit and provides techniques for dealing with them more rigorously than does casual human inquiry. It is these qualities that most distinguish science from casual inquiry. What I want to do, then, is to sharpen skills you already have, making you more conscious, rigorous, and explicit in your inquiries.

In looking at native human inquiry, it is important to distinguish between prediction and understanding. Often, we are able to predict without understanding—you may be able to predict rain when your trick knee aches. And often, even if we don't understand why, we are willing to act on the basis of a demonstrated predictive ability. The race track buff who finds that the third-ranked horse in the third race of the day always wins will probably keep betting without knowing, or caring, why it works out that way.

Whatever the primitive drives or instincts are that motivate human beings and other animals, satisfying them depends heavily on the ability to predict future circumstances. For humans, however, the attempt to predict is often placed in a context of knowledge and understanding. If you can understand why things are related to one another, why certain regular patterns occur, you can predict even better than if you simply observe and remember those patterns. Thus, human inquiry aims at answering both what and why questions, and we pursue these goals by observing and figuring out.

As I suggested earlier in the chapter, our attempts to learn about the world are only partly linked to direct, personal inquiry or experience. Another, much larger, part comes from the agreed-upon knowledge that others give us. This agreement reality both assists and hinders our attempts to find out for ourselves. Two important sources of our secondhand knowledge—tradition and authority—deserve brief consideration here.

Tradition

Each of us inherits a culture made up, in part, of firmly accepted knowledge about the workings of the world. We may learn from others that planting corn in the spring will gain the greatest assistance from the gods, that sugar from too much candy will decay our teeth, that the circumference of a circle is approximately twenty-two sevenths of its diameter, or that masturbation will blind us. We may test a few of these "truths" on our own, but we simply accept the great majority of them. These are the things that "everybody knows."

Tradition, in this sense of the term, has some clear advantages for human inquiry. By accepting what everybody knows, you are spared the overwhelming task of starting from scratch in your search for regularities and understanding. Knowledge is cumulative, and an inherited body of infor-

The Inscrutable American Economy

The 1980 presidential election campaign in the United States had a great deal in common with previous political campaigns. Then-president Jimmy Carter and challenger Ronald Reagan differed in many ways: party, ideology, programs, promises, and partners. All that was understandable and reasonable. The nature of democracy centers on the people choosing between competing orientations. Less reasonably, and more frustratingly, the two candidates disagreed on the *facts*.

On 28 October 1980, Carter and Reagan met before an international television audience of tens of millions to contest their different points of view. They differed in almost every regard. Carter argued that his administration had been good for the working people of America; Reagan said it had been disastrous. To substantiate his contention, Carter said 9 million new jobs had been created during the course of his administration. In bold contrast, Reagan charged that 8 million Americans were unemployed: 2 million, he said, had lost their jobs during 1980. Who was right? The *Washington Post* news service reconciled the apparent contradiction succinctly:

Both things are true. There were about 87.5 million jobs in this country in 1976, the year of the past presidential election. There are nearly 97 million now. But the number of jobs has not increased as fast as the number of people wanting them. There were 6.1 million people unemployed last December, 5.9 percent of the work force. There were 8.2 million out of work in July, 7.8 percent.

The competing presidential candidates apparently disagreed on the facts of inflation as well. Carter said that in the third quarter of 1980, the inflation rate had been 7 percent. More gloomily, Reagan said inflation was 12.7 percent.

mation and understanding is the jumping-off point for the development of more knowledge. We often speak of "standing on the shoulders of giants," that is, of previous generations.

At the same time, tradition may be detrimental to human inquiry. If you seek a fresh and different understanding of something that everybody already understands and has always understood, you may be marked the fool for your efforts. You may be sent to live in one of those special hospitals I mentioned earlier. More to the point, however, it will probably never occur to you to seek a different understanding of something that is already understood and obvious.

Authority

Despite the power of tradition, new knowledge appears every day. Quite aside from your own personal inquiries, throughout your life you will be the beneficiary of new discoveries and understandings produced by others. Often, acceptance of these new acquisitions will depend on the status of the discoverer. You're more likely to believe the epidemiologist who declares that the common cold can be transmitted through kissing, for example, than to believe your maiden aunt.

Like tradition, authority can both assist and hinder human inquiry. We do well to

Who was right? Again, the *Washington Post* resolved the puzzle:

Both are right. Consumer prices have risen 12.7 percent in the last year, and rose at an annual rate of 12.7 last month. But in the last three months the annual rate was 7 percent.

National defense was an issue of contention during the 1980 presidential campaign: Reagan argued for more defense expenditures, Carter for relatively less. As with unemployment and inflation, however, the two men seemed to have examined two radically different realities. Reagan challenged Carter's commitment to defense by alleging the president had sharply reduced the five-year defense budget projected by Republican President Gerald Ford. Carter countered by contending that defense spending had actually declined during seven of the eight Republican years of the Nixon-Ford administra-

tions prior to his own. Who was right? You guessed it.

Defense spending did fall in seven of those eight years, not in dollars—the defense budget rose from $75.8 billion to $105.2 billion—but in so-called "real" terms, after allowing for inflation. In 1972 dollars, defense outlays fell from $81.2 billion in fiscal 1971 to $66.5 billion in fiscal 1977. It rose the next year to $66.6 billion. But Carter did chop back the Ford defense budget to which he fell heir. . . .

This interchange should lead you to look at the authoritative pronouncements of authorities with a degree of skepticism. Perhaps you already do that. In either case, you can see the value of mastering the logic of social scientific research. The purpose of this book is to support you in that.

Source: "Different Facts—Both Were Correct," *San Francisco Chronicle*, 29 October 1980.

trust in the judgment of the person who has special training, expertise, and credentials in the matter, especially in the face of contradictory positions on a given question. At the same time, inquiry can be greatly hindered by the legitimate authority who errs within his or her own special province. Biologists, after all, do make mistakes in the field of biology. Biological knowledge changes over time. The box entitled "The Inscrutable American Economy" illustrates how authorities citing research findings can run amok.

Inquiry is also hindered when we depend on the authority of experts speaking outside their realm of expertise. For example, con-

sider the political or religious leader, lacking in any biochemical expertise, who declares marijuana to be a dangerous drug. The advertising industry plays heavily on this misuse of authority by having popular athletes discuss the nutritional value of breakfast cereals, having movie actors evaluate the performance of automobiles, and using other similar tactics.

Both tradition and authority, then, are two-edged swords in the search for knowledge about the world. Most simply put, they provide us with a starting point for our own inquiry, but they may lead us to start at the wrong point and push us off in the wrong direction.

ERRORS IN PERSONAL HUMAN INQUIRY

Quite aside from the potential dangers of tradition and authority, you and I often stumble and fall down when we set out to learn for ourselves. I'm going to mention some of the common errors we make in our casual inquiries and look at the ways in which science provides safeguards against those errors.

Inaccurate Observation

The keystone of inquiry is observation. We can never understand the way things are without first having something to understand. We have to know *what* before we can explain *why*. On the whole, however, you and I are pretty sloppy, even unconscious, observers of the flow of events in life. Recall, for example, the last person you talked to today. What kind of shoes was that person wearing? Are you even certain the person was wearing shoes? On the whole, we are pretty casual in observing things, and as a result we make mistakes. We fail to observe things right in front of us and mistakenly observe things that aren't so.

An American tourist in France may be treated rudely by several strangers and conclude that the French are a rude people, even though the offenders were actually German tourists. A meteor streaking across the sky may be mistaken for a flying saucer and held responsible for the earthquake that occurs the following day.

In contrast to casual human inquiry, scientific observation is a *conscious* activity. Simply making observation more deliberate helps to reduce error. You probably don't recall, for example, what your instructor was wearing on the first day of this class. If you had to guess now, you'd probably make a mistake. If you had gone to the first class meeting with a conscious plan to observe and record what your instructor was wearing, however, you'd have been more accurate.

In many cases, both simple and complex measurement devices help to guard against inaccurate observations. At the same time, they add a degree of precision well beyond the capacity of the unassisted human senses. Suppose, for example, that you had taken color photographs of your instructor that day.

Overgeneralization

When we look for patterns among the specific things we observe around us, we often fall into assuming that a few similar events are evidence of a general pattern. Probably the tendency to overgeneralize is greatest when the pressure to arrive at a general understanding is high. Yet it also occurs casually in the absence of pressure. Whenever overgeneralization does occur, it can misdirect or impede inquiry.

Imagine that you are a reporter covering an anti-nuclear demonstration. You have orders to turn in your story in just two hours, and you need to know why the demonstrators are demonstrating. Rushing to the scene, you start interviewing demonstrators, asking them for their reasons. If the first two demonstrators you interview give you essentially the same reason, you may simply assume that the other 3,000 are demonstrating for that reason.

Scientists guard against overgeneralization by committing themselves in advance to a sufficiently large sample of observations (see Chapter 7). The **replication*** of inquiry provides another safeguard. Basi-

---

*Words in **boldface** are defined in the Glossary at the end of the book.

cally, this means repeating a study, checking to see if the same results are produced each time. Then, the study may be repeated under slightly varied conditions. Thus, when a social scientist discovers that educated people are less prejudiced than uneducated people, that's only the beginning. Is the relationship true for both men and women? For both old and young? Among people from different regions of the country? This extension of the inquiry seeks to find the breadth and the limits of the generalization about education and prejudice.

Totally independent replications by other researchers extend the safeguards. Suppose that I do the original study that shows education and prejudice to be related. Later, you might conduct a study of your own. You would study different people, and perhaps you'd measure education and prejudice somewhat differently. If your independent study produced exactly the same conclusion as mine, we'd both feel more confident in the generalizability of the relationship. If you obtained somewhat different results or found a subgroup of people among whom it didn't hold at all, you'd have saved me from overgeneralizing.

Selective Observation

One danger of overgeneralization is that it may lead to selective observation. Once you have concluded that a particular pattern exists and have developed a general understanding of why, you will be tempted to pay attention to future events and situations that correspond with the pattern and ignore those that don't. Racial and ethnic prejudices depend heavily on selective observation for their persistence.

Suppose you were once cheated by a shopkeeper you thought to be Jewish. You might conclude from that one event that Jewish shopkeepers are dishonest in gen-

eral. Subsequently, you'd probably take special note of dishonest actions by other Jewish shopkeepers, while ignoring honest Jews and dishonest non-Jews. Some people take special note of all the lazy blacks they come across and ignore energetic blacks and lazy whites. Others notice irrational and emotional women while overlooking stable women as well as unstable men.

Usually, a research design will specify in advance the number and kind of observations to be made as a basis for reaching a conclusion. If you and I wanted to learn whether women were more likely than men to support the Equal Rights Amendment, we'd commit ourselves to making a specified number of observations on that question in a research project. We might select a thousand people to be interviewed on the issue. Even if the first ten women supported ERA and the first ten men opposed it, we'd interview everyone selected for the study, recognize and record each observation. Then, we'd base our conclusion on an analysis of all the observations.

There is a second safeguard against selective observation in science that also works against most of the other pitfalls. If you overlook something that contradicts your conclusion about the way things are, your colleagues will notice it and bring it to your attention. That's a service scientists provide to one another and to the enterprise of science itself. The box entitled "Popular Press Reporting of Social Science Research" exemplifies the practice of scientists checking on the representativeness of the observations upon which research findings are based.

Made-Up Information

Sometimes you just can't ignore the events that contradict your general conclusions about the way things are. Suppose, for

Popular Press Reporting of Social Science Research

by William R. Todd-Mancillas
Department of Human Communication, Rutgers University

The public learns much about science in newspapers and magazines, but these popular media cannot be relied upon to provide accurate or complete information. Take, for instance, the article written in the *National Enquirer* entitled "Hairy Men Are Smarter." This is how the reporter, Dick Robinson, described the study done by a staff psychiatrist at the St. Louis, Missouri, state hospital:

> Dr. Aikarakudy G. Alias compared the body hair of 117 men in Mensa, an organization of people with extremely high I.Q.'s, with men from the general population and found that the incidence of noticeable body hair is about double in the Mensa members.
>
> Mensa members rated themselves by comparing their body hair with the amount of hair observed on a total of 246 men—105 nude men pictured in *Playgirl* magazine and 141 men photographed on a Miami Beach, FL, public beach.

There are several problems with this brief description of Dr. Alias's study. First, you might wonder why anyone would be interested in doing this study in the first place. Without additional information, the casual reader might get the impression this is just the sort of silly research conducted by many social scientists. But if you were to read Dr. Alias's original research report you would find that this study is only one of several he has conducted attempting to identify physiological signs of personality characteristics. This line of research is based on the known fact that both your skin and brain develop from the same embryonic tissues. Because of their common origin, Dr. Alias thinks (hypothesizes) that features of one of these organs (such as hair on the skin) may vary in a systematic way with features of the other organ (intellectual capacity of the brain). None of this is

example, you had decided that all Jewish shopkeepers were dishonest, and then one of them walked four miles to return the wallet that you left on the store counter. What would you do? In our casual, day-to-day handling of such matters, we often make up information that would resolve the contradiction. Maybe the shopkeeper isn't really Jewish after all. Or maybe the shopkeeper was just casing your house with a later burglary in mind.

Perhaps that hard-working and energetic black at work is just trying to get promoted to a soft executive post. Perversely, people often doubt the general femininity of the woman who is tough-minded, logical, and unemotional in getting the job done. Concluding that she's not really a woman protects the general conclusion that women are irrational and flighty.

Just as you and I make up probable information in our day-to-day inquiries as a way of explaining away confusion, scientists engaged in scientific inquiry do also. When our scientific observations and analyses don't turn out the way we expect, we often think up reasons to explain away the surprise.

Suppose you and I had the idea that people

explained in the brief article appearing in the *National Enquirer*.

A second problem with popular press stories is that they seldom help the reader to think critically about how the research was done. Take, for instance, the way data was collected in Dr. Alias's study. Mensa members were given a page with nine male torsos arrayed from least to most hairy. Mensa members then identified the torso most closely resembling their own torsos. No similar information was collected for men representing populations with lower IQs. Instead, Dr. Alias only compared Mensa members' self-reports with actual photographs of men shown in *Playgirl* photographs or with photographs of men on a Miami beach. Note that it is possible the Mensa members reported themselves as being hairier than they actually were. It is also possible that for aesthetic reasons *Playgirl* photographers may use male models with only slight-to-moderate as opposed to moderate-to-heavy body hair. In short, since data was not collected the same way

for men of average IQ as for men with above average IQ, you simply can't interpret the results without a very large grain of salt.

These aren't the only problems with the study done by Dr. Alias or with the *National Enquirer* account of this study. In fact, when reading any popular press account of behavioral science you need to be suspicious. Suggestion: Why don't you try making a similar comparison yourself? It only takes three steps: (1) find a newspaper or magazine article describing a study done by a social scientist; (2) write away for the original report; (3) make comparisons between the popular press story and the scientist's report of the study.

Source: "Hairy Men Are Smarter," *National Enquirer*, 1 November 1977, p. 28. "Positive Correlations between Body Hair and Intelligence . . . ?" (Copy of research report made available through the courtesy of A. G. Alias, M.D.)

who knew a lot about world affairs would feel less alienated politically than people who knew little or nothing about world affairs. We might test that idea by administering a questionnaire to a group of college students. In the questionnaire, we'd find out (1) how much they knew about world affairs and (2) how politically alienated they felt. We'd then examine the relationship between those two variables. But suppose the informed and the uninformed turned out to be equally alienated. What a disappointment. "Aha!" you say, "The reason we didn't discover a difference is that college

students are generally quite knowledgeable about world affairs, so our distinction between 'informed' and 'uninformed' wasn't much of a distinction after all. Surely the expected relationship would hold among the general public, where we'd find some people who were *really* uninformed."

The exercise I've just described is sometimes called *ex post facto hypothesizing*, and it's perfectly acceptable in science *if it doesn't stop there*. The argument you proposed clearly suggests that we need to test our hypothesis among a broader spectrum of people. The line of reasoning doesn't prove our hypothesis is correct, only that there's still some hope for it. Later observations may prove its accuracy. Thus, scientists very often engage in deducing information, and they follow up on their deductions by looking at the facts again.

Illogical Reasoning

There are other ways of handling observations that contradict our conclusions about the way things are. Surely one of the most remarkable creations of the human mind is "the exception that proves the rule." That idea doesn't make any sense at all. An exception can draw attention to a rule or to a supposed rule, but in no system of logic can it prove the rule it contradicts. Yet, we often use this pithy saying to brush away contradictions with a simple stroke of illogic.

What statisticians have called the *gambler's fallacy* is another illustration of illogic in day-to-day reasoning. A consistent run of either good or bad luck is presumed to foreshadow its opposite. An evening of bad luck at poker may kindle the belief that a winning hand is just around the corner, and many a poker player has stayed in a game much too long because of that mistaken belief. Or, conversely, an extended period of good weather may lead you to worry that it is certain to rain on the weekend picnic.

The simple fact is that even the best of us get a little funny in our reasoning from time to time. Worse yet, we can get defensive when others point out our error of logic.

Although all of us sometimes fall into embarrassingly illogical reasoning in day-to-day life, scientists avoid this pitfall by using systems of logic consciously and explicitly. Chapter 2 will examine the logic(s) of science in more depth. For now, it is sufficient to note that logical reasoning is a conscious activity for scientists, and they

always have their colleagues around to keep them honest in that regard as in others.

Ego-Involvement in Understanding

The search for regularities and generalized understanding is not a trivial intellectual exercise. It critically affects our personal lives. Our understanding of events and conditions, then, is often of special psychological significance to us. If you lose your job or fail to get a promotion, you may be tempted to conclude that your boss wants to get you out of the way to promote a personal friend. That explanation would save you from examining your own abilities and worth.

Any challenge to that explanation, consequently, is also a challenge to your abilities and worth.

In countless ways, we link our understandings of how things are to the image of ourselves that we present to others. Because of this linkage any disproof of these understandings tends to make us look stupid, gullible, and generally not okay. So we commit ourselves all the more unshakably to our understanding of how things are and create a formidable barrier to further inquiry and more accurate understanding.

Scientists, being human, run the risk of becoming personally involved in and committed to the conclusions they reach in scientific inquiry. Sometimes it's worse than in nonscientific life. Imagine, for example, that you have discovered an apparent cure for cancer and have been awarded the Nobel prize. How do you suppose you'll feel when somebody else publishes an article arguing that your cure doesn't really work? You might not be totally objective.

A firm commitment to the other norms of science that we have been examining works against too much ego-involvement. Failing that, you will find that your colleagues can evaluate a critical article more objectively than you can. Ultimately, then, although ego-involvement is a problem sometimes for individual scientists, it is less of a problem for science in general.

The Premature Closure of Inquiry

Overgeneralization, selective observation, made-up information, and the defensive uses of illogical reasoning all conspire to produce a premature closure of inquiry. This whole discussion began with our desire to understand the world around us, and the various errors detailed above often lead us to stop looking at it too soon.

The anti-Semite who says, "I already understand Jews, so don't confuse me with facts," has achieved a personal closure on the subject. Sometimes this closure of inquiry is a social, rather than individual, act. For example, the private foundation or government agency that refuses to support further research on a topic that is "already understood" effects closure as a social act, as does the denominational college that prohibits scholarship and research that might challenge the existence of God.

The danger of premature closure of inquiry is obvious. It brings a halt to attempts to understand things before that understanding is complete. If you review the history of human knowledge, however, you will reach a startling conclusion: we keep changing the things we know—even the things we know for certain. In an important sense, then, any closure of inquiry is premature.

At its base, science is an open-ended enterprise in which conclusions are constantly being modified. That is an explicit norm of science. Experienced scientists, therefore, accept it as a fact of life and expect established theories to be overturned eventually. And if one scientist considers a line of inquiry to be completed forever, others

will not. Even if a whole generation of scientists closes inquiry on a given topic, a later generation of scientists is likely to set about testing the old ideas and changing many of them.

In part, the reward structure of science supports this openness. While you may have to overcome a great deal of initial resistance and disparagement, imagine how famous you would be if you could demonstrate persuasively that something people have always believed simply isn't true. What if you could *prove* that carbon monoxide was really *good* for people? The potential rewards for astounding discoveries keep everything fair game for inquiry in science.

Mystification

None of us can hope to understand everything. No matter how intelligent or how diligent you and I may be in our inquiry, there will always be countless events and situations that we do not understand. We may never fully understand the origin of the universe; a particular individual may never know why he or she failed calculus in college.

One common response to this problem is to attribute supernatural or mystical causes to the phenomena that humans cannot understand. It is simply asserted that some things are ultimately beyond human comprehension. Quite possibly that may be true of some events and situations; perhaps some things are totally random. Nonetheless, accepting that a phenomenon is ultimately unknowable brings a halt to inquiry, whether the thing is actually knowable or not.

The same comments just made in connection with the premature closure of inquiry can be made about the scientific safeguards against mystification. It is an article of faith in science that everything is knowable, or—waffling slightly—that everything is *poten-*

tially knowable. Even if one scientist is willing to concede that a particular phenomenon is beyond human comprehension, another will recognize the rewards to be gained in making that phenomenon comprehensible. If I were to publicly announce my feeling that we can never hope to understand love, say, that would probably give you an added incentive to find a way to understand it.

To Err Is Human

These, then, are some of the ways in which you and I go astray in our attempts to know and understand the world and some of the ways that science protects its inquiries from these pitfalls. For the most part, science differs from our casual, day-to-day inquiry in two important respects. First, scientific inquiry is a conscious activity. Although you and I engage in continuous observation in daily life, much of it is unconscious or semiconscious. In scientific inquiry, we make a conscious decision to observe, and we stay awake while we do it. Second, scientific inquiry is more careful than our casual efforts. In scientific inquiry, we are more wary of making mistakes and take special precautions to avoid error.

Nothing I've said should lead you to conclude that science offers total protection against the errors that nonscientists commit in day-to-day inquiry. Not only do individual scientists make every kind of error we've looked at, scientists as a group fall into the pitfalls and stay trapped for long periods of time.

Not long ago, when most of us felt it would be extremely difficult for people to travel to the moon, it was the physicists who could *prove* that such a trip would be *impossible*. I think it had something to do with the weight of the fuel it would take to lift the amount of fuel it would take to lift

the amount of fuel it would take. . . . Only the physicists really understood it.

But who put us on the moon in 1969? The physicists! In fact it was the same physicists who could prove it was impossible. The NASA story provides an excellent illustration of how science operates. The scientists involved were able to view the proven impossibility of going to the moon within a larger context. Given that it's impossible, how can we do it?

THE FOUNDATIONS OF SOCIAL SCIENCE

Science is sometimes characterized as *logico-empirical*. This ugly term carries an important message: the two pillars of science are (1) logic or rationality and (2) observation. A scientific understanding of the world must make sense and correspond with what we observe. Both of these elements are essential to science.

As a gross generalization, scientific theory deals with the logical aspect of science, and research deals with the observational aspect. A scientific theory describes the logical relationships that appear to exist among parts of the world, and research offers means for seeing whether those relationships actually exist in the real world. Though too simplistic, perhaps, this statement provides a useful jumping-off point for the examination of theory and research. Here I will present some of the foundations of social science inquiry. Then, Chapter 2 will examine theory in detail and show its links to research.

Theory, Not Philosophy or Belief

Social scientific theory has to do with what *is*, not with what *should be*. I point that out at the start, since social theory for many centuries has combined these two orientations. Social philosophers mixed liberally their observations of what happened around them, their speculations as to why, and their ideas about how things ought to be. Although modern social scientists may do the same from time to time, it is important to realize that social *science* has to do with how things are and why.

This means that scientific theory—and, more broadly, science itself—cannot settle debates on value. Science cannot determine whether capitalism is better or worse than socialism except in terms of some set of agreed-on criteria. We could only determine scientifically whether capitalism or socialism most supported human dignity and freedom if we were able to agree on some measures of dignity and freedom, and our conclusion in that case would depend totally on the measures we had agreed on. The conclusions would have no general meaning beyond that.

By the same token, if we could agree that suicide rates, say, or perhaps giving to charity were good measures of a religion's quality, then we would be in a position to determine scientifically whether Buddhism or Christianity was the better religion. Again, however, our conclusion would be inextricably tied to the criteria agreed on. As a practical matter, people are seldom able to agree on criteria for determining issues of value, so science is seldom of any use in settling such debates. Moreover, people's convictions in matters of value are more nonrational than rational, making science, which deals in rational proofs, all the more inappropriate.

This issue will be considered in more detail in Chapter 12 when we look at *evaluation research*. As you'll see, social scientists have become increasingly involved in studying programs that reflect ideological points of view, and one of the biggest problems faced by researchers is getting people to agree on

criteria of success and failure. Yet such criteria are essential if social scientific research is to tell us anything useful about matters of value. By analogy, a stopwatch cannot tell us if one sprinter is better than another unless we can agree that speed is the critical criterion.

Thus, social science can assist us in knowing only what is and why. It can be used to address the question of what ought to be only when people agree on the criteria for deciding what's better than something else. Furthermore, this agreement seldom occurs. With that understanding, let's turn now to some of the fundamental bases upon which social science allows us to develop theories about what is and why.

Social Regularities

Ultimately, social scientific theory aims to determine the logical and persistent patterns of regularity in social life. Lying behind that aim is the fundamental assumption that life *is* regular, not totally chaotic or random. That assumption, of course, applies to all science, but it is sometimes a barrier for people when they first approach *social* science.

Certainly at first glance, it would appear that the subject matter of the physical sciences is more regular than that of the social sciences. A heavy object, after all, falls to earth *every* time we drop it, while a person may vote for a particular candidate in one election and against that same candidate in the next election. Similarly, ice *always* melts when heated enough, while seemingly honest people sometimes steal. Examples like these, although true, can lead us to lose sight of the high degree of regularity in social affairs.

To begin, a vast number of formal norms in society create a considerable degree of regularity. For example, only persons who have reached a certain age are permitted to vote in elections. In the American military, only men are allowed to participate in combat. Such formal prescriptions, then, regulate, or regularize, social behavior.

Aside from formal prescriptions, other social norms can be observed that create more regularities. Registered Republicans are more likely to vote for Republican candidates than are registered Democrats. University professors tend to earn more money than unskilled laborers. Men earn more than women. Whites earn more than blacks. The list of regularities could go on and on.

To review, all science is based on the fundamental assumption that regularity exists in what is to be studied, and we have noted that regularities exist in social life. Therefore, logically, social behavior should be susceptible to scientific analysis. But is that necessarily the case? After all, you probably know an unskilled laborer who earns more than most college professors. Or are those kinds of irregularities worthy of scientific study? So Republicans vote for Republicans more than Democrats do. So what. Isn't that pretty obvious? We don't need scientific theories and research to understand something like that.

Three major objections can be raised in regard to the kinds of social regularities that we've been looking at, and those should be dealt with before we proceed. First, some of the regularities may seem trivial; everyone is aware of them. Second, contradictory cases may be cited, indicating that the "regularity" isn't totally regular anyway. And third, it may be argued that the people involved in the regularity could upset the whole thing if they wanted to. Let's handle the business of triviality first, those things that "everybody knows."

During World War II, Samuel Stouffer, one of the greatest of social science researchers, organized a research branch in the U. S. Army to conduct studies in support of the war effort (Stouffer 1949, 1950). Many of the studies concerned the morale among soldiers. Stouffer and his colleagues found there was a great deal of "common wisdom" regarding the bases of military morale. Much of their research was devoted to testing the "obvious."

For example, it has been recognized for a long time that promotions affect morale in the military. When people get promotions and the promotion system seems fair, morale rises. Moreover, it makes sense that people who are getting promoted will tend to think the system is fair, whereas those passed over are likely to think the system unfair. By extension, it seems sensible that soldiers in units with slow promotion rates would tend to think the system unfair, while those in units with rapid promotions would think the system fair. Was this the way they really felt though?

Stouffer and his colleagues focused their studies on two units: the Military Police (MPs), where promotions were the slowest in the Army, and the Army Air Corps (forerunner of the U. S. Air Force), which had the fastest promotions. It stood to reason that those in the MPs would say the promotion system was unfair, while those in the Air Corps would say it was fair. The studies, however, showed just the opposite.

Notice the dilemma faced by a researcher in a situation such as this one. On the one hand, the observations don't make any sense. On the other hand, an explanation that makes obvious good sense isn't supported by the facts. A lesser person would have set the problem aside "for further study." Stouffer, however, looked for an explanation that did make sense of this observation.

Eventually he found it. Robert Merton and some other sociologists at Columbia had begun thinking and writing about something they called *reference group theory*. This theory says that people judge their lot in life not so much by objective conditions as by comparing themselves with others around them—those people who constitute their reference group. (If you lived among poor people, a salary of $50,000 a year would make you feel like a millionaire. But if you lived among people who earned $500,000 a year, however, you'd probably feel impoverished.)

Stouffer applied this line of reasoning to the soldiers he had studied. Even if a particular MP had not been promoted for a long time, it was unlikely that he knew some less deserving person who had gotten promoted faster. Nobody got promoted in the MPs. Had he been in the Air Corps—even if he had gotten several promotions in rapid succession—he would probably be able to point to someone less deserving who had gotten even faster promotion. An MP's reference group, then, was his fellow MPs, while the air corpsman compared himself with fellow corpsmen. Ultimately, then, Stouffer reached an understanding of soldiers' attitudes toward the promotion system that (1) made sense and (2) corresponded to the facts.

This story shows that documenting the obvious is a valuable function of any science, physical or social. All too often, the obvious turns out to be wrong, and apparent triviality is not a legitimate objection to any scientific endeavor. (Darwin coined the phrase *fool's experiment* in ironic reference to much of his own research—research in which he tested things that everyone else already knew.)

The objection that there are always exceptions to any social regularity is also inappropriate. It is not important that a particular woman earns more money than a particular man if men earn more than women overall. The pattern still exists. Social regularities represent *probabilistic* patterns, and a general pattern need not be reflected in 100 percent of the observable cases.

This rule applies in the physical sciences as well as in social science, by the way. In

genetics, for example, the mating of a blue-eyed person with a brown-eyed person will *probably* result in a brown-eyed offspring. The birth of a blue-eyed child does not challenge the observed regularity, however, since the geneticist states only that the brown-eyed offspring is more likely and, further, that brown-eyed offspring will be born in a certain percentage of the cases. The social scientist makes a similar, probabilistic prediction—that women overall are likely to earn less than men. And the social scientist has grounds for asking why that is the case.

Finally, the objection that observed social regularities could be upset through the conscious will of the actors is not a serious challenge to social science, even though there does not seem to be a parallel situation in the physical sciences. (Presumably an object cannot resist falling to earth "because it wants to.") There is no denying that a religious, right-wing bigot could go to the polls and vote for an agnostic, left-wing radical black if he or she wanted to upset the political scientist studying the election. All voters in an election could suddenly switch to the underdog just to frustrate the pollster. Similarly, workers could go to work early or stay home from work and thereby prevent the expected rush-hour commuter traffic. But these things do not happen often enough to seriously threaten the observation of social regularities.

The fact remains that social norms do exist, and the social scientist can observe the effects of those norms. When norms change over time, the social scientist can observe and explain those changes. Ultimately, social regularities persist because they tend to make sense for the people involved in them. When the social scientist suggests that it is logical to expect a given type of person to behave in a certain manner, that type of person may very well agree with the logical basis for the expectation. Thus, although a religious, right-wing bigot *could* vote for an agnostic, left-wing radical black candidate, such a voter would be the first to consider it stupid to do so.

Aggregates, Not Individuals

Social regularities do exist, then, and they are both susceptible to and worthy of theoretical and empirical study. Implicit in the above comments, however, is a point that needs to be made explicit. Social scientists study *social* patterns rather than individual ones. All the regular patterns I've mentioned have reflected the *aggregate* actions and situations of many individuals. Although social scientists often study motivations that affect individuals, the individual per se is seldom the subject of social science. We do not create theories about individuals, only about the nature of group life.

Sometimes the aggregated regularities are amazing. Consider the birthrate, for example. People have babies for an incredibly wide range of personal reasons. Some do it because their own parents want them to. Some feel it's a way of completing their womanhood or manhood. Others want to hold their marriages together. Still others have babies by accident.

If you have had a baby, you could probably tell a much more detailed, idiosyncratic story. Why did you have the baby when you did, rather than a year earlier or later? Maybe your house burned down and you had to delay a year before you could afford to have the baby. Maybe you felt that being a family person would demonstrate maturity that would support a promotion at work.

Everyone who had a baby last year had a different set of reasons for doing so. Yet despite this vast diversity, despite the idiosyncrasy of each individual's reasons, the overall birthrate in a society is remarkably consistent from year to year. If the rate is 19.1 per 1,000 this year, it is likely to be very close to 19.1 per 1,000 next year, even though the rate may be gradually rising or declining over a longer period of time. If the birthrate of a society were to be 19.1, 35.6, 7.8, 28.9, and 16.2 in five successive years, demographers would begin dropping like flies.

Ultimately, then, *social* scientific theories deal with aggregated, not individual, behavior. Their purpose is to explain why aggregated patterns of behavior are so regular even when the individuals participating in them may change over time. In another important sense, social science doesn't even seek to explain *people*. Our aim is to understand the *systems* within which people operate, the systems that explain why people do what they do. The elements in such a system are not people but *variables*.

A Variable Language

The idea of a system composed of variables is somewhat complex, and I want to introduce this subtle aspect of social scientific theory with an analogy that tells the story. The subject of a physician's attention is the patient. If the patient is ill, the physician's purpose is to assist that patient in getting well. By contrast, a medical researcher's subject matter is different: a disease, for example. The medical researcher may study the physician's patient, but for the researcher that patient is relevant only as a carrier of the disease, which is what the researcher is really studying.

That is not to say that medical researchers don't care about real people. They certainly do. Their ultimate purpose in studying diseases is to protect people from them. But in their actual research, patients are directly relevant only for what they reveal about the disease under study. In fact, when a disease can be studied meaningfully without studying actual patients, medical researchers do so.

By the same token, social science involves the study of **variables** and the **attributes** that compose them. Social scientific theories are written in a variable language, and people get involved only as the carriers of those variables. Here's what social scientists mean by variables and attributes.

Attributes are characteristics or qualities that describe an object—in this case, a person. Examples include *female, oriental, alienated, conservative, dishonest, intelligent, farmer,* and so forth. Anything you might say to describe yourself or someone else involves an attribute.

Variables, on the other hand, are logical groupings of attributes. Thus, for example, *male* and *female* are attributes, while *sex* or *gender* are the variables composed of those two attributes. The variable *occupation* is composed of attributes such as *farmer, professor, truck driver,* and so forth. *Social class* is a variable composed of a set of attributes such as *upper class, middle class, lower class,* or some similar set of divisions.

The relationship between attributes and variables lies at the heart of both description and explanation in science. For example, we might describe a college class in terms of the variable *sex* by reporting the observed frequencies of the attributes *male* and *female*: "The class is 60 percent men and 40 percent women." An unemployment rate can be thought of as a description of the variable *employment status* of a labor force in terms of the attributes *employed* and *unemployed*. Even the report of family income for a city is a summary of attributes composing that variable: $3,124; $10,980; $35,000; and so forth.

The relationship between attributes and variables is more complicated in the case of explanation and gets to the heart of the variable language of scientific theory. Here's a simple example, involving two variables, *education* and *prejudice*. For the sake of

simplicity, let's assume that the variable *education* has only two attributes: *educated* and *uneducated*. (Chapters 5 and 6 will address the issue of how such things are defined and measured.) Similarly, let's give the variable *prejudice* two attributes: *prejudiced* and *unprejudiced*.

Now let's suppose that 90 percent of the uneducated are prejudiced, while the other 10 percent are unprejudiced. And let's suppose that 30 percent of the educated people are prejudiced, while the other 70 percent are unprejudiced. This is illustrated graphically in Figure 1-1A.

Figure 1-1A illustrates a *relationship* or *association* between the variables *education* and *prejudice*. This relationship can be seen in terms of the pairings of attributes on the two variables. There are two predominant pairings: (1) those who are educated and unprejudiced and (2) those who are uneducated and prejudiced. Here are two other useful ways of seeing that relationship.

First, let's suppose that we play a game in which we bet on your ability to guess whether a person is prejudiced or unprejudiced. I'll pick the people one at a time (not telling you which one I've picked) and you have to guess whether the person is prejudiced. We'll do it for all 20 people in Figure 1-1A. Your best strategy in that case would be to always guess *prejudiced*, since 12 out of the 20 are categorized that way. Thus, you'll get 12 right and 8 wrong, for a net success of 4.

Now let's suppose that when I pick a person from the figure, I have to tell you whether the person is educated or uneducated. Your best strategy now would be to guess *prejudiced* for each uneducated person and *unprejudiced* for each educated person. If you followed that strategy, you'd get 16 right and 4 wrong. Your improvement in guessing prejudice by knowing education is an illustration of what I mean by the variables being related. (This procedure, by the way, provides the basis for the statistical

Figure 1-1   Illustration of Relationships between Two Variables (two possibilities)

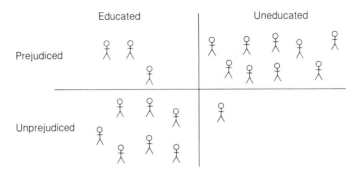

A. The uneducated are more prejudiced than the educated.

B. There is no apparent relationship between education and prejudice.

calculation *lambda*, to be discussed in Chapter 17.)

Second, by contrast, let's consider how the 20 people would be distributed if education and prejudice were *unrelated* to one another. This is illustrated in Figure 1-1B. Notice that half the people are educated and half are uneducated. Also notice that 12 of the 20 (60 percent) are prejudiced. If 6 of the 10 people in each group were prejudiced, we would conclude that the two variables were unrelated to each other. Then knowing a person's education would not be of any value to you in guessing whether that person was prejudiced.

We're going to be looking at the nature of relationships between variables in some depth in Part Four of this book. In particular, we'll see some of the ways in which

relationships can be discovered and interpreted in research analysis. It is important that you have a general understanding of relationships now, however, in order to appreciate the logic of social scientific theories.

Theories describe the relationships that might logically be expected among variables. Often, the expectation involves the notion of *causation*. A person's attributes on one variable are expected to cause, predispose, or encourage a particular attribute on another variable. In the example just illustrated, it appeared that a person's being educated or uneducated caused that person to be unprejudiced or prejudiced, respectively. It seems that there is something about being educated that leads people to be less prejudiced than if they are uneducated.

As I'll discuss in more detail later in the book, education and prejudice in this example would be regarded as **independent** and **dependent variables**, respectively. These two concepts are implicit in deterministic, causal models, and we'll devote all of Chapter 3 to the notion of causation. In this example, we assume that levels of prejudice are determined or caused by something; prejudice depends on something, hence it is called the dependent variable. That which the dependent variable depends on is called the independent variable; in this case, prejudice depends on education. Although the educational levels of the people being studied vary, that variation is independent of prejudice.

Notice, at the same time, that educational variations can be found to depend on something else—such as our subjects' parents' educational levels. People whose parents have a lot of education are more likely to get a lot of education themselves than those whose parents have little education. In this latter relationship, the subject's education would be the dependent variable, and the parents' education would be the independent variable. In "cause/effect" terms, the independent variable is the cause and the dependent variable the effect.

Returning to our example, the discussion of Figure 1–1 has involved the interpretation of data. We looked at the distribution of the 20 people in terms of the two variables. In the construction of a social scientific theory, we would derive an expectation regarding the relationship between the two variables based on what we know about each. We know, for example, that education exposes people to a wide range of cultural variation, to diverse points of view—in short, it broadens their perspectives. Prejudice, on the other hand, represents a narrower perspective. Logically, then, we would expect that education and prejudice would be somewhat incompatible. We might arrive at an expectation, therefore,

that increasing education would reduce prejudice, an expectation that would be supported by the observations to be made later.

Notice that the theory has to do with the two variables, education and prejudice, not with people per se. People are, as I indicated before, the carriers of those two variables, so the relationship between the variables can only be seen by observing people. Ultimately, however, the theory is constructed of a variable language. It describes the associations that might logically be expected to exist between particular attributes of different variables.

These, then, are some of the presuppositions upon which social scientific theories and research are based. Chapter 2 will show you the nature of the theories and research methods that have been created on that foundation. Then the remainder of the book will be devoted to an elaboration of the research methods themselves.

MAIN POINTS

- Inquiry is a natural human activity.

- People seek general understanding about the world around them.

- Much of what we know, we know by agreement rather than by experience.

- Tradition and authority are important sources of understanding.

- When we understand through experience, we make observations and seek patterns of regularities in what we observe.

- In day-to-day inquiry, we often make mistakes. Science offers protection against such mistakes.

- Whereas people often observe inaccurately, such errors are avoided in science by making observation a careful and deliberate activity.

■ Sometimes we jump to general conclusions on the basis of only a few observations. Scientists avoid overgeneralization through replication, the repeating of studies.

■ Once a conclusion has been reached, we sometimes ignore evidence that contradicts that conclusion, only paying attention to evidence that confirms it. Scientists commit themselves in advance to a set of observations to be made regardless of whether a pattern seems to be emerging early.

■ When confronted with contradictory evidence, all of us make up explanations to explain away the contradictions. Often this involves making assumptions about facts not actually observed. Scientists, however, make further observations to test those assumptions.

■ Sometimes people simply reason illogically. Scientists avoid this by being as careful and deliberate in their reasoning as in their observations. Moreover, the public nature of science means that scientists have their colleagues looking over their shoulders.

■ The same support of colleagues protects scientists from being too ego-involved in their conclusions.

■ Where people often decide they understand something and stop looking for new answers, scientists—as a group—ultimately regard all issues as open.

■ Science has no place for the common human conclusion that some things are ultimately unexplainable.

■ Social scientific theory addresses what is, not what should be. Theory should not be confused with philosophy or belief.

■ Social science is focused on logical and persistent regularities in social life.

■ Social scientists are interested in explaining human aggregates, not individuals.

■ An attribute is a characteristic, such as male or young.

■ A variable is a logical set of attributes. Sex, for example, is a variable made up of the attributes male and female.

■ While social scientists observe people, they are primarily interested in finding relationships that connect variables.

REVIEW QUESTIONS AND EXERCISES

1. Review the common errors of human inquiry discussed in the chapter. Find a magazine or newspaper article, or perhaps a letter to the editor, that illustrates one of those errors. Discuss how a scientist would avoid making that error.

2. List five social variables and the attributes making up those variables.

ADDITIONAL READINGS

Babbie, Earl, *Observing Ourselves: Essays in Social Research* (Belmont, CA: Wadsworth, 1986). A collection of essays that expand some of the philosophical issues raised in this book, including objectivity, paradigms, determinism, concepts, reality, causation, values.

Butterfield, Herbert, *The Origins of Modern Science* (New York: Macmillan, 1960). An excellent, readable history of the development of science that illustrates many of the central issues involved in scientific inquiry. Understanding some of the stages through which science has passed can clarify what it is that now distinguishes scientific inquiry from nonscientific inquiry.

Irvine, William, *Apes, Angels, and Victorians* (New York: Meridian Books, 1959). An account of the social and religious furor that surrounded Darwin's publications on evolution and natural selection and Thomas Huxley's propounding of Darwin's ideas.

In addition to casting science within a social context, this engaging little book offers excellent insights into the personal doubts and vacillations of a great scientist at work.

Toben, Bob, *Space-Time and Beyond* (New York: E. P. Dutton, 1975). An absolutely delightful look at the tentativeness of what we know about physical reality. Using a cartoon format, Toben has presented some of the frontier issues of contemporary physics. I've included this book both because it's so much fun and because it fosters a healthy openness as you set about mastering the logic and skills of social science.

Watson, James, *The Double-Helix* (New York: New American Library, 1968). An informal and candid research biography describing the discovery of the DNA molecule, written by a principal in the drama. This account should serve as a healthy antidote to the traditional view of science as totally cool, rational, value-free, and objectively impersonal.

2

Theory and Research

INTRODUCTION

One of the livelier academic debates of recent years has concerned the scientific status of those disciplines gathered under the heading of social sciences: sociology, political science, social psychology, economics, anthropology, and sometimes fields such as geography, history, communications, and other composite and specialty fields. Basically at issue is whether human behavior can be studied scientifically, and academicians have disagreed about calling these disciplines *sciences*.

Opposition to the idea of social sciences has risen both within the fields and outside them. Within the fields, the movement toward social science has represented a redirection and, in some cases, a renaming of established academic disciplines. Increasingly, departments of government have been replaced by departments of political science. There are today few university departments of social studies, while sociology departments abound.

In many cases, the movement toward social science has represented a greater emphasis on systematic explanation where the previous emphasis was on description. In political science, it has meant a greater emphasis on explaining political behavior rather than describing political institutions. In anthropology, it has represented a lessening of the emphasis on ethnography. The growth of such subfields as econometrics has had this effect in economics, as has historiography in history. Some geographers have moved from the enumeration of imports and exports to mathematical models of migration. Quite understandably, professionals trained and experienced in the more traditional orientations of these fields have objected to the new directions.

This book is grounded in the position that human social behavior can be subjected to scientific study as legitimately as can the physicist's atoms, the biologist's cells, and

so forth. This view needs to be seen in the context of the earlier discussion of what science is, however. This chapter describes the overall logic of social scientific inquiry. We'll look more closely at the structure of social scientific theories and how they are created. In particular, we'll examine the links between theory and research.

By the time you complete this chapter, you should have a clear understanding of what is meant by the phrase "social science" and of what can and cannot be done in social scientific inquiry.

THE CREATION OF SOCIAL SCIENCE THEORY

In Chapter 1, we looked at some of the foundations of social scientific research as a mode of inquiry involving both logic and observation. Now we'll examine the relationship between theory and research. First comes a look at "the scientific method" as it is traditionally taught. Following that, we'll see there are actually two models describing the relationship between theory and research in the practice of social science. Having introduced those two models, later sections of the chapter will examine each in more detail.

The Traditional Model of Science

In my experience as a teacher, I've found that university instruction in "the scientific method"—especially in the physical sciences—tends to create a particular picture in students' minds of how science operates. Although this traditional model of science tells only a part of the story, it is important that you understand the basic logic of that model.

There are three main elements in the traditional model of science, which are typically presented in a chronological order of execution. They are *theory, operationalization,* and *observation.* Let's look at each in turn.

Theory   According to the traditional model of science, the scientist begins with an interest in some aspect of the real world. Suppose, for example, you were interested in discovering some of the broad social factors that affect the stability of families. What kinds of major events in society at large threaten the stability and survival of existing families and produce marriages that do not last?

As you thought about those questions, you'd probably come eventually to "mass crises" as one possible answer. Wars, droughts, floods, mass unemployment, and similar society-wide problems would seem to be an important source of instability in marriages and families. That's an idea Sam Stouffer (1937) had when he looked at the topic. Stouffer found a number of logical reasons why mass crises could affect family stability. Most obviously, major crises required a great many adjustments in the daily lives of individuals and families. To the extent that stability is supported by routine and habit, mass crises would upset that pattern. Moreover, in some crises, such as disasters, government and other agencies often step in to take over some of the functions of families and family members. When the disaster results in families' being unable to support themselves economically, the government—through welfare or similar programs—may take on the job of economic support. Since that takes away the customary function of the family's breadwinner, it is likely to produce repercussions.

Stouffer's primary interest, however, concerned the formation of new families. Did broad social crises lead to marriages that would not last? Even more specifically, he was interested in what he called impul-

sive marriages: those entered into "mainly as a device to legalize sexual intercourse, carrying few obligations and no necessary expectation of union or of children to carry on the family name" (1937:138). In addition, did social crises produce more marriages that crossed religious, ethnic, and socioeconomic lines—and more forced marriages, those in which the bride was pregnant at the time of marriage?

If you had been Sam Stouffer studying this matter in the late 1930s, you would have had little trouble selecting a particular crisis for testing your ideas. The Great Depression of 1929 and the early 1930s would have been your obvious choice, as it was Stouffer's. On a theoretical level, Stouffer found it was possible to derive two contradictory expectations regarding the relationship between the depression and impulsive marriages.

On the one hand, "the depression presumably weakened the respect for custom and tradition with respect to economic matters; therefore it might be inferred that this weakening carried over to other aspects of life" (1937:139). He also reasoned that the depression could have weakened parental authority, through the increase of mobility and other factors. It could produce more marriages entered into without the knowledge of the brides' or grooms' parents. Finally, with the assurance of "relief" (the forerunner of welfare), young people might get married even if they were not sure they could afford it. Thus, there were a number of reasons for expecting that the depression would produce an increase in the number of impulsive marriages.

At the same time, Stouffer saw a counterargument. The same factors that produced a weakening of young people's commitment to tradition and custom might lead them to avoid marriage altogether. Stouffer reasoned:

Why, indeed, it may be asked, should couples whose principal object in marriage was the legalization of sexual intercourse bother about those legalities, once the older conceptions of marriage had been altered? Would not the effect of the depression be to increase casual and extra-legal unions rather than marriages with lightly assumed obligations?

(1937:139)

In terms of theoretical logic, two contradictory expectations could be argued for. It could be argued that the depression would increase or decrease the number of impulsive marriages. Although Stouffer's theoretical analysis had greatly clarified the possible relationships among variables, the reasoning alone could not answer his question with certainty. He needed to test his theory with empirical observation.

Operationalization   To settle the question of depressions and impulsive marriages, then, it would make sense to simply observe whether more such marriages happen during depressions. But how would you recognize an impulsive marriage if you saw one? Even if you thought you'd recognize one, where would you look for it? The second step in the traditional model of science is addressed to such questions.

Operationalization refers simply to a specification of the steps, procedures, or operations that you will go through in actually measuring and identifying the variables you want to observe. Chapter 6 of this book is devoted solely to that topic. In the present example, it involves (1) how you'll go about looking for an impulsive marriage and (2) how you'll know one when you find it. Let's begin with the strategy for looking.

When Stouffer initially decided to study families and the depression, he planned to undertake a large-scale survey. He would have selected a large sample of people—perhaps a sample purposely designed to include people who got married before, during, and after the depression. He would have designed a questionnaire asking them about their marriages and the events leading up to these

marriages, and he would then have been in a position to see any changes that took place during the depression. Like other researchers, he requested a research grant to cover the costs of his proposed study. Like many other researchers, he was turned down—no money.

Stouffer now realized that he wouldn't be able to conduct the study he had envisioned. Still, he was interested in answering his research question. What Sam Stouffer did next is a mark of his special genius as a researcher—he turned his attention to thinking up studies he could conduct. Would it be possible, he asked, to recognize impulsive marriages among all the marriages routinely reported in official government statistics? He found that a reasonable approximation was at least possible, as the following statement shows:

No single index would seem adequate. Only if all, or most, of several indexes showed a strong tendency in the same direction, would there be a basis for inference that the shift during the depression was toward, or away from, "impulsive" marriages. Among such indexes might be the following:
    1. Marriage in a community other than residence of the bride and groom. . . .
    2. Marriage by a magistrate rather than a clergyman.
    3. Divorce or separation within five years of marriage, especially if no children had been born.

(1937:140)

Stouffer used the same operationalization process for mixed and forced marriages. In each case, he was able to find indicators of what he had in mind. Some were found in regularly published government statistics (foreign, U.S., state, local); some, such as indicators for religiously mixed marriages, appeared in nongovernment publications.

In operationalizing his inquiry into the effects of the depression on the family, Stouffer had to handle one additional problem. Many of the indicators he intended to examine had been changing steadily over time, quite aside from the depression. The number of religiously mixed marriages had been increasing, for example. His research question, then, had to be refined: Did the rate of increase go up during the depression years? Ultimately, Stouffer had a clear plan about how to look for the answer to his research questions and how to recognize and interpret the answers once he found them.

Observation   The final step in the traditional model of science involves actual observation, looking at the world and making measurements of what is seen. Having developed theoretical clarity and expectations and having created a strategy for looking, all that remains is to look at the way things are. Sometimes this step involves conducting experiments, sometimes interviewing people, sometimes visiting what you're interested in and watching it. Sometimes the observations are structured around the testing of specific hypotheses; sometimes the inquiry is less structured. In Stouffer's case, it meant poring through published statistics in search of data relevant to his operationalization.

In the case of nonresident marriages, he found an increase, followed by a reversal as the depression receded. For civil marriages (as distinguished from religious ones), he found that although the information was recorded on marriage licenses, it was not tabulated and reported in published statistics in the United States. The depression, however, was hardly limited to the United States: much of the world suffered, and Stouffer discovered that such statistics were reported in Australia. There, moreover, the percentage of civil marriages increased rapidly during the depression years and decreased as the depression waned. Other variables were found in data relating to other states and countries.

Notice the format of Stouffer's research at this point. As he approached each set of statistics, he had certain expectations about the pattern he would find in the numbers if a particular theoretical explanation was accurate. He had operationalized forced marriages, for example, as those that resulted in births within seven months. He found data on this question available on Australia. If the depression increased forced marriages, he would expect to find a higher percentage of marriages resulting in early births during the depression years. Here's what he found (1937:151):

Year	Percentage of Marriages Resulting in Early Births
1921	22.2
1922	21.6
1923	21.0
1924	20.8
1925	20.9
1926	21.4
1927	22.0
1928	23.5
1929	23.3
1930	25.7
1931	27.6
1932	24.3
1933	23.6
1934	20.8

The dramatic increase in the number of forced marriages—as operationalized by Stouffer—in the years immediately following the onset of the depression (1930 and 1931) supported the theoretical expectation. In themselves, of course, these particular data did not prove the case; they did not provide definitive evidence that the

Figure 2-1 The Traditional Image of Science

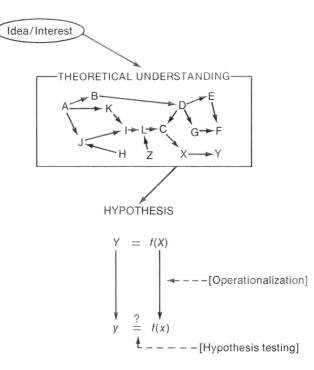

depression weakened the stability of the family. These data, however, were part of a weight of evidence that Stouffer amassed. To recall his earlier words, he discovered that "several indexes showed a strong tendency in the same direction." As you can see, observation in social science can take many forms other than simply looking at events with your eyes.

I have chosen this illustration for several reasons. First, it demonstrates the traditional model of scientific research, moving from theory to operationalization to observation. Second, it is more realistic than the hypothetical example of a simple physics experiment. Primarily, I suppose, I have wanted to share Stouffer's special genius with you.

Figure 2-1 provides a schematic diagram of the traditional model of scientific inquiry. In it, we see the researcher beginning with an interest in something or an idea about it. Next comes the development of a theoretical understanding. The theoretical considerations result in a **hypothesis**, or an expectation about the way things ought to be in the world if the theoretical expectations are correct. The notation $Y = f(X)$ is a conventional way of saying that Y (for example, forced marriages) is a function of (is in some way affected by) X (for example, the depression). At that level, however, X and Y have general rather than specific meanings.

In the operationalization process, general concepts are translated into specific indicators and procedures. The lowercase x, for example, is a concrete indicator of capital X. This operationalization process results in the formation of a testable hypothesis: for example, did the percentage of marriages resulting in early births actually increase with the onset of the depression? Observations aimed at finding out are part of what is typically called **hypothesis testing**.

Although this traditional model of science provides a clear and understandable guide to how you could study something carefully and logically, it presents only a part of the picture. Let's look at the other parts now.

Two Logical Systems

The traditional model of science discussed above uses what is called *deductive logic* (see **deduction** in Glossary). In this section, I will examine deductive logic as it fits into social scientific research and, particularly, contrast it with *inductive logic* (see **induction** in Glossary). W. I. B. Beveridge, a philosopher of science, describes these two systems of logic as follows:

Logicians distinguish between inductive reasoning (from particular instances to general principles, from facts to theories) and deductive reasoning (from the general to the particular, applying a theory to a particular case). In induction one starts from observed data and develops a generalization which explains the relationships between the objects observed. On the other hand, in deductive reasoning one starts from some general law and applies it to a particular instance.

(Beveridge 1950:113)

The classical illustration of deductive logic is the familiar syllogism "All men are mortal; Socrates is a man; therefore Socrates is mortal." This syllogism presents a theory and its operationalization. To prove it, you might then perform an empirical test of Socrates' mortality. That is essentially the approach discussed as the traditional model above.

Using inductive logic, you might begin by noting that Socrates is mortal and observing a number of other men as well. You might then note that all the *observed* men were mortals, thereby arriving at the tentative conclusion that *all* men are mortal.

Figure 2-2 shows a graphic comparison of the deductive and inductive methods. In both cases, we are interested in the relationship between the number of hours spent studying for an exam and the grade earned on that exam. Using the deductive method, we would begin by examining the matter logically. Doing well on an exam reflects a student's ability to recall and manipulate information. Both of these abilities should be increased by exposure to the information before the exam. In this sort of fashion, we would arrive at a *hypothesis* suggesting a positive relationship between the number of hours spent studying and the grade earned on the exam. We say *positive* because we expect grades to increase as the hours of studying increase. If increased hours produced decreased grades, that would be called a *negative* relationship. The hypothesis is represented by the line in Part I(a) of Figure 2-2.

Our next step, using the deductive method, would be to make observations relevant to testing our hypothesis. The shaded area in Part I(b) of the figure represents perhaps hundreds of observations of different students, noting how many hours they studied and what grades they got. Finally, in Part I(c) of the figure, we compare the hypothesis and the observations. Since observations in the real world seldom if ever match our expectations perfectly, we must decide whether the match is close enough to consider the hypothesis confirmed. Put differently, can we conclude that the hypothesis describes the general pattern that exists, granting some variations in real life?

Now let's turn to addressing the same research question, using the inductive method. In this case, we would begin—as

Figure 2-2   Deductive and Inductive Methods

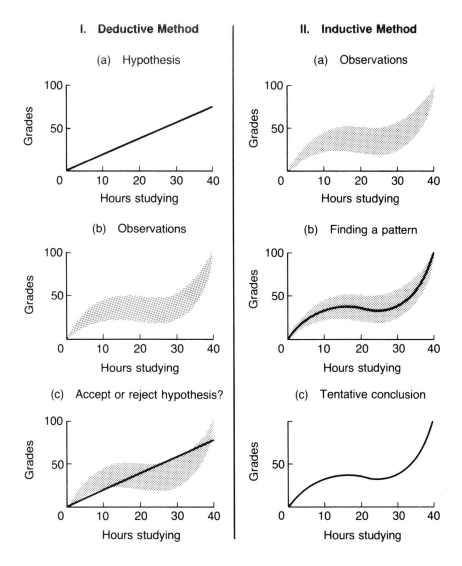

in Part II(a) of the figure—with a set of observations. Curious about the relationship between hours spent studying and grades earned, we might simply arrange to collect some relevant data. Then we'd look for a pattern that best represented or summarized our observations. In Part II(b) of the figure, the pattern is shown as a curved line running through the center of the curving mass of points.

The pattern found among the points in this case suggests that with 1 to 15 hours of studying, each additional hour generally produces a higher grade on the exam. With 15 to about 25 hours, however, more study seems to slightly lower the grade. Studying more than 25 hours, on the other hand, results in a return to the initial pattern: more hours produce higher grades. Using the inductive method, then, we end up with

Figure 2-3 The Wheel of Science

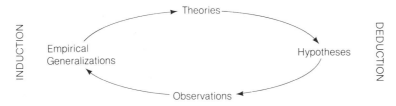

a *tentative* conclusion as to the pattern of the relationship between the two variables. The conclusion is tentative because the observations we have made cannot be taken as a test of the pattern—those observations are the *source* of the pattern we've created.

What do you suppose would happen next in an actual research project? We'd try to find a logical explanation for the pattern discovered in the data, just as Stouffer tried to find a logical explanation for the discovery that the MPs were more likely than the air corpsmen to think the promotion system was fair (recall Chapter 1). Eventually, we'd arrive at an explanation—one that would generate further expectations about what should be observed in the real world. Then, we'd look again.

In actual practice, then, theory and research interact through a never-ending alternation of deduction, induction, deduction, and so forth. Walter Wallace (1971) has represented this process nicely as a circle, which is presented in a modified form in Figure 2-3.

In the Wallace model, theories generate hypotheses, hypotheses suggest observations, observations produce generalizations, and those generalizations result in modifications of the theory. The modified theory then suggests somewhat modified hypotheses and a new set of observations, which produce somewhat revised generali-

zations, further modifying the theory. What I like most about this model is that there is clearly no beginning or ending point. You can begin anywhere in examining what interests you.

Thus, when Stouffer began wondering whether the Great Depression would have any consequences on the stability of families, he turned to a logical derivation of hypotheses, making observations later for the purpose of testing those hypotheses. When Emile Durkheim (1897) looked at suicide, on the other hand, he pored through table after table of official statistics on suicide rates in different areas, and he was struck by the fact that Protestant countries consistently had higher suicide rates than Catholic ones. Why should that be the case? His initial observations led him to create a theory of religion, social integration, anomie, and suicide. His theoretical explanations led to further hypotheses and further observations.

In summary, the scientific norm of logical reasoning provides a bridge between theory and research—a two-way bridge. (The box entitled "Components of Scientific Theory" illustrates its "bridge" more graphically.) Scientific inquiry in practice typically involves an alternation between deduction and induction. During the deductive phase, we reason *toward* observations; during the inductive phase, we rea-

Components of Scientific Theory

by Michael R. Leming
Department of Sociology, St. Olaf College

According to George Homans, scientific theory is an explanation of a phenomenon by the use of a deductive system of empirical propositions. The three basic components of scientific theory are (1) a conceptual scheme, (2) a set of propositions stating relationships between properties or variables, and (3) a context for verification.

The model of a suspension bridge serves as a good illustration of the relationship between scientific theory's three components. Bridges are constructed out of girders and rivets and tied into both banks of the river. In similar fashion, a theory consists of concepts ("rivets") and propositions ("girders") tied into an empirical base of support. It is the relationship between the components that makes for a bridge or theory. A disorganized pile of girders and rivets are not sufficient components for what we would call a bridge. Likewise concepts, propositions, and observations are not sufficient in themselves for scientific theory.

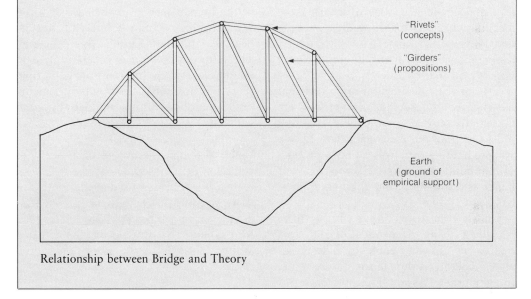

Relationship between Bridge and Theory

son *from* observations. Both logic and observation are essential. In practice, both deduction and induction are routes to the construction of social theories. Let's look a little more closely at how each of the two methods operates in that regard.

DEDUCTIVE THEORY CONSTRUCTION

What's involved in deductive theory construction and hypothesis testing? To begin, here's an overview of some of the terminology associated with deductive theory construction. Then we'll look at how you might go about constructing a deductive theory.

Terms Used in Theory Construction

In this section, I want to provide definitions of some of the terms used in connection with the creation of scientific theories. I've already been using some of these terms, because I knew you had a general idea of what they meant in normal language. Now, however, it is important to examine their meanings with some attention.

Reality   This seems as good a place to begin as anywhere. I suspect you already know that philosophers have been debating the meaning of reality for thousands of years, and they haven't come to a satisfactory, lasting conclusion about it yet. I won't improve on that record.

One of the fundamental questions that has engaged philosophers is whether there is actually anything out there, existing independent of our experience. Is the book you are holding real, or is it only a product of your mind? Your mind tells you that your hands feel the book, but then your mind has lied to you before.

Unable ultimately to prove whether there is *really* a reality independent of our experience, we all—laypeople and scientists alike—operate as though there were something out there. As you'll see, however, this sticky issue will keep recurring.

Objectivity and Subjectivity   Another way of stating the issue of reality is in terms of objectivity and subjectivity. We recognize that some things fall in the realm of attitudes, opinions, and points of view: we say that the question of whether Beethoven or Mozart was the better composer is a *sub-*

jective matter: dependent on the experiences of the person making such a judgment. But we feel that the existence of the book in your hands is an *objective* matter: independent of your experience of it. But whereas *objective* is typically defined as "independent of mind," our awareness of what might objectively exist comes to us through our minds. As a working principle, we substitute **intersubjectivity** for objectivity. If several of us agree that something exists, we treat that thing as though it had objective existence. This book can be seen as a discussion of the logic and procedures by which social scientists come to agree on what's real.

Observation   In the above discussions, the "experience" of whatever may or may not really exist typically refers to the operation of the human senses: in the case of social research, this is typically limited to seeing, hearing, and—less commonly—touching. The term *observation* is generally used in reference to such information gathering. (Part 3 of this book is devoted to the many "modes of observation" employed by social scientists.)

Fact   Although the notion of a *fact* is as complex for philosophers as the notion of reality, it is generally used in the context of social scientific research to mean some phenomenon that has been observed. It is a fact, for example, that Ronald Reagan defeated Walter Mondale in the 1984 presidential election.

Law   Abraham Kaplan (1964:91) defines laws as universal generalizations about classes of facts. The law of gravity is a classical example: bodies are attracted to each other in proportion to their masses and inversely proportionate to the distance separating them.

Laws must be truly universal, however, and not merely accidental patterns found among a specific set of facts. It is a fact, Kaplan points out (1964:92), that in each of the U. S. presidential elections from 1920 to 1960, the major candidate with the longest name won. That is not a law, however, as shown in four of the next five elections. It was a coincidence.

Laws are sometimes also called *principles* and are important statements about what is so, and we speak of them as being "discovered." Laws are not created by scientists. Also, laws in and of themselves do not explain anything. They just summarize the way things are. Explanation is a function of theory, and theories *are* created, as we'll see next.

Theory A *theory* is a systematic explanation for the observed facts and laws that relate to a particular aspect of life: juvenile delinquency, for example, or perhaps social stratification, political revolution, or the like. Jonathan Turner (1974:2) has examined several elements of theory. We are going to consider three of those briefly: concepts, variables, and statements.

Concepts Turner calls *concepts* the "basic building blocks of theory" (1974:3). They are abstract elements representing classes of phenomena within the field of study. The concepts relevant to a theory of juvenile delinquency, for example, would include *juvenile* and *delinquency* for starters. *Peer group*—the people you hang around with and identify with—would be another relevant concept. *Social class* and *ethnicity* would undoubtedly be relevant concepts in a theory of juvenile delinquency. *School performance* might also be relevant to a theory of juvenile delinquency.

Variables A variable is a concept's empirical counterpart. Where concepts are in the domain of theory, variables are a matter of observation and measurement. Thus, variables require more specificity than con-

cepts. For example, as a variable, income might be specified as annual family income, as reported in response to a survey question. Chapters 5 and 6 will pursue this matter in considerable detail.

Statements There are several types of statements comprising a theory. Principles or laws, as discussed above, are one type. *Axioms* are fundamental assertions—taken to be true—upon which the theory is grounded. *Propositions* are conclusions drawn about the relationships among concepts, based on the logical interrelationships among the axioms.

In a theory of juvenile delinquency, we might begin with axioms such as "Everyone desires material comforts" and "The ability to obtain material comforts legally is greater for the upper class than for the working class." From these axiomatic beginnings, we might reasonably conclude that working class youths would be more likely to break the law to gain material comforts than would upper class youths. This conclusion would constitute a proposition. *Hypotheses* are specified expectations about empirical reality, derived from propositions. Pursuing our present example, a theory might contain the hypothesis "Working class youths have higher delinquency rates than upper class youths." Such a hypothesis could then be tested through research, as we saw in the earlier example of family stability and the depression.

We'll return shortly to an examination of how theories are actually created, and we'll see these various elements in action. Prior to that, however, I want to consider the contexts from which theories emerge.

Paradigm No one ever starts out with a completely clean slate to create a theory. The concepts that are the building blocks of theory are not created out of nothing. I know that when I mentioned juvenile delinquency as an example of a topic for theory construction you already had some implicit ideas about it. If I had asked you to list some concepts that would be relevant to a theory of juvenile delinquency, you would have been able to make suggestions. We might say that you already have a general point of view or frame of reference.

A *paradigm* is a fundamental model or scheme that organizes our view of something. While a paradigm doesn't necessarily answer important questions, it tells us where to look for the answers. And, as we'll see repeatedly, where you look largely determines the answers you'll find.

Thomas Kuhn describes the importance of paradigms this way:

. . . one of the things a scientific community acquires with a paradigm is a criterion for choosing problems that, while the paradigm is taken for granted, can be assumed to have solutions. To a great extent these are the only problems that the community will admit as scientific or encourage its members to undertake. Other problems, including many that had previously been standard, are rejected as metaphysical, as the concern of another discipline, or sometimes as just too problematic to be worth the time. A paradigm can, for that matter, even insulate the community from those socially important problems that are not reducible to the puzzle form, because they cannot be stated in terms of the conceptual and instrumental tools the paradigm supplies.

(1970:37)

Kuhn's chief interest was in how science advances. While some progress is the slow, steady, and incremental improvement of established paradigms—Kuhn calls this "normal science"—he suggests that major scientific progress takes the form of "paradigm shifts," as established, agreed-on paradigms are thrown out in favor of new ones. Thus, for example, Newtonian physics was replaced by Einstein's relativity in what Kuhn calls a "scientific revolution."

Three major paradigms—interaction-ism, functionalism, and conflict theory—dominate inquiry in sociology at the present. The *interactionist* paradigm sees social life as a process of interactions among individuals. Coming from this paradigm to address juvenile delinquency, for example, you might focus on the ways in which young people interact as peers. How do young people gain approval in the eyes of friends, for example? How do juvenile gangs recruit and initiate new members? Or, differently, how do parents go about providing good or bad role models for their children? These are examples of the kinds of questions you might ask if you were approaching juvenile delinquency from the interactionist paradigm.

The *functionalist* or *social systems* paradigm focuses on the organizational structure of social life. What are the components of society, and how are those components interrelated? From this paradigm, you might pay special attention to the impact of broad economic conditions on delinquency rates: does delinquency increase during periods of high unemployment, for example? Or does the increased complexity of modern society make it harder for young people to understand what's right and what's wrong? Attention might be paid to the causes of failure in social control, the breakdown of law and order.

The *conflict* paradigm describes social life as a struggle among competing individuals and groups. It is, for example, a competition between the haves and the have-nots, as in the Marxist "class struggle." From this paradigm, you might see juvenile delinquency as a response of the working class to their oppression by the rulers of society. Or, quite differently, you might see delinquency among young people as a way of competing for status.

Notice that the "class struggle" example has a social systems flavor to it, just as the "competition for status" example has an interactionist element. These three paradigms are not mutually exclusive. Nonetheless, each casts a somewhat different light (as well as shadow) on social life. Paradigms such as these provide the source of concepts and axioms upon which to build theories.

Getting Started

The first step in deductive theory construction is to pick a topic that interests you. It can be broad, such as "What's the structure of society?" or narrower, as in "Why do people support the Moral Majority?" Whatever the topic, it should be something you're interested in understanding and explaining.

Once you've picked your topic, you should undertake an inventory of what is known or thought about it. In part, this means writing down your own observations and ideas about it. Beyond that, you'll want to learn what other scholars have said about it. You can talk to other people, and you'll want to read what others have written about it. Appendix B of this book provides guidelines for using the library, and you'll probably spend a lot of time there.

As part of this process, you should be identifying the key concepts involved in your topic. If you want to learn why people support the Moral Majority, for example, you'll need to specify the concept of *supporting*. You may want to distinguish (1) formal membership in the organization, (2) taking actions aligned with the organization, and (3) holding opinions associated with the Moral Majority. In the realm of opinions, you'll probably deal with the concepts of *liberalism* and *conservatism*, and you'll want to distinguish social, economic, religious, and foreign policy liberalism/conservatism.

Here's what pollster Daniel Yankelovich had to say about precisely this problem:

Last year, 14 months after the Reverend Jerry Falwell founded the organization, the *New York Times* reported its membership at 400,000. Soon after, the Moral Majority claimed that it registered 3 million new voters in the 1980 Presidential election. This year, an ABC-TV survey concluded that 2.9 percent of those interviewed —or a projected 4.6 million Americans— supported the Moral Majority's "attempt to influence [TV] programs to conform to their standards and values" and tentatively projected a membership of 10.6 million. A *New York Times*/ CBS Poll suggested the Moral Majority could be equated with evangelical Christians and thereby implied that the number of people who share the organization's outlook might extend to the stratospheric height of 67 million.

(1981:5)

After noting the large gap separating 400,000 and 67 million, Yankelovich went on to say, "What we really want to know is whether the Moral Majority is a passing fad or will take hold in the mainstream of American life" (1981:6). This example points to the importance of *specifying* the variable you wish to study.

Your research will also identify variables that will be relevant to the topic under consideration: age, sex, race, social class, education, etc. If you are asking why people support the Moral Majority, you'll need to identify variables that may hold the answer. (Yankelovich, incidentally, suggested that parents' concern for their children lay at the heart of support for the Moral Majority.)

By the same token, your preliminary research will probably uncover consistent patterns discovered by prior scholars. In general, older people are more conservative than younger ones. Upper-class people tend to be more economically conservative and more socially liberal than working-class people. Findings such as these will be very useful to you in creating your own theory.

In this context, I want to say a word or two on the value of introspection. If you are able to look at your own personal processes—including reactions, fears, and prejudices you aren't especially proud of—

you may be able to gain important insights into human behavior in general. I don't mean to say that everyone thinks like you, but introspection can be a useful source of insights.

Constructing Your Theory

While theory construction is not a lockstep affair, the following list of elements in theory construction should organize the activity for you.

1. Specify the topic.

2. Specify the range of phenomena your theory addresses. Will your theory apply to all of human social life, will it apply only to Americans, only to young people, or what?

3. Identify and specify your major concepts and variables.

4. Assemble what is known (propositions) about the relationships among those variables.

5. Reason logically from those propositions to the specific topic you are examining.

We've already discussed items (1) through (3) above, so let's focus now on (4) and (5). As you identify the relevant concepts and discover what has already been learned about them, you can begin creating a propositional structure that explains the topic under study. For the most part, social scientists have not created formal, propositional theories. Still, it is useful to look at a well-reasoned example.

George Homans is a sociologist who has concerned himself with the formal development of *exchange theory*—looking at human behavior in terms of the relative costs and benefits of alternative actions. Here's a portion of Homans's theoretical reasoning regarding levels of education in industrial and preindustrial societies.

1. Men are more likely to perform an activity, the more valuable they perceive the reward of that activity to be.

2. Men are more likely to perform an activity, the more successful they perceive the activity to be in getting that reward.

3. Compared with agricultural societies, a higher proportion of men in industrial societies are prepared to reward activities that involve literacy. (Industrialists want to hire bookkeepers, clerks, persons who can make and read blueprints, manuals, etc.)

4. Therefore, a higher proportion of men in industrial societies will perceive the acquisition of literacy as rewarding.

5. And (by (1)) a higher proportion will attempt to acquire literacy.   (1971:23)

Next, Homans notes the importance of wealth as it is directly and indirectly related to getting an education. With more wealthy people in industrial societies than in agricultural ones, Homans ultimately concludes "the literacy rate is apt to be higher in an industrial than in an agricultural society" (1971:23).

That's enough discussion of the pieces of deductive theory construction. Let's look now at an example of how those pieces fit together in deductive theory construction and empirical research.

An Example of Deductive Theory

The early civil rights movement, beginning in the mid-1950s, was reasonably peaceful outside the deep South, and even there the main acts of violence were perpetrated by whites against blacks. Blacks were, for the most part, nonviolent. All that changed during the summer of 1965. Beginning on August 11, 35 people died and about $200 million in damages were incurred in nearly a week of rioting, burning, and looting in the predominantly black suburb of Watts in Los Angeles.

Although the Watts rioting was triggered by a specific incident involving black residents and white police, that event couldn't account for the extent of the rioting that followed. Most of those who participated in the rioting had nothing to do with the original incident. Who were they, and why did they participate? Many people asked those questions. H. Edward Ransford (1968), a sociologist, was one who suggested an answer.

As he addressed the aftermath of Watts, Ransford found a body of theoretical literature dealing with extreme political behavior. Specifically, social isolation and powerlessness had been linked to political violence by previous scholars. As he surveyed the violent events of Watts, Ransford found it reasonable to expect that those two variables might lie at the base of participation in the rioting. It made sense to imagine that blacks who were isolated from the mainstream white society would feel they had little opportunity for communication. They would, moreover, have little investment in the system, so it was reasonable to expect that they would be more likely to riot than those blacks who were already participating in the mainstream society.

Similarly, the psychological feeling of being powerless to effect peaceful changes in society should further encourage them to seek violent redress of grievances. Thus, Ransford reasoned that blacks who felt powerless would be more likely to riot than those who felt they already had some chance of improving things.

Ransford, then, had theoretical grounds for expecting that isolation and powerlessness would produce political violence. But that's only half of science, as we've already discussed. Very often, the things that seem to make sense don't turn out to be true. So Ransford undertook a research project to find out if his theoretical expectations were borne out by empirical reality.

Ransford chose to find out if isolation and powerlessness produced violence by interviewing a sample of black residents in Watts. To find out the extent to which the subjects in his study were isolated from the mainstream white society, Ransford had his interviewers ask about contacts with whites in the community. Subjects were asked about contacts with whites at work, in their neighborhoods, in organizations, and in other situations. Other questions probed the extent to which they socialized with whites.

Feelings of powerlessness were measured by other questions in the study. For example, subjects were asked whether they agreed or disagreed with the statement "The world is run by the few people in power, and there is not much the little guy can do about it." Similar statements had been used in previous research projects and had been found to give a good indication of general feelings of powerlessness and alienation.

The answers that subjects gave to all these questions made it possible for Ransford to characterize each in terms of (1) isolation and (2) powerlessness. In the simplest characterization, any particular subject could be described as being high or low in terms of isolation from whites and high or low in the feeling of powerlessness. How did these characterizations relate to participation in the rioting?

It seemed unlikely that many subjects would admit to participating in the actual rioting in Watts, since they might fear criminal prosecution. Therefore, Ransford had his interviewers ask two questions. First, subjects were asked: "Would you be willing to use violence to get Negro rights?" About one-fourth of the subjects said they would be willing. The second question asked if they had ever done so. Only 5 percent said they had.

If Ransford's theoretical expectations were correct, he should have found that subjects with high isolation and high powerlessness were more likely to report a willingness to use violence and to report actually doing so than those who rated low on isolation and powerlessness. That's exactly what he found. Of the subjects rated high on isolation, 44 percent said they would be willing to use violence, contrasted with only 17 percent of those rated low on isolation. Similarly, 41 percent of those rated high on powerlessness and only 16 percent of those rated low said they would be willing to use violence. Ransford also found that the reports of actually using violence were strongly related to isolation and powerlessness. Of the 16 people who said they had used violence, for example, all but one scored high on powerlessness, and nearly three-fourths scored high on isolation from whites.

Ransford's conclusions regarding the causes of political violence had both logical and empirical support. His theoretical expectations made sense, and their sense was borne out by the facts. That's not always the case, as you'll recall from the Chapter 1 discussion of Stouffer's study of morale in the Army.

There are two important elements in science, as we've seen: logical integrity and empirical verification. Both are essential to scientific inquiry and discovery. Logic alone is not enough, since what initially seems a logical expectation may not be the case in fact. On the other hand, the mere observation and collection of empirical facts does not provide understanding—the telephone directory, for example, is not a scientific conclusion. Observation, however, can be the jumping off point for the construction of a social scientific theory, as we now see in the case of inductive theory.

INDUCTIVE THEORY CONSTRUCTION

Very often, social scientists begin constructing a theory by observing aspects of social life, seeking to discover patterns that may point to more or less universal principles. Barney Glaser and Anselm Strauss (1967) coined the term *grounded theory* in reference to this inductive method of theory construction.

Field research—the direct observation of events in progress (discussed in depth in Chapter 10)—is frequently used to develop theories through observation. A long and rich anthropological tradition has seen this method used to good advantage.

Among contemporary social scientists, no one was more adept at seeing the patterns of human behavior through observation than Erving Goffman:

A game such as chess generates a habitable universe for those who can follow it, a plane of being, a cast of characters with a seemingly unlimited number of different situations and acts through which to realize their natures and destinies. Yet much of this is reducible to a small set of interdependent rules and practices. If the meaningfulness of everyday activity is similarly dependent on a closed, finite set of rules, then explication of them would give one a powerful means of analyzing social life.   (1974:5)

In a variety of researches, Goffman uncovered the rules of such diverse behaviors as living in a mental institution (1961) and managing the "spoiled identity" of disfiguration (1963). In each case, Goffman observed the phenomenon in depth and has teased out the rules governing behavior. Goffman's research provides an excellent example of field research as a source of grounded theory.

Field research is not the only method of observation appropriate to the development of inductive theory. Two detailed examples—on religion and on drugs—should illustrate the process of inductive theory construction.

The Sources of Religiosity

Everyone has noticed that some people are more religious than others, but what do you suppose accounts for those differences? To answer that question, Charles Glock and his colleagues (1967) conducted a large-scale survey of Episcopal church members across the country. The survey questionnaire asked questions about religious practices that would permit the researchers to distinguish degrees of religiosity.

As sociologists, Glock and his colleagues were first interested in learning whether different types of people varied in degree of religiosity. Sex was the first variable examined: women in the study were substantially more religious than the men. Next it was found that old people were more religious than the young. Then the researchers found a negative relationship between social class and religiosity: poor people were more religious than rich ones.

Finally, family status was examined. It was discovered that persons living in "traditional" families—married and with children—were less religious than those with incomplete families, and those with no families were the most religious of all. This latter discovery was surprising, given the family orientation of American churches, exemplified in the phrase "The family that prays together stays together."

To review, then, the researchers had uncovered four variables, each of which was strongly related to religiosity:

1. Women more religious than men

2. Old people more religious than the young

3. Poor people more religious than rich people

4. Single people more religious than those with families

It is worth noting that each of the findings listed above—with the exception of (4)—had been found consistently in prior studies of religiosity. In the terms of this chapter, the differences noted could be considered laws of religiosity, at least within the realm of mainstream American religion. You'll recall, however, that laws don't explain anything; they just describe what's so.

When Glock and his colleagues examined the joint effects of the four variables, they discovered something new. Each of the four variables contributed independently to the degree of religiosity observed. That is, the poor old women living alone were the most religious of all, while the rich young men with complete families were the least religious. Moreover, people with three of the characteristics associated with religiosity were more religious than those with only two of the characteristics. And the range of religiosity separating the two extreme types was very large.

Findings such as these encouraged the researchers to believe they had unlocked the social sources of religiosity. They had discovered a powerful explanation for why some people were religious and others weren't. Only one problem remained: why did the four characteristics have the effects they had? To repeat: laws don't explain anything.

Take a moment to review the list of four characteristics associated with religiosity. Can you see anything they have in common? What could each of them reflect that would result in varying degrees of religiosity?

After years of pondering the puzzling finding, Glock and his colleagues saw the pattern. Each of the characteristics associated with religiosity was generally devalued in American society. For example, men enjoyed a generally higher status in American society than women did, and women were more religious than men. Similarly, we are a youth-oriented society—with young people accorded higher status than the elderly—and old people were more religious than young people. Rich people clearly have more status than poor people, and the poor were the more religious. Finally, family life—at least at the time of the study—was highly valued in American society, and those without families were more religious than those with them.

Recognizing this pattern, Glock and his colleagues concluded, "Parishioners whose life situations most deprive them of satisfaction and fulfillment in the secular society turn to the church for comfort and substitute rewards" (1967:107–8). In this fashion, they developed what they called a "social deprivation theory of church involvement."

Why Do People Smoke Marijuana?

During the 1960s and 1970s, marijuana use on America's college campuses was a subject of considerable discussion in the popular press. Some people were troubled by marijuana's popularity, while others welcomed it. What interests us here is why some students smoked marijuana and others didn't. A survey of students at the University of Hawaii (Takeuchi 1974) provided the data needed to answer that question.

At the time of the study, countless explanations were being offered for drug use. People who opposed drug use, for example, often suggested that marijuana smokers were academic failures who turned to drugs rather than face the rigors of college life. Those in favor of marijuana, on the other hand, often spoke of the search for new values: marijuana smokers, they said, were people who had seen through the hypocrisy of middle-class values.

David Takeuchi's (1974) analysis of the data gathered from University of Hawaii students, however, did not support any of

the explanations being offered. Those who reported smoking marijuana had essentially the same academic records as those who didn't smoke it, and both groups were equally involved in traditional "school spirit" activities. Both groups seemed to feel equally well integrated into campus life.

There were differences, however:

1. Women were less likely than men to smoke marijuana.

2. Asian students (a large proportion of the UH student body) were less likely to smoke marijuana than non-Asians.

3. Students living at home were less likely to smoke marijuana than those living in apartments.

As in the case of religiosity, the three variables independently affected the likelihood of a student's smoking marijuana. About 10 percent of the Asian women living at home had smoked marijuana, as contrasted with about 80 percent of the non-Asian men living in apartments. And, as in the religiosity study, the researchers discovered a powerful pattern of drug use before they had an explanation for that pattern.

In this instance, the explanation took a peculiar turn. Instead of explaining why some students smoked marijuana, the researchers explained why some *didn't*. Assuming that all students had some motivation for trying drugs, the researchers suggested that students differed in the degree of "social constraints" preventing them from following through on that motivation.

American society is, on the whole, more permissive with men than with women when it comes to deviant behavior. Consider, for example, a group of men getting drunk and boisterous. We tend to dismiss such behavior with references to "camaraderie" and "having a good time," whereas a group of women behaving similarly would probably be regarded with great disapproval. We have an idiom "Boys will be boys," but no comparable idiom for girls. The researchers reasoned, therefore, that women would have more to lose by smoking marijuana than men would. Being female, then, provided a constraint against smoking marijuana.

Students living at home had obvious constraints against smoking marijuana in comparison with students living on their own. Quite aside from differences in opportunity, those living at home were seen as being more dependent on their parents—hence more vulnerable to additional punishment for breaking the law.

Finally, the Asian subculture in Hawaii has traditionally placed a higher premium on obedience to the law than other subcultures, so Asian students would have more to lose if they were caught violating the law by smoking marijuana.

Overall, then, a "social constraints" theory was offered as the explanation for observed differences in the likelihood of smoking marijuana. The more constraints a student had, the less likely he or she would be to smoke marijuana. It bears repeating that the researchers had no thoughts about such a theory when their research began. The theory was developed out of an examination of the data.

THE LINKS BETWEEN THEORY AND RESEARCH

Throughout this chapter, we have seen various aspects of the links between theory and research in social scientific inquiry. In the deductive model, research is used to test theories. And in the inductive model, theories are developed from the analysis of research data. In this final section, I want to look a little more closely at the ways in which theory and research are related in actual social scientific inquiry.

Whereas we have discussed two logical models for the linking of theory and research,

actual social scientific inquiries have developed a great many variations on these themes. Sometimes, theoretical issues are introduced merely as a background for empirical analyses. Other studies cite selected empirical data to bolster theoretical arguments. In neither case is there really an interaction between theory and research for the purpose of developing new explanations. And some studies make no use of theory at all.

Rather than simply discuss the possible relationships between theory and research, let's take a look at the ways social scientists have actually linked them in their studies. To do this, we're going to examine four decades of articles published in the *American Sociological Review* (ASR), the main research journal for American sociologists.

To find out how theory has figured in sociological research, Richard H. Wells and J. Steven Picou (1981) conducted a *content analysis*—the rigorous examination of communications (see Chapter 11)—of a sample of 707 articles from the 2,619 published in the ASR between 1936 and 1978. One of the first things Wells and Picou discovered was that sociologists have increasingly employed theory in their research articles. Between 1936 and 1949, only 34 percent of the ASR articles included any use of theory, with the percentage increasing to 66 percent in the period from 1965 to 1978 (1981:103). Table 2-1 reports the various uses made of theory during the entire period from 1936 to 1978.

Among the many different uses made of theory in connection with sociological research, notice that only 24.5 percent of the articles involved the testing of theoretically derived hypotheses: the traditional model of scientific inquiry. Of these, 22.5 percent presented findings in support of the hypotheses, and 2 percent refuted the hypotheses. Taken together, these two items amounted to 38 percent of those articles that used theory at all.

Table 2-1   How Theory Was Utilized in the ASR, 1936–78

Primary Theory Utilization	Percent
Not theoretically related research	35.8%
Theory is used to support author's idea	1.9
Theory is used to focus research problem	3.3
Concepts are used to discuss and interpret findings	20.8
Theory is used to discuss and interpret findings	0.9
Modification or extension of existing theory	4.5
Development of theory	2.1
Theory is used to develop testable hypotheses and findings support the hypotheses	22.5
Theory is used to develop testable hypotheses and findings refute the hypotheses	2.0
Unfavorable discussion of theory	2.7
Favorable discussion of theory	3.8
TOTAL	100.0
	(707)

Source: Richard H. Wells and J. Steven Picou, *American Sociology: Theoretical and Methodological Structures* (Washington, D.C.: University Press of America, 1981), p. 105. Used by permission.

When Wells and Picou examined the uses of theory over time, they found a substantial increase in the traditional hypothesis-testing model. During the period 1936–49, this model was used for only 16 percent of the articles making any use of theory, 36 percent used it during the period 1950–64, and 54 percent during 1965–78 (1981:106).

The data we've seen in this section should complete your recognition that there is no simple cookbook recipe for conducting social science research. It is far more open-ended than the traditional view of science would suggest. Ultimately, science rests on two pillars: logic and observation. As we'll see throughout this book, they can be fit together in many patterns.

MAIN POINTS

■ Whether human social behavior can be studied "scientifically" has been debated for some time. It can.

■ The traditional image of science includes theory, operationalization, and observation.

■ The traditional image of science is not a very accurate picture of how scientific research is actually done.

■ Social scientific theory and research are linked through two logical methods:

—*Deduction* involves the derivation of expectations or hypotheses from theories.

—*Induction* involves the development of generalizations from specific observations.

■ Science is a process involving an alternation of deduction and induction.

■ While people speak of science as being "objective," that quality is difficult to define and demonstrate. More accurately, *intersubjectivity* means that different scientists—even with different points of view—can agree in their observations and conclusions.

■ A fact usually refers to something that has been observed.

- A law is a universal generalization about a class of facts.

- A theory is a systematic explanation for a set of facts and laws.

- A paradigm is a fundamental model or scheme which organizes our view of something.

- The three major paradigms informing social scientific inquiry today are interactionism, functionalism, and conflict theory.

- Grounded theory is a term used in reference to the creation of theory based on observation more than deduction.

REVIEW QUESTIONS AND EXERCISES

1. Consider the possible relationship between education and prejudice (mentioned in Chapter 1). Describe how that relationship might be examined through (a) deductive and (b) inductive methods.

2. Review the relationships between theory and research described in Table 2-1. Select a research article in some academic journal and classify the relationship between theory and research in that article.

ADDITIONAL READINGS

Babbie, Earl, *Survey Research Methods* (Belmont, Calif.: Wadsworth, 1973), Chapter 3. An application of the basic ideas developed in this chapter to the method of survey research. This short discussion should further clarify your understanding of the characteristics of science and social science as these appear in practice.

Chavetz, Janet, *A Primer on the Construction and Testing of Theories in Soci-*ology (Itasca, Ill.: Peacock, 1978). One of few books on theory construction written expressly for undergraduates. Chavetz provides a rudimentary understanding of the philosophy of science through simple language and everyday examples. She describes the nature of explanation, the role of assumptions and concepts, and the building and testing of theories.

Franklin, Billy, and Osborne, Harold (eds.), *Research Methods: Issues and Insights* (Belmont, Calif.: Wadsworth, 1971), Parts One and Two. An excellent collection of papers dealing with various aspects of social research. The selections in Parts One and Two provide a variety of stimulating perspectives on the general logic of social research, asking whether social science is "scientific," where it fits into our comprehensive understanding of people, and the links between theory and research in the social sciences.

Glazer, Myron, *The Research Adventure: Promise and Problems of Field Work* (New York: Random House, 1972). An eminently readable and informal biography of social research. I've included this book among the more technical and theoretical references to give you a flavor of what social inquiry is like in the flesh.

Kaplan, Abraham, *The Conduct of Inquiry* (San Francisco: Chandler, 1964). A standard reference volume on the logic and philosophy of science and social science. Though rigorous and scholarly, it is eminently readable and continually related to the real world of inquiry.

Kuhn, Thomas, *The Structure of Scientific Revolution* (Chicago: University of Chicago Press, 1970). An exciting and innovative recasting of the nature of scientific development. Kuhn disputes the notion of gradual change and modification in science, arguing instead that established "paradigms" tend to persist until the weight of contradictory evidence brings their rejection and replacement by new paradigms. This short book is at once stimulating and informative.

Wallace, Walter, *The Logic of Science in Sociology* (Chicago: Aldine-Atherton, 1971). An eminently readable overview of the logic connecting the several stages of social research. This remarkable little book leads you around the unending circle of observation to generalization to theory to hypothesis to observation and on and on.

3

The Nature of Causation

What You'll Learn in This Chapter

Here you'll see how the notions of cause and effect relate to explanatory social science. You'll learn about both the technical and philosophical aspects of the issue.

INTRODUCTION

Implicit in much of what has been said so far in this book are the notions of *cause* and *effect*. One of the chief goals of the scientist, social or other, is to explain why things are the way they are. Typically, we do that by specifying the causes for the way things are: some things are caused by other things.

The general notion of *causation* is at once very simple and very complex. I imagine, on the one hand, that I could have ignored the issue altogether in this book—simply using the terms *cause* and *effect*—and you would have had little difficulty understanding the use of the terms. On the other hand, an adequate discourse on causation would require a whole book in its own right, or a series of books. However, let me attempt a middle-ground treatment of the subject, providing something more than a common-sense perspective on causation without attempting to be definitive.

We'll begin with the subject of *determinism* in social science. Having done that, we'll return briefly to the topic of deductive and inductive logic, with deterministic assumptions added. Next we'll consider some appropriate and inappropriate criteria for causality. The chapter will conclude with a discussion of the links between measurement and association.

DETERMINISM AND SOCIAL SCIENCE

The deterministic perspective to be discussed now contrasts with a *freewill* image of human behavior that you and I take for granted in our daily lives. The fundamental issue is this: Is your behavior the product of your own, personal willpower or the product of forces and factors in the world that you cannot control and may not even rec-ognize? We are going to look at that issue in more depth here. Once we have completed our examination, we'll be in a position to look at the place of causation in social scientific research. We'll start with an example outside the social sciences altogether.

Causation in the Natural Sciences

Let's do an experiment. Take a pencil or some other small object, hold it up in the air, and let it go. What happens? It falls down, right? Why does it do that? As you probably learned in high school, one of the laws of the universe is that masses attract with a force reflecting their distance from one another and their masses. In practical terms, we say the gravitational force of the earth pulled the pencil to the ground.

What if the pencil didn't *want* to fall to the ground? That may strike you as a bizarre question, and well it should. Obviously, the pencil's feelings—assuming it could have any—make no difference. In fact, if we were to substitute a human being for the pencil, we know that gravity would win out over any feelings that person might have in the matter. The operation of gravity illustrates our commonsense view of cause-and-effect determinism in the world. We accept the limitation that gravity places on our freedom.

The deterministic model of explanation is in evidence throughout the natural sciences. Growth, for example, is *caused* by a number of factors. We can affect the growth of plants by varying the amount of light, water, and nutrients they receive. We also know that the rate of growth of human beings is affected by the nutrients they receive. And returning to the "bizarre" question asked earlier, the desire to grow or not to grow is irrelevant—for humans just as for plants. We acknowledge that nutrition greatly overshadows our free will in the matter.

The point of these examples is to show that the natural sciences operate on the basis of a cause/effect, deterministic model, and that model is often applied to human beings as well as to plants and inanimate objects. For the most part, moreover, we accept the deterministic model as appropriate in such cases. We recognize that our free will is limited by certain determinist constraints.

Finding Causes in Social Science

Essentially the same cause/effect, deterministic model is used in the social sciences. It is usually so implicit that we may forget the nature of the model we are using, so let me illustrate how social science might proceed with that model. Imagine that you have managed to obtain a million-dollar grant from the National Science Foundation to find out the causes of prejudice. That's certainly a laudable aim, and various government and private foundations are often willing to support such research. Let's suppose you receive the money and spend it doing your research. Now you are ready to send your project report off to the foundation. Here's how the report reads:

After an exhaustive examination of the subject, we have discovered that some people are prejudiced, and the reason for that is that they *want* to be prejudiced. Other people are not prejudiced, and the reason is that they *don't* want to be prejudiced.

Obviously, this paragraph would not be a satisfactory conclusion for a research project aimed at finding out what *causes* prejudice. When we look for the causes of prejudice, we look for the reasons: the things that make some people prejudiced and others

unprejudiced. Satisfactory reasons would include economic competition, religious ideology, political views, childhood experiences, amount and kind of education, and so forth. We know, for example, that education tends to reduce prejudice. That's the kind of causal explanation that we accept as the end product of social research.

Now let's look at the logic of such an explanation a little more closely. What does it say about the people involved in the research conclusion—the subjects of study? Fundamentally, it says that they turned out prejudiced or unprejudiced as a result of something they did not, themselves, control or choose. It's as though they came to a fork in the road—one turn represents prejudice and the other represents no prejudice—and they were propelled down one or the other road by forces such as childhood experiences, their inherited religious affiliation, and similar factors they neither controlled nor were even aware of. They turned out prejudiced or unprejudiced for reasons beyond their control.

When social scientists study juvenile delinquency, the basic model is the same: delinquency is *caused* by factors other than the delinquent's free choice. It is further assumed that those factors can be discovered and perhaps modified, regardless of whether the delinquent wants to change or not.

The same model applies when social scientists study "nice" behaviors. What are the factors that cause a person to be altruistic, considerate, responsible? If we knew the answer, we could *make* more people that way—so the implicit reasoning goes.

Reasons Have Reasons

Sometimes people protest this reasoning by arguing that individuals personally choose those things that determine how prejudiced, delinquent, or altruistic they are. For example, let's say that you are quite unprejudiced, and we conclude from research that your lack of prejudice is probably a function of all the education you've received. Didn't *you* choose to go to school? Aren't you, therefore, the source of your being unprejudiced?

The problem with this view is that reasons have reasons. *Why* did you go to school? If you and I were discussing this subject, I know that you'd be able to give me reasons for having continued going to school up to this point. Let's say that you wanted to learn about the world around you, and you thought college would be a good way to do that. That makes sense.

That makes so much sense in fact that we might even say that your desire to learn about the world *caused* you to continue going to school. It's as if your desire *forced* you to go to school. Given that you had such a desire, how could you *not* go to school?

"I might not have gone if I hadn't had enough money," you say. That's true. If you hadn't had enough money to go to school, that factor would have *forced* you to stay out of school. But then suppose your desire to learn about the world around you was so powerful that you overcame the lack of money—maybe you got a scholarship or went to work for a while. In that case, we are back to your powerful desire forcing you to go to school.

Ah, but *why* did you have such a strong desire to go to school? If I could ask you that in person, I know you'd have a reason. Perhaps you grew up in a family where everyone had gone to college generation after generation, and you'd feel you were letting your family down if you didn't go to college. Or perhaps you come from a family where nobody had ever gone to college before, and they were all proud of the fact that you

might be the first. In both cases, we can see that those factors *forced* you to have the powerful desire to go to college, and that powerful desire *forced* you to go to college, and going to college *forced* you to be unprejudiced.

Clearly I can't—through a book—deal with all the particular reasons *you* had for doing something like going to college, but I think you'll be able to see that you did it for *reasons*, and that those reasons caused you to go. Moreover, no matter what reason you had at any specific step in the process, your reason would have a reason. The ultimate implication of this discussion is that your being prejudiced or unprejudiced can be traced back through a long and complex chain of reasons that explain why you turned out the way you did.

Recall how silly it seemed to think about whether the pencil wanted to fall when you let go of it. The pencil's feelings had nothing to do with it; gravity caused it to fall. The same thing would have happened to any pencil, so the one we dropped certainly couldn't take any pride in how well it fell. Questions of feeling and pride in accomplishment seem unimportant when we are dealing with a pencil being pulled around by gravity.

However, whether *you* turned out to be prejudiced or unprejudiced seems like a different matter. I know that if you consider yourself to be tolerant or honest or hardworking, you feel that such qualities are a reflection of who you are, of the kind of person you are deep down inside. They seem intimately woven into your experience of yourself.

Whenever we undertake explanatory social science research, however—when we set out to discover the causes of prejudice, for example—we adopt a model of human behavior that assumes people have no more individual freedom of choice than the pencil did. We don't say that, of course, but if you look at the implications of asking "Why are people prejudiced?" you'll see that it's so.

Determinism in Perspective

As you no doubt know, the issue of determinism and freedom is a complex one, which philosophers have debated for thousands of years and will probably debate for thousands more. It is perhaps ultimately one of those "open questions" that is more valuable in the asking than it would be in the answering. We are not going to resolve it here.

My purpose in raising the issue of determinism is to engage you in the question and to alert you to its place in social research. I have observed that when people set out to learn the skills of explanatory social research, that implicit assumption disturbs them. Somewhere, new researchers harbor a concern about whether they are learning to demonstrate that *they* themselves have no free will, no personal freedom in determining the course of their own lives. To the extent that this concern grows and festers, it interferes with the learning of analytic skills and techniques. My purpose in this discussion has been to confront the issue head-on rather than leaving it for you to discover later on.

Having said all that, let me clarify what is not part of the model. First, social scientists do not *believe* all human actions, thoughts, and feelings are determined, nor do they lead their lives as though they believed that. Second, the deterministic model does not assume that the causal patterns are simple ones, as I've already suggested in the discussions of reasons causing reasons. Nor does the model assume we are all controlled by the same factors and forces:

your reasons for going to college were surely somewhat different from mine.

Moreover, the deterministic model lying at the base of explanatory social science does not suggest that we now know all the answers about what causes what, or that we ever will. Realize, however, that this is different from the error of "mystification" discussed in Chapter 1.

Finally, as we'll see later, social science typically operates on the basis of a _proba-bilistic_ causal model. Rather than predicting, for example, that a particular person will attend college, we say that certain factors make attending college more or less likely within groups of people. Thus, high school students whose parents attended college are more likely to attend college themselves than those students whose parents didn't attend college. This does not mean that all of the former will attend college and none of the latter.

To summarize, the kind of understanding we seek as we analyze social research data inevitably involves a deterministic model of human behavior. In looking for the reasons why people are the way they are and do the things they do, we implicitly assume that their characteristics and actions are determined by forces and factors operating on them. You do not need to *believe* that human beings are totally determined, nor do you have to lead your life as though you were, but you must be willing to use deterministic logic in looking for explanations when you engage in social science research.

IDIOGRAPHIC AND NOMOTHETIC MODELS OF EXPLANATION

Social scientists use two models of explanation in coming to grips with the reasons for human behavior. The preceding discussions, which probed the multiplicity of reasons that would account for a specific behavior, illustrated the *idiographic model of explanation*. This model aims at explanation through the enumeration of the very many, perhaps unique, considerations that lie behind a given action. Of course, we never truly exhaust those reasons in practice. Nevertheless, it is important to realize that the idiographic model is employed frequently in many different contexts.

Traditional historians, for example, tend to use the idiographic model, enumerating all the special causes of the French Revolution, or of the United States's decision to enter World War II. Clinical psychologists may employ this model in seeking an explanation for the aberrant behavior of a patient. A criminal court, in response to a plea of extenuating circumstances, may seek to examine all the various considerations that have resulted in the crime in question. And most of us employ the idiographic model in attempting to understand the actions of the people around us.

Scientists, including social scientists, often employ a different model, called the *nomothetic model of explanation*. This model does not involve an exhaustive enumeration of all the considerations that result in a *particular* action or event, as I've already indicated above in the discussion of *probabilistic* causation. Rather, this model is consciously designed to discover those considerations that are most important in explaining general classes of actions or events.

Suppose we wanted to find out why people voted the way they did in the 1984 presidential election. Each individual we talked to could give a great many reasons why he or she voted for either Mondale or Reagan. Suppose someone gave us 99 different reasons for voting for Mondale. We'd probably feel we had a pretty complete explanation for that person's vote. In fact, if we found someone else with those same 99 reasons, we would feel pretty confident in predicting that *that* person also voted for Mondale. This approach represents the idiographic model of explanation.

The nomothetic model of explanation, on the other hand, involves the isolation of those *relatively few* considerations that will provide a *partial* explanation for the voting behavior of *many* people or of all people. For example, political orientation—liberal or conservative—would probably be a consideration of great *general* importance in determining the voting behavior of the electorate as a whole. Most of those sharing the attribute *liberal* probably voted for Mondale, while most of those sharing the attribute *conservative* probably voted for Reagan. Realize that this single consideration would not provide a complete explanation for all voting behavior. Some liberals voted for Reagan; some conservatives voted for Mondale. The goal of the nomothetic model of explanation is to provide the greatest amount of explanation with the fewest number of causal variables to uncover general patterns of cause and effect.

The nomothetic model of explanation is inevitably *probabilistic* in its approach to causation. Being able to name a few considerations seldom if ever provides a complete explanation. (We might discover, of course, that everyone who believed Reagan was the best man voted for him, but that would not be a very satisfying explanation.) In the best of all practical worlds, the nomothetic model indicates there is a very high (or very low) probability or likelihood that a given action will occur whenever a limited number of specified considerations are present. Adding more specified considerations to the equation typically increases the degree of explanation, but the basic simplicity of the model calls for a balancing of a high degree of explanation with a small number of considerations being specified.

Social scientists sometimes are criticized for *dehumanizing* the people they study.

This charge is lodged specifically against the nomothetic model of explanation; the severity of the charge is increased when social scientists analyze matters of great human concern. Religious people, for example, are likely to feel robbed of their human individuality when a social scientist reports that their religiosity is largely a function of their sex, age, marital status, and social class. Any religious person will quickly report there is much more than that to the strength of his or her convictions. And indeed there is, as the use of the idiographic model in the case of any individual person would reveal. Is the idiographic model any less *dehumanizing* than the nomothetic model, however?

If everything—including being religious—is a product of prior considerations, is it any more dehumanizing to seek partial but general explanations using only a few of those considerations than to seek total explanation using them all? I suspect the true source of concern, underlying the charges of dehumanization, is based on the more direct confrontation with determinism that the nomothetic model represents. It is important to realize, however, that a careful listing of all the private individual reasons for being religious, or for voting for Candidate X, or for any other action, involves the acknowledgment of a deterministic perspective: one that is logically no different from the deterministic perspective that permits us to specify the four variables that are most important in causing religiosity.

CRITERIA FOR CAUSALITY

None of the preceding discussion provides much practical guidance to the discovery of causal relationships in scientific research. This section will discuss three specific criteria for causality as suggested by Paul Lazarsfeld (1959). The actual use of these criteria in research practice will be illustrated in Chapter 16 on the *elaboration model*.

The first requirement in a causal relationship between two variables is that the cause precede the effect in time. It makes no sense, in science, to imagine something being caused by something else that happened later on. A bullet leaving the muzzle of a gun does not cause the gunpowder to explode; it works the other way around.

As simple and obvious as this criterion may seem, we will discover endless problems in this regard in the analysis of social science data. Often, the time order connecting two variables is simply unclear. Which comes first: authoritarianism or prejudice? Even when the time order seems essentially clear, exceptions can often be found. For example, we would normally assume that the educational level of parents would be a cause of the educational level of their children. Yet, some parents may return to school as a result of the advanced education of their own children.

The second requirement in a causal relationship is that the two variables be empirically correlated with one another. It would make no sense to say that exploding gunpowder causes bullets to leave muzzles of guns if, in observed reality, bullets did not come out after the gunpowder exploded.

Again, social science research has difficulties in regard to this seemingly obvious requirement. In the probabilistic world of nomothetic models of explanation at least, there are few perfect correlations. Most conservatives voted for Reagan, but some didn't. We are forced to ask, therefore, how great the empirical relationship must be for that relationship to be considered causal.

The third requirement for a causal relationship is that the observed empirical correlation between two variables cannot be explained away as being due to the influence of some third variable that causes both of them. For example, I may observe that

Correlation and Causality

by Charles Bonney

Department of Sociology, Eastern Michigan University

Having demonstrated a statistical relationship between a hypothesized "cause" and its presumed "effect," many people (sometimes including researchers who should know better) are only too eager to proclaim "proof" of causation. Let's take an example to see why "it ain't necessarily so."

Imagine you have conducted a study on college students and have found an inverse correlation between marijuana smoking (variable M) and grade point average (variable G)—that is, those who smoke tend to have lower GPAs than those who do not, and the more smoked, the lower the GPA. You might therefore claim that smoking marijuana lowers one's grades (in symbolic form, $M \rightarrow G$), giving as an explanation, perhaps, that marijuana adversely affects memory, which would naturally have detrimental consequences on grades.

However, if an inverse correlation is all the evidence you have, a second possibility exists. Getting poor grades is frustrating; frustration often leads to escapist behavior; getting stoned is a popular means of escape; ergo, low grades cause marijuana smoking ($G \rightarrow M$)! Unless you can establish which came first, smoking or low grades, this explanation is supported by the correlation just as plausibly as the first.

Let's introduce another variable into the picture: the existence and/or extent of emotional problems (variable E). It could certainly be plausibly argued that having emotional problems may lead to escapist behavior, including marijuana smoking. Likewise it seems reasonable to suggest that emotional problems are likely to adversely affect grades. That correlation of marijuana smoking and low grades may exist for the same reason that runny noses and sore throats tend to go together—*neither* is the cause of the other, but rather, both are the consequences of some third variable ($E \overset{M}{\underset{G}{\rightrightarrows}}$). Unless you can rule out such third variables, this explanation too is just as well supported by the data as is the first (or the second).

Then again, perhaps students smoke marijuana primarily because they have

my left knee generally aches just before it rains, but this does not mean that my joints affect the weather. A third variable, relative humidity, is the cause of both my aching knee and the rain. (This requirement of causality will be one of the main topics of discussion in Chapter 16. The terms *spuriousness* and *explanation* will be used in that context.)

The box entitled "Correlation and Causality" illustrates the point that correlation does not necessarily point to a particular causal relationship.

To review, most social researchers consider two variables to be causally related—that is, one causes the other—if (a) the cause precedes the effect in time, (b) there is an empirical correlation between them, and (c) the relationship is not found to be the result of the effects of some third variable on each

friends who smoke, and get low grades because they are simply not as bright or well prepared or industrious as their classmates, and the fact that it's the same students in each case in your sample is purely coincidental. Unless your correlation is so strong and so consistent that mere coincidence becomes highly unlikely, this last possibility, while not supported by your data, is not precluded either.

Incidentally, this particular example was selected for two reasons. First of all, *every one* of the above explanations for such an inverse correlation has appeared in a national magazine at one time or another. And second, *every one* of them is probably doomed to failure because it turns out that, among college students, most studies indicate a *direct* correlation, i.e., it is those with higher GPAs who are more likely to be marijuana smokers! Thus, with tongue firmly in cheek, we may reanalyze this particular finding:

1. Marijuana relaxes a person, clearing away other stresses, thus allowing more effective study; hence, M → G.

or

2. Marijuana is used as a reward for really hitting the books or doing well ("Wow, man! An 'A'! Let's go get high!"); hence, G → M.

or

3. A high level of curiosity (E) is definitely an asset to learning and achieving high grades and may also lead one to investigate "taboo" substances; hence, $E \rightrightarrows {}^M_G$.

or

4. Again coincidence, but this time the samples just happened to contain a lot of brighter, more industrious students whose friends smoke marijuana!

The obvious conclusion is this: if *all* of these are possible explanations for a relationship between two variables, then no *one* of them should be too readily singled out. Establishing that two variables tend to occur together is a *necessary* condition for demonstrating a causal relationship, but it is not by itself a *sufficient* condition. It is a fact, for example, that human birthrates are higher in areas of Europe where there are lots of storks, but as to the meaning of that relationship . . . !

of the two initially observed. Any relationship satisfying *all* these criteria is causal, and these are the only criteria.

To emphasize this point more strongly, let's briefly examine some other—inappropriate—criteria that are sometimes employed, especially by nonscientists. In this discussion, I am indebted to Travis Hirschi and Hanan Selvin for an excellent article on this subject and its later expansion in

their book *Principles of Survey Analysis* (1973:114–36).

Necessary and Sufficient Causes

First, to review a point made earlier in the chapter, a *perfect* correlation between variables is *not* a criterion of causality in social science research (or in science generally for that matter). Put another way, exceptions, although they do not prove the rule, do not necessarily deny the rule either. In probabilistic models, there are almost always exceptions to the posited relationship. If a few liberals voted for Reagan and a few conservatives voted for Mondale, that would not deny the general causal relationship between political orientations and voting in the election.

Within this probabilistic model, it is useful to distinguish two types of causes: *necessary* and *sufficient* causes. A *necessary cause* represents a condition that must be present for the effect to follow. For example, it is necessary for a person to be a woman to become pregnant, even though not all women do become pregnant. A *sufficient cause* represents a condition which, if it is present, inevitably results in the effect. Enlisting in the army is a sufficient cause for being given a uniform, even though there are other ways of acquiring uniforms.

The discovery of a *necessary and sufficient cause* is, of course, the most satisfying outcome in research. If cancer were the effect under examination, it would be nice to discover a single condition that (a) had to be present for cancer to develop and (b) always resulted in cancer. In such a case, you would surely feel that you knew precisely what caused cancer. Unfortunately, we seldom discover causes that are both necessary and sufficient, nor, in practice, are the causes perfectly necessary or perfectly sufficient. In social science, *either* necessary *or* sufficient causes—even imperfect ones—can be the basis for concluding there is a causal relationship.

You may have greater difficulty accepting the notion of a necessary cause than of a sufficient one. For example, you would no doubt feel more comfortable saying that enlisting in the army causes you to be given a uniform than saying that being a woman causes you to become pregnant. Everyone

who enlists is given a uniform, but not every woman becomes pregnant. The difficulty in accepting necessary causes is usually even greater when a majority of those *caused* to do something do not do it. Let's postulate, for example, that being an anti-Semite is a necessary cause of murdering Jews in the streets. Non-anti-Semites don't do it. This causal relationship is not at all diminished by the fact that the vast majority of anti-Semites do not murder Jews in the streets.

LINKING MEASUREMENT AND ASSOCIATION

As we have seen, one of the key elements determining causation in science is an empirical correlation between the *cause* and the *effect*. All too often, however, the process of *measuring* variables is seen as separate from that of determining the *associations* between variables. This view is incorrect, I think, or at the very least misleading.

This section addresses the intimate links between measurement and association within the context of causal inference. To do that, we'll review the traditional, deductive model of science. Then we'll examine some alternative images of science. In this latter regard, we'll consider the notions of the interchangeability of indexes and fixed-point analysis.

The Traditional Deductive Model

The traditional perspective on the scientific method, as you'll recall, is based on a set of serial steps which may be summarized as follows:

1. Theory construction
2. Derivation of theoretical hypotheses

3. Operationalization of concepts

4. Collection of empirical data

5. Empirical testing of hypotheses

Let's illustrate this view of the scientific research process with an example.

Theory Construction   Faced with an aspect of the natural or social world that interests him or her, the scientist creates an abstract deductive theory to describe it. This is a largely logical exercise. Let's assume for the moment that a social scientist is interested in deviant behavior. He or she constructs— on the basis of existing sociological theory—a theory of deviant behavior. Among other things, this theory includes a variety of concepts relevant to the causes of deviant behavior.

Derivation of Theoretical Hypotheses   On the basis of this total theory of deviant behavior, the scientist derives hypotheses relating to the various concepts composing the theory. Following the above example, let us suppose that the scientist logically derives the hypothesis that juvenile delinquency is a function of supervision: as supervision increases, juvenile delinquency decreases.

Operationalization of Concepts   The next step is the specification of empirical indicators to represent the theoretical concepts. Although theoretical concepts must be somewhat abstract and perhaps vague, the empirical indicators must be precise and specific (as we'll examine in detail in Chapters 5 and 6). Thus, in our example, the scientist might operationalize the concept *juvenile* as anyone under 18 years of age; *delinquency* might be operationalized as being arrested for a criminal act; and *supervision* might be operationalized as the presence of a nonworking adult in the home.

The effect of operationalization is to convert the theoretical hypothesis into an empirical one. In the present case, the empirical hypothesis would be that among persons under 18 years of age, those living in homes with a nonworking adult will be less likely to be arrested for a criminal act than will those without a nonworking adult in the home.

Collection of Empirical Data   Based on the operationalization of theoretical concepts, the researcher collects data relating to the empirical indicators. In the present example, he or she might conduct a survey of persons under 18 years of age. Among other things, the survey questionnaire would ask of each whether the person lived in a home with a nonworking adult and whether the person had ever been arrested for a criminal act.

Empirical Testing of Hypotheses   Once the data have been collected, the final step is the statistical testing of the hypothesis. The scientist determines, empirically, whether those juveniles with a nonworking adult in the home are less likely to have been arrested for criminal acts than those with no nonworking adult. The confirmation or disconfirmation of the empirical hypothesis is then used for purposes of accepting or rejecting the theoretical hypothesis.

Although this traditional image of scientific research can be a useful model for you to have in mind, it tends to conceal some of the practical problems that crop up in most actual research. In particular, there are two basic problems that prevent the easy application of this model in practice.

First, theoretical concepts seldom if ever permit unambiguous operationalization. Because concepts are abstract and general, every specification of empirical indicators must be an approximation. In the previous example, it is unlikely that the general concept of *supervision* is adequately represented by the presence of a nonworking adult in the home. The presence of such an adult does not assure supervision of the juvenile; in some homes lacking such an adult, other arrangements may be made for the juvenile's supervision.

Being arrested for a criminal act cannot be equated with the abstract concept of *delinquency*. Some juveniles may engage in delinquent behavior without being arrested. Others may be arrested falsely. Moreover, the specification of *juvenile* as a person under 18 years of age is an arbitrary one. Other specifications might have been made, and probably none would be unambiguously correct. Every empirical indicator has some defects; all could be improved upon, and the search for better indicators is an endless one.

Second, the empirical associations between variables are almost never perfect. In the previous example, if all juveniles with nonworking adults in the home had never been arrested and all those without such adults had been arrested, we might conclude that the hypothesis had been confirmed. Or if both groups had exactly the same records, we might conclude that the hypothesis had been rejected. Neither eventuality is likely in practice, however. Nearly all variables are related empirically to one another to some extent. Specifying the extent that represents acceptance of the hypothesis and the extent that represents rejection, however, is also an arbitrary act. (See Chapter 17 for a discussion of tests of statistical significance.)

Ultimately, then, scientists use approximate indicators of theoretical concepts to discover partial associations. And these imperfections conspire with one another against us. Suppose that you specify a degree of association that will constitute acceptance of the hypothesis, and the empirical analysis falls short. You will quite naturally ask yourself whether different indicators of the concepts might have produced the specified extent of association.

Measurement and association are interrelated concepts. The scientist must handle both simultaneously and logically. Rather than moving through a fixed set of steps, the scientist moves back and forth through them endlessly. Often theoretical constructions are built around the previously observed associations between empirical indicators. Partial theoretical constructions may suggest new empirical data to be examined, and so forth. After each activity, you hope to understand your subject matter a little better. The "critical experiment" that ultimately determines the fate of an entire theory is rare indeed.

Scientific research, then, is a never-ending enterprise aimed at the understanding of some phenomenon. To that end, you continually measure and examine associations, and you must constantly be aware of the relationships between them.

The Interchangeability of Indexes

Paul Lazarsfeld (1959), in his discussions of the **interchangeability of indexes,** has provided an important conceptual tool for our understanding of the relationship between measurement and association, and has partially resolved the two problems discussed in the previous section. His comments grew out of the recognition that there are several possible indicators for any concept.

Let's suppose that you have an idea that religiosity may affect marital fidelity. That's something that could be researched, but what do you mean by religiosity? Here are but a few of the possible indicators: attending church, reading religious books, praying before meals, avoiding certain types of food, believing in God, wearing jewelry in the form of religious symbols, and so forth. How can you determine whether religion affects marital fidelity unless you can specify what you mean by religiosity? Let us return for the moment to the notion of a theoretical hypothesis: $Y = f(X)$, first introduced in Figure 2-1. It suggests that some dependent variable (Y)—marital fidelity in this case—can be explained as an effect of the independent variable X—religiosity. Lazarsfeld recognized that a concept like religiosity can have several possible indicators; we might write these as X_1, X_2, X_3, and so forth. Although there may be reasons for believing that some of the indicators are better than others, Lazarsfeld argued, if they all are indicators of the same concept, they should be essentially interchangeable in testing relationships. Thus, whereas the traditional model of science suggests that we test one relationship—represented by the equation $y = f(x)$—we can use *all* the possible indicators of religiosity. Thus, we test the following empirical hypotheses: $y = f(x_1)$, $y = f(x_2)$, $y = f(x_3)$, and so forth. Rather than having one test of the hypothesis, we have several, as indicated schematically in Figure 3-1.

In the terms of our present example, we might be asking (1) whether those who attend church regularly are more faithful in marriage than those who do not attend church, (2) whether those who believe in God are more faithful than those who do not, (3) whether those who pray before meals are more faithful than those who do not, and so forth. You may already have antici-

pated a new dilemma. If following the traditional view of the scientific method created the problem that the single empirical association might not be perfect, now we may be faced with several empirical associations, none of which will be perfect and some of which may conflict with one another. Thus, even if we have specified a particular extent of association that will be sufficient to confirm the hypothesis, we may discover that the tests involving x_1, x_3, and x_5 meet that specified criterion, but the tests involving x_2 and x_4 do not. Our dilemma is seemingly compounded. In fact, however, the situation really may be clarified.

Using the notion of the interchangeability of indexes, a theoretical hypothesis is accepted as a *general* proposition if it is confirmed by all the specified empirical tests. If, for example, marital fidelity is a function of religiosity in a broadly generalized sense, then fidelity should be empirically related to every empirical indicator of religiosity.

If, however, we discover that only certain indicators of religiosity have this property, then we have specified the kinds of religiosity for which the proposition holds. In practice, this may help us to reconceptualize *religiosity* in more precise terms.

It is very important to realize what we have accomplished through this process. Rather than routinely testing a fixed hypothesis relating to religiosity and marital fidelity, we will have gained a better-defined understanding of the nature of that association. That will make sense, however, only if we view the goal of science as understanding rather than simply as theory construction and hypothesis testing.

Figure 3-1 The Interchangeability of Indexes

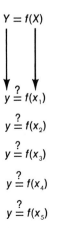

$$Y = f(X)$$

$$y \stackrel{?}{=} f(x_1)$$

$$y \stackrel{?}{=} f(x_2)$$

$$y \stackrel{?}{=} f(x_3)$$

$$y \stackrel{?}{=} f(x_4)$$

$$y \stackrel{?}{=} f(x_5)$$

Fixed-Point Analysis

One additional step is required, however, before our understanding of the scientific process can be clear. That is to comprehend what I have called *fixed-point analysis*. The notion of interchangeable indexes discussed above focused on the variability of *one* of the concepts, when in fact *all* concepts have this property.

In the preceding section, we saw that a given theoretical hypothesis $Y = f(X)$ has several possible indicators of X written as x_1, x_2, x_3, and so forth. It may have occurred to you that the discussion of the interchangeability of indexes seemed incomplete. If X can be measured in many ways, isn't the same likely to be true of Y? If, for example, we want to find out whether wealth produces conservatism, both wealth and conservatism can be measured variously. Here are some examples:

Wealth (X)	Conservatism (Y)
x_1 = annual income	y_1 = foreign affairs
x_2 = savings accounts	y_2 = domestic issues
x_3 = property/ investments	y_3 = economic issues
x_4 = parents' wealth	y_4 = social issues
x_5 = life-style	y_5 = morality

With so many ways to measure wealth and so many ways to measure conservatism, how do we set about discovering if the two variables are related? If we had begun with clear and specific concepts of what we mean by *wealth* and *conservatism*, we would simply have created two operational measures appropriate to those concepts. Very often, however, we lack such clarity at the beginning of a research project. Indeed, a common purpose of research is to provide clarity, and it is necessary to create many different measures of variables in order to clarify their relationship to one another. As a result, we often begin our analysis with something that might be called, in paraphrase of William James, "a buzzing, whirling mess of indicators." This state is illustrated schematically in Part I of Figure 3-2.

In such a situation, there is no safe anchoring point from which to build your analysis. If you knew what *wealth* really meant, you could play with the different measures of conservatism; or if you knew what *conservatism* really meant, you could play around with the various measures of wealth. Given such total uncertainty, however, you may be tempted to give up in despair and wish you had made even arbitrary measurement decisions earlier in your study.

It's possible to extricate yourself from this morass, however, and even experience the thrill of scientific discovery in the process. To do that, you need to drum up some healthy pragmatism and a large shot of tolerance for ambiguity. I've labeled this approach fixed-point analysis.

With all the possible indicators of the two variables floating around with no fixed, anchoring point, you need to begin by "fixing" one. Let's start with wealth. Granting that we don't know the best way of measuring wealth in terms of learning whether it's related to conservatism, let's simply agree to start by measuring it as annual income. With that decision made, we can now begin to examine how wealth relates to the several measures of conservatism. This task is illustrated in Part II of Figure 3-2, where $y_1, \ldots, y_5$ are various indicators of conservatism, and x_1 is annual income.

Let's suppose that this analysis indicates that wealth (measured as annual income) is strongly related to conservatism in foreign affairs, economic issues, and social issues. Suppose that our measures of conservatism in domestic issues and morality aren't as strongly related to wealth. As a result of this discovery, we tentatively decide to measure conservatism as some combination (creating a scale or index) of indicators y_1, y_3, and y_4.

With this working measure of conservatism, we now examine the various indicators of wealth ($x_1, \ldots, x_5$). This task is

Figure 3-2 Fixed-Point Analysis

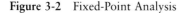

I	II
y_3	$y_1 \stackrel{?}{=} f(x_1)$
$x_1 \qquad x_3$	$y_2 \stackrel{?}{=} f(x_1)$
x_4	$y_3 \stackrel{?}{=} f(x_1)$
y_5	$y_4 \stackrel{?}{=} f(x_1)$
$y_1 \qquad x_2$	$y_5 \stackrel{?}{=} f(x_1)$
$y_2 \quad y_4 \quad x_5$	
III	**IV**
$y_{134} \stackrel{?}{=} f(x_1)$	$y_i = x_j$
$y_{134} \stackrel{?}{=} f(x_2)$	
$y_{134} \stackrel{?}{=} f(x_3)$	
$y_{134} \stackrel{?}{=} f(x_4)$	
$y_{134} \stackrel{?}{=} f(x_5)$	

illustrated in Part III of Figure 3-2. This latest set of analyses will give us a better idea of which measure of wealth is most appropriate to study in association with conservatism. Once we decide on the most useful measure of wealth, we can use *it* to reexamine the various possible measures of conservatism. Ultimately, we conclude this process with the creation of measures of wealth and conservatism that shed some light on the relationship between the two variables. I've illustrated this in Part IV, using *i* and *j* to indicate the measures arrived at.

In this fashion, then, you can extricate yourself from the confusion of too much variation. Make a decision, see what it tells you, then revise your initial decision. You should realize that the ultimate outcome of this procedure is quite different from what is suggested by the traditional view of the scientific method and hypothesis testing. It neither asks nor answers the question, "Is *Y* a function of *X*?" Rather, we ask, "*How* is *Y* a function of *X*?" (Under what operationalizations is *Y* a function of *X*?) We do not address the straightforward question of *whether* conservatism increases with wealth; instead the question is "What kinds of conservatism are produced by what kinds of wealth?"

In practice, of course, we might arrive at several answers to this question. That shouldn't be viewed as a problem, however. When you think about it, such questions probably *have* several answers.

The implication of the preceding comments is that measurement and association are importantly intertwined. The measurement of a variable makes little sense outside the empirical and theoretical contexts of the associations to be tested. Asked "How should I measure social class?" the experienced scientist will reply, "What is your purpose for measuring it?" The "proper" way of measuring a given variable depends very heavily on the variables to be associated with it. One further example should make this point clearer.

An Example of Measurement and Association

A recent controversy in the sociology of religion concerns the relationship between religiosity and prejudice. A book by Charles Y. Glock and Rodney Stark entitled *Christian Beliefs and Anti-Semitism* (1967) reported empirical data indicating that Christian church members holding orthodox beliefs (in God, Jesus, the Bible, etc.) were more likely to be anti-Semitic than were less orthodox members. The book's findings stirred considerable discussion within the churches, and other researchers did follow-up projects on the same topic.

One of these research projects arrived at a conclusion directly opposite that of Glock and Stark. The researchers reported that as orthodoxy increased, prejudice decreased. Upon closer examination, however, it was noted that orthodoxy in that study was measured by acceptance of questionnaire statements of the traditional Christian doctrines of "All men are brothers" and "Love thy neighbor." Not surprisingly, survey respondents who accepted the statements based on these doctrines appeared less prejudiced than those who rejected them. Normally, these research findings would be (and were) challenged on the grounds of "con-

tamination": the indicators used to operationalize religious orthodoxy and prejudice actually measured the same or similar qualities. Calling one set of indicators "orthodoxy" and the other "prejudice" does not prove that prejudice decreases with increasing orthodoxy in a general sense. (Of course, measuring orthodoxy in terms of brotherly love and equality might be extremely useful in some other context.)

The discussions of this chapter suggest a somewhat different reaction to the two kinds of research findings. Asking *how* orthodoxy and prejudice are associated with each other rather than *whether* they are associated, we would conclude that orthodoxy measured in terms of the Glock-Stark indicators is positively associated with prejudice, while orthodoxy measured as commitment to the norms of brotherly love and equality is negatively associated with prejudice. Both conclusions are empirically correct; neither conclusion answers the more general question of *whether* religion and prejudice are related. The final remaining step, of course, is to evaluate the relative utility of the conclusions. The finding that orthodoxy and prejudice are negatively associated would probably be disregarded as either tautological or trivial.

The various discussions of this chapter should have given you a sense of the explanatory purpose of social research. Though not our only purpose in research, we very often wish to explain why people think and act as they do. Typically, we ask what causes what. I have introduced the notion of causation early in the book so that you can hold it as a backdrop for the technical discussions that follow.

MAIN POINTS

■ Explanatory scientific research depends implicitly on the notion of cause and effect.

- Explanatory *social* scientific research depends implicitly on a *deterministic image* of human behavior, at least in part.

- The *idiographic* model of explanation aims at a complete understanding of a particular phenomenon, utilizing all relevant causal factors.

- The *nomothetic* model of explanation aims at a general understanding—not necessarily complete—of a *class* of phenomena, utilizing the smallest number of most relevant causal factors. The nomothetic model is more parsimonious than the idiographic model, and it is the one most typically employed in social scientific research.

- Although social scientists may seem to take a rather dehumanized view of the people they study, that merely reflects their parsimonious point of view. When a social scientist says that political party affiliation is the best predictor of voting behavior, this does not mean that he or she disregards or denies all other influences; the social scientist is simply interested in discovering the most important ones.

- Most explanatory social research utilizes a *probabilistic* model of causation. X may be said to *cause* Y if it is seen to have *some* influence on Y.

- There are two important types of causal factors: *necessary* causes and *sufficient* causes. X is a necessary cause of Y if Y cannot happen without X having happened. X is a sufficient cause of Y if Y always happens when X happens. The scientifically most satisfying discovery is a necessary *and* sufficient cause.

- There are three basic criteria for the determination of causation in scientific research: (1) The independent (cause) and dependent (effect) variables must be empirically related to one another, (2) the independent variable must occur earlier in time than the dependent variable, and (3) the observed relationship cannot be explained away as the artificial product of the effect of another, earlier variable. (This final criterion will be discussed more fully in Chapter 16.)

- A perfect statistical relationship between two variables is *not* an appropriate criterion for causation in social research. We may say that a causal relationship exists between X and Y, then, even though X is not the *total* cause of Y.

- The *interchangeability of indexes* suggests that if several specific, though imperfect, indicators of one variable are similarly related to another variable, then we may assume that the first variable—*in general*—is related to the second. Thus, we may conclude that X is related to Y, even though we cannot satisfactorily define X.

- *Fixed-point analysis* is a logical model for varying the definitions of variables in such a way as to discover the *different* relationships that exist between variables according to the operational definitions employed. This model suggests that it is more fruitful to ask, "In what ways are X and Y related?" than it is to ask, "Are X and Y related?"

- *Contamination* of indicators means that the operational measure of one of two variables whose relationship is being examined may be construed as a measure of the other variable as well. For example, it would be an inappropriate test of the relationship between religiosity and prejudice if the measure of religiosity might be seen as a measure of prejudice as well.

REVIEW QUESTIONS AND EXERCISES

1. Several times we have discussed the relationship between education and prejudice. Describe the conditions that would lead us to conclude that education was

   a. a necessary cause

b. a sufficient cause
c. a necessary and sufficient cause

2. A recent newspaper article (Perlman 1982) discussed arguments linking fluoridation to acquired immune deficiency syndrome (AIDS), citing this evidence: ". . . while half the country's communities have fluoridated water supplies, and half do not, 90 percent of AIDS cases are coming from fluoridated areas and only 10 percent are coming from nonfluoridated areas." Discuss this in terms of what you have learned about the criteria of causation, indicating what other variables might be involved.

ADDITIONAL READINGS

Hirschi, Travis, and Selvin, Hanan, *Principles of Survey Analysis* (New York: Free Press, 1973), especially Part II. Excellent statements on causation within a practical framework. I can think of no better discussions of causation within the context of particular research findings than these.

The book is readable, stimulating, and generally just plain excellent.

Kaplan, Abraham, *The Conduct of Inquiry* (San Francisco: Chandler, 1964). A philosopher's perspective on social research. Especially in his discussions of explanation (Part 9), Kaplan lays the logical foundation for an understanding of the nature and analysis of causal relationships in social science.

Lazarsfeld, Paul, Foreword in Hyman, Herbert, *Survey Design and Analysis* (New York: Free Press, 1955). A classic and still valid statement of causation in social science. In the context of the elaboration model, Lazarsfeld provides a clear statement of the criteria for determining causation.

Rosenberg, Morris, *The Logic of Survey Analysis* (New York: Basic Books, 1968). A clear and practical statement of how the social researcher addresses causation. In his opening chapter, Rosenberg discusses the general meaning of causal relationships. In the concluding two chapters, he describes the process through which a researcher may arrive at causal conclusions.

PART 2

The Structuring of Inquiry

Posing problems properly is often more difficult than answering them. Indeed, a properly phrased question often seems to answer itself. You may have discovered the answer to a question just in the process of making the question clear to someone else.

At base, scientific research is a process for achieving generalized understanding through observation. Part 3 of this book describes some of the specific methods of social scientific observation. Part 2 deals with what should be observed. Put differently, Part 2 considers the posing of proper scientific questions, the structuring of inquiry.

Chapter 4 addresses the beginnings of research. It examines some of the purposes of inquiry, the units of analysis and topics of social scientific research, and the reasons scientists get involved in research projects.

Chapter 5 deals with the specification of what it is you want to study—a process called *conceptualization*. We're going to look at some of the terms that you and I use quite casually in everyday life—terms like *prejudice, liberalism, happiness,* and so forth—and we're going to see how essential it is to get clear about what we really mean by such terms when we do research.

Chapter 6 is an extension of Chapter 5. Once we have gotten clear on what we mean when we use certain terms, we are then in a position to create measurements of what those terms refer to. The process of devising steps or operations for measuring what we want to study is called *operationalization*. Chapter 6 deals with the topic of operationalization in general and with the concrete application of the process in the framing of questions to ask people.

Finally, we'll look at how social scientists go about selecting people or things for observation. Chapter 7, on *sampling,* addresses the fundamental scientific issue of *generalizability*. As we'll see, it is possible for us to select a few people or things for observation and then apply what we observe to a much larger group of people or things than we actually observed. It is possible, for example, to ask 1,000 Americans whom they favor for president of the United States and accurately predict how tens of millions will vote.

What you learn in Part 2 will bring you to the verge of making controlled social scientific observations. Part 3 will then show you how to take that next step.

4

Research Design

What You'll Learn in This Chapter

Here you'll learn the wide variety of research designs available to social science researchers: variatons as to who *or* what *is to be studied* when, how, *and for what* purpose.

INTRODUCTION

Science is an enterprise dedicated to "finding out." No matter what you want to find out, though, there are likely to be a great many ways of doing it. That's true in life generally. Suppose, for example, that you want to find out whether a particular automobile—say, the new Burpo-Blasto—would be a good car for you. You could, of course, buy one and find out that way. You could talk to a lot of B-B owners, or talk to people who considered buying one and didn't. You might check the classified ads to see if there were a lot of B-Bs being sold cheap. You could read a consumer magazine evaluation of Burpo-Blastos, or you could find out in a number of other ways. The same situation occurs in scientific inquiry.

Research design, the topic of this chapter, addresses the planning of scientific inquiry—designing a strategy for finding out something. Although the special details vary according to what you wish to study, there are two major aspects of research design. First, you must specify precisely what you want to find out. Second, you must determine the best way to do that. Interestingly, if you can handle the first consideration fully, you'll probably handle the second in the same process. As mathematicians say, a properly framed question contains the answer within it.

Ultimately, scientific inquiry comes down to making observations and interpreting what you've observed. (Parts 3 and 4 of this book deal with those two major aspects of social research.) Before you can observe and analyze, however, you need a plan. You need to determine what you're going to observe and analyze: why and how. That's what research design is all about.

Let's say that you are interested in studying corruption in government. That's certainly a worthy and appropriate topic for social research. But what *specifically* are you interested in? What do you mean by *corruption?* What kinds of behavior do you have in mind? And what do you mean by *government?* *Who* do you want to study: all public employees? only civilian employees? elected officials? civil servants? Finally, what is your purpose? Do you want to find out *how much* corruption there is? Do you want to learn *why* corruption exists? These are the kinds of questions that need to be answered in the course of research design.

This chapter provides a general introduction to research design, and the other chapters in Part 2 elaborate on specific aspects. In practice, *all* aspects of research design are interrelated. I have separated them here to permit a reasonably coherent picture of research by doing that. In this chapter, I want to lay out the various possibilities for social research. In later chapters, the interrelationships among parts will become clearer.

We'll start with a brief examination of some main purposes for social research. Then, we'll consider **units of analysis**—the what or whom you want to study. This topic will be elaborated further in Chapter 7, which deals with sampling.

Next, we'll look at some topics of research. We'll see some of the things you can study when you observe the units of analysis you've chosen. Chapters 5 and 6 elaborate on this topic by discussing the process of refining your measurements of the things you want to study. As we'll see, this aspect of research design is inextricably tied to the method of observation that you'll use.

There are two additional topics dealing with research design covered in this chapter. First, I want to draw your attention to alternative ways of handling *time* in social research. As we'll see, it is sometimes appropriate to examine a static cross section of social life, but other studies follow social processes across time.

Next comes a discussion of the various motivations that can and do lie behind social research. Although these do not represent design decisions in the way that the other topics of the chapter do, they will give you a broader understanding of the reasons social researchers have for engaging in social research.

Finally, the brief overview of the research process serves two purposes: (1) it gives you a sense of how *you* might go about designing a study, and (2) it gives you a map to the remainder of this book.

So, let's get started. We'll begin with the various purposes of social research.

PURPOSES OF RESEARCH

Social research, of course, serves many purposes. Three of the most common and useful purposes are *exploration, description,* and *explanation.* Although a given study can have more than one of these purposes—and most do—it will be useful to examine them separately because each has different implications for other aspects of research design.

Exploration

Much of social research is conducted to explore a topic, to provide a beginning familiarity with that topic. This purpose is typical when a researcher is examining a new interest or when the subject of study is itself relatively new and unstudied.

As an example, let's suppose that widespread taxpayer dissatisfaction with the government erupts into a taxpayer's revolt. People begin refusing to pay their taxes and they organize themselves around that issue. You might like to learn more about the movement: How widespread is it? What levels and degrees of support are there within the community? How is the movement organized? What kinds of people are active

in it? You might undertake an exploratory study to obtain at least approximate answers to some of these questions. You might check figures with tax-collecting officals, collect and study the literature of the movement, attend meetings, and interview leaders.

Exploratory studies are also appropriate in the case of more persistent phenomena. Perhaps a college student is unhappy with the college's dormitory regulations and wants to work toward changing them. He or she might study the history of dormitory regulations at the college, meet with college officials to learn the reasons for the regulations, and talk to a number of students to get a rough idea of student sentiments on the subject. This latter activity would not necessarily yield a precise and accurate picture of student opinion, but it could suggest what the results of a more careful study might be.

Exploratory studies are most typically done for three purposes: (1) simply to satisfy the researcher's curiosity and desire for better understanding, (2) to test the feasibility of undertaking a more careful study, and (3) to develop the methods to be employed in a more careful study. As an example of the last of these, a number of researchers at a major university, during the mid- to late-1960s, were interested in studying the extent, sources, and consequences of the changes in student attitudes occurring at about that time. It was evident to a casual observer that many students were becoming active in radical politics, others were becoming "flower children," and still others seemed to have maintained a commitment to the more traditional collegiate orientations. The researchers were interested in learning the relative proportions of the student body in each category, the reasons for commitment to the various positions, and the possible consequences for school performance, occupational plans, and so forth.

They ultimately planned to do a large-scale survey of students, but realized how difficult it would be to devise a questionnaire that measured the several student orientations. In view of this difficulty, they made a small-scale exploratory study, conducting open-ended interviews with approximately 50 students who were selected so that some seemed to fit into each of the initial categories. In the interviews, respondents were asked general questions about their orientations to college and to society and were encouraged to give their answers in depth and in their own words. The answers given in the exploratory study provided many insights into the complexities of the different major orientations and suggested ways in which those complexities could be tapped in a more structured questionnaire to be administered to a much larger sample.

Exploratory studies are very valuable in social scientific research. They are essential whenever a researcher is breaking new ground, and they can almost always yield new insights into a topic for research. Exploratory studies are also a source of grounded theory as discussed in Chapter 2.

The chief shortcoming of exploratory studies is that they seldom provide satisfactory answers to research questions. They can hint at the answers and can give insights into the research methods that could provide definitive answers. The reason exploratory studies are seldom definitive in themselves is the issue of **representativeness,** discussed at length in Chapter 7 in connection with sampling. Once you understand sampling and representativeness, you will be able to know whether a given exploratory study actually answered its research problem or only pointed the way toward an answer.

The researcher observes and then describes what was observed. Since scientific observation is careful and deliberate, however, scientific descriptions are typically more accurate and precise than casual descriptions.

The U.S. Census is an excellent example of a descriptive social scientific research project. The goal of the census is to describe accurately and precisely a wide variety of characteristics of the U.S. population, as well as the populations of smaller areas such as states and counties. Other examples of descriptive studies are the computation of age-sex profiles of populations done by demographers and the computation of crime rates for different cities.

A Gallup Poll conducted during a political election campaign has the purpose of describing the voting intentions of the electorate. A product marketing survey normally has the purpose of describing the people who use, or would use, a particular product. A researcher who carefully chronicles the events that take place on a labor union picket line has, or at least serves, a descriptive purpose. A researcher who computes and reports the number of times individual legislators voted for or against organized labor also has or serves a descriptive purpose.

Two aspects of social scientific description discussed in more detail in later chapters are worth mentioning at this point. They are the *quality* of descriptions and the **generalizability** of them. The first of these considerations will be examined in Chapter 5, which deals, among other things, with the quality criteria for measurement. The second consideration will be dealt with in Chapter 7 on sampling.

Description

A major purpose of many social scientific studies is to describe situations and events.

Explanation

The third general purpose of social scientific research is to explain things. Reporting the voting intentions of an electorate is a descriptive activity, but reporting *why* some people plan to vote for Candidate A and others for Candidate B is an explanatory activity. Reporting *why* some cities have higher crime rates than others is a case of explanation, but simply reporting the different crime rates is a case of description. A researcher has an explanatory purpose if he or she wishes to know why an anti-nuclear demonstration ended in a violent confrontation with police, as opposed to simply describing what happened.

Although it is useful to distinguish the three purposes of research, it bears repeating that most studies will have elements of all three. Suppose, for example, that you have set out to evaluate a new form of psychotherapy. Your study will have exploratory aspects, as you map out the impacts of the therapy. You will want to describe recovery rates, and you will undoubtedly seek to explain why the therapy works better for some types of people than for others.

You will see these several purposes at work in the following discussions of other aspects of research design. Let's turn now to a consideration of whom or what you want to explore, describe, and explain.

UNITS OF ANALYSIS

In social scientific research, there is a wide range of variation in what or whom is studied. By this, I do not mean the *topics* of research but what are technically called the **units of analysis.** Social scientists most typically perhaps have individual people as their units of analysis. You may make observatioons describing the characteristics of a large number of individual people, such as their sexes, ages, regions of birth, attitudes, and so forth. You then aggregate the descriptions of the many individuals to provide a

descriptive picture of the population that those individuals comprise.

For example, you may note the age and sex of each individual student enrolled in Political Science 110 and then characterize the students as a group as being 53 percent men and 47 percent women, and as having a mean age of 18.6 years. This is a descriptive analysis of the students taking Political Science 110. Although the final description would be of the class as a whole, the individual characteristics are aggregated for purposes of describing some larger group.

The same situation would exist in an explanatory study. Suppose that you wished to discover whether students with a high grade point average received better grades in Political Science 110 than did students with a low grade point average. So you would measure the grade point averages and the P.S. 110 grades of individual students. You might then aggregate all those students with a high grade point average and aggregate all those with a low grade point average and see which group received the best grades in the course. The purpose of the study would be to explain why some students do better in the course than others (looking at overall grade point averages as a possible explanation), but individual students would still be the units of analysis.

Units of analysis, then, are those units that we initially describe for the ultimate purpose of aggregating their characteristics in order to describe some larger group or explain some abstract phenomenon. This concept should be clarified further as we now consider some possible social science units of analysis.

Individuals

As mentioned above, individual human beings are perhaps the most typical units of analysis for social scientific research. We tend to describe and explain social groups and interactions by aggregating and manipulating the descriptions of individuals.

Any variety of individuals may be the unit of analysis for social scientific research. This point is more important than it may seem at first reading. The norm of *generalized understanding* in social science should suggest that scientific findings are most valuable when they apply to *all* kinds of people. In practice, however, social scientists seldom study all kinds of people. At the very least, their studies are typically limited to the people living in a single country, though some comparative studies stretch across national boundaries. Often, our studies are even more circumscribed.

Examples of circumscribed groups whose members may be units of analysis—at the individual level—would be students, residents, workers, voters, parents, and faculty members. Note that each of these terms implies some population of individual persons. The term *population* will be considered in some detail in Chapter 7 on sampling. At this point, it is enough to realize that descriptive studies having individuals as their units of analysis typically aim to describe the population that those individuals comprise, whereas explanatory studies aim to discover the social dynamics operating within that population.

Individuals, as the units of analysis, may be characterized in terms of their membership in social groupings. Thus, an individual may be described as belonging to a rich family or to a poor one, or a person may be described as having a college-educated mother or not. We might examine in a research project whether people with college-educated mothers are likely to attend college than are those with non-college-educated mothers, or whether high school graduates in rich families are more likely to attend college than are those in poor families. In each case, the individual would be the unit of analysis—not the mother or the family.

Groups

Social groups themselves may also be the units of analysis for social scientific research. Realize that this case is not the same as studying the individuals within a group. If you were to study the members of a criminal gang in order to learn about gangsters, for example, the individual (gangster) would be the unit of analysis; but if you studied all the gangs in a city in order to learn the differences, say, between big gangs and small ones, between "uptown" and "downtown" gangs, and so forth—the unit of analysis would be the *gang*, a social group.

Families might be the units of analysis in a study. You might describe each family in terms of its total annual income and according to whether or not it had a videotape recorder. You could aggregate families and describe the mean income of families and the percentage with color television sets. You would then be in a position to determine whether families with higher incomes were more likely to have color television sets than those with lower incomes. The individual *family* in such a case would be the unit of analysis.

Other units of analysis at the group level could be friendship cliques, married couples, census blocks, cities, or geographic regions. Each of these terms also implies some population. *Street gangs* implies some population that includes all street gangs. The population of street gangs could be described, say, in terms of its geographical distribution throughout a city, and an explanatory study of street gangs might discover, say, whether large gangs were more likely than small ones to engage in inter-gang warfare.

Formal social organizations may also be the units of analysis in social scientific research. An example would be corporations, implying, of course, a population of all corporations. Individual corporations might be characterized in terms of their number of employees, net annual profits, gross assets, number of defense contracts, percentage of employees who are from racial or ethnic minority groups, and so forth. We might determine whether large corporations hire a larger or smaller percentage of minority group employees than small corporations do. Other examples of formal social organizations suitable as units of analysis would be churches, colleges, army divisions, academic departments, and supermarkets.

When social groups are the units of analysis, their characteristics may be derived from the characteristics of their individual members. Thus, a family might be described in terms of the age, race, or education of its head. In a descriptive study, then, we might find the percentage of all families that have a college-educated head of family. In an explanatory study, we might determine whether families with a college-educated head have, on the average, more or fewer children than families with heads who have not graduated from college. In each of these examples, however, the family would be the unit of analysis. (Had we asked whether college graduates—college-educated *individuals*—have more or fewer children than their less educated counterparts, then the individual *person* would have been the unit of analysis.)

Social groups (and also individuals) may be characterized in other ways: for instance, according to their environments or their membership in larger groupings. Families, for example, might be described in terms of the type of dwelling unit they reside in, and we might want to determine whether rich families are more likely to reside in single-family houses (as opposed, say, to apartments) than poor families are. The unit of analysis would still be the family.

If all this seems unduly complicated, be assured that in most research projects you are likely to undertake, the unit of analysis

will be relatively clear to you. When the unit of analysis is not so clear, however, it is absolutely essential to determine what it is; otherwise, you will be unable to determine what observations are to be made about whom or what.

Some studies have the purpose of making descriptions or explanations pertaining to more than one unit of analysis. In these cases, it is imperative that the researcher anticipate what conclusions he or she wishes to draw with regard to what units of analysis.

Social Artifacts

Another large group of possible units of analysis may be referred to generally as *social artifacts*, or the products of social beings or their behavior. One class of artifacts would include social objects such as books, poems, paintings, automobiles, buildings, songs, pottery, jokes, and scientific discoveries.

Each of these objects implies a population of all such objects: all books, all novels, all biographies, all introductory sociology textbooks, all cookbooks. An individual book might be characterized by its size, weight, length, price, content, number of pictures, volume of sale, or description of its author. The population of all books or of a particular kind of book could be analyzed for the purpose of description or explanation.

A social scientist could analyze whether paintings by Russian, Chinese, or American artists showed the greatest degree of working-class consciousness, taking paintings as the units of analysis and describing each, in part, by the nationality of its creator. You might examine a local newspaper's editorials regarding a local university for purposes of describing, or perhaps explaining, changes in the newspaper's editorial position on the university over time; individual editorials would be the units of analysis.

Social interactions form another class of social artifacts suitable for social scientific research. Weddings would be an example. Weddings might be characterized as racially or religiously mixed or not, religious or secular in ceremony, resulting in divorce or not, or they could be characterized by descriptions of one or both of the marriage partners. Realize that when a researcher reports that weddings between partners of different religions are more likely to be performed by secular authorities than those between partners of the same religion, the weddings are the units of analysis and not the individual partners to them.

Other examples of social interactions that might be the units of analysis in social scientific research are friendship choices, court cases, traffic accidents, divorces, fistfights, ship launchings, airline hijackings, race riots, and congressional hearings.

Units of Analysis in Review

The purpose of this section has been to stretch your imagination somewhat regarding possible units of analysis for social scientific research. Although individual human beings are typically the units of analysis, that need not be the case. Indeed, many research questions can more appropriately be answered through the examination of other units of analysis.

The concept of the unit of analysis may seem more complicated than it needs to be. It is irrelevant whether you classify a given unit of analysis as a group, a formal organization, or a social artifact. It is essential, however, that you be able to identify what your unit of analysis *is*. You must decide whether you are studying marriages or marriage partners, crimes or criminals, corpo-

rations or corporate executives. Unless you keep this point in mind constantly, you run the risk of making assertions about one unit of analysis based on the examination of another.

To test your grasp of the concept of units of analysis, here are some examples of real research topics. See if you can determine the unit of analysis in each. (The answers are at the very end of this chapter.)

[1] . . . women watch TV more than men because they are likely to work fewer hours outside the home than men. . . . Black people watch an average of approximately three-quarters of an hour more television per day than white people.

(Hughes 1980:290)

[2] Of the 130 incorporated U.S. cities with more than 100,000 inhabitants in 1960, 126 had at least two short-term nonproprietary general hospitals accredited by the American Hospital Association.

(Turk 1980:317)

[3] The early TM organizations were small and informal. The Los Angeles group, begun in June 1959, met at a member's house where, incidentally, Maharishi was living.

(Johnston 1980:337)

[4] However, it appears that the nursing staffs exercise strong influence over . . . a decision to change the nursing care system. . . . Conversely, among those decisions dominated by the administration and the medical staffs. . .

(Comstock 1980:77)

[5] In 1958, there were 13 establishments with 1,000 employees or more, accounting for 60 percent of the industry's value added. In 1977, the number of this type of establishment dropped to 11, but their share of industry value added had fallen to about 48 percent.

(York and Persigehl 1981:41)

[6] Though 667,000 out of 2 million farmers in the United States are women, women historically have not been viewed as farmers, but rather, as the farmer's wife.

(Votaw 1979:8)

The Ecological Fallacy

At this point it is appropriate to introduce briefly two important concepts related to units of analysis: the **ecological fallacy** and **reductionism.** The first of these concepts, the ecological fallacy, means the danger, just mentioned, of making assertions about individuals as the unit of analysis based on the examination of groups or other aggregations. Let's consider a hypothetical illustration of this fallacy.

Suppose we are interested in learning something about the nature of electoral support received by a female political candidate in a recent city-wide election. Let's assume that we have the vote tally for each precinct so that we can tell which precincts gave her the greatest support and which gave her the least. Assume also that we have census data describing some of the characteristics of those precincts. Our analysis of such data might show that precincts whose voters were relatively young gave the female candidate a greater proportion of their votes than precincts whose voters had an older average age. We might be tempted to conclude from these findings that young voters were more likely to vote for the female candidate than older voters—that age affected support for the woman. In reaching such a conclusion, we run the risk of committing the *ecological fallacy* because it may have been the older voters in those "young" precincts who voted for the woman. Our problem is that we have examined *precincts* as our units of analysis and wish to draw conclusions about *voters*.

The same problem would arise if we discovered that crime rates were higher in cities having large black populations than in those with few blacks. We would not know if the crimes were actually committed by blacks. Or if we found suicide rates higher in Protestant countries than in Catholic ones, we still could not know for sure that more Protestants than Catholics committed suicide.

Notice that very often the social scientist must address a particular research question through an ecological analysis such as those mentioned above. Perhaps the most appropriate data are simply not available. For example, the precinct vote tallies and the precinct characteristics mentioned in our initial example might be easy to obtain, but we may not have the resources to conduct a post-election survey of individual voters. In such cases, we may reach a tentative conclusion, recognizing and noting the risk of committing the ecological fallacy.

Don't let these warnings against the ecological fallacy lead you into committing what we might call an *individualistic fallacy.* Some students approaching social research for the first time have trouble reconciling general patterns of attitudes and actions with individual exceptions they know of. If you know a rich Democrat, for example, that doesn't deny the fact that most rich people vote Republican—as individuals. The ecological fallacy deals with something else altogether—drawing conclusions about individuals based solely on the observation of groups.

Reductionism

A second concept related to units of analysis is *reductionism*. Basically, *reductionism* refers to an overly strict limitation on the kinds of concepts and variables to be considered as causes in explaining a broad range of human behavior. Sociologists may tend to consider only sociological variables (values, norms, roles); economists may consider only economic variables (supply and demand, marginal value); psychologists may consider only psychological variables (personality types, traumas). For example, what caused the American Revolution? A shared commitment to the value of individual liberty? The economic plight of the colonies in relation to Britain? The megalomania of the Founding Fathers? Scientists from different disciplines tend to look at different types of answers and ignore the others. Explaining all or most human behavior in terms of economic factors is called *economic reductionism*; explaining all or most human behavior in terms of psychological factors is called *psychological reductionism*; and so forth. Note how this issue relates to the Chapter 2 discussion of theoretical paradigms.

Reductionism of any type tends to suggest that particular units of analysis or variables are more relevant than others. If we were to regard shared values as the cause of the American Revolution, our unit of analysis would be the individual colonist. An economist, though, might choose the thirteen different colonies as units of analysis and examine the economic organizations and conditions of each colony. A psychologist might choose individual leaders as the units of analysis for purposes of examining their personalities.

Reductionism, like the ecological fallacy, occurs with the use of inappropriate units of analysis. The appropriate unit of analysis for a given research question, however, is not always clear, and it is often debated by social scientists, especially across disciplinary boundaries.

TOPICS FOR RESEARCH

The preceding discussion of different possible units of analysis has frequently mentioned ways of describing or characterizing them. These represent the *topics* for research. To present a general overview of this, I'll consider three classes: *characteristics, orientations,* and *actions*. While these do not exhaust the possibilities for research topics, nor are the three rigidly separate from each other, they should suggest some of the possibilities for social research.

Characteristics

To begin, the various units of analysis may be characterized in terms of their characteristics or their states of being. Individual persons might be characterized by such states as sex, age, height, marital status, deformities, region of origin, or hearing ability. Social groups and formal organizations might be characterized by size, structure, location, and aggregated descriptions of their members. Physical objects as social artifacts might be described physically—by size, weight, and color for example—or by the characteristics of the humans associated with them. Social interactions as units of analysis might be characterized in terms of where they occur, when they occur, or what the people involved are like.

These examples are not intended to represent an exhaustive list of possibilities. Nevertheless, they should suggest some of the ways to characterize units of analysis.

Orientations

When individual people are the units of analysis, we frequently investigate what are called *orientations*: attitudes, beliefs, personality traits, prejudices, predispositions, and the like. Individuals might be characterized as religious, politically liberal, anti-Semitic, intellectually sophisticated, superstitious, scientific.

Social groups and formal organizations, similarly, might be characterized in terms of their purposes, policies, regulations, or procedures, or in terms of the aggregated orientations of their members.

Social interactions might be similarly characterized. Airline hijackings might be characterized as politically or nonpolitically motivated. So could court cases and congressional hearings.

Actions

Sometimes social *action* is the focus of research. We may observe directly or accept secondhand accounts of individual human actions such as voting, bond buying, investing, striking, dropping out of school, going to church, or buying Brand X toothpaste. Secondhand accounts of actions may come from the participants themselves or from other sources. Thus, to find out whether people have registered to vote, we might ask them, or we might check the list of registered voters.

Social groups and formal organizations act as well. Families may go on picnics, pray together, fight over money, or move to another city. Fraternities may sponsor concerts; sororities may collect money to send girls to camp. Corporations may contribute to political campaigns, merge with other corporations, fix prices, or go bankrupt.

Since social interactions are actions themselves, it is a little more difficult to imagine them engaging in actions. Nevertheless, marriages succeed or fail, court cases result in conviction or acquittal, and fistfights cool off or get out of hand.

Like the earlier discussion of units of analysis, the present section on topics for research is intended as a mind-expanding exercise, not as a definitive statement of all the possible or legitimate topics. It matters little at this point whether you regard a

person's score on an IQ test as a characteristic, an orientation, or an action—only that you recognize it as a possible focus of study.

Chapters 5 and 6 will return to these issues with a more rigorously analytical perspective.

THE TIME DIMENSION

Time plays a number of roles in the design and execution of research, quite aside from the time it takes to do research. When we examine causation in detail in Part 4, we'll find that the time sequence of events and situations is a critical element in determining causation. Time is also involved in the issue of the generalizability of research findings. Do the descriptions and explanations that result from a particular study accurately represent the situation of 10 years ago, 10 years from now, or do they represent only the present state of affairs?

Thus far in this chapter, we have regarded research design as a process for deciding *what aspects* we shall observe, *of whom,* and *for what purpose.* Now we must consider a set of time-related options that cuts across each of these earlier considerations. Our observations may be made more or less at one time, or they may be deliberately stretched over a long period.

Cross-Sectional Studies

Many research projects are designed to study some phenomenon by taking a cross section of it at one time and analyzing that cross section carefully. Exploratory and descriptive studies are often **cross-sectional**. A single U.S. Census, for instance, is a study aimed at describing the U.S. population at a given time.

Many explanatory studies are also cross-sectional. A researcher who conducted a large-scale national survey to examine the sources of racial and religious prejudice would, in all likelihood, be dealing with a single time frame in the ongoing process of prejudice.

Explanatory cross-sectional studies have an inherent problem. Typically, their aim is to understand causal processes that occur over time, yet their conclusions are based on observations made at only one time. This problem is somewhat akin to that of determining the speed of a moving object on the basis of a high-speed, still photograph that freezes the movement of the object. Some of the ways in which you can deal with this difficult problem will be discussed a little later.

Longitudinal Studies

Other research projects called **longitudinal studies** are designed to permit observations over an extended period. An example is a researcher who participates in and observes the activities of a radical political group from the time of its inception to its demise. Analyses of newspaper editorials or Supreme Court decisions over time are other examples. In the latter instances, it would be irrelevant whether the researcher's observations and analyses were made at one time or over the course of the actual events under study.

Three special types of longitudinal studies should be noted here. **Trend studies** are those that study changes within some general population over time. Examples would be a comparison of U.S. Censuses over time, showing growth in the national population, or a series of Gallup Polls during the course of an election campaign, showing trends in the relative strengths and standing of different candidates.

Cohort studies examine more specific subpopulations (cohorts) as they change over time. Typically, a cohort is an age group, such as those people born during the 1920s, but it can also be based on some other time grouping, such as people attending college during the Vietnam War, people who got married in 1964, and so forth. An example of a cohort study would be a series of national surveys, conducted perhaps every 10 years, to study the economic attitudes of the cohort born during the depression of the early 1930s. A sample of persons 20–25 years of age might be surveyed in 1950, another sample of those 30–35 years of age in 1960, and another sample of those 40–45 years of age in 1970. Although the specific set of people studied in each of those surveys would be different, each sample would represent the survivors of the cohort born between 1930 and 1935.

Panel studies are similar to trend and cohort studies except that the same set of people is studied each time. One example would be a voting study in which the same sample of voters was interviewed every month during an election campaign and asked for whom they intended to vote. Such a study would make it possible to analyze overall trends in voter preferences for different candidates, but it would have the added advantage of showing the precise patterns of persistence and change in intentions. For example, a trend study that showed that Candidates A and B each had exactly half of the voters on September first and on October first as well could indicate that none of the electorate had changed voting plans, that all of the voters had changed their intentions, or something in between. A panel study would eliminate this confusion by showing what kinds of voters switched from A to B and what kinds switched from B to A, as well as other facts.

Since the distinctions between trend, cohort, and panel studies are sometimes difficult to grasp at first, let's contrast the three study designs in terms of the same variable: political party affiliation. A trend study might look at shifts in the affiliations of the American electorate over time, as the Gallup Poll does on a regular basis. A cohort study might follow shifts in party affiliations among "the Depression generation," specifically, say, people who were between 20 and 30 in 1932. We could study a sample of people 30–40 years old in 1942, a new sample of people aged 40–50 in 1952, and so forth. A panel study could start with a sample of the whole population or of some special subset and study those specific individuals over time. Notice that only the panel study would give a full picture of the shifts in party affiliations: from Democrat to Republican, from Republican to Democrat, and so forth. Cohort and trend studies would only uncover *net* changes.

Longitudinal studies have an obvious advantage over cross-sectional ones in providing information describing processes over time. But very often this advantage comes at a heavy cost in both time and money, especially in a large-scale survey. Observations may have to be made at the time events are occurring, and the method of observation may require many research workers.

Approximating Longitudinal Studies

Often it is possible to draw approximate conclusions about processes that take place over time even when only cross-sectional data are available. It is worth noting some of the ways to do that.

Sometimes, cross-sectional data imply processes over time on the basis of simple logic. For example, a study of student drug use was conducted at the University of Hawaii in 1969 (mentioned in Chapter 2). Students were asked to report whether they

had ever tried each of a number of illegal drugs. With regard to marijuana and LSD, it was found that some students had tried both drugs, some had tried only one, and others had not tried either. Since these data were collected at one time, and since some students presumably would experiment with drugs later on, it would appear that such a study could not tell the *order* in which students were likely to experiment with marijuana and LSD: were students more likely to try marijuana or LSD first?

A closer examination of the data showed, however, that although some students reported having tried marijuana but not LSD, there were no students in the study who had tried only LSD. From this finding it was inferred—as common wisdom suggested—that marijuana use preceded LSD use. If the process of drug experimentation occurred in the opposite time order, then a study at a given time should have found some students who had tried LSD but not marijuana, and it should have found no students who had tried only marijuana.

Logical inferences may also be made whenever the time order of variables is clear. If we discover in a cross-sectional study of college students that those educated in private high schools received better college grades than those educated in public high schools, we would conclude that the type of high school attended affected college grades, not the other way around. Thus, even though our observations were made at only one time, we would feel justified in drawing conclusions about processes taking place across time.

Very often, age differences discovered in a cross-sectional study form the basis for inferring processes across time. Suppose you are interested in the pattern of worsening health over the course of the typical life cycle. You might examine that by studying the results of annual checkups in a large hospital. You could group health records according to the ages of those examined and rate each age group in terms of several health conditions—sight, hearing, blood pressure, and so forth. By reading across the age group ratings for each health condition, you would have something approximating the health history of individuals. Thus, you might conclude that the average person develops vision problems earlier in life than hearing problems, for example. You would need to be cautious in this assumption, however, since the differences might reflect society-wide trends. Perhaps improved hearing examinations were instituted in the schools, but only the young people in your study had had the benefit of them.

Asking people to *recall* their pasts is another common way of approximating observations over time. We use that method when we ask people where they were born or when they graduated from high school or whom they voted for in 1976. The danger in this technique is evident. Sometimes people have faulty memories; sometimes they lie. When people are asked in post-election polls whom they voted for, the results inevitably show more people voting for the winner than did so on election day. Thus, although recall may be the only way of approximating observations across time, it must be used with caution.

These, then, are some of the ways in which time figures into social research and some of the ways social scientists have learned to cope with it. In designing any study, you need to look at both the explicit and implicit assumptions you are making about time in whatever you are studying. Are you interested in describing some process that occurs over time, or are you simply going to describe what exists now? If you want to describe a process occurring over time, will you be able to make observations at different points in the process, or will you have to approximate such observations—drawing logical inferences from what you can observe now?

Unless you pay attention to questions like these, you are likely to end up in trouble. The box entitled "The Time Dimension and Aging" explores this issue further.

HOW TO DESIGN A RESEARCH PROJECT

You've now seen some of the options available to social researchers in designing projects, but what if *you* were to undertake research? Where would you start? Then, where would you go? These are the topics of this final section of the chapter.

Although research design occurs at the beginning of a research project, it involves all the steps of the subsequent project. The comments to follow, then, (1) should give you some guidance on how to start a research project and (2) will provide an overview of the topics that follow in later chapters of the book. Ultimately, the research process needs to be seen as a *whole*, and you need to grasp it as a whole in order to create a research design. Unfortunately, both textbooks and human cognition operate on the basis of sequential *parts*.

Figure 4-1 presents a schematic view of the social science research process. I present this view reluctantly, since it may suggest more of a "cookbook" order to research than is the case in practice. Nonetheless, as I've said, it should be useful to you to have some overview of the whole process before we launch into the specific details of particular components of research.

At the top of the diagram are interests, ideas, and theories, the possible beginning points for a line of research. The letters (A, B, X, Y, and so forth) represent variables or concepts such as prejudice, alienation, and so on. Thus, you might have a general *interest* in finding out what causes some

The Time Dimension and Aging

by Joseph J. Leon

Behavioral Science Department, California State Polytechnic
University, Pomona

One way to identify the type of time dimension used in a study is to imagine a number of different research projects on growing older in the American society. If we studied a sample of individuals in 1990 and compared the different age groups, the design would be termed *cross-sectional*. If you or another researcher drew another sample of individuals using the same study instrument in the year 2000 and compared the new data with the 1990 data, the design would be termed *trend*.

Let's suppose you or another researcher wished to study only those individuals from the new sample in the year 2000 who were 51–60 and wished to compare them with the 1990 sample of 41–50-year-old persons (the 41–50 age cohort); this study design would be termed *cohort*. The comparison could be made for the 51–60 and 61–70 age cohorts as well. Now, if we as researchers desired to do a *panel* study on growing older in America, we would draw a sample in the year 1990 and, using the same sampled individuals in the year 2000, do the study again. It must be remembered that there would be fewer people in the year 2000 study because all the 41–50-year-old people in 1990 are 51–60 and there would be no 41–50-year-old individuals in the year 2000

study. Furthermore, some of the sampled individuals in 1990 would no longer be alive in the year 2000.

CROSS-SECTIONAL STUDY

1990
41–50
51–60
61–70
71–80

COHORT STUDY

1990	2000
41–50	41–50
51–60	51–60
61–70	61–70
71–80	71–80

TREND STUDY

1990	2000
41–50	41–50
51–60	51–60
61–70	61–70
71–80	71–80

PANEL STUDY

1990	2000
41–50*	41–50
51–60*	51–60*
61–70*	61–70*
71–80*	71–80*
	+81*

⟷ *Denotes comparison*
* *Denotes same individuals*

Figure 4-1 The Research Process

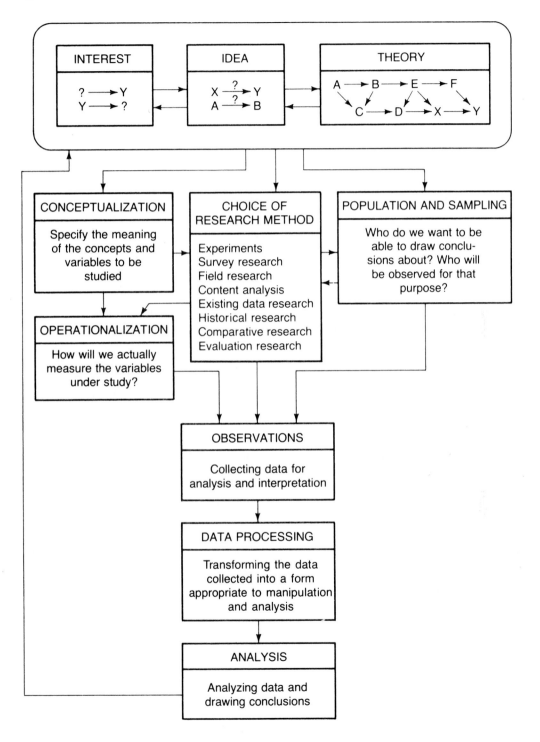

people to be more prejudiced than others, or you might want to know some of the consequences of alienation, say. Alternatively, your inquiry might begin with a specific *idea* about the way things are. You might have the idea that working on an assembly line causes alienation, for example. I have put a question mark in the diagram to indicate that you aren't sure things are the way you suspect they are. Finally, I have represented a *theory* as a complex set of relationships among several variables.

Notice, moreover, that there is often a movement back and forth across these several possible beginnings. An initial interest may lead to the formulation of an idea, which may be fit into a larger theory, and the theory may produce new ideas and create new interests.

Any or all of these three may suggest the need for empirical research. The purpose of such research can be to explore an interest, test a specific idea, or validate a complex theory. Whatever the purpose, a variety of decisions needs to be made, as indicated in the remainder of the diagram.

To make this discussion more concrete, let's take a specific research example. Suppose you are concerned about the nuclear-arms race and have a special interest in learning why some college students are in favor of the United States initiating a nuclear freeze, while others oppose a freeze. Going a step further, let's say you have the impression that students in the humanities and social sciences seem generally more inclined to support the idea of a freeze than those in the natural sciences. That kind of situation often leads people to design and conduct social research.

In terms of the options we've discussed earlier in the chapter, your research would be pretty much exploratory. You probably have both descriptive and explanatory interests: what percentage of the student body favors the freeze, and what causes some to favor it and others to oppose it? The units

of analysis are individuals: college students. You might decide that a cross-sectional study would suit your purposes; let's assume you'd be satisfied to learn something about the way things are now. While this would provide you with no direct evidence of processes taking place over time, you might be able to approximate some longitudinal analyses as discussed earlier.

Getting Started The topmost portion of Figure 4-1 contains a number of possible activities. In pursuing your interest in student attitudes about the nuclear freeze, you would undoubtedly want to read something about the issue. If you have a hunch that attitudes are somehow related to college major, you might want to find out what other researchers may have written about that. Appendix A of this book will give you some assistance in using your college library. In addition, you would probably want to talk to people—some who support the freeze and some who don't. You would probably want to attend meetings of freeze-related groups. The purpose of all these activities is to prepare you to handle the various decisions of research design we are about to examine. As you review the previous research literature regarding the freeze, you should note the design decisions other researchers have made, always asking whether the same decisions would satisfy your purpose.

What *is* your purpose, by the way? It's important that you get clear about that before designing your study. Do you plan to write a paper based on your research to satisfy a course requirement or as an honors thesis? Is your purpose to gain information that will support you in arguing for or against the freeze? Do you want to write an article for the campus newspaper or for an academic journal?

Usually, your purpose for undertaking research can be expressed in the form of a *report*. Appendix B of this book will help you with the organization of research reports, and I would recommend that you outline such a report as the *first* step in the design of your project. Specifically, you should get clear about the kinds of statements you will want to make when the research is complete. Here are two examples of such statements: "_____ percent of State U. students favor a nuclear freeze." "Engineers are (more/less) likely than sociologists to favor the freeze."

While your final report may not look much like your initial image of it, this exercise will give you something against which to test the appropriateness of different research designs.

Conceptualization We often talk pretty casually about social science concepts such as prejudice, alienation, religiosity, liberalism, and so forth, but it's necessary to specify what we mean by these concepts in order to do research on them. Chapter 5 examines this process of **conceptualization** in depth. For now, let's see what it might involve in the case of our hypothetical example.

If you are going to study how college students feel about a nuclear freeze and why, the first thing you'll have to specify is what you mean by the "freeze." This highly charged term has come to mean very different things to different people: ranging from unilateral disarmament and surrender, to the United States telling the USSR, "we'll stop building nuclear arms if you will."

Obviously, you will need to specify what you mean by the term in your research, but this doesn't necessarily mean you have to settle for a single definition. In fact, an excellent strategy would be to present students with several different (but clear) possible meanings of a nuclear freeze and ask them how they feel about each. You might even want to ask them which comes closest to what they mean by the "freeze."

You will, of course, need to specify all the concepts you plan to study. If you want to study the possible effect of college major, you'll have to decide whether you want to limit that to officially declared majors or to also include students' intentions in that regard. What will you do with those who have no major?

Choice of Research Method As we'll see in Part 3 of this book, there are a variety of research methods available to the social scientist. Each of those methods has strengths and weaknesses, and certain concepts are more appropriately studied by some methods than by others.

The Wells and Picou study of sociological theory mentioned in Chapter 2 offers some idea of the relative popularity of the various research methods as well. Table 4-1 shows the frequency with which three classes of methods were used in articles published in the *American Sociological Review* between 1936 and 1978. The table also shows the trends in popularity over time.

The conclusions to be drawn from Table 4-1 are clear. In the earliest period, interpretative methods and surveys each accounted for about half the articles published. The years since have witnessed a substantial growth in the popularity of surveys and a corresponding decline for interpretative methods. Experimental studies have been relatively rare throughout the period. While these figures represent only one journal in one social science discipline, they provide some sense of the popularity of the data collection methods from which social scientists can choose.

In terms of our hypothetical study of attitudes toward a nuclear freeze, a survey might be the most appropriate method: either interviewing students or asking them to fill out a questionnaire. As you'll see in Chapter 9, surveys are particularly well suited to the study of individuals' attitudes. This is not to say that you couldn't make good use of the other methods presented in Part 3.

Table 4-1   Classification of *ASR* Articles by Primary Method of Data Collection

Method of Data Collection	Time Period			Total	
	1936–1949	1950–1964	1965–1978	1936–1978	
Interpretative*	51%	27%	17%	31%	
Survey	48	70	80	67	
Experimental	1	3	3	2	
	(137)	(200)	(152) =	(489) =	100%

*Interpretative includes historical review of documents, books, etc.; systematic content analysis; informant; observation; unstructured interview.

Source: Adapted from Richard H. Wells and J. Steven Picou, *American Sociology: Theoretical and Methodological Structure* (Washington D.C.: University Press of America, 1981), p. 115. Used by permission.

Through *content analysis* (discussed in Chapter 11), for example, you might examine letters to the editor and analyze the different images letter-writers have of the freeze. *Field research* (Chapter 10) would provide an avenue to understanding how people interact with one another regarding the freeze, how they discuss it, and how they change their minds. As you read Part 3, you'll see ways in which other research methods might be used in studying this topic. Usually, the very best study design is one that uses more than one research method—taking advantage of their different strengths.

Operationalization   Having specified the concepts to be studied and having chosen the research method to be used, we must create concrete measurement techniques. **Operationalization,** discussed in Chapter 6, refers to the concrete steps or operations that will be used to measure specific concepts.

If you had decided to study attitudes toward a nuclear freeze by a survey, your operationalization would take the form of questionnaire items. Thus, you would operationalize attitudes toward a nuclear freeze, perhaps, with the statement, "Listed below are several different ways people have described what 'nuclear freeze' means to

them. Beside each description, indicate whether you would generally favor or oppose the actions described." This would be followed by several different descriptions of the freeze and "Favor" and "Oppose" boxes beside each.

Population and Sampling   In addition to refining concepts and measurements, decisions must be made about *who* or *what* to study. The *population* for a study is that group (usually of people) about whom we want to be able to draw conclusions. We are almost never able to study all the members of the population that interests us, however. In virtually every case, we must sample subjects for study. Chapter 7 describes methods for selecting samples that give an adequate reflection of the whole population that interests us. Notice in the diagram that decisions about population and sampling are related to decisions about the research method to be used.

In the study of freeze attitudes we've been discussing, the relevant population is the student population of your college. As you'll discover in Chapter 7, however, selecting a sample will require you to get more specific than that. Will you include part-time as well as full-time students? Only degree-candidates or everyone? Foreign as well as American citizens? Undergraduates, graduate students, or both? There are many such questions—each of which must be answered in terms of your research purpose. If your purpose is to predict how students would vote in a local referendum on the freeze, you might want to limit your population to those eligible and likely to vote.

Observations   Having decided what to study among whom by what method, we are now ready to make observations—to collect empirical data. The chapters of Part 3, which describe the various research methods, give the different observation methods appropriate to each.

In the case of the nuclear freeze survey, you might want to print questionnaires and mail them to a sample selected from the student body, or you could arrange to have a team of interviewers conduct the survey over the telephone. The relative advantages and disadvantages of these and other possibilities are discussed in Chapter 9.

Data Processing   Depending on the research method chosen, you will have amassed a volume of observations in a form that probably isn't easily interpretable. Chapter 13 describes some of the ways in which social scientific data are processed or transformed for quantitative analysis.

In the case of a survey, the "raw" observations are typically in the form of questionnaires with boxes checked, answers written in spaces, and the like. The data-processing phase for a survey typically involves the classification (*coding*) of written-in answers, and the transformation of all information to some computer format: on magnetic diskettes, tapes, punched cards, etc.

Analysis   Finally we manipulate the collected data for the purpose of drawing conclusions that reflect on the interests, ideas, and theories that initiated the inquiry. Chapters 14 through 18 describe a few of the many options available to you in analyzing data. Notice that the results of your analyses feed back into your initial interests, ideas, and theories. In practice, this feedback may very well represent the beginning of another cycle of inquiry.

In the study of student attitudes about a nuclear freeze, the analysis phase would pursue both descriptive and explanatory aims. You might begin by calculating the percentages of students who favored or opposed each of the several different versions of a nuclear freeze. Taken together, these several percentages would provide a good picture of student opinion on the issue.

Moving beyond simple description, you might describe the opinions of different subsets of the student body: men versus women; freshmen, sophomores, juniors, seniors, graduate students; engineering majors, sociology majors, English majors, and so forth. The description of subgroups could then lead you into an explanatory analysis, as explained in Chapter 14.

Review   As this overview shows, research design involves a set of decisions regarding *what topic* is to be studied among *what population* with *what research methods* for *what purpose*. Whereas the earlier sections of this chapter—dealing with research purposes, units of analysis, topics—aimed at broadening your perspective in all these regards, research design is the process of narrowing, of focusing, your perspective for purposes of a particular study.

If you are doing a research project for a course you are taking, many aspects of research design may have been specified for you in advance. If you must do a project for a course in experimental methods, the method of research will have been specified for you. If the project is for a course in voting behavior, the research topic will have been somewhat specified. Since it would not be feasible for me to anticipate all such con-straints, the following discussion will assume there are none.

In designing a research project, you will find it useful to begin by assessing three things: your own interests, your abilities, and the resources available to you. Each of these considerations will suggest a large number of possible studies.

Simulate the beginning of a somewhat conventional research project: ask yourself what you are interested in understanding. Surely you have several questions about social behavior and attitudes. Why are some people politically liberal and others politically conservative? Why are some people more religious than others? Are college students becoming more vocationally oriented or less so? Do colleges and universities still dis-criminate against women faculty members? Are interracial marriages more or less suc-cessful than others? Do students learn more in large classes or small ones? Is the United States's economy more or less dependent on war and defense than in the past? Sit for a while and think about the kinds of ques-tions that interest and concern you.

Once you have a few questions you would be interested in answering for yourself, think about the kind of information that would be needed to answer them. What research units of analysis would provide the most relevant information: college students, cor-porations, voters, cities, or what? This question will probably be inseparable in your thoughts from the question of research top-ics. Then ask which *aspects* of the units of analysis would provide the information you need to answer your research question?

Once you have some ideas about the kind of information relevant to your purpose, ask yourself how you might go about get-ting that information. Are the relevant data likely to be already available somewhere (say, in a government publication), or would you have to collect them yourself? If you think you would have to collect them, how would

you go about doing that? Would it be nec-essary to interview a large number of people? Could you learn what you need to know by attending meetings of certain groups? Could you glean the data you need from books in the library?

As you answer these questions, you are well into the process of research design. Keep in mind your own research abilities and the resources available to you, however. Do not design the perfect study if you will be un-able to carry it out. You may want to try a research method you have not used before, since research should be a learning expe-rience in many ways, but you should not put yourself at too great a disadvantage.

Once you have a general idea of what you want to study and how, carefully review previous research in journals and books to see how other researchers have addressed the topic and what they have learned about it. Your review of the literature may lead you to revise your research design: perhaps you will decide to use a previous research-er's method or even *replicate* an earlier study. The independent replication of research projects is a standard procedure in the phys-ical sciences, and it is just as important in the social sciences, although we tend to overlook that. Or, you might want to go beyond replication and study some aspect of the topic that you feel previous research-ers have overlooked.

Here's another approach you might take. Suppose a topic has been studied previously using field research methods. Can you design an experiment that would test the findings those earlier researchers produced? Or, can you think of existing statistics that could be used to test their conclusions? The use of several different research methods to test the same finding is sometimes called *trian-gulation*, and you should always keep it in mind as a valuable research strategy. Since each research method has particular strengths and weaknesses, there is always a danger that research findings will reflect, at least in part, the method of inquiry. In the best of all worlds, your own research design should bring more than one research method to bear on the topic.

Having refined your ideas about what you will study and how, you should turn to the remaining chapters in this book and learn exactly how to proceed. If you have found a topic that really interests you, you will have made an excellent start on a successful project.

MAIN POINTS

■ Exploration is the attempt to develop an initial, rough understanding of some phenomenon.

■ Description is the precise measurement and reporting of the characteristics of some population or phenomenon under study.

■ Explanation is the discovery and reporting of relationships among different aspects of the phenomenon under study. Whereas descriptive studies answer the question "What's so?" explanatory ones tend to answer the question "Why?"

■ Units of analysis are the people or things whose characteristics social researchers observe, describe, and explain. Typically, the unit of analysis in social research is the individual person, but it may also be a group or a social artifact.

■ Cross-sectional studies are those based on observations made at one time. While such studies are limited by this characteristic, inferences can be made about processes that occur over time.

■ Longitudinal studies are those in which observations are made at many times. Such observations may be made of samples drawn from general populations (trend studies), samples drawn from more specific subpopulations (cohort studies), or the same sample of people each time (panel studies).

■ A theory is a general and more or less comprehensive set of statements relating different aspects of some phenomenon.

■ A hypothesis is a statement of specific expectations about the nature of things, derived from a theory. Much research is devoted to hypothesis testing to determine whether theoretical expectations are confirmed by what goes on in the real world.

REVIEW QUESTIONS AND EXERCISES

1. Make up a research example—different from those discussed in the text—that would illustrate a researcher falling into the trap of the *ecological fallacy.* Then describe a modified research project that would avoid that trap.

2. Look through an academic research journal and find examples of at least three different units of analysis. Identify each unit of analysis and present a quotation from the journal in which that unit of analysis is reported on.

ADDITIONAL READINGS

Bart, Pauline, and Frankel, Linda, *The Student Sociologist's Handbook* (Morristown, N.J.: General Learning Press, 1976). A handy little reference book to assist you in getting started on a research project. Written from the standpoint of a student term paper, this volume gives a particularly good guide to the periodical literature of the social sciences that's waiting for you in your campus library.

Hammond, Phillip (ed.), *Sociologist at Work* (New York: Basic Books, 1964). A collection of candid research biographies written by several eminent social science researchers, discussing the studies that made them eminent. A variety of research motivations and designs are illustrated in these honest reports of how the research actually came about and unfolded. Take two chapters every four hours to relieve the discomfort of believing that social science research is routine and dull.

Miller, Delbert, *Handbook of Research Design and Social Measurement* (New York: Longman, 1983). A useful reference book for introducing or reviewing numerous issues involved in design and measurement. In addition, the book contains a wealth of practical information relating to foundations, journals, and professional associations.

Stouffer, Samuel, *Social Research to Test Ideas* (New York: Free Press of Glencoe, 1962). A stimulating and downright inspirational posthumous collection of research articles by one of the giants of social research. In these reports, you will see how an ingenious man formulates an idea, designs the perfect study for testing it, is prevented from conducting the study, and then devises another feasible method for testing the same idea. Especially enlightening are Paul Lazarsfeld's introduction and Chapter 6, in which Stouffer reports on the effects of the Great Depression on the family.

ANSWERS TO UNITS OF ANALYSIS EXERCISE (page 77)

1. individuals
2. cities
3. groups, organizations
4. groups
5. companies
6. individuals

5

Conceptualization and Measurement

What You'll Learn in This Chapter

In this chapter, you'll discover that most of the words used in everyday language communicate vague, unspecified meanings. In science, it's essential to specify exactly what we mean (and don't mean) by the terms we use.

INTRODUCTION

This chapter is the first of two dealing with the process of moving from vague ideas about what you want to study to being able to recognize it and measure it in the real world. In this chapter we deal with the general issue of *conceptualization*, which sets up a foundation for the discussions of *operationalization* in Chapter 6. The issues raised in Chapters 5 and 6 will return in Chapter 15 which deals with more complex types of measurements.

I want to begin the chapter with a frontal attack on the hidden concern people sometimes have as to whether it's possible to measure the stuff of life: love, hate, prejudice, radicalism, alienation, and things like that. The answer is yes, but it will take a few pages for me to make that point. Once you see that we can measure anything that exists, we'll turn to the steps involved in doing that.

MEASURING ANYTHING THAT EXISTS

It seems altogether possible to me that you may have some reservations about the ability of science to measure the really important aspects of human social existence. You may have read research reports dealing with something like liberalism or religion or prejudice, and you may have been dissatisfied with the way the researchers measured whatever they were studying. You may have felt they were too superficial, that they missed the aspects that really matter most. Maybe they measured *religiosity* as the number of times a person went to church, or maybe they measured *liberalism* by how people voted in a single election. Your dissatisfaction would surely have been increased if you found yourself being misclassified by the

measurement system. People often have that experience.

Or, you may have looked up the definition of a word like *compassionate* in the dictionary and found the definition wanting. You may have heard yourself muttering, "There's more to it than that." In fact, whenever you look up the definition of something you already understand well, you can probably see ways people might misunderstand the term if they had only that definition to go on.

Earlier in this book, I have said that one of the two pillars of science is *observation*. Since this word can suggest a rather casual, passive activity, scientists often use *measurement* instead: meaning careful, deliberate observations of the real world for the purpose of describing objects and events in terms of the attributes comprising a variable. If the variable under study were *political party affiliation*, we might consult the list of registered voters to note whether the people we were studying were registered as Democrats or Republicans. In this fashion, we would have measured their political party affiliation.

Although measurement would seem to present a special problem for social science, this section of the chapter makes the point that *we can measure anything that exists*. There are no exceptions. If it exists, we can measure it.

How Do You Know?

To demonstrate to you that social scientists can measure anything that exists, I'd like you to imagine that we are discussing the matter. I'll write the script, but feel free to make substitutions for your side of the dialogue as you see fit. Here goes.

ME: Social scientists can measure anything that exists.

YOU: Hah! Betcha can't.

ME: Tell me something that exists, and I'll tell you how to measure it.

YOU: Okay, let's see you measure prejudice.

ME: Good choice. Now, I'm not willing to waste our time trying to measure something that doesn't exist. So, tell me if it exists.

YOU: Yes, of course it exists. Everybody knows that.

ME: How do you *know* that prejudice exists?

YOU: *Everybody* knows that.

ME: Everybody used to think the world was flat, too. I want to know how *you* know that prejudice really exists.

YOU: I've seen it in action.

ME: What have you seen that proves prejudice exists?

YOU: Well, a businessman told me that he'd never hire a woman for an executive position because he thought all women were flighty and irrational. How's that?

ME: Great! That sounds like prejudice to me, so I guess we can assume that prejudice exists. I am now prepared to measure prejudice. Ready?

YOU: Ready.

ME: You and I will circulate quietly through the business community, talking to businessmen about hiring. Whenever a businessman tells us that he would never hire a woman for an executive position because he thinks all women are flighty and irrational, we'll count that as a case of prejudice. Whenever we are not told that, we'll count the conversation as a case of nonprejudice. When we finish, we'll be able to classify all the businessmen we've talked to as either prejudiced or nonprejudiced.

YOU: Wait a minute! That's not a very good measure of prejudice. We're going to miss a lot of prejudice that way. All we'll measure is blatant prejudice against women in hiring.

ME: I see what you mean. But your comment also means that the situation you described before proves only that blatant prejudice against women in hiring exists. We'd better reconsider whether *prejudice* exists. Does it?

YOU: Of course it does. I was just giving you one example. There are hundreds of other examples of prejudice.

ME: Give me one that proves prejudice exists.

YOU: Okay, try this for size. I was in a bar the other night, and two guys—one white and one black—were arguing about politics. Finally, the white guy got so angry, he yelled, "You stupid nigger. All you niggers ought to be sent back to Africa." Is that prejudiced enough for you?

ME: Suits me. That would seem to prove that prejudice exists, so I'm ready again to measure prejudice. This will be more fun. You and I will split up and start touring bars every night. We'll keep our ears open and listen for a white person saying, "You stupid nigger. All you niggers—"

YOU: Hold it! I see where this is headed, and that's not going to do it either. A person who said that would be prejudiced, but we're going to classify a lot of prejudiced people as nonprejudiced just because they don't happen to get carried away and talk dirty.

ME: All of which brings me back to my original question. Does prejudice really exist, or have you been just stringing me along?

YOU: Yes, it exists!

ME: Well, I'm not sure any longer. You persuaded me that businessmen who discriminate against women in hiring exist, because you saw that and I believe you. You persuaded me that there are people who call black people niggers and say they should all go back to Africa. But I'm not so sure *prejudice* exists. I'd sure like to track it down so I can show you that I can measure it. To be honest, though, I'm beginning to doubt that it really exists. I mean, have you ever seen a prejudice? What color are they? How much do they weigh? Where are they located?

YOU: What on earth are you talking about?

The point of this dialogue, as you may have guessed, is to demonstrate that *prejudice doesn't exist*. We don't know what a prejudice looks like, how big it is, or what color. None of us has ever touched a prejudice or ridden in one. But we do talk a lot about prejudice. Here's how that came about.

As you and I wandered down the road of life, we observed a lot of things and knew they were real through our observations. We heard about a lot of other things that other people said they observed, and those other things seemed to have existed. Someone reported seeing a lynching and described the whole thing in great detail.

With additional experience, we noticed something more. We noticed that people who participate in lynchings are also quite likely to call black people niggers. A lot of them, moreover, seemed to want women to "stay in their place." Eventually, we began to get the feeling that there was a certain kind of person running around the world that had those several tendencies. When we discussed the people we'd met, it was sometimes appropriate to identify someone in terms of those tendencies. We used to say a person was "one of those who participate in lynchings, call black people niggers, and wouldn't hire a woman for an executive position." After a while, however, it got pretty clumsy to say all of that, and you had a bright idea: "Let's use the word *prejudiced* as a shorthand notation for people like that. We can use the term even if they don't do all those things—as long as they're pretty much like that."

Being basically agreeable and interested in efficiency, I agreed to go along with the system. That's where *prejudice* came from. It never really existed. We never saw it. We just made it up as a shortcut for talking behind people's backs. Ultimately, *prejudice* is merely a *term* we have agreed to use in communication: a name we use to represent a whole collection of apparently related phenomena that we've each observed in the course of life. Each of us developed his or her own mental image of what the set of real phenomena we've observed represent in general and what they have in common.

When I say the word *prejudice* I know that it evokes a mental image in your mind, just as it evokes a mental image for me. It's as though we have file drawers in our minds containing thousands of sheets of paper, and each sheet of paper has a label in the upper right-hand corner. One sheet of paper in your file drawer has the term *prejudice* on it, and I have one too. On your sheet are all the things you were told about prejudice and everything you've observed that seemed to be an example of it. My sheet has what I was told about *prejudice* plus all the things I've observed that seemed to be examples of it.

Conceptions and Concepts

The technical term for those mental images, those sheets of paper in our mental file drawers, is *conception*. Each sheet of paper is a conception. Now, those mental images cannot be communicated directly. There is no way I can directly reveal to you what's written on mine. So we use the *terms* written in the upper right-hand corner as a way of communicating about our conceptions and the things we observe that are related to those conceptions.

Let's suppose that I'm going to meet someone named Pat whom you already know. I ask you what Pat is like. Now suppose that you have seen Pat help lost children find their parents and put a tiny bird back in its nest. Pat got you to take turkeys to poor families on Thanksgiving and to visit a children's hospital on Christmas. You've seen Pat weep in a movie about a mother overcoming adversities to save and protect her child. As you search through your mental file drawer, you may find all or most of those phenomena recorded on a single sheet labeled *compassionate* in the upper right-hand corner. You look over the other entries on the page, and you find they seem to provide an accurate description of Pat. So, you say, "Pat is compassionate."

Now I leaf through my own mental file drawer until I find a sheet marked *compassionate*. I then look over the things written on my sheet, and say, "Oh, that's nice." I now feel I know what Pat is like, but my expectations in that regard reflect the entries on *my* file sheet, not yours. Later, when I meet Pat, I may find that my own, personal experiences correspond to the entries I have on my *compassionate* file sheet, and I'll say you were sure right. Or, my observations of Pat may contradict the things I have on my file sheet, and I'll tell you that I don't think Pat is very compassionate. If the latter happens, we may begin to compare notes.

You say, "I once saw Pat weep in a movie about a mother overcoming adversity to save and protect her child." I look at my *compassionate* sheet and can't find anything like that. Looking elsewhere in my file, I locate that sort of phenomenon on a sheet labeled *sentimental*. I retort, "That's not compassion. That's just sentimentality."

To further strengthen my case, I tell you that I saw Pat refuse to give money to an organization dedicated to saving the whales from extinction. "That represents a lack of compassion," I argue. You search through your files and find saving the whales on a sheet marked *environmental activism,* and you say so. Eventually, we set about comparing the entries we have on our respective sheets labeled *compassionate*. We may discover that we have quite different mental images represented by that term.

In the big picture, language and communication only work to the extent that you and I have considerable overlap in the kinds of entries we have on our corresponding mental file sheets. The similarities we have on those sheets represent the agreements existing in the society we both occupy. When we were growing up, we were both told approximately the same thing when we were first introduced to a particular term. Dictionaries formalize the agreements our society has about such terms. Each of us, then, shapes his or her mental images to correspond with those agreements, but since all of us have different experiences and observations, no two people end up with exactly the same set of entries on any sheet in their file systems.

Returning to the assertion made at the outset of this chapter, we *can* measure anything that is real. We can measure, for example, whether Pat actually puts the little bird back in its nest, visits the hospital on Christmas, weeps at the movie, or refuses to contribute to saving the whales. All of those things exist, so we can measure them. But is Pat really compassionate? We can't answer that question, we can't measure compassion in that sense, because compassion doesn't exist the way those things I just described exist.

Compassion as a *term* does exist. We can measure the number of letters it contains and agree that there are 10. We can agree that it has three syllables and that it begins with the letter C. In short, we can measure those aspects of it that are real.

Some aspects of our conceptions are real also. Whether you *have* a mental image associated with the term *compassion* is real. When an elementary school teacher asks a class how many know what *compassion* means, those who raise their hands can be counted. The presence of particular entries on the sheets bearing a given label is also real, and that can be measured. We could measure how many people do or do not associate giving money to save the whales with their conception of compassion. About the only thing we cannot measure is what compassion really means, because compassion isn't real. Compassion exists only in the form of the agreements we have about how to use the term in communicating about things that are real.

In this context, Abraham Kaplan (1964) distinguishes three classes of things that scientists measure. The first class is *direct observables:* those things we can observe rather simply and directly, like the color of an apple or the check mark made in a questionnaire. *Indirect observables* require "relatively more subtle, complex, or indirect observations" (1964:55). We note a person's check mark beside *female* in a questionnaire and have indirectly observed that person's sex. Finally, *constructs* are theoretical creations based on observations but which cannot be observed directly or indirectly. IQ is a good example. It is constructed mathematically from observations of the answers given to a large number of questions on an IQ test.

Kaplan (1964:49) defines *concept* as a "family of conceptions." A concept is, as Kaplan notes, a construct. The concept of *compassion,* then, is a construct created from your conception of it, mine, and the conceptions of all those who have ever used the term. It cannot be observed directly or indirectly, because it doesn't exist. We made it up.

Conceptualization

Day-to-day communication usually occurs through a system of vague and general agreements about the use of terms. Usually, people do not understand exactly what we wish to communicate, but they get the general drift of our meaning. Although you and

I do not agree completely about the use of the term *compassionate,* I'm probably safe in assuming that Pat won't pull the wings off flies. A wide range of misunderstandings and conflict—from the interpersonal to the international—is the price we pay for our imprecision, but somehow we muddle through. Science, however, aims at more than muddling, and it cannot operate in a context of such imprecision.

Conceptualization is the process through which we specify precisely what we will mean when we use particular terms. Suppose we want to find out, for example, whether women are more compassionate than men. I suspect most of us assume that is the case, but it might be interesting to find out if it's really so. We can't meaningfully study the question, let alone agree on the answer, without some precise working agreements as to the meaning of the term. They are working agreements in the sense that they allow us to work on the question. We don't need to agree or even pretend to agree that a particular specification might be worth using.

Indicators and Dimensions

The end product of this conceptualization process is the specification of a set of *indicators* of what we have in mind, indicating the presence or absence of the concept we are studying. Thus, we may agree to use visiting children's hospitals at Christmas as an indicator of compassion. Putting little birds back in their nests may be agreed on as another indicator, and so forth. If the unit of analysis for our study were the individual person, we could then observe the presence or absence of each indicator for each person under study. Going beyond that, we could add up the number of indicators of compassion observed for each individual.

We might agree on 10 specific indicators, for example, and find 6 present in our study of Pat, 3 for John, 9 for Mary, and so forth.

Returning to our original question, we might calculate that the women we studied had an average of 6.5 indicators of compassion, and the men studied had an average of 3.2. We might therefore conclude on the basis of that group difference that women are, on the whole, more compassionate than men. Usually, it's not that simple.

Very often, when we take our concepts seriously and set about specifying what we mean by them, we discover disagreements and inconsistencies. Not only do you and I disagree, but each of us is likely to find a good deal of muddiness within our own, individual mental images. If you take a moment to look at what *you* mean by compassion, you'll probably find that your image contains several *kinds* of compassion. The entries on your file sheet can be combined into groups and subgroups, and you'll even find several different strategies for making the combinations. For example, you might group the entries into feelings and actions.

The technical term for such groupings is *dimension,* and we might speak of the "feeling dimension" of compassion and the "action dimension" of compassion. In a different grouping scheme, we might distinguish "compassion for humans" from "compassion for animals." Or, compassion might center on helping people be and have what *we* want for them or what *they* want for themselves. Still differently, we might distinguish "compassion as forgiveness" from "compassion as pity."

Thus, it would be possible for us to subdivide the concept of compassion according to several sets of dimensions. Specifying dimensions and identifying the various indicators for each of those dimensions are both parts of conceptualization.

Specifying the different dimensions of a concept often paves the way for a more sophisticated understanding of what we are studying. We might observe, for example, that women are more compassionate in terms of feelings, and men are more compassionate in terms of actions—or vice versa. Noting that this was the case, we would not be able to say whether men or women are really more compassionate. Our research, in fact, would have shown that there is no single answer to the question.

The Interchangeability of Indicators

Recall for a moment the Chapter 3 discussion of the *interchangeability of indexes.* In the present context, Lazarsfeld's earlier point suggests that we may be able to answer a general question such as whether men or women are the more compassionate—even when we cannot agree on the ultimate or even the best way of measuring it.

Suppose, for the moment, that you and I have compiled a list of 100 indicators of the concept *compassion* and its various dimensions. Suppose further that we disagree widely on which indicators give the clearest evidence of compassion or its absence. If we pretty much agree on some indicators, we could focus our attention on those, and we would probably agree on the answer they provided. But suppose we don't really agree on any of the possible indicators. It is still possible for us to reach an agreement on whether men or women are the more compassionate.

If we disagree totally on the value of the indicators, one solution would be to study all of them. Now, suppose that women turn out to be more compassionate than men on all 100 indicators—on all the indicators you favor and on all of mine. Then we would be able to agree that women are more compassionate than men even though we still disagree on what compassion means in general.

The **interchangeability of indicators** means that if several different indicators all represent, to some degree, the same concept, then all of them will behave the same way that the concept would behave if it were real and could be observed. Thus, if women are generally more compassionate than men, we should be able to observe that difference by using any reasonable measure of compassion.

You now have the fundamental logic of conceptualization and measurement. The discussions that follow in this chapter and the next one are mainly refinements and extensions of what I've just presented. Before turning to more technical elaborations on the main framework, however, it may be useful to cover more general topics.

First, I know that the discussions above may not fit exactly with your previous understanding of the meaning of such terms as *prejudice* and *compassion*. We tend to operate in daily life as though such terms have real, ultimate meanings. In the next subsection, then, I want to comment briefly on how we came to that understanding.

Second, lest this whole discussion create a picture of anarchy in the meanings of words, I will describe some of the ways in which scientists have organized the confusion so as to provide standards, consistency, and commonality in the meaning of terms. You should come away from this latter discussion with a recaptured sense of order— but one based on a conscious understanding rather than the casual acceptance of common usage.

The Confusion over Definitions and Reality

Reviewing briefly, our concepts are derived from the mental images (conceptions) that summarize collections of seemingly related observations and experiences. Although the observations and experiences are real, our concepts are only mental creations. The terms associated with concepts are merely devices created for purposes of filing and communication. The word *prejudice* is an example. Ultimately, that word is only a collection of letters and has no intrinsic meaning. We could have as easily and meaningfully created the word *slanderice* to serve the same purpose.

Very often, however, we fall into the trap of believing that terms have real meanings. That danger seems to grow stronger when we begin to take terms seriously and attempt to use them precisely. And the danger is all the greater in the presence of experts who appear to know more than you do about what the terms really mean. It's very easy to yield to the authority of experts in such a situation.

Once we have assumed that terms have real meanings, we begin the tortured task of discovering what those real meanings are and what constitutes a genuine measurement of them. Figure 5-1 illustrates the history of this process. We make up conceptual summaries of real observations because the summaries are convenient. They prove to be *so* convenient, however, that we begin to think they are real. The process of regarding as real things that are not is called **reification,** and the reification of concepts in day-to-day life is very common.

Creating Conceptual Order

In all this confusion, logicians and scientists have found it useful to distinguish three kinds of definitions: *real, nominal,* and *operational.* The first of these reflects the reification of terms, and as Carl G. Hempel has cautioned,

A "real" definition, according to traditional logic, is not a stipulation determining the meaning of

Figure 5-1   The Process of Conceptual Entrapment

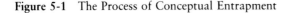

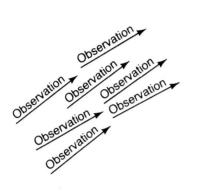

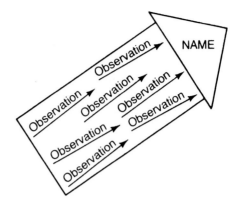

1. Many of our observations in life seem to have something in common. We get the sense that they represent something more general than the simple content of any single observation. We find it useful, moreover, to communicate about the general concept.

2. It is inconvenient to keep describing all the specific observations whenever we want to communicate about the general concept they seem to have in common, so we give a name to the general concept—to stand for whatever it is the specific observations have in common.

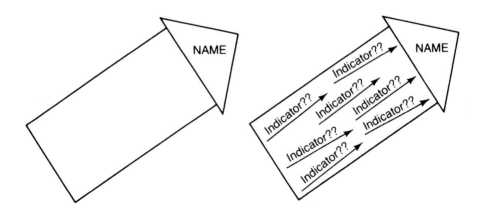

3. As we communicate about the general concept, using its term, we begin to think that the concept is some*thing* that really exists, not just a summary reference for several concrete observations in the world.

4. The belief that the concept itself is real results in irony. We now begin discussing and debating whether specific observations are "really" sufficient indicators of the concept.

some expression but a statement of the "essential nature" or the "essential attributes" of some entity. The notion of essential nature, however, is so vague as to render this characterization useless for the purposes of rigorous inquiry.

(1952:6)

The specification of concepts in scientific inquiry depends on nominal and operational definitions. A *nominal* definition is one that is *assigned* to a term. In the midst of disagreement and confusion over what a term really means, the scientist specifies a working definition for the purposes of the inquiry. Wishing to examine socioeconomic status (SES) in a study, for example, we may simply specify that we are going to treat it as a combination of income and educational attainment. In that definitional decision, we rule out many other possible aspects of SES: occupational status, money in the bank, property, lineage, life-style, and so forth.

The specification of nominal definitions focuses our observational strategy, but it does not allow us to observe. As a next step we must specify exactly what we are going to observe, how we will do it, and what interpretations we are going to place on various possible observations. All of these further specifications make up what is called the **operational definition** of the concept— a definition that spells out precisely how the concept will be measured. Strictly speaking, an operational definition is a description of the "operations" that will be undertaken in measuring a concept.

Pursuing the case of SES, we might decide to ask the people we are studying two questions:

1. What was your total family income during the past twelve months?

2. What is the highest level of school you completed?

Here, we would probably want to specify a system for categorizing the answers people give us. For income, we might use categories such as "under $5,000"; "$5,000 to $10,000"; and so forth. Educational attainment might be similarly grouped in categories. Finally, we would specify the manner in which a person's responses to these two questions would be combined in creating a measure of socioeconomic status. Chapter 15, on index and scale construction, will present some of the methods for doing that.

Ultimately, we would have created a working and workable definition of SES. Others might disagree with our conceptualization and operationalization, but the definition would have one essential scientific virtue: it would be absolutely specific and unambiguous. Even if someone disagreed with our definition, that person would have a good idea how to interpret our research results, since what we meant by the term SES—reflected in our analyses and conclusions—would be clear.

Here is a diagram showing the progression of measurement steps from our vague sense of what a term means to specific measurements in a scientific study:

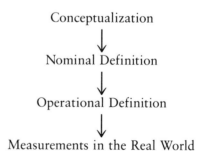

A Conceptualization Example

I want to bring the preceding discussions together now through a brief history of a social scientific concept. You may recall from Chapter 2 that Edward Ransford, in his study of the Watts riots, was particularly interested in the part played by feelings of "powerlessness." Social scientists sometimes use the term *anomie* in this context. This term was first introduced into social science by Emile Durkheim, the great French sociologist, in his classic 1897 study, *Suicide.*

Using only government publications on suicide rates in different regions and countries, Durkheim wrote a work of analytical genius. To determine the effects of religion on suicide, he compared the suicide rates of predominantly Protestant countries with predominantly Catholic ones, Protestant regions of Catholic countries with Catholic regions of Protestant countries, and so forth. To determine the possible effects of the weather, he compared suicide rates in northern and southern countries and regions, and he examined the different suicide rates across the months and seasons of the year. Thus, he was able to draw conclusions about a supremely individualistic and personal act without having any data about the individuals engaging in it.

At a more general level, Durkheim suggested that suicide also reflected the extent to which a society's agreements were clear and stable. Noting that times of social upheaval and change often present the individual with grave uncertainties about what is expected of him or her, Durkheim suggested that such uncertainties cause confusion, anxiety, and even self-destruction. To describe this societal condition of normlessness, Durkheim chose the term *anomie.* It is worth noting that Durkheim did not make this word up out of thin air. Used in both German and French, it meant, literally, *without law,* and the English term *anomy* had been used for at least three centuries before Durkheim to mean *disregard for divine law.* Still, Durkheim created anomie as a social scientific concept.

In the years that have followed the publication of *Suicide,* social scientists have found anomie a useful concept, and many have expanded on Durkheim's use. Robert Merton, in a classic article entitled "Social Structure and Anomie" (1938), concluded that anomie results from a disparity between the goals and means prescribed by a society. Monetary success, for example, is a widely shared goal in our society, yet not all individuals have the resources to achieve it through acceptable means. An emphasis on the goal itself, Merton suggested, produces normlessness, because those denied the traditional avenues to wealth go about getting it through illegitimate means. Merton's discussion, then, could be considered a further conceptualization of the concept of anomie.

Although Durkheim originally intended the concept of anomie to be a characteristic of societies, as did Merton after him, other social scientists have used it to describe individuals. (To clarify this distinction, some scholars have chosen to use the term *anomie* in its original, societal meaning and to use *anomia* in reference to the individual characteristic.) In a given society, then, some individuals experience anomia, while others do not. Elwin Powell, writing 20 years after Merton, provided the following conceptualization of anomia (though using the term *anomie*) as a characteristic of individuals:

When the ends of action become contradictory, inaccessible or insignificant, a condition of anomie arises. Characterized by a general loss of orientation and accompanied by feelings of "emptiness" and apathy, anomie can be simply conceived as meaninglessness.

(1958:132)

Powell went on to suggest there were two distinct kinds of anomia and to examine how the two rose out of different occupational experiences to result, sometimes, in suicide. In his study, however, Powell did not measure anomia per se; he studied the relationship between suicide and occupation, making inferences about the two kinds of anomia. Thus, the study did not provide an operational definition of anomia, only a further conceptualization.

The Origins of *Anomia*

by Leo Srole
Center for Geriatrics and Gerontology, Columbia University

My career-long fixation on anomie began with reading Durkheim's *Le Suicide* as a Harvard undergraduate. Later, as a graduate student at Chicago, I studied under two Durkheimian anthropologists: William Lloyd Warner and Alfred Radcliffe-Brown. Radcliffe-Brown had carried on a lively correspondence with Durkheim, making me a collateral "descendant" of the great French sociologist.

For me, the early impact of Durkheim's work on suicide was mixed but permanent. On the one hand, I had serious reservations about his strenuous, ingenious, and often awkward efforts to force the crude, bureaucratic records on suicide rates to fit with his unidirectional sociological determinism. On the other hand, I was moved by Durkheim's unswerving preoccupation with the moral force of the inter-personal ties that bind us to our time, place, and past, and also his insights about the lethal consequences that can follow from shrinkage and decay in those ties.

My interest in anomie received an eye-witness jolt at the finale of World War II, when I served with the United Nations Relief and Rehabilitation Administration, helping to rebuild a war-torn Europe. At the Nazi concentration camp of Dachau, I saw firsthand the depths of dehumanization that macro-social forces, such as those that engaged Durkheim, could produce in individuals like Hitler, Eichmann, and the others serving their dictates at all levels in the Nazi death factories.

Returning from my UNRRA post, I felt most urgently that the time was long overdue to come to an understanding

---

Many other researchers *have* offered operational definitions, but one name stands out over all the others. Two years before Powell's article appeared, Leo Srole (1956) published a set of questionnaire items that he said provided a good measure of anomia as experienced by individuals. It consists of five statements that subjects are asked to agree or disagree with.

1. In spite of what some people say, the lot of the average man is getting worse.
2. It's hardly fair to bring children into the world with the way things look for the future.
3. Nowadays a person has to live pretty much for today and let tomorrow take care of itself.
4. These days a person doesn't really know who he can count on.
5. There's little use writing to public officials because they aren't really interested in the problems of the average man.

(1956:713)

In the decades that followed its publication, the Srole scale has become a research staple for social scientists. You are likely to find this particular operationalization of

of the dynamics underlying disintegrated social bonds. We needed to work expeditiously, de-emphasizing proliferation of macro-level theory in favor of a direct exploratory encounter with individuals, using newly developed state-of-the-art survey research methodology. Such research, I also felt, should focus on a broader spectrum of behavioral pathologies than suicide.

My initial investigations were a diverse effort. In 1950, for example, I was able to interview a sample of 401 bus riders in Springfield, Mass. Four years later, the Midtown Manhattan Mental Health Study provided a much larger population reach. These and other field projects gave me scope to expand and refine my measurements of that quality in individuals which reflected the macro-social quality Durkheim had called *anomie*.

While I began by using Durkheim's term in my own work, I soon decided that it was necessary to limit the use of that concept to its macro-social meaning and to sharply segregate it from its individual manifestations. For the latter purpose, the cognate but hitherto obsolete Greek term, *anomia* readily suggested itself.

I first published the *anomia* construct in a 1956 article in the *American Sociological Review*,* describing ways of operationalizing it, and presenting the results of its initial field application research. By 1982, the Science Citation Index and Social Science Citation Index had listed some 400 publications in political science, psychology, social work, and sociology journals here and abroad that had cited use of that article's instruments or findings, warranting the American Institute for Scientific Information to designate it a "citation classic."

---

* Leo Srole, "Social Integration and Certain Corollaries: An Exploratory Study," *American Sociological Review*, Vol. 21, 709–16, 1956.

anomie used in many of the research projects you'll find reported in academic journals. (Professor Srole touches on this in the accompanying box, "The Origins of *Anomia*," in which he discusses the history of his research in this area.)

I've presented this greatly abbreviated history of anomie and anomia as social scientific concepts for several reasons. First, they illustrate the process through which general concepts become operationalized measurements, though I wouldn't want you to think that the issue of anomie/anomia has been resolved once and for all. Scholars

will surely continue to reconceptualize and reoperationalize them for years to come—continually seeking more useful measures.

I've ended the story with the Srole scale, however, because it illustrates another important point. Letting conceptualization and operationalization be open-ended does not necessarily produce anarchy and chaos as you might expect. Order emerges. There are several elements in this order. First, although you *could* define anomia any way you chose—in terms of, say, shoe size—you are likely to define it in ways not too different from other people's mental images.

If you were to use a really offbeat definition, people would probably ignore you.

Second, as researchers discover the *utility* of a particular conceptualization and operationalization of a concept, they are likely to adopt it, and standardized definitions of concepts appear. Besides the Srole scale, examples include IQ tests and a whole host of demographic and economic measures developed by the Bureau of the Census. Using such established measures has two advantages: they have been extensively pretested and debugged, and studies using the same scales can be compared. If you and I do separate studies of two different groups, and if each of us uses the Srole scale, we will be able to compare our two groups on the basis of anomia.

Thus, social scientists can measure anything that's real, and we can even do a pretty good job of measuring things that aren't. Granting that such concepts as socioeconomic status, prejudice, compassion, and anomia aren't real ultimately, we've now seen that social scientists are able to create order in handling them. It is an order based on utility, however, and not on ultimate truth.

The remainder of this chapter is devoted to some of the considerations and alternatives involved in the creation of *useful* definitions and measurements. First, we're going to look at the relationship between definitions and research purposes; then the chapter concludes with an examination of some criteria used in determining the *quality* of the measurements we create.

DEFINITIONS AND RESEARCH PURPOSES

Recall from Chapter 4 that two of the general purposes of research are *description* and *explanation*. The distinction between them has important implications for the process of definition and measurement. If you have formed the opinion that description is a simpler task than explanation, you will be surprised to learn that definitions are more problematic for descriptive research than for explanatory research. This point will be discussed more fully in Part 4, but it is important that you have a basic understanding of why it is so before we turn to other aspects of measurement.

The importance of definitions for descriptive research should be clear. If our task is to describe and report the unemployment rate in a city, our definition of *being unemployed* is critical. That definition will depend on our definition of another term: the *labor force*. If it seems patently absurd to regard a 3-year-old child as being unemployed, it is because such a child is not considered a member of the labor force. Thus, we might follow the U.S. Census Bureau's convention and exclude all persons under 14 years of age from the labor force.

This convention alone, however, would not give us a satisfactory definition, since it would count as unemployed such people as high school students, the retired, the disabled, and homemakers. We might follow the census convention further by defining the labor force as "all persons 14 years of age and over who are employed, looking for work, or waiting to be called back to a job from which they have been laid off or furloughed." Unemployed persons, then, would be those members of the labor force who are not employed. If a student, homemaker, or retired person is not looking for work, such a person would not be included in the labor force.

But what does "looking for work" mean? Must a person register with the state employment service or go from door to door asking for employment? Or would it be sufficient to want a job or be open to an offer of employment? Conventionally, "looking for work" is defined operationally as saying yes in response to an interviewer's asking "Have you been looking for a job during the past seven days?" (Seven days is the time period most often specified, but for some research purposes it might make more sense to shorten or lengthen it.)

I have spelled out these considerations in some detail so that you will realize that the conclusion of a descriptive study about the unemployment rate, for example, depends directly on how each issue is resolved. Increasing the period of time during which people are counted as looking for work would have the effect of adding more unemployed persons to the labor force as defined, thereby increasing the reported unemployment rate. If we follow another convention and speak of the *civilian* labor force and the *civilian* unemployment rate, we are excluding military personnel; that, too, increases the reported unemployment rate, since military personnel would be employed—*by definition.*

Thus the descriptive statement that the unemployment rate in a city is 3 percent, or 9 percent, or whatever it might be, depends directly on the operational definitions used. If that seems clear in this example, it is because there are a number of accepted conventions relating to the labor force and unemployment. Consider how difficult it would be to get agreement about the definitions needed to make the descriptive statement "45 percent of the students are politically conservative." This percentage, like the unemployment rate above, would depend directly on your definition of what is being measured. A different definition might result in the conclusion "5 percent of the student body are politically conservative."

Ironically, definitions are less problematical in the case of explanatory research. Let's suppose that we are interested in explaining political conservatism. Why are some people conservative and others not?

More specifically, let's suppose we are interested in whether old people are generally more conservative than young people. What if you and I have 25 different operational definitions of *conservative,* and we can't agree on which definition is the best one? As we've already seen, this is not necessarily an insurmountable obstacle to our research. Suppose, for example, that we found old people more conservative than young people in terms of *all 25 definitions!* (Recall the earlier discussion of compassion in men and women.) Suppose that we found old people more conservative than young people by *every* reasonable definition of conservatism we could think of. It wouldn't matter what our definition was. We would conclude that old people are generally more conservative than young people—even though we couldn't agree about what a conservative really was.

In practice, explanatory research seldom results in findings quite as unambiguous as the above example suggests; nonetheless, the general pattern is quite common in actual research. There *are* consistent patterns of relationships in human social life, and they result in consistent research findings. The important point here, however, is that such consistency does not appear in a descriptive situation. Changing definitions almost inevitably result in different descriptive conclusions.

The box "The Importance of Variable Names" explores this issue in connection with the variable "citizen participation."

CRITERIA FOR MEASUREMENT QUALITY

This chapter has come some distance. It began with the bald assertion that social scientists can measure anything that exists. Then we discovered that most of the things

The Importance of Variable Names

by Patricia Fisher
Graduate School of Planning, University of Tennessee

Operationalization is one of those things that's easier said than done. It is quite simple to explain to someone the purpose and importance of operational definitions for variables, and even to describe how operationalization typically takes place. However, until you've tried to operationalize a rather complex variable, you may not appreciate some of the subtle difficulties involved. Of considerable importance to the operationalization effort is the particular name that you have chosen for a variable. Let's consider an example from the field of Urban Planning.

A variable of interest to planners is citizen participation. Planners are convinced that participation in the planning process by citizens is important to the success of plan implementation. Citizen participation is an aid to planners' understanding of the real and perceived needs of a community, and such involvement by citizens tends to enhance their cooperation with and support for planning efforts. Although many different conceptual definitions might be offered by different planners, there would be little misunderstanding over what is *meant* by citizen participation. The name of the variable seems adequate.

However, if we asked different planners to provide very simple operational measures for citizen participation, we are likely to find a variety among their

we might want to measure and study don't really exist. Next we learned that it is possible to measure them anyway. I want to conclude the chapter with a discussion of some of the yardsticks against which we judge our relative success or failure in measuring things—even things that don't exist.

To begin, measurements can be made with varying degrees of *precision:* representing the fineness of distinctions made between attributes comprising a variable. The description of a woman as "43 years old" is more precise than "in her forties." Saying "11 1/2 inches long" is a more precise description than "about a foot long."

As a general rule, precise measurements are superior to imprecise ones, as common sense would dictate. There are no condi-

tions under which imprecise measurements would be intrinsically superior to precise ones. Precision is not always necessary or desirable, however. If your research purpose is such that knowing a woman to be in her forties is sufficient, then any additional effort invested in learning her precise age is wasted. The operationalization of concepts, then, must be guided partly by an understanding of the degree of precision required. If your needs are not clear, be more precise rather than less.

Don't confuse precision with *accuracy,* however. Describing someone as "born in Stowe, Vermont," is more precise than "born in New England"—but suppose the person in question was actually born in Boston. The less precise description, in this instance,

responses that does generate confusion. One planner might keep a tally of attendance by private citizens at city commission and other local government meetings; another might maintain a record of the different topics addressed by private citizens at similar meetings; while a third might record the number of local government meeting attendees, letters and phone calls received by the mayor and other public officials, and meetings held by special interest groups during a particular time period. As skilled researchers, we can readily see that each planner would be measuring (in a very simplistic fashion) a different *dimension* of citizen participation: extent of citizen participation, issues prompting citizen participation, and form of citizen participation. Therefore, the original *naming* of our variable, citizen participation, which was quite satisfactory from a conceptual point of view, proved inadequate for purposes of operationalization.

The precise and exact naming of variables is important in research. It is both essential to and a result of good operationalization. Variable names quite often evolve from an iterative process of forming a conceptual definition, then an operational definition, then renaming the concept to better match what can or will be measured. This looping process continues (our example above illustrates only one iteration), resulting in a gradual refinement of the variable name and its measurement until a reasonable fit is obtained. Sometimes the concept of the variable that you end up with is a bit different from the original one that you started with, but at least you are measuring what you are talking about, if only because you are talking about what you are measuring!

would have been more accurate, a better reflection of the real world.

Precision and accuracy are obviously important qualities in research measurement, and they probably need no further explanation. When social scientists construct and evaluate measurements, however, they pay special attention to two technical considerations: **reliability** and **validity**.

Reliability

In the abstract, *reliability* is a matter of whether a particular technique, applied repeatedly to the same object, would yield the same result each time. Suppose, for example, that I asked you to estimate how much I weigh. You look me over carefully and guess that I weigh 165 pounds. (Thank you.) Now let's suppose I ask you to estimate the weights of 30 or 40 other people, and while you're engrossed in that, I slip back into line wearing a clever disguise. When my turn comes again, you guess 180 pounds. Gotcha! That little exercise would have demonstrated that having you estimate people's weights was not a very reliable technique.

Suppose, however, that I had loaned you my bathroom scale to use in weighing people. No matter how clever my disguise, you would presumably announce the same weight for me both times, indicating that the scale provided a more reliable measure of weight than guessing.

Reliability, however, does not ensure accuracy any more than precision does. Suppose I've set my bathroom scale to shave five pounds off my weight just to make me feel better. Although you would (reliably) report the same weight for me each time, you would always be wrong. This new element is called *bias,* and it is discussed in more detail in Chapter 7 on sampling. For now, just be warned that reliability does not ensure accuracy.

Here's an example illustrating the problem of reliability. Jeffrey Sacks and his colleagues (1980) focused their attention on Health Hazard Appraisal (HHA), part of a preventive medicine. Their purpose was to determine the risks associated with various background and life-style factors, making it possible for physicians to counsel their patients appropriately. By knowing patients' life situations, physicians could advise them on their potential for survival and how to improve it. This purpose, of course, depended heavily on the accuracy of the information gathered about each subject in the study.

To test the reliability of their information, Sacks and his colleagues had all 207 subjects complete a baseline questionnaire that asked about their characteristics and behavior. Three months later, a follow-up questionnaire asked the same subjects for the same information, and the results of the two surveys were compared. Overall, only 15 percent of the subjects reported the same information in both studies.

Sacks reports (1980:730): "Almost 10 percent of subjects reported a different height at follow-up examination. Parental age was changed by over one in three subjects. One parent reportedly aged 20 chronologic years in three months. One in five ex-smokers and ex-drinkers have apparent difficulty in reliably recalling their previous consumption pattern."

Some subjects erased all trace of previously reported heart murmur, diabetes, emphysema, arrest record, and thoughts of suicide. One subject's mother, deceased in the first questionnaire, was apparently live and well in time for the second. One subject had one ovary missing in the first study but present in the second. In another case, an ovary present in the first study was missing in the second study—and had been for 10 years! One subject was reportedly 55 years old in the first study and 50 years old 3 months later. You have to wonder if the physician-counselors could have had nearly the impact on their patients as their patients' memories did. Thus, the data-collection method was not especially reliable.

Here's another example, a hypothetical one. Let's suppose that we are interested in studying morale among factory workers in two different kinds of factories. In one set of factories, workers do very specialized jobs, reflecting an extreme division of labor. Each worker contributes a tiny part to the overall process performed on a long assembly line. In the other set of factories, each worker performs many tasks and small teams of workers complete the whole process.

How should we measure morale? Following one strategy, we could spend more time observing the workers in each factory, noticing such things as whether they joke with one another, whether they smile and laugh a lot, and so forth. We could ask them how they like their work and even ask them whether they think they would prefer their current arrangement or the other one being studied. By comparing what we observed in the different factories, we might reach a conclusion as to which assembly process produced the higher morale.

Now let's look at some of the possible problems of reliability inherent in this method. First of all, how you and I are feeling when we do the observing is likely to color what we see. We may misinterpret what we see. We may see workers kidding each other and think they are having an argument. Or, maybe we'll catch them on an off day. If we were to observe the same group of workers several days in a row, we might arrive at different evaluations on each day.

If several observers evaluated the same behavior, on the other hand, they too might arrive at different conclusions about the workers' morale.

Here's another strategy for assessing morale. Suppose we check the company records to see how many grievances have been filed with the union during some fixed period of time. Presumably that would be an indicator of morale: the more grievances, the lower the morale. This measurement strategy would appear to be more reliable: we could count up the grievances over and over and we should keep arriving at the same number.

If you find yourself saying "Wait a minute" over the second measurement strategy, you're worrying about validity, not reliability. Let's complete the discussion of reliability, and then we'll handle validity.

Reliability problems crop up in many forms in social research. Survey researchers have known for a long time that different interviewers get different answers from respondents as a result of their own attitudes and demeanor. If we were to conduct a study of editorial positions on some public issue, we might create a team of coders to take on the job of reading hundreds of editorials and classifying them in terms of their position on the issue. Different coders would code the same editorial differently. Or we might want to classify a few hundred specific occupations in terms of some standard coding scheme, say a set of categories created by the Department of Labor or by the Bureau of the Census. You and I would not code all those occupations into the same categories.

Each of these examples illustrates problems of reliability. Similar problems arise whenever we ask people to give us information about themselves. Sometimes we ask questions that people don't know the answers to. (How many times have you been to church?) Sometimes we ask people about things that are totally irrelevant to them. (Are you satisfied with China's current rela-

tionship with Albania?) And sometimes we ask questions that are so complicated that a person who had a clear opinion in the matter might arrive at a different interpretation of the question upon being asked a second time.

How do you create reliable measures? There are a number of techniques. First, in asking people for information—if your research design calls for that—be careful to ask only about things the respondents are likely to know the answer to. Ask about things relevant to them and be clear in what you're asking. The danger in these instances is that people *will* give you answers—reliable or not. People will tell you how they feel about China's relationship with Albania even if they haven't the foggiest idea what that relationship is.

In addition to this commonsense advice, there are a number of more technical methods for coping with the problem of reliability in asking people for information. Sometimes researchers ask for the same information more than once, using either the same or a similar question. By the same token, you should always ask several questions aimed at measuring alienation, and if one of them classifies people very differently from the other nine, that should be a tip-off that the variant item is unreliable (or invalid—coming up soon).

Sometimes, it will be appropriate for you to ask people questions at different times, and it may be possible to ask the same question each time, thereby testing the reliability of their answers. Experiments, for example, often involve a test and retest, and you might repeat some of the earlier questions the second time around. Be careful about those things that might actually change during the interval between the test and retest, however, or you could misjudge the reliability of your measure. Somebody might get married during the course of the study, and you'd then doubt the reliability of your data on marital status.

Another way to handle the problem of

reliability in getting information from people is to use measures that have proven their reliability in previous research. If you want to measure anomia, for example, you might very well want to follow Srole's lead. There are other ways of handling this problem, and you'll probably be able to think of some new ones.

In the case of unreliability generated by research workers, there are also several solutions. To guard against interviewer unreliability, it is common practice in surveys to have a supervisor call a subsample of the respondents on the telephone and verify selected pieces of information. Replication works in other situations also. If you are worried that newspaper editorials or occupations may not be classified reliably, why not have each independently coded by several coders? Those that generate disagreement should be evaluated more carefully and resolved.

Finally, clarity, specificity, training, and practice will avoid a great deal of unreliability and grief. If you and I were to spend some time reaching a clear agreement on how we were going to evaluate editorial positions on an issue—discussing the various positions that might be represented and reading through several together—we'd probably be able to do a good job of classifying them in the same way independently.

We'll return to the issue of reliability more than once in the chapters ahead. For now, however, let's recall that even total reliability doesn't ensure that our measures measure what we think they measure. Now let's plunge into the question of validity.

Validity

In conventional usage, the term *validity* refers to the extent to which an empirical measure adequately reflects the *real meaning* of the concept under consideration. Whoops! I've

already committed us to the view that concepts don't have real meanings. How can we ever say whether a particular measure adequately reflects the concept's meaning, then? Ultimately, of course, we can't. At the same time, I've already suggested some of the ways in which researchers deal with this issue.

First, there's something called **face validity**. Particular empirical measures may or may not jibe with our common agreements and our individual mental images associated with a particular concept. You and I might quarrel about the adequacy of measuring worker morale by counting the number of grievances filed with the union, but we'd surely agree that the number of grievances has *something* to do with morale. If I were to suggest that we measure morale by finding out how many books the workers took out of the library during their off-duty hours, you'd undoubtedly raise a more serious objection: that measure wouldn't have any face validity.

Second, I've already pointed to many of the more concrete agreements researchers have reached in the case of some concepts. The Bureau of the Census, for example, has created operational definitions of such concepts as family, household, and employment status that seem to have a workable validity in most studies using those concepts.

Edward Carmines and Richard Zeller (1979) discuss three types of validity: *criterion-related validity*, *content validity*, and *construct validity*.

Criterion-related validity is sometimes called *predictive validity* and is based on some external criterion. For example, the validity of the college board is shown in its ability to predict the college success of students. The validity of a written driver's test is determined, in this sense, by the relationship between the scores people get on the test and how well they drive. In these examples, college success and driving ability are the *criteria*.

Content validity refers to the degree to which a measure covers the range of meanings included within the concept. For example, a test of mathematical ability, the authors point out, cannot be limited to addition alone but would also need to cover subtraction, multiplication, divison, and so forth. Finally, construct validity is based on the way a measure relates to other variables within a system of theoretical relationships. Let's suppose, for example, that you are interested in studying "marital satisfaction"— its sources and consequences. As part of your research, you develop a measure of marital satisfaction, and you want to assess its validity.

In addition to developing your measure, you will have also developed certain theoretical expectations about the way marital satisfaction "behaves" in relation to other variables. To take a trivial example, you may have concluded that satisfied husbands will be less likely than dissatisfied husbands to beat their wives. If your measure of marital satisfaction relates to wife-beating in the expected fashion, that constitutes evidence of your measure's construct validity. If "satisfied" and "dissatisfied" husbands were equally likely to beat their wives, however, that would challenge the validity of your measure.

Figure 5-2 presents a graphic portrayal of the difference between validity and reliability. If you can think of measurement as analogous to hitting the bull's-eye on a target, you'll see that reliability looks like a "tight pattern," regardless of where it hits, since reliability is a function of consistency. Validity, on the other hand, is a function of shots being arranged around the bull's-eye. The failure of reliability in the figure can be seen as a random error, whereas the failure of validity is a systematic error. Notice that neither an unreliable nor an invalid measure is likely to be very useful.

Tension between Reliability and Validity

As a footnote to these discussions, I want to point out briefly that a certain tension often exists between the criteria of reliability and validity. Often we seem to face a trade-off between the two.

If you'll recall for a moment the earlier example of measuring morale in different factories, I think you'll see that the strategy

Figure 5-2 An Analogy to Validity and Reliability

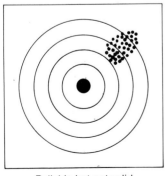
Reliable but not valid

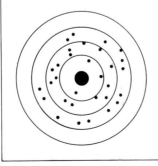
Valid but not reliable

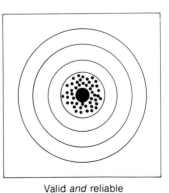
Valid *and* reliable

Suggested by an anonymous reviewer

of immersing yourself in the day-to-day routine of the assembly line, observing what went on, and talking to the workers seems to provide a more valid measure of morale than counting grievances. It just seems obvious that we'd be able to get a clearer sense of whether the morale was high or low in that fashion than we would get from counting the number of grievances filed with the union.

As I pointed out earlier, however, the counting strategy would be more reliable. This situation reflects a more general strain in research measurement. Most of the really interesting concepts that we want to study have many subtle nuances, and it's hard to specify precisely what we mean by them. Researchers sometimes speak of such concepts as having a "richness of meaning." Scores of books and articles have been writtten on the topic of anomie/anomia, and they still haven't exhausted the interesting aspects of that concept.

Yet, science needs to be specific to generate reliable measurements. Very often, then, the specification of reliable operational definitions and measurements seems to rob such concepts of their richness of meaning. I mean, morale is much more than a lack of grievances filed with the union; anomie is much more than the five items created by Leo Srole.

That is a persistent and inevitable dilemma for the social researcher, and you will be effectively forearmed against it by being forewarned. Be prepared for it and deal with it. If there is no clear agreement on how to measure a concept, measure it several different ways. If the concept has several different dimensions, measure them all. And above all, know that the concept does not have any meaning other than what you and I give it. And the only justification for giving any concept a particular meaning is utility. Measure concepts in ways that help us understand the world around us.

MAIN POINTS

■ Concepts are mental images we use as summary devices for bringing together observations and experiences that seem to have something in common.

■ Our concepts do not exist in the real world, so they can't be measured directly.

■ It *is* possible to measure the things that our concepts summarize.

■ Conceptualization is the process of specifying the vague mental imagery of our concepts, sorting out the kinds of observations and measurements that will be appropriate for our research.

■ The interchangeability of indicators permits us to study and draw conclusions about concepts even when we can't agree on how those concepts should be defined.

■ Precision refers to the exactness of the measure used in an observation or description of an attribute. For example, the description of a person as being "six feet, one and three-quarters inches tall" is more precise than the description "about six feet tall."

■ Reliability refers to the likelihood that a given measurement procedure will yield the same description of a given phenomenon if that measurement is repeated. For example, estimating a person's age by asking his or her friends would be less reliable than asking the person or checking the birth certificate.

■ Validity refers to the extent to which a specific measurement provides data that relate to commonly accepted meanings of a particular concept. There are numerous yardsticks for determining validity: face validity, criterion-related validity, content validity, and construct validity.

■ The creation of specific, reliable measures often seems to diminish the richness of meaning our general concepts have. This problem is inevitable. The best solution is to use several different measures, tapping the different aspects of the concept.

REVIEW QUESTIONS AND EXERCISES

1. Pick a social science concept such as liberalism, alienation, etc., and specify that concept so that it could be studied in a research project. Be sure to specify the dimensions you wish to include (and those you wish to exclude) in your conceptualization.

2. In a newspaper or magazine, find an instance of invalid and/or unreliable measurement. Justify your choice.

ADDITIONAL READINGS

Carmines, Edward G., and Zeller, Richard A., *Reliability and Validity Assessment* (Beverly Hills, Calif.: Sage, 1979). In this chapter, we've examined the basic logic of validity and reliability in social science measurement. Carmines and Zeller explore those issues in more detail and examine some of the ways for calculating reliability mathematically.

Gould, Julius, and Kolb, William, *A Dictionary of the Social Sciences* (New York: Free Press, 1964). A primary reference to the social scientific agreements on various concepts. Although the terms used by social scientists do not have ultimately "true" meanings, this reference book lays out the meanings social scientists have in mind when they use those terms.

Lazarsfeld, Paul, and Rosenberg, Morris (eds.), *The Language of Social Research* (New York: Free Press of Glencoe, 1955), Section I. An excellent and diverse collection of descriptions of specific measurements in past social research. These 14 articles present extremely useful accounts of actual measurement operations performed by social researchers as well as more conceptual discussions of measurement in general.

Wallace, Walter, *The Logic of Science in Sociology* (Chicago: Aldine-Atherton, 1971), Chapter 3. A brief and lucid presentation of concept formation within the context of other research steps. This discussion relates conceptualization to observation on the one hand and to generalization on the other.

6

Operationalization

What You'll Learn in This Chapter

Now we'll go from conceptualization to the next step in measurement—seeing how social scientists find concepts reflected in the real world. In particular, we'll look at some of the skills involved in asking questions.

INTRODUCTION

The preceding chapter discussed and described various aspects of the conceptualization process. In the course of that discussion, we frequently talked about operationalization, since the two are intimately linked. I have distinguished the two as follows: *conceptualization* is the refinement and specification of abstract concepts, and *operationalization* is the development of specific research procedures (operations) that will result in empirical observations representing those concepts in the real world.

The purpose of this chapter—moving squarely into the operationalization process—is to get closer to the nitty-gritty of concrete measurements in social research. Even so, our coverage here will still be a little abstract and general. Ultimately, operationalization is inseparable from actual data collection, and we'll get even more specific and concrete in this regard when we examine the different modes of observations available to social researchers in Part 3. In that sense, the present chapter is partly a preview of what is to come. Nonetheless, I'm going to present some issues in operationalization that apply to most or all types of studies you might undertake.

We'll begin with an overview of some of the operationalization choices you have in organizing the business of observation and measurement: what range of variation to consider, what levels of measurement to use, and whether to depend on a single indicator or several. Then, I'll give you some illustrations of the different ways we might measure a given variable. The purpose of that will be to broaden your imagination and vision.

Next, since social research often involves asking people for information—in surveys, experiments, and field research—I'll present some general guidelines for doing that in a useful way. As you'll see, there are many styles of questions—only some of which will give you useful information about how human social life operates. One danger in observation is that your magnifying glass will turn into a mirror, and all you'll see is yourself.

The chapter ends with a discussion of operationalization as a continuing process throughout a research project. Although I've discussed it in the context of research design—gearing up for the collection of data—we'll see that concepts are also operationalized when these data are analyzed. This concluding discussion, then, should round out your introduction to how social scientists measure things. We'll return to measurement in Chapter 15 on composite measures.

OPERATIONALIZATION CHOICES

As I've indicated above, the social researcher has a wide variety of options available when it comes to measuring a concept. Most obvious are the several methods of data collection: surveys, experiments, etc. These were introduced in Chapter 4 and will be discussed in depth in Part 3. As we'll see in this section, however, there are numerous other options available to researchers. Although the several choices are intimately interconnected, I've separated them for purposes of discussion. Please realize, however, that operationalization does *not* proceed through a systematic checklist.

Range of Variation

In operationalizing any concept, it is essential that you be clear about the range of variation that interests you in your research. To what extent are you willing to combine attributes in fairly gross categories?

Let's suppose you want to measure people's incomes in a study—either collecting the information from records or in interviews. The highest annual incomes people receive run into the millions of dollars, but not many people get that much. Unless you are studying the very rich, it probably wouldn't be worth much to allow for and keep track of extremely high categories. Depending on whom you are studying, you'll probably want to establish a highest income category with a much lower floor—maybe $50,000 or more. Although this decision will lead you to throw together people who earn a trillion dollars a year with paupers earning only $50,000, they'll survive it, and that mixing probably won't hurt your research any. The same decision faces you at the other end of the income spectrum. In studies of the general American population, a cutoff of $5,000 or less usually works just fine.

In the study of attitudes and orientations, the question of range of variation has another dimension. Unless you're careful, you may end up measuring only half an attitude without really meaning to. Here's an example of what I mean.

Suppose you're interested in people's attitudes toward the expanded use of nuclear power generators. You'd anticipate in advance that some people consider it the greatest thing since the wheel, while other people have absolutely no interest in it whatever. Given that anticipation, it would seem to make sense to ask people how much they favor expanding the use of nuclear energy. You might give them answer categories ranging from "Favor it very much" to "Don't favor it at all."

This operationalization, however, conceals half of the attitudinal spectrum regarding nuclear energy. Many people have feelings that go beyond simply not favoring it: they are absolutely *opposed* to it. In this instance, there is considerable variation on the left side of zero. Some oppose it a little,

some quite a bit, and others a great deal. To measure the full range of variation, then, you'd want to operationalize attitudes toward nuclear energy with a range from favoring it very much, through no feelings one way or the other, to opposing it very much.

This consideration applies to many of the variables we study in social science. Virtually any public issue involves both support and opposition, each in varying degrees. Political orientations range from very liberal to very conservative, and depending on the people you are studying, you may want to allow for radicals on one or both ends. People are not just more or less religious, some are antireligious.

I do not mean that you must measure the full range of variation in any given case. You should, however, consider whether that's needed in the light of your research purpose. If the difference between *not religious* and *antireligious* isn't relevant to your research, forget it. Someone has defined pragmatism as "any difference that makes no difference is no difference." Be pragmatic.

Finally, your decision on the range of variation should be governed also by the expected distribution of attributes among your subjects of study. That is what I meant earlier when I said range depends on whom you are studying. In a study of college professors' attitudes toward the value of higher education, you could probably stop at *no value* and not worry about those who might consider higher education dangerous to students' health. (If you were studying students, however . . .)

Variations between the Extremes

In Chapter 5, I briefly discussed precision as a criterion of quality in measurement. It arises again as a consideration in operationalizing variables. What it boils down to is how fine you will make distinctions among the various possible attributes composing a given variable. Does it really matter whether a person is 17 or 18 years old, or could you conduct your inquiry by throwing them together in a group labeled 10 to 19 years old? Don't answer too quickly. If you wanted to study rates of voter registration and participation, you'd definitely want to know whether the people you studied were old enough to vote.

If you are going to measure age, then, you must look at the purpose and procedures of your study and decide whether fine or gross differences in age are important to you. If you measure political affiliation, will it matter to your inquiry whether a person is a conservative Democrat rather than a liberal Democrat, or is it sufficient to know the party? In measuring religious affiliation, is it enough to know that a person is a Protestant, or do you need to know the denomination? Do you simply need to know whether a person is married or not, or will it make a difference to know if he or she has never married or is separated, widowed, or divorced?

There is, of course, no general answer to questions like these. The answers come out of the purpose of your study, the purpose you have in making a particular measurement. I can mention a useful guideline, however. Whenever you're not sure how much detail to get in a measurement, get too much rather than too little. During the analysis of data, it will always be possible to combine precise attributes into more general categories, but it will never be possible to separate out the variations that were lumped together during observation and measurement.

A Note on Dimensions

When people get down to the business of creating operational measures of variables, they often discover—or worse, never notice—that they are not exactly clear about which dimensions of a variable they are really interested in. In Chapter 5, I dealt with this to some degree, and now I want to look at it more closely. Here's one example to illustrate what I mean.

Let's suppose you and I are studying people's attitudes toward government, and we want to include an examination of how people feel about corruption. Here are just a few of the different dimensions we might examine:

- Do people think there is corruption in government?
- How much corruption do they think there is?
- How certain are they in their judgment of how much corruption there is?
- How do they feel about corruption in government as a problem in society?
- What do they think causes it?
- Do they think it's inevitable?
- What do they feel should be done about it?
- What are they willing to do personally to eliminate corruption in government?
- How certain are they that they would be willing to do what they say they would do?

The list could go on and on. How people feel about corruption in government has many dimensions, and it's essential that you be clear about which ones are important in your inquiry. Otherwise, you may measure how people feel about it when you really wanted to know how much they think there is, or vice versa.

Once you have determined how you are going to collect your data (e.g., survey, field research) and have decided on the relevant range of variation, the degree of precision needed between the extremes of variation, and the specific dimensions of the variables that interest you, you may have another choice: a mathematical-logical one. You may need to decide what level of measurement to use, and to discuss that question we need to take another look at attributes and their relationship to variables. (See Chapter 1 for the first discussion of this topic.)

Levels of Measurement

An attribute, you'll recall, is a characteristic or quality of something. *Female* would be an example. So would *old* or *student*. Variables, on the other hand, are logical sets of attributes. Thus, *sex* or *gender* is a variable composed of the attributes *female* and *male*.

The conceptualization and operationalization processes can be seen as the specification of variables and the attributes composing them. Thus, in one of the examples given in the preceding chapter, employment status would be a variable having the attributes *employed* and *unemployed* and perhaps expanded to include the other possibilities discussed.

Every variable should have two important qualities. First, the attributes composing it should be *exhaustive*. If the variable is to have any utility in research, you should be able to classify every observation in terms of one of the attributes composing the variable. You will run into trouble if you conceptualize the variable *political party affiliation* in terms of the attributes *Republican* and *Democrat*, because some of the people you set out to study will belong to the Socialist Workers Party, the American Independent Party, the Peace and Freedom Party, or some other party, and some (often a large percentage) will tell you they have no party affiliation. You could make the list of attributes exhaustive by adding *other* and *no affiliation*. Whatever you do, you must be able to classify every observation.

At the same time, attributes composing a variable must be *mutually exclusive*. You must be able to classify every observation in terms of one and *only one* attribute. Thus, for example, you need to define *employed* and *unemployed* in such a way that nobody can be both at the same time. That means being able to handle the person who is working at a job *and* is looking for work. (You might run across an employed economist who is looking for the glamour and excitement of being a sociologist.) In this case, you might define your attributes so that *employed* takes precedence over *unemployed* and anyone working at a job is employed regardless of whether he or she is looking for something better.

These qualities must be present among the attributes composing any variable. However, attributes may be related in other ways as well. Because of these additional relationships among their attributes, different variables may represent different *levels of measurement*. We are going to examine four levels of measurement in this section: *nominal, ordinal, interval,* and *ratio*.

Nominal Measures   Variables whose attributes have *only* the characteristics of exhaustiveness and mutual exclusiveness are **nominal measures.** Examples of these would be sex, religious affiliation, political party affiliation, birthplace, college major, and hair color. Although the attributes composing each of these variables—*male* and *female* composing the variable *sex*—are distinct from one another (and exhaust the possibilities of gender among people), they have none of the additional structures mentioned below.

It might be useful to imagine a group of people being characterized in terms of one such variable and physically grouped by the applicable attributes. Imagine asking a large gathering of people to stand together in groups according to the states in which they were born: all those born in Vermont in one group, those born in California in another, and so forth. (The variable would be *place of birth;* the attributes would be *born in California, born in Vermont,* etc.) All the people standing in a given group would share at least one thing in common; the people in any one group would differ from the people in all other groups in that same regard. Where the individual groups formed, how close they were to one another, or how the groups were arranged in the room would be irrelevant. All that would matter would be that all the members of a given group share the same state of birth and that each group has a different shared state of birth.

Ordinal Measures Variables whose attributes may be logically *rank-ordered* are **ordinal measures.** The different attributes represent relatively more or less of the variable. Variables of this type are social class, conservatism, alienation, prejudice, intellectual sophistication, and the like.

Note that each of these examples would be subject to serious differences of opinion as to its definition. Many of the ordinal variables used in social scientific research have this quality, but that need not be the case. In the physical sciences, *hardness* is the most frequently cited example of an ordinal measure. We may say that one material (for example, diamond) is harder than another (say, glass) if the former can scratch the latter and not vice versa (that is, diamond scratches glass, but glass does not scratch diamond). By attempting to scratch various materials with other materials, we might eventually be able to arrange several materials in a row, ranging from the softest to the hardest. It would not ever be possible to say how hard a given material was in absolute terms, but only in relative terms—which materials it was harder than, and which it was softer than.

Let's pursue the earlier example of grouping the people at a social gathering

and imagine that we asked all the people who had graduated from college to stand in one group, all those with a high school diploma (but who were not also college graduates) to stand in another group, and all those who had not graduated from high school to stand in a third group. This manner of grouping peotple would satisfy the requirements for exhaustiveness and mutual exclusiveness discussed earlier. In addition, however, we might logically arrange the three groups in terms of the relative amount of formal education (the shared attribute) each had. We might arrange the three groups in a row, ranging from most to least formal education. This arrangement would provide a physical representation of an ordinal measure. If we knew which groups two individuals were in, we could determine that one had more, less, or the same formal education as the other; in a similar way, one individual object could be ranked as harder, softer, or of the same hardness as another object.

It is important to note that in this example it would be irrelevant how close or far apart the educational groups were from one another. They might stand 5 feet apart or 500 feet apart; the college and high school groups could be 5 feet apart, while the less-than-high-school group might be 500 feet farther down the line. These actual distances would not have any meaning. The high school group, however, should be between the less-than-high-school group and the college group, or else the rank order would be incorrect.

Interval Measures For the attributes composing some variables, the actual distance separating those attributes does have meaning. Such variables are **interval measures.** For these, the logical distance between attributes can be expressed in meaningful standard intervals. A physical science example would be the Fahrenheit or the Celsius temperature scale. The difference, or distance, between 80 degrees and 90 degrees is the same as that between 40 degrees and 50 degrees. However, 80 degrees Fahrenheit is not twice as hot as 40 degrees, since the zero point in the Fahrenheit and Celsius scales are arbitrary; zero degrees does not really mean lack of heat, nor does −30 degrees represent 30 degrees less than no heat. (The Kelvin scale is based on an *absolute zero*, which does mean a complete lack of heat.)

About the only interval measures commonly used in social scientific research are constructed measures such as standardized intelligence tests that have been more or less accepted. The interval separating IQ scores of 100 and 110 may be regarded as the same as the interval separating scores of 110 and 120 by virtue of the distribution of observed scores obtained by many thousands of people who have taken the tests over the years. (A person who received a score of 0 on a standard IQ test could not be regarded, strictly speaking, as having *no* intelligence, although we might feel he or she was unsuited to be a college professor or even a college student.)

Ratio Measures   Most of the social scientific variables meeting the minimum requirements for interval measures also meet the requirements for **ratio measures.** In ratio measures, the attributes composing a variable, besides having all the structural characteristics mentioned above, are based on a true zero point. I have already mentioned the Kelvin temperature scale in contrast to the Fahrenheit and Celsius scales. Examples from social scientific research would include age, length of residence in a given place, number of organizations belonged to, number of times attending church during a particular period of time, number of times married, and number of Arab friends.

Returning to the illustration of methodological party games at a social gathering, we might ask people to group themselves by age. All the one-year-olds would

stand (or sit or lie) together, the two-year-olds together, the three-year-olds, and so forth. The fact that members of a single group share the same age and that different groups have different shared ages satisfies the minimum requirements for a nominal measure. Averaging the several groups in a line from youngest to oldest meets the additional requirements of an ordinal measure and permits us to determine if one person is older than, younger than, or the same age as, another. If we arrange the groups to have the same distance between each pair of adjacent groups, we satisfy the additional requirements of an interval measure and will be able to say *how much* older one person is than another. Finally, since one of the attributes included in age represents a true zero (babies carried by women about to give birth), the phalanx of hapless party goers also meets the requirements for a ratio measure, permitting us to say that one person is twice as old as another.

To review this discussion, Figure 6-1 presents a graphic illustration of the four levels of measurement.

Implications of Levels of Measurement
Since it is unlikely that you will undertake the physical grouping of people described above (try it once, and you won't be invited to many parties), I should draw your attention to some of the practical implications of the differences that have been distinguished. Primarily, these implications appear in the analysis of data (discussed in Part 4), but those analytical implications should be anticipated in the structuring of your research project.

Certain analytical techniques require variables that meet certain minimum levels of measurement. To the extent that the variables to be examined in your research project are limited to a particular level of measurement—say, ordinal—you should plan your analytical techniques accordingly. More precisely, you should anticipate drawing

Figure 6-1   Levels of Measurement.

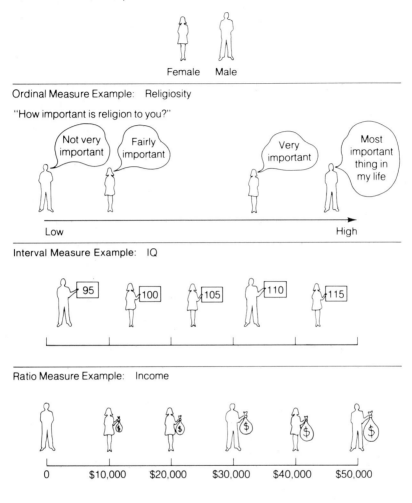

Nominal Measure Example: Sex

Female   Male

Ordinal Measure Example: Religiosity

"How important is religion to you?"

Not very important   Fairly important   Very important   Most important thing in my life

Low   High

Interval Measure Example: IQ

95   100   105   110   115

Ratio Measure Example: Income

0    $10,000 $20,000 $30,000 $40,000 $50,000

research conclusions appropriate to the levels of measurement used in your variables. For example, you might reasonably plan to determine and report the mean age of a population under study (add up all the individual ages and divide by the number of people), but you should not plan on reporting the mean religious affiliation, since that is a nominal variable, and the mean requires ratio level data. (You could report the *modal*—the most common—religious affiliation.)

At the same time, it is important to realize that some variables may be treated as representing different levels of measurement. Ratio measures are the highest level, descending through interval and ordinal to nominal, the lowest level of measurement. A variable representing a given level of measurement—say, ratio—may also be treated as representing a lower level of measurement—say, ordinal. Recall for example, that age is a ratio measure. If you wished to examine only the relationship between age and some ordinal-level variable—say, self-perceived religiosity: high, medium, and low—you might choose to treat age as an ordinal-level variable as well. You might characterize the subjects of your study as being *young, middle-aged,* and *old,* specifying what age range composed each of those groupings. Finally age might be used as a nominal-level variable for certain research purposes. People might be grouped as being born during the depression of the 1930s or not. Another nominal measurement, based on birth date rather than just age, would be the grouping of people by astrological signs.

The analytical uses planned for a given variable, then, should determine the level of measurement to be sought, with the realization that some variables are inherently limited to a certain level. If a variable is to be used in a variety of ways, requiring different levels of measurement, the study should be designed to achieve the highest level required. (For example, if the subjects in a study are asked their exact ages, they can later be organized into ordinal or nominal groupings.)

You need not necessarily measure variables at their highest level of measurement, however. If you are sure to have no need for ages of people at higher than the ordinal level of measurement, you may simply ask people which among several age ranges they belong in: for example, their twenties, thirties, and so forth. In a study of the wealth of corporations, you may use Dun & Bradstreet data to rank corporations rather than seek more precise information. Whenever your research purposes are not altogether clear, however, it is advisable to seek the highest level of measurement possible. Although ratio measures can later be reduced to ordinal ones, it is not possible to convert an ordinal measure to a ratio one. More generally, you cannot convert a lower level measure to a higher level one. That is a one-way street worth remembering.

Single or Multiple Indicators

In presenting so many alternatives and choices for you to make in operationalizing social scientific variables, I realize that I may create a sense of uncertainty and insecurity. You may find yourself worrying about whether you will make the right choices. To counterbalance this possible feeling, let me add a momentary dash of certainty and stability.

Many social scientific variables have pretty obvious, straightforward measures. No matter how you cut it, gender usually turns out to be a matter of male or female: a nominal-level variable that can be measured by a single observation—either looking or asking a question. Although you'll want to think about adopted and foster children, it's usually pretty easy to find out how many children a family has. And although some fine tuning is possible, for most research purposes, the resident population of a country is the resident population of that country—you can look it up in an almanac and know the answer. A great many variables, then, have obvious single indicators. If you can get one piece of information, you have what you need.

Sometimes, however, there is no single indicator that will give you the measure of a variable that you really want. As discussed in Chapter 5, many concepts are subject to varying interpretations—each with several possible indicators. In these cases, you will want to make several observations for a given variable. You can then combine the several pieces of information you've collected to create a *composite* measurement of the variable in question. All of Chapter 15 (Indexes, Scales, and Typologies) is devoted to ways of doing that, so I'll give you only a simple illustration at this point.

Consider the concept *college performance.* All of us have noticed that some students do well in college and others don't do so well—in terms of their performance in courses. It might be useful to study that, perhaps asking what characteristics and experiences are related to high levels of performance, and many researchers have done just that. How should we measure overall performance? Each grade in any single course is a potential indicator of college performance, but we run a risk in using any single course grade that the one used will not be typical of the student's general performance. The solution to this problem is so firmly established that it is, of course, obvious to you: the *grade point average*. We assign numerical scores to each letter grade, total the points earned by a given student and divide by the number of courses taken to obtain a composite measure. (If the courses vary in number of credits, adjustments are made in that regard.) It is often appropriate to create such composite measures in social research.

SOME OPERATIONALIZATION ILLUSTRATIONS

To bring together all the operationalization choices available to the social researcher and to show you the potential in those possibilities, I want to take just a little time to illustrate some of the ways you might address certain research problems. My purpose here is to stretch your imagination just a bit further and demonstrate the challenge that social research can present to your ingenuity. To simplify matters, I have not attempted to describe all the research conditions that would make one alternative superior to the others, though you should realize that in a given situation, they would not all be equally appropriate. Let's look at specific research questions, then, and some of the ways you could address them. We'll begin with an example that was discussed at length in Chapter 5. It has the added advantage that one of the variables is reasonably straightforward.

1. *Are women more compassionate than men?*
   a. Select a group of subjects for study. Present them with hypothetical situations that involve someone's being in trouble. Ask them what *they* would do if they were confronted with that situation. What would they do, for example, if they came across a small child who was lost and crying for its parents? Consider any answer that involves helping the child or comforting it to be compassionate, and count whether men or women are more likely to indicate they would be compassionate.
   b. Set up an experiment in which you pay a small child to pretend that he or she is lost. Put the kid to work on a busy sidewalk, and count whether men or women are more likely to offer assistance. Be sure to count how many men and women walk by, also, since there may be more of one than the other. If that's the case, simply calculate the percentage of men and the percentage of women who help.
   c. Select a sample of people and do a survey in which you ask them what organizations they belong to. Calculate whether women or men are more likely to belong to those that seem to reflect compassionate feelings. To take account of men belonging to more organizations than women in general—or vice versa—do this: for each person you study, calculate the *percentage* of his or her organizational memberships that reflect compassion. See if men or women have a higher average percentage.
   d. Watch your local newspaper for a special feature on some issue involving compassion—the slaughter of baby

seals, for example. In the days to follow, keep a record of all letters to the editor on the subject. See whether men or women are the more likely to express their compassion in the matter—making the necessary adjustments for one gender writing more letters to the editor than the other in general.

2. *Are sociology students or psychology students better informed about world affairs?*

   a. Prepare a short quiz on world affairs and arrange to administer it to the students in a sociology class and in a comparable psychology class. If you want to compare sociology and psychology *majors,* be sure to ask them what they are majoring in.
   b. Get the instructor of a course in world affairs to give you the average grades of sociology and psychology students in the course.
   c. Take a petition to sociology and psychology classes which urges that "the United Nations headquarters be moved to New York City." Keep a count of how many in each class sign the petition and how many inform you that the UN headquarters is already located in New York City.

3. *Do people consider New York or California the better place to live?*

   a. Consulting the *Statistical Abstract of the United States* or a similar publication, check the migration rates into and out of each state. See if you can find the numbers moving directly from New York to California and vice versa.
   b. The national polling companies—Gallup, Harris, Roper, and so forth—often ask people what they consider the best state to live in. Look up some recent results in the library or through your local newspaper.
   c. Compare suicide rates in the two states.

4. *Who are the most popular instructors on your campus: those in the social sciences, the natural sciences, or the humanities?*

   a. If your school has a provision for student evaluation of instructors, review some recent results and compute the average ratings given the three groups.
   b. Begin visiting the introductory courses given in each group of disciplines and count the numbers of students attending classes. Get the enrollment figures for the classes you study and calculate the average absentee rates.
   c. Around Christmas, select a group of faculty in each of the three divisions and ask them to keep a record of the numbers of cards and presents they receive from admiring students. See who wins.
   d. Read the obituary column in your campus newspaper every day and keep a record of all the faculty who are lynched after class by mobs of irate students—taking care to always note their departmental affiliation. Be sure to adjust your figures to take account of the total number of faculty in each division: the percentages lynched are more appropriate than the numbers lynched.

We could continue moving from the ridiculous to the more ridiculous, but the point of these illustrations has been to broaden your vision of the many ways variables can be operationalized, not necessarily to suggest respectable research projects. When you think about it, absolutely everything you see around you is already an operationalized measure of some variable. Most are measures of more than one variable, so all you have to do is pick the ones you want and decide what they will represent in your particular study. Usually, you will want to use more than one measure for each variable in the inquiry.

GUIDELINES FOR ASKING QUESTIONS

In several of the illustrations above—and in the actual practice of social research—variables are often operationalized by asking people questions as a way of getting data for analysis and interpretation. That is always the case in survey research, and such "self-report" data are often collected in experiments, field research, and other modes of observation. Sometimes the questions are asked by an interviewer; sometimes they are written down and given to respondents for completion (these are called *self-administered questionnaires*).

Since questionnaires represent a common and concrete illustration of the operationalization process, they are a fit topic for completing our general examination. As we'll see, several general guidelines can assist you in framing and asking questions that serve as excellent operationalizations of variables. There are also pitfalls that can result in useless and even misleading information. This section should assist you in distinguishing the two. Let's begin with some of the options available to you in creating questionnaires.

Questions and Statements

The term **questionnaire** suggests a collection of questions, but an examination of a typical questionnaire will probably reveal as many statements as questions. That is not without reason. Often, the researcher is interested in determining the extent to which respondents hold a particular attitude or perspective. If you are able to summarize the attitude in a fairly brief statement, you will often present that statement and ask respondents whether they agree or disagree with it. Rensis Likert has greatly formalized this procedure through the creation of the Likert scale, a format in which respondents are asked to strongly agree, agree, disagree, or strongly disagree, or perhaps strongly approve, approve, and so forth.

Both questions and statements may be used profitably. Using both in a given questionnaire gives you more flexibility in the design of items and can make the questionnaire more interesting as well.

Open-Ended and Closed-Ended Questions

In asking questions, researchers have two options. We may ask *open-ended* questions, in which case the respondent is asked to provide his or her own answer to the question. For example, the respondent may be asked, "What do you feel is the most important issue facing the United States today?" and be provided with a space to write in the answer (or be asked to report it verbally to an interviewer).

In the other case, *closed-ended* questions, the respondent is asked to select an answer from among a list provided by the researcher. Closed-ended questions are very popular, since they provide a greater uniformity of responses and are more easily processed. Open-ended responses must be coded before they can be keypunched, as will be discussed in Chapter 13. This coding process often requires that the researcher interpret the meaning of responses, opening the possibility of misunderstanding and researcher bias. There is also a danger that some respondents will give answers that are essentially irrelevant to the researcher's intent. Closed-ended responses, on the other hand, can often be keypunched directly from the questionnaire and in some cases can be marked directly on optical-sensing sheets by respondents for automatic punching.

The chief shortcoming of closed-ended questions lies in the researcher's structuring of responses. When the relevant answers to a given question are relatively clear, there should be no problem. In other cases, however, the researcher's structuring of responses may overlook some important responses. In asking about "the most important issue facing the United States," for example, your checklist of issues might omit certain issues that respondents would have said were important.

In the construction of closed-ended questions, you should be guided by the two structural requirements discussed earlier. The response categories provided should be *exhaustive:* they should include all the possible responses that might be expected. Often, researchers ensure this by adding a category labeled something like Other (Please specify: _____).

Second, the answer categories must be *mutually exclusive:* the respondent should not feel compelled to select more than one. (In some cases, you may wish to solicit multiple answers, but these may create difficulties in data processing and analysis later on.) To ensure that your categories are mutually exclusive, you should carefully consider each combination of categories, asking yourself whether a person could reasonably choose more than one answer. In addition, it is useful to add an instruction to the question asking the respondent to select the *one best* answer, but this technique is not a satisfactory substitute for a carefully constructed set of responses.

Make Items Clear

It should go without saying that questionnaire items should be clear and unambiguous, but the broad proliferation of unclear and ambiguous questions in surveys makes the point worth stressing here. Often you can become so deeply involved in the topic under examination that opinions and perspectives are clear to you but will not be clear to your respondents—many of whom

have given little or no attention to the topic. Or if you have only a superficial understanding of the topic, you may fail to specify the intent of your question sufficiently. The question "What do you think about the proposed nuclear freeze?" may evoke in the respondent a counterquestion: *"Which* nuclear freeze proposal?" Questionnaire items should be precise so that the respondent knows exactly what the researcher wants an answer to.

Avoid Double-Barreled Questions

Very frequently, researchers ask respondents for a single answer to a combination of questions. That seems to happen most often when the researcher has personally identified with a complex question. For example, you might ask respondents to agree or disagree with the statement "The United States should abandon its space program and spend the money on domestic programs." Although many people would unequivocally agree with the statement and others would unequivocally disagree, still others would be unable to answer. Some would want to abandon the space program and give the money back to the taxpayers. Others would want to continue the space program, but also put more money into domestic programs. These latter respondents could neither agree nor disagree without misleading you.

As a general rule, whenever the word *and* appears in a question or questionnaire statement, you should check whether you are asking a *double-barreled question.*

Respondents Must Be Competent to Answer

In asking respondents to provide information, you should continually ask yourself whether they are able to do so reliably. In a study of child rearing, you might ask respondents to report the age at which they first talked back to their parents. Quite aside from the problem of defining *talking back to parents,* it is doubtful if most respondents would remember with any degree of accuracy.

As another example, student government leaders occasionally ask their constituents to indicate the manner in which students' fees ought to be spent. Typically, respondents are asked to indicate the percentage of available funds that should be devoted to a long list of activities. Without a fairly good knowledge of the nature of those activities and the costs involved in them, the respondents cannot provide meaningful answers. (*Administrative costs* will receive little support although they may be essential to the program as a whole.)

One group of researchers examining the driving experience of teenagers insisted on asking an open-ended question concerning the number of miles driven since receiving a license. Although consultants argued that few drivers would be able to estimate such information with any accuracy, the question was asked nonetheless. In response, some teenagers reported driving hundreds of thousands of miles.

Questions Should Be Relevant

Similarly, questions asked in a questionnaire should be relevant to most respondents. When attitudes are requested on a topic that few respondents have thought about or really care about, the results are not likely to be very useful. Of course, the respondents may express attitudes even though they have never given any thought to the issue, and you run the risk of being misled.

This point is illustrated occasionally when you ask for responses relating to fictitious

persons and issues. In one political poll I conducted, I asked respondents whether they were familiar with each of 15 political figures in the community. As a methodological exercise, I made up a name: Tom Sakumoto. In response, 9 percent of the respondents said they were familiar with him. Of those respondents familiar with him, about half reported seeing him on television and reading about him in the newspapers.

When you obtain responses to fictitious issues, you can disregard those responses. But when the issue is real, you may have no way of telling which responses genuinely reflect attitudes and which reflect meaningless answers to an irrelevant question.

Short Items Are Best

In the interest of being unambiguous and precise and pointing to the relevance of an issue, the researcher is often led into long and complicated items. That should be avoided. Respondents are often unwilling to study an item in order to understand it. The respondent should be able to read an item quickly, understand its intent, and select or provide an answer without difficulty. In general, you should assume that respondents *will* read items quickly and give quick answers; therefore, you should provide clear, short items that will not be misinterpreted under those conditions.

Avoid Negative Items

The appearance of a negation in a questionnaire item paves the way for easy misinterpretation. Asked to agree or disagree with the statement "The United States should not recognize Cuba," a sizable portion of the respondents will read over the word *not* and answer on that basis. Thus, some will

Learning from Bad Examples

by Charles Bonney
Department of Sociology, Eastern Michigan University

Here's a questionnaire I've used to train my students in some of the problems of question construction. These are questions that might be asked in order to test the hypothesis "College students from high-status family backgrounds are more tolerant toward persons suffering mental or emotional stress" (where "status" has been operationally defined as the combined relative ranking on family income, parents' educational level, and father's occupational prestige—or mother's, *if* father not present or employed). Each question has one or more flaws in it. See if you can identify these problems. (A critique of the questionnaire appears at the end of the box.)

Questionnaire

1. What is your reaction to crazy people? _____

_____

2. What is your father's income? _____

3. As you were growing up, with whom were you living?
_____ both parents
_____ mother only
_____ father only
_____ other (please specify) _____

4. What is your father's occupation?

_____

(If father is deceased, not living at home, or unemployed or retired, is your mother employed?
_____ yes   _____ no)

5. Did your parents attend college?
_____ yes   _____ no

6. Wouldn't you agree that people with problems should be sympathized with?
_____ yes   _____ no

7. The primary etiology of heterophilic blockage is unmet dependency gratification.
_____ agree
_____ undecided
_____ disagree

8. If a friend of yours began to exhibit strange and erratic behavior, what do you think your response would be?

_____

9. Has anyone in your immediate family ever been institutionalized?
_____ yes   _____ no

Critique

The most fundamental critique of any questionnaire is simply, "Does it get the information necessary to test the

agree with the statement when they are in favor of recognition, while others will agree when they oppose it. And you may never know which is which.

In a study of civil liberties support, respondents were asked whether they felt "the following kinds of people should be prohibited from teaching in public schools," and were presented with a list including such items as a Communist, a Ku Klux

hypothesis?" While questions can be bad in and of themselves, they can be good only when seen in terms of the needs of the researcher. Good questionnaire construction is probably about as much an art as a science, and even "good" questions may contain hidden pitfalls or be made even better when the overall context is considered, but the following flaws definitely exist:

1. Derogatory and vague use of a slang term. Because it's the first question it's even worse: it may contaminate your results either by turning off some people enough to affect your response rate or it may have a "funneling effect" on later responses.

2. The operational definition of status calls for *family* income, not just father's. Also, it's been found that people are more likely to answer a question as personal as income if categories are provided for check-off, rather than this open-ended format.

3. "As you were growing up" is a vague time period. Also, the question is of dubious relevance or utility in the current format, although it *could* have been used to organize questions 2, 4, and 5.

4. While the format (asking about mother's employment only if there's no employed father) may well be sexist, it

follows the operational definition. There are still two problems, however. First, a checklist nearly always works better for occupation—open-ended questions often get answers that are too vague to be categorized. Also, in cases where status *will* be measured by mother's occupation, the question only elicits whether or not she's employed at all.

5. Limited measure of educational levels. Also, it's double-barreled: what if one parent attended college and the other didn't?

6. "Wouldn't you agree" is leading the respondent. Also, "sympathized" and "problems" are vague.

7. Technical jargon. No one will know what it means. (In fact, *I'm* not even sure what it means, and I wrote it! As close as I can translate it, it says, "the main reason you can't get a date is because your folks ignored you.")

8. Asks for speculation regarding a vague, hypothetical situation—which is not *always* bad, but there's usually a better way. Note, however, that the question is *not* double-barreled as many have said: it asks only about behavior which is *both* "strange" *and* "erratic."

9. "Institutionalized" is a vague term. Many types of institutionalization would clearly be irrelevant.

Klansman, and so forth. The response categories "yes" and "no" were given beside each entry. A comparison of the responses to this item with other items reflecting support for civil liberties strongly suggested that

many respondents gave the answer yes to indicate willingness for such a person to teach, rather than to indicate that such a person should be prohibited from teaching. (A later study in the series giving as answer categories "permit" and "prohibit" produced much clearer results.)

Avoid Biased Items and Terms

Recall from the earlier discussion of conceptualization and operationalization that there are no ultimately true meanings for any of the concepts that we typically study in social science. *Prejudice* has no ultimately correct definition, and whether a given person is prejudiced depends on our definition of that term. This same general principle applies to the responses that we get from persons completing a questionnaire.

The meaning of someone's response to a question depends in large part on the wording of the question that was asked. That is true of every question and answer. Some questions seem to encourage particular responses more than other questions. Questions that encourage respondents to answer in a particular way are called **biased.**

Most researchers recognize the likely effect of a question that begins "Don't you agree with the President of the United States that . . ." and no reputable researcher would use such an item. Unhappily, the biasing effect of items and terms is far subtler than this example suggests.

The mere identification of an attitude or position with a prestigious person or agency can bias responses. The item "Do you agree or disagree with the recent Supreme Court decision that . . ." would have a similar effect. I should make it clear that I am not suggesting that such wording will necessarily produce consensus or even a majority in support of the position identified with the prestigious person or agency, only that support would likely be increased over what would have been obtained without such identification.

Questionnaire items can be biased negatively as well as positively. "Do you agree or disagree with the position of Adolf Hitler when he stated that . . ." is an example. Since 1949, asking American questions about China has been tricky. Identifying the country as "China" can still result in confusion between mainland China and Taiwan. Not all Americans recognize the official name: The People's Republic of China. Referring to "Red China" or "Communist China" evokes negative response from many respondents, though that might be desirable if your purpose were to study anticommunist feelings.

In this context, you need to be generally wary of what researchers call the *social desirability* of questions and answers. Whenever you ask people for information, they answer through a filter of what will make them look good. That is especially true if they are being interviewed in a face-to-face situation. Thus, for example, a particular man may feel that things would be a lot better if women were kept in the kitchen, not allowed to vote, forced to be quiet in public, and so forth. Asked whether he supports equal rights for women, however, he may want to avoid looking like a male chauvinist pig. Recognizing that his views might have been progressive in the fifteenth century but are out of step with current thinking, he may choose to say yes. The main guidance I can offer you in relation to this problem is to suggest that you imagine how *you* would feel giving each of the answers you offered to respondents. If you'd feel embarrassed, perverted, inhumane, stupid, irresponsible, or anything like that, you should give some serious thought to whether others will be willing to give those answers.

As in all other examples, you must carefully examine the purpose of your inquiry and construct items that will be most useful to it. You should never be misled into thinking there are ultimately "right" and "wrong" ways of asking the questions. When you are in doubt as to the best question to ask, moreover, remember that you should ask more than one.

These, then, are some general guidelines for writing questions to elicit data for analysis and interpretation. I'll have more to say about questionnaires in Chapter 9 (Survey Research) when we look at some nitty-gritty details such as questionnaire layout, interviewing guidelines, and so forth. For now, the discussion of question construction should have filled out your understanding of the operationalization process. There's only one more general comment to be made.

OPERATIONALIZATION GOES ON AND ON

Although I've discussed conceptualization and operationalization as activities that precede data collection and analysis—you design your operational measures before you observe—you should realize that these two processes continue throughout a research project, even after data have been collected and analyzed. Here's what I mean by that.

You'll recall that I have repeatedly suggested that you measure a given variable in several different ways in your research. That is essential if the concept lying in the background is at all ambiguous and open to different interpretations and definitions. By measuring the variable in several different ways, you will be in a position to examine alternative operational definitions during your analysis. You will have several single indicators to choose from and many ways of creating different composite measures. Thus, you'll be able to experiment with different measures—each representing a somewhat different conceptualization and operationalization—to decide which gives the clearest and most useful answers to your research questions.

This doesn't mean that you should select the measurement that confirms your expec-

tations or proves your point. That's clearly not appropriate and doesn't do much to advance our understanding of social life. Instead, operationalization is a continuing process, not a blind commitment to a particular measure that may turn out to have been poorly chosen. Suppose, for example, that you decide to measure compassion by asking people whether they give money to charity, and everybody says yes. Where does that leave you? Nowhere. Your study of why some people are more compassionate than others would be in deep trouble unless you had included some other possible measures in designing your observations.

The ultimate purpose of social research is to clarify the nature of social life. The validity and utility of what you learn in that regard doesn't depend on when you first figured out how to look at things, any more than it matters whether you got the idea from a learned textbook, a dream, or your brother-in-law.

MAIN POINTS

- Operationalization is an extension of the conceptualization process.

- In operationalization, concrete empirical procedures are specified that will result in measurements of variables.

- Operationalization is the final specification of how we would recognize the different attributes of a given variable in the real world.

- In determining the range of variation for a variable, be sure to consider the opposite of the concept. Will it be sufficient to measure *religiosity* from "very much" to "none," or should you go past "none" to measure "anti-religiosity" as well?

- Nominal measures refer to those variables whose attributes are simply different from one another. An example would be *sex*.

■ Ordinal measures refer to those variables whose attributes may be rank-ordered along some progression from more to less. An example would be the variable *prejudice* as composed of the attributes "very prejudiced," "somewhat prejudiced," "slightly prejudiced," and "not at all prejudiced."

■ Interval measures refer to those variables whose attributes are not only rank-ordered but also are separated by a uniform distance between them. An example would be IQ.

■ Ratio measures are the same as interval measures except that ratio measures are also based on a true zero point. Age would be an example of a ratio measure, since that variable contains the attribute *zero years old*.

■ A given variable can sometimes be measured at different levels of measurement. Thus, age, potentially a ratio measure, may also be treated as interval, ordinal, or even nominal. The most appropriate level of measurement employed depends on the purpose of the measurement.

■ Questionnaires provide a method of collecting data by (a) asking people questions or (b) asking them to agree or disagree with statements representing different points of view.

■ Questions may be open-ended (respondents supply their own answers) or closed-ended (they select from a list of answers provided them).

■ Usually, short items in a questionnaire are better than long ones.

■ Negative items and terms should be avoided in questionnaires because they may confuse respondents.

■ Bias is the quality in questionnaire items that encourages respondents to answer in a particular way or to support a particular point of view. Avoid it.

■ Operationalization begins in study design and continues throughout the research project, including the analysis of data.

REVIEW QUESTIONS AND EXERCISES

1. What level of measurement—nominal, ordinal, interval, or ratio—describes each of the following variables:
   a. Race (white, black, Asian, etc.)
   b. Order of finish in a race (1st, 2nd, 3rd, etc.)
   c. Number of children in families
   d. Populations of nations
   e. Attitudes toward nuclear energy (strongly approve, approve, disapprove, strongly disapprove)
   f. Region of birth (Northeast, Midwest, etc.)
   g. Political orientation (very liberal, somewhat liberal, somewhat conservative, very conservative)

2. For each of the open-ended questions listed below, construct a closed-ended question that could be used in a questionnaire.
   a. What was your family's total income last year?
   b. How do you feel about the MX missile system?
   c. How important is religion in your life?
   d. What was your main reason for attending college?
   e. What do you feel is the biggest problem facing this community?

ADDITIONAL READINGS

Miller, Delbert, *Handbook of Research Design and Social Measurement* (New York: Longman, 1983). A useful reference work. This book, especially Part IV, cites and describes a wide variety of operational measures used in earlier social research. In a number of cases, the questionnaire formats used are presented. Though the quality of these illustrations is uneven, they provide excellent examples of the variations possible.

Oppenheim, A. N., *Questionnaire Design and Attitude Measurement* (New York: Basic Books, 1966). An excellent and com-

prehensive treatment of the construction of questionnaires and their relation to measurement in general. Although the illustrations of questionnaire formats are not always the best, this comes the closest of any book available to being the definitive work on questionnaires. Its coverage ranges from the theoretical to the nitty-gritty.

7

The Logic of Sampling

INTRODUCTION

In November 1984, Ronald Reagan was elected president of the United States with 59 percent of the popular vote, as against 41 percent for Walter Mondale: representing a political landslide. Prior to the election, a number of political polls had predicted a sizeable Reagan victory. Let's see how well they predicted the election.

Here are the results of several national polls conducted in late October or early November on the eve of the election. For purposes of comparability, I've assigned the "undecideds" proportionately to the percentages who chose one of the candidates (*Public Opinion* 1984:40).

	Reagan	Mondale
Time/Yankelovich	64	36
Gordon Black/USA Today	63	37
CBS/New York Times	61	39
Gallup Poll	59	41
ACTUAL VOTE	**59**	**41**
Gallup/Newsweek	59	41
ABC/Washington Post	57	43
Harris Poll	56	44
Roper Poll	55	45

Although the poll estimates varied, you can see how they were clustered around the actual election-day results. Now, how many interviews do you suppose it took each of these pollsters to come within a few percentage points in estimating the behavior of about a hundred million voters? Fewer than 2,000! In this chapter, we are going to find out how it's possible for social researchers to pull off such wizardry.

We've been talking a lot about observation in recent chapters. Those discussions have omitted the question of *what* or *who* will be observed. If you think about it for a minute, you'll see that a social researcher has a whole world of potential observations. Yet nobody can observe everything. A critical part of social research, then, is the decision as to what will be observed and what won't. If you want to study voters, for example, which voters should you study? That's the subject of this chapter.

Sampling is the process of selecting observations. After a brief history of social scientific sampling, the key section of this chapter discusses the logic and the skills of **probability sampling**. As we'll see, probability sampling techniques—involving *random sampling*—allow a researcher to make relatively few observations and generalize from those observations to a much wider population. We'll examine the requirements for generalizability. As you'll discover, random selection is a scientific procedure, not the haphazard choosing people often have in mind when they say "selected at random."

Although probability sampling is central to social research today, we'll take some time to examine a variety of nonprobability methods as well. While not based on random selection, these methods have their own logic and can provide useful samples for social inquiry. We'll examine both the advantages and the shortcomings of such methods, and we'll see where they fit within the social scientific enterprise.

THE HISTORY OF SAMPLING

Sampling in social research has developed hand in hand with political polling. This is the case, no doubt, because political polling is one of the few opportunities social researchers have to discover the accuracy of their estimates. On election day, they find out how well or how poorly they did.

President Alf Landon

You may have heard about the *Literary Digest* in connection with political polling. The *Digest* was a popular news magazine published between 1890 and 1938 in America. In 1920, *Digest* editors mailed postcards to people in six states, asking them who they were planning to vote for in the presidential campaign between Warren Harding and James Cox. Names were selected for the poll from telephone directories and automobile registration lists. Based on the postcards sent back, the *Digest* correctly predicted that Harding would be elected. In elections that followed, the *Literary Digest* expanded the size of its poll, and made correct predictions in 1924, 1928, and 1932.

In 1936, the *Digest* conducted their most ambitious poll: ten million ballots were sent to people listed in telephone directories and on lists of automobile owners. Over two million responded, giving Republican contender Alf Landon a stunning 57 to 43 percent landslide over incumbent President Franklin Roosevelt. The editors modestly cautioned:

We make no claim to infallibility. We did not coin the phrase "uncanny accuracy" which has been so freely applied to our Polls. We know only too well the limitations of every straw vote, however enormous the sample gathered, however scientific the method. It would be a miracle if every State of the forty-eight behaved on Election Day exactly as forecast by the Poll.

(1936a:6)

Two weeks later, the *Digest* editors knew the limitations of straw polls even better: voters gave Roosevelt a third term in office by the largest landslide in history, with 61 percent of the vote. Landon won only 8 electoral votes to Roosevelt's 523. The editors were puzzled by their unfortunate turn of luck.

A part of the problem surely lay in the 22 percent return rate garnered by the poll. The editors asked:

Why did only one in five voters in Chicago to whom the *Digest* sent ballots take the trouble to reply? And why was there a preponderance of Republicans in the one-fifth that did reply? . . . We were getting better cooperation in what we have always regarded as a public service from Republicans than we were getting from Democrats. Do Republicans live nearer to mail-boxes? Do Democrats generally disapprove of straw polls?   (1936b:7)

A part of the answer to these questions lay in the sampling frame used by the *Digest*: telephone subscribers and automobile owners. Such a sampling design selected a disproportionately wealthy sample, especially coming on the tail end of the worst economic depression in the nation's history. The sample effectively excluded poor people, and the poor people predominantly voted for Roosevelt's New Deal recovery program.

President Thomas E. Dewey

The 1936 election also saw the emergence of a young pollster whose name was to become synonymous with public opinion. In contrast to the *Literary Digest*, George Gallup correctly predicted that Roosevelt would beat Landon. Gallup's success in 1936 hinged on his use of **quota sampling**, which I'll have more to say about later in the chapter. For now, you need only know that quota sampling is based on a knowledge of the characteristics of the population being sampled: what proportion are men, what proportion women, what proportions are of various incomes, ages, etc. People are selected to match the population characteristics: the right number of poor, white, rural men; the right number of rich, black, urban women,

etc. The quotas are based on those variables most relevant to the study. By knowing the numbers of people with various incomes in the nation, Gallup selected his sample so as to ensure the right proportion of respondents at each income level.

Gallup and his American Institute of Public Opinion used quota sampling to good effect in 1936, 1940, and 1944—correctly picking the presidential winner each of those years. Then, in 1948, Gallup and most political pollsters suffered the embarrassment of picking New York Governor Thomas Dewey over incumbent President Harry Truman. A number of factors accounted for the 1948 failure. First, most of the pollsters stopped polling in early October despite a steady trend toward Truman during the campaign. In addition, many voters were undecided throughout the campaign, and they went disproportionately for Truman when they stepped in the voting booth. More important for our present purposes, however, Gallup's failure rested on the unrepresentativeness of his samples.

Quota sampling—which had been effective in earlier years—was Gallup's undoing in 1948. Recall that this technique requires that the researcher know something about the total population (of voters in this instance). For national political polls, such information came primarily from census data. By 1948, however, a world war, producing a massive movement from country to city, had radically changed the character of the American population from what the 1940 Census showed. City dwellers, moreover, were more likely to vote Democratic, hence the over-representation of rural voters also underestimated the number of Democratic votes.

Two Types of Sampling Methods

In 1948, a number of academic researchers had been experimenting with *probability sampling* methods. By and large, they were far more successful than those using quota samples. Today, probability sampling remains the primary method for selecting samples for social science research. To appreciate the logic of probability sampling, it is useful to distinguish it from **nonprobability sampling.** The bulk of this chapter will be devoted to probability sampling, since it is currently the most respected and useful method. A smaller portion of this chapter will consider the various methods of nonprobability sampling.

I'll begin with a discussion of the logic of probability sampling and a brief glossary of sampling concepts and terminology. Then we'll look at the concept of sampling distribution: the basis of estimating the accuracy of findings based on samples. Following these theoretical discussions, we'll consider populations and sampling frames—focusing on practical problems of determining the target group of the study and the way to begin selecting a sample. Next, we'll examine the basic types of sample designs: simple random samples, systematic samples, stratified samples, and cluster samples. Finally, a short discussion and description of nonprobability sampling is presented.

THE LOGIC OF PROBABILITY SAMPLING

If all members of a population were identical in all respects—all demographic characteristics, attitudes, experiences, behaviors, etc.—there would be no need for careful sampling procedures. In such a case, any sample would indeed be sufficient. In this extreme case of homogeneity, in fact, *one* case would be sufficient as a sample to study characteristics of the whole population.

In fact, of course, the human beings who compose any real population vary in many ways. A sample of individuals from a population, if it is to provide useful descriptions of the total population, must contain essentially the same variations that exist in the population. Probability sampling provides an efficient method for selecting a sample that should adequately reflect variations that exist in the population.

Conscious and Unconscious Sampling Bias

Of course anyone could select a sample, even without any special training or care. To select a sample of 100 university students, a person might go to the university campus and interview students found walking around campus. This kind of sampling method is often used by untrained researchers, but it has very serious problems.

To begin, the researcher's own personal biases may affect the sample selected in this manner; hence the sample would not truly represent the student population. Suppose that you are personally somewhat intimidated by "hippie-looking" students, feeling that they would ridicule your research effort. You might consciously or semiconsciously avoid interviewing such people. Or, you might feel that the attitudes of "straight-looking" students would be irrelevant to your research purposes and avoid interviewing them. Even if you sought to interview a balanced group of students, you probably would not know the proper proportions of different types of students making up such a balance, or you might be unable to identify the different types just by watching them walk by.

Even if you made a conscientious effort to interview every tenth student entering the university library, you could not be sure of a *representative* sample, since different types of students visit the library with different frequencies. Your sample would overrepresent students who visit the library more often.

Representativeness and Probability of Selection

While the term *representativeness* has no precise, scientific meaning, it carries a commonsense meaning that makes it a useful concept in the discussion of sampling. As I'll use the term here, a sample will be representative of the population from which it is selected if the aggregate characteristics of the sample closely approximate those same aggregate characteristics in the population. (Samples need not be representative in all respects; representativeness is limited to those characteristics that are relevant to the substantive interests of the study, though you may not know which are relevant.) If the population, for example, contains 50 percent women, then a representative sample would also contain "close to" 50 percent women. Later in this chapter, we'll discuss "how close" in detail.

A basic principle of probability sampling is that *a sample will be representative of the population from which it is selected if all members of the population have an equal chance of being selected in the sample.* (We'll see shortly that the size of the sample selected also affects the *degree* of representativeness.) Samples that have this quality are often labeled **EPSEM** samples (equal probability of selection method). I'll discuss variations of this principle later, but it is primary and forms the basis of probability sampling.

Moving beyond this basic principle, we must realize that samples—even carefully selected EPSEM samples—are seldom if ever *perfectly* representative of the populations

from which they are drawn. Nevertheless, probability sampling offers two special advantages.

First, probability samples, although never perfectly representative, are typically *more representative* than other types of samples because the biases discussed in the preceding section are avoided. In practice, there is a greater likelihood that a probability sample will be representative of the population from which it is drawn than that a nonprobability sample will be.

Second, and more important, probability theory permits us to estimate the accuracy or representativeness of the sample. Conceivably, an uninformed researcher might, through wholly haphazard means, select a sample that nearly perfectly represents the larger population. The odds are against doing so, however, and we would be unable to estimate the likelihood that he or she has achieved representativeness. The probability sampler, on the other hand, can provide an accurate estimate of success or failure.

Following a brief glossary of sampling terminology, we'll examine the means the probability sampler uses to estimate the representativeness of the sample.

SAMPLING CONCEPTS AND TERMINOLOGY

The following discussions of sampling theory and practice use a number of technical terms. To make it easier for you to understand those discussions, it is important to quickly define these terms. For the most part, I'll employ terms commonly used in sampling and statistical textbooks so that readers may better understand those other sources.

In presenting this glossary of sampling concepts and terminology, I would like to acknowledge a debt to Leslie Kish and his excellent textbook *Survey Sampling*. Although I have modified some of the conventions used by Kish, his presentation is easily the most important source of this discussion.

Element An *element* is that unit about which information is collected and which provides the basis of analysis. Typically, in survey research, elements are people or certain types of people. However, other kinds of units can constitute the elements for social research; families, social clubs, or corporations might be the elements of a study. (*Note:* Elements and units of analysis are often the same in a given study, though the former refers to sample selection while the latter refers to data analysis.)

Population A *population* is the theoretically specified aggregation of study elements. While the vague term *Americans* might be the target for a study, the delineation of the population would include the definition of the element *Americans* (for example, citizenship, residence) and the time referent for the study (Americans as of when?). Translating the abstract *adult New Yorkers* into a workable population would require a specification of the age defining *adult* and the boundaries of *New York*. Specifying the term *college student* would include a consideration of full-time and part-time students, degree candidates and non-degree candidates, undergraduate and graduate students, and similar issues.

While researchers must begin with careful specification of their population, poetic license usually permits them to phrase their reports in terms of the hypothetical universe. For ease of presentation, even the most conscientious researcher normally speaks of "Americans" rather than "resident citizens of the United States of America as of November 12, 1985." The primary guide in this matter, as in most others, is that you should not mislead or deceive your readers.

Study Population A *study population* is that aggregation of elements from which the sample is actually selected. As a practical matter, you are seldom in a position to guarantee that every element meeting the theoretical definitions laid down actually has a chance of being selected in the sample. Even where lists of elements exist for sampling purposes, the lists are usually somewhat incomplete. Some students are always omitted, inadvertently, from student rosters. Some telephone subscribers request that their names and numbers be unlisted. The study population, then, is the aggregation of elements from which the sample is selected.

Often researchers decide to limit their study populations more severely than indicated in the above examples. National polling firms may limit their national samples to the 48 adjacent states, omitting Alaska and Hawaii for practical reasons. A researcher wishing to sample psychology professors may limit the study population to those who are serving in psychology departments, omitting those serving in other departments. (In a sense, we might say that these researchers have redefined their universes and populations, in which case they must make the revisions clear to their readers.)

Sampling Unit A *sampling unit* is that element or set of elements considered for selection in some stage of sampling. In a simple, single-stage sample, the sampling units are the same as the elements. In more complex samples, however, different levels of sampling units may be employed. For example, you might select a sample of census blocks in a city, then select a sample of households on the selected blocks, and finally select a sample of adults from the selected households. The sampling units for these three stages of sampling are, respectively, census blocks, households, and adults, of which only the last of these are the elements. More specifically, the terms *primary sampling units, secondary sampling units,* and *final sampling units* are used to designate the successive stages.

Sampling Frame   A **sampling frame** is the actual list of sampling units from which the sample, or some stage of the sample, is selected. If a simple sample of students is selected from a student roster, the roster is the sampling frame. If the primary sampling unit for a complex population sample is the census block, the list of census blocks composes the sampling frame—either in the form of a printed booklet, a card file, or a magnetic tape file.

In a single-stage sample design, the sampling frame is a list of the elements composing the study population. In practice, existing sampling frames often define the study population rather than the other way around. We often begin with a population in mind for our study; then we search for possible sampling frames. The frames available for our use are examined and evaluated, and we decide which frame presents a study population most appropriate to our needs.

The relationship between populations and sampling frames is critical and one that has not been given sufficient attention. A later section of this chapter will pursue this issue in greater detail.

Observation Unit   An *observation unit,* or unit of data collection, is an element or aggregation of elements from which information is collected. Again, the unit of analysis and unit of observation are often the same—the individual person—but that need not be the case. Thus the researcher may interview heads of households (the observation units) to collect information

about all members of the households (the units of analysis).

Our task is simplified when the unit of analysis and the observation unit are the same. Often that is not possible or feasible, however, and in such situations we need to exercise some ingenuity in collecting data relevant to our units of analysis without actually observing those units.

Variable   As discussed earlier, a *variable* is a set of mutually exclusive attributes: sex, age, employment status, and so forth. The elements of a given population may be described in terms of their individual attributes on a given variable. Often social research aims to describe the distribution of attributes composing a variable in a population. Thus a researcher may describe the age distribution of a population by examining the relative frequency of different ages among members of the population.

A variable, by definition, must possess *variation;* if all elements in the population have the same attribute, that attribute is a *constant* in the population, rather than part of a variable.

Parameter   A *parameter* is the summary description of a given variable in a *population.* The mean income of all families in a city and the age distribution of the city's population are parameters. An important portion of social research involves the estimation of population parameters on the basis of sample observations.

Statistic   A *statistic* is the summary description of a given variable in a sample. Thus the mean income computed from a sample and the age distribution of that sample are statistics. Sample statistics are used to make estimates of population parameters.

Sampling Error   Probability sampling methods seldom, if ever, provide statistics exactly equal to the parameters that they are used to estimate. Probability theory, however, permits us to estimate the degree of error to be expected for a given sample design. *Sampling error* will be discussed in more detail later.

Confidence Levels and Confidence Intervals The two key components of sampling error estimates are **confidence levels** and **confidence intervals**. We express the accuracy of our sample statistics in terms of a level of confidence that the statistics fall within a specified interval from the parameter. For example, we may say we are 95 percent confident that our sample statistics (for example, 50 percent favor Candidate X) are within plus or minus 5 percentage points of the population parameter. As the confidence interval is expanded for a given statistic, our confidence increases and we may say that we are 99.9 percent confident that our statistic falls within ± 7.5 percentage points of the parameter. I'll describe how sampling intervals and levels are calculated in the next section, making these two concepts even clearer.

PROBABILITY SAMPLING THEORY AND SAMPLING DISTRIBUTION

With definitions presented, we can now examine the basic theory of probability sampling as it applies to social research. We'll also consider the logic of sampling distribution and sampling error with regard to a **binomial variable**—a variable composed of two attributes.

Probability Sampling Theory

The ultimate purpose of sampling is to select a set of elements from a population in such a way that descriptions of those elements (statistics) accurately portray the parameters of the total population from which the elements are selected. Probability sampling enhances the likelihood of accomplishing this aim and also provides methods for estimating the degree of probable success.

Random selection is the key to this process. In random selection each element has an equal chance of selection that is independent of any other event in the selection process. Flipping a perfect coin is the most frequently cited example: the "selection" of a head or a tail is independent of previous selections of heads or tails. Rolling a perfect set of dice is another example. Such images of random selection seldom apply directly to social research sampling methods, however. The social researcher more typically uses tables of random numbers or computer programs that provide a random selection of sampling units.

The reasons for using random selection methods—random-number tables or computer programs—are twofold. First, this procedure serves as a check on conscious or unconscious bias on the part of the researcher. The researcher who selects cases on an intuitive basis might very well select cases that would support his or her research expectations or hypotheses. Random selection erases this danger. More important, random selection offers access to the body of probability theory, which provides the basis for estimates of population parameters and estimates of error. Let's turn now to an examination of this latter aspect.

The Sampling Distribution of Ten Cases

To introduce the statistics of probability sampling, let's begin with a simple example of only ten cases.* Suppose there are ten

---

*I want to thank Hanan Selvin for suggesting this method of introducing probability sampling.

people in a group, and each has a certain amount of money in his or her pocket. To simplify, let's assume that one person has no money, another has one dollar, another has two dollars, and so forth up to the person with nine dollars. Figure 7-1 presents the population of ten people.

Our task is to determine the average amount of money one person has: specifically, the *mean* number of dollars. If you simply add up the money shown in Figure 7-1, you'll find that the total is $45, so the mean is $4.50. Our purpose in the rest of this exercise is to estimate that mean without actually observing all ten individuals. We'll do that by selecting random samples from the population and use the means of those samples to estimate the mean of the whole population.

To start, suppose we were to select—at random—a sample of only *one* person from the ten. Depending on which person we selected, we'd estimate the group's mean as anywhere from $0 to $9. Figure 7-2 gives a graphic display of those ten possible samples.

The ten dots shown on the graph in Figure 7-2 represent the ten "sample" means we would get as estimates of the population. The distribution of the dots on the graph is called the *sampling distribution*. Obviously, it would not be a very good idea to select a sample of only one, since we stand a very good chance of missing the true mean of $4.50 by quite a bit.

But what if we take samples of 2 each? As you can see from Figure 7-3, increasing the sample size improves our estimations.

Figure 7-1   A Population of Ten People with $0–$9

Figure 7-2   The Sampling Distribution of Samples of 1

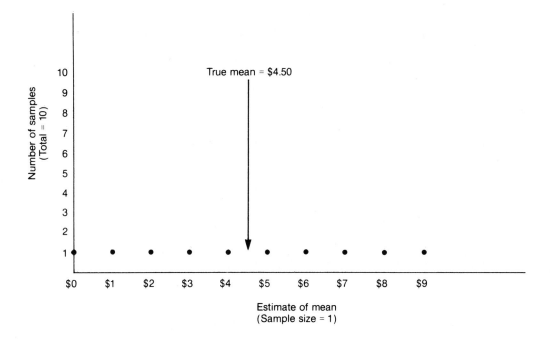

Figure 7-3   The Sampling Distribution of Samples of 2

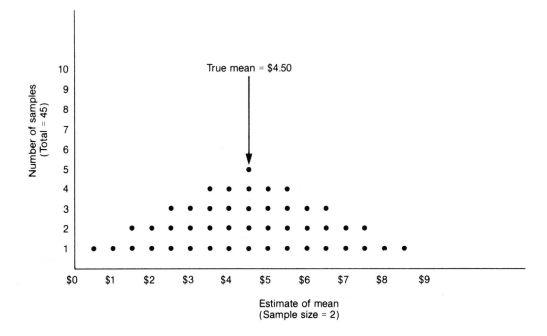

There are now 45 possible samples: $0/$1, $0/$2, . . . $7/$8, $8/$9. Moreover, some of those samples produce the same means. For example, $0/$6, $1/$5, and $2/$4 all produce means of $3. In Figure 7-3, the three dots shown above the $3 mean represent those three samples.

The 45 sample means are not evenly distributed, as you can see. Rather, they are somewhat clustered around the true value of $4.50. Only two samples deviate by as much as four dollars from the true value ($0/$1 and $8/$9), whereas five of the samples would give the true estimate of $4.50; another eight samples miss the mark by only fifty cents (plus or minus).

Now suppose we select even larger samples. What do you suppose that will do to our estimates of the mean? Figure 7-4 presents the sampling distributions of samples of 3, 4, 5, and 6.

The progression of sampling distributions is clear. Every increase in sample size improves the distribution of estimates of the mean. The limiting case in this procedure, of course, is to select a sample of ten. There would be only one possible sample (everyone) and it would give us the true mean of $4.50.

Binomial Sampling Distribution

Let's turn now to a more realistic sampling situation and see how the notion of sampling distribution applies, using a simple example involving a population much larger than ten. Let's assume for the moment that we wish to study the student population of State University to determine approval or disapproval of a student conduct code pro-

Figure 7-4   The Sampling Distributions of Samples of 3, 4, 5, and 6

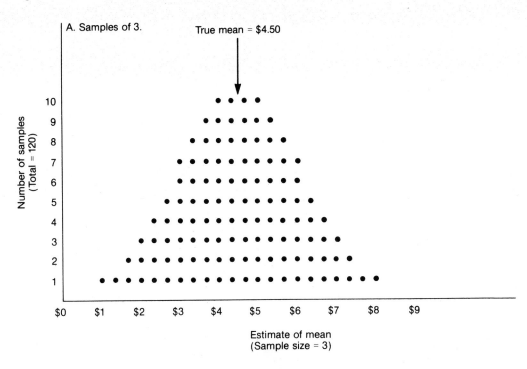

Figure 7-4   *(Continued)*

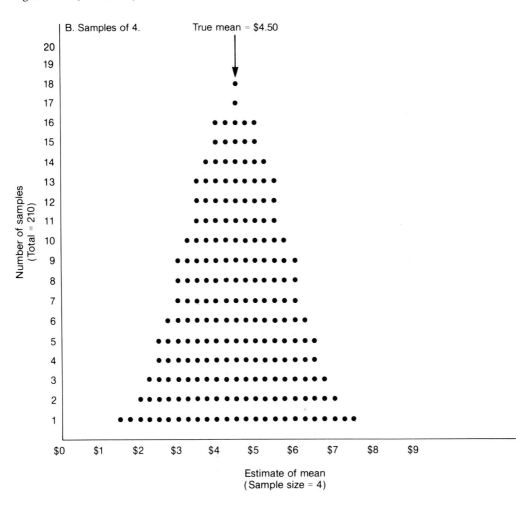

posed by the administration. The study population will be that aggregation of, say, 20,000 students contained in a student roster: the sampling frame. The elements will be the individual students at SU. The variable under consideration will be attitudes toward the code, a binomial variable: approve and disapprove. We'll select a random sample of, say, 100 students for purposes of estimating the entire student body.

The horizontal axis of Figure 7-5 presents all *possible* values of this parameter in the population—from 0 percent approval

to 100 percent approval. The midpoint of the axis—50 percent—represents half the students approving of the code and the other half disapproving.

To choose our sample, we give each student on the student roster a number and select 100 random numbers from a table of random numbers. Then we interview the 100 students whose numbers have been selected and ask for their attitudes toward the student code: whether they approve or disapprove. Suppose that this operation gives us 48 students who approve of the code and

Figure 7-4 *(Continued)*

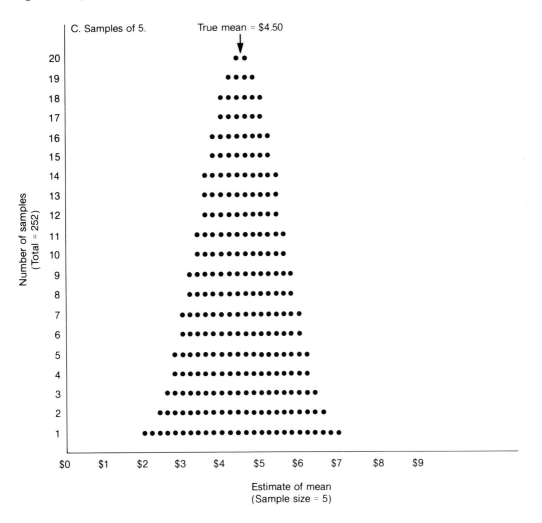

52 who disapprove. We present this statistic by placing a dot on the *x* axis at the point representing 48 percent.

Now let's suppose that we select another sample of 100 students in exactly the same fashion and measure their approval or disapproval of the student code. Perhaps 51 students in the second sample approve of the code, and that we place another dot in the appropriate place on the *x* axis. Repeating this process once more, we may discover

that 52 students in the third sample approve of the code.

Figure 7-6 presents the three different sample statistics representing the percentages of students in each of the three random samples who approved of the student code. The basic rule of random sampling is that such samples drawn from a population give estimates of the parameter that pertains in the total population. Each of the random samples, then, gives us an estimate of the

Figure 7-4   *(Continued)*

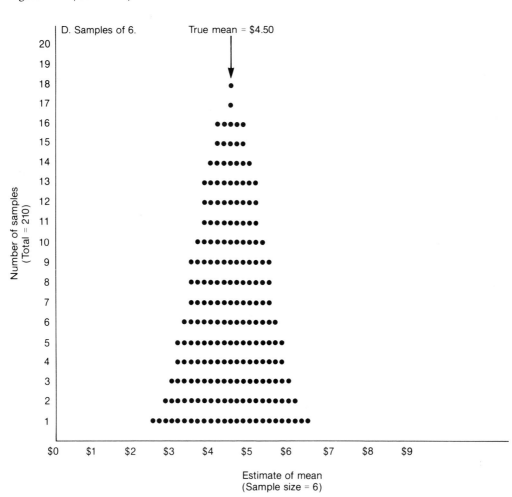

percentage of students in the total student body who approve of the student code. Unhappily, however, we have selected three samples and now have three separate estimates.

To retrieve ourselves from this dilemma, let's draw more and more samples of 100 students each, question each of the samples as to their approval or disapproval of the code, and plot the new sample statistics on our summary graph. In drawing many such samples, we discover that some of the new

samples provide duplicate estimates, as in the illustration of ten cases. Figure 7-7 shows the sampling distribution of, say, hundreds of samples. This is often referred to as a normal curve.

Note that by increasing the number of samples selected and interviewed, we have also increased the range of estimates provided by the sampling operation. In one sense we have increased our dilemma in attempting to guess the parameter in the population. Probability theory, however,

Figure 7-5   Range of Possible Sample Study Results

Percent of students approving of the student code

provides certain important rules regarding the sampling distribution presented in Figure 7-7.

First, if many independent random samples are selected from a population, the sample statistics provided by those samples will be *distributed around the population parameter* in a known way. Thus, although Figure 7-7 shows a wide range of estimates, more of them are in the vicinity of 50 percent than elsewhere in the graph. Probability theory tells us, then, that the true value is in the vicinity of 50 percent.

Second, probability theory gives us a formula for estimating *how closely* the sample statistics are clustered around the true value. This formula contains three factors: the parameter, the sample size, and the *standard error* (a measure of sampling error):

$$s = \sqrt{\frac{P \times Q}{n}}$$

Symbols: P,Q = the population parameters for the binomial; if 60 percent of the student body approves of the code and 40 percent disapproves, P and Q are 60 percent and 40 percent, or .6 and .4. Note that $Q = 1 - P$ and $P = 1 - Q$.

n = the number of cases in each sample.

s = the standard error.

Let's assume that the population parameter in the student example is 50 percent approving of the code and 50 percent disapproving. Recall that we have been selecting samples of 100 cases each. When these numbers are put into the formula, we find that the standard error equals .05, or 5 percent.

In probability theory, the standard error is a valuable piece of information, for it indicates the extent to which the sample estimates will be distributed around the population parameter. Specifically, probability theory indicates that certain proportions of the sample estimates will fall within specified increments—each equal to one standard error—from the population parameter. Approximately 34 percent (.3413) of the sample estimates will fall within one standard error increment above the population parameter, and another 34 percent will fall within one standard error below the parameter. In our example, the standard error increment is 5 percent, so we know that 34 percent of our samples will give estimates of student approval between 50 percent (the parameter) and 55 percent (one standard error above); another 34 percent of the samples will give estimates between 50 percent and 45 percent (one standard error below the parameter). Taken

Figure 7-6   Results Produced by Three Hypothetical Studies

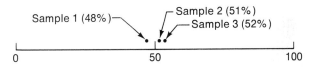

Percent of students approving of the student code

Figure 7-7   The Sampling Distribution

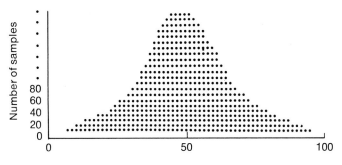

Percent of students approving of the student code

together, then, we know that roughly two-thirds (68 percent) of the samples will give estimates within ± 5 percent of the parameter.

Moreover, probability theory dictates that roughly 95 percent of the samples will fall within plus or minus two standard errors of the true value, and 99.9 percent of the samples will fall within plus or minus three standard errors. In our present example, then, we know that only one sample out of a thousand would give an estimate lower than 35 percent approval or higher than 65 percent.

The proportion of samples falling within one, two, or three standard errors of the parameter is constant for any random sampling procedure such as the one just described, providing that a large number of samples are selected. The size of the standard error in any given case, however, is a function of the population parameter and the sample size. If we return to the formula for a moment, we note that the standard error will increase as a function of an increase in the quantity P times Q. Note further that this quantity reaches its maximum in the situation of an even split in the population. If $P = .5$, $PQ = .25$; if $P = .6$, $PQ = .24$; if $P = .8$, $PQ = .16$; if $P = .99$, $PQ = .0099$. By extension, if P is either 0.0 or 1.0 (either 0 percent or 100 percent

approve of the student code), the standard error will be 0. If everyone in the population has the same attitude (no variation), then every sample will give exactly that estimate.

The standard error is also a function of the sample size—an *inverse* function. As the sample size increases, the standard error *decreases*. As the sample size increases, the several samples will be clustered nearer to the true value. Another rule of thumb is evident in the formula: because of the square root formula, the standard error is reduced by half if the sample size is *quadrupled*. In our present example, samples of 100 produce a standard error of 5 percent; to reduce the standard error to 2.5 percent, we must increase the sample size to 400.

All of this information is provided by established probability theory in reference to the selection of large numbers of random samples. If the population parameter is known and very many random samples are selected, we are able to predict how many of the samples will fall within specified intervals from the parameter. These conditions do not typically pertain in social research, however.

Usually, we do not know the parameter, but we conduct a sample survey to estimate that value. Moreover, we do not typically select large numbers of samples; we select only one sample. Nevertheless, the preceding discussion of probability theory provides the basis for inferences about the typical social research situation.

Whereas probability theory specifies that 68 percent of the samples will produce estimates falling within one standard error of the parameter, the social researcher infers that a given random sample has a likelihood of 68 percent of falling within that range. In this regard we speak of *confidence levels:* we are 68 percent confident that our sample estimate is within one standard error of the parameter. Or we may say that we are 95 percent confident that the sample statistic is within two standard errors of the parameter, and so forth. Quite reasonably, our confidence increases as the margin for error is extended. We are virtually positive (99.9 percent) that we are within three standard errors of the true value.

Although we may be confident (at some level) of being within a certain range of the parameter, we have already noted that we seldom know what the parameter is. To resolve this dilemma, we substitute our sample estimate for the parameter in the formula; lacking the true value, we substitute the best available guess.

The result of these inferences and estimations is that we are able to estimate a population parameter and also the expected degree of error on the basis of one sample drawn from a population. Beginning with the question "What percentage of the student body approves of the student code?" you could select a random sample of 100 students and interview them. You might then report that your best estimate is that 50 percent of the student body approves of the code, and that you are 95 percent confident that between 40 and 60 percent (plus or minus two standard errors) approve. The range from 40· to 60 percent is called the *confidence interval.* (At the 68 percent confidence level, the confidence interval would be 45–55 percent.)

The logic of confidence levels and confidence intervals also provides the basis for determining the appropriate sample size for a study. Once you have decided on the degree of sampling error you can tolerate, you will be able to calculate the number of cases needed in your sample. Thus, for example, if you want to be 95 percent confident that your study findings are accurate within plus or minus five percentage points of the population parameters, you should select a sample of at least 400. (Appendix G is a convenient guide in this regard.)

This then is the basic logic of probability sampling. Random selection permits the researcher to link findings from a sample to the body of probability theory so as to estimate the accuracy of those findings. All statements of accuracy in sampling must specify both a confidence level and a confidence interval. The researcher may report that he or she is *x* percent confident that the population parameter is between two specific values.

Here's how George Gallup (1984:7) described his sampling error in a newspaper report of a recent Gallup Poll regarding attitudes of children and parents:

The adult findings are based on in-person interviews with 1520 adults, 18 and older, conducted in more than 300 scientifically selected localities across the nation during the period October 26–29. For results based on samples of this size, one can say with 95 percent confidence that the error attributable to sampling and other random effects could be three percentage points in either direction.

Or hear what the *New York Times* (1984:12) had to say about a poll they conducted among Democrats during the 1984 political campaigns:

In theory, in 19 cases out of 20, the results from a poll such as this should differ by no more than three percentage points, in either direction, from what would have been obtained by interviewing all Democratic voters.

The next time you read statements like these in the newspaper, they should make more sense to you. Be wary, however, that such statements are sometimes made when they are not warranted, but you are now able to make that determination.

The foregoing discussion has considered only one type of statistic: the percentages produced by a *binomial* or **dichotomous variable**. The same logic, however, would apply to the examination of other statistics, such as mean income, for example. Since the computations are somewhat more complicated in such a case, I have chosen to consider only binomials in this introduction.

You should be cautioned that the survey uses of probability theory as discussed above are not wholly justified technically. The theory of sampling distribution makes assumptions that almost never apply in survey conditions. The number of samples contained within specified increments of standard errors, for example, assumes an infinitely large population, an infinite number of samples, and sampling with replacement. Moreover, the inferential jump from the distribution of several samples to the probable characteristics of one sample has been grossly oversimplified in the above discussion.

These cautions are offered to give you perspective. Researchers often appear to overestimate the precision of estimates produced by use of probability theory in connection with social research. As will be mentioned elsewhere in this chapter and throughout the book, variations in sampling techniques and nonsampling factors may further reduce the legitimacy of such estimates. Nevertheless, the calculations discussed in this section can be extremely valuable to you in understanding and evaluating your data. Although the calculations do not provide as precise estimates as some researchers might assume, they can be quite valid for practical purposes; they are unquestionably more valid than less rig-

orously derived estimates based on less rigorous sampling methods.

Most important, you should be familiar with the basic *logic* underlying the calculations. If you are so informed, you will be able to react sensibly to your own data and to those reported by others.

POPULATIONS AND SAMPLING FRAMES

The immediately preceding section has dealt with the theoretical model for social research sampling. Although it is necessary for the research consumer, student, and researcher to understand that theory, it is no less important that they appreciate the less-than-perfect conditions that exist in the field. The present section is devoted to a discussion of one aspect of field conditions that requires a compromise with regard to theoretical conditions and assumptions. Here we'll consider the congruence of or disparity between populations of sampling frames.

Simply put, a sampling frame is the list or quasi-list of elements from which a probability sample is selected. Here are some reports of sampling frames appearing in research journals:

The data for this research were obtained from a random sample of parents of children in the third grade in public and parochial schools in Yakama County, Washington.
(Petersen & Maynard 1981:92)

The sample at Time 1 consisted of 160 names drawn randomly from the telephone directory of Lubbock, Texas.
(Tan 1980:242)

The data reported in this paper . . . were gathered from a probability sample of adults aged 18 and over residing in households in the 48 contiguous United States. Personal interviews with 1,914 respondents were conducted by the

Survey Research Center of the University of Michigan during the fall of 1975.

(Jackman and Senter 1980:345)

Properly drawn samples provide information appropriate for describing the population of elements composing the sampling frame—nothing more. It is necessary to make this point in view of the all-too-common tendency for researchers to select samples from a given sampling frame and then make assertions about a population similar to, but not identical to, the study population defined by the sampling frame.

For an example of an overgeneralized sampling frame, take a look at this report, which is discussing the drugs most frequently prescribed by American physicians:

> Information on prescription drug sales is not easy to obtain. But Rinaldo V. DeNuzzo, a professor of pharmacy at the Albany College of Pharmacy, Union University, Albany, NY, has been tracking prescription drug sales for 25 years by polling nearby drugstores. He publishes the results in an industry trade magazine, *MM&M*.
>
> DeNuzzo's latest survey, covering 1980, is based on reports from 66 pharmacies in 48 communities in New York and New Jersey. Unless there is something peculiar about that part of the country, his findings can be taken as representative of what happens across the country.

(Moskowitz 1981:33)

The main thing that should strike you is the casual comment about whether there is anything peculiar about New York and New Jersey. There is. The life-style in these two states is hardly typical of the other 48. We cannot assume that residents in these large, urbanized, Eastern seaboard states necessarily have the same drug-use patterns as residents of Mississippi, Utah, New Mexico, and Vermont.

Does the survey even represent prescription patterns in New York and New Jersey? To determine that, we would have to know something about the manner in which the 48 communities and the 66 pharmacies were selected. We should be wary in this regard, in view of the reference to "polling nearby drugstores." As we'll see, there are several methods for selecting samples that ensure representativeness, and unless they are used, we should not generalize from the study findings.

Studies of organizations are often the simplest from a sampling standpoint because organizations typically have membership lists. In such cases, the list of members constitutes an excellent sampling frame. If a random sample is selected from a membership list, the data collected from that sample may be taken as representative of all members—*if all members are included in the list*.

Populations that can be sampled from good organizational lists include elementary school, high school, and university students and faculty; church members; factory workers; fraternity or sorority members; members of social, service, or political clubs; and members of professional associations.

The above comments apply primarily to local organizations. Often statewide or national organizations do not have a single membership list easily available. There is, for example, no single list of Episcopalian church members. However, a slightly more complex sample design could take advantage of local church membership lists by first sampling churches, and then subsampling the membership lists of those churches selected. (More about that later.)

Other lists of individuals may be especially relevant to the research needs of a particular study. Government agencies maintain lists of registered voters, for example, that might be used if you wanted to conduct a preelection poll or an in-depth examination of voting behavior—but you must ensure that the list is up-to-date. Similar lists contain the names of automobile owners, welfare recipients, taxpayers, business permit holders, licensed professionals, and so forth. Although it may be difficult to gain access to some of these lists, they provide excellent sampling frames for specialized research purposes.

Realizing that the sampling elements in a study need not be individual persons, we may note that the lists of other types of elements also exist: universities, businesses of various types, cities, academic journals, newspapers, unions, political clubs, professional associations, and so forth.

Telephone directories are frequently used for "quick and dirty" public opinion polls. Undeniably they are easy and inexpensive to use, and that is no doubt the reason for their popularity. And, if you want to make assertions about telephone subscribers, the directory is a fairly good sampling frame. (Realize, of course, that a given directory will not include new subscribers or those who have requested unlisted numbers. Sampling is further complicated by the inclusion in directories of nonresidential listings.) Unfortunately, telephone directories are all too often taken to be a listing of a city's population or of its voters. There are many defects in this reasoning, but the chief one involves a social-class bias. Poor people are less likely to have telephones; rich people may have more than one line; a telephone directory sample, therefore, is likely to have a middle- or upper-class bias.

The class bias inherent in telephone directory samples is often hidden. Preelection polls conducted in this fashion are sometimes quite accurate, perhaps because of the class bias evident in voting itself: poor people are less likely to vote. Frequently, then, these two biases nearly coincide and the results of a telephone poll may come very close to the final election outcome. Unhappily, the pollster never knows for sure until after the election. And sometimes, as in the case of the 1936 *Literary Digest* poll, you may discover that the voters have not acted according to the expected class biases. The ultimate disadvantage of

this method, then, is the researcher's inability to estimate the degree of error to be expected in the sample findings.

Street directories and tax maps are often used for easy samples of households, but they may also suffer from incompleteness and possible bias. For example, in strictly zoned urban regions, illegal housing units are unlikely to appear on official records. As a result, such units would have no chance for selection, and sample findings could not be representative of those units, which are often poorer and more overcrowded than the average.

Review of Populations and Sampling Frames

Surprisingly little attention has been given to the issues of populations and sampling frames in social research literature. With this in mind, I've devoted special attention to them here. To further emphasize the point, here is a summary of the main guidelines to remember:

1. Findings based on a sample can be taken as representative only of the aggregation of elements that compose the sampling frame.

2. Often, sampling frames do not truly include all the elements that their names might imply. Omissions are almost inevitable. Thus a first concern of the researcher must be to assess the extent of the omissions and to correct them if possible. (Realize, of course, that the researcher may feel he or she can safely ignore a small number of omissions that cannot easily be corrected.)

3. Even to generalize to the population composing the sampling frame, it is necessary for all elements to have equal representation in the frame: typically, each element should appear only once. Elements that appear more than once will have a greater

probability of selection, and the sample will, overall, overrepresent those elements.

Other, more practical matters relating to populations and sampling frames will be treated elsewhere in this book. For example, the form of the sampling frame—such as a list in a publication, a 3×5 card file, mailing address plates, machine-readable cards, or magnetic tapes—can affect how easy it is to use. And ease of use may often take priority over scientific considerations: an "easier" list may be chosen over a "harder" one, even though the latter is more appropriate to the target population. We should not take a dogmatic position in this regard, but every researcher should carefully weigh the relative advantages and disadvantages of such alternatives.

TYPES OF SAMPLING DESIGNS

Introduction

Up to this point, we have focused on **simple random sampling** (SRS). And, indeed, the body of statistics typically used by social researchers assumes such a sample. As we shall see shortly, however, you have a number of options in choosing your sampling method, and you will seldom if ever choose simple random sampling. There are two reasons for that. First, with all but the simplest sampling frame, simple random sampling is not feasible. Second, and probably surprisingly, simple random sampling may not be the most accurate method available. Let's turn now to a discussion of simple random sampling and the other options available.

Simple Random Sampling

As noted above, *simple random sampling* is the basic sampling method assumed in the statistical computations of social research. The mathematics of random sampling are especially complex, so we'll detour around them in favor of describing the ways of employing this method in the field.

Once a sampling frame has been established in accord with the discussion above, to employ *simple random sampling* the researcher assigns a single number to each element in the list, not skipping any number in the process. A table of random numbers (Appendix D) is then used to select elements for the sample. The box entitled "Using a Table of Random Numbers" explains its use.

If your sampling frame is in a machine-readable form—cards or magnetic tape—a simple random sample can be selected automatically by computer. (In effect, the computer program numbers the elements in the sampling frame, generates its own series of random numbers, and prints out the list of elements selected.)

Systematic Sampling

Simple random sampling is seldom used in practice. As we shall see, it is not usually the most efficient sampling method, and it can be rather laborious if done manually. SRS typically requires a list of elements; when such a list is available, researchers usually employ **systematic sampling** rather than simple random sampling.

In *systematic sampling*, every kth element in the total list is chosen (systematically) for inclusion in the sample. If the list contains 10,000 elements and you want a sample of 1,000, you select every tenth element for your sample. To ensure against any possible human bias in using this method, you should select the first element at random. Thus, in the above example you would begin by selecting a random number between 1 and 10. The element having that number is included in the sample, plus every tenth element following it. This method is tech-

Using a Table of Random Numbers

In social research, it is often appropriate to select a set of random numbers from a table such as the one presented in Appendix D. Here's how to do that.

Suppose that you want to select a simple random sample of 100 people (or other units) out of a population totaling 980.

1. To begin, number the members of the population: in this case, from 1 to 980. Now the problem is to select 100 random numbers. Once you've done that, your sample will consist of the people having the numbers you've selected. (Note: It's not essential to actually number them, as long as you're sure of the total. If you have them in a list, for example, you can always count through the list after you've selected the numbers.)

2. The next step is to determine the number of digits you will need in the random numbers you select. In our example, there are 980 members of the population, so you will need 3-digit numbers to give everyone a chance of selection. (If there were 11,825 members of the population, you'd need to select 5-digit numbers.) Thus, we want to select 100 random numbers in the range from 001 to 980.

3. Now turn to the first page of Appendix D. Notice that there are several rows and columns of 5-digit numbers, and there are several pages. The table represents a series of random numbers in the range from 00001 to 99999. To use the table for your hypothetical sample, you have to answer these questions:
a. How will you create 3-digit numbers out of 5-digit numbers?
b. What pattern will you follow in moving through the table to select your numbers?
c. Where will you start?
Each of these questions has several satisfactory answers. The key is to create a plan and follow it. Here's an example.

4. To create 3-digit numbers from 5-digit numbers, let's agree to select 5-digit numbers from the table but consider only the left-most 3 digits in each case. If we picked the first number on the first page—10480—we would only consider the 104. (We could agree to

---

nically referred to as *a systematic sample with a random start*. Two terms are frequently used in connection with systematic sampling. The **sampling interval** is the standard distance between elements selected in the sample: 10 in the sample above. The **sampling ratio** is the proportion of elements in the population that are selected: 1/10 in the example.

$$\text{sampling interval} = \frac{\text{population size}}{\text{sample size}}$$

$$\text{sampling ratio} = \frac{\text{sample size}}{\text{population size}}$$

In practice, systematic sampling is virtually identical to simple random sampling. If the list of elements is indeed randomized before sampling, one might argue that a systematic sample drawn from that list is in fact a simple random sample. By now, debates over the relative merits of simple random sampling and systematic sampling

take the digits furthest to the right, 480, or the middle three digits, 048, and any of these plans would work.) The key is to make a plan and stick with it. For convenience, let's use the left-most 3 digits.

5. We can also choose to progress through the tables any way we want: down the columns, up them, across to the right or to the left, or diagonally. Again, any of these plans will work just fine so long as we stick to it. For convenience, let's agree to move down the columns; when we get to the bottom of one column, we'll go to the top of the next; when we exhaust a given page, we'll start at the top of the first column of the next page.

6. Now, where do we start? You can close your eyes and stick a pencil into the table and start wherever the pencil point lands. (I know it doesn't sound scientific, but it works.) Or, if you're afraid you'll hurt the book or miss it altogether, close your eyes and make up a column number and a row number. ("I'll pick the number in the fifth row of column 2.") Start with that number.

7. Let's suppose we decide to start with the fifth number in column 2. If you look on the first page of Appendix D, you'll see that the starting number is 39975. We have selected 399 as our first random number, and we have 99 more to go. Moving down the second column, we select 069, 729, 919, 143, 368, 695, 409, 939, and so forth. At the bottom of column 2, we select number 104 and continue to the top of column 3: 015, 255, and so on.

8. See how easy it is? But trouble lies ahead. When we reach column 5, we are speeding along, selecting 816, 309, 763, 078, 061, 277, 988 . . . Wait a minute! There are only 980 students in the senior class. How can we pick number 988? The solution is simple: ignore it. Any time you come across a number that lies outside your range, skip it and continue on your way: 188, 174, and so forth. The same solution applies if the same number comes up more than once. If you select 399 again, for example, just ignore it the second time.

9. That's it. You keep up the procedure until you've selected 100 random numbers. Returning to your list, your sample consists of person number 399, person number 69, person number 729, and so forth.

have been resolved largely in favor of the simpler method: systematic sampling. Empirically, the results are virtually identical. And, as we shall see in a later section, systematic sampling, in some instances, is slightly more accurate than simple random sampling.

There is one danger involved in systematic sampling. The arrangement of elements in the list can make systematic sampling unwise. Such an arrangement is usually called *periodicity*. If the list of elements is arranged in a cyclical pattern that coincides with the sampling interval, a grossly biased sample may be drawn. Two examples will illustrate.

In one study of soldiers during World War II, the researchers selected a systematic sample from unit rosters. Every tenth soldier on the roster was selected for the study. The rosters, however, were arranged in a table of organizations: sergeants first, then corporals and privates, squad by squad— and each squad had 10 members. As a result, every tenth person on the roster was a squad sergeant. The systematic sample selected contained only sergeants. It could, of course, have been the case that no sergeants were selected for the same reason.

As another example, suppose we select a sample of apartments in an apartment building. If the sample is drawn from a list of apartments arranged in numerical order (for example, 101, 102, 103, 104, 201, 202, and so on), there is a danger of the sampling interval coinciding with the number of apartments on a floor or some multiple thereof. Then the samples might include only northwest-corner apartments or only apartments near the elevator. If these types of apartments have some other particular characteristic in common (for example, higher rent), the sample will be biased. The same danger would appear in a systematic sample of houses in a subdivision arranged with the same number of houses on a block.

In considering a systematic sample from a list, then, you should carefully examine the nature of that list. If the elements are arranged in any particular order, you should figure out whether that order will bias the sample to be selected and take steps to counteract any possible bias (for example, take a simple random sample from cyclical portions).

In summary, however, systematic sampling is usually superior to simple random sampling, in convenience if nothing else. Problems in the ordering of elements in the sampling frame can usually be remedied quite easily.

Stratified Sampling

In the two preceding sections we have discussed two methods of sample selection from a list: random and systematic. **Stratification** is not an alternative to these methods, but it represents a possible modification in their use.

Simple random sampling and systematic sampling both ensure a degree of representativeness and permit an estimate of the error present. Stratified sampling is a method for obtaining a greater degree of representativeness—decreasing the probable sampling error. To understand why that is the case, we must return briefly to the basic theory of sampling distribution.

We recall that sampling error is reduced by two factors in the sample design. First, a large sample produces a smaller sampling error than a small sample. Second, a homogeneous population produces samples with smaller sampling errors than does a heterogeneous population. If 99 percent of the population agrees with a certain statement, it is extremely unlikely that any probability sample will greatly misrepresent the extent of agreement. If the population is split 50-50 on the statement, then the sampling error will be much greater.

Stratified sampling is based on this second factor in sampling theory. Rather than selecting your sample from the total population at large, you ensure that appropriate numbers of elements are drawn from homogeneous subsets of that population. To get a stratified sample of university students, for example, you would first organize your population by college class and then draw appropriate numbers of freshmen, sophomores, juniors, and seniors. In a nonstratified sample, representation by class would be subjected to the same sampling error as other variables. In a sample stratified by class, the sampling error on this variable is reduced to zero.

Even more complex stratification methods are possible. In addition to stratifying by class, you might also stratify by sex, by grade point average, and so forth. In this fashion you might be able to ensure that your sample would contain the proper numbers of freshman men with a 4.0 average, of freshman women with a 4.0 average, and so forth.

The ultimate function of stratification, then, is to organize the population into homogeneous subsets (with heterogeneity between subsets) and to select the appropriate number of elements from each. To the extent that the subsets are homogeneous on the stratification variables, they may be homogeneous on other variables as well. Since age is related to college class, a sample stratified by class will be more representative in terms of age as well. Since occupational aspirations still seem to be related to sex, a sample stratified by sex will be more representative in terms of occupational aspirations.

The choice of stratification variables typically depends on what variables are available. Sex can often be determined in a list of names. University lists are typically arranged by class. Lists of faculty members may indicate their departmental affiliation. Government agency files may be arranged by geographical region. Voter registration lists are arranged according to precinct.

In selecting stratification variables from among those available, however, you should be concerned primarily with those that are presumably related to variables that you want to represent accurately. Since sex is related to many variables and is often available for stratification, it is often used. Education is related to many variables, but it is often not available for stratification. Geographical location within a city, state, or nation is related to many things. Within a city, stratification by geographical location usually increases representativeness in social class, ethnic group, and so forth. Within a nation, it increases representativeness in a broad range of attitudes as well as in social class and ethnicity.

Methods of stratification in sampling vary. When you are working with a simple list of all elements in the population, two are predominant. One method is to sort the population elements into discrete groups based on whatever stratification variables are being used. On the basis of the relative proportion of the population represented by a given group, you select—randomly or systematically—a number of elements from that group constituting the same proportion of your desired sample size. For example, if freshman men with a 4.0 average compose 1 percent of the student population and you desire a sample of 1,000 students, you would select 10 freshman men with a 4.0 average.

The other method is to group students as described above and then put those groups together in a continuous list: beginning with all freshman men with a 4.0 average and ending with all senior women with a 1.0 or below. You would then select a systematic sample, with a random start, from the entire list. Given the arrangement of the list, a systematic sample would select proper numbers (within an error range of 1 or 2) from each subgroup. (Note: A simple random sample drawn from such a composite list would cancel out the stratification.)

Stratified sampling ensures the proper representation of the stratification variables to enhance representation of other variables related to them. Taken as a whole, then, a stratified sample is likely to be more representative on a number of variables than a simple random sample. Although the simple random sample is still regarded as somewhat sacred, it should now be clear that you can often do better.

Implicit Stratification in Systematic Sampling

It was mentioned above that systematic sampling can, under certain conditions, be more accurate than simple random sampling. That is the case whenever the arrangement of the list creates an implicit stratification. As already noted, if a list of university students is arranged by class, then a systematic sample provides a stratification by class where a simple random sample would not.

In a study of students at the University of Hawaii, after stratification by school class, the students were arranged by their student identification numbers. These numbers, however, were their social security numbers. The first three digits of the social security number indicate the state in which the number was issued. As a result, within a class, students were arranged by the state in which they were issued a social security number, providing a rough stratification by geographical origins.

You should realize, therefore, that an ordered list of elements may be more useful to you than an unordered, randomized list. This point has been stressed here in view of an unfortunate belief that lists should be randomized before systematic sampling. Only if the arrangement presents the problems discussed earlier should the list be rearranged.

ILLUSTRATION: SAMPLING UNIVERSITY STUDENTS

Let's put these principles into practice by looking at an actual sampling design used to select a sample of university students. The purpose of the study was to survey, with a mail-out questionnaire, a representative cross section of students attending the main campus of the University of Hawaii in 1968. The following sections will describe the steps and decisions involved in selecting that sample.

Study Population and Sampling Frame

The obvious sampling frame available for use in this sample selection was the mag-

netic registration tape maintained by the university administration. The tape contained students' names, local and permanent addresses, social security numbers, and a variety of other information such as field of study, class, age, sex, and so forth.

The registration tape, however, contains files on all persons who could, by any conceivable definition, be called students, many of whom seemed inappropriate to the purposes of the study. As a result, it was necessary to define the *study population* in a somewhat more restricted fashion. The final definition included those 15,225 day-program degree candidates registered for the fall 1968 semester on the Manoa campus of the university, including all colleges and departments, both undergraduate and graduate students, and both American and foreign students. The computer program used for sampling, therefore, limited consideration to students fitting this definition.

Stratification

The sampling program also permitted stratification of students before sample selection. The researchers decided that stratification by college class would be sufficient, although the students might have been further stratified within class, if desired, by sex, college, major, and so forth.

Sample Selection

Once the students had been arranged by class, a systematic sample was selected across the entire rearranged list. The sample size for the study was initially set at 1,100. To achieve this sample, the sampling program was set for a 1/14 sampling ratio. The program generated a random number between 1 and 14; the student having that number and every fourteenth student thereafter was selected in the sample.

Once the sample had been selected, the computer was instructed to print each student's name and mailing address on six self-adhesive mailing labels. These labels were then simply transferred to envelopes for mailing the questionnaires.

Sample Modification

This initial design of the sample had to be modified. Before the mailing of questionnaires, the researchers discovered that unexpected expenses in the production of the questionnaires made it impossible to cover the costs of mailing to all 1,100 students. As a result, one-third of the mailing labels were systematically selected (with a random start) for exclusion from the sample. The final sample for the study was thereby reduced to about 770.

This modification to the sample is mentioned here to illustrate the frequent necessity to change aspects of the study plan in midstream. Since the excluded students were systematically omitted from the initial systematic sample, the remaining 770 students could still be taken as reasonably representing the study population. The reduction in sample size did, of course, increase the range of sampling error.

MULTISTAGE CLUSTER SAMPLING

The preceding sections have dealt with reasonably simple procedures for sampling from lists of elements. Such a situation is ideal. Unfortunately, however, much interesting social research requires the selection of samples from populations that cannot be easily listed for sampling purposes. Examples would be the population of a city, state,

or nation; all university students in the United States; and so forth. In such cases, the sample design must be much more complex. Such a design typically involves the initial sampling of *groups* of elements—clusters—followed by the selection of elements within each of the selected clusters.

Cluster sampling may be used when it is either impossible or impractical to compile an exhaustive list of the elements composing the target population. All church members in the United States would be an example of such a population. It is often the case, however, that the population elements are already grouped into subpopulations, and a list of those subpopulations either exists or can be created practically. Thus, church members in the United States belong to discrete churches, and it would be possible to discover or create a list of those churches. Following a cluster sample format, then, the list of churches would be sampled in some manner as discussed above (for example, a stratified, systematic sample). Next, you would obtain lists of members from each of the selected churches. Each of the lists would then be sampled, to provide samples of church members for study. (For an example, see Glock, Ringer, and Babbie 1967.)

Another typical situation concerns sampling among population areas such as a city. Although there is no single list of a city's population, citizens reside on discrete city blocks or census blocks. It is possible, therefore, to select a sample of blocks initially, create a list of persons living on each of the selected blocks, and subsample persons on each block.

In a more complex design, you might sample blocks, list the households on each selected block, sample the households, list the persons residing in each household, and, finally, sample persons within each selected household. This multistage sample design would lead to the ultimate selection of a sample of individuals but would not require the initial listing of all individuals in the city's population.

Multistage cluster sampling, then, involves the repetition of two basic steps: listing and sampling. The list of primary sampling units (churches, blocks) is compiled and, perhaps, stratified for sampling. Then a sample of those units is selected. The selected primary sampling units are then listed and perhaps stratified. The list of secondary sampling units is then sampled, and so forth.

Cluster sampling is highly recommended by its efficiency, but the price of that efficiency is a less accurate sample. A simple random sample drawn from a population list is subject to a single sampling error, but a two-stage cluster sample is subject to two sampling errors. First, the initial sample of clusters will represent the population of clusters only within a range of sampling error. Second, the sample of elements selected within a given cluster will represent all the elements in that cluster only within a range of sampling error. Thus, for example, you run a certain risk of selecting a sample of disproportionately wealthy city blocks, plus a sample of disproportionately wealthy households within those blocks. The best solution to this problem lies in the number of clusters selected initially and the number of elements selected within each.

Typically, you'll be restricted to a total sample size; for example, you may be limited to conducting 2,000 interviews in a city. Given this broad limitation, however, you have several options in designing your cluster sample. At the extremes you might choose one cluster and select 2,000 elements within that cluster; or you might select 2,000 clusters with one element selected within each. Of course, neither of these extremes is advisable, but a broad range of choices lies between them. Fortunately, the logic of sampling distributions provides a general guideline to be followed.

Recall that sampling error is reduced by two factors: an increase in the sample size and increased homogeneity of the elements being sampled. These factors operate at each level of a multistage sample design. A sample of clusters will best represent all clusters if a large number are selected and if all clusters are very much alike. A sample of elements will best represent all elements in a given cluster if a large number are selected from the cluster and if all the elements in the cluster are very much alike.

With a given total sample size, however, if the number of clusters is increased, the number of elements within a cluster must be decreased. In this respect, the representativeness of the clusters is increased at the expense of more poorly representing the elements composing each cluster, or vice versa. Fortunately, the factor of homogeneity can be used to ease this dilemma.

Typically, the elements composing a given natural cluster within a population are more homogeneous than are all elements composing the total population. The members of a given church are more alike than are all church members; the residents of a given city block are more alike than are all the residents of a whole city. As a result, relatively fewer elements may be needed to adequately represent a given natural cluster, while a larger number of clusters may be needed to adequately represent the diversity found among the clusters. This fact is most clearly seen in the extreme case of very different clusters that are composed of identical elements within each. In such a situation, a large number of clusters would adequately represent all its members. Although this extreme situation never exists in reality, it is closer to the truth in most cases than its opposite: identical clusters composed of grossly divergent elements.

The general guideline for cluster design, then, is to maximize the number of clusters selected while decreasing the number of elements within each cluster. It must be noted, however, that this scientific guideline must be balanced against an administrative constraint. The efficiency of cluster sampling is based on the ability to minimize the listing of population elements. By initially selecting clusters, you need only list the elements composing the selected clusters, not all elements in the entire population. Increasing the number of clusters, however, goes directly against this efficiency factor in cluster sampling. A small number of clusters may be listed more quickly and more cheaply than a large number. (Remember that all the elements in a selected cluster must be listed even if only a few are to be chosen in the sample.)

The final sample design will reflect these two constraints. In effect, you will probably select as many clusters as you can afford. Lest this issue be left too open-ended at this point, one rule of thumb may be presented. Population researchers conventionally aim for the selection of 5 households per census block. If a total of 2,000 households are to be interviewed, you would aim at 400 blocks with 5 household interviews on each. Figure 7-8 presents a graphic overview of this process.

Before turning to more detailed procedures available to cluster sampling, it bears repeating that this method almost inevitably involves a loss of accuracy. The manner in which this appears, however, is somewhat complex. First, as noted earlier, a multistage sample design is subject to a sampling error at each stage. Since the sample size is necessarily smaller at each stage than the total sample size, the sampling error at each stage will be greater than would be the case for a single-stage random sample of elements. Second, sampling error is estimated on the basis of observed variance among the sample elements. When those elements are drawn from among relatively homogeneous clusters, the estimated sampling error will be too optimistic and must be corrected in the light of the cluster sample design.

Multistage Cluster Sampling, Stratification

Thus far, we have looked at cluster sampling as though a simple random sample were selected at each stage of the design. In fact, stratification techniques can be used to refine and improve the sample being selected.

The basic options available are essentially the same as those possible in single-stage sampling from a list. In selecting a national sample of churches, for example, you might initially stratify your list of churches by denomination, geographical region, size, rural or urban location, and perhaps by some measure of social class.

Once the primary sampling units (churches, blocks) have been grouped according to the relevant, available stratification variables, either simple random or systematic sampling techniques can be used to select the sample. You might select a specified number of units from each group or *stratum*, or you might arrange the stratified clusters in a continuous list and systematically sample that list.

To the extent that clusters are combined into homogeneous strata, the sampling error at this stage will be reduced. The primary goal of stratification, as before, is homogeneity.

There is no reason why stratification could not take place at each level of sampling. The elements listed within a selected cluster might be stratified before the next stage of sampling. Typically, however, that is not done. (Recall the assumption of relative homogeneity within clusters.)

Figure 7-8   Multistage Cluster Sampling

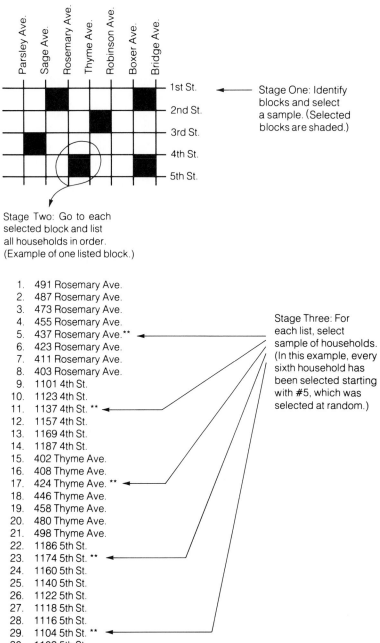

Stage One: Identify blocks and select a sample. (Selected blocks are shaded.)

Stage Two: Go to each selected block and list all households in order. (Example of one listed block.)

1.   491 Rosemary Ave.
2.   487 Rosemary Ave.
3.   473 Rosemary Ave.
4.   455 Rosemary Ave.
5.   437 Rosemary Ave.**
6.   423 Rosemary Ave.
7.   411 Rosemary Ave.
8.   403 Rosemary Ave.
9.   1101 4th St.
10.   1123 4th St.
11.   1137 4th St. **
12.   1157 4th St.
13.   1169 4th St.
14.   1187 4th St.
15.   402 Thyme Ave.
16.   408 Thyme Ave.
17.   424 Thyme Ave. **
18.   446 Thyme Ave.
19.   458 Thyme Ave.
20.   480 Thyme Ave.
21.   498 Thyme Ave.
22.   1186 5th St.
23.   1174 5th St. **
24.   1160 5th St.
25.   1140 5th St.
26.   1122 5th St.
27.   1118 5th St.
28.   1116 5th St.
29.   1104 5th St. **
30.   1102 5th St.

Stage Three: For each list, select sample of households. (In this example, every sixth household has been selected starting with #5, which was selected at random.)

Probability Proportionate
to Size (PPS) Sampling

In this section, I want to give you an introduction to a more sophisticated form of cluster sampling that is used in many large-scale survey sampling projects. In the discussion above, I talked about selecting a random or systematic sample of clusters and then a random or systematic sample of elements within each cluster that was selected. Notice that this produces an overall sampling scheme in which every element in the whole population has the same probability of selection.

Let's say that we are selecting households within a city. If there are 1,000 city blocks and we initially select a sample of 100, that means that each block has a 100/1,000 or .1 chance of being selected. If we next select 1 household in 10 from those residing on the selected blocks, each household has a .1 chance of selection within its block. To calculate the overall probability of a household being selected, we simply multiply the probabilities at the individual steps in sampling. That is, each household has a 1/10 chance of its block being selected and a 1/10 chance of that specific household being selected *if* the block is one of those chosen. Each household, in this case, has a $1/10 \times 1/10 = 1/100$ chance of selection overall. Since each household would have the same chance of selection, the sample so selected should be representative of all households in the city.

There are dangers in this procedure, however. In particular, the varying sizes of blocks (measured in numbers of households) present a problem. Let's suppose that half the city's population resides in 10 densely packed blocks filled with high-rise apartment buildings, and suppose that the rest of the population lives in single-family dwellings spread out over the remaining 900 blocks. When we first select our sample of 1/10 of the blocks, it is quite possible that we'll miss all of the 10 densely packed high-rise blocks. No matter what happens in the second stage of sampling, our final sample of households will be grossly unrepresentative of the city, being composed only of single-family dwellings.

Whenever the clusters sampled are of greatly differing sizes, it is appropriate to use a modified sampling design called *probability proportionate to size*—**PPS**. This design (1) guards against the problem I've just described and (2) still produces a final sample in which each element has the same chance of selection.

As the name suggests, each cluster is given a chance of selection proportionate to its size. Thus, a city block with 200 households has twice the chance of selection as one with only 100 households. The method for doing this is demonstrated in the illustration that follows in the next section. Within each cluster, however, a fixed *number* of elements is selected, say, 5 households per block. Notice how this procedure results in each household having the same probability of selection overall.

Let's say that Household A is located on a block containing 100 households altogether, and Household B is located on a block containing 25 households. Suppose that we plan to select 5 households from whatever blocks are picked. This means that if the block containing Household A is picked, that household has a 5/100 chance of selection in the second stage of sampling. If the block containing Household B is picked, it has a 5/25 or 20/100 chance of being selected in the second stage of sampling. At the second stage of sampling, then, Household B has four times as good a chance of having its block selected in the first stage as did Household A. In the overall sampling design, then, both Household A and Household B have the same chance of being selected.

In a PPS sample design, the overall probability of selection for elements is calculated as follows:

1. The probability of a cluster being selected is equal to its proportional share of all the elements in the population *times* the number of clusters to be selected.

2. The probability of an element being selected within a cluster is equal to the number to be selected within each cluster divided by the number of elements contained within that particular cluster.

3. The overall probability of an element being selected equals (1) times (2).

Here's an example. Suppose a city is composed of 2,000 blocks and 100,000 households and that we want to select 1,000 households. That means that each household should have a 1,000/100,000 or .01 chance of selection. We decide to accomplish this by picking 200 blocks PPS and selecting 5 households on each of the blocks chosen.

Now consider a block containing 100 households. The block has a probability of selection equal to:

$$\frac{200 \text{ blocks to be chosen}}{} \times \frac{100 \text{ (households on the block)}}{100,000 \text{ (households in the city)}} = .2$$

If that block is selected, each household has a second-stage probability of selection equal to:

$$\frac{5 \text{ (to be selected on each block)}}{100 \text{ (households on that block)}} = .05$$

Multiplying .2 times .05, we get an overall probability of selection equal to .01, as required.

Now let's consider a block with only 20 households on it. The block's chance of

selection is only $200 \times 20/100,000$ or .04, much less than the earlier example. If this block is selected, however, each household has a chance of 5/20 or .25 of selection in the second stage. Overall, its probability of selection is .04 times .25, or .01: the same as the earlier case and as required by the overall sample design.

If you examine the method for calculating overall probabilities carefully, you'll see why the result is always going to be the same.

Example 1: $200 \times 100/100,000 \times 5/100$
         $= .01$
Example 2: $200 \times 20/100,000 \times 5/20$
         $= .01$

The only thing that differs in the two examples is the number of households on the blocks, and that number appears in both numerator and denominator, thus canceling itself out. No matter what the block size, then, the overall probability of a household being selected will be equal to 200 times 5/100,000, or .01. See how neat and clean it is?

As a practical matter, PPS cluster sampling is never quite this neat in the field. For example, the estimates of the number of households on blocks are seldom totally accurate, so that blocks are given too high or too low probabilities of selection. There are several statistical solutions to this problem, however, although it's probably not necessary for you to know them for purposes of this introduction to sampling. Other problems arise because some households selected cannot be interviewed—either the people are never home or they refuse to be interviewed. Again, the structure of PPS sampling makes adjustments possible, so that the data collected from households that are selected and interviewed can be taken as representative of all households in the city.

I began this section on PPS sampling by pointing to the danger of missing very large blocks altogether. There is another benefit inherent in this more sophisticated design. If you recall the earlier discussion of homogeneity and heterogeneity, you'll remember that sampling is less of a problem if all the elements being selected are pretty much alike, that is, homogeneous. PPS sampling takes advantage of that fact, in the sense that households composing a single city block or similar geographical groupings are likely to be quite similar to one another, as are the families residing in them. Specifically, the similarity of households on a block is greater than the similarity among households in a whole city. This means that it takes relatively few households on a single block to describe all the households on that block. As a rule of thumb, 5 is usually enough in the context of a large multistage cluster sample. Observing more than 5 households on a single block would improve the description of the block slightly, but the description of the city as a whole would be better improved by adding more blocks to the sample than adding more households on fewer blocks. Given that you can only interview, say, 1,000 households altogether, it would be better to interview 5 each on 200 blocks than to interview 20 each on 50 blocks. In addition to guarding against specific dangers, then, PPS sampling is an efficient use of limited resources.

Disproportionate Sampling and Weighting

Ultimately, a probability sample is representative of a population if all elements in the population have an equal chance of selection in that sample. Thus, in each of the preceding discussions we have noted that the various sampling procedures result in an equal chance of selection—even though the ultimate selection probability is the product of several partial probabilities.

More generally, however, a probability sample is one in which each population element has a *known nonzero* probability of selection—even though different elements may have different probabilities. If controlled probability sampling procedures have been used, any such sample may be representative of the population from which it is drawn if each sample element is assigned a weight equal to the inverse of its probability of selection. Thus, where all sample elements have had the same chance of selection, each is given the same weight: 1. (This is called a *self-weighting* sample.)

Disproportionate sampling and **weighting** come into play in two basic ways. First, you may sample subpopulations disproportionately to ensure sufficient numbers of cases from each for analysis. For example, a given city may have a suburban area containing one-fourth of its total population. Yet you might be especially interested in a detailed analysis of households in that area and may feel that one-fourth of this total sample size would be too few. As a result, you might decide to select the same number of households from the suburban area as from the remainder of the city. Households in the suburban area, then, are given a disproportionately better chance of selection than those located elsewhere in the city.

As long as you analyze the two area samples separately or comparatively, you need not worry about the differential sampling. If you want to combine the two samples to create a composite picture of the entire city, however, you must take the disproportionate sampling into account. If n is the number of households selected from each area, then the households in the suburban area had a chance of selection equal to n divided by one-fourth of the total city population. Since the total city population and the sample size are the same for both areas, the suburban-area households should be given a weight of $1/4n$ while the remaining households should be given a weight of $3/4n$. This weighting procedure could be simplified by merely giving a weight of 3 to each of the households selected outside the suburban area. (This procedure gives a proportionate representation to each sample element. The population figure would have to be included in the weighting if population estimates were desired.)

Here's an example of the problems that can be created when disproportionate sampling is not accompanied by a weighting scheme. When the *Harvard Business Review* decided to survey its subscribers on the issue of sexual harassment at work, for example, it seemed appropriate to oversample women. Here's how Collins and Blodgett explained the matter:

> We also skewed the sample another way: to ensure a representative response from women, we mailed a questionnaire to virtually every female subscriber, for a male/female ratio of 68% to 32%. This bias resulted in a response to 52% male and 44% female (and 4% who gave no indication of gender)—compared to HBR's U. S. subscriber proportion of 93% male and 7% female.
>
> (1981:78)

You should have noticed a couple of things in this quotation. First, it would be nice to know a little more about what "virtually every female" means. Evidently, they didn't send questionnaires to all female subscribers, but there's no indication of who was omitted and why. Second, they didn't use the term "representative" in its normal social science usage. What they mean, of course, is that they want to get a substantial or "large enough" response from women, and oversampling is a perfectly acceptable way of accomplishing that.

By sampling more women than a straightforward probability sample would have produced, they have gotten enough women (812) to compare with the men (960). Thus, when the authors report, for example, that 32 percent of the women and 66 percent of the men agree that "the amount

of sexual harassment at work is greatly exaggerated," we know that the female response is based on a substantial number of cases. That's good. There are problems, however.

To begin, subscriber surveys are always problematic. In this case, the best the researchers can hope to talk about is "what subscribers to *Harvard Business Review* think." In a loose way, it might make sense to think of that population as representing the more sophisticated portion of corporate management. Unfortunately, the overall response rate was 25 percent. Although that is quite good for subscriber surveys, it is a low response rate in terms of generalizing from probability samples.

Beyond that, however, the disproportionate sample design creates a further problem. When the authors state that 73 percent favor company policies against harassment (Collins and Blodgett 1981:78), that figure is undoubtedly too high, since the sample contains a disproportionately high percentage of women—who are more likely to favor such policies. And, when the researchers report that top managers are more likely to feel that claims of sexual harassment are exaggerated than are middle- and lower-level management (1981:81), that finding is also suspect. As the researchers report, women are disproportionately represented in lower management. That alone might account for the apparent differences in different levels of management. In short, the failure to take account of the oversampling of women confounds all survey results that don't separate findings by sex.

Degrees of Precision in Weighting

In any complex sample design, you face a number of options with regard to weighting of purposively or inadvertently disproportionate samples. You may compute weights for each element to several decimal places, or you may assign rough weights to account for only the grossest instances of disproportionate sampling. In the previous case of the city in which the suburban area was oversampled, it is unlikely that the population of that area was exactly one-fourth of the city's population: suppose it actually was .25001, .2600, or .2816 of the total population. In each of these instances, whether you choose to apply the rough overall weighting of one-fourth or decide to be more precise will depend on the precision you desire in your findings. If your research purposes can tolerate errors of a few percentage points, you will probably not waste your time and effort in weighting exactly. In deciding the degree of precision required, moreover, you should take into account the degree of error to be expected from normal sampling distribution, plus all the various types of nonsampling error.

Ultimately, there is no firm guideline for you to follow in determining the precision to be sought in weighting. As in so many other aspects of study design, you have considerable latitude. At the same time, however, you should bear your decision in mind when reporting your findings. You should not employ only a rough weighting procedure and then suggest that your findings are accurate within a miniscule range of error.

Methods for Weighting

Having outlined the scientific concerns for determining the degree of precision desired in weighting, I should note that the choice will often be made on the basis of available methods for weighting. There are three basic methods for weighting.

1. For the rough weighting of samples drawn from subpopulations, weighted tables can be constructed from the unweighted tables for each of the subsamples. In the earlier example, you could create a raw table of distributions for the suburban sample and for the nonsuburban sample separately, triple the number of cases in each cell of the nonsuburban table, add the cases across the two tables, and compute percentages for the composite table.

2. If the data are to be analyzed by computer, a special program may be designed to assign a precise weight to each case in the data file. This way, the computer does all the work of weighting.

It bears repeating that complex weighting methods are usually not necessary in social research. Understanding the logic of weighting, however, will strengthen your grasp of the logic of sampling in general.

ILLUSTRATION: SAMPLING CHURCHWOMEN

Now let's see what cluster sampling looks like in practice. The illustration that follows is not as complex as the **area probability samples** that are employed in studies of geographic areas such as cities, states, or the nation. Nonetheless, it should be a useful example of the various principles of cluster sampling.

The purpose of this study was to examine the attitudes of women members of churches in a diocese of the Episcopal church. A representative sample of all churchwomen in the diocese was desired. Since there was no single list of such women, a multistage sample design was created. In the initial stage of sampling, churches were selected with probability proportionate to size (PPS), and then women were selected from each.

Table 7-1   Form Used in Listing of Churches

Church	Membership	Cumulative Membership
Church A	3,000	3,000
Church B	5,000	8,000
Church C	1,000	9,000

Selecting the Churches

The diocese in question publishes an annual report that lists the 100 or so diocesan churches and their membership sizes. This listing constituted the sampling frame for the first stage of sampling.

A total of approximately 500 respondents was desired for the study, so the decision was made to select 25 churches with probability proportionate to size and take 20 women from each of those selected. To accomplish this, the list of churches was arranged geographically, and then a table was created similar to the partial listing shown in Table 7-1.

Beside each church in the table, its membership was entered, and that figure was used to compute the cumulative total running through the list. The final total came to approximately 200,000. The object at this point was to select a sample of 25 churches in such a way that each would have a chance of selection proportionate to the number of its members. To accomplish this, the cumulative totals were used to create ranges of numbers for each church equaling the number of members in that church. Church A in the table above was assigned the numbers 1 through 3,000; Church B was assigned 3,001 through 8,000; Church C was assigned 8,001 through 9,000; and so forth.

By selecting 25 numbers ranging between 1 and 200,000, it would be possible to select 25 churches for the study. The 25 numbers were selected in a systematic sample as follows. The sampling interval was set at 8,000 (200,000/25) and a random start was selected between 1 and 8,000. Let us say the random number was 4,538. Since that number fell within the range of numbers assigned to Church B (3,001–8,000), Church B was selected.

Increments of 8,000 (the sampling interval) were then added to the random start, and every church within whose range one of the resultant numbers appeared was selected into the sample of churches. It should be apparent that in this fashion, each church in the diocese had a chance of selection directly proportionate to its membership size. A church with 4,000 members had twice the chance of selection as a church of 2,000 and 10 times the chance of selection as one with only 400 members.

Selecting the Churchwomen

Once the sample of churches was selected, arrangements were made to get lists of the women members of each. It is worth noting here that in practice the lists varied greatly in their form and content. In some cases, lists of all members (men and women) were provided, and it was necessary to sort out the women before sampling the lists. The form of the lists varied from typed lists to 3 × 5 cards printed from mailing address plates.

As the list arrived from a selected church, a sampling interval for that church was computed on the basis of the number of women members and the number desired (20). If a church contained 2,000 women, the sample interval, therefore, was set at 100. A random number was selected and incremented by the sampling interval to select the sample of women from that church. This procedure was repeated for each church.

Note that this sample design ultimately gives every woman in the diocese an equal chance of selection *only* if the assumption is made that each church has the same ratio of men to women. That is due to the fact that churches were given a chance of selection based on their *total* membership with an assumption that half the members of each church were women. In fact, of course, women made up more than half the members of some churches and less than half of others. Given the aims of this particular study, the slight inequities of selection were considered insignificant.

A more sophisticated sample design for the second stage would have resolved this possible problem. Since each church was given a chance of selection based on an assumed number of women (assuming 1,000 women in a church of 2,000), the sampling interval could have been computed on the basis of that assumption rather than on the actual number of women listed. If it were assumed in the first stage of sampling that a church had 1,000 women (out of a membership of 2,000), the sampling interval could have been set at 50 (1,000/20). Then this interval could have been used in the selection of respondents regardless of the actual number of women listed for that church. If 1,000 women were in fact listed, then their church had the proper chance of selection and 20 women would be selected from it. If 1,200 women were listed, that would mean that the church had too small a chance of selection, but this would have been remedied through the selection of 24 women using the preestablished sampling interval. If only 800 women were listed, on the other hand, only 16 would have been selected.

Probability Sampling in Review

The preceding discussions have been devoted to the key sampling method used in controlled survey research: probability sampling. In each of the variations examined, we have seen that elements are chosen for study from a population on a basis of random selection with known nonzero probabilities.

Depending on the field situation, probability sampling can be very simple, or it can be extremely difficult, time-consuming, and expensive. Whatever the situation, however, it remains the most effective method for the selection of study elements. There are two reasons for this.

First, probability sampling avoids conscious or unconscious biases in element selection on the part of the researcher. If all elements in the population have an equal (or unequal and subsequently weighted) chance of selection, there is an excellent chance that the sample so selected will closely represent the population of all elements.

Second, probability sampling permits estimates of sampling error. Although no probability sample will be perfectly representative in all respects, controlled selection methods permit the researcher to estimate the degree of expected error in that regard.

In spite of the above comments, it is sometimes not possible to use standard probability sampling methods. Sometimes it isn't even appropriate to do so. In those cases, nonprobability sampling is used. The remainder of this chapter is devoted to a brief discussion of the different forms of nonprobability sampling available to you as a researcher.

NONPROBABILITY SAMPLING

I'm sure you can envision situations in which it would be either impossible or unfeasible to select the kinds of probability samples described above. Suppose you wanted to study embezzlers: there is no list of all embezzlers nor are you likely to create such a list. Moreover, as we'll see, there are times when probability sampling wouldn't be appropriate if possible. In many such situations, nonprobability sampling procedures are called for, and we'll examine three types in this section: purposive or **judgmental sampling**, quota sampling, and the reliance on available subjects.

Purposive or Judgmental Sampling

Occasionally it may be appropriate for you to select your sample on the basis of your own knowledge of the population, its elements, and the nature of your research aims: in short, based on your judgment and the purpose of the study. Especially in the initial design of your questionnaire, you might wish to select the widest variety of respondents to test the broad applicability of questions. Although the study findings would not represent any meaningful population, the test run might effectively uncover any peculiar defects in your questionnaire. This situation would be considered a pretest, however, rather than a final study.

In some instances, you may wish to study a small subset of a larger population in which many members of the subset are easily identified but the enumeration of all of them would be nearly impossible. For example, you might want to study the leadership of a student protest movement; many of the leaders are easily visible, but it would not be feasible to define and sample all leaders. In studying all or a sample of the most visible leaders, you may collect data sufficient for your purposes.

In a multistage sample design, you might want to compare left-wing and right-wing students. Since you may not be able to enumerate and sample from all such students, you might decide to sample the member-

ships of Students for a Democratic Society and Young Americans for Freedom. Although such a sample design would not provide a good description of either left-wing or right-wing students as a whole, it might suffice for general comparative purposes.

Sampling of *selected precincts* for political polls is a somewhat refined judgmental process. On the basis of previous voting results in a given area (city, state, nation), you purposively select a group of voting precincts that, in combination, produces results similar to those of the entire area. Then, in later polls, you select your samples solely from those precincts. The theory is that the selected precincts provide a cross section of the entire electorate, so you need to know what you're doing.

Each time an election is held, permitting you to evaluate the adequacy of your group of precincts, you would consider revisions, additions, or deletions. Your goal is to update the group of precincts to ensure that it will provide a good representation of all precincts.

To be done effectively, selected precinct sampling requires considerable political expertise. You should be well versed in the political and social history of the area under consideration so that the selection of precincts is based on an *educated* guess as to its persistent representativeness. In addition, this system of sampling requires continuing feedback to be effective. You must be in a position to conduct frequent polls and must have periodic electoral validations.

Quota Sampling

Quota sampling, mentioned earlier, is the method that helped George Gallup avoid disaster in 1936—and set up the disaster of 1948. Like probability sampling, quota sampling addresses the issue of representativeness though the two methods approach the issue quite differently.

Quota sampling begins with a matrix describing the characteristics of the target population. You need to know what proportion of the population is male and what proportion female, for example, and for each sex, what proportions fall into various age categories, educational levels, ethnic groups, and so forth. In establishing a national quota sample, you would need to know what proportion of the national population is urban, eastern, male, under 25, white, working class, and the like, and all the other permutations of such a matrix.

Once such a matrix has been created and a relative proportion assigned to each cell in the matrix, you collect data from persons having all the characteristics of a given cell. All the persons in a given cell are then assigned a weight appropriate to their portion of the total population. When all the sample elements are so weighted, the overall data should provide a reasonable representation of the total population.

Quota sampling has several inherent problems. First, the quota frame (the proportions that different cells represent) must be accurate, and it is often difficult to get up-to-date information for this purpose. The Gallup failure to predict Truman as the presidential victor in 1948 was due partly to this problem.

Second, biases may exist in the selection of sample elements within a given cell— even though its proportion of the population is accurately estimated. An interviewer, instructed to interview five persons meeting a given, complex set of characteristics, may still avoid persons living at the top of seven-story walk-ups, having particularly run-down homes, or owning vicious dogs.

In recent years, attempts have been made to combine probability and quota sampling methods, but the effectiveness of this effort remains to be seen. At present, you would be advised to treat quota sampling warily.

Reliance on Available Subjects

Relying on available subjects, that is stopping people at a street corner or some other location, is almost never an adequate sampling method, although it is employed all too frequently. It is justified only if the researcher wants to study the characteristics of people passing the sampling point at specified times.

University researchers frequently conduct surveys among the students enrolled in large lecture classes. The ease and inexpense of such a method explains its popularity, but it seldom produces data of any general value. It may be useful to pretest a questionnaire, but such a sampling method should not be used for a study purportedly describing students as a whole.

Consider this report on the sampling design in an examination of knowledge and opinions about nutrition and cancer among medical students and family physicians:

The fourth-year medical students of the University of Minnesota Medical School in Minneapolis comprised the student population in this study. The physician population consisted of all physicians attending a "Family Practice Review and Update" course sponsored by the University of Minnesota Department of Continuing Medical Education.

(Cooper-Stephenson and Theologides 1981:472)

After all is said and done, what will the results of this study represent? They do not provide a meaningful comparison of medical students and family physicians in the United States or even in Minnesota. Who were the physicians who attended the course? We can guess that they were probably more concerned about their continuing education than other physicians, but we can't say that for sure. Ultimately, we don't know what to do with the results of a study like this.

MAIN POINTS

■ A sample is a special subset of a population that is observed for purposes of making inferences about the nature of the total population itself.

■ Although the sampling methods used earlier in this century often produced misleading inferences, current techniques are far more accurate and reliable.

■ The chief criterion of the quality of a sample is the degree to which it is representative—the extent to which the characteristics of the sample are the same as those of the population from which it was selected.

■ Probability sampling methods provide one excellent way of selecting samples that will be quite representative.

■ The most carefully selected sample will almost never provide a perfect representation of the population from which it was selected. There will always be some degree of sampling error.

■ Probability sampling methods make it possible for you to estimate the amount of sampling error that should be expected in a given sample.

■ The chief principle of probability sampling is that every member of the total population must have some known nonzero probability of being selected into the sample.

■ An EPSEM sample is one in which every member of a population has the same probability of being selected.

■ A sampling frame is a list or quasi-list of the members of a population. It is the resource used in the selection of a sample. A sample's representativeness depends directly on the extent to which a sampling frame contains all the members of the total population that the sample is intended to represent.

■ Simple random sampling is logically the most fundamental technique in probability sampling, though it is seldom used in practice.

■ Systematic sampling involves the selection of every kth member from a sampling frame. This method is functionally equivalent to simple random sampling, with a few exceptions, and it is a more practical method.

■ Stratification is the process of grouping the members of a population into relatively homogeneous strata before sampling. This practice has the effect of improving the representativeness of a sample by reducing the degree of sampling error.

■ Multistage cluster sampling is a more complex sampling technique that is frequently used in those cases in which a list of all the members of a population does not exist. An initial sample of groups of members (clusters) is selected first. Then, all the members of the selected cluster are listed, often through direct observation in the field. Finally, the members listed in each of the selected clusters are subsampled, thereby providing the final sample of members.

■ Probability proportionate to size (PPS) is a special efficient method for multistage cluster sampling.

■ If the members of a population have unequal probabilities of selection into the sample, it is necessary to assign weights to the different observations made in order to provide a representative picture of the total population. Basically, the weight assigned to a particular sample member should be the inverse of its probability of selection.

■ Purposive sampling is a type of nonprobability sampling method in which the researcher uses his or her own judgment in the selection of sample members. It is sometimes called a judgmental sample.

■ Quota sampling is another nonprobability sampling method. You begin with a detailed description of the characteristics of the total population (quota matrix) and then select your sample members in such a fashion as to include different composite profiles that exist in the population. The representativeness of a quota sampling depends in large part on the accuracy of the quota matrix as a reflection of the characteristics of the population.

■ In general, nonprobability sampling methods are regarded as less reliable than probability sampling methods. On the other hand, they are often easier and cheaper to use.

REVIEW QUESTIONS AND EXERCISES

1. Review the discussion of the 1948 Gallup Poll that predicted that Thomas Dewey would defeat Harry Truman for president. Discuss some ways in which Gallup could have modified his quota sample design so as to have avoided the error.

2. Using Appendix D of this book, select a simple random sample of 10 numbers in the range from 1 to 9876. Describe each step in the process.

3. In a paragraph or two, describe the steps involved in selecting a multistage cluster sample of students taking Freshman English in the nation's colleges and universities.

ADDITIONAL READING

Kish, Leslie, *Survey Sampling* (New York: John Wiley, 1965). Unquestionably the definitive work on sampling in social research. Let's not beat around the bush: if you need to know something more about sampling than was contained in this chapter, there is only one place to go. Kish's coverage ranges from the simplest matters to the most complex and mathematical. He is both highly theoretical and downright practical. Easily readable and difficult passages intermingle as Kish exhausts everything you could want or need to know about each aspect of sampling.

PART 3

Modes of Observation

I have a hunch that you may have grown impatient. If you began this book with a view that doing research means making observations and analyzing what you've observed, the preliminary discussions of various aspects of research design may have seemed overlong. It bears repeating, however, that the structuring of inquiry is an integral part of research. With that point firmly in mind, let's dive into the various observational techniques available to social scientists.

Experiments are usually thought of in connection with the physical sciences. In Chapter 8 we will see how social scientists use experiments. This is the most rigorously controllable of the methods we'll examine, and you should come away from this chapter with a better understanding of the general logic of social scientific research.

Chapter 9 will describe survey research, one of the most popular of methods in social science. As we'll see, this type of research involves collecting data through asking people questions—either in self-administered questionnaires or through interviews.

Chapter 10, on field research, examines what is perhaps the most natural form of data collection employed by social scientists: the direct observation of social phenomena in natural settings. As we shall see, some researchers go beyond mere observation to participate in what they are studying so as to get a more intimate view and fuller understanding.

Chapter 11 discusses three forms of unobtrusive data collection that take advantage of some of the data that are available all around us. Content analysis is a method of collecting social data through carefully specifying and counting social artifacts such as books, songs, speeches, and paintings. Without making any personal contact with people, you can use this method to examine a wide variety of social phenomena. The analysis of existing statistics offers another way of studying people without having to talk to them. Governments and a variety of private organizations regularly compile great masses of data, and these data can often be used with little or no modification to answer properly posed questions. Finally, historical documents are a valuable resource for social scientific analysis.

Chapter 12, on evaluation research, looks at a rapidly growing subfield in social science, involving the application of experimental and quasi-experimental models to the testing of social interventions in real life. Evaluation research, for example, might be used to test the effectiveness of a drug rehabilitation program or the efficiency of a new school cafeteria. In the same chapter, we'll look briefly at social indicators as a way of assessing broader social processes.

Before we turn to the actual descriptions of the several methods, two points should be made. First, you will probably discover that you have been using these scientific methods quite casually in your daily life for as long as you can remember. You use some form of field research every day. You are employing a crude form of content analysis every time you judge an author's motivation or orientation from his or her writings. You engage in at least casual experiments frequently. The chapters in Part 3 will show you how to improve your use of these methods so as to avoid the pitfalls of casual, uncontrolled observation.

Second, none of the data-collection methods described in the following chapters is appropriate to all research topics and situations. I have tried to give you some ideas, early in each chapter, of when a given method might be appropriate. Still, it would not be possible to anticipate all the possible research topics that may one day interest you. As a general guideline, it is always best to employ a variety of techniques in the study of any topic. Since each of the methods has its weaknesses, the use of several methods can help fill in any gaps; and if the different, independent approaches to the topic all yield the same conclusion, that can constitute a form of replication.

8

Experiments

What You'll Learn in This Chapter

This chapter examines the experimental method. Besides learning about a specific mode of observation, you'll see a logic of inquiry that applies to other modes as well.

INTRODUCTION

TOPICS APPROPRIATE TO EXPERIMENTS

THE CLASSICAL EXPERIMENT
Independent and Dependent Variables
Pretesting and Posttesting
Experimental and Control Groups
The Double-Blind Experiment

SELECTING SUBJECTS
Probability Sampling
Randomization
Matching

VARIATIONS ON EXPERIMENTAL DESIGN
Sources of Internal Invalidity
Sources of External Invalidity

AN ILLUSTRATION OF EXPERIMENTATION
Experimenting with Computer Dating

"NATURAL" EXPERIMENTS

STRENGTHS AND WEAKNESSES OF THE EXPERIMENTAL METHOD

MAIN POINTS

REVIEW QUESTIONS AND EXERCISES

ADDITIONAL READINGS

INTRODUCTION

This chapter addresses a research method that is probably most frequently associated with structured science in general. Here, we'll discuss the *experiment* as a mode of scientific observation. At base, experiments involve (1) taking action and (2) observing the consequences of that action. Social scientific researchers typically select a group of subjects, do something to them, and observe the effect of what was done. In this chapter, we'll examine both the logic and the various techniques involved in social scientific experiments.

It is worth noting at the outset that experiments also are used often in nonscientific human inquiry. In preparing a stew, for example, we add salt, taste, add more salt, and taste again. In defusing a bomb, we clip a wire, observe whether the bomb explodes, and clip another.

We also experiment copiously in our attempt to develop generalized understanding about the world we live in. All adult skills are learned through experimentation: eating, walking, talking, riding a bicycle, swimming, and so forth. Students discover how much studying is required for academic success through experimentation. Professors learn how much preparation is required for successful lectures through experimentation. This chapter will discuss some ways in which social scientists use experiments to develop generalized understandings. We'll see that, like other methods available to the social scientist, experimenting has special strengths and weaknesses.

TOPICS APPROPRIATE TO EXPERIMENTS

Experiments are especially well suited to research projects involving relatively limited and well-defined concepts and propositions. The traditional image of science, discussed earlier in this book, and the *experimental model* are closely related to one another. Experimentation, then, is especially appropriate for hypothesis testing. It is better suited to explanatory than to descriptive purposes. Let's assume, for example, that we are interested in studying antiblack prejudice and in discovering ways of reducing it. We hypothesize that acquiring an understanding of the contribution of blacks to American history will have the effect of reducing prejudice. We can test this hypothesis experimentally. To begin, we might test the level of antiblack prejudice among a group of experimental subjects. Next, we might show them a documentary film depicting the many ways in which blacks have contributed importantly to the scientific, literary, political, and social development of the nation. Finally, we measure the levels of antiblack prejudice among our subjects to determine whether the film has actually reduced prejudice.

Experimentation is also appropriate and has been successful in the study of small group interaction. Thus, we might bring together a small group of experimental subjects and assign them a task, such as making recommendations for popularizing carpools. We observe, then, the manner in which the group organizes itself and deals with the problem. Over the course of several such experiments, we might vary the nature of the task or the rewards for handling the task successfully. By observing differences in the way groups organize themselves and operate under these varying conditions, we can learn a great deal about the nature of small group interaction.

We typically think of experiments as being conducted in laboratories. Indeed, most of the examples to be used in this chapter will involve such a setting. That need not be the case, however. As we'll see, social scientists often study what are called *natural experiments*: "experiments" that occur in the regular course of social events. The latter portion of this chapter will deal with such research.

THE CLASSICAL EXPERIMENT

The most conventional type of experiment, in the natural as well as social sciences, involves three major pairs of components: (1) independent and dependent variables, (2) experimental and control groups, and (3) pretesting and posttesting. This section of the chapter will deal with each of those components and the way they are put together in the execution of the experiment.

Independent and Dependent Variables

Essentially, an experiment examines the effect of an **independent variable** on a **dependent variable.** Typically, the independent variable takes the form of an experimental *stimulus,* which is either present or absent: that is, a *dichotomous variable*, having two attributes. (That need not be the case, however, as later sections of this chapter will indicate.) In the example concerning antiblack prejudice mentioned above, prejudice is the dependent variable, and exposure to black history is the independent variable. The researcher's hypothesis suggests that prejudice depends, in part, on a lack of knowledge of black history. The purpose of the experiment is to test the validity of this hypothesis. The independent and dependent variables appropriate to experimentation are nearly limitless. It should be noted, moreover, that a given variable might serve as an independent variable in one experiment and as a dependent variable in another. For example, prejudice would be the dependent variable in the previous example, whereas it might be the

independent variable in an experiment examining the effect of prejudice on voting behavior.

It is essential that both independent and dependent variables be operationally defined for purposes of experimentation. Such operational definitions might involve a variety of observation methods. Responses to a questionnaire, for example, might be the basis for defining antiblack prejudice. Speaking to black subjects, agreeing with black subjects, disagreeing with black subjects, or ignoring the comments of black subjects might be elements in the operational definition of interaction with blacks in a small group setting.

Conventionally, in the experimental model dependent and independent variables must be operationally defined before the experiment begins. However, as will be seen in connection with survey research and other methods, it is sometimes appropriate to first make a wide variety of observations during data collection and then determine the most useful operational definitions of variables during later analyses. Ultimately, however, experimentation, like other quantitative methods, requires specific and standarized measurements and observations.

Pretesting and Posttesting

In the simplest experimental design, subjects are measured in terms of a dependent variable (pretested), exposed to a stimulus representing an independent variable, and then remeasured in terms of the dependent variable (posttested). Differences noted between the first and last measurements on the dependent variable are then attributed to the influence of the independent variable.

In the example of antiblack prejudice and exposure to black history, we would begin by pretesting the extent of prejudice among our experimental subjects. Using a questionnaire asking about attitudes toward blacks, for example, we could measure the extent of prejudice exhibited by each individual subject and the average prejudice level of the whole group. After exposing the subjects to the black history film, we could administer the same questionnaire again. Responses given in this posttest would permit us to measure the later extent of prejudice for each subject and the average prejudice level of the group as a whole. If we discovered a lower level of prejudice during the second administration of the questionnaire, we might conclude that the film had indeed reduced prejudice.

In the experimental examination of attitudes such as prejudice, we face a special practical problem relating to *validity*. As you may have already imagined, it is possible that the subjects would respond differently to the questionnaires the second time, even if their attitudes remained unchanged. During the first administration of the questionnaire, the subjects may have been unaware of its purpose. By the time of the second measurement, they might have figured out that the researchers were interested in measuring their prejudice. Since no one wishes to seem prejudiced, the subjects might "clean up" their answers the second time around. Thus, the film would seem to have reduced prejudice, although, in fact, it had not.

This is an example of a more general problem that plagues many forms of social scientific research. The very act of studying something may change it. The techniques for dealing with this problem in the context of experimentation will be discussed in various places throughout the chapter.

Experimental and Control Groups

The foremost method of offsetting the effects of the experiment itself is the use of a **control group.** Laboratory experiments seldom if ever involve only the observation of an experimental group to which a stimulus has been administered. In addition, the researchers also observe a control group to which the experimental stimulus has *not* been administered.

In the example of prejudice and black history, two groups of subjects might be examined. To begin, each group is administered a questionnaire designed to measure their antiblack prejudice. Then, one of the groups—the experimental group—is shown the film. Later, the researcher administers a posttest of prejudice to *both* groups. Figure 8-1 illustrates this basic experimental design.

Using a control group allows the researcher to control for the effects of the experiment itself. If participation in the experiment were to lead the subjects to exhibit, or even to have, less prejudice against blacks, that should occur in both experimental and control groups. If the overall level of prejudice exhibited by the control group is reduced between the pretest and posttest as much as for the experimental group, then the apparent reduction in prejudice must be a function of the experiment or of some external factor rather than a function of the film specifically. If, on the other hand, prejudice were reduced *only* in the experimental group, such reduction would seem to be a consequence of exposure to the film (because that's the only difference between the two groups). Or, alternatively, if prejudice were reduced *more* in the experimental group than in the control group, that, too, would be grounds for assuming that the film reduced prejudice.

The need for control groups in social research became clear in connection with a series of studies of employee satisfaction conducted by F. J. Roethlisberger and W. J. Dickson (1939) in the late 1920s and early 1930s. These two researchers studied working conditions in the telephone "bank wiring room" of the Western Electric Works in Chicago, attempting to discover what changes in working conditions would im-

Figure 8-1   Diagram of Basic Experimental Design

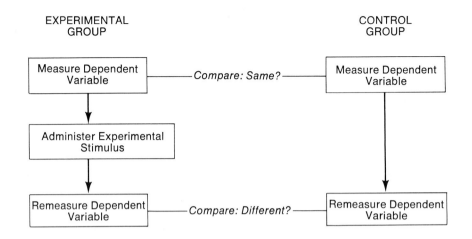

prove employee satisfaction and productivity.

To the researchers' great satisfaction, they discovered that making working conditions better consistently increased satisfaction and productivity. As the workroom was brightened up through better lighting, for example, productivity went up. Lighting was further improved, and productivity went up again. To further substantiate their scientific conclusion, the researchers then dimmed the lights: *productivity again improved!*

It became evident then that the wiring room workers were responding more to the *attention* given them by the researchers than to improved working conditions. As a result of this phenomenon, often called the **Hawthorne effect**, social researchers have become more sensitive to and cautious about the possible effects of experiments themselves. The use of a proper control group—studied intensively without any of the working conditions changed otherwise—would have pointed to the existence of this effect in the wiring room study.

The need for control groups in experimentation has been nowhere more evident than in medical research. Time and again, patients who participate in medical experiments have appeared to improve, and it has

been unclear how much of the improvement has come from the experimental treatment and how much to the experiment. In testing the effects of new drugs, then, medical researchers frequently administer a *placebo* (for example, sugar pills) to a control group. Thus, the control group patients believe they, like the experimental group, are receiving an experimental drug. Often, they improve. If the new drug is effective, however, those receiving that drug will improve more than those receiving the placebo.

In social scientific experiments, control groups are important as a guard not only against the effects of the experiments themselves but also against the effects of events that may occur outside the laboratory during the course of experiments. In the example of the study of antiblack prejudice, suppose that a very popular black leader were assassinated in the middle of, say, a week-long experiment. Such an event might very well horrify the experimental subjects, requiring them to examine their own attitudes toward blacks, with the result of reduced prejudice. Since such an effect should happen about equally for members of the control and experimental groups, a *greater* reduction of prejudice among the experimental group would, again, point to the impact of the experimental stimulus: the documentary film.

The Double-Blind Experiment

Mention was made earlier of the problem in medical experimentation of patients often improving when they *think* they are receiving a new drug; thus it is often necessary to administer a placebo to a control group.

Sometimes, experimenters are subject to this same tendency to prejudge results. In medical research, the experimenters may be more likely to "observe" improvements among patients receiving the experimental drug than among those receiving the placebo. (That would be most likely, perhaps, for the researcher who developed the drug.) A double-blind experiment eliminates the possibility because neither the subjects nor the experimenters know which is the experimental group and which the control. In the medical case, those researchers who were responsible for administering the drug and for noting improvements would not be told which subjects were receiving the drug and which were receiving the placebo. Conversely, the researcher who knew which subjects were in which group would not be responsible for administering the experiment.

In social scientific experiments, as in medical experiments, the danger of experimenter bias is further reduced to the extent that the operational definitions of the dependent variables are clear and precise. Thus, medical researchers would be less likely to unconsciously bias their reading of a patient's temperature than they would be to unconsciously bias their assessment of how lethargic the patient was. For the same reason, the small group researcher would be less likely to misperceive which subject spoke, or to whom he or she spoke, than whether the subject's comments were in a spirit of cooperation or competition.

As indicated several times already in this book, it is seldom possible to devise operational definitions and measurements that are wholly precise and unambiguous. It may be appropriate sometimes, therefore, to employ a double-blind design in social research experiments.

SELECTING SUBJECTS

It seems very likely that most social scientific laboratory experiments are conducted with college undergraduates as subjects. Typically, the experimenter asks students enrolled in his or her classes to participate in experiments or advertises for subjects in a college newspaper. Subjects may or may not be paid for participating in such experiments.

In relation to the norm of *generalizability* in science, it is clear that this tendency represents a potential defect in social scientific research. Most simply put, college undergraduates are not typical of the public at large. There is a danger, therefore, that we may become knowledgeable about the attitudes and actions of college undergraduates without learning very much about social attitudes and actions in general.

However, this potential defect is less significant in explanatory research than it would be in descriptive research. Having noted the level of antiblack prejudice that existed among a group of college undergraduates, we would have little confidence that the same level existed among the public at large. If a documentary film, on the other hand, were found to reduce prejudice among those undergraduates, we would have more confidence—without being certain—that it would have a similar effect in the community at large. Social processes and *patterns* of causal relationships appear to be more generalizable and more stable than *specific* characteristics.

Aside from the question of generalizability, the cardinal rule of subject selection and experimentation concerns the comparability of experimental and control groups. Ideally, the control group represents what the experimental group would have been like had it not been exposed to the experimental stimulus. It is essential, therefore, that experimental and control groups be as similar as possible. There are several ways of accomplishing that.

Probability Sampling

The earlier discussions of the logic and techniques of probability sampling provide one method for selecting two groups of people very similar to each other. Beginning with a sampling frame composed of all the people in the population under study, the researcher might select two probability samples. If two probability samples each resemble the total population from which they are selected, they will also resemble each other.

Recall also, however, that the degree of resemblance (representativeness) achieved by probability sampling is largely a function of the sample size. As a rule of thumb, probability samples of less than 100 are not likely to be terribly representative, and social scientific experiments seldom involve that many subjects in either experimental or control groups. As a result, then, probability sampling is seldom used in experiments to select subjects from a larger population. The logic of random selection is used in a modified fashion, however.

Randomization

Having recruited, by whatever means, a total group of subjects, the experimenter may

randomly (see **randomization** in Glossary) assign those subjects to either the experimental or control group. That might be accomplished by numbering all of the subjects serially and selecting numbers by means of a random number table, or the experimenter might assign the odd-numbered subjects to the experimental group and the even-numbered subjects to the control group.

Let's return again to the basic concept of probability sampling. If the experimenter has recruited forty subjects altogether, in response to a newspaper advertisement, for example, there is no reason to believe that the forty subjects are necessarily representative of the entire population from which they have been drawn. Nor can we assume that the twenty subjects randomly assigned to the experimental group represent that larger population. We may have greater confidence, however, that the twenty subjects randomly assigned to the experimental group will be reasonably similar to the twenty assigned to the control group.

Within the logic of our earlier discussions of sampling, it is as though the forty subjects in this instance are a population from which we select two probability samples—each consisting of half the population. Since each sample will reflect the characteristics of the total population, so the two samples will mirror each other. And, as we saw in Chapter 7, the *number* of subjects involved is important. In the extreme, if we recruited only two subjects and assigned, by the flip of a coin, one as the experimental subject and one as the control, there would be no reason to assume that the two subjects are similar to each other. With larger numbers of subjects, however, randomization makes good sense.

Matching

The comparability of experimental and control groups can sometimes be achieved more directly through a **matching** process similar to the *quota sampling* methods discussed in Chapter 7. If twelve of your subjects are young white men, you might assign six of those at random to the experimental group and the other six to the control group. If fourteen are middle-aged black women, you might assign seven to each group. The overall matching process could be most efficiently achieved through the creation of a *quota matrix* constructed of all the most relevant characteristics. (Figure 8-2 provides a simplified illustration of such a matrix.) Ideally, the quota matrix would be contructed to result in an even number of subjects in each cell of the matrix. Then, half the subjects in each cell would go into the experimental group, and half into the control group.

Alternatively, you might recruit more subjects than are required by your experimental design. You might then examine many characteristics of the large initial group of subjects. Whenever you discover a pair of very similar subjects, you might assign one at random to the experimental group and the other to the control group. Poten-

tial subjects who were unlike anyone else in the initial group might be left out of the experiment altogether.

Whatever method is employed, the desired result is the same. The overall average description of the experimental group should be the same as that of the control group. For example, they should have about the same average age, the same sex composition, the same racial composition, and so forth. This same test of comparability should be employed whether the two groups are created through probability sampling or through randomization.

Thus far, I have referred to the "important" variables without saying clearly what those variables are. I cannot, of course, give a definite answer to this question, any more than I could specify, earlier, which variables should be used in stratified sampling. The answer, ultimately, depends on the nature and purpose of the experiment. As a general rule, however, the two groups should be comparable in terms of those variables that are likely to be related to the dependent variable under study. In a study of prejudice, for example, the two groups should

Figure 8-2   Quota Matrix Illustration

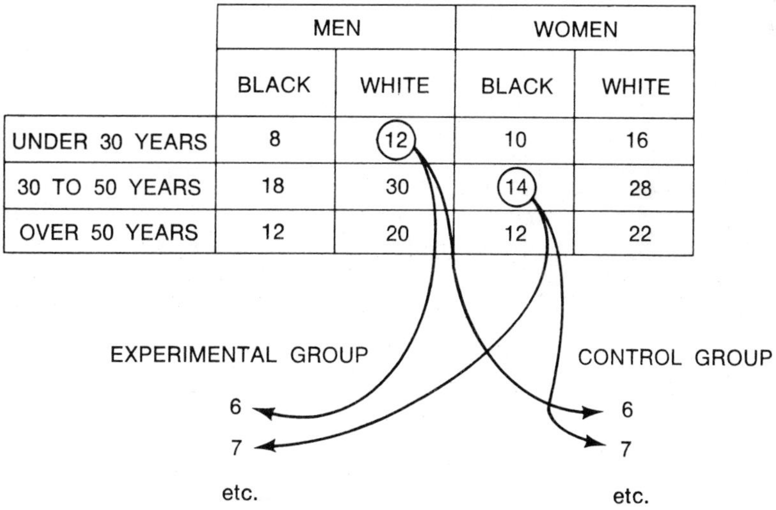

be alike in terms of education, ethnicity, and age, among other variables. In some cases, moreover, you may delay assigning subjects to experimental and control groups until you have initially measured the dependent variable. Thus, for example, you might administer a questionnaire measuring subjects' prejudice and then match the experimental and control groups so as to assure yourself that the two groups exhibited the same overall level of prejudice.

When considering the assignment of subjects to the experimental and control groups, you should be aware of two arguments in favor of randomization over matching. First, you may not be in a position to know in advance what the relevant variables are for the matching process. Second, there's a more technical reason for randomization. Most of the statistics used to evaluate the results of experiments assume randomization. Failure to design your experiment that way, then, makes your later use of those statistics less meaningful.

Sometimes it is possible to combine matching and randomization. When conducting an experiment in the educational enrichment of young adolescents, Milton Yinger and his colleagues (1977) needed to assign a large number of students, aged 13 and 14, to several different experimental and control groups so as to ensure the comparability of students composing each of the groups. They achieved this goal by the following method.

Beginning with a pool of subjects, the researchers first created strata of students nearly identical to one another in terms of some fifteen variables. From each of the strata, students were randomly assigned to the different experimental and control groups. In this fashion, the researchers actually improved on conventional randomization. Essentially, they had used a *stratified* sampling procedure (recall Chapter 7), except that they had employed far more stratification variables than are typically used in, say, survey sampling.

Thus far, I have described the classical experiment—the experimental design that best represents the logic of causal analysis in the laboratory. In practice, however, social researchers use a great variety of experimental designs. Let's look at some of the variations on the basic theme.

VARIATIONS ON EXPERIMENTAL DESIGN

Donald Campbell and Julian Stanley (1963), in an excellent little book on research design, describe some 16 different experimental and quasi-experimental designs. In this section, I'm going to describe some of those briefly to give you a broader view of the potential for experimentation in social research.

To begin, Campbell and Stanley discuss three preexperimental designs, not to recommend them but because they are frequently used in less than professional research. In the first such design—the *one-shot case study*—a single group of subjects is measured on a dependent variable following the administration of some experimental stimulus. Suppose, for example, that we show the black history film mentioned earlier to a group of people and then administer a questionnaire that seems to measure antiblack prejudice. Suppose further that the answers given to the questionnaire seem to represent a low level of prejudice. We might be tempted to conclude that the film reduced prejudice. Lacking a pretest, however, we can't be sure. Perhaps the questionnaire doesn't really represent a very sensitive measure of prejudice, or perhaps the group we are studying was low in prejudice to begin with. In either case, the film might have made no difference, though our experimental results might have misled us into thinking it did.

The second preexperimental design discussed by Campbell and Stanley adds a pretest for the experimental group but lacks a control group. This design—which the authors call the *one-group pretest-posttest design*—suffers from the possibility that some factor other than the independent variable might cause a change between the pretest and posttest results, as in the case of the assassination of a respected black leader mentioned earlier. Thus, while we can see that prejudice has been reduced, we can't be sure the film caused that reduction.

To round out the possibilities for preexperimental designs, Campbell and Stanley point out that some research is based on experimental and control groups but has no pretests. They call this design the *static-group comparison*. In the case of the black history film, we might show the film to one group and not to another; then measure prejudice in both groups. If the experimental group had less prejudice at the conclusion of the experiment, we might assume the film was responsible. But unless we had randomized our subjects as described above, we would have no way of knowing that the two groups had the same degree of prejudice initially; perhaps the experimental group started out with less.

Figure 8-3 graphically illustrates these three preexperimental research designs. See if you can visualize where the potentially confounding and misleading factors could intrude into each design.

In discussing the disadvantages or weaknesses of the three preexperimental research designs and in the initial discussion of the classical experiment, I have pointed to a number of factors that affect experimental research. Now, I want to review those, adding additional factors, in a more systematic fashion. We are going to look at what Campbell and Stanley call the sources of **internal invalidity**, reviewed and expanded in a follow-up book by Cook and Campbell (1979). Later, we'll look at the problem of generalizing experimental results to the "real" world, referred to as **external invalidity**. Having examined those, we will be in a position to appreciate the advantages of some of the more sophisticated experimental and quasi-experimental designs social science researchers sometimes use.

Sources of Internal Invalidity

The problem of *internal invalidity* refers to the possibility that the conclusions drawn from experimental results may not accurately reflect what has gone on in the experiment itself. Campbell and Stanley (1963:5–6) and Cook and Campbell (1979:51–55) point to several sources of the problem. Here are twelve:

1. *History.* Historical events may occur during the course of the experiment that will confound the experimental results. The assassination of a black leader during the course of an experiment on reducing anti-black prejudice would be an example.

2. *Maturation.* People are continually growing and changing, whether in an experiment or not, and those changes affect the results of the experiment. In a long-term experiment, the fact that the subjects grow older (and wiser?) may have an effect. In shorter experiments, they will grow tired, sleepy, bored, or hungry, or change in other ways that may affect their behavior in the experiment.

3. *Testing.* Often the process of testing and retesting will influence people's behavior, thereby confounding the experimental results. Suppose we administer a questionnaire to a group as a way of measuring their prejudice. Then we administer an experimental stimulus and remeasure their prejudice. By the time we conduct the posttest, the subjects will probably have gotten more sensitive to the issue of prejudice and will be more thoughtful in their answers. In fact, they may have figured out that we are trying to find out how prejudiced they are, and,

Figure 8-3 Three Preexperimental Research Designs

1. THE ONE-SHOT CASE STUDY

Administer the experimental stimulus to a single group and measure the dependent variable in that group afterward. Make an intuitive judgment as to whether the posttest result is "high" or "low."

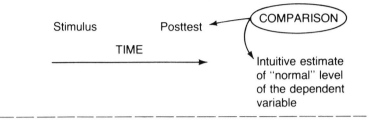

2. THE ONE-GROUP PRETEST-POSTTEST DESIGN

Measure the dependent variable in a single group, administer the experimental stimulus, and then remeasure the dependent variable. Compare pretest and posttest results.

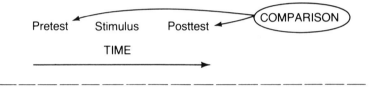

3. THE STATIC-GROUP COMPARISON

Administer the experimental stimulus to one group (the experimental group), then measure the dependent variable in both the experimental group and a control group.

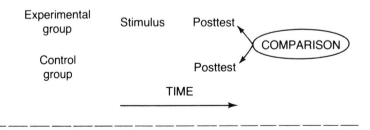

Source: Adapted from Donald Campbell and Julian Stanley, *Experimental and Quasi-Experimental Designs for Research* (Chicago: Rand McNally, 1963), pp. 6–13. Copyright 1963 American Educational Research Association, Washington, D.C. Used by permission.

since no one likes to appear prejudiced, they will be on their best behavior and give answers that they think we want or that will make them look good.

4. *Instrumentation.* Thus far, I haven't said very much about the process of measurement in pretesting and posttesting, and it's appropriate to remind you of the problems of conceptualization and operationalization discussed earlier. If we use different measures of the dependent variable (say, different questionnaires about prejudice), how can we be sure that they are comparable to one another? Perhaps prejudice will seem to have decreased simply because the pretest measure was more sensitive than the posttest measure. Or if the measurements are being made by the experimenters, their standards or their abilities may change over the course of the experiment. This is a problem of reliability.

5. *Statistical regression.* Sometimes it's appropriate to conduct experiments on subjects who start out with extreme scores on the dependent variable. If you were testing a new method for teaching math to hardcore failures in math, you'd want to conduct your experiment on people who have done extremely poorly in math previously. But consider for a minute what is likely to happen to the math achievement of such people over time without any experimental interference. They are starting out so low that they can only stay at the bottom or improve: they can't get worse. Even without any experimental stimulus, then, the group as a whole is likely to show some improvement over time. Referring to a *regression to the mean,* statisticians often point out that extremely tall people as a group are likely to have children shorter than themselves, whereas extremely short people as a group are likely to have children taller than themselves. There is a danger, then, that changes occurring by virtue of subjects starting out in extreme positions will be

attributed erroneously to the effects of the experimental stimulus.

6. *Selection biases.* We discussed bias in selection earlier when we examined different ways of selecting subjects for experiments and assigning them to experimental and control groups. Comparisons don't have any meaning unless the groups are *compare-able.*

7. *Experimental mortality.* Although some social experiments could, I suppose, kill subjects, this problem refers to a more general and less extreme form of mortality. Often, experimental subjects will drop out of the experiment before it is completed, and the statistical comparisons and conclusions drawn can be affected by that. In the classical experiment involving an experimental and a control group, each with a pretest and posttest, suppose that the bigots in the experimental group are so offended by the black history film that they tell the experimenter to forget it and leave. Those subjects sticking around for the posttest will have been less prejudiced to start with, and the group results will reflect a substantial "decrease" in prejudice.

8. *Causal time-order.* Though seldom the case in social research, there is a possibility of ambiguity as to the time-order of the experimental stimulus and the dependent variable. Whenever this occurs, the research conclusion that the stimulus caused the dependent variable can be challenged with the explanation that the "dependent" variable actually caused changes in the stimulus. As you'll recall, Chapter 3 examined this issue in depth.

9. *Diffusion or imitation of treatments.* In the event that experimental and control group subjects are in communication with each other, it's possible that experimental subjects will pass on some elements of the experimental stimulus to the control group. Members of the experimen-

tal group might tell control-group subjects about the black-history film. In that case, the control group becomes affected by the stimulus and is not a real control. Sometimes we speak of the control group having been "contaminated."

10. *Compensation.* As we'll see in Chapter 12 on program evaluation, in experiments in real-life situations—such as a special educational program, for example—subjects in the control group are often deprived of something considered to be of value. In such cases, there may be pressures to offer some form of compensation. For example, hospital staff might feel sorry for medical control group patients and give them extra "tender loving care." In such a situation, the control group is no longer a genuine control group.

11. *Compensatory rivalry.* In real-life experiments, the subjects deprived of the experimental stimulus may try to compensate for the missing stimulus by working harder. Suppose an experimental math program is the experimental stimulus; the control group may work harder than before on their math in the attempt to beat the "special" experimental subjects.

12. *Demoralization.* On the other hand, feelings of deprivation among the control group may result in their giving up. In educational experiments, demoralized control group subjects may stop studying, act up, and get angry.

These, then, are the sources of internal invalidity cited by Campbell, Stanley, and Cook. Aware of these, experimenters have devised designs aimed at handling some or all of them. The classical experiment, discussed earlier in the chapter, if coupled with proper subject selection and assignment, handles each of the twelve problems of internal invalidation. Let's look again at that study design, presented graphically in Figure 8-4.

Pursuing the example of the black history film as an attempt to reduce antiblack prejudice, if we use the experimental design shown in Figure 8-4, we should expect two findings. For the experimental group, the level of prejudice measured in their posttest should be less than was found in their pretest. In addition, when the two posttests are compared, less prejudice should be found in the experimental group than in the control.

This design also guards against the problem of history in that anything occurring outside the experiment that might affect the experimental group should also affect the control group. There should still be a difference in the two posttest results. The same comparison guards against problems of maturation as long as the subjects have been

Figure 8-4   Another Look at the Classical Experiment

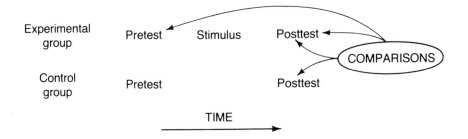

randomly assigned to the two groups. Testing and instrumentation can't be problems, since both the experimental and control groups are subject to the same tests and experimenter affects. If the subjects have been assigned to the two groups randomly, statistical regression should affect both equally, even if people with extreme scores on prejudice (or whatever the dependent variable is) are being studied. Selection bias is ruled out by random assignment of subjects. The problems of experimental mortality are more complicated to handle, but the data provided in this study design offer a number of ways for dealing with them. Slight modifications to the design—administering a placebo to the control group, for example—can make the problems even easier to manage.

The remaining five problems of internal invalidity are avoided through the careful administration of a controlled experimental design. The experimental design we've been discussing facilitates the clear specification of independent and dependent variables. Experimental and control subjects can be kept separate, reducing the possibility of diffusion or imitation of treatments. Administrative controls can avoid compensations being given to the control group, and compensatory rivalry can be watched for and taken into account in evaluating the results of the experiment, as can the problem of demoralization.

Sources of External Invalidity

The problems of internal invalidity are only a part of the complications faced by experimenters, however. In addition, there are problems of what Campbell and Stanley call *external invalidity*. This second class of problems relates to the *generalizability* of experimental findings to the "real" world.

Even if the results of an experiment are an accurate gauge of what happened during that experiment, do they really tell us anything about life in the wilds of society?

Campbell and Stanley describe four forms of this problem, and I want to present one of them to you as an illustration. The generalizability of experimental findings is jeopardized, as the authors point out, if there is an interaction between the testing situation and the experimental stimulus (Campbell and Stanley 1963:18). Here's an example of what they mean.

Staying with the study of prejudice and the black history film, let's suppose that our experimental group—in the classical experiment—has less prejudice in its posttest than in its pretest and that its posttest shows less prejudice than that of the control group. We can be confident that the film actually reduced prejudice among our experimental subjects. But would it have the same effect if the film were shown in theaters or on television? We can't be sure, since the film might only be effective when people have been sensitized to the issue of prejudice, as the subjects may have been in taking the pretest. That is an example of interaction between the testing and the stimulus. The classical experimental design cannot control for that possibility. Fortunately, experimenters have devised other designs that can.

The *Solomon four-group design* (Campbell and Stanley 1963:24–25) handles the problem of testing interaction with the stimulus. As the name suggests, it involves four groups of subjects, assigned randomly from a pool. Figure 8-5 presents this design graphically.

Notice that Groups 1 and 2 in Figure 8-5 compose the classical experiment. Group 3 is administered the experimental stimulus without a pretest and Group 4 is only posttested. This latest experimental design permits four meaningful comparisons. If the black history film really reduces preju-

Figure 8-5 The Solomon Four-Group Design

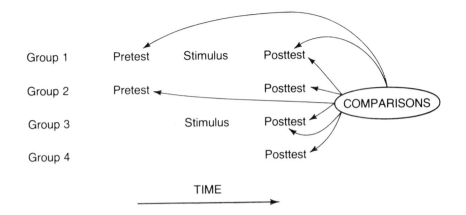

dice—unaccounted for by the problem of internal validity *and* unaccounted for by an interaction between the testing and the stimulus—we should expect four findings:

1. In Group 1, posttest prejudice should be less than pretest prejudice.

2. There should be less prejudice evident in the Group 1 posttest than in the Group 2 posttest.

3. The Group 3 posttest should show less prejudice than the Group 2 pretest.

4. The Group 3 posttest should show less prejudice than the Group 4 posttest.

Notice that findings (3) and (4) rule out any interaction between the testing and the stimulus. And remember that these comparisons are meaningful only if subjects have been assigned randomly to the different groups, thereby providing groups of equal prejudice initially, even though their pre-experiment prejudice is only measured in Groups 1 and 2.

There is a side benefit to this research design, as the authors point out. Not only does the Solomon four-group design rule out interactions between testing and the stimulus, it provides data for comparisons

that will reveal the amount of such interaction that occurs in the classical experimental design. This knowledge would allow a researcher to review and evaluate the value of any prior research that used the simpler design.

The last experimental design I want to mention is what Campbell and Stanley (1963:25–26) call the *posttest-only control group design;* it consists of the second half—Groups 3 and 4—of the Solomon design. As the authors argue persuasively, with proper randomization only Groups 3 and 4 are needed for a true experiment that controls for the problems of internal invalidity as well as the interaction between testing and the stimulus. With randomized assignment to experimental and control groups (which distinguishes this design from the static-group comparison discussed earlier), the subjects will be initially comparable on the dependent variable—comparable enough to satisfy the conventional statistical tests used to evaluate the results—and it is not necessary to measure them. Indeed, Campbell and Stanley suggest the only justification for pretesting in this situation is tradition. Experimenters have simply grown accustomed to pretesting and feel more secure with research designs that include it.

I trust that this discussion has given you a sense of the intricacies of experimental design, its problems, and some solutions. There are, of course, a great many other possible experimental designs in use. Some involve more than one stimulus and combinations of stimuli. Others involve several tests of the dependent variable over time and the administration of the stimulus at different times for different groups. If you are interested in pursuing this topic, you should look at the Campbell and Stanley book, since such variations go beyond the scope of this discussion.

AN ILLUSTRATION OF EXPERIMENTATION

I have the fear that technical discussions of research methods—no matter how clear, charming, and witty—tend to take the life out of what is really an exciting enterprise. In each of the chapters in Part 3, therefore, I want to give you some illustrations of the method under consideration, adding a little more reality and life to it.

The example of experimentation I have chosen differs from the neat rigor of the previous discussions, but it seems to give an excellent picture of how logical-empirical inquiry can progress along the path to understanding social life. In the process, it demonstrates how experiments can be incorporated into a broader package of research methods, and you should get a sense of how appropriate experimentation can be in the course of tracking down elusive explanations of social phenomena.

Experimenting with Computer Dating

In the folklore of courtship, there is a long and cross-cultural tradition concerning the desirability of the hard-to-get woman. Sages have advised young men to seek her out and win her heart, and young women, in turn, have been encouraged to play the part. By contrast, the too-easy woman is likely to be scorned, spurned, and slandered. But why, exactly, is that the case? That's the question that started Elaine Walster, Jane Allyn Piliavin, and G. William Walster (1973) off on a winding and often frustrating search.

They began in a logical enough fashion: they asked a number of college men what they found so attractive about hard-to-get women. The answers came easily. If a woman could afford to play hard-to-get, she must be very popular and have desirable characteristics. Moreover, she was a challenge to male egos. Winning her brought fame if not fortune. Aside from the reports of college men, a number of psychological theories supported the desirability of the hard-to-get woman. People most appreciate those things they have to work hardest for. Also, sexual frustration can provide a strong motivation and hot passion. In short, everything supported the notion that hard-to-get women were especially desirable. But the researchers wanted a clearer understanding of the phenomenon.

In their initial experiment, the researchers showed pictures and biographies of teenage couples to a group of high school juniors and seniors. The key element in the biographies concerned the extent to which one member of the couple "liked" the other. Then students were asked how desirable the various partners pictured and described were. Everything suggested, of course, that those who were described as not caring very much for his or her partner would be the most desirable. Everything, that is, except the results of the experiment. Consistently, those described as caring very much were said to be the most desirable by the student-subjects.

Back at the drawing boards, the researchers decided to approach the matter from a different direction and in a different fashion. Rather than using pictures and stories they chose to be more realistic. Teaming up with a computer dating service, they hired as experimenters a number of women recently enrolled in the program. When the women began receiving calls and offers of dates from men matched with them, they had specific instructions on how to behave. Half the time, they were to pause three seconds before accepting; half the time they were to accept right away. It was expected, then, that the men would develop a greater liking for the dates who had subjected them to three seconds of being hard to get than for those who had been easy. Not so. The pause didn't seem to make any difference.

Rethinking the problem, and getting increasingly frustrated with the repeated failures, the researchers added two new dimensions. First, they wanted to rule out the actual experience of the date, forcing their subjects to react only to others' assessments of the woman. Second, they had begun to think that the men's own self-esteem and self-confidence might matter. Specifically, they hypothesized that men lacking in self-confidence would be the most susceptible to the judgments of others that a woman was hard to get and thereby desirable. Here's how they tested that hypothesis.

This time, each man was given a standard test of self-esteem when he signed up for the dating service. All his data were entered into the computer, and the counselor then gave him a telephone number, saying that it was the number of a woman the computer had matched him with. The man then called the woman for a date and, after talking to her, reported his first impressions to the counselor. As you might guess, all the "dates" were members of the research team. Half the time, the "dates" accepted eagerly. The rest of the time, they responded to the invitation saying, "Mmmm. (slight pause) No, I've got a date then. It seems like I signed up for that Date Match thing a long time ago, and I've met more

people since then. . . . I'm really busy this week" (Walster et al. 1973:822). If the man suggested another time, she paused slightly and then agreed. If he didn't, she suggested getting together the next week and accepted whatever time he proposed. Alas, no positive results were forthcoming from the new experiment. The men did not have a more favorable impression of the hard-to-get woman than of the others, and their own level of self-esteem didn't make the difference. The desirability of the hard-to-get woman was now becoming an increasingly hard-to-get research finding. But the researchers persevered.

It next occurred to them that the experiment needed a heavier sexual component. After all, much of the folklore surrounding the hard-to-get woman had to do with sexuality and sexual attractiveness. So they set about adding sex to the study. How do you suppose you would do that? Walster, Piliavin, and Walster hired a prostitute as a new member of the research team.

The easy-to-get condition was operationalized as the prostitute's normal mode of business. When playing hard to get, on the other hand, she would mix her client-subject a drink and warn him that she wasn't necessarily going to let him call her any time he wanted, adding that she was starting school soon and would only be able to see the men she liked best. She measured her perceived desirability on the basis of (1) how much she got paid by the man and (2) the number of times he returned during the next month.

Though the experimentation was certainly getting more exciting, it didn't get any more successful. Being hard to get didn't seem to make the prostitute any more desirable. If anything, it seemed to put a chill on business.

At this point, the researchers concluded that the desirability of the hard-to-get woman was at least more complicated than they had imagined. Perhaps it only appeared under particular conditions. Not knowing what new dimensions to pursue, they went back to interviewing college men on the subject. But this time, there was an important difference in their questioning. Instead of merely asking what made the hard-to-get woman desirable, they asked about both the advantages and disadvantages she presented, and they repeated the expanded question in reference to the easy-to-get woman. It quickly became apparent that men perceived advantages and disadvantages in both kinds of women. While there was certainly prestige to be gained by dating a woman generally regarded as hard-to-get, there was the accompanying danger that she'd stand her date up or call him a turkey in front of his friends. Eventually the full picture began to emerge.

A man was most likely to consider a woman desirable if she was impossibly hard-to-get for all other men but easy for *him,* subsequently labeled the *selectively elusive* woman. Now they were ready to conduct what would be the final experiments in the study.

Returning to the computer-dating gambit, 71 college men were asked to participate in a test of computer matching as compared with random matching. Initially, each man completed a form describing himself. Then, later, he returned to the office to examine the files of some (fictitious) women in the study. Each man was given five folders, and each of the folders contained a woman's self-description plus her evaluations of five men, including the subject. Each of the self-descriptions was close enough to what the subject said about himself to make each woman a reasonable date. The five differed from one another as follows:

- One woman indicated she was willing to date any of the five men but was not very enthusiastic about any of them.

- One woman was enthusiastic about all the men, including the subject.

- One woman gave low marks to all the men *except* the subject, about whom she was really enthusiastic.

- The other two women were described, but the subject was told they had not returned to the office to evaluate the prospective dates.

Virtually every man in the experiment picked the selectively elusive woman: the one who liked them but didn't like any of the other men. They tended to reject the uniformly hard-to-get woman as too picky or stuck-up, and they tended to suspect that the uniformly easy-to-get woman must have trouble getting dates. The selectively elusive woman was sometimes complimented for her good judgment, and some men simply said, "She made me feel good."

As I indicated at the outset of this section, the study of the hard-to-get woman has a special merit for my purpose here. It demonstrates nicely the pursuit of understanding in real-life social research. Failing repeatedly to confirm their hypothesis, the researchers returned again and again, rethinking their topic, adding new dimensions, and redesigning their observations. This is the process—often frustrating, always challenging—that can give social research the fascination and excitement of detective work.

"NATURAL" EXPERIMENTS

Although we tend to equate the terms *experiment* and *laboratory experiment,* many important social scientific experiments occur outside laboratories, often in the course of normal social events. Sometimes nature designs and executes experiments that we are able to observe and analyze; sometimes social and political decision makers serve this natural function.

Let's imagine, for example, that a hurricane has struck a particular town. Some residents of the town suffer severe financial damages while others escape relatively lightly. What, we might ask, are the behavioral consequences of suffering a natural disaster? Are those who suffer most more likely to take precautions against future disasters than those who suffer less? To find the answers to these questions, we might interview residents of the town some time after the hurricane. We might question them regarding their precautions before the hurricane and precautions that they are currently taking, comparing those who suffered greatly from the hurricane with those who suffered relatively little. In this fashion, we might take advantage of a natural experiment, which we could not have arranged even if we were perversely willing to do so.

A similar example may be taken from the annals of social research surrounding World War II. After the war ended, social researchers undertook retrospective surveys of wartime morale among civilians in a number of German cities. One of the chief purposes of this research was to determine the effect of mass bombing on the morale of civilians, and the reports of wartime morale were compared for residents of heavily bombed cities and cities that received relatively little bombing. (*Note:* Bombing did not reduce morale.)

Because the researcher must take things pretty much as they occur, natural experiments raise many of the validity problems discussed earlier. Thus when Stanislav Kasl and his colleagues (1981) chose to study the impact of the Three Mile Island (TMI) nuclear accident on plant workers, they had to be especially careful in the study design:

Disaster research is necessarily opportunistic, quasi-experimental, and after-the-fact. In the terminology of Campbell and Stanley's classical analysis of research designs, our study falls into

the "static-group comparison" category, considered one of the weak research designs. However, the weaknesses are potential and their actual presence depends on the unique circumstances of each study.

(1981:474)

The foundation of this study was a survey of the people who had been working at Three Mile Island at the time of the accident. The survey was conducted five to six months after the accident. Among other things, the survey questionnaire measured workers' attitudes toward working at nuclear power plants. If they had measured only the TMI workers' attitudes after the accident, the researchers would have had no idea whether attitudes had changed as a consequence of the accident. But they improved their study design by selecting another, nearby—seemingly comparable—nuclear power plant (abbreviated as PB) and surveyed workers there as a control group: hence their reference to a "static-group comparison."

Even with an experimental and a control group, the authors were wary of potential problems with their design. In particular, their design was based on the idea that the two sets of workers were equivalent to one another, except for the single fact of the accident. The researchers could have assumed this if they had been able to assign workers to the two plants randomly, but of course that was not the case. Instead, they needed to compare characteristics of the two groups and infer whether they were equivalent. Ultimately, Kasl et al. concluded that the two sets of workers were very much alike, and the plant they worked at was merely a function of where they lived.

Even granting that the two sets of workers were equivalent, the researchers faced another problem of comparability. They were not able to contact all the workers who had been employed at TMI at the time of the accident. The researchers discuss the problem thusly:

One special attrition problem in this study was the possibility that some of the no-contact non-respondents among the TMI subjects, but not PB subjects, had permanently left the area because of the accident. This biased attrition would, most likely, attenuate the estimated extent of the impact. Using the evidence of disconnected or "not in service" telephone numbers, we estimate this bias to be negligible (< 1 percent).

(Kasl et al. 1981:475)

The TMI example points both to the special problems involved in natural experiments and to the possibility for taking those problems into account. Social research generally requires ingenuity and insight, and natural experiments call for a little more than the average.

Earlier in the chapter, I introduced experimental design with a hypothetical example of using a black history film to reduce prejudice. Sandra Ball-Rokeach and colleagues (1981) were able to address that topic in real life through a natural experiment. In 1977, the television dramatization of Alex Haley's *Roots* was presented by ABC on eight consecutive nights. It garnered the largest audiences in television history up to that time. Ball-Rokeach and her colleagues wanted to know if *Roots* changed white-American attitudes toward blacks. Their opportunity arose in 1979, when a sequel—*Roots: The Next Generation*—was televised. While it would have been nice (from a researcher's point of view) to assign random samples of Americans to either watch or not watch the show, that wasn't possible. Instead, the researchers selected four samples in Washington state and mailed questionnaires that measured attitudes toward blacks. Following the last episode of the show, respondents were called and asked how many, if any, episodes they had watched. Subsequently, questionnaires were sent to respondents, remeasuring their attitudes toward blacks.

By comparing before and after attitudes for both those who watched the show and those who didn't, the researchers were able to reach several conclusions. For example, they found that people with already egalitarian attitudes were much more likely to watch the show than those who were more prejudiced toward blacks: a *self-selection* phenomenon. Comparing the before and after attitudes of those who watched the show, moreover, suggested the show itself had little or no effect. Those who watched it were no more egalitarian afterward than they had been before.

The Ball-Rokeach example anticipates the subject of Chapter 12, *evaluation research*, which can be seen as a special type of natural experiment. As we'll see, it involves taking the logic of experimentation into the field to observe and evaluate the effects of stimuli in real life. Since it is an increasingly important form of social research, I'll devote a whole chapter to it.

STRENGTHS AND WEAKNESSES OF THE EXPERIMENTAL METHOD

The chief advantage of a controlled experiment lies in the isolation of the experimental variable and its impact over time. That is seen most clearly in terms of the basic experimental model. A group of experimental subjects are found, at the outset of the experiment, to have a certain characteristic; following the administration of an experimental stimulus, they are found to have a different characteristic. To the extent that subjects have experienced no other stimuli, we may conclude that the change of characteristics is attributable to the experimental stimulus.

Another advantage is that, since individual experiments are often rather limited in scope, requiring relatively little time and money and relatively few subjects, it is often possible to replicate a given experiment several times using several different groups of subjects. (That is not always the case, of course, but it is usually easier to repeat experiments than, say, survey research.) As in all other forms of scientific research, replication of research findings strengthens our confidence in the validity and generalizability of those findings.

The greatest weakness of laboratory experiments lies in their artificiality. Social processes that occur in a laboratory setting might not necessarily occur in more natural social settings. If we may return to the example used frequently in this chapter, a black history film might genuinely reduce prejudice among a group of experimental subjects. That would not necessarily mean, however, that the same film shown in neighborhood movie theaters throughout the country would reduce prejudice among the general public. Artificiality is not as much of a problem, of course, for natural experiments as for those conducted in the laboratory.

I've already discussed several of the sources of internal and external invalidity mentioned by Campbell, Stanley, and Cook. As we saw in that context, it is possible to create experimental designs that logically control those problems. This possibility points to one of the great advantages of experiments: they lend themselves to a logical rigor that is often much more difficult to achieve in other modes of observation.

MAIN POINTS

■ Experiments are an excellent vehicle for the controlled testing of causal processes.

■ The classical experiment tests the effect of an experimental stimulus on some dependent variable through the pretesting and posttesting of experimental and control groups.

■ It is generally less important that a group of experimental subjects be representative of some larger population than that experimental and control groups be similar to one another.

■ Randomization is the generally preferred method for achieving comparability in the experimental and control groups.

■ Campbell and Stanley describe three forms of preexperiments: the one-shot case study, the one-group pretest-posttest design, and the static-group comparison.

■ There are 12 sources of internal invalidity in experimental design:
   a. history
   b. maturation
   c. testing
   d. instrumentation
   e. regression
   f. selection
   g. mortality
   h. causal time-order
   i. diffusion or imitation of treatments
   j. compensation
   k. compensatory rivalry
   l. demoralization

■ The classical experiment with random assignment of subject guards against each of the sources of internal invalidity.

■ Experiments also face problems of external invalidity: experimental findings may not reflect real life.

■ The interaction of testing with the stimulus is an example of external invalidity, and the classical experiment does not guard against that problem.

■ The Solomon four-group design and other variations on the classical experiment can safeguard against the problems of external invalidity.

■ Campbell and Stanley suggest that, given proper randomization in the assignment of subjects to the experimental and control groups, there is no need for pretesting in experiments.

■ Natural experiments often occur in the course of social life in the real world, and social researchers can study those in somewhat the same way they would design and conduct laboratory experiments.

REVIEW QUESTIONS AND EXERCISES

1. Pick 6 of the 12 sources of internal invalidity discussed in the book and make up examples (not discussed in the book) to illustrate each.

2. Think of a recent natural disaster you have witnessed or read about. Frame a research question that might be studied by treating that disaster as a natural experiment. In two or three paragraphs, outline how the study might be done.

ADDITIONAL READINGS

Bales, Robert, *Interaction Process Analysis: A Method for the Study of Small Groups* (Reading, Mass.: Addison-Wesley, 1950). An old but classic overview of small group research. Bales discusses the theory and techniques appropriate to the examination of social interaction in small groups under controlled laboratory conditions.

Campbell, Donald, and Stanley, Julian, *Experimental and Quasi-Experimental Designs for Research* (Chicago: Rand McNally, 1963). An excellent analysis of the logic and methods of experimentation in social research. This book is especially useful in its application of the logic of experiments to other social research methods.

Cook, Thomas D., and Campbell, Donald T., *Quasi-Experimentation: Design and Analysis Issues for Field Settings* (Chicago: Rand McNally, 1979). An expanded and updated version of Campbell and Stanley, above.

Martin, David W., *Doing Psychology Experiments* (Monterey, Calif.: Brooks/Cole, 1985). Thorough explanations of the logic behind research methods, often in a humorous style. The book emphasizes ideas of particular importance to the beginning researcher, such as getting an idea for an experiment, reviewing the literature, etc.

Ray, William, and Ravizza, Richard, *Methods Toward a Science of Behavior and Experience* (Belmont, Calif.: Wadsworth, 1985). A comprehensive examination of social science research methods, with a special emphasis on experimentation. This book is especially strong in the philosophy of science.

9

Survey Research

INTRODUCTION

Survey research is a very old research technique. In the Old Testament, for example, we find:

> After the plague the Lord said to Moses and to Eleazar the son of Aaron, the priest, "Take a census of all the congregation of the people of Israel, from twenty old and upward. . . ."
>
> (Numbers 26:1–2)

Ancient Egyptian rulers conducted censuses for the purpose of administering their domains. Jesus was born away from home because Joseph and Mary were journeying to Joseph's ancestral home for a Roman census.

A little-known survey was attempted among French workers in 1880. A German political sociologist mailed some 25,000 questionnaires to workers to determine the extent of their exploitation by employers. The rather lengthy questionnaire included items such as these:

> Does your employer or his representative resort to trickery in order to defraud you of a part of your earnings?
>
> If you are paid piece rates, is the quality of the article made a pretext for fraudulent deductions from your wages?

The survey researcher in this case was not George Gallup but Karl Marx (1880:208). Though 25,000 questionnaires were mailed out, there is no record of any being returned.

Today, survey research is perhaps the most frequently used mode of observation in the social sciences. As we saw in Chapter 4, it is far and away the most common method reported in recent articles of the *American Sociological Review*. I am certain that you have been a **respondent** in a survey more than once, and it is quite possible that you have done a survey of your own. In a typical survey, the researcher selects a sample of respondents and administers a standardized questionnaire to them.

Chapter 7 has already covered the topic of sampling, referring most often to survey situations. In this chapter, we look at questionnaire construction and then at the two primary methods for administering questionnaires. Sometimes it's appropriate to have respondents complete questionnaires themselves, and other times it's more appropriate to have interviewers ask the questions and record the answers given. We'll examine both methods and then compare their relative advantages and disadvantages.

The chapter concludes with a short discussion of **secondary analysis,** the analysis of survey data collected by someone else, perhaps for some purpose other than that of subsequent analyses. This use of survey results has become an important aspect of survey research in recent years, and it's especially useful for students and others with scarce research funds.

Let's begin by looking at the kinds of topics you could study using survey research.

TOPICS APPROPRIATE TO SURVEY RESEARCH

Surveys may be used for descriptive, explanatory, and exploratory purposes. They are chiefly used in studies that have individual people as the units of analysis. Although this method can be used for other units of analysis, such as groups or interactions, it is necessary that some individual persons are used as respondents or informants. Thus, it would be possible to undertake a survey in which divorces were the unit of analysis, but the survey questionnaire would need to be administered to the participants in the divorces (or to some other informants).

Survey research is probably the best method available to the social scientist interested in collecting original data for describing a population too large to observe directly. Careful probability sampling provides a group of respondents whose characteristics may be taken to reflect those of the larger population, and carefully constructed standardized questionnaires provide data in the same form from all respondents. The U.S. Decennial **Census** differs from surveys primarily in that all members of the U.S. population are studied rather than a sample. (The Census Bureau also conducts numerous sample surveys in addition to the decennial censuses.)

Surveys are also excellent vehicles for measuring attitudes and orientations in a large population. Public opinion polls—e.g., Gallup, Harris, Roper, Yankelovich—are well-known examples of this use.

QUESTIONNAIRE CONSTRUCTION

Questionnaires are used in connection with many modes of observation in social research, but they are essential to and most directly associated with survey research. Thus, it's appropriate that questionnaires be dealt with in this chapter, though you should bear in mind that what you learn here might be useful in doing experiments, field research, and so forth.

This section is, in a sense, a continuation of the operationalization discussion in Chapter 6. You recall that I covered some of the guidelines and techniques for writing *questions* as a culmination of the conceptualization-operationalization process. This section will continue that discussion, showing some of the ways questions are organized and presented in a questionnaire.

As in the earlier discussion of question wording, I'll run the risk of offending you, perhaps, by presenting some nitty-gritty details that may seem unworthy of scientific

attention and other details that seem so obvious as to be not worth mentioning. I take the risk, however, because I have made each of the mistakes I'll warn against and have seen others do the same. Let's begin with some issues of questionnaire *format*.

General Questionnaire Format

The format of a questionnaire is just as important as the nature and wording of the questions asked. An improperly laid out questionnaire can lead respondents to miss questions, can confuse them as to the nature of the data desired, and in the extreme, may lead them to throw the questionnaire away. Both general and specific guidelines can be suggested.

As a general rule, the questionnaire should be spread out and uncluttered. Inexperienced researchers tend to fear that their questionnaire will look too long, and as a result, they squeeze several questions onto a single line, abbreviate questions, and try to use as few pages as possible. All these efforts are ill-advised and even dangerous. Putting more than one question on a line will cause some respondents to miss the second question altogether. Some respondents will misinterpret abbreviated questions. And more generally, respondents who find they have spent considerable time on the first page of what seemed a short questionnaire will be more demoralized than respondents who quickly completed the first several pages of what initially seemed a rather long form. Moreover, the latter will have made fewer errors and will not have been forced to reread confusing, abbreviated questions. Nor will they have been forced to write a long answer in a tiny space.

The desirability of spreading questions out in the questionnaire cannot be overemphasized. Squeezed-together questionnaires are disastrous whether they are to be completed by the respondents themselves or to be administered by trained interviewers. And the processing of such questionnaires is another nightmare. I'll have more to say about this in Chapter 13.

Formats for Respondents

In one of the most common questionnaire formats, the respondent is expected to check one response from a series. Of the variety of methods that are available, it has been my experience that *boxes* adequately spaced apart are the best. If the questionnaire is to be set in type, this can be accomplished easily and neatly. It is also possible to create boxes on a typewriter, however.

If the questionnaire is typed on a typewriter with brackets, excellent boxes can be produced by a left bracket, a space, and a right bracket: [ ]. If brackets are not available, parentheses work reasonably well in the same fashion: ( ). I'd discourage the use of slashes and underscores, however. First, this technique requires considerably more typing effort; and second, the result is not very neat, especially if the response categories must be single-spaced. Figure 9-1 provides a comparison of the different methods.

Of the three methods shown, the brackets and the parentheses are clearly the neatest; the slash-and-underscore method simply looks sloppy. Since every typewriter at least has parentheses, there is no excuse for using slashes and underscores. The worst method of all is to provide open blanks for check marks, since respondents will often enter rather large check marks and it will not be possible to determine which response was intended.

A very different method might also be considered. Rather than providing boxes to be checked, the researcher might print a code number beside each response and ask the respondent to *circle* the appropriate number (see Figure 9-2). This method has the added advantage of specifying the number to be punched later in the processing stage (see Chapter 13). If numbers are to be circled, however, you should provide clear and prominent instructions to the respondent, because many will be tempted to cross out the appropriate number, which makes punching even more difficult. (*Note:* The technique can be used more safely when interviewers administer the questionnaires, since they can be specially instructed and supervised.)

Contingency Questions

Quite often in questionnaires, certain questions will be clearly relevant only to some of the respondents and irrelevant to others. In a study of birth control methods, for instance, you would probably not want to ask men if they take birth control pills.

Frequently, this situation—realizing that the topic is relevant only to some respondents—will arise when you wish to ask a series of questions about a certain topic.

Figure 9-1   Three Answer Formats

```
[ ] Yes          ( ) Yes
[ ] No           ( ) No
[ ] Don't know   ( ) Don't know
```

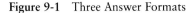
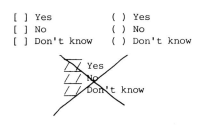

Figure 9-2   Circling the Answer

```
1.   Yes
②.   No
3.   Don't know
```

You may want to ask whether your respondents belong to a particular organization and, if so, how often they attend meetings, whether they have held office in the organization, and so forth. Or, you might want to ask whether respondents have heard anything about a certain political issue and then learn the attitudes of those who have heard of it.

The subsequent questions in series such as these are called **contingency questions:** whether they are to be asked and answered is contingent on responses to the first question in the series. The proper use of contingency questions can facilitate the respondents' task in completing the questionnaire, because they are not faced with trying to answer questions that are irrelevant to them.

There are several formats for contingency questions. The one shown in Figure 9-3 is probably the clearest and most effective. Note two key elements in this format. First, the contingency question is isolated from the other questions by being set off to the side and enclosed in a box. Second, an arrow connects the contingency question to the answer upon which it is contingent. In the illustration, only those respondents answering yes are expected to answer the contingency question. The rest of the respondents should simply skip it.

It should be noted that the questions shown in Figure 9-3 could have been dealt with in a single question. The question might have read: "How many times, if any, have you smoked marijuana?" The response categories, then, might have read: "Never," "Once," "2 to 5 times," and so forth. Such a single question would apply to all respondents, and each would find an appropriate answer category. Such a question, however, might put some pressure on respondents to report having smoked marijuana, since the main question asks how many times they have smoked it, even though it allows for those *exceptional cases* who have *never smoked marijuana even once.* (The emphases used in the previous sentence give a fair indication of how respondents might read the question.) The contingency question format illustrated in Figure 9-3 should reduce the subtle pressure on respondents to report having smoked marijuana. The foregoing discussion should show how seemingly theoretical issues of *validity* and *reliability* are involved in so mundane a matter as how to put questions on a piece of paper.

Used properly, even rather complex sets of contingency questions can be constructed without confusing the respondent. Figure 9-4 illustrates a more complicated example.

Sometimes a set of contingency questions is long enough to extend over several pages. Suppose you are studying political

Figure 9-3   Contingency Question Format

```
23.   Have you ever smoked marijuana?
      [ ] Yes ─────────┐
      [ ] No           │
                       ↓
         ┌──────────────────────────────────┐
         │ If yes: About how many times have │
         │         you smoked marijuana?     │
         │         [ ] Once                  │
         │         [ ] 2 to 5 times          │
         │         [ ] 6 to 10 times         │
         │         [ ] 11 to 20 times        │
         │         [ ] More than 20 times    │
         └──────────────────────────────────┘
```

Figure 9-4   Complex Contingency Question

```
14.  Have you ever heard anything about
     the Model Cities Program?
     [ ] Yes ─────────────────────┐
     [ ] No                       │
                                  ▼
        ┌────────────────────────────────────────┐
        │ If yes:                                 │
        │                                         │
        │ a. Do you generally approve or          │
        │    disapprove of that program?          │
        │    [ ] Approve                          │
        │    [ ] Disapprove                       │
        │    [ ] No opinion                       │
        │                                         │
        │ b. Have you ever attended a Model       │
        │    Cities resident meeting?             │
        │    [ ] Yes ──────────────┐              │
        │    [ ] No                │              │
        │                          ▼              │
        │     ┌──────────────────────────────┐   │
        │     │ If yes: When did you last     │   │
        │     │         attend a meeting?     │   │
        │     │                               │   │
        │     │ ────────────────────────────  │   │
        │     └──────────────────────────────┘   │
        └────────────────────────────────────────┘
```

activities of college students, and you wish to ask a large number of questions of those students who had voted in a national, state, or local election. You could separate out the relevant respondents with an initial question such as "Have you ever voted in a national, state, or local election?" but it would be confusing to place the contingency questions in a box stretching over several pages. It would make more sense to enter instructions in parentheses after each answer telling respondents to answer or skip the contingency questions. Figure 9-5 provides an illustration of this method.

In addition to these instructions, it would be worthwhile to place an instruction at the top of each page containing only the con-

tingency questions. For example, you might say, "This page is only for respondents who have voted in a national, state, or local election." Clear instructions such as these spare respondents the frustration of reading and puzzling over questions that are irrelevant to them as well as increasing the likelihood of responses from those for whom the questions are relevant.

Matrix Questions

Quite often, you will want to ask several questions that have the same set of answer categories. This is typically the case when-

Figure 9-5   Instructions to Skip

```
13.  Have you ever voted in a national, state, or local
     election?
     [ ] Yes  (Please answer questions 14-25)
     [ ] No   (Please skip questions 14-25.  Go directly
              to question 26 on page 8.)
```

ever the Likert response categories are used. In such cases, it is often possible to construct a matrix of items and answers as illustrated in Figure 9-6.

This format has a number of advantages. First, it uses space efficiently. Second, respondents will probably find it faster to complete a set of questions presented in this fashion. In addition, this format may increase the comparability of responses given to different questions for the respondent as well as the researcher. Since respondents can quickly review their answers to earlier items in the set, they might choose between, say, "strongly agree" and "agree" on a given statement by comparing their strength of agreement with their earlier responses in the set.

There are some dangers inherent in using this format as well. Its advantages may encourage you to structure an item so that the responses fit into the matrix format when a different, more idiosyncratic, set of responses might be more appropriate. Also, the matrix question format can foster a *response-set* among some respondents—they may develop a pattern of, say, agreeing with all the statements. That would be especially likely if the set of statements began with several that indicated a particular orientation (for example, a liberal political perspective) with only a few, later ones representing the opposite orientation. Respon-

dents might assume that all the statements represented the same orientation and, reading quickly, misread some of them, thereby giving the wrong answers. This problem can be reduced somewhat by alternating statements representing different orientations and by making all statements short and clear.

Ordering Questions in a Questionnaire

The *order* in which questions are asked can also affect the answers given. First, the appearance of one question can affect the answers given to later ones. For example, if a number of questions have been asked about the dangers of communism to the United States and then a question asks respondents to volunteer (open-ended) what they believe to represent dangers to the United States, communism will receive more citations than would otherwise be the case. In this situation, it is preferable to ask the open-minded question first.

If respondents are asked to assess their overall religiosity ("How important is your religion to you in general?"), their responses to later questions concerning specific aspects of religiosity will be aimed at consistency with the prior assessment. The converse would be true as well. If respondents are first asked specific questions about different

Figure 9-6   Matrix Question Format

```
17.  Beside each of the statements presented below,
     please indicate whether you Strongly Agree (SA),
     Agree (A), Disagree (D), Strongly Disagree (SD),
     or are Undecided (U).

                                 SA    A    D    SD    U
      a. What this country
         needs is more law and
         order. . . . . . . . .  [ ]  [ ]  [ ]  [ ]  [ ]
      b. The police should be
         disarmed in America. .  [ ]  [ ]  [ ]  [ ]  [ ]
      c. During riots, looters
         should be shot on
         sight. . . . . . . . .  [ ]  [ ]  [ ]  [ ]  [ ]
      etc.
```

aspects of their religiosity, their subsequent overall assessment will reflect the earlier answers.

Some researchers attempt to overcome this effect by randomizing the order of questions. This is usually a futile effort. To begin, a randomized set of questions will probably strike respondents as chaotic and worthless. It will be difficult to answer, moreover, since they must continually switch their attention from one topic to another. And, finally, even a randomized ordering of questions will have the effect discussed above—except that you will have no control over the effect.

The safest solution is sensitivity to the problem. Although you cannot avoid the effect of question order, you should attempt to estimate what that effect will be. Thus, you will be able to interpret results in a meaningful fashion. If the order of questions seems an especially important issue in a given study, you might construct more than one version of the questionnaire containing the different possible ordering of questions. You would then be able to determine the effects. At the very least, you should pretest your questionnaire in the different forms.

The desired ordering of questions differs somewhat between self-administered questionnaires and interviews. In the former, it is usually best to begin the questionnaire with the most interesting set of questions. The potential respondents who glance casually over the first few questions should *want* to answer them. Perhaps the questions will ask for attitudes that they are aching to express. At the same time, however, the initial questions should not be threatening. (It might be a bad idea to begin with questions about sexual behavior or drug use.) Requests for duller, demographic data (age, sex, and the like) should generally be placed at the end of a self-administered questionnaire. Placing these questions at the beginning, as many inexperienced researchers are tempted to do, gives the questionnaire the initial appearance of a routine form, and the person receiving it may not be motivated to complete it.

Just the opposite is generally true for interview surveys. When the potential respondent's door first opens, the interviewer must begin gaining rapport quickly. After a short introduction to the study, the interviewer can best begin by enumerating the members of the household, getting demographic data about each. Such questions are easily answered and generally nonthreatening. Once the initial rapport has been established the interviewer can then move into the area of attitudes and more sensitive matters. An interview that began with the question "Do you believe in God?" would probably end rather quickly.

Instructions

Every questionnaire, whether it is to be completed by respondents or administered by interviewers, should contain clear instructions and introductory comments where appropriate.

It is useful to begin every self-administered questionnaire with basic instructions to be followed in completing it. Although many people these days are pretty familiar with forms and questionnaires, you should begin by telling them exactly what you want: that they are to indicate their answers to certain questions by placing a check mark or an X in the box beside the appropriate answer, or by writing in their answer when asked to do so. If many open-ended questions are used, respondents should be given some guide as to whether brief or lengthy answers are expected. If you wish to encourage your respondents to elaborate on their responses to closed-ended questions, that should be noted.

If a questionnaire is arranged into content subsections—political attitudes, religious attitudes, background data—introduce each section with a short statement concerning its content and purpose. For example, "In this section, we would like to know what people around here consider the most important community problems." Demographic items at the end of a self-administered questionnaire might be introduced thus: "Finally, we would like to know just a little about you so we can see how different types of people feel about the issues we have been examining."

Short introductions such as these help make sense out of the questionnaire for the respondent. They make the questionnaire seem less chaotic, especially when it taps a variety of data. And they help put the respondent in the proper frame of mind for answering the questions.

Some questions may require special instructions to facilitate proper answering. That is especially true if a given question varies from the general instructions pertaining to the whole questionnaire. Some specific examples will illustrate this situation.

Despite the desirability for mutually exclusive answer categories in closed-ended questions, it is often the case that more than one answer will apply for respondents. If you want a single answer, you should make this perfectly clear in the question. An example would be, "From the list below, please check the *primary* reason for your decision to attend college." Often the main question can be followed by a parenthetical note: "Please check the *one* best answer." If, on the other hand, you want the respondent to check as many answers as apply, that should be made clear as well.

When a set of answer categories are to be rank-ordered by the respondent, the instructions should indicate as much, and a different type of answer format should be used (for example, blanks instead of boxes). These instructions should indicate how many answers are to be ranked (for example, all, first and second, first and last, most important and least important) and the order of

ranking (for example, "Place a 1 beside the most important, a 2 beside the next most important, and so forth"). Rank-ordering of responses is often difficult for respondents, however, since they may have to read and reread the list several times, so this technique should only be used in those situations where no other method will produce the desired result.

In multiple-part matrix questions, it is useful to give special instructions unless the same format is used throughout the questionnaire. Sometimes respondents will be expected to check one answer in each *column* of the matrix, while in other questionnaires they will be expected to check one answer in each *row*. Whenever the questionnaire contains both types, it will be useful to add an instruction clarifying which is expected in each case.

There are countless other tips and guidelines that I could give you in connection with questionnaire construction, but this section of this single chapter would soon be longer than the rest of the book. There is also the danger that you'd be bored silly. Somewhat reluctantly, then, I'm going to complete this discussion with an illustration of a real questionnaire, showing you how some of these comments find substance in practice.

Before turning to the illustration, however, I want to mention a critical aspect of questionnaire design that I will delay discussing until Chapter 13: *precoding*. Since the information collected by questionnaires is typically transferred into punch cards or magnetic tapes, it is usually appropriate to include data-processing instructions on the questionnaire itself. These instructions indicate where specific pieces of information will be stored in the machine-readable data files. In Chapter 13, I'll discuss the nature of such storage and point out the kinds of questionnaire notations that would be appropriate. As a preview, however, notice that the following illustration has been precoded with the mysterious numbers that appear near questions and answer categories.

A Composite Illustration

Figure 9-7 is a portion of a 32-page student survey questionnaire developed by University of Hawaii students in 1969. The purpose of the survey was to create a comprehensive file of information about student attitudes and orientations in a variety of areas: politics, religion, education, and others.

I have chosen this questionnaire because it employed no expensive production techniques—it was typed and then photo-offset—and because it covers subject matter that you might want to study sometime yourself. On the whole, it is a pretty good questionnaire. Still, it is not perfect. As you read through the questionnaire, you will find marginal notations (*Note 1* and so on). Whenever such a notation appears, you might try to figure out how the questionnaire could have been improved at that point. In the notes below the illustration questionnaire, I have told how I feel it could have been improved.

To improve your critical skills in questionnaire construction, you should also look for mistakes that I have *not* marked.

SELF-ADMINISTERED QUESTIONNAIRES

There are two main methods of administering survey questionnaires to a sample of respondents. This section will deal with the method in which respondents are asked to complete the questionnaires themselves—*self-administered* questionnaires—and the following section will deal with surveys that are administered by staff interviewers.

Although the mail survey is the typical method used in self-administered studies, there are several other common methods. In some cases, it may be appropriate to administer the questionnaire to a group of respondents gathered at the same place at the same time. A survey of students taking introductory psychology might be conducted in this manner during class. High school students might be surveyed during homeroom period.

Some recent experimentation has been conducted with regard to the home delivery of questionnaires. A research worker delivers the questionnaire to the home of sample respondents and explains the study. Then the questionnaire is left for the respondent to complete, and the researcher picks it up later.

Home delivery and the mail can be used in combination as well. Questionnaires can be mailed to families, and then research workers visit homes to pick up the questionnaires and check them for completeness. In just the opposite method, questionnaires have been hand delivered by research workers with a request that the respondents mail the completed questionnaires to the research office.

On the whole, when a research worker either delivers the questionnaire, picks it up, or both, the completion rate seems higher than for straightforward mail surveys. Additional experimentation with this method is likely to point to other techniques for improving completion while reducing costs. Mail surveys are the typical form of self-administered survey, however, and the remainder of this section is devoted specifically to that type of study.

Mail Distribution and Return

The basic method for data collection through the mail has been transmittal of a ques-

Figure 9-7   A Sample Questionnaire

> GENERAL INSTRUCTIONS: Either a pen or pencil may be used
> to complete this questionnaire. Most of the questions may be
> answered by simply placing an X in the appropriate box; other
> questions ask for written-in answers. However, you may write
> in additional comments whenever you wish to do so. Please ignore
> the numbers beside the questions and answers; they are for machine
> tabulation only.

A.   POLITICAL ORIENTATIONS   NOTE 1

(1-4, 5/1)

1. Beside each of the statements listed below, please indicate
    whether you strongly agree (SA), agree (A), disagree (D),
    strongly disagree (SD), or don't know (DK).

	SA 1	A 2	D 3	SD 4	DK 5
(6-15)					
a. It would be a good thing if the United Nations were someday converted into a world government. .	[ ]	[ ]	[ ]	[ ]	[ ]
b. People who defile the American flag should be put in prison. . .	[ ]	[ ]	[ ]	[ ]	[ ]
c. The United States is too ready to interpret the actions of communist nations as threatening . . .	[ ]	[ ]	[ ]	[ ]	[ ]
d. The United States is spending too much money on defense	[ ]	[ ]	[ ]	[ ]	[ ]
e. Communism is probably the best form of government for some countries	[ ]	[ ]	[ ]	[ ]	[ ]
f. The Central Intelligence Agency has too much power.	[ ]	[ ]	[ ]	[ ]	[ ]
g. The NLF (Viet Cong) are mostly invaders from North Vietnam . . .	[ ]	[ ]	[ ]	[ ]	[ ]
h. The United States was justified in using nuclear weapons against Japan in 1945	[ ]	[ ]	[ ]	[ ]	[ ]
i. If it were not for the power of the United States, most nations of the world would be taken over by the communists	[ ]	[ ]	[ ]	[ ]	[ ]
j. We should support our country's policies even when they are wrong	[ ]	[ ]	[ ]	[ ]	[ ]

Note 1.   This is not a serious problem, but since the full questionnaire dealt with a variety of topics, it would have been useful to insert a short introductory comment at this point to inform respondents of what was contained in the section. Such introductions would have been even more useful in later sections, where respondents were asked implicitly to switch their thinking to different topics. An appropriate introduction might have been, "In this first section, we are interested in learning how you feel about a variety of foreign and domestic political issues."

Figure 9-7 *(Continued)*

2. In general, how do you feel about each of the following possible U.S. policies regarding the war in Vietnam? Please indicate beside each whether you approve (A), disapprove (D), or don't know (DK).

	A 1	D 2	DK 3
(16-25)			
a. Maintenance of present level of U.S. military activities	[ ]	[ ]	[ ]
b. Immediate beginning of unilateral withdrawal of U.S. forces	[ ]	[ ]	[ ]
c. Withdrawal of U.S. forces into strategic hamlets in South Vietnam.	[ ]	[ ]	[ ]
d. Bombing of strategic targets in North Vietnam	[ ]	[ ]	[ ]
e. Invasion of North Vietnam by U.S. ground forces.	[ ]	[ ]	[ ]
f. Invasion of North Vietnam by South Vietnamese ground forces.	[ ]	[ ]	[ ]
g. Use of nuclear weapons against North Vietnam if recommended by U.S. military leaders	[ ]	[ ]	[ ]
h. Cessation of all U.S. bombing in South Vietnam	[ ]	[ ]	[ ]
i. Granting U.S. military leaders complete freedom to handle the war as they see fit .	[ ]	[ ]	[ ]
j. Continuation of the Paris peace talks . . .	[ ]	[ ]	[ ]

3. As a general rule, do you personally tend to believe or doubt the validity of *official* U.S. government reports regarding the following aspects of the war in Vietnam?

	Believe 1	Doubt 2	Don't know 3
(26-28)			
a. Reports of enemy casualties	[ ]	[ ]	[ ]
b. Reports of Viet Cong atrocities . .	[ ]	[ ]	[ ]
c. Proclamations of U.S. goals in Vietnam	[ ]	[ ]	[ ]

4. Is there anything else you would like to say about the war in Vietnam? (Additional space is provided at the end of the questionnaire.)
   (29-30)

Figure 9-7   *(Continued)*

5. Listed below are some statements people have made regarding
    the student peace movement in America. Beside each, please
    indicate whether you strongly agree (SA), agree (A), disagree
    (D), strongly disagree (SD), or don't know how you feel (DK).

	SA	A	D	SD	DK
(31-36)	1	2	3	4	5
a. Peace demonstrators threaten the peace more than they enhance it .	[ ]	[ ]	[ ]	[ ]	[ ]
b. A person's moral convictions should take precedence over national policies of war.	[ ]	[ ]	[ ]	[ ]	[ ]
c. Peace demonstrators are primarily interested in personal publicity.	[ ]	[ ]	[ ]	[ ]	[ ]
d. Pacifism is simply not a practical philosophy in the world today.	[ ]	[ ]	[ ]	[ ]	[ ]
e. Burning one's draft card should *not* be considered a crime	[ ]	[ ]	[ ]	[ ]	[ ]
f. Peace demonstrators should be drafted and sent to Vietnam . . .	[ ]	[ ]	[ ]	[ ]	[ ]

6. In November, 1968, two U.S. Marines sought sanctuary on the
    UH campus as a protest against the war in Vietnam. Which of
    the following do you believe *should* have been the policy of
    the university administration?
    (37)   NOTE 2
        1 [ ] The university should have granted official sanctuary.
        2 [ ] The university should have permitted them to stay on
               campus without granting official sanctuary.
        3 [ ] The university should have forced them to leave the
               campus.
                                                                            NOTE 3
7. There has been disagreement recently as to whether the uni-
    versity should permit military recruiters and antidraft
    counselors to come on the UH campus to talk with students.
    Do you personally feel the university should permit both,
    only one, or neither to come on campus to talk with students?
    (38)
        1 [ ] Should permit *both* military recruiters and antidraft
               counselors
        2 [ ] Should permit only *military* recruiters
        3 [ ] Should permit only *antidraft* counselors
        4 [ ] Should permit *neither*
        5 [ ] I don't know

Note 2. Since Question 5 has its answer spaces to the right of the answers, it would have been better to follow the same pattern with Questions 6 and 7. Switching the placement of answer spaces on the same page will make processing somewhat difficult for keypunchers and will increase the likelihood of errors.

Note 3. The list of response categories for Question 6 is probably not exhaustive. In fact, some respondents wrote in answers of their own. It would have been better to provide an "Other (Please specify): _____ _____ " category for this purpose. (Incidentally, the university administration chose the second alternative, and everything worked out just fine.)

Figure 9-7 *(Continued)*

8. Which of the following, if any, do you believe should be sufficient grounds for exemption from military service? (Please
check 'yes' if you believe it should be sufficient and 'no'
if you believe it should not be sufficient.)

	(39-43)	Yes 1	No 2	Don't know 3
a.	Membership in a religious group with strong pacifist principles.	[ ]	[ ]	[ ]
b.	Strong personal religious pacifist principles.	[ ]	[ ]	[ ]
c.	Strong personal moral or philosophical (nonreligious) pacifist principles. . . .	[ ]	[ ]	[ ]
d.	Strong objections to a particular war . .	[ ]	[ ]	[ ]
e.	Other (Please specify: _____ _____) . .	[ ]	[ ]	[ ]

9. Have you personally supported the current peace movement in
any of the following ways?

	(44-50)	Yes 1	No 2
a.	Attended a peace rally.	[ ]	[ ]
b.	Participated in a peace march	[ ]	[ ]
c.	Written a letter intended for publication . . .	[ ]	[ ]
d.	Spoken at a peace rally	[ ]	[ ]
e.	Written a letter to a public official	[ ]	[ ]
f.	Campaigned for a peace candidate.	[ ]	[ ]
g.	Distributed peace literature.	[ ]	[ ]
h.	Participated in *mild* direct action subject to arrest (trespassing, disturbing the peace, etc.)	[ ]	[ ]
i.	Participated in *strong* direct action subject to arrest (destruction of property, inter- fering with military operations, etc.).	[ ]	[ ]
j.	Was arrested for peace movement activities. . .	[ ]	[ ]
k.	Other (Please specify: _____ _____)	[ ]	[ ]

10. Which government would you prefer to have represented in the
United Nations: the Nationalist government on Taiwan or the
Communist government on the mainland of China?
(55)   NOTE 4
    1 [ ] Only the Nationalist government on Taiwan
    2 [ ] Only the Communist government on the mainland
    3 [ ] Both governments should be represented

Note 4. Rather whimsically, the answer spaces for Question 10 have been placed to the left, while those for
Questions 11 and 12 are on the right. See Note 2 if you've forgotten why this is a bad idea.

Figure 9-7 *(Continued)*

11. Please indicate whether you agree (A), disagree (D), or are undecided (U) about each of the following possible United States' policies toward mainland China.

(56-61)	A 1	D 2	U 3
a. Granting diplomatic recognition to China. .	[ ]	[ ]	[ ]
b. Seeking economic trade with China	[ ]	[ ]	[ ]
c. Offering economic aid to China.	[ ]	[ ]	[ ]
d. Seeking cultural exchange programs with China	[ ]	[ ]	[ ]
e. Seeking to contain China militarily	[ ]	[ ]	[ ]
f. Seeking to destroy China's military power .	[ ]	[ ]	[ ]

12. The question of military intervention has come up many times in the past. The following is a list of instances in which the U.S. had to decide whether or not to intervene militarily. In each case, please indicate whether or not you feel the U.S. should have intervened with military force.

(62-72)	Should have intervened 1	Should not have intervened 2	Not sure 3
a. Chinese Communist Revolution, 1948-49	[ ]	[ ]	[ ]
b. Korean conflict, 1950	[ ]	[ ]	[ ]
c. Hungarian revolt, 1956. . . .	[ ]	[ ]	[ ]
d. Bay of Pigs invasion, 1961. .	[ ]	[ ]	[ ]
e. Vietnam buildup, 1964-65. . .	[ ]	[ ]	[ ]
f. Dominican Republic revolt, 1965.	[ ]	[ ]	[ ]
g. Rhodesian independence, 1965.	[ ]	[ ]	[ ]
h. Greek military coup d'etat, 1965.	[ ]	[ ]	[ ]
i. Israeli-Arab conflict, 1967 .	[ ]	[ ]	[ ]
j. Capture of U.S.S. Pueblo, 1968.	[ ]	[ ]	[ ]
k. Russian occupation of Czechoslovakia, 1968.	[ ]	[ ]	[ ]

Figure 9-7   *(Continued)*

13. In general, how would you characterize your own political
     orientation? How would you characterize the political orien-
     tations of your parents? (Please answer for each.)

		Yourself	Your Father	Your Mother	NOTE 5
Right radical.	(73-75)	1 [ ]	1 [ ]	1 [ ]	
Very conservative.		2 [ ]	2 [ ]	2 [ ]	
Moderately conservative.		3 [ ]	3 [ ]	3 [ ]	
Moderately liberal		4 [ ]	4 [ ]	4 [ ]	
Left radical		5 [ ]	5 [ ]	5 [ ]	
Other (Please specify: _____					
_____). .		6 [ ]	6 [ ]	6 [ ]	
Don't know		7 [ ]	7 [ ]	7 [ ]	

14. Do you normally identify yourself with any particular politi-
     cal party? (Please indicate *which party*, if any, you identi-
     fy with.)
     (76)   NOTE 6

     1 [ ] Democratic party
     2 [ ] Republican party
     3 [ ] American Independent party
     4 [ ] Peace and Freedom party
     5 [ ] Other (Please specify: _____)
     6 [ ] No party identification, independent

15. Were you eligible to vote in the November, 1968, general
     election?
     (77-78)   NOTE 7
     1 [ ] Yes**   15a. ** If *yes*, did you vote? 1 [ ] Yes
     2 [ ] No   2 [ ] No

16. Whether or not you were eligible to vote in November, 1968,
     which of these Presidential candidates, if any, did you
     prefer?
     (79)

     1 [ ] Hubert Humphrey
     2 [ ] Richard Nixon
     3 [ ] George Wallace
     4 [ ] Eldridge Cleaver
     5 [ ] None of these

     (80/R)

Note 5. "Very liberal" is missing from the list of response categories. As a result, the spectrum of political orientations is unbalanced. This omission is the result of a simple typing error and the failure to proofread the questionnaire carefully enough. It is worth noting that this error occurred after hours of considered debate over the proper terms to be used in labeling different political orientations—especially the extremes. The most careful conceptualization can go for naught unless every step in the research process is taken with sufficient caution.

Note 6. There go the answer spaces across the page again. Since Question 15 contains a contingency question, making it awkward to place the answer spaces to the right, it would have been better to place those for Question 13 on the left.

Note 7. This is not a very good format for the contingency question. See Figure 9-5 earlier in this chapter for a better format. Also, note how crowded the questionnaire is at this point. There is a danger that many respondents would get confused and miss the contingency question altogether. Can you determine why the researchers crowded questions together so much here?

tionnaire, accompanied by a letter of explanation and a self-addressed, stamped envelope for returning the questionnaire. I imagine you have received one or two in your lifetime. As a respondent, you are expected to complete the questionnaire, put it in the envelope, and return it. If, by any chance, you've received such a questionnaire and failed to return it, it would be extremely valuable for you to recall the reasons you had for *not* returning it—and keep those in mind any time you plan to send questionnaires to others.

One big reason for not returning questionnaires is the complaint that it seems like too much trouble. To overcome this problem, researchers have developed a number of ways to make the return of questionnaires easier. One development is a *self-mailing* questionnaire, requiring no return envelope. The questionnaire is designed so that when it is folded in a particular fashion, the return address appears on the outside. That way, the respondent doesn't have to worry about losing the envelope.

Use this method with caution, however. One of the first surveys I conducted was an enormous one with some 70,000 respondents. To save money and simplify the logistics, I had the questionnaire printed on a long sheet of paper and had it prefolded so that my return address and business-reply permit showed on the outside. To facilitate several follow-up mailings (see below), I had nearly a quarter of a million questionnaires printed. Since we were going to be receiving a lot of mail, we decided to warn the local post office and see if we could arrange to have the questionnaires delivered to us in mail bags. When the postal officials saw the questionnaire, however, they announced that it violated postal regulations! Since I had made no provisions for the folded questionnaire to be sealed (required for first class mail), the local officials indicated they couldn't handle it. Only an inspirational discussion of social research and a tearful

appeal to save my graduate career got the questionnaires into the mail.

More elaborate designs are available also. The student questionnaire described and illustrated earlier in this chapter was bound in a booklet with a special, two-panel back cover. Once the questionnaire was completed, the respondent needed only to fold out the extra panel, wrap it around the booklet, and seal the whole thing with the adhesive strip running along the edge of the panel. The foldout panel contained my return address and postage. When I repeated the study a couple of years later, I improved on the design further. Both the front and back covers had foldout panels: one for sending the questionnaire out and the other for getting it back—thus avoiding the use of envelopes altogether.

The point here is that anything you can do to make the job of completing and returning the questionnaire easier will improve your study. Imagine receiving a questionnaire that made no provisions for its return to the researcher. Suppose you had to (1) find an envelope, (2) write the address on it, (3) figure out how much postage it required, and (4) put the stamps on it. How likely is it that you would return the questionnaire?

A few brief comments are in order here on the postal options available to you. You have options for mailing questionnaires out and for getting them returned. On outgoing mail, your choices are essentially between first-class postage and bulk rate. First is more certain, but bulk rate is far cheaper. (Check your local post office for rates and procedures.) On return mail, your choice is between postage stamps and business-reply permits. Here, the cost differential is more complicated. If you use stamps, you pay for them whether people return their questionnaires or not. With the business-reply permit, you only pay for those that are used, but you pay an additional surcharge of about a nickel. This means that stamps are cheaper if a lot of questionnaires are returned, but business-reply permits are cheaper if fewer are returned (and you won't know in advance how many will be returned).

There are many other considerations involved in choosing among the several postal options. Some researchers, for example, feel that the use of postal stamps communicates more "human-ness" and sincerity than bulk rate and business-reply permits. Others worry that respondents will steam off the stamps and use them for some purpose other than returning the questionnaires. Since both bulk rate and business-reply permits require establishing accounts at the post office, you'll probably find stamps much easier in small surveys.

Monitoring Returns

The mailing of questionnaires sets up a new research question that may prove very valuable to the study. As questionnaires are returned, you should not sit back idly, but should undertake a careful recording of the varying rates of return among respondents.

An invaluable tool in this activity will be a return rate graph. The day on which questionnaires were mailed should be labeled Day 1 on the graph, and every day thereafter, the number of returned questionnaires should be logged on the graph. Since this is a minor activity, it is usually best to compile two graphs. One should show the number returned each day—rising, then dropping. Another should report the *cumulative* number or percentage. In part, this activity provides you with gratification, as you get to draw a picture of your successful data collection. More important, however, it is your guide to how the data collection is going. If you plan follow-up mailings, the graph provides a clue as to when such mailings should be launched. (The dates of subsequent mailings should be noted on the graph.)

As completed questionnaires are returned, each should be opened, scanned, and assigned an identification number. These numbers should be assigned serially as the questionnaires are returned—even if other identification (ID) numbers have already been assigned. Two examples should illustrate the important advantages of this procedure.

Let's assume that you are studying attitudes toward a political figure. In the middle of the data collection, let's say the politician is discovered to be supporting a mistress. By knowing the date of that public disclosure and the dates when questionnaires have been received, you will be in a position to determine the effects of the disclosure. (Recall the discussion of history in connection with experiments.)

In a less sensational way, serialized ID numbers can be valuable in estimating nonresponse biases in the survey. Barring more direct tests of bias, you may wish to assume that those who failed to answer the questionnaire will be more like respondents who delayed answering than like those who answered right away. An analysis of questionnaires received at different points in the data collection might then be used for estimates of sampling bias. For example, if the grade point averages (GPAs) reported by student respondents decrease steadily through the data collection, with those replying right away having higher GPAs and those replying later having lower GPAs, then you might tentatively conclude that those who failed to answer at all have lower GPAs yet. Although it would not be advisable to make statistical estimates of bias in this fashion, you could take advantage of approximate estimates.

If respondents have been identified for purposes of follow-up mailing, then preparations for those mailings should be made as the questionnaires are returned. The case study later in this chapter will discuss this process in greater detail.

Follow-up Mailings

Follow-up mailings may be administered in a number of ways. In the simplest, nonrespondents are simply sent a letter of additional encouragement to participate. A better method, however, is to send a new copy of the survey questionnaire with the follow-up letter. If potential respondents have not returned their questionnaires after two or three weeks, the questionnaires probably have been lost or misplaced. Receiving a follow-up letter might encourage them to look for the original questionnaire, but if they can't find it easily, the letter may go for naught.

The methodological literature on follow-up mailings strongly suggests that it is an effective method for increasing return rates in mail surveys. In general, the longer a potential respondent delays replying, the less likely he or she is to do so at all. Properly timed follow-up mailings, then, provide additional stimuli to respond.

The effects of follow-up mailings will be seen in the response rate curves recorded during data collection. The initial mailings will be followed by a rise and subsequent subsiding of returns, the follow-up mailings will spur a resurgence of returns, and more follow-ups will do the same. In practice, three mailings (an original and two follow-ups) seem the most efficient.

The timing of follow-up mailings is also important. Here the methodological literature offers less precise guides, but it has been my experience that two or three weeks is a reasonable space between mailings. (This period might be increased by a few days if the mailing time—out and in—is more than two or three days.)

When researchers conduct several surveys of the same population over time, they will be able to develop more specific guidelines in this regard. The Survey Research Office at the University of Hawaii conducts frequent student surveys and has been able to refine the mailing and remailing procedure considerably. Indeed, a consistent pattern of returns has been found, which appears to transcend differences of survey content, quality of instrument, and so forth. Within two weeks after the first mailing, approximately 40 percent of the questionnaires are returned; within two weeks after the first follow-up, an additional 20 percent are received; and within two weeks after the final follow-up, an additional 10 percent are received. (These response rates all involved the sending of additional questionnaires, not just letters.) There are no grounds for assuming that a similar pattern would appear in surveys of different populations, but this illustration should indicate the value of carefully tabulating return rates for every survey conducted.

If the individuals in the survey sample are not identified on the questionnaires, it may not be possible to remail only to nonrespondents. In such a case, you should send your follow-up mailing to all members of the sample, thanking those who may have already participated and encouraging those who have not to do so. (The case study reported in a later section of this chapter describes another method that may be used in an anonymous mail survey.)

Acceptable Response Rates

A question that new survey researchers frequently ask concerns the percentage return rate that should be achieved in a mail survey. It should be pointed out here that the body of inferential statistics used in connection with survey analysis assumes that *all* members of the initial sample complete and return their questionnaires. Since this almost never happens, response bias becomes a concern, with the researcher testing (and hoping for) the possibility that the respondents look essentially like a random sample of the initial sample, and thus a somewhat smaller random sample of the total population. (For more detailed discussions of response bias, you might want to read Donald [1960] and Brownlee [1975].)

Nevertheless, overall **response rate** is one guide to the representativeness of the sample respondents. If a high response rate is achieved, there is less chance of significant response bias than if a low rate is achieved. But what is a *high* response rate?

A quick review of the survey literature will uncover a wide range of response rates. Each of these may be accompanied by a statement something like "This is regarded as a relatively high response rate for a survey of this type." (A U.S. senator made this statement regarding a poll of constituents that achieved a 4-percent return rate.) Even so, it's possible to state some rules of thumb about return rates. I feel that a response rate of at least 50 percent is *adequate* for analysis and reporting. A response of at least 60 percent is *good*. And a response rate of 70 percent is *very good*. You should bear in mind, however, that these are only rough guides; they have no statistical basis, and a demonstrated lack of response bias is far more important than a high response rate.

As you can imagine, one of the more persistent discussions among survey researchers concerns ways of increasing response rates. You'll recall that this was a chief concern in the earlier discussion of options for mailing out and receiving questionnaires. Survey researchers have developed a number of ingenious techniques addressing this problem. Some have experimented with novel formats. Others have tried paying respondents to participate. The problem with paying, of course, is that it's expensive to make meaningfully high payment to hundreds or thousands of repondents, but some imaginative alternatives have been used. Some researchers have said, "We want to get your two-cents worth on some issues, and we're willing to pay"—enclos-

ing two pennies. Another enclosed a quarter, suggesting that the respondent make some little child happy.

Don Dillman (1978) has undertaken an excellent review of the various techniques survey researchers have used to increase return rates on mail surveys, and he evaluates the impact of each. More important, Dillman stresses the necessity of paying attention to *all* aspects of the study—what he calls the "Total Design Method"—rather than one or two special gimmicks.

A Case Study

The steps involved in the administration of a mail survey are many and can best be appreciated in a walk-through of an actual study. I'll conclude this section, then, with a detailed description of the University of Hawaii student survey mentioned earlier. As you'll see shortly, the study did not represent the theoretical ideal for such studies, but in that regard it serves present purposes all the better. The study was conducted by the students in my graduate seminar in survey research methods.

By way of general overview, approximately 1,100 students were selected from the university registration tape through a stratified, systematic sampling procedure. For each student selected, six self-adhesive mailing labels were printed by the computer.

By the time we were ready to distribute the questionnaires, it became apparent that our meager research funds were inadequate to cover several mailings to the entire sample of 1,000 students. (Questionnaire printing costs were higher than anticipated.) As a result, a systematic two-thirds sample of the mailing labels was chosen, yielding a subsample of 770 students.

Earlier, we had decided to keep the survey anonymous in the hope of encouraging more candid responses to some sensitive questions. (Later surveys of the same issues among the same population indicated this anonymity was unnecessary.) Thus, the questionnaires would carry no identification of students on them. At the same time, we hoped to reduce the follow-up mailing costs by mailing only to nonrespondents.

To achieve both of these aims, a special postcard method was devised. Each student was mailed a questionnaire that carried no identifying marks, plus a postcard addressed to the research office—with one of the student's mailing labels affixed to the reverse side of the card. The introductory letter asked the student to complete and return the questionnaire—assuring anonymity—and to return the postcard simultaneously. Receiving the postcard would tell us that the student had returned his or her questionnaire—without indicating *which* questionnaire it was. This procedure would then facilitate follow-up mailings.

The 32-page questionnaire was printed in booklet form (photo-offset and saddle-stitched). A three-panel cover—described earlier in this chapter—permitted the questionnaire to be returned without an additional envelope.

A letter introducing the study and its purposes was printed on the front cover of the booklet. It explained why the study was being conducted (to learn how students feel about a variety of issues), how students had been selected for the study, the importance of each student's responding, and the mechanics of returning the questionnaire.

Students were assured that their responses to the survey were anonymous, and the postcard method was explained. A statement followed about the auspices under which the study was being conducted, and a telephone number was provided for those who might want more information about the study. (About five students called for information.)

By printing the introductory letter on the questionnaire, we avoided the necessity of enclosing a separate letter in the outgoing envelope, thereby simplifying the task of assembling mailing pieces.

The materials for the initial mailing were assembled in the following steps. (1) One mailing label for each student was stuck on a postcard. (2) Another label was stuck on an outgoing manila envelope. (3) One postcard and one questionnaire were placed in each envelope—with a glance to ensure that the name on the postcard and on the envelope were the same in each case.

These steps were accomplished through an assembly line procedure involving several members of the research team. Although the procedure was somewhat organized in advance, it took a certain amount of actual practice before the best allocation of tasks and persons was discovered.

It is also worth noting that the entire process was delayed several days while the initial batch of manila envelopes was exchanged for larger ones. This delay could have been avoided if we had walked through the assembly process in advance.

The distribution of the survey questionnaires had been set up for a bulk rate mailing. Once the questionnaires had been stuffed into envelopes, they were grouped by zip codes, tied in bundles, and delivered to the post office.

Shortly after the initial mailing, questionnaires and postcards began arriving at the research office. Questionnaires were opened, scanned, and assigned identification numbers as described earlier in this chapter. For every postcard received, a search was made for that student's remaining labels, and they were destroyed.

After a period of two or three weeks, all the remaining mailing labels were used to organize a follow-up mailing. The assembly procedures described above were repeated with one exception. A special, separate letter of appeal was included in the mailing piece. The new letter indicated that many students had returned their questionnaires already, but that it was very important for all others to do so as well.

The follow-up mailing stimulated a resurgence of returns, as expected, and the same logging procedures were continued. The returned postcards told us which additional mailing labels to destroy. Unfortunately, time and financial pressures made it impossible to undertake a third mailing, as had been initially planned, but the two mailings resulted in an overall return rate of 62 percent.

I trust this illustration will give you a fairly good sense of what's involved in the execution of mailed self-administered questionnaires—a very popular survey method. Let's turn now to the other method of conducting surveys.

INTERVIEW SURVEYS

The **interview** is an alternative method of collecting survey data. Rather than asking respondents to read questionnaires and enter their own answers, researchers send interviewers to ask the questions orally and record respondents' answers. Interviewing is typically done in a face-to-face encounter, but telephone interviewing, as we'll see, follows most of the same guidelines. Also, most interview surveys require more than one interviewer, although you might undertake a small-scale interview survey yourself. Portions of this section will discuss methods for training and supervising a staff of interviewers assisting you on the survey.

The Role of the Interviewer

There are a number of advantages in having a questionnaire administered by an interviewer rather than the respondent. To begin, interview surveys typically attain higher response rates than mail surveys. A properly designed and executed interview survey ought to achieve a completion rate of at least 80 to 85 percent. (Federally funded surveys often require one of these response rates.) Respondents seem more reluctant to turn down an interviewer standing on their doorstep than they are to throw away a mail questionnaire.

Within the context of the questionnaire, the presence of an interviewer generally decreases the number of "don't knows" and "no answers." If minimizing such responses is important to the study, the interviewer can be instructed to probe for answers ("If you had to pick one of the answers, which do you think would come closest to your feelings?").

Interviewers can also provide a guard against confusing questionnaire items. If the respondent clearly misunderstands the intent of a question or indicates that he or she does not understand, the interviewer can clarify matters, thereby obtaining relevant responses. (Such clarifications must be strictly controlled, however, through formal *specifications*. See "Coordination and Control.")

Finally, the interviewer can observe as well as ask questions. For example, the interviewer can note the respondent's race if this is considered too delicate a question to ask. Similar observations can be made regarding the quality of the dwelling, the presence of various possessions, the respondent's ability to speak English, the respondent's general reactions to the study, and so forth. In one survey of students, respondents were given a short, self-administered questionnaire to complete—concerning sexual attitudes and behavior—during the course of the interview. While a student completed the questionnaire, the interviewer made detailed notes regarding the dress and grooming of the respondent.

Before leaving this example, there is an ethical issue that should be raised. Some researchers have objected that such practices violate the spirit of the agreement by which the respondent has allowed the interview. While ethical issues seldom are open and shut in social research, it is important for you to be sensitive to that aspect of research, and we'll examine ethical issues in detail in Chapter 19.

Survey research is of necessity based on an unrealistic *stimulus-response* theory of cognition and behavior. It must be assumed that a questionnaire item will mean the same thing to every respondent, and every given response must mean the same when given by different respondents. Although this is an impossible goal, survey questions are drafted to approximate the ideal as closely as possible.

The interviewer must also fit into this ideal situation. The interviewer's presence should not affect a respondent's perception of a question or the answer given. The interviewer, then, should be a *neutral* medium through which questions and answers are transmitted.

If this goal is successfully accomplished, different interviewers will obtain exactly the same responses from a given respondent. (Recall earlier discussions of reliability.) This neutrality has a special importance in area samples. To save time and money, a given interviewer is typically assigned to complete all the interviews in a particular geographical area—a city block or a group of nearby blocks. If the interviewer does anything to affect the responses obtained, then the bias thus interjected might be interpreted as a characteristic of that area.

Let's suppose that a survey is being done to determine attitudes toward low-cost housing, to help in the selection of a site for a new government-sponsored development. An interviewer assigned to a given neighborhood might—through word or gesture—communicate his or her own distaste for low-cost housing developments. Respondents might therefore tend to give responses generally in agreement with the interviewer's own position. The results of the survey would indicate that the neighborhood in question strongly resisted construction of the development in its area whereas their apparent resistance might only reflect the interviewer's attitudes.

General Rules for Interviewing

The manner in which interviews ought to be conducted will vary somewhat by survey population and will be affected somewhat by the nature of the survey content as well. Nevertheless, it is possible to provide some general guidelines that apply to most if not all interviewing situations.

Appearance and Demeanor As a general rule, the interviewer should dress in a fashion similar to that of the people he or she will be interviewing. A richly dressed interviewer will probably have difficulty getting good cooperation and responses from poorer respondents. And a poorly dressed interviewer will have similar difficulties with richer respondents.

To the extent that the interviewer's dress and grooming differ from those of the respondents, it should be in the direction of cleanliness and neatness in modest apparel. If cleanliness is not next to godliness, it appears to be next to neutrality. Although middle-class neatness and cleanliness may not be accepted by all sectors of American society, they remain the primary norm and are more likely to be acceptable to the largest number of respondents.

Dress and grooming are typically regarded as signals to a person's attitudes and orientations. At the time this is being written, a man wearing colorful clothes, beads, and sandals, and sporting long hair, sideburns, and a beard may communicate—correctly or incorrectly—that he is politically on the

How Much Is "Very"?

by Keith Crew
Department of Sociology, University of Kentucky

Last summer I spent some time interviewing rural and small-town Appalachian residents for a large survey project. The person who trained and pretested me on the interview schedule related the following experience which she had while interviewing in the same area on a previous survey. Many of the questions on the interview schedule were Likert-type items ranging from "very much" to "very little" or "very good" to "very poor." The problem was that in the colloquial language of the region, the word "very" apparently has an idiomatic usage which is closer to what we mean by "fairly" or even "poorly." For instance, if you inquired about someone's health and they responded that they were doing "very well," they do not mean that their health is excel-lent, but quite the contrary, that they are just getting along.

One assumption of surveys, which seems so obvious that it is usually ignored, is that the researcher and the respondent are speaking the same language. In this case, the sponsors of the survey (who shall remain nameless) refused to consider the difference in language usage: they told their interviewers to code "very well" if that was what the respondent said. In other words, in many cases the coded response was quite likely the exact opposite of the respondent's opinion; furthermore, since we are discussing a regional-cultural variation it is not really "legit" to simply toss it into the category of "random error."

left, sexually permissive, favorable to drug use, and so forth.

In demeanor, interviewers should be pleasant if nothing else. Since they will be prying into the respondent's personal life and attitudes, they must communicate a genuine interest in getting to know the respondent without appearing to spy. They must be relaxed and friendly without being too casual or clinging. Good interviewers also have the ability to determine very quickly the kind of person the respondent will feel most comfortable with, the kind of person the respondent would most enjoy talking to. There are two aspects of this. Clearly, the interview will be more successful if the interviewer can become the kind of person the respondent is comfortable with. Second, since respondents are asked to volunteer a portion of their time and to divulge personal information about themselves, they deserve the most enjoyable experience that the researcher and interviewer can provide.

Familiarity with Questionnaire If an interviewer is unfamiliar with the questionnaire, the study suffers and an unfair burden is placed on the respondent. The interview is likely to take more time than necessary and be generally unpleasant. Moreover, the interviewer cannot acquire familiarity by skimming through the questionnaire two or three times. It must be studied carefully, question by question, and the interviewer must practice reading it aloud.

Ultimately, the interviewer must be able to read the questionnaire items to respondents without error, without stumbling over words and phrases. A good model for interviewers is the actor reading lines in a play or motion picture. The lines must be read as naturally as though they constituted a natural conversation, but that conversation must follow exactly the language set down in the questionnaire.

By the same token, the interviewer must be familiar with the specifications prepared in conjunction with the questionnaire. Inevitably some questions will not exactly fit a given respondent's situation, and the interviewer must determine how the question should be interpreted in that situation. The specifications provided to the interviewer should give adequate guidance in such cases, but the interviewer must know the organization and contents of the specifications well enough to refer to them efficiently. It would be better for the interviewer to leave a given question unanswered than to spend five minutes searching through the specifications for clarification or trying to interpret the relevant instructions.

Following Question Wording Exactly In Chapter 6, I discussed the significance of question wording for the responses obtained. A slight change in the wording of a given question may lead a respondent to answer yes rather than no.

Even though you have very carefully phrased your questionnaire items so as to obtain the information you need and to ensure that respondents will interpret items precisely as you intend, all this effort will be wasted if interviewers rephrase questions in their own words.

Recording Responses Exactly Whenever the questionnaire contains open-ended

questions, those soliciting the respondent's own answer, it is very important that the interviewer record that answer exactly as given. No attempt should be made to summarize, paraphrase, or correct bad grammar.

This exactness is especially important because the interviewer will not know how the responses are to be coded before processing. Indeed, the researchers may not know the coding until they have read a hundred or so responses. For example, the questionnaire might ask respondents how they feel about the traffic situation in their community. One respondent might answer that there are too many cars on the roads and that something should be done to limit their numbers. Another might say that more roads are needed. If the interviewer recorded these two responses with the same summary—"congested traffic"—the researchers would not be able to take advantage of the important differences in the original responses.

Sometimes, the respondent may be so inarticulate that the verbal response is too ambiguous to permit interpretation. However, the interviewer may be able to understand the intent of the response through the respondent's gestures or tone. In such a situation, the exact verbal response should still be recorded, but the interviewer should add marginal comments giving both the interpretation and the reasons for arriving at it.

More generally, researchers can use any marginal comments explaining aspects of the response not conveyed in the verbal recording, such as the respondent's apparent uncertainty in answering, anger, embarrassment, and so forth. In each case, however, the exact verbal response should also be recorded.

Probing for Responses Sometimes respondents will respond to a question with an inappropriate answer. For example, the question may present an attitudinal statement and ask the respondent to strongly agree, agree somewhat, disagree somewhat, or strongly disagree. The respondent, however, may reply: "I think that's true." The interviewer should follow this reply with: "Would you say you strongly agree or agree somewhat?" If necessary, interviewers can explain that they must check one or the other of the categories provided. If the respondent adamantly refuses to choose, the interviewer should write in the exact response given by the respondent.

Probes are more frequently required in eliciting responses to open-ended questions. For example, in response to a question about traffic conditions, the respondent might simply reply, "Pretty bad." The interviewer could obtain an elaboration on this response through a variety of probes. Sometimes the best probe is silence; if the interviewer sits quietly with pencil poised, the respondent will probably fill the pause with additional comments. (This technique is used effectively by newspaper reporters.) Appropriate verbal probes might be "How is that?" or "In what ways?" Perhaps the most generally useful probe is "Anything else?"

It is frequently necessary to probe for answers that will be sufficiently informative for analytical purposes. In every case, however, it is imperative that such probes be completely *neutral*. The probe must not in any way affect the nature of the subsequent response. Whenever you anticipate that a given question may require probing for appropriate responses, you should present one or more useful probes next to the question in the questionnaire. This practice has two important advantages. First, you will have more time to devise the best, most neutral probes. Second, all interviewers will use the same probes whenever they are needed. Thus, even if the probe is not perfectly neutral, all respondents will be presented with the same stimulus. This is the same logical guideline discussed for ques-

tion wording. Although a question should not be loaded or biased, it is essential that every respondent be presented with the same question, even a biased one.

Coordination and Control

Most interview surveys require the assistance of several interviewers. In the large-scale surveys, of course, such interviewers are hired and paid for their work. As a student researcher, you might find yourself recruiting friends to assist you in interviewing. Whenever more than one interviewer is involved in a survey, it is essential that efforts be carefully controlled. There are two aspects of this control: training interviewers and supervising them after they begin work.

Interviewers should be trained in a group, rather than individually. The latter approach will inevitably result in more superficial training.

The interviewer training session should begin with the description of what the study is all about. Even though the interviewers may be involved only in the data collection phase of the project, it will be useful to them to understand what will be done with the interviews they conduct and what purpose will be served. Morale and motivation are usually low when interviewers do not know what is going on.

The training on how to interview should begin with a discussion of general guidelines and procedures, such as those discussed earlier in this chapter. Then you should turn to the questionnaire itself. The whole group should go through the questionnaire together—question by question. Do not simply ask if anyone has any questions about the first page of the questionnaire. Read the first question aloud, explain the purpose of the question, and then entertain any questions or comments the interviewers may have. Once all their questions and comments have been handled, go on to the next question in the questionnaire.

It is always a good idea to prepare what are called **specifications** to accompany an interview questionnaire. Specifications are explanatory and clarifying comments about handling of difficult or confusing situations that may occur with regard to specific questions in the questionnaire. When you are drafting the questionnaire, you should try to think of all the problem cases that might arise—the bizarre circumstances that might make a question difficult to answer. The survey specifications should provide detailed guidelines on how to handle such situations. As an example, such a simple matter as age might present problems. Suppose a respondent says he or she will be 25 next week. The interviewer might not be sure whether to take the respondent's current age or the nearest one. The specifications for that question should explain what should be done. (Probably, you would specify that age as of last birthday should be recorded in all cases.)

If you have prepared a set of specifications, you should go over them with the interviewers when you go over the individual questions in the questionnaire. Make sure that your interviewers fully understand the specifications as well as the questions themselves and the reasons for them.

This portion of the interviewer training is likely to generate a number of troublesome questions from your interviewers. They will ask: "What should I do if . . . ?" In such cases, you should never give a quick answer. If you have specifications, be sure to show how the solution to the problem could be determined from the specifications. If you do not have specifications prepared, show how the preferred handling of the situation fits within the general logic of the question and the purpose of the study. Giving offhand, unexplained answers to such ques-

tions will only confuse the interviewers, and they will probably not take their work very seriously. If you do not know the answer to such a question when it is asked, admit it and ask for some time to decide on the best answer. Then think out the situation carefully and be sure to give all the interviewers your answer, explaining your reasons.

Once you have gone through the whole questionnaire as described above, you should conduct one or two demonstration interviews in front of everyone. Preferably, *you* should interview someone else. Realize that your interview will be a model for those you are training, and make it good. It would be best, moreover, if the demonstration interview were done as realistically as possible. Do not pause during the demonstration to point out how you have handled a complicated situation: handle it, and then explain later. It is irrelevant if the person you are interviewing gives real answers or takes on some hypothetical identity for the purpose, just so long as the answers are consistent.

After the demonstration interviews, you should pair off your interviewers and have them practice on each other. When they have completed the questionnaire, have them reverse roles and do it over again. Interviewing is the best training for interviewing. As your interviewers are practicing on each other, you should try to wander around, listening in on the practice so that you will know how well they are doing. Once the practice is completed, the whole group should discuss their experiences and ask any other questions they may have.

The final stage of the training for interviewers should involve some "real" interviews. Have them conduct some interviews under the actual conditions that will pertain to the final survey. You may want to assign them people to interview, or perhaps they may be allowed to pick people themselves. Do not have them practice on people you have selected in your sample, however. After each interviewer has completed three to five interviews, have him or her check back with you. Look over the completed questionnaires to see if there is any evidence of misunderstanding. Again, answer any questions that individual interviewers may have. Once you are convinced that a given interviewer knows what to do, assign some actual interviews—using the sample you have selected for the study.

It is essential that you continue supervising the work of interviewers over the course of the study. It is probably unwise to let them conduct more than 20 or 30 interviews without seeing you. You might assign 20 interviews, have the interviewer bring back those questionnaires when they are completed, look them over, and assign another 20 or so. Although that may seem overly cautious, you must continually protect yourself against misunderstandings that may not be evident early in the study.

If you are the only interviewer in your study, these comments may not seem relevant to you. That is not wholly the case, however. You would be advised, for example, to prepare specifications for potentially troublesome questions in your questionnaire. Otherwise, you run the risk of making ad hoc decisions during the course of the study that you will later regret or forget. Also, the emphasis that has been placed on *practice* applies equally to the one-person project and to the complex funded survey with a large interviewing staff.

Telephone Surveys

Pluses and Minuses   I want to conclude the discussion of interview surveys with some comments on an increasingly popular technique, sometimes ironically called *telephone polls*. For years telephone surveys had a rather bad reputation among professional researchers. Among the diverse sources of their bad press were the sampling problems discussed in Chapter 7. Telephone surveys are limited by definition to people who have telephones. Years ago, then, this method produced a substantial social-class bias by excluding poor people from the surveys. Over time, however, the telephone has become a standard fixture in almost all American homes. The Census Bureau (1979:582) estimates that 97 percent of all households had telephones in 1978. So, class bias has been substantially reduced.

A related sampling problem involved unlisted numbers. If the survey sample was selected from the pages of a local telephone directory, it would totally omit all those people—typically richer—who requested that their numbers not be published. This potential bias has been erased through a technique that has advanced telephone sampling substantially: *random-digit dialing*. Chaffee and Choe report a random sample survey of Wisconsin adults as follows:

All interviews were conducted by telephone, and sampling was based on a probability sample of area codes and telephone prefixes, followed by four random digits. Three callbacks were tried before a number was abandoned. Within households, adults were selected randomly according to a predetermined schedule.   (1980:58)

The final sampling problem concerns *who* should be interviewed at the number called. There are a variety of ways for handling this decision. Carefully selecting the hours for calling will increase the chances of all family members being at home and will guard against interviewing only homemakers. Going even further, a quota-sampling design can ensure that you interview sufficient numbers of all kinds of family members overall. Or, finally, you can specify, through random assignment as Chaffee and Choe did, who is to be interviewed at each specific number called.

As a general rule, telephone interviews should be shorter than face-to-face, household interviews. As a rough rule of thumb, you should limit telephone interviews to 10 to 15 minutes at most, although it is sometimes possible to conduct longer ones.

Telephone surveys have many advantages that underlie the growing popularity of this method. Probably the greatest advantages are money and time, in that order. In a face-to-face, household interview, you may drive several miles to a respondent's home, find no one there, return to the research office, and drive back the next day—possibly finding no one there again. It's cheaper and quicker to let your fingers make the trips.

Interviewing by telephone, you can dress any way you please without affecting the answers respondents give. And, sometimes respondents will be more honest in giving socially disapproved answers if they don't have to look you in the eye. Similarly, it may be possible to probe into more sensitive areas, though that is not necessarily the case. (People are, to some extent, more suspicious when they can't see the person asking them questions—perhaps a legacy of "surveys" aimed at selling magazine subscriptions.)

Finally, telephone surveys can give you greater control over data collection if several interviewers are engaged in the project. If all the interviewers are calling from the research office, they can get clarification from the person in charge whenever problems occur, as they inevitably do. Alone in the boondocks, an interviewer may have to wing it between weekly visits with the interviewing supervisor.

Computer-Assisted Telephone Interviewing
A telephone survey method sure to become more popular in the years to come is *computer-assisted telephone interviewing* (CATI). Though there are variations in practice, here's what it can look like. The interviewer sits in front of a computer terminal and its video screen. The central computer randomly selects a telephone number and dials it on behalf of the telephone headset the interviewer is wearing. On the video screen is an introduction ("Hello, my name is . . .") and the first question to be asked ("Could you tell me how many people live at this address?"). When the respondent answers the phone, the interviewer says hello and introduces the study. Then, the interviewer reads the first question as displayed on the screen, and types the respondent's answer into the computer terminal. The respondent's answer is immediately stored within the central computer. The second question to be asked instantly appears on the video screen, and the interview continues.

This is not science fiction but is being used increasingly by commercial survey firms. Largely developed at the University of California's Survey Research Center in Berkeley, it is now being adapted for use by the U.S. Census Bureau.

An advertising brochure from the commercial research firm Audits & Surveys details some of the advantages of CATI. Respondents can be selected randomly by the computer. The order of questions making up the questionnaire can be rotated automatically to avoid any biases due to question order—as discussed in Chapter 6—and the order of answers to particular questions can also be rotated.

Since respondents' answers are typed into the computer by the interviewer, the growing body of data can be analyzed continuously. Moreover, the computer maintains a continuing check on unacceptable answers, insisting on acceptable ones. If a series of numerical answers is supposed to total 100 percent, the computer checks the arithmetic automatically.

The company points to several cost savings as well:

- Elimination of printed questionnaires
- Reduced interviewing time

■ Automatic editing and cleaning (see Chapter 13)

■ Automatic coding on all structured questions

■ No keypunching

■ No hand tabulations

These are some of the reasons why you are likely to be reading more reports on CATI surveys in the future. It is important, therefore, that you understand the particular strengths and weaknesses of telephone surveys.

COMPARISON OF TWO SURVEY METHODS

We have now examined two methods of data collection appropriate for survey research. Although I touched on some of the relative advantages of each, it will be worth looking at this issue directly.

Self-administered questionnaires are generally cheaper and quicker than interview surveys. These considerations are likely to be important for an unfunded student wishing to undertake a survey in connection with a term paper or a thesis. Moreover, if you use the self-administered mail format, it costs no more to conduct a national survey than a local one; the cost difference between a local and a national interview survey would be enormous. Also, mail surveys typically require a small staff: one person can conduct a reasonably good mail survey alone, although you should not underestimate the work involved.

Self-administered surveys are also more appropriate in dealing with especially sensitive issues, if they offer complete anonymity. Respondents might be reluctant to report controversial or deviant attitudes or behavior in a face-to-face interview, but might be more willing to respond to an anonymous self-administered questionnaire.

Interview surveys have many advantages, also. For example, they generally produce fewer incomplete questionnaires. Although respondents may skip questions in a self-administered questionnaire, interviewers are trained not to do so. Interview surveys, moreover, typically achieve higher return rates than self-administered ones.

Although self-administered questionnaires may be more effective in dealing with sensitive issues, interview surveys are definitely more effective in dealing with complicated ones. Prime examples would be the enumeration of household members and the determination of whether a given household address contained more than one housing unit. Although the concept *housing unit* has been refined and standardized by the Bureau of the Census and interviewers can be trained to deal with the concept in the field, it would be extremely difficult to devise a self-administered questionnaire dealing with this issue that could be understood by respondents. This advantage of interview surveys pertains more generally to all complicated contingency questions.

With interviewers, it is possible to conduct a survey based on a sample of addresses. An interviewer can arrive at an assigned address, introduce the survey, and even—following instructions—choose the appropriate person at that address to respond to the survey. Self-administered mail questionnaires addressed to "occupant" receive a notoriously low response.

Finally, interviewers are able to make important observations aside from responses to questions asked in the interview. In a household interview, they may note the characteristics of the neighborhood, the dwelling unit, and so forth. They may also note characteristics of the respondents or of their interaction with the respondents, such as that a respondent had difficulty communicating or was hostile.

Ultimately, you must balance all these advantages and disadvantages of the two methods in relation to (1) your research needs and (2) your resources.

STRENGTHS AND WEAKNESSES OF SURVEY RESEARCH

Like other modes of observation in social scientific research, surveys have special strengths and weaknesses. It is important to know these in determining whether the survey format is appropriate to your research goals.

Surveys are particularly useful in describing the characteristics of a large population. A carefully selected probability sample in combination with a standardized questionnaire offers the possibility of making refined descriptive assertions about a student body, a city, a nation, or other large population. Surveys determine unemployment rates, voting intentions, and the like with uncanny accuracy. Although the examination of official documents—such as marriage, birth, or death records—can provide equal accuracy for a few topics, no other method of observation can provide this general capability.

Surveys—especially self-administered ones—make very large samples feasible. Surveys of 2,000 respondents are not unusual. A large number of cases is very important for both descriptive and explanatory analyses. Whenever several variables are to be analyzed simultaneously, it is essential to have a large number of cases.

In one sense, surveys are flexible. Many questions may be asked on a given topic, giving you considerable flexibility in your analyses. Although experimental design may require you to commit yourself in advance to a particular operational definition of a concept, surveys let you develop operational definitions from actual observations.

Finally, standardized questionnaires have an important strength in regard to measurement generally. Earlier chapters have discussed the ambiguous nature of most concepts: they have no ultimately *real* meanings. One person's religiosity is quite different from another's. Although you must be able to define concepts in ways most relevant to your research goals, you may not find it easy to apply the same definitions uniformly to all subjects. The survey researcher is bound to this requirement by having to ask exactly the same questions of all subjects and having to impute the same intent to all respondents giving a particular response.

Survey reseach has a number of weaknesses. First, the requirement for standardization just mentioned often seems to result in the fitting of round pegs into square holes. Standardized questionnaire items often represent the least common denominator in assessing people's attitudes, orientations, circumstances, and experiences. By designing questions that will be at least minimally appropriate to all respondents, you may miss what is most appropriate to many respondents. In this sense, surveys often appear superficial in their coverage of complex topics. Although this problem can be partly offset through sophisticated analyses, it is inherent in survey research.

Similarly, survey research can seldom deal with the *context* of social life. Although questionnaires can provide information in this area, the survey researcher can seldom develop the feel for the total life situation in which respondents are thinking and acting that, say, the participant observer can (see Chapter 10).

Although surveys are flexible in the sense mentioned earlier, they are inflexible in other ways. Studies involving direct observation can be modified as field conditions warrant, but surveys typically require that an initial study design remain unchanged throughout. As a field researcher, for example, you can become aware of an important new variable operating in the phenomenon you are studying and begin making careful observations of it. The survey researcher would likely be unaware of the new variable's importance and could do nothing about it in any event.

Finally, surveys are subject to the artificiality mentioned earlier in connection with experiments. Finding out that a person gives conservative answers to a questionnaire does not necessarily mean the person is conservative; finding out that a person gives prejudiced answers to a questionnaire does not necessarily mean that the person is prejudiced. This shortcoming is especially salient in the realm of action. Surveys cannot measure social action; they can only collect self-reports of recalled past action, or of prospective or hypothetical action. There are two aspects of this problem. First, the topic of study may not be amenable to measurement through questionnaires. Second, the act of studying that topic—an attitude, for example—may affect it. A survey respondent may have given no thought to whether the governor should be impeached until asked for his or her opinion by an interviewer. He or she may, at that point, form an opinion on the matter.

Survey research is generally weak on validity and strong on reliability. In comparison with field research, for example, the artificiality of the survey format puts a strain on validity. As an illustration, people's opinions on issues seldom take the form of strongly agreeing, agreeing, disagreeing, or strongly disagreeing with a specific statement. Their survey responses in such cases, then, must be regarded as approximate indicators of what we have in mind initially in framing the questions. This comment, however, needs to be held in the context of earlier discussions of the ambiguity of *validity* itself. To say something is a valid

or an invalid measure assumes the existence of a "real" definition of what is being measured, and many scholars now reject that assumption.

Reliability is a clearer matter. Survey research, by presenting all subjects with a standardized stimulus, goes a long way toward eliminating unreliability in observations made by the researcher. Moreover, careful wording of the questions can also reduce significantly the subject's own unreliability.

As with all methods of observation, a full awareness of the inherent or probable weaknesses of survey research can partially resolve them in some cases. Ultimately, though, you are on the safest ground when you can employ a number of different research methods in studying a given topic.

SECONDARY ANALYSIS

As a mode of observation, survey research involves the following steps: (1) questionnaire construction, (2) sample selection, and (3) data collection, through either interviewing or self-administered questionnaires. As you will have gathered, surveys are usually major undertakings. It is not unusual for a large-scale survey to take several months or even more than a year to progress from conceptualization to having data in hand. (Smaller-scale surveys can, of course, be done more quickly.) At the same time, however, it is possible for you to pursue your particular social research interests—analyzing survey data from, say, a national sample of 2,000 respondents—while avoiding the enormous expenditure of time and money such a survey entails. *Secondary analysis* makes such work possible.

With the development of computer-based analyses in social research, it has become easily possible for social researchers to *share* their data with one another. Suppose, for example, that I have obtained the money and time to conduct large-scale surveys on the topic of political socialization and the nature of political participation in five different nations. Perhaps I want to learn something about the various faces of democracy as a form of political organization in the United States, Germany, Mexico, England, and Italy. It has taken me a few years and a very large, international staff to design and execute such a set of surveys. Once the interviews are completed, I process the data (see Chapter 13) and analyze them, answering the research questions that led to the study in the first place.

Now suppose further that you have some research interests in the same general area as mine. You have questions you would have addressed had you been able to get the resources necessary for the five-nation survey I conducted. Unfortunately, you couldn't get the money to do such a survey. But here's what you *can* do. For very little money—and assuming my cooperation—you can get a copy of the punch cards or magnetic tape that contains all the data collected in my study. If I have collected the data appropriate to answering your research questions, you are off and running.

The hypothetical situation I've just described is not hypothetical at all. In the late 1950s and early 1960s, Gabriel Almond and Sidney Verba designed and executed the five-nation study I've been describing. They reported their research results in 1963 in a book called *The Civic Culture*. Once their own analyses were completed, the researchers made the data available to others for what is appropriately called *secondary analysis*. In the years that followed, the Almond-Verba data have probably become the most analyzed set of data in existence. Individual researchers have pursued particular research interests, and the data have also been used for teaching purposes in

research methods classes. Let me illustrate this use with a short personal example.

As a graduate student at Berkeley, I became interested in Charles Glock's notions about the causes of religious involvement (discussed in Chapter 2). In part, Glock had suggested that people who saw, and felt capable of achieving, secular solutions to social problems would seek those means. Those who did not see secular solutions would turn to the church. I wanted to test that notion, though I didn't have the resources necessary to conduct a large-scale survey. The Almond-Verba data, however, contained information about both religious and political activities—and about people's perceptions of political solutions to problems. As a result, I was able to examine whether people who did not see political solutions were more religiously involved than those who did see political solutions. Since the data set had been purchased for use in my research methods class, I was able to undertake my study at absolutely no cost to me.

Beginning in the 1960s, the potential for secondary analysis was developed on an international scale. A consortium of research centers collaborated with one another to form a network of *data archives*, each of which would collect and administer data sets from various parts of the United States and the world. Decks of punch cards and magnetic tapes were shelved the way books are shelved in a conventional library, and the holdings were available for broad circulation and use. Whereas library books are loaned, however, the data sets are reproduced and sold—you get to keep your copy and use it again and again for as long as you find new things to study.

The advantages of secondary analysis are obvious and enormous: cheaper and faster than doing original surveys, and depending on who did the original survey, you may benefit from the work of top-flight professionals. There are disadvantages, however.

The key problem involves the recurrent question of validity. When one researcher collects data for one particular purpose, you have no assurance that those data will be appropriate to *your* research interests. Typically, you'll find that the original researcher asked a question that "comes close" to measuring what you are interested in, but you'll wish the question had been asked just a little differently—or that another, related question had also been asked. Your question, then, is whether the question that *was* asked provides a valid measure of the variable you want to analyze.

Notice that this problem resembles closely one of the key problems in the analysis of existing statistics. Recall that Stouffer had to ask whether out-of-state marriages provided a valid measure of what he was calling, on theoretical grounds, impulsive marriages. As with existing statistics, this dilemma in secondary analysis can be lessened through replication. Perhaps a particular set of data do not provide a totally satisfactory measure of what interests you. But there are other sets of data available. Even if no one set of data provides totally valid measures, you can build up a weight of evidence by analyzing all the possibilities. If each of the imperfect measures points to the same research conclusion, you will have developed considerable support for its accuracy.

In this book, the discussion of secondary analysis has a special purpose. As we continue our examination of modes of observation in social research, you should have developed a full appreciation of the range of possibilities available to you in finding the answers to questions about social life. There is no single method of getting information that unlocks all puzzles. Yet there is no limit to the ways you can find out about things. And, more powerfully, you can zero in on an issue from several independent directions, gaining an even greater mastery of it.

MAIN POINTS

- Survey research, a popular social research method, is the administration of questionnaires to a sample of respondents selected from some population.

- Survey research is especially appropriate for making descriptive studies of large populations; survey data may be used for explanatory purposes as well.

- Contingency questions are those that should be answered only by those persons giving a particular response to some preceding question. The contingency question format is very useful in that it saves asking people to answer questions that have no meaning for them. For example, a question about the number of times a person has been pregnant should be asked only of women.

- Matrix questions are those in which a standardized set of closed-ended response categories are to be used in answering several questionnaire items. This format can facilitate the presentation and completion of items.

- Questionnaires may be administered in two basically different ways: self-administered questionnaires may be completed by the respondents themselves; interviewers may administer questionnaires, reading the items to respondents and recording the answers.

- It is generally advisable to plan follow-up mailings in the case of self-administered questionnaires: sending new questionnaires to those respondents who fail to respond to the initial appeal.

- A proper monitoring of questionnaire returns will provide a good guide as to when a follow-up mailing is appropriate.

- The essential characteristic of interviewers is that they be neutral; their presence in the data-collection process must not have any effect on the responses given to questionnaire items.

■ Interviewers must be carefully trained to be familiar with the questionnaire, to follow the question wording and question order exactly, and to record responses exactly as they are given.

■ A probe is a neutral, nondirective question designed to elicit an elaboration on an incomplete or ambiguous response, given in an interview in response to an open-ended question. Examples would include: "Anything else?" "How is that?" "In what ways?"

■ The advantages of a self-administered questionnaire over an interview survey are economy, speed, lack of interviewer bias, and the possibility of anonymity and privacy to encourage more candid responses on sensitive issues.

■ The advantages of an interview survey over a self-administered questionnaire are fewer incomplete questionnaires and fewer misunderstood questions, generally higher return rates, and greater flexibility in terms of sampling and special observations.

■ Survey research in general has advantages in terms of economy and the amount of data that can be collected. The standardization of the data collected represents another special strength of survey research.

■ Survey research has the weaknesses of being somewhat artificial and potentially superficial. It is difficult to gain a full sense of social processes in their natural settings through the use of surveys.

■ Secondary analysis refers to the analysis of data collected earlier by another researcher for some purpose other than the topic of the current study.

REVIEW QUESTIONS AND EXERCISES

1. Construct a set of contingency questions for use in a self-administered questionnaire that would solicit the following information:

a. Is the respondent employed?
b. If unemployed, is the respondent looking for work?
c. If the unemployed respondent is not looking for work, is he or she retired, a student, or a homemaker?
d. If the respondent is looking for work, how long has he or she been looking?

2. Find a questionnaire printed in a magazine or newspaper (for a reader survey, for example). Bring the questionnaire to class and critique it. Critique other aspects of the survey design.

ADDITIONAL READINGS

Babbie, Earl, *Survey Research Methods* (Belmont, Calif.: Wadsworth, 1973). A comprehensive overview of survey methods. (You thought I'd say it was lousy?) This textbook, although overlapping somewhat with the present one, covers aspects of survey techniques that are omitted here.

Dillman, Don A., *Mail and Telephone Surveys: The Total Design Method* (New York: John Wiley & Sons, 1978). An excellent review of the methodological literature on mail and telephone surveys. Dillman makes many good suggestions for improving response rates.

Glock, Charles (ed.), *Survey Research in the Social Sciences* (New York: Russell Sage Foundation, 1967). An excellent collection of essays on the use of survey methods in the several social sciences. This book is especially useful in illustrating the somewhat different ways in which different disciplines regard and utilize a given research method. The several chapters also provide extensive bibliographies, citing examples of survey projects.

Hyman, Herbert, *Secondary Analysis of Sample Surveys* (New York: John Wiley & Sons, 1972). A comprehensive overview of secondary analysis. Hyman examines the role of this method within the broader context of social scientific inquiry, discusses methods of secondary analysis, and provides many illustrations.

Rossi, Peter; Wright, James; and Anderson, Andy (eds.), *Handbook of Survey Research* (New York: Academic Press, 1983). A useful reference book on various aspects of survey design and execution.

Stouffer, Samuel, *Communism, Conformity, and Civil Liberties* (New York: John Wiley & Sons, 1955). An old but classic survey. This massive survey examined the impact of (Joe) McCarthyism on the attitudes of both the general public and community leaders, asking whether the repression of the early 1950s affected support for civil liberties.

Sudman, Seymour, and Bradburn, Norman, *Asking Questions* (San Francisco: Jossey-Bass, 1982). Practical suggestions and samples of use in designing questionnaires.

10

Field Research

What You'll Learn in This Chapter

You'll improve your ability to observe social life in its natural habitat: going where the action is and watching. You'll learn how to prepare for the field, how to observe, how to take notes, and how to analyze what you observe.

INTRODUCTION

Several chapters ago, I said that you had been doing social research all your life. That should become even clearer to you as we turn now to what probably seems like the most obvious method of making observations: field research. If you want to know about something, why not just go where it's happening and watch it happen? That's what this chapter is all about. I have used the term *field research* to include methods of research sometimes referred to as *participant observation, direct observation,* and *case studies.*

Most of the observation methods discussed in this book are designed to produce data appropriate for *quantitative* (statistical) analysis. Thus, surveys provide data from which to calculate the percentage unemployed in a population, mean incomes, and so forth. Field research more typically yields *qualitative* data: observations not easily reduced to numbers. Thus, for example, a field researcher may note the "paternalistic demeanor" of leaders at a political rally or the "defensive evasions" of a public official at a public hearing without being able to express either the paternalism or the defensiveness as numerical quantities or degrees.

Field research is at once very old and very new in social science. Many of the techniques to be discussed in this chapter have been used by social researchers for centuries. Within the social sciences, anthropologists are especially associated with this method and have contributed to its development as a scientific technique. It should be noted, moreover, that something similar to this method is employed by many people who might not, strictly speaking, be regarded as social science researchers. Newspaper reporters are one example; welfare department case workers are another.

It bears repeating that field research is constantly used in everyday life, by all of us. In a sense, we do field research whenever we observe or participate in social behavior and try to understand it, whether at a corner tavern, in a doctor's waiting room, on an airplane, or anywhere. Whenever we report our observations to others, we are reporting our field research efforts. The purpose of this chapter is to discuss this method in some detail, providing a logical overview of the method, and suggesting some of the specific skills and techniques that make scientific field research more useful than the casual observation we all engage in.

Field observation differs from some other models of observation in that it is not only a data-collecting activity. Frequently, perhaps typically, it is a theory-generating activity as well. As a field researcher you will seldom approach your task with precisely defined hypotheses to be tested. More typically, you will attempt to make sense out of an ongoing process that cannot be predicted in advance—making initial observations, developing tentative general conclusions that suggest particular types of further observations, making those observations and thereby revising your conclusions, and so forth. The alternation of induction and deduction discussed in Part 1 of this book is perhaps nowhere more evident and essential than in good field research.

TOPICS APPROPRIATE TO FIELD RESEARCH

One of the key strengths of field research is the comprehensiveness of perspective it gives the researcher. By going directly to the social phenomenon under study and observing it as completely as possible, you can develop a deeper and fuller understanding of it. This mode of observation, then, is especially, though not exclusively, appropriate to research topics and social studies that appear to defy simple quantification. The field researcher may recognize several nuances of attitude and behavior that might escape researchers using other methods.

Somewhat differently, field research is especially appropriate to the study of those topics for which attitudes and behaviors can best be understood within their natural setting. Experiments and surveys may be able to measure behaviors and attitudes in somewhat artificial settings, but not all behavior is best measured this way. For example, field research provides a superior method for studying the dynamics of religious conversion at a revival meeting.

Finally, field research is especially appropriate to the study of social processes over time. Thus, the field researcher might be in a position to examine the rumblings and final explosion of a riot as events actually occur rather than trying to reconstruct them afterward.

Other good uses of field research methods would include campus demonstrations, courtroom proceedings, labor negotiations, public hearings, or similar events taking place within a relatively limited area and time. Several such observations must be combined in a more comprehensive examination across time and space.

In his *Analyzing Social Settings* (1984: 71–92), John Lofland discusses several appropriate kinds of focuses for field research. He calls them *thinking units*.

1. *Meanings*. This includes linguistic devices such as culture, norms, world views, etc.

2. *Practices*. This refers to various kinds of behavior.

3. *Episodes*. Here Lofland includes a variety of events such as divorce, crime, and illness.

4. *Encounters*. This involves two or more people meeting and interacting in immediate proximity with one another.

5. *Roles*. Field research is also appropriate to the analysis of the positions people occupy and the behavior associated with those positions: occupations, family roles, ethnic groups.

6. *Relationships*. Much social life can be examined in terms of the kinds of behavior appropriate to pairs or sets of roles: mother-son relationships, friendships, and the like.

7. *Groups*. Moving beyond relationships, field research can also be used to study small groups, such as friendship cliques, athletic teams, work groups.

8. *Organizations*. Beyond small groups, field researchers also study formal organizations, such as corporations, schools, and so forth.

9. *Settlements*. Finally, while it is difficult to study large societies such as nations, field researchers often study smaller scale "societies" such as villages, ghettos, and neighborhoods.

In all these social settings, field research can reveal things that would not otherwise be apparent. Let me give you a concrete example.

Recently, I've become increasingly interested in the nature of responsibility for public matters: Who's responsible for making the things we share work? Who's responsible for keeping public spaces—parks, malls, buildings, and so on—clean? Who's responsible for seeing that broken street signs get fixed? Or, if a strong wind knocks over garbage cans and rolls them around the street, who's responsible for getting them out of the street? (See Babbie 1985.)

On the surface, the answer to these questions is pretty clear. We have formal and informal agreements in our society that assign responsibility for these activities. Government custodians are responsible for keeping public places clean. Transportation department employees are responsible for the street signs, and perhaps the police are responsible for the garbage cans rolling around the street on a windy day. And when these responsibilities are not fulfilled, we tend to look around for someone to blame.

What fascinates me is the extent to which the assignment of responsibility for public things to specific individuals not only relieves others of the responsibility but actually *prohibits* them from *taking* responsibility. It's my notion that it has become unacceptable for someone like you or me to take personal responsibility for public matters that haven't been assigned to us.

Let me illustrate what I mean. If you were walking through a public park and you threw down a bunch of trash, you'd discover that your action was unacceptable to those around you. People would glare at you, grumble to each other, and perhaps someone would say something to you about it. Whatever the form, you'd be subjected to definite, negative sanctions for littering. Now here's the irony. If you were walking through that same park, came across a bunch of trash that someone else had dropped, and cleaned it up, it's likely that your action would also be unacceptable to those around you. You'd probably be subjected to definite, negative sanctions for cleaning it up.

When I first began discussing this pattern with students, most felt the notion was absurd. Although we would be negatively sanctioned for littering, cleaning up a public place would obviously bring positive sanctions. People would be pleased with us for doing it. Certainly, all my students said *they* would be pleased if someone cleaned up a public place. It seemed likely that everyone else would be pleased, too, if we asked them how they would react to someone's cleaning up litter in a public place or otherwise taking personal responsibility for fixing some social problem.

To settle the issue, I suggested that my students start fixing the public problems they came across in the course of their everyday activities. As they did so, I asked them to note the answers to two questions:

1. How did they feel while they were fixing a public problem they had not been assigned responsibility for?

2. How did others around them react?

My students picked up litter, fixed street signs, put knocked-over traffic cones back in place, cleaned and decorated communal lounges in their dorms, trimmed trees that blocked visibility at intersections, repaired public playground equipment, cleaned public restrooms, and took care of a hundred other public problems that weren't "their responsibility."

Most reported feeling very uncomfortable doing whatever they did. They felt foolish, goody-goody, conspicuous, and all the other feelings that keep us from performing these activities normally. In almost every case, their personal feelings of discomfort were increased by the reactions of those around them. One student was removing a damaged and long-unused newspaper box from the bus stop where it had been a problem for months when the police arrived, having been summoned by a neighbor. Another student decided to clean out a clogged storm drain on his street and found himself being yelled at by a neighbor who insisted that the mess should be left for the street cleaners. Everyone who picked up litter was sneered at, laughed at, and generally put down. One young man was picking up litter scattered around a trash can when a passerby sneered, "Clumsy!" It became clear to us that there are only three acceptable explanations for picking up litter in a public place:

1. You did it and got caught—somebody forced you to clean up your mess.

2. You did it and got a guilty conscience.

3. You're stealing litter.

In the normal course of things, it is simply not acceptable for people to take responsibility for public things.

Clearly, we could not have discovered the nature and strength of agreements about taking personal responsibility for public things except by field research. Social norms suggest that taking responsibility is a good thing—sometimes referred to as *good citizenship*. Asking people what they thought about it would have produced a solid consensus that it was good. Only going out into life, doing it, and watching what happened gave an accurate picture.

As an interesting footnote to this story, we found that whenever people could get past their initial reactions and discover that the students were simply taking responsibility for fixing things for the sake of having them work, the tendency was for the passersby to assist. Although there are some very strong agreements making it "unsafe" to take responsibility for public things, the willingness of one person to rise above those agreements seemed to make it safe for others to do so, and they did.

In summary, then, field research offers the advantage of probing social life in its natural habitat. Although some things can be studied adequately in questionnaires or in the laboratory, others cannot. And direct observation in the field lets you observe subtle communications and other events that might not be anticipated or measured otherwise.

THE VARIOUS ROLES OF THE OBSERVER

The students who fixed public things were definitely *participating* in what they wanted

to observe. In this chapter, I have used the term *field research* rather than the frequently used term *participant observation*, since field researchers need not always participate in what they are studying, though they usually will study it directly at the scene of the action. Raymond Gold (1969:30–39) has discussed four different positions on a continuum of roles that field researchers may play in this regard: *complete participant, participant-as-observer, observer-as-participant,* and *complete observer*. Gold described the *complete participant* as follows:

The true identity and purpose of the complete participant in field research are not known to those whom he observes. He interacts with them as naturally as possible in whatever areas of their living interest him and are acceptable to him in situations in which he can play or learn to play requisite day-to-day roles successfully.

(1969:33)

The complete participant, in this sense, may be a genuine participant in what he or she is studying (for example, a participant in a campus demonstration) or may pretend to be a genuine participant. In any event, if you are acting as the complete participant you let people see you *only* as a participant, not a researcher.

Clearly, if you are not a genuine participant in that which you are studying, you must learn to behave as though you were. If you are studying a group made up of uneducated and inarticulate people, it would not be appropriate for you to talk and act like a university professor or student.

Here let me recall your attention to an ethical issue, one on which social researchers themselves are divided. Is it ethical to deceive the people you are studying in the hope that they will confide in you as they will not confide in an identified researcher? Do the interests of science—the scientific values of the research—offset such ethical considerations? Although many professional associations have addressed this issue, the norms to be followed remain somewhat ambiguous when applied to specific situations.

Related to this ethical consideration is a scientific one. No researcher deceives his or her subjects solely for the purpose of deception. Rather, it is done in the belief that the data will be more valid and reliable, that the subjects will be more natural and honest if they do not know that the researcher is doing a research project. If the people being studied know they are being studied, they might modify their behavior in a variety of ways. First, they might expel the researcher. Second, they might modify their speech and behavior so as to appear more respectable than would otherwise be the case. Third, the social process itself might be radically changed. Students making plans to burn down the university administration building, for example, might give up the plan altogether once they learn that one of their group is a social scientist conducting a research project.

On the other side of the coin, if you are a complete participant, you may affect what you are studying. To play the role of participant, you must *participate*. Yet, your participation may importantly affect the social process you are studying. Suppose, for example, that you are asked for your ideas as to what the group should do next. No matter what you say, you will affect the process in some fashion. If the group follows your suggestion, your influence on the process is obvious. If the group decides not to follow your suggestion, the process whereby the suggestion is rejected may importantly affect what happens next. Finally, if you indicate that you just don't know what should be done next, you may be adding to a general feeling of uncertainty and indecisiveness in the group.

Ultimately, *anything* that the participant observer does or does not do will have some effect on that which is being observed; it is simply inevitable. More seriously, what you do or do not do may have an *important* effect on what happens. There is no complete protection against this effect, though sensitivity to the issue may provide a partial protection. (This influence, called the Hawthorne effect, was discussed more fully in Chapter 8.)

Because of these several considerations, ethical and scientific, the field researcher frequently chooses a different role from that of complete participant. In Gold's terminology, you might choose the role of *participant-as-observer*. In this role, you would participate fully with the group under study, but you would make it clear that you were also undertaking research. There are dangers in this role also, however. The people being studied may shift much of their attention to the research project rather than focusing on the natural social process, and the process being observed may no longer be typical. Or, conversely, you yourself may come to identify too much with the interests and viewpoints of the participants. You may begin to "go native" and lose much of your scientific detachment.

The *observer-as-participant* is one who identifies himself or herself as a researcher and interacts with the participants in the social process but makes no pretense of actually being a participant. A good example of that would be a newspaper reporter who is learning about a social movement, for instance, the unionization of migrant farm workers. The reporter might interview leaders and also visit workers where they live, watch strawberry picking, go with an injured worker to the hospital, and so on.

The *complete observer*, at the other extreme, observes a social process without becoming a part of it in any way. Quite possibly, the subjects of study might not realize they are being studied because of the researcher's unobtrusiveness. Sitting at a bus stop to observe jaywalking behavior at a nearby intersection would be an example.

While the complete observer is less likely to affect that which is being studied and less likely to "go native" than the complete participant, he or she is also less likely to develop a full appreciation of what is being studied. Observations may be more sketchy and transitory.

Different situations require different roles for the researcher. Unfortunately, there are no clear guidelines for making this choice, and you must rely on your understanding of the situation and your own good judgment. In making your decision, however, you must be guided by both methodological and ethical considerations. Since these often conflict with one another, your decision will frequently be a difficult one, and you may find sometimes that your role limits your study.

PREPARING FOR THE FIELD

Suppose for the moment that you have decided to undertake field research on a campus political organization. Let's assume further that you are not a member of that group, that you do not know a great deal about it, and that you will identify yourself to the participants as a researcher. This section will discuss some of the ways in which you might prepare yourself before undertaking direct observation of the group.

As is true of all research methods, you would be well advised to begin with a search of the relevant literature, filling in your knowledge of the subject and learning what others have said about it. Since library research is discussed at length in Appendix A, I won't say anything further at this point.

In the next phase of your research, you may wish to make use of **informants.** You might wish to discuss the student political group with others who have already studied it, or with anyone else who is likely to be familiar with it. In particular, you might find it useful to discuss the group with one of its members. Perhaps you have a friend who is a member, or you can meet someone who is. This aspect of your preparation is likely to be more effective if your relationship with the informant extends beyond your research role. In dealing with members of the group as informants, you should take care that your initial discussions do not compromise or limit later aspects of your research. Realize that the impression you make on the member-informant, the role you establish for yourself, may carry over into your later effort. For example, creating the initial impression that you may be an undercover FBI agent is unlikely to facilitate later observations of the group.

You should also be wary about the information you get from informants. Although they may have more direct, personal knowledge of the subject under study than you, what they "know" is probably a mixture of fact and point of view. Members of the political group in our example are unlikely to give you completely unbiased information (nor would members of opposing political groups). Before making your first contact with the student group, then, you should be already quite familiar with it, and you should understand the general, theoretical context within which it exists.

There are a variety of ways in which to establish your initial contact with the people you plan to study. How you do it will depend, in part, on the role you intend to play. Especially if you are to take on the role of complete participant, you must find a way of developing an identity with the people to be studied. If you wish to study dishwashers in a restaurant, the most direct method would be to get a job as a dishwasher. In the case of the student political group, you might simply join the group.

Many of the social processes appropriate to field research are sufficiently open to make your contact with the people to be studied rather simple and straightforward. If you wish to observe a mass demonstration, just be there. If you wish to observe patterns in jaywalking, hang around busy streets.

Whenever you wish to make a more formal contact with the people and wish to identify yourself as a researcher, you must be able to establish a certain rapport with them. You might contact a participant with whom you feel comfortable and gain that person's assistance. If you are studying a formal group, you might approach the group leaders. Or you may find that one of your informants who has studied the group can introduce you.

In making a direct, formal contact with the people you want to study, you will be required to give them some explanation of the purpose of your study. Here again, you face an ethical dilemma. Telling them the complete purpose of your research might lose their cooperation altogether or importantly affect their behavior. On the other hand giving only what you believe would be an acceptable explanation may involve outright deception. Realize in all this that your decisions—in practice—may be largely determined by the purpose of your study, the nature of what you are studying, observations you wish to use, and other such factors.

Previous field research offers no fixed rule—methodological or ethical—to follow in this regard. Your appearance as a researcher, regardless of stated purpose, may result in a warm welcome from people who are flattered that a scientist finds them important enough to study. Or, it may result in your being totally ostracized or worse. (Do not, for example, burst into a meeting of an organized crime syndicate and announce that you are writing a term paper on organized crime.)

SAMPLING IN FIELD RESEARCH

Earlier chapters of this book discussed the logic and the more conventional techniques involved in probability sampling in social research. Although the general principles of representativeness in that context should be remembered in field research, controlled sampling techniques are normally inappropriate. This section will discuss the matter of sampling as it typically applies in field research.

To begin, the population and the units of analysis in the field research project may be somewhat ambiguous. In studying the campus political group mentioned above, are you interested in studying that group only, the members of the group, student political behavior in general, political behavior more generally, or what? If you are studying three juvenile gangs in a particular city, are the gangs your units of analysis, the individual juveniles, or the city? Are you interested only in describing the gangs, or does your interest extend to juvenile peer relations in general? It is important that you ask yourself what population you wish to make general assertions about when you are finished with your research. The answer to this question will not always be obvious to you, and it may change over the course of your research. A limited initial concern may be expanded later, as you conclude that certain of the phenomena that you are observing apply well beyond your specific subjects of study. Although this general issue may not be easy to resolve in practice, sensitivity to it should help clarify your goals and methods.

The concept of sampling in connection with field research is more complicated than for the kinds of research dealt with in the earlier chapters. Field researchers attempt to observe everything within their field of study; thus, in a sense, they do not sample at all. In reality, of course, it is impossible to observe everything. To the extent that field researchers observe only a portion of what happens, then, what they do observe is a de facto sample of all the possible observations that might have been made. If several people are shouting support for the speaker in a religious revival meeting, those shouts that the researcher hears and understands represent a sample of all such shouts. Or if a researcher observes acts of violence during a riot, the observed acts are a sample of all such acts of violence. You will seldom be able to select a controlled sample of such observations, but you should bear in mind the general principles of representativeness and interpret your observations accordingly.

Sometimes, however, you will be in a position to sample among possible observations. If you are studying the development of a student political organization over time, for example, you may choose to interview different members of that organization by listing all the members and then selecting a probability sample. This might not be the best method of sampling for your purposes, however. McCall and Simmons (1969) suggest three types of sampling methods that are specifically appropriate to field research: the *quota* sample, the *snowball* sample, and *deviant cases*.

To begin, if the group or social process under study has fairly clearly defined categories of participants, some kind of *quota sample* might be employed: persons representing all different participation categories should be studied. (Review Chapter 7 for a more detailed discussion of quota sampling as a general procedure.) In the study of a formal group, for example, you might wish to interview both leaders and nonleaders. In studying a student political organization, it might be useful to interview both radical and more moderate members of that group. In general, whenever representativeness is desired, you should use quota sampling and interview both men and women, young people and old people, and the like.

Second, McCall and Simmons mention the **snowball sample.** If you wish to learn the pattern of recruitment to a religious organization over time, you might begin by interviewing fairly recent converts, asking them who introduced them to the group. You might then interview the persons named,

asking them who introduced them to the group. You might then interview the persons named, asking, in part, who introduced *them*. In studying a loosely structured political group, you might ask one of the participants who he or she believes to be the most influential members of the group. You might interview those people and, in the course of the interviews, ask who *they* believe to be the most influential. In each of these examples, your sample would "snowball" as each of your interviewees suggested others.

Finally, McCall and Simmons draw attention to the importance of *deviant cases*. Often, our understanding of fairly regular patterns of attitudes and behaviors is further improved by examining those cases that do not fit into the regular pattern. You might gain important insights into the nature of school spirit as exhibited at a pep rally by interviewing people who did not appear to be caught up in the emotions of the crowd or by interviewing students who did not attend the rally at all.

Aside from sampling individuals for interviewing, there are other field research situations in which it may be possible to undertake a conscious sampling procedure. In a study of jaywalking, you might wish to make observations on a number of different city streets. You could pick the sample of locations through standard probability methods; or, more likely, you could employ a rough quota system, observing wide streets and narrow ones, busy streets and quiet ones, or including samples from different times of day, or of common types of pedestrians. In a study of the way in which people interact or fail to interact at a bus stop, you would observe different kinds of bus stops in various neighborhoods, for example.

In practice, controlled probability sampling is seldom employed in field research. If you consciously sample at all, you are most likely to use a **purposive sample.** Here, you select a sample of observations that you believe will yield the most comprehensive understanding of your subject of study, based on the intuitive feel for the subject that comes from extended observation and reflection. Nonetheless, understanding the principles and logic of more formal sampling methods is likely to produce more effective intuitive sampling in field research.

In field research, bear in mind two stages of sampling. First, to what extent are the total situations *available* for observation representative of the more *general class* of phenomena you wish to describe and explain? Are the three juvenile gangs you are observing representative of all gangs? Second, are your *actual* observations within those total situations representative of all the *possible* observations? Have you observed a representative sample of the members of the three gangs? Have you observed a representative sample of the interactions that have taken place? Even when controlled probability sampling methods are impossible or inappropriate, the logical link between representativeness and generalizability still holds.

ASKING QUESTIONS

In part, field research is a matter of going where the action is and simply watching and listening. You can learn a lot merely by being attentive to what's going on. At the same time, as I've already indicated, field research can involve more active inquiry. Sometimes it's appropriate to ask people questions and record their answers. Your on-the-spot observations of a full-blown riot will lack something if you don't know why people are rioting. Ask somebody.

We have already discussed interviewing in Chapter 9 on survey research. The interviewing that you will do in connection with field observation, however, is different enough to demand a separate treatment here. In surveys, questionnaires are always structured, while *unstructured* interviews are usually more appropriate to field research.

An unstructured interview is an interaction between an interviewer and a respondent in which the interviewer has a general plan of inquiry but not a specific set of questions that must be asked in particular words and in a particular order. An unstructured interview is essentially a conversation in which the interviewer establishes a general direction for the conversation and pursues specific topics raised by the respondent. Ideally, the respondent does most of the talking.

Asking questions and noting answers is a natural process for us all, and it seems simple enough to add that to your bag of tricks as a field researcher. Be a little cautious, however. There is a danger that, to paraphrase comedian Flip Wilson, "what you ask is what you get." As I've already discussed in Chapter 6, question wording is a tricky business. All too often, the way we ask questions subtly biases the answers we get. Sometimes we put our respondent under pressure to look good. Sometimes we put the question in a particular context that omits altogether the most relevant answers.

Pursuing the above example of student political action, suppose you want to find out why a group of students is rioting and pillaging on campus. You might be tempted to focus your questioning on how students feel about the dean's recent ruling that requires students always to carry *The Practice of Social Research* with them on campus. (Makes sense to me.) Although you may collect a great deal of information about students' attitudes toward the infamous ruling, they may be rioting for some other reason. Or perhaps most are simply joining in for the excitement. Properly done, field research interviewing would enable you to find out.

Although you may set out to conduct interviews with a pretty clear idea of what you want to ask, one of the special strengths of field research is its flexibility in the field. The answers evoked by your initial questions should shape your subsequent ones. It doesn't work, in this situation, merely to ask preestablished questions and record the answers. You need to ask a question, hear the answer, interpret its meaning for your general inquiry, frame another question either to dig into the earlier answer in more depth or to redirect the person's attention to an area more relevant to your inquiry. In short, you need to be able to listen, think, and talk almost at the same time.

The discussion of *probes* in Chapter 9 provides a useful guide to getting answers in more depth without biasing later answers. Learn the skills of being a good listener. Be more interested than interesting. Learn to say things like "How is that?" "In what ways?" "How do you mean that?" "What would be an example of that?" Learn to look and listen expectantly, and let the person you are interviewing fill in the silence.

At the same time, you can't afford to be a totally passive receiver in the interaction. You'll go into your interviews with some general (or specific) questions you want answered, some topics you want addressed, and you will have to learn the skills of subtly directing the flow of conversation.

There's something you can learn here from the Far Eastern martial arts. The aikido master never resists an opponent's blow but rather accepts it, joins with it, and then subtly redirects it in a more appropriate direction. You should master a similar skill for interviewing. Don't try to halt your respondent's line of discussion, but learn to take what he or she has just said and branch that comment back in the direction appropriate to your purposes. Most people love to talk to anyone who's really interested. Stopping their line of conversation tells them you aren't interested; asking them to elaborate in a particular direction tells them you are. Consider this hypothetical example in which you are interested in why college students chose their majors.

YOU: What are you majoring in?

RESP: Engineering.

YOU: I see. How did you come to choose engineering?

RESP: I have an uncle who was voted the best engineer in Arizona in 1981.

YOU: Gee, that's great.

RESP: Yeah. He was the engineer in charge of developing the new civic center in Tucson. It was written up in most of the engineering journals.

YOU: I see. Did you talk to him about *your* becoming an engineer?

RESP: Yeah. He said that he got into engineering by accident. He needed a job when he graduated from high school, so he went to work as a laborer on a construction job. He spent eight years working his way up from the bottom, until he decided to go to college and come back nearer the top.

YOU: So is your main interest in civil engineering, like your uncle, or are you more interested in some other branch of engineering?

RESP: Actually, I'm leaning more toward electrical engineering—computers, in particular. I started messing around with microcomputers when I was in high school, and my long-term plan is . . .

Notice how the interview first begins to wander off into a story about the respondent's uncle. The first attempt to focus things back on the student's own choice of major failed. The second attempt succeeded. Now the student is providing the kind of information you're looking for. It's important for you to develop the ability to "control" conversations in that fashion.

Since field research interviewing is so much like normal conversations, it is essential that you keep reminding yourself that you are *not* having a normal conversation. In normal conversations, each of us wants to come across as an interesting, worthwhile person. If you'll watch yourself the next time you are chatting with someone you don't know too well, I think you'll find that much of your attention is spent on thinking up interesting things to *say*—contributions to the conversation that will make a good impression. Often, we don't really hear each other, because we're too busy thinking of what we'll say next. As an interviewer, the desire to appear interesting is counter-productive to your job. You need to make the *other* person seem interesting, by being interested. (Do this, by the way, and people will actually regard you as a great conversationalist.)

Interviewing needs to be an integral part of your whole field research process. Later, I stress the need to review your notes every night—making sense out of what you've observed, getting a clearer feel for the situation you're studying, and finding out what you should pay more attention to in further observations. In this same fashion, you need to review your notes on interviews, detecting all those things you should have asked but didn't. Start asking those things when you next interview people.

As with all other aspects of field research, interviewing improves with practice. Fortunately, it is something you can practice any time you want. Practice on your friends.

RECORDING OBSERVATIONS

Finally, the basic tools of field research are the notebook—or *field journal*—and a pencil. Even tape recorders and cameras cannot capture all the relevant aspects of social processes. The greatest advantage of the field research method is the presence of an observing, thinking researcher on the scene of the action. If possible, you should take notes on your observations *as you observe*. When that is not possible, you should write down your notes as soon as possible afterward.

Your notes should include both your empirical observations and your interpretations of them. You should record what you "know" has happened and what you "think" has happened. It is important, however, that these different kinds of notes be identified for what they are. For example, you might note that Person X spoke out in opposition to a proposal made by a group leader, that you *think* this represents an attempt by Person X to take over leadership of the group, and you *think* you heard the leader comment to that effect in response to the opposition.

Just as you cannot hope to observe everything, neither can you record everything that you do observe. Just as your observations represent a de facto sample of all possible observations, so do your notes represent a sample of your observations. Rather than recording a random sample of your observations, you should, of course, record the most important ones.

Some of the most important observations can be anticipated before beginning the study; others will become apparent as your observations progress. Sometimes your note taking can be made easier if you prepare standardized recording forms in advance. In a study of jaywalking, for example, you might anticipate the characteristics of pedestrians that are the most likely to be useful for analysis—age, sex, social class, ethnicity, and so forth—and prepare a form in which actual observations can be recorded easily. Or, you might develop a symbolic shorthand in advance to speed up recording. For studying audience participation at a mass meeting, you might want to construct a numbered grid representing the different sections of the meeting room; then you would be able to record the location of participants easily, quickly, and accurately.

None of this advance preparation should limit your recording of unanticipated events and aspects of the situation. Quite the contrary, speedy handling of anticipated observations can give you more freedom to observe the unanticipated.

I know that you are familiar with the process of taking notes. Every student is. And as I've said earlier, everybody is somewhat familiar with field research in general. Like *good* field research, however, *good* note taking requires more careful and deliberate attention, and involves some specific skills. I'll provide some guidelines below, and you can learn more about this in John Lofland's *Analyzing Social Settings* (1984:62–68), which was mentioned earlier in the chapter.

First, don't trust your memory any more than you have to; it's untrustworthy. If I'm being too unkind to your mind, try this experiment. Recall the last few movies you saw that you really liked. Now, name five of the actors or actresses. Which had the longest hair? Which was the most likely to start conversations? Which was the most likely to make suggestions that others followed? ("Quick! Bring the wagons into a circle!") Now, if you didn't have any trouble answering any of those questions (and think you outsmarted me), how *sure* are you of your answers? Would you be willing to bet a hundred dollars that a panel of impartial judges would observe what you recall? If you are absolutely certain of your answers, then what color shoes was your methods instructor wearing three class meetings ago? Gotcha!

Even if you pride yourself on having a photographic memory, it's a good idea to take notes either during the observation or as soon afterward as possible. If you are taking notes during observation, do it unobtrusively, since people are likely to behave differently if they see you taking down everything they say or do.

Second, it's usually a good idea to take notes in stages. In the first stage, you may need to take sketchy notes (words and phrases) in order to keep abreast of what's happening. Then get off by yourself and rewrite your notes in more detail. If you do this soon after the events you've observed, the sketchy notes should allow you to recall most of the details. The longer you delay, the less likely it is that you'll recall things accurately and fully.

I know this method sounds logical, and you've probably made a mental resolve to do it that way if you're ever involved in field research. Let me warn you, however, that you'll need some self-discipline to keep your resolution in practice. Careful observation and note taking can be tiring, especially if it involves excitement or tension and if it extends over a long period of time. If you've just spent eight hours straight observing and making notes on how people have been coping with a disastrous flood, your first thought afterward is likely to be directed toward getting some sleep, dry clothes, or a drink. You may need to take some inspiration from newspaper reporters who undergo the same sorts of hardships, then write their stories, and meet their deadlines.

Third, you will inevitably wonder *how much* you should record. Is it really worth the effort to write out all the details you can recall right after the observation session? The general guideline here is *yes*. Generally, in field research you can't be really sure of what's important and what's unimportant until you've had a chance to review and analyze a great volume of information, so you should even record things that don't seem important at the outset. They may turn out to be significant after all. Also, the act of recording the details of something "unimportant" may jog your memory on something that *is* important.

You should realize that *most* of your field notes will not be reflected in your final report on the project. Put more harshly, most of the notes you take will be "wasted." But take heart: even the richest gold ore yields only about 30 grams of gold per metric ton, meaning that 99.997 percent of the ore is wasted. Yet, that 30 grams of gold can be hammered out to cover an area 18 feet square—the equivalent of about 685 book pages. So take a ton of notes and plan to select and use only the gold.

Like other aspects of field research (and all research for that matter), proficiency comes with practice. The nice thing about field research is that you can begin practicing now and can continue practicing in almost any situation. You don't have to be engaged in an organized research project to practice observation and recording. You might start by volunteering to take the minutes at committee meetings, for example.

DATA PROCESSING

The preceding section of this chapter dealt with the ways you, as a field researcher, would make observations and record them. Now, we're going to look at what you might do with those recorded observations afterward. In large part, this discussion will focus on the process of *filing* and organizing. I'll give you a brief overview of the process, but you'd do well to study some of the specific techniques field researchers have developed also before actually undertaking a project. Again, an excellent source of nitty-gritty, detailed suggestions is John Lofland's *Analyzing Social Settings* (1984:131–37).

Rewriting Your Notes

Hot on the trail of some social phenomenon, you are likely to end a day of observations with a mass of scribbled notes in your notebook, on the backs of envelopes, or on wine-stained cocktail napkins. Depending on how late in the day or night you complete your observations, you may be tempted to set the notes aside and sleep on them. Don't. Field researchers can't work on a 9 to 5 schedule, and it is vital that you rewrite your notes as soon as possible after making a set of observations.

It's far better to type up your full notes than to write them longhand. They'll be more legible, and as your typing improves it will be faster than longhand. Use your notes as a stimulus to recreate as many details of the day's experiences as possible. Your goal should be to produce typed notes as comprehensive and detailed as you would have taken in the first place if it had been possible to record everything that seemed potentially relevant. If you regard your scribbled on-the-spot notes as a trigger for your memory, then you'll see the importance of retyping each night and you'll have a clear sense of how to proceed.

Also, you should make at least two copies of your notes, whether carbons, photocopies, or dittos. When you analyze your data and prepare your report, you will need to be able to cut and paste without losing information. With at least two copies, you can cut up one and have the other as a backup. (If you have access to a word processor for computer editing, by the way, that's better yet. You'll be able to duplicate files, create combinations, and move them around with ease. In my remaining comments, however, I'll assume you'll be using a typewriter and paper.) Let's see next how you will use the multiple copies of your typed notes.

Creating Files

Your typed notes will probably represent a more or less chronological record of your observations in the project, and you should be sure to include notations of the dates and times you made them. You should keep one complete set of notes in this form. It will serve as a master file that you can fall back on to establish the chronological order of events later on and to get more copies of certain notes if you need them. You don't need to store your master file in a bank safe-deposit box (unless you're studying organized crime), but you should take care of it.

The copies of your typed notes are for cutting up, underlining, scribbling on, circling, and filing. So far in this chapter, we have focused on making observations. A mass of raw observations, however, doesn't tell us much of general value about social life. Ultimately, you must analyze and interpret your observations, discerning *patterns* of behavior, finding the underlying *meaning* in the things you observed. The organization and filing of your notes is the first step in discovering that meaning.

Files can be organized in endless ways, so what I'll do here is suggest some possibilities you might otherwise overlook. As you undertake your own research project, however, you'll find that deciding what files to create is a part of your analysis of the data.

As a start, you should create some background files. If you are studying a social movement, for example, it would be useful to have a separate file on its history. You'll probably begin the file with notes from your initial reading about the movement: When and where did it begin? How many people were in it initially? What have been the major events in the history of the movement? What were the dates? Although you'll probably begin this file before making observations in the field, you should plan to add to it over the course of your study, since you'll be continually learning more about the history of your subject.

You'll probably want to create a biographical file, too. Who are the key figures in the movement? You may want to have separate files for the most important figures. In any event, you should keep all the information on a particular individual together. That will allow you to get a fuller sense of the person, and it may also help you to understand the links between diverse events.

Lest you forget, you should also create a bibliographical file to keep track of all the things you will have read in the course of your study. When you write your report, you will want to make references to what other people have written, and it will be both wasteful and frustrating if you have to return continually to the library to relocate sources.

The creation of background files represents a pretty straightforward housekeeping function, but the creation of *analytical* files depends more on the nature of what you are studying and what you "see" in what you observe. As you begin to develop a sense of the different aspects of what you're observing, you'll want to establish files to deal with those different aspects.

Suppose, for example, that you begin to sense that the political movement you're studying has a religious or quasi-religious significance for the people participating in it. You'll want to establish a file for data relating to that aspect. You might do that as follows. Write "Religious Significance" on a manila file folder. Every time you find an entry in your notes that's relevant to the religious aspect of the movement—perhaps a participant will tell you that the movement has provided a new meaning to life—you should cut out that entry (recall the multiple copies?) and stick it in the file folder.

Perhaps one of your interests in the political movement concerns the varying degrees of violence considered, proposed, or engaged in by movement members. Sometimes they seem peaceful and willing to compromise; at other times they are more oriented toward hard-line aggression. Perhaps you will want to explain why those differences occur. Create a file on "Degrees of Violence" and clip and file all entries from your notes that are relevant.

I could continue endlessly with illustrations of the kinds of analytical files you might want to create, but I think you've gotten a sense of what's involved. I can't give you a blueprint of what files will be appropriate in your project—you get to do that. I should add, however, that the creation of analytical files is a continuous process. Do not create a filing system at the beginning of the project and stick doggedly to it throughout. Stay flexible and keep modifying the system as new topics appear to be relevant.

The flexibility of your filing system suggests another important step in the data processing of field research notes and other materials. As you modify your view of how best to organize your files, you should frequently review the materials already filed to see if certain notes should be moved to a newly created file. Sometimes, it will work to merely *cross-reference* your notes. You can jot a note to yourself indicating that the notes on X in File A are also relevant to the topic in File G. Stick the jotted note in File G.

As I've indicated, the creation and use of analytical files is part and parcel of the interpretation of your data. Let's turn now to that topic specifically.

DATA ANALYSIS

Throughout the previous discussions, I have omitted a direct discussion of the most critical aspects of field research: how you determine what is important to observe, and how you formulate your analytical conclusions on the basis of those observations. I have indicated that observations and analysis are interwoven processes in field research. Now it is time to say something about that interweaving.

As perhaps the most general guide, you look especially for *similarities* and *dissimilarities*. (That just about covers everything you are likely to see.) On the one hand, you look for those patterns of interaction and events that are generally common to what you are studying. In sociological terms, you look for *norms* of behavior. What behavior patterns do all the participants in a situation share? Do all jaywalkers check for police officers before darting across the street? Do all the participants in a campus political rally join in the same forms of supportive behavior during speeches? Do all the participants in a religious revival meeting shout "amen" at the appropriate times? Do all prostitutes dress seductively? In this sense, then, the field researcher is especially attuned to the discovery of *universals*. As you first notice these, you become more deliberate in observing whether they are truly universal in the situation you are observing. If they are essentially universal, you ask why that should be the case. What function do they serve, for example? This explanation may suggest conditions under which the "universals" would not appear, and you may look around for those conditions in order to test your expectations.

On the other hand, the field researcher is constantly alert to *differences*. You should be on the watch for deviation from the general norms you may have noted. Although most of the participants in a religious revival meeting murmur "amen" throughout the leader's sermon, you may note a few who do not. Why do they deviate from the norm? In what other ways are they different from the other participants?

Sometimes you will find aspects of behavior for which there is no easily identifiable norm. How do different people handle the problem of standing in a line for tickets at a movie theatre? Some stare into space, some strike up conversations with strangers, some talk to themselves, some keep standing on tiptoes to see if the line is really moving, some keep counting their money, some read, and so forth. An important part of a field researcher's initial task in such situations is to create a classification of behaviors: an organized list of the variety of types. Having done that, you then seek to discover other characteristics associated with those different types of behavior. Are the "rich-looking" or "poor-looking" moviegoers more likely to recount their money? Do men strike up more conversations with strangers than women? Do old people talk to themselves more than young people? Your purpose is to discover general patterns.

To the field researcher, the formulation of theoretical propositions, the observation of empirical events, and the evaluation of theory are typically all part of the same ongoing process. While your actual field observations may be preceded by deductive theoretical formulas, you seldom if ever merely test a theory and let it go at that. Rather, you develop theories, or generalized understandings, over the course of your observations. You ask what each new set of empirical observations represents in terms of general social scientific principles. Your tentative conclusions, so arrived at, then provide the conceptual framework for further observations. In the course of your observations of jaywalking, for example, it may strike you that whenever a well-dressed and important-looking person jaywalks, others are encouraged to follow suit. Having noticed this apparent pattern, you might pay more attention to this aspect of the phenomenon, thereby testing more carefully your initial impression. You might later observe that your initial impression held true only when the jaywalking "leader" was also middle-aged, for example, or perhaps only when he or she was Caucasian. These more specific impressions would simultaneously lead you to pay special attention to the new variables and require that you consider what general principle might be underlying the new observations.

An inherent advantage of field research is that interaction between data collection and data analysis affords a greater flexibility than is typical for other research methods. Survey researchers, for example, must at some point commit themselves to a questionnaire, thus limiting the kind of data that will be collected. If subsequent analyses indicate that they have overlooked the most important variable of all, they are out of luck. The field researcher, on the other hand, can continually modify the research design as indicated by the observations, the developing theoretical perspective, or changes in what he or she is studying.

This advantage in field research comes at the price of an accompanying danger. As you develop theoretical understanding of what you are observing, there is a constant risk that you will observe only those things that support your theoretical conclusions. You'll recall that this problem has already been discussed in connection with selective perception.

This danger may be at least partially avoided in a number of ways. First, you can augment your qualitative observations with quantitative ones. If you expect religious proselytization to be greater under some conditions than others, you might formulate a concrete operational definition of proselytization and begin counting under the different conditions. For example, you might note the number of group members who raised this topic, the number of members assigned to the task, or perhaps the number of new converts added to the group. Even rough quantifications such as these might provide a safeguard against selective perception and misinterpretation.

Second, we should recall that one of the norms of science is its *intersubjectivity*. As a field researcher, then, you might enlist the assistance of others as you begin to refine your theoretical conclusions. In the case of religious conversion, for example, you might ask colleagues to attend several meetings of the group over time and indicate their observations about the relative stress placed on proselytization in each of the meetings.

Finally, as with all such problems, sensitivity and awareness may provide sufficient safeguards. Merely by being aware of the problem, you may be able to avoid it.

This last comment points to a more general aspect of field research analysis. *Introspection*—examining your own thoughts and feelings—is a natural and crucial process for understanding what you observe. Since you will have been observing social life close up and all its details, you should be able to put yourself in the place of those you are studying—George Herbert Mead called this "taking the role of the other"—and ask yourself how you would have felt and behaved. Can you imagine yourself acting the way the person you observed acted? Why do you suppose you would have done that?

Introspection, then, can protect against many of the pitfalls of inquiry. And, when leavened with some role taking, it can give you insights into what you see going on around you.

In all social science research methods, there is a large gap between understanding the skills of data analysis and actually using those skills effectively. Typically, experience is the only effective bridge across the gap. This situation applies more to field research than to any other method. It is worth recalling the parallel between the activities of the scientist and those of the investigative detective. While fledgling detectives can be taught the technical skills and can be given general guidelines, insight and experience separate good detectives from mediocre ones. The same is true of field researchers.

To assist you further in logical reasoning in your analysis of field research (and other) data, the next section contains a brief examination of some errors people com-

monly make in logic. I trust these examples will help steer you away from such mistakes and alert you to such mistakes in the reasoning of others.

DRAWING CONCLUSIONS: SOME LOGICAL PITFALLS

While no one can give you a neat set of logical rules for analyzing qualitative data, I want to draw your attention to an excellent book—Howard Kahane's *Logic and Contemporary Rhetoric* (1980)—which outlines many of the errors people commonly make. Here are some of the pitfalls Kahane discusses.

Provincialism All of us look at the world through glasses framed by our particular histories and current situations. There is always a danger, then, that the field researcher—or any researcher for that matter—will interpret people's behavior so that it makes sense from the researcher's own point of view. For example, a Christian researcher may see things in Christian terms, a socialist within socialist terms, and so forth. This problem is particularly evident in cross-cultural research.

Hasty Conclusion Researchers as well as other people are susceptible to this error. Whenever the researcher offers an interpretation of data, be sure to evaluate the "weight" of evidence leading to that interpretation. Is the conclusion essentially inevitable given the data lying behind it, or are other conclusions just as reasonable?

Questionable Cause Whenever it seems to you that X caused Y, ask yourself if that is necessarily the case. What else could have caused Y? Kahane (1980:63) gives several economic examples. If a business goes

Are Black Children Undernourished?

Here's an example of faulty reasoning to help you refine your analytical skills. In the midst of national concern over the persistence of hunger in America, President Reagan appointed a 13-member Task Force on Food Assistance to determine the nature and extent of the problem and to recommend government action. One of the panel's members, Dr. George Graham, attracted considerable attention by indicating his belief that the problem of malnutrition among children had been exaggerated—especially with regard to black children. He was quoted as stating his view thusly:

"National data show that black children are now taller than white children—obviously, they must be getting more to eat," he said yesterday, echoing comments he made Wednesday. "If you think that blacks as a group are undernourished, look around at the black athletes on television—they're a pretty hefty bunch."

As you can see, Dr. Graham cites two pieces of evidence—one statistical, one impressionistic—to support his thesis that black Americans are no more likely to suffer malnutrition than other Americans. Are you convinced by his arguments? If not, how would you respond? Think about it, and then continue reading.

First, Graham says black children are taller, on the average, than white children. But does this mean "they must be getting more to eat"? What other factors might affect height? If you said "genetics," you can go to the head of the class. Racial and ethnic groups differ in average height. Consider the African Watusi tribesmen, for example. These poor cattle-herders of Burundi and Rwanda are noted for their spectacular height, commonly over seven feet tall. It would be absurd to conclude that they must eat more than Americans.

Second, how about the black athletes on television? Does their heftiness mean that black Americans as a whole must be getting a lot to eat? In this instance, you might have asked whether the black athletes are typical of all black Americans. Of course not. They are no more typical of blacks in general than white athletes are typical of all white Americans. Otherwise, we would need to look at Japanese Sumo wrestlers and conclude that the Japanese people in general must be bigger and better fed than Americans.

Source: "Big Changes Made in Hunger Report," *San Francisco Chronicle*, 30 December 1983, p. 10.

bankrupt, people often conclude that the company's president lacked business skills—even when the bankruptcy occurred during a severe recession, marked by a great many business failures.

Suppressed Evidence   Field researchers, as you've undoubtedly gathered, amass a great deal of information through direct observations, interviews, library work, etc. To reach conclusions requires dismissing information as much as selecting it. On the whole, the researcher will dismiss information that is "not relevant," but that is obviously a matter of judgment.

In particular, take note of observations you've noted that do not figure in the conclusions, as well as observations not mentioned that you can reasonably assume were made. If a researcher concludes that members of a neo-nazi group opposed blacks out of a fear of economic competition, for example, we would expect that most members were working class or lower middle class. But if the researcher has not indicated the occupations of the members, you might well wonder about the conclusion.

False Dilemma Research conclusions, like nonscientific opinions, often represent the selection of one position from among alternatives. Selecting one often seems to rule out all others, but this need not be the case. Kahane offers this example: "Economics, not biology, may explain male domination." This bold assertion seems to rule out the influence of politics, education, custom, religion, and a host of other possibilities.

This statement suggests that there are just two possibilities: either biology explains male dominance, or economic success does so. And it suggests that the second possibility, economic success, "may" (weasel word) be the true explanation of male domination. Yet there are many other possibilities, such as social custom, religious conviction, and various *combinations* of economic and biological factors. By tempting us to think of the cause of male domination as either economics or biology, the quote leads us to overlook other possibilities and thus to commit the fallacy of *false dilemma*.

(1980:81)

Be wary of this pitfall in reading the works of others, but also be wary of falling into it yourself.

I suspect these few examples of logical pitfalls will have sharpened your critical

faculties somewhat, and I encourage you to read Kahane's book for more guidance and insights. As with observation, note taking, filing, and the other skills of field research, your ability to reason logically will also improve with practice.

ILLUSTRATIONS OF FIELD RESEARCH

Before concluding this chapter on field research, let's examine two illustrations of the method in action. I hope these two descriptions will give you a clearer sense of how you might use field research in your own examination of social life.

Studying the Satanists

As a part of a broad-based study of the "new religious consciousness," sociology graduate student Randy Alfred (1976) was given the task of studying and reporting on the Church of Satan. Pronouncing itself in league with Satan and opposed to Christ, the church is headquartered in San Francisco and operates under the charismatic leadership of Anton LaVey. You can probably imagine how you'd handle an assignment to study the local Methodist or Episcopalian congregation, but how would you go about studying the Satanists? Here's what Alfred did:

I approached the group in April 1968 as an outsider and indicated an immediate interest in joining. My feigned conversion to Satanism was accepted as genuine and I made rapid progress in the group, as measured by my advancement in ritual rank, my being given administrative as well as magical responsibilities, and my appointment to the "ruling" body of the church.

From April 1968 to August 1969 I attended fifty-two of the group's weekly rituals, participating in all but eight of these early on. I was also present at twelve meetings of the ruling council, at twelve classes on various aspects of Satanism, and at six parties.

(1976:183–84)

Alfred studied the church until 1973, having some one hundred contacts with members, lasting a total of perhaps 600 hours and resulting in about as many pages of notes. In addition, he read books and articles about the group, including publications of the church itself. Right up to the end, he played the role of complete participant, concealing his research identity from those he was studying.

Alfred's total immersion in church life gave him insights into the nature of Satanism that would have been hard to gain from the outside. He was able to discover and distinguish many different motivations that led people to the group. Some were attracted by the prospect of sexual indulgence, others by the powers they might gain from magic, and others seemed primarily intent on rebelling against conventional religiosity and conventionality even more generally. Still others saw Satanism as a wave of the future, a new millennium.

Through his *participation* in the church —he ultimately became the official church historian—Alfred was able to learn details of rituals and other practices that would have been kept secret from outsiders. He observed LaVey and other church leaders close up and studied the dynamics of interpersonal relations in the church. There simply would have been no other way of gaining such information.

In reading Alfred's report, you also have the sense that many of his analytical insights would have escaped an outsider. For example, the popular view of Satanism is one of total self-indulgence. Freed from all conventional social norms, Satanists would be expected to be completely hedonistic, indulging their every urge and desire. That is not what Alfred observed, however. In the case of sex, for example, Satanists limit sexual indulgence to acts that don't hurt others against their will. LaVey further distinguishes between indulgence freely chosen and compulsive acts. Satanists should be free to indulge their desires, but they should not be run by those desires. By the same token, Satanists have a negative view of drug use. Even more unexpectedly, perhaps, LaVey strongly urges his followers to work hard at their jobs and succeed.

As a closing note, Alfred reported that he eventually found himself regretting the initial decision to conceal his research identity—he felt increasingly unethical. After all, he had been admitted to the inner circles of the church and been given a position of trust and responsibility. As he approached the final stages of wrapping up and reporting the project, he went to LaVey to tell him the truth and to request permission to publish an article about what he had learned. LaVey indicated that he had suspected all along that Alfred was doing research. Did he feel Alfred had been unethical in attempting deception? Not at all: it was an appropriately satanic thing to do!

Life in the Streets

Elliot Liebow's modern classic study *Tally's Corner* (1967) differs from Alfred's study in many ways. There is an initial similarity, however. Like Alfred, Liebow was assigned to his task as part of a larger research project. In this instance, Liebow, an anthropology graduate student, was hired to work on an ongoing study of childrearing practices among low-income families in the District of Columbia. Liebow's task was to do field work among low-income adult males to fill out the picture created by numerous interviews with families.

Liebow prepared for the field work through a series of meetings with the project staff, learning the kinds of materials that were needed. He read the reports already written on the project. Then, one day,

having partially digested the project literature, I told the director that I was ready to get started. He suggested a neighborhood that might be "a good place to get your feet wet." His instructions were: "Get out there and make like an anthropologist."

(1967:245)

Arriving in the suggested neighborhood, Liebow discovered a white police detective scuffling with an angry black woman. Approaching two black male onlookers, Liebow asked them what happened. They answered cautiously. The conversation continued, warming somewhat as each expressed negative feelings about the police. Eventually convinced that Liebow was not himself a policeman, one of the men spent the next several hours talking to him over coffee.

Unlike Alfred, Liebow revealed his identity as a researcher and the purpose of his research from the start. Though recognized as an "outsider," he was accepted as a friend, and he became more and more a part of the street corner life as the research progressed. Like Alfred, Liebow soon found himself deeply involved in the lives of his subjects. He reports:

I went to three different jails during this time, sat through one murder trial and two hearings in judges' chambers, testifying at one of them. I went to bondsmen's offices, to the United Employment Services, to the Blessed Martin de Porres Hostel (for homeless men) and into several private homes.

(1967:245)

Whenever his new friends ran afoul of the law, Liebow's legal advice was sought and respected. He reports that he stayed in close touch with the project director about this participation, weighing the consequences of his actions for his research. There was certainly a danger that his own participation would change the character of the events and situations he had set out to study in the first place.

Liebow's description of his record keeping nicely illustrates the procedures described earlier in this chapter:

Throughout this period, my field observations were focused on individuals: what they said, what they did, and the contexts in which they said them or did them. I sought them out and was sought out by them.

My field notes contain a record of what I saw when I looked at Tally, Richard, Sea Cat and the others. I have only a small notion—and one that I myself consider suspect—of what they saw when they looked at me.

(1967:248)

Ultimately, Liebow was able to gain a personal experience of street corner life in a black, urban ghetto that few white people have. To an unusual extent, he was able to see and understand the men as they saw and understood themselves. He was able to learn their views and experiences of family life, employment, and—more to the point—unemployment.

These two short accounts scarcely do justice to the projects they describe, but they should give a more concrete view of what field research entails. Both original reports are interesting and eminently readable, so you might like to read them for yourself.

THE STRENGTHS AND WEAKNESSES OF FIELD RESEARCH

It's time now to wrap up the discussion of field research and move on to some of the other methods available to social researchers. I want to conclude the chapter by assessing the relative strengths and weaknesses of this particular method. This examination will be somewhat longer than those of earlier chapters, since I want to spend part of the time comparing field research with experiments and surveys.

As I've already indicated, field research is especially effective for studying the subtle nuances of attitudes and behaviors, and for examining social processes over time. For these reasons, the chief strength of this method lies in the depth of understanding that it may permit. Although other research methods may be challenged as "superficial," that charge is seldom lodged against field research.

Flexibility is another advantage of field research. In this method, you may modify your research design at any time, as discussed earlier. Moreover, you are always prepared to engage in field research, whenever the occasion should arise, whereas you could not as easily initiate a survey or an experiment.

Field research can be relatively inexpensive. Other social scientific research methods may require expensive equipment or an expensive research staff, but field research typically can be undertaken by one researcher with a notebook and a pencil. This is not to say that field research is never expensive. The nature of the research project, for example, may require a large number of trained observers. Expensive recording equipment may be needed. Or the researcher may wish to undertake participant observation of interactions in expensive Paris nightclubs.

Field research has a number of weaknesses as well. First, being qualitative rather than quantitative, it seldom yields precise descriptive statements about a large population. Observing casual political discussions in laundromats, for example, would not yield trustworthy estimates of the future voting behavior of the total electorate. Nevertheless, the study could provide

important insights into the process of political attitude formation.

More generally, the conclusions drawn from qualitative field research are often regarded as suggestive rather than definitive. This is due to certain problems of validity, reliability, and generalizability, and I'll say a little about each of those.

You'll recall that validity and reliability are both qualities of measurements. Validity concerns whether measurements actually measure what they are supposed to rather than measuring something else. Reliability, on the other hand, is a matter of dependability: if you made the same measurement again and again, would you get the same result? Finally, generalizability refers to whether specific research findings apply to people, places, and things not actually observed. Let's see how field research stacks up in these respects.

Validity

Compared with criticisms that survey and experimental measurements are often superficial and not really valid, field research seems to provide more valid measures. Let's review a couple of field research examples to see why this is so.

"Being there" is a powerful technique for gaining insights into the nature of human affairs. Listen, for example, to what this nurse reports about the impediments to patients' coping with cancer:

Common fears that may impede the coping process for the person with cancer can include the following:
—Fear of death—for the patient, and the implications his or her death will have for significant others.
—Fear of incapacitation—because cancer can be a chronic disease with acute episodes that may result in periodic stressful periods, the variabil-

ity of the person's ability to cope and constantly adjust may require a dependency upon others for activities of daily living and may consequently become a burden.

—Fear of alienation—from significant others and health care givers, thereby creating helplessness and hopelessness.

—Fear of contagion—that cancer is transmissible and/or inherited.

—Fear of losing one's dignity—losing control of all bodily functions and being totally vulnerable.

(Garant 1980:2167)

Observations and conceptualizations such as these are valuable in their own right. In addition, they can provide the basis for further research—both qualitative and quantitative.

Now listen to what Joseph Howell (1973) has to say about "toughness" as a fundamental ingredient of life on Clay Street, a white, working-class neighborhood in Washington, D.C.

Most of the people on Clay Street saw themselves as fighters in both the figurative and literal sense. They considered themselves strong, independent people who would not let themselves be pushed around. For Bobbi, being a fighter meant battling the welfare department and cussing out social workers and doctors upon occasion. It meant spiking Barry's beer with sleeping pills and bashing him over the head with a broom. For Barry it meant telling off his boss and refusing to hang the door, an act that led to his being fired. It meant going through the ritual of a duel with Al. It meant pushing Bubba around and at times getting rough with Bobbi.

June and Sam had less to fight about, though if pressed they both hinted that they, too, would fight. Being a fighter led Ted into near conflict with Peg's brothers, Les into conflict with Lonnie, Arlene into conflict with Phyllis at the bowling alley, etc.

(1973:292)

Even without having heard the episodes Howell refers to in this passage, you have the distinct impression that Clay Street is a tough place to live. That "toughness" comes through far more powerfully than would a set of statistics on the median number of fistfights occurring during a specified period of time.

These examples point to the superior validity of field research, as compared with surveys and experiments. The kinds of comprehensive measurements available to the field researcher tap a depth of meaning in our concepts, such as liberal and conservative, that are generally unavailable to surveys and experiments. Instead of defining concepts, field researchers will commonly give some detailed illustrations.

Reliability

Field research does have a potential problem with reliability, however. Suppose you were to characterize your best friend's political orientations based on everything you know about him or her. There's certainly no question about your assessment of that person's politics being superficial. The measurement you arrived at would appear to have considerable validity. We can't be sure, however, that someone else would characterize your friend's politics the same way you did, even with the same amount of observation.

Field research measurements—while indepth—are also often very personal. How I judge your friend's political orientation depends very much on my own, just as your judgment would depend on your political orientation. Conceivably, then, you would describe your friend as middle-of-the-road while I felt I'd been observing a fire-breathing radical.

Be wary, therefore, of any purely descriptive measurements in field research. If a researcher reports that the members of a club are pretty conservative, know that such a judgment is unavoidably linked to the researcher's own politics. You can be more trusting, however, of comparative evaluations: identifying who is more conservative than whom, for example. Even if you and I had different political orientations, we would probably agree pretty much in ranking the relative conservatism of the members of a group.

In any event, study the characterizations offered by field researchers to get a full sense yourself of what the people characterized are like. Even if you disagree with the researcher, you will be able to get some value out of the research he or she has done.

In a sense, we've been talking above about the issue of generalizability. I want to look at that more directly now.

Generalizability

One of the chief goals of science is generalization. Social scientists study particular situations and events in order to learn about social life in general. Usually, nobody would be interested in knowing about the specific subjects observed by the researcher. Who cares, after all, how George Gallup's sample of 1,500 voters are going to vote? We are interested only if their voting intentions can be generalized to the total electorate. (This was the key issue in Chapter 7 on sampling.)

Generalizability is a problem for field research. It crops up in three forms. First, as I've already suggested above, the personal nature of the observations and measurements made by the researcher can produce results that would not necessarily be replicated by another, independent researcher. If the observation depends in part on the particular observers, then it becomes more valuable as a source of insight than as proof or truth.

Second, because field researchers get a full and in-depth view of their subject mat-

ter, they can reach an unusually comprehensive understanding. By its very comprehensiveness, however, this understanding is less generalizable than results based on rigorous sampling and standardized measurements. Let's say you set out to *fully* understand how your city council operates. You study each of the members in great depth, learning about their ideological positions, how they came to public life, how they got elected, who their friends and enemies are. You could learn about their family lives, seeing how personal feelings enter into their public acts. After such an in-depth study, you could probably understand the actions of the council really well. But would you be able to say much about city councils in general? Surely your study would have provided you with some general insights, but you wouldn't be able to carry over everything you learned from the specific to the general. Having mastered the operations of the Dayton City Council, you might not be able to say much about Cleveland's. You should, however, be in a position to organize a great study of the Cleveland City Council.

In reviewing reports of field research projects, you should determine where and to what extent the researcher is generalizing beyond his or her specific observations to other settings. Such generalizations may be in order, but you need to judge that. Nothing in this research method guarantees it.

Finally, there is often a problem of generalizability even within the specific subject matter being observed. As an illustration, let's imagine you were interested in learning about the Unification Church of Reverend Sun Myung Moon—the "Moonies." Suppose you were particularly interested in their recruitment practices: how does the group attract new members, what kinds of people are attracted, etc.? One way to find the answers to such questions would be for you to express interest in the church yourself. Talk to members, attend meetings and retreats. In this fashion, you'd be able to get a first-hand experience of what you wanted to study. You could observe the manner in which you were treated after expressing interest, and you could observe the treatment of other newcomers. By getting to know the other people who were considering joining the church, you would get an idea of the kinds of people who were joining.

Here's the problem of generalizability. Although you might talk to a number of church members, you couldn't be sure how "typical" they were. You might end up talking only to those people assigned the job of talking to potential recruits. Or perhaps you make your contact through your English class and meet mostly members majoring in the humanities and none majoring in the sciences. The potentials for biased sampling are endless. The same would apply to the new recruits you got to know. They might not be typical of new recruits in general.

As we've seen, field research is a potentially powerful tool for social scientists, one that provides a useful balance to the strengths and weaknesses of experiments and surveys. These are not the only modes of observation available, however, as we'll see in the remaining chapters of Part 3.

MAIN POINTS

■ Field research is a social research method that involves the direct observation of social phenomena in their natural settings.

■ You may or may not identify yourself as a researcher to the people you are observing. Identifying yourself as a researcher may have some effect on the nature of what you are observing, but concealing your identity may involve deceit.

■ You may or may not participate in that which you are observing. Participating in the events may make it easier for you to conceal your identity as a researcher, but participation is likely to affect what is being observed.

■ Since controlled probability sampling techniques are usually impossible in field research, a rough form of quota sampling may be used in the attempt to achieve better representativeness in observations.

■ Snowball sampling is a method through which you develop an ever-increasing set of sample observations. You ask one participant in the event under study to recommend others for interviewing, and each of the subsequently interviewed participants is asked for further recommendations.

■ Often, the careful examination of deviant cases in field research can yield important insights into the "normal" patterns of social behavior.

■ The field journal is the backbone of field research, for that is where the researcher records his or her observations. Journal entries should be detailed, yet concise. If possible, observations should be recorded as they are made; otherwise, they should be recorded as soon afterward as possible.

■ Field research is a form of qualitative research, although it is sometimes possible to quantify some of the observations that are being recorded.

■ In field research, observation, data processing, and analysis are interwoven and cyclical processes.

■ Some of the logical pitfalls of data analysis are provincialism, hasty conclusions, questionable causes, suppressed evidence, and false dilemmas.

■ Compared with surveys and experiments, field research measurements generally have more validity but less reliability, and field research results cannot be generalized as safely as those based on rigorous sampling and standardized questionnaires.

REVIEW QUESTIONS AND EXERCISES

1. Think of some group or activity you participate in or are very familiar with. In two or three paragraphs, describe how an outsider might effectively go about studying that group or activity. What should he or she read, what contacts should be made, etc.?

2. To show that you appreciate the differing strengths and weaknesses of experiments, surveys, and field research, give brief descriptions of two studies especially appropriate to each method. Be sure that each study would be most appropriately studied by the method you identify it with.

ADDITIONAL READINGS

Becker, Howard; Geer, Blanche; Hughes, Everett; and Strauss, Anselm, *Boys in White: Student Culture in Medical School* (Chicago: University of Chicago Press, 1961). An excellent and important illustration of field research methods. This study, involving continued interaction with medical school students over the course of their professional training, examines the impact of their experiences on their values and orientations. An informal biography of this project, by Blanche Geer, may be found in Phillip Hammond (ed.), *Sociologists at Work* (New York: Basic Books, 1964) and is also reprinted in McCall and Simmons (see below).

Emerson, Robert M. (ed.), *Contemporary Field Research* (Boston: Little, Brown, 1983). A diverse and interesting collection of articles on how field research contributes to understanding, the role of theory in such research, personal and relational issues that emerge, and ethical and political issues.

Lofland, John, *Analyzing Social Settings* (Belmont, Calif.: Wadsworth, 1984). An unexcelled presentation of field research methods from beginning to end. This eminently readable little book manages successfully to draw the links between the logic of scientific inquiry and the nitty-gritty practicalities of observing, communicating, recording, filing, reporting, and everything else involved in field research. In addition, the book contains a wealth of references to field research illustrations.

Lofland, John, *Doomsday Cult: A Study of Conversion, Proselytization, and Maintenance of Faith* (Englewood Cliffs, N.J.: Prentice-Hall, 1966). Another excellent illustration of field research methods in practice. This study examines the dynamic development of a deviant religious movement still active today. A shorter report of this study may be found in John Lofland and Rodney Stark, "Becoming a World-Saver: Conversion to a Deviant Perspective," *American Sociological Review*, Vol. 30 (December 1965) 862–75.

McCall, George, and Simmons, J. L. (eds.), *Issues in Participant Observation: A Text and Reader* (Reading, Mass.: Addison-Wesley, 1969). An excellent collection of important articles dealing with field research. The 32 selections cover most aspects of field research, both theoretical and practical. Moreover, many of the selections provide illustrations of actual research projects.

Shostak, Arthur (ed.), *Our Sociological Eye: Personal Essays on Society and Culture* (Port Washington, N.Y.: Alfred, 1977). An orgy of social scientific introspection. This delightful collection of first-person research accounts offers concrete, inside views of the thinking process in sociological research, especially field research.

11

Unobtrusive Research

What You'll Learn in This Chapter

This chapter will present overviews of three unobtrusive research methods: content analysis, the analysis of existing statistics, and historical/comparative analysis. Each of these methods allows researchers to study social life from afar, without influencing it in the process.

INTRODUCTION

With the exception of the complete observer in field research, each of the modes of observation discussed so far requires the researcher to intrude to some degree into whatever he or she is studying. This is most obvious in the case of experiments, followed closely by survey research. Even the field researcher, as we've seen, can change things in the process of studying them.

Two previous examples in this book, however, were totally exempt from that danger. In his examination of the effects of the depression on family life, for example, Stouffer could have no impact because he merely analyzed government statistics. For the same reason, Durkheim's analysis of suicide did nothing to affect suicides one way or the other.

As a major part of this chapter, we'll examine three different research methods: content analysis, the analysis of existing statistics, and historical/comparative analysis. In *content analysis,* researchers examine a class of social artifacts, typically written documents (recall Chapter 4). Suppose, for example, you wanted to contrast the relative importance of foreign versus domestic problems for Americans in the 1930s and the 1980s. One way, as we saw in Chapter 9, would be to examine the results of public opinion polls in those two periods. Another method would be to analyze, say, newspaper articles during the two periods. This latter design would be an example of content analysis: the analysis of communications.

The Stouffer and Durkheim studies mentioned above are examples of the *analysis of existing statistics,* another form of unobtrusive research to be examined in this chapter. As you'll see, there are great masses of data all around you, awaiting your use in the understanding of social life.

Finally, we consider *historical/comparative analysis,* a form of research with a ven-erable history in the social sciences and one that is enjoying a resurgence of popularity at present. Like field research, historical/comparative analysis is a qualitative method, one in which the researcher attempts to master many subtle details. The main resources for observation and analysis are historical records. While a historical/comparative analysis might include content analysis, it is not limited to communications. The method's name includes the word *comparative* because social scientists—in contrast to historians who may simply describe a particular set of events—seek to discover common patterns that recur in different times and places.

To set the stage for our examination of these three research methods, I want to draw your attention to an excellent book that should sharpen your senses about the potential for unobtrusive measures in general. It is, among other things, the book from which I take the term *unobtrusive measures.*

A COMMENT ON UNOBTRUSIVE MEASURES

In 1966, Eugene J. Webb and three colleagues published an ingenious little book on social research (revised in 1981) that has become a classic. It focuses on the idea of *unobtrusive* or *nonreactive* research. Webb and his colleagues have played freely with the task of learning about human behavior by observing what people inadvertently leave behind them. Want to know what exhibits are the most popular at a museum? You could conduct a poll, but people might tell you what they thought you wanted to hear or what might make them look more intellectual and serious. You could stand by different exhibits and count the viewers that came by, but people might come over to see what you were doing. Webb and his colleagues suggest that you check the wear and tear on the floor in front of various exhibits. Those where the tiles have been worn down the most are probably the most popular. Want to know which exhibits are popular with little kids? Look for mucus on the glass cases. To get a sense of the most popular radio stations, you could arrange with an auto mechanic to check the radio dial settings for cars brought in for repair.

The possibilities are limitless. Like an investigative detective, the social researcher looks for clues, and clues of social behavior are all around you. In a sense, everything you see represents the answer to some important social scientific question—all you have to do is think of the question.

While problems of validity and reliability crop up in unobtrusive measures like those mentioned above, a little ingenuity can either handle them or put them in perspective. I'd encourage you to look at Webb's book. It's enjoyable reading, and it should be a source of stimulation and insight for you in taking on social inquiry through the use of the data that already exist. For now, let's turn our attention to three unobtrusive methods often employed by social scientists.

TOPICS APPROPRIATE TO CONTENT ANALYSIS

Content analysis methods may be applied to virtually any form of communication. Among the possible artifacts for study are books, magazines, poems, newspapers, songs, paintings, speeches, letters, laws, and constitutions, as well as any components or collections thereof. Are popular French novels more concerned with love than American ones? Was the popular American music of the 1960s more politically cynical than the popular German music during that period? Do political candidates who pri-

marily address "bread and butter" issues get elected more often than those who address issues of high principle? Each of these questions addresses a social scientific research topic: the first might address national character, the second political orientations, and the third political process. While such topics might be studied through observation of individual people, content analysis provides another approach.

John Naisbitt's best-selling *Megatrends* (1982) used content analysis to determine the major trends in modern American life. Naisbitt and his staff regularly monitored 6,000 local newspapers a month in order to discover local and regional trends for publication in a series of quarterly reports. His book examined some of the trends they observed in the nation at large.

Some topics are more appropriately addressed by content analysis than by any other method of inquiry. Suppose for a moment that you're interested in violence on television. Maybe you suspect that the manufacturers of men's products are more likely to sponsor violent TV shows than are other kinds of sponsors. Content analysis would be the best way of finding out if it's true.

Briefly, here's what you would do. First, you'd develop operational definitions of the two key variables in your inquiry: *men's products* and *violence*. The section on coding, later in this chapter, will discuss some of the ways you could do that. Ultimately, you'd need a plan that would allow you to watch television, classify sponsors, and rate the degree of violence on particular shows.

Next, you'd have to decide what to watch. Probably you would decide (1) what stations to watch, (2) for what days or period, and (3) at what hours. Then, you'd stock in some beer and potato chips and start watching, classifying, and recording. Once you had completed your observations, you'd be able to analyze the data you collected and determine whether men's product manufacturers sponsored more blood and gore than other sponsors.

Content analysis, then, is particularly well suited to the study of communications and to answering the classic question of communications research: "Who says what, to whom, why, how, and with what effect?" As a mode of observation, content analysis requires a considered handling of the *what*, and the analysis of data collected in this mode, as in others, addresses the *why* and *with what effect*.

SAMPLING IN CONTENT ANALYSIS

In the study of communications, as in the study of people, it is often impossible to observe directly all that you are interested in. In your study of television violence and sponsorship, I'd advise against attempting to watch everything that's broadcast. It wouldn't be possible, and your brain would probably short-circuit before you got close to discovering that for yourself. Usually, then, it's appropriate to sample. Let's begin by looking again at units of analysis and then review some of the sampling techniques that might be applied to them in content analysis.

Units of Analysis

You'll recall from Chapter 4 that determining appropriate units of analysis, the individual units about which or whom descriptive and explanatory statements are to be made, can be a complicated task. For example, if we wished to compute the average family income, the individual family would be the unit of analysis. But we would have to ask individual members of families how much money they make. So individuals

would be the units of observation, while the individual family would still be the unit of analysis. Similarly, we may wish to compare crime rates of different cities in terms of their sizes, geographical regions, racial composition, and other differences. Even though the characteristics of these cities are partly a function of the behaviors and characteristics of their individual residents, the cities would ultimately be the units of analysis.

The complexity of this issue is often more apparent in content analysis than in other research methods. That is especially the case when the units of observation differ from the units of analysis. A few examples should clarify this distinction.

Let's suppose that we want to find out whether criminal law or civil law makes the most distinctions between men and women. In this instance, individual laws would be both the units of observation and the units of analysis. We might select a sample of a state's criminal and civil laws, and then categorize each law by whether it makes a distinction between men and women. In this fashion, we would be able to determine whether criminal or civil law distinguishes most by sex.

Somewhat differently, we might wish to determine whether states that enact laws distinguishing between different racial groups are also more likely than other states to enact laws distinguishing between men and women. Although the examination of this question would also involve the coding of individual acts of legislation, the unit of analysis in this latter case is the individual state, not the law.

Or, changing topics radically, let's suppose we are interested in representationalism in painting. If we wish to compare the relative popularity of representational and nonrepresentational paintings, the individual paintings would be our units of analysis. If, on the other hand, we wish to discover whether representationalism in painting is more characteristic of wealthy or impoverished painters, of educated or un-educated painters, of capitalist or socialist painters, the individual painters would be our units of analysis.

It is essential that this issue be clear, since sample selection depends largely on what the unit of analysis is. If individual writers are the units of analysis, the sample design should select all or a sample of the writers appropriate to the research question. If books are the units of analysis, we should select a sample of books, regardless of their authors.

I am not suggesting that sampling should be based solely on the units of analysis. Indeed, we may often subsample—select samples of subcategories—for each individual unit of analysis. Thus, if writers are the units of analysis, we might (1) select a sample of writers from the total population of writers, (2) select a sample of books written by each writer selected, and (3) select portions of each selected book for observation and coding.

Finally, let's look at a trickier example: the study of television violence and sponsors. What is the unit of analysis for the research question, "Are men's products manufacturers more likely to sponsor violent shows than other sponsors?" Is it the TV show? The sponsor? The instance of violence? In the simplest study design, it would be none of these.

Though you might structure your inquiry in various ways, the most straightforward design would be based on the *commercial* as the unit of analysis. You would use two kinds of observational units: the commercial and the program (the show that gets squeezed in between commercials). You'd want to observe both units. You would classify commercials by whether they advertised men's products and the programs by their violence. The program classifications would be transferred to the commercials occurring near them. Figure 11-1 is an example of the kind of record you might keep.

Notice that in the research design illustrated in Figure 11-1, all the commercials occurring together are bracketed and get the same scores. Also, the number of violent instances recorded as following one commercial is the same as the number preceding the next commercial. This simple design allows us to classify each commercial by its sponsorship and the degree of violence associated with it. Thus, for example, the first Grunt Aftershave commercial is coded as being a men's product and as having 10 instances of violence associated with it. The Buttercup Bra commercial is coded as not being a men's product and as having no violent instances associated with it.

In the illustration, we have four men's product commercials with an average of 7.5 violent instances each. The four commercials classified as definitely not men's products have an average of 1.75, and the two that might or might not be considered men's products have an average of 1 violent instance each. If this pattern of differences persisted across a much larger number of observations, we'd probably conclude that men's products manufacturers are more likely to sponsor TV violence than other sponsors.

The point of this illustration is to demonstrate how units of analysis figure into the data collection and analysis. You need to be clear about your unit of analysis before planning your sampling strategy, but in this case you can't sample commercials. Unless you have access to the stations' broadcasting logs, you won't know when the commercials are going to occur. Moreover, you need to observe the programming as well as the commercials. As a result, you must set up a sampling design that will include everything you need to observe.

In designing the sample, you would need to establish the universe to be sampled from. In this case, what TV stations will you observe? What will be the period of the study—number of days? And what hours of each day will you observe? Then, how many

Figure 11-1   Example of Recording Sheet for TV Violence

Sponsor	Men's Product?			Number of Instances of Violence	
	Yes	No	?	Before	After
Grunt Aftershave	✓			6	4
Brute Jock Straps	✓			6	4
Roperot Cigars	✓			4	3
Grunt Aftershave	✓			3	0
Snowflake Toothpaste		✓		3	0
Godliness Cleanser		✓		3	0
Big Thumb Hammers			✓	0	1
Snow flake Toothpaste		✓		1	0
Big Thumb Hammers		✓		1	0
Buttercup Bras		✓		0	0

commercials do you want to observe and code for analysis? Watch television for a while and find out how many commercials occur each hour, then you can figure out how many hours of observation you'll need.

Now you're ready to design the sample selection. As a practical matter, you wouldn't have to sample among the different stations if you had assistants—each of you could watch a different channel during the same time period. But let's suppose you are working alone. Your final sampling frame, from which a sample will be selected and watched, might look something like this:

Jan. 7, Channel 2, 7–9   P.M.
Jan. 7, Channel 4, 7–9   P.M.
Jan. 7, Channel 9, 7–9   P.M.
Jan. 7, Channel 2, 9–11   P.M.

Jan. 7, Channel 4, 9–11   P.M.
Jan. 7, Channel 9, 9–11   P.M.
Jan. 8, Channel 2, 7–9   P.M.
Jan. 8, Channel 4, 7–9   P.M.
Jan. 8, Channel 9, 7–9   P.M.
Jan. 8, Channel 2, 9–11   P.M.
Jan. 8, Channel 4, 9–11   P.M.
Jan. 8, Channel 9, 9–11   P.M.
Jan. 9, Channel 2, 7–9   P.M.
Jan. 9, Channel 4, 7–9   P.M.
etc.

Notice that I've made several decisions for you in the illustration. First, I have assumed that channels 2, 4, and 9 are the ones appropriate to your study. I've assumed that you found the 7 to 11 P.M. prime time hours to be the most relevant, and that two-hour periods would do the job. I picked January 7 out of the hat for a starting date. In practice, of course, all of these decisions should be based on your careful consideration of what would be appropriate to your particular study.

Once you have become clear as to your units of analysis and the observations appropriate to those units and have created a sampling frame like the one I've illustrated, sampling is simple and straightforward. The alternative procedures available to you are the same ones described earlier in Chapter 7: random, systematic, stratified, and so on.

Sampling Techniques

In content analysis of written prose, sampling may occur at any or all of the following levels: words, phrases, sentences, paragraphs, sections, chapters, books, writers, or the contexts relevant to the works. Other forms of communication may also be sampled at any of the conceptual levels appropriate to them.

Any of the conventional sampling techniques discussed in Chapter 7 may be employed in content analysis. We might select a *random* or *systematic* sample of French and American novelists, of laws passed in the state of Mississippi, or of Shakespearean soliloquies. We might select (with a random start) every twenty-third paragraph in Tolstoy's *War and Peace*. Or, we might number all of the songs recorded by the Beatles and select a random sample of 25.

Stratified sampling is also appropriate to content analysis. To analyze the editorial policies of American newspapers, for example, we might first group all newspapers by region of the country, size of the community in which they are published, frequency of publication, or average circulation. We might then select a stratified random or systematic sample of newspapers for analysis.

Having done so, we might select a sample of editorials from each selected newspaper, perhaps stratified chronologically.

Cluster sampling is equally appropriate to content analysis. Indeed, if individual editorials were to be the unit of analysis in the previous example, then the selection of newspapers at the first stage of sampling would be a cluster sample. In an analysis of political speeches, we might begin by selecting a sample of politicians; each politician would represent a cluster of political speeches. The TV commercial study described above is another example of cluster sampling.

It should be repeated that sampling need not end when we reach the unit of analysis. If novels are the unit of analysis in a study, we might select a sample of novelists, subsamples of novels written by each selected author, and a sample of paragraphs within each novel. We would then analyze the content of the paragraphs for the purpose of describing the novels themselves.

Let us turn now to a more direct examination of analysis which has been mentioned frequently in the previous discussions. At this point, *content analysis* will refer to the coding or classification of material being observed. Part 4 will deal with the manipulation of those classifications to draw descriptive and explanatory conclusions.

CODING IN CONTENT ANALYSIS

Content analysis is essentially a coding operation. Communications—oral, written, or other—are coded or classified according to some conceptual framework. Thus, for example, newspaper editorials may be coded as liberal or conservative. Radio broadcasts might be coded as propagandistic or not. Novels might be coded as romantic or not. Paintings might be coded as representational or not. Political speeches might be coded as containing character assassinations or not. Recall that terms such as these are subject to many interpretations, and the researcher must specify definitions clearly.

Coding in content analysis involves the logic of conceptualization and operationalization as these have been discussed in Chapters 5 and 6. In content analysis, as in other research methods, you must refine your conceptual framework and develop specific methods for observing in relation to that framework.

Manifest and Latent Content

In the earlier discussions of field research, we found that the researcher faces a fundamental choice between *depth* and *specificity* of understanding. Often, this represents a choice between *validity* and *reliability,* respectively. Typically, field researchers opt for depth, preferring to base their judgments on a broad range of observations and information, even at the risk that another observer might reach a different judgment of the situation. But survey research—through the use of standardized questionnaires—represents the other extreme: total specificity, even though the specific measures of variables may not be fully satisfactory as valid reflections of those variables. The content analyst has more of a choice in this matter.

Coding the **manifest content**—the visible, surface content—of a communication more closely approximates the use of a standardized questionnaire. To determine, for example, how erotic certain novels are, you might simply count the number of times the word *love* appears in each novel, or the average number of appearances per page. Or, you might use a list of words, such as *love, kiss, hug,* and *caress,* each of which might serve as an indicator of the erotic

nature of the novel. This method would have the advantage of ease and *reliability* in coding and of letting the reader of the research report know precisely how eroticism was measured. It would have a disadvantage, on the other hand, in terms of *validity.* Surely the term *erotic novel* conveys a richer and deeper meaning than the number of times the word *love* is used.

Alternatively, you may code the **latent content** of the communication: its underlying meaning. In the present example, you might read an entire novel or a sample of paragraphs or pages and make an overall assessment of how erotic the novel was. Although your total assessment might very well be influenced by the appearance of words such as *love* and *kiss,* it would not depend fully on the frequency with which such words appeared.

Clearly, this second method seems better designed for tapping the underlying meaning of communications, but its advantage comes at a cost of reliability and specificity. Especially if more than one person is coding the novel, somewhat different definitions or standards may be employed. A passage that one coder regards as erotic may not seem erotic to another. Even if you do all of the coding yourself, there is no guarantee that your definitions and standards will remain constant throughout the enterprise. Moreover, the reader of your research report would be generally uncertain as to the definitions you have employed.

Wherever possible, the best solution to this dilemma is to use *both* methods. A given unit of observation should receive the same characterization from both methods to the extent that your coding of manifest and latent content has been reasonably valid and reliable. If the agreement achieved by the two methods is fairly close, though imperfect, the final score might reflect the scores assigned in the two independent methods. If, on the other hand, coding manifest and latent content produces gross disagreement, you would be well advised to reconsider your theoretical conceptualization.

Conceptualization and the Creation of Code Categories

For all research methods, conceptualization and operationalization typically involve the interaction of theoretical concerns and empirical observations. If, for example, you believe some newspaper editorials to be liberal and others to be conservative, ask yourself *why* you think so. Read some editorials, asking yourself which ones are liberal and which ones are conservative. Was the political orientation of a particular editorial most clearly indicated by its manifest content or by its tone? Was your decision based on the use of certain terms (for example, *pinko, right-winger,* and so on) or on the support or opposition given to a particular issue or political personality?

Both inductive and deductive methods should be used in this activity. If you are testing theoretical propositions, your theories should suggest empirical indicators of concepts. If you have begun with specific empirical observations, you should attempt to derive general principles relating to them and then apply those principles to the other empirical observations.

Throughout this activity, you should remember that the operational definition of any variable is composed of the *attributes* included in it. Such attributes, moreover, should be mutually exclusive and exhaustive. A newspaper editorial, for example, should not be described as both liberal and conservative, though you should probably allow for some to be middle-of-the-road. It may be sufficient for your purposes to code novels as being erotic or nonerotic, but you may also want to consider that some could be anti-erotic. Paintings might be classified as representational or not, if that satisfied

your research purpose, or you might wish to further classify them as impressionistic, abstract, allegorical, and so forth.

Realize further that different levels of measurement may be employed in content analysis. You may, for example, use the *nominal* categories of liberal and conservative for characterizing newspaper editorials, or you might wish to use a more refined *ordinal* ranking that ranged from extremely liberal to extremely conservative. It is important that you bear in mind, however, that the level of measurement implicit in your coding methods—nominal, ordinal, interval, or ratio—does not necessarily reflect the nature of your variables. If the word *love* appeared 100 times in Novel A and 50 times in Novel B, you would be justified in saying that the word *love* appeared twice as often in Novel A, but not that Novel A was twice as erotic as Novel B. Similarly, agreeing with twice as many anti-Semitic statements in a questionnaire does not make one twice as anti-Semitic.

No coding scheme should be used in content analysis until it has been carefully *pretested*. You should decide what manifest or latent contents of communications will be regarded as indicators of the different attributes composing your research variables, write down these operational definitions, and then use them in the actual coding of several units of observation. If you plan to use more than one coder in the final project, each of them should independently code the same set of observations, so that you can determine the extent of agreement produced. In any event, you should take special note of any difficult cases: those observations that were not easily classified using the operational definition. Finally, you should review the overall results of the pretest to ensure that they will be appropriate to your analytical concerns. If, for example, all of the pretest newspaper editorials have been coded as liberal, you may want to reconsider your definition of that attribute.

As with other types of quantitative research, it is not essential that you commit yourself in advance to a specific definition of each concept. Often you will do better to devise the most appropriate definition of a concept on the basis of your subsequent quantitative analyses. In the cases of erotic novels, for example, you might count separately the frequency with which different erotic words appear. This procedure would allow you to determine, during your later analysis, which words or combinations of words provided the most useful indication of your variable. (Part 4 of this book will tell you how to do that.)

Counting and Record Keeping

If you plan to evaluate your content analysis data quantitatively, it is essential that your coding operation be amenable to data processing.

First, the end product of your coding must be *numerical*. If you are counting the frequency of certain words, phrases, or other manifest content, that will necessarily be the case. Even if you are coding latent content on the basis of overall judgments, it will be necessary to represent your coding decision numerically: 1 = very liberal, 2 = moderately liberal, 3 = moderately conservative, and so on.

Second, it is essential that your record keeping clearly distinguishes between your units of analysis and your units of observation, especially if these two are different. The initial coding, of course, must relate to your units of observation. If novelists are your units of analysis, for example, and you wish to characterize them through a content analysis of their novels, your primary records will represent novels. You may then combine your scoring of individual novels to characterize each novelist.

Third, when counting, it will normally be important to record the *base* from which

the counting is done. It would probably be useless to know the number of realistic paintings produced by a given painter without knowing the number that he or she had painted altogether; the painter would be regarded as realistic if a high percentage of paintings were of that genre. Similarly, it would tell us little that the word *love* appeared 87 times in a novel if we did not know about how many words there were in the novel altogether. The issue of observation base is most easily resolved if *every* observation is coded in terms of one of the attributes making up a variable. Rather than simply counting the number of liberal editorials in a given collection, for example, code each editorial by its political orientation, even if it must be coded "no apparent orientation."

Let's suppose that we want to describe and explain the editorial policies of different newspapers. Figure 11-2 illustrates a portion of a tally sheet that might result from the coding of newspaper editorials. Note that newspapers are the units of analysis. Each newspaper has been assigned an identification number to facilitate mechanized processing. The second column has a space for the number of editorials coded for each newspaper. That will be an important piece of information, since we want to be able to say, for example, "22 percent of all the editorials were pro–United Nations," not just "there were eight pro–United Nations editorials."

One column in Figure 11-2 is for assigning a subjective overall assessment of the newspapers' editorial policies. (Such assignments might later be compared with the several objective measures.) Other columns provide space for recording numbers of editorials reflecting specific editorial positions. In a real content analysis, there would be spaces for recording other editorial positions plus noneditorial information about each newspaper, such as the region in which it is published, its circulation, and so forth.

Figure 11-2   Sample Tally Sheet (partial)

Newspaper ID	Number of editorials evaluated	SUBJECTIVE EVALUATION 1. Very liberal 2. Moderately liberal 3. Middle-of-road 4. Moderately conservative 5. Very conservative	Number of "anticommunist" editorials	Number of "pro-UN" editorials	Number of "anti-UN" editorials
001	37	2	0	8	0
002	26	5	10	0	6
003	44	4	2	1	2
004	22	3	1	2	3
005	30	1	0	6	0

ILLUSTRATIONS OF CONTENT ANALYSIS

Let's look at some examples of content analysis in action. The first illustration uses content analysis in conjunction with public opinion polling to find out what the key issues of the 1960s were in America. The second example describes a content analysis of the underground press to shed some light on the nature of the early counterculture movement of the 1960s.

Isolating Issues

The 1960s were turbulent years for the United States. The decade opened with a civil rights movement in full swing. Midway, popular attention turned to the war in Vietnam, and the decade ended with the appearance of social movements focused on the environment and on equality for women. The decade began with the romantic Camelot period of the Kennedy administration, experienced the tragedy of assassination, and witnessed a steady decline in popular faith in government. If you were a historian writing the history of the 1960s, how would you go about *finding* the key issues of the decade?

For G. Ray Funkhouser (1973), a communications researcher, the problem was to find the key *public opinion* issues of the 1960s. He approached the problem from two directions, using two different research methods: survey research and content analysis. For the survey research portion, Funkhouser turned to the Gallup Polls conducted during the decade, looking at answers people gave when asked for "the most important problem facing America." The three issues cited most often during the 1960s were (1) the Vietnam war, (2) race relations (and urban riots), and (3) crime.

For the content analysis part of his research, Funkhouser turned to an important source of public opinion: the mass media, in particular weekly news magazines. His intention here was to discover which issues were given the most coverage by weekly news magazines during the decade. These he would compare with the results shown in the Gallup Polls.

Here are the decisions Funkhouser had to make:

1. What period would he cover?

2. What magazines would he observe?

3. What sampling design would he use?

4. What issues would he consider?

5. How would he code the issues?

The period to be covered was already specified in Funkhouser's research: the 1960s. More specifically, he looked at 1960 through 1970. He chose to examine the three most popular weekly news magazines: *Newsweek, Time*, and *U.S. News and World Report*. Here's his rationale for focusing on news magazines from among the many forms of mass media:

It would clearly be impossible to carry out a completely representative, content-analytic study of the full range of informational stimuli carried by television and newspapers to the nationwide public during the years 1960 through 1970. The sheer volume of material *available* would overwhelm, to say nothing of the material no longer available (for example, the nightly network newscasts) or the problem of generalizing from the available (mostly local) material to the potential nationwide audience. Therefore, a strategy of indicators was used. Although news magazines are not cited as primary sources of information by most people, it seems likely that their content reflects the nationwide content of the prominent news media—television and newspapers. That is, if television and newspapers were presenting abundant material concerning ecology (or drugs, or whatever), the news magazines probably would be doing so also.

(Funkhouser 1973:64)

Funkhouser's sampling design was simplicity itself: he took 'em all, every edition of each magazine during the period specified. Given that decision, you can probably envision the observation procedures appropriate once the code categories were established: scan some 1,716 magazines, coding each of the thousands of articles. Suddenly content analysis may not seem so much fun. Actually, Funkhouser created code categories and grossly simplified the observation at the same time. I'll let him tell you what he did.

The source of data for the content analysis of these publications was the *Readers' Guide to Periodical Literature*. Articles (but not book reviews) were tallied, by publication by year, for the following issues (using *only* the topics listed under the headings):

Vietnam: *Vietnam* . . . American participation . . . peace and mediation (except negotiation meetings) . . . politics and government . . . protests, demonstrations, etc., against . . . public opinion

Race Relations: *Negro* . . . militants . . . students . . . student demonstrations . . . student militants . . . in U.S. . . . civil rights . . . culture . . . education . . . history . . . politics and suffrage . . . segregation . . . resistance to segregation . . . social conditions . . . *Race Relations* . . . in U.S. . . . prejudice

Inflation: *Inflation* (financial)

Crime: *Crime and Criminals* . . . in U.S. . . . prevention . . . procedure . . . criminal statistics . . . *Law Enforcement*

Urban Riots (covering the general topic only— not specific cities, which were in some years listed separately): *United States* . . . riots

Campus Unrest: *Student* . . . demonstrations . . . militants . . . movement . . . SDS . . . SNCC

... opinion (all in U.S. only) ... *Kent State* (in 1970 only)

Environment: *Ecology* ... study and teaching ... *Environment* ... environmental movement ... environmental policy ... pollution ... control ... laws and legislation ... *Air Pollution* ... *Water Pollution*

Drugs: *Drugs* ... abuse ... laws and legislation ... *Hallucinogenic Drugs* ... LSD ... *Marijuana* ... *Narcotics* habit ... addicts ... control of ... and youth

Sex: *Sex* ... (psychology) ... in literature ... in moving pictures ... in art and the arts ... in the performing arts ... instruction ... and laws ... relations ... sexual behavior ... sexual ethics

Mass Media: *Mass Media* ... *Television Broadcasting* ... and children ... censorship ... moral aspects ... news ... in politics ... laws and regulations ... in U.S. ... social aspects

Population: *Population* ... overpopulation ... increase of ... distribution of

Poverty: *Poor* ... in U.S. ... *poverty* ... *slums*

Smoking: *Smoking Cigarettes* ... advertising

Science: *Research* ... federal aid ... in U.S. ... *science* ... and civilization ... social aspects ... and state ... *Technology* ... technological change ... and civilization

Women's Rights: *Woman, Women* ... equal rights ... in U.S. ... and men ... social and moral questions ... liberation movement ... marches, rallies ... suffrage

(Funkhouser 1973:64–65)

Rather than creating his own coding scheme and poring through thousands of magazine articles, Funkhouser chose to use the coding scheme developed by the *Readers' Guide* editors, and he used their coding of articles as well. All he needed to do, then, was count the number of entries under each code category for the three magazines.

In simplifying the research effort, of course, Funkhouser ran certain risks, and he discussed those in his report. He had no control over the validity and reliability of what the editors had done. Similarly, he noted the difficulty involved in multiple entries—

a single article being listed under more than one heading. All in all, however, he felt that the data generated from the index listings gave him a good measure of the mass media coverage of various issues during the 1960s.

Table 11-1 presents his summary data. Besides showing the number of articles and ranking of issues in terms of news magazine coverage, the table also presents the issues as ranked by the Gallup Poll. Notice the close—though imperfect—correspondence between the two rankings.

The Funkhouser study combines content analysis and the analysis of existing data, demonstrating how a social researcher can find out about social life through an examination of information already collected and compiled by others. The next illustration focuses solely on content analysis.

Understanding the Underground

Growing up in the 1940s and 1950s, Jack Levin and James Spates attended college and graduate school during the appearance and development of the hippie movement of the 1960s. Not surprisingly, they found themselves personally interested in that social movement and its implications for mainstream American culture. As their sociological training progressed in graduate school, they were able to use their new professional skills to pursue their personal interest and contribute to our scientific understanding of the hippie movement (Levin and Spates 1970, 1976).

The thing that most interested Levin and Spates was a value difference that had been discussed on a general theoretical level by Talcott Parsons and others years before: the difference between *instrumental* and *expressive* values and orientations. To put it simply, instrumental values are those having to do with rationality and achievement, and expressive values lie more in the realm

Table 11-1 News Magazine Coverage of Various Issues
during the 1960s and Importance Ranking of the Issues

Issue	Number of Articles	Coverage Rank	Importance Rank
Vietnam War	861	1	1
Race relations (and urban riots)	687	2	2
Campus unrest	267	3	4
Inflation	234	4	5
Television and mass media	218	5	12*
Crime	203	6	3
Drugs	173	7	9
Environment and pollution	109	8	6
Smoking	99	9	12*
Poverty	74	10	7
Sex (declining morality)	62	11	8
Women's rights	47	12	12*
Science and society	37	13	12*
Population	36	14	12*

Note: Rank-order correlation between coverage and importance = .78 (p = .001).

*These items were never noted as "the most important problem" in the Gallup findings, so are ranked equally below the items that were.

Source: G. Ray Funkhouser, "The Issues of the Sixties: An Exploratory Study," *Public Opinion Quarterly,* Vol. 37 (Spring 1973), p. 66. Used by permission.

of feelings. Thus, an engineer building a bridge is engaged in an instrumental activity, and the profession of engineering is heavily imbued with instrumental values. A romantic poet writing of love, on the other hand, is engaged in a more expressive activity.

Though not simply favoring poetry over engineering, the hippie movement—like the beat movement before it—represented a challenge to the predominant emphasis on instrumental achievement that has characterized mainstream American society throughout our national history. The movement produced critics who spoke of the meaningless superficiality of middle-class American concerns for material possessions and social status. It was often charged that Americans had for the most part lost touch

with their feelings and were unable to relate to one another in a meaningful, human way. Clearly, it looked as though the hippie movement represented a commitment to expressive values, in contrast to the instrumental values of mainstream American society. Levin and Spates wanted to find out if that was so, and—if it was—whether the hippie movement was having any impact on the values of the host society.

One place where the movement values could be observed was in its literature—for example, in the undergound press made up of such newspapers as the *East Village Other, Avatar,* and the *San Francisco Oracle.* But two problems immediately arose: (1) How would the authors recognize an expressive orientation in contrast to an instrumental one? (2) *How much* expressiveness would be "really" expressive? Put differently, they needed some definitions of expressiveness and instrumentality and a standard for comparison.

They found the answer to their first need in the research literature. Ralph White (1951) had published a value catalog several years before that seemed to specify the different orientations sufficiently for the research project. Levin and Spates adapted White's work to create the following definitions and categories:

Instrumental
a. *Achievement:* Values which produce achievement motivation for the individual in terms of hard work, practicality, or economic value are often expressed by means of contributions to society through occupation and high regard for ownership.

b. *Cognitive:* These represent the drive for learning as an end in itself as well as the means for achieving success, welfare or happiness.

c. *Economic:* Economic values are at the collective level (such as national, state, industrial), thus differing from individual goals as achievement.

Expressive
d. *Self-expressive:* This area includes all the self-expressive values and goals. The main ones are humor, play, and fun in general, relaxation, or exciting new discoveries, and travel. Art and beauty are included as well as other creative-expressive activities.

e. *Affiliative:* These may be the product of social conditioning, or a result of the need to belong to a group, to affiliate with another person. This category focuses upon the gregariousness of individuals and the friendships which they develop. These affiliative aims may be expressed as conformity, loyalty to the group, friendship, or other-directedness.

f. *Concern for others:* Concern for others does not depend upon a drive to interact. Unlike the affiliative values, this category focuses upon attitudes and feelings toward particular groups or toward humanity in general. Therefore, this cat-

egory tends to include more abstract objectives than those associated with affiliation.

g. *Religious-philosophical:* This category includes goals dealing with ultimate meaning in life, the role of deity, concerns with after-life, and so on.

Other
h. *Individualistic:* This category is concerned with values which stress the importance of the individual, the development of his unique personality, individual independence, and the achievement of individualized personal fulfillment including rebellion.

i. *Physiological:* These are goals created by simple physiological drives such as hunger, sex, physical health, and physical safety.

j. *Political:* This category includes collective goals (such as state, community, national, international objectives) in their central reference to group decision-making processes.

k. *Miscellaneous:* Any other goals not covered above (such as hope, honesty, purity, modesty, and manners).

(Levin and Spates 1976:395)

Notice that the categorization scheme was not totally specific, calling for the coding of latent more than manifest content. Although this lack of specificity perhaps strengthened the *validity* of the coding, it presented a potential problem in terms of *reliability*. To check this danger, the researchers selected 30 sample articles and had three coders independently code each. In 90 percent of the cases, two out of three coders agreed as to whether a particular article was *expressive, instrumental,* or *other;* in 78 percent, all three agreed in their coding. On the basis of this test, the researchers concluded that the coding scheme provided a high enough reliability to permit a meaningful study and analysis.

To satisfy their second need—for a way of determining how much expressiveness ought to be considered expressive—they turned to the mainstream periodical literature of America. Specifically, they compared the underground press with the *Reader's Digest*. If the common assumptions about the predominantly instrumental orientation of mainstream American society and about the contrasting expressive orientation of the hippie movement were true, the difference should show up in the comparison proposed.

Here is the authors' description of how they specified their sampling design for the study:

To obtain a representative sample of underground newspapers, the following most widely circulated periodicals were selected from major centers of . . . hippie activities, including both eastern and western regions: *Avatar* (Boston), *Distant Drummer* (Philadelphia), *East Village Other* (New York), *Los Angeles Free Press, San Francisco Oracle,* and *Washington Free Press.* A single issue of each UPS periodical from every month in the time from September 1967 to August 1968 was selected on a random basis. Every second nonfictional article appearing in this sample of issues, excluding poetry and letters to the editor, was subjected to analysis ($n = 316$).

To provide a comparable sample of articles representative of middle-class values, an analysis was also conducted of concurrently published issues of the *Reader's Digest,* selected for its variety of middle-class articles from diverse sources. . . . Excluding fiction and poetry, each article appearing in every other issue of *Reader's Digest* was studied ($n = 162$).

(Levin and Spates 1976:394)

Table 11-2 presents the results of the comparison. As expected, the sample of undergound press papers was clearly and strongly more expressive than was the *Reader's Digest*. The initial question asked by Levin and Spates was thus answered.

But how about the possibility that the hippie movement would have an impact on the mainstream values of American society? The impact on music, dress, and other aspects of culture was too obvious to require study. But would the movement bring about a trend toward expressiveness and away from instrumentalism?

To gauge the historical consequences, the researchers repeated their study on a larger scale, examining three time periods: 1957 to 1959 (the "beat" era), 1967 to 1969, and 1970 to 1972. If the hippie movement—through the underground press and in other ways—was strengthening expressive values in America, the predominance of expressive values in the underground press should have been maintained over time, and the mainstream media, such as the *Reader's Digest*, should be found to have shifted from instrumental to expressive values.

For the expanded study, *Life, Look, True, Redbook,* and *Cosmopolitan* were added to the *Reader's Digest*. A sampling design was created to produce a larger number of observations from both the underground press and mainstream magazines, running to several thousand observations altogether. To further refine the study design, the researchers shifted from articles to paragraphs as the unit of analysis. In the initial study, they had coded whole articles as either expressive, instrumental, or other. Now they selected a sample of paragraphs from articles in both the underground press and mainstream magazines, and coded the paragraphs.

Once the sampling and coding were complete, the tabulations were done, and the surprises appeared. First, no significant change was found in the value orientations of the mainstream magazines over the course of the three time periods. They stayed predominantly instrumental. However, Levin and Spates discovered that "the real *coup de grace* concerning high hopes for the counterculture came in the underground press figures themselves. These indicated that a major value priority shift had occurred within the counterculture *itself*" (Levin and Spates 1976:408). Table 11-3 presents the data producing that conclusion.

Table 11-2   Value-Themes in the Underground Press and *Reader's Digest*

Value-Theme	Underground Press		*Reader's Digest*	
Expressive	46%		23%	
Self-expressive		28%		9%
Concern for others		8		6
Affiliative		4		3
Religious-philosophical		6		5
Instrumental	10		42	
Achievement		3		28
Cognitive		5		7
Economic		2		7
Other	44		35	
Individual		20		10
Political*		19		12
Physiological†		4		12
Miscellaneous		1		1
Total		100		100
(n = 478)		(316)		(162)

Note: A chi-square analysis was conducted by comparing the underground press and *Reader's Digest* on the two major value-themes, Expressive and Instrumental (x^2 = 61.17 df = 1, $p<.001$).

*The distribution of political values reveals an important aspect of the nature of the underground press: a secondary appeal of these newspapers is often to politically radical or New Left types, though most of the material is designed for hippie consumption . . . a group known for its apolitical stance. . . .

†In the *Reader's Digest,* this category consisted primarily of health-related topics such as methods of weight reduction, physical diseases such as cancer, and aging. In the underground press, it contained references to physiological sex.

Source: Adapted from Jack Levin and James Spates, "Hippie Values: An Analysis of the Underground Press," *Youth and Society,* Vol. 2 (1970), p. 396. Used by permission.

Rather than finding that the mainstream American press moved from instrumental to expressive concerns, the researchers discovered that the underground press had moved in an instrumental direction. As the researchers noted in their second report, this finding from the content analysis was supported by other observations. In particular, it was being widely reported that the leaders of the counterculture were dropping back into the mainstream society as they reached their late twenties and early thirties.

These two illustrations of content analysis in action should give you a clearer picture of the procedures and potential that characterize this research method. Let's conclude the discussion of content analysis with an overview of its particular strengths and weaknesses.

STRENGTHS AND WEAKNESSES OF CONTENT ANALYSIS

Probably the greatest advantage of content analysis is its economy in terms of both time and money. A single college student could

Table 11-3   Changes in Value Orientations

	Percentage of Instrumental Paragraphs from Those Coded as Either Instrumental or Expressive	
	Underground Press	Mainstream Magazines
1957–1959	25%*	73%
1967–1969	30%	78%
1970–1972	55%	78%

*The authors report this figure is "approximately one-quarter instrumental" in the text of their report, and I have taken the liberty of showing it as 25% for the sake of readability in the table.

Source: Adapted from Jack Levin and James Spates, "Hippie Values: An Analysis of the Underground Press," *Youth and Society,* Vol. 2 (1970), pp. 407–08. Used by permission.

undertake a content analysis, whereas undertaking a survey, for example, might not be feasible. There is no requirement for a large research staff; no special equipment is required. As long as you have access to the material to be coded, you can undertake content analysis.

Safety is another advantage of content analysis. If you discover that you have botched up a survey or an experiment, you may be forced to repeat the whole research project with all the attendant costs in time and money. If you botch up your field research, it may be impossible to redo the project; the event under study may no longer exist. In content analysis, it is usually easier to repeat a portion of the study than for other research methods. You might be required, moreover, to recode only a portion of your data rather than to repeat the entire enterprise.

Also important, content analysis permits you to study processes occurring over long periods of time. You might focus on the imagery of blacks conveyed in American novels of 1850 to 1860, for example, or

you might examine changing imagery from 1850 to present.

Finally, content analysis has the advantage, mentioned at the outset of the chapter, of being *unobtrusive.* That is, the content analyst seldom has any effect on the subject *being studied.* Since the novels have already been written, the paintings already painted, the speeches already presented, content analyses can have no effect on them. This advantage is not present in all research methods.

Content analysis has disadvantages as well. For one thing, content analysis is limited to the examination of *recorded* communications. Such communications may be oral, written, or graphic, but they must be recorded in some fashion to permit analysis.

Content analysis, as we have seen, has both advantages and disadvantages in terms of validity and reliability. For validity, problems are likely unless you happen to be studying communication processes per se. For example, did the appearance of expressive/instrumental values in the underground press represent the most valid measure of those values in the hippie movement in general? Probably not. Even if the researchers achieved a high degree of validity in their coding of value orientations in the underground press and mainstream magazines, there's still a question of whether they had a valid measure of the *cultures* those media were taken to represent. This is a common problem with content analysis.

On the other side of the ledger, the concreteness of materials studied in content analysis strengthens the likelihood of reliability. You can always code and recode and even recode again if you want, making certain that the coding is consistent. In field research, by contrast, there's probably nothing you can do after the fact to ensure greater reliability in observation and categorization.

Let's move from content analysis now and turn to a related research method: the analysis of existing data. Although numbers rather than communications are the substance analyzed in this case, I think you'll see the similarity to content analysis.

ANALYZING EXISTING STATISTICS

Frequently it is possible or necessary to undertake social scientific inquiry through the use of official or quasi-official statistics. Recall, for example, Samuel Stouffer's study of the consequences of the Great Depression on the family, which used government statistics on marriages, divorces, and the like. This differs from secondary analysis, in which you obtain a copy of someone else's data and undertake your own statistical analysis. In this section, we're going to look at ways of using the data analyses others have already done.

Before getting into the nuts and bolts of this research method, I'd like to point out that existing statistics should always be considered at least a *supplemental* source of data. If you were planning a survey of political attitudes, for example, you would do well to examine and present your findings within a context of voting patterns, rates of voter turnout, or similar statistics relevant to your research interest. Or, if you were doing evaluation research on an experimental morale-building program on an assembly line, probably statistics on absenteeism, sick leave, and so on would be interesting and revealing in connection with the data your own research would generate. Existing statistics, then, can very often provide a historical or conceptual context within which to locate your original research.

Existing statistics can also provide the main data for a social scientific inquiry. In contrast to the structure of preceding discussions, I want to begin here with an illustration: Durkheim's classic study, *Suicide*

(1897). Then we'll look at some of the special problems this method presents in terms of units of analysis, validity, and reliability. I'll conclude the discussion by mentioning some useful sources of data.

Studying Suicide

Why do people kill themselves? Undoubtedly every suicide case has a unique history and explanation, yet all such cases could no doubt be grouped according to certain common causes: financial failure, trouble in love, disgrace, and other kinds of personal problems. French sociologist Emile Durkheim had a slightly different question in mind when he addressed the matter of suicide, however. He wanted to discover the environmental conditions that encouraged or discouraged it, especially social conditions.

The more he examined the available records, the more patterns of differences became apparent to Durkheim. All of these patterns interested him. One of the first things to attract his attention was the relative *stability* of suicide rates. Looking at several countries, he found suicide rates to be about the same year after year. He also discovered that a disproportionate number of suicides occurred during the hot summer months, leading him to hypothesize that temperature might have something to do with suicide. If that were the case, suicide rates should be higher in the southern European countries than in the temperate ones. However, Durkheim discovered that the highest rates were found in countries in the central latitudes, so temperature couldn't be the answer.

He explored the role of age (35 was the most common suicide age), sex (men outnumbered women around four to one), and numerous other factors. Eventually, a general pattern emerged from different sources.

In terms of the stability of suicide rates over time, for instance, Durkheim found the pattern was not *totally* stable. He found spurts in the rates during times of political turmoil, which occurred in a number of European countries around 1848. This observation led him to hypothesize that suicide might have something to do with "breaches in social equilibrium." Put differently, social stability and integration seemed to be a protection against suicide.

This general hypothesis was substantiated and specified through Durkheim's analysis of a different set of data. The different countries of Europe had radically different suicide rates. The rate in Saxony, for example, was about ten times that of Italy, and the relative ranking of various countries persisted over time. As Durkheim considered other differences in the various countries, he eventually noticed a striking pattern: predominantly Protestant countries had consistently higher suicide rates than Catholic ones. The predominantly Protestant countries had 190 suicides per million population; mixed Protestant-Catholic countries, 96; and predominantly Catholic countries, 58 (Durkheim 1897:152).

It was possible, Durkheim reasoned, that some other factor, such as level of economic and cultural development, might explain the observed differences. If religion had a genuine effect on suicide, then the religious difference would have to be found *within* given countries. To test this idea, Durkheim first noted that the German state of Bavaria had both the most Catholics and the lowest suicide rates in that country, whereas heavily Protestant Prussia had a much higher suicide rate. Not content to stop there, however, Durkheim examined the provinces composing each of those states. Table 11-4 shows what he found.

As you can see, in both Bavaria and Prussia, provinces with the highest propor-

Table 11-4 Suicide Rates in Various German Provinces, Arranged in Terms of Religious Affiliation

Religious Character of Province	Suicides per Million Inhabitants
*Bavarian Provinces (1867–1875)**	
Less than 50% Catholic	
Rhenish Palatinate	167
Central Franconia	207
Upper Franconia	204
Average	192
50% to 90% Catholic	
Lower Franconia	157
Swabia	118
Average	135
Over 90% Catholic	
Upper Palatinate	64
Upper Bavaria	114
Lower Bavaria	19
Average	75
Prussian Provinces (1883–1890)	
More than 90% Protestant	
Saxony	309.4
Schleswig	312.9
Pomerania	171.5
Average	264.6
68% to 89% Protestant	
Hanover	212.3
Hesse	200.3
Bradenberg and Berlin	296.3
East Prussia	171.3
Average	220.0
40% to 50% Protestant	
West Prussia	123.9
Silesia	260.2
Westphalia	107.5
Average	163.6
28% to 32% Protestant	
Posen	96.4
Rhineland	100.3
Hohenzollern	90.1
Average	95.6

Note: The population below 15 years has been omitted.

Source: Adapted from Emile Durkheim, *Suicide* (Glencoe, Ill.: Free Press, 1897, 1951), p. 153.

tion of Protestants also had the highest suicide rates. Increasingly, Durkheim became confident that religion played a significant role in the matter of suicide.

Returning eventually to a more general theoretical level, Durkheim combined the religious findings with the earlier observation about increased suicide rates during times of political turmoil. Put most simply, Durkheim suggested that many suicides are a product of *anomie,* "normlessness," or a general sense of social instability and disintegration. During times of political strife, people might feel that the old ways of society were collapsing. They would become demoralized and depressed, and suicide was one answer to the severe discomfort. Seen from the other direction, social integration and solidarity—reflected in personal feelings of being part of a coherent, enduring social whole—would offer protection against depression and suicide. That was where the religious difference fit in. Catholicism, as a far more structured and integrated religious system, would give people a greater sense of coherence and stability than would the more loosely structured Protestantism.

From these theories, Durkheim created the concept of *anomic suicide* and, more importantly, added the concept of *anomie* to the lexicon of the social sciences. Please realize that I have given you only the most superficial picture of Durkheim's classic study, and I think you'd enjoy looking through the original. In any event, this study gives you a good illustration of the possibilities for research contained in the masses of data regularly gathered and reported by government agencies.

Units of Analysis

As we have already seen in the case of *Suicide,* the unit of analysis involved in the analysis of existing statistics is often *not* the individual. Thus, Durkheim was required to work with political-geographical units: countries, regions, states, and cities. The same situation would probably appear if you were to undertake a study of crime rates, accident rates, disease, and so forth. By their nature, most existing statistics are *aggregated:* they describe groups.

The aggregate nature of existing statistics can present a problem, though not an insurmountable one. As we saw, for example, Durkheim wanted to determine whether Protestants or Catholics were more likely to commit suicide. None of the records available to him indicated the religion of those people who committed suicide, however. Ultimately, then, it was not possible for him to say whether Protestants committed suicide more often than Catholics, though he *inferred* as much. Since Protestant countries, regions, and states had higher suicides than Catholic countries, regions, and states, he drew the obvious conclusion.

There's danger in drawing that kind of conclusion, however. It is always possible that patterns of behavior at a group level do not reflect corresponding patterns on an individual level. Such errors are said to be due to an *ecological fallacy.* It was altogether possible, for example, that it was Catholics who committed suicide in the predominantly Protestant areas. Perhaps Catholics in predominantly Protestant areas were so badly persecuted that they were led into despair and suicide. Then it would be possible for Protestant countries to have high suicide rates without any Protestants committing suicide.

Durkheim avoided the danger of the ecological fallacy in two ways. First, his general conclusions were based as much on rigorous, theoretical deductions as on the empirical facts. The correspondence between theory and fact made a counter-explanation, such as the one I just made up, less likely.

Constructing Indicators of Quality of Life

by Ira M. Wasserman
Department of Sociology, Eastern Michigan University

Within the social sciences there has been a recent concern with constructing quality of life indicators for various political-geographical areas (e.g., states, standard metropolitan statistical areas). Studies of this type (Liu 1973, 1975; Smith 1973) have differentiated various topical areas related to the overall quality of life of a population within a political boundary (e.g., health, education, economics, public safety, individual status) and have then proceeded to select individual indicator measures of these categories which are then equally aggregated together to form an overall measure for that area. The overall quality of life for the political region is then computed by equally weighting the various topical measures. For example, Liu (1973:18) measures the health and welfare index for American states by the use of such individual variables as the number of physicians, dentists, and nurses per 100,000 population, as well as by the number of admissions to mental hospitals in the state per 100,000 population. Employing the previous variables, as well as other selected variables, he then constructed a health and welfare index for the 50 states, weighting each of the selected variables equally. He then constructed an overall quality of life index for the fifty states by aggregating together equally the 11 topical indices which he had differentiated.

As Gehrmann (1978) has demonstrated, there are a number of methodological difficulties with this type of index construction. First, the quality of life index for the various topical areas will be a function of the individual variables selected for the various topical areas. For example, in his construction of indices Liu (1973) tended to select input variables (e.g., physicians per capita, which is an input into the health system), while Smith (1973) tended to select output variables (e.g., mortality per capita, which is an output of any health system in an area). Also, it is

Second, by extensively retesting his conclusions in a variety of ways, Durkheim further strengthened the likelihood that they were correct. Suicide rates were higher in Protestant countries than in Catholic ones; higher in Protestant regions of Catholic countries than in Catholic regions of Protestant countries; and so forth. The replication of findings added to the weight of evidence in support of his conclusions.

Problems of Validity

Whenever you base your research on an analysis of data that already exist, you are obviously limited to what exists. Often, the existing data don't cover exactly what you are interested in, and your measurements may not be altogether valid representations of the variables and concepts you want to draw conclusions about.

possible that the selected variables may have no policy relation to the topical area. For example, hospital beds or physicians per capita may not be a good indicator of the health quality of life in an area if these facilities are used by a national population (e.g., location of the Mayo Clinic in Minnesota or the location of Veterans Hospitals in various large metropolitan areas). Thus, even though the measure may be relatively high for a given geographical area, it may not reflect the health facilities available to the population in the area, since the individuals from many other areas may use these facilities quite extensively. A second methodological difficulty with the construction of quality of life indices is the aggregation of the selected variables, i.e., the problem of weighting of the individual variables. For example, health facilities and climate are variables that are likely to be weighted high by individuals over 60, but are likely to be given a lower weighting by individuals under 60. In the construction of quality of life indices the manner in which the population of an area is likely to weight the various individual variables must be taken into account in constructing the overall measure.

In summary, the construction of objective quality of life indicators has been hindered by the inability of social investigators to solve key methodological problems. First, no consensus has developed concerning the individual variables that are to be selected for the construction of the various indices. Second, no consensus has been developed concerning the manner in which the various selected variables are to be aggregated together employing some weighting scheme.

References:

Gehrmann, Friedhelm. 1978. " 'Valid' Empirical Measurement of Quality of Life?" *Social Indicators Research* 5 (January): 73–109.

Liu, Ben-Chieh. 1973. *The Quality of Life in the United States, 1970: Index, Ratings, and Statistics.* Kansas City, MO: Midwest Research Institute.

Liu, Ben-Chieh. 1975. *Quality of Life Indicators in U.S. Metropolitan Areas, 1970: A Comprehensive Assessment.* Washington, DC: Environmental Protection Agency.

Smith, David M. 1973. *The Geography of Social Well-Being in the United States: An Introduction to Territorial Social Indicators.* New York: McGraw-Hill Book Company.

You'll recall that Stouffer wanted to look at the consequences of the depression on what he called "impulsive marriages." Had he been able to interview married couples at length, he probably would have been able to categorize each couple as representing an impulsive marriage or not, and we might all have agreed that his categorizations were valid ones. Official statistics, however, didn't indicate whether the couples were getting married impulsively. As a result, he had to find data that *were* recorded and could be taken as an *indicator* of impulsiveness. In this case, he chose to analyze rates of out-of-state marriages. Notice that this procedure involves the following line of reasoning:

1. Assume that out-of-state marriages are more impulsive than in-state marriages.

2. If the depression produced a greater number of impulsive marriages, then we should expect to find more out-of-state marriages during the depression.

3. Finding that out-of-state marriages *did* increase during the depression confirms the hypothesis about impulsive marriages *only if* the assumption about out-of-state marriages being more impulsive is correct.

Two additional characteristics of science are used to handle the problem of validity in analysis of existing statistics: logical reasoning and replication. First, you'll recall that Stouffer didn't grab out-of-state marriages out of the hat; he had a carefully reasoned theoretical basis for assuming that they could be taken to represent impulsiveness. Second, the increase in out-of-state marriages during the depression was only one of several findings supporting Stouffer's general conclusions about the consequences of the depression on the family. Had none of his other hypotheses turned out as expected, he would have questioned whether the increase in out-of-state marriages really meant what he thought it did.

Replication, in this sense, is a general solution to problems of validity in social research. Recall the earlier discussion of the interchangeability of indexes. Crying in sad movies isn't necessarily a valid measure of compassion, so if women cry more than men, that doesn't *prove* they are more compassionate. Neither is putting little birds back in their nests a valid measure of compassion, so that wouldn't *prove* women to be more compassionate. And giving money to charity could represent something other than compassion, and so forth. None of these things, *taken alone,* would prove that women were more compassionate than men. But if women appeared more compassionate than men by *all* these measures, that would create a weight of evidence in support of the conclusion. In the analysis of existing sta-

tistics, a little ingenuity and reasoning can usually turn up several independent tests of your hypothesis, and if all the tests seem to confirm it, then the weight of evidence supports the view you are advancing.

Problems of Reliability

The analysis of existing statistics depends heavily on the quality of the statistics themselves: are they accurate reports of what they claim to report? That can be a substantial problem sometimes, since the weighty tables of government statistics are sometimes grossly inaccurate.

Since a great deal of the research into crime is dependent on official crime statistics, this body of data has come under critical evaluation. The results have not been too encouraging. Suppose, for purposes of illustration, that you were interested in tracing the long-term trends in marijuana use in the United States. Official statistics on the numbers of people arrested for selling or possessing it would seem to be a reasonable measure of use. Right? Not necessarily.

To begin, you face a hefty problem of validity. Before the passage of the Marihuana Tax Act in 1937, grass was legal in the United States, so arrest records would not give you a valid measure of use. But even if you limited your inquiry to the post-1937 era, you would still have problems of reliability, stemming from the nature of law enforcement and crime record keeping.

Law enforcement, for example, is subject to various pressures. A public outcry against marijuana, led perhaps by a vocal citizens' group, often results in a police "crackdown on drug trafficking"—especially if it occurs during an election or budget year. A sensational story in the press can have a similar effect. In addition, the volume of other business facing police has an effect on marijuana arrests.

Lois DeFleur (1975) has traced the pattern of drug arrests in Chicago between 1942 and 1970 and has demonstrated that the official records present a far more accurate history of police practices and political pressure on police than a history of drug use. On a different level of analysis, Donald Black (1970) and others have analyzed the factors influencing whether an offender is actually arrested by police or let off with a warning. Ultimately, official crime statistics are influenced by whether specific offenders are well or poorly dressed, whether they are polite or abusive to police officers, and so forth. Consider unreported crimes, sometimes estimated to be as much as ten times the number of crimes known to police, and the reliability of crime statistics gets even shakier.

These comments concern crime statistics at a local level. Often it is useful to analyze national crime statistics, such as those reported in the FBI's annual *Uniform Crime Reports*. Additional problems are introduced at the national level. Different local jurisdictions define crimes differently. Also, participation in the FBI program is voluntary, so the data are incomplete.

Finally, the process of record keeping affects the records that are kept and reported. Whenever a law enforcement unit improves its record-keeping system—computerizing it, for example—the apparent crime rates always increase dramatically. That can happen even if the number of crimes committed, reported, and investigated does not increase.

Your first protection against the problems of reliability in the analysis of existing statistics is awareness—knowing that the problem may exist. Investigating the nature of the data collection and tabulation may enable you to assess the nature and degree of unreliability so that you can judge its potential impact on your research interest.

If you also use logical reasoning and replication, as discussed above, you can usually cope with the problem.

Sources of Existing Statistics

It would take a whole book just to list the sources of data available for analysis. In this section, I want to mention a few sources and point you in the direction of finding others relevant to your research interest.

Undoubtedly, the single most valuable book you can buy is the annual *Statistical Abstract of the United States*, published by the United States Department of Commerce. It is unquestionably the single best source of data about the United States, and it includes statistics on the individual states and (less extensively) cities as well as on the nation as a whole. Where else can you learn the number of work stoppages in the country year by year, residential property taxes of major cities, the number of water pollution discharges reported around the country, the number of business proprietorships in the nation, and hundreds of other such handy bits of information? To make things even better, Grosset & Dunlap, a commercial publisher, currently offers the same book in soft cover for less cost. The commercial version is entitled *The U.S. Fact Book: The American Almanac* and shouldn't be confused with other almanacs that are less reliable and less useful for social scientific research.

Federal agencies—the Departments of Labor, Agriculture, Transportation, and so forth—publish countless data series. To find out what's available, go to your library, find the government documents section, and spend a few hours browsing through the shelves. You'll come away with a clear sense of the wealth of data available for your insight and ingenuity.

World statistics are available through the United Nations. Its *Demographic Yearbook* presents annual vital statistics (births, deaths, and other data relevant to population) for the individual nations of the world. Other publications report a variety of other kinds of data. Again, a trip to your library is the best introduction to what's available.

The amount of data provided by non-government agencies is as staggering as the amount your taxes buy. Chambers of commerce often publish data reports on business, as do private consumer groups. Ralph Nader has information on automobile safety, and *Common Cause* covers politics and government. And, as mentioned earlier, George Gallup publishes reference volumes on public opinion as tapped by Gallup Polls since 1935.

My temptation is to continue listing data sources, but I suspect that you have already gotten the idea. I will suggest that you visit the government documents section the next time you're at your college library. You'll be amazed by the data waiting for your analysis. The lack of funds to support expensive data collection is no reason for not doing good and useful social research.

HISTORICAL/COMPARATIVE ANALYSIS

In this final section of the chapter, we are going to examine historical/comparative research, a method that differs substantially from those previously discussed, though it overlaps somewhat with field research, content analysis, and the analysis of existing statistics. It involves the use of historical methods by sociologists, political scientists, and other social scientists.

The discussion of longitudinal research designs in Chapter 4 notwithstanding, our examination of research methods to date has focused primarily on studies anchored in one point in time and in one locale, whether a particular small group or a nation. This focus, while accurately portraying the main thrust of contemporary social scientific research, conceals the fact that social scientists are also interested in tracing the development of social forms over time and comparing those developmental processes across cultures. So in this section, after describing some major instances of historical and comparative research in the past, I'll turn to the key elements of this method with the purpose of empowering you to use it.

Examples of Historical/ Comparative Analysis

August Comte, who coined the term *sociologie,* saw that new discipline as the final stage in a historical development of ideas. With his broadest brush, he painted an evolutionary picture that took humans from a reliance on religion to metaphysics to science. With a finer brush, he portrayed science as evolving from the development of biology and the other natural sciences to the development of psychology and, finally, to the development of scientific sociology.

A great many later social scientists have also turned their attention to broad historical processes. A number have examined the historical progression of social forms from the simple to the complex, from rural-agrarian to urban-industrial societies. The American anthropologist Lewis Morgan, for example, saw a progression from "savagery" to "barbarism" to "civilization" (1870). Robert Redfield, a more recent anthropologist, has written of a shift from "folk society" to "urban society" (1941). Durkheim saw social evolution largely as a process of ever-greater division of labor (1893). In a more specific analysis, Karl Marx examined economic systems progressing historically from primitive to feudal to capitalistic forms (1867). All history, he wrote in this context, was a history of class struggle—the "haves" struggling to maintain their advantages and the "have-nots" struggling for a better lot in life. Looking beyond capitalism, Marx saw the development of socialism and finally communism.

Not all historical studies in the social sciences have had this evolutionary flavor, however. Some social scientific readings of the historical record, in fact, point to grand cycles rather than linear progressions. No scholar better represents this view than Pitirim A. Sorokin. A participant in the Russian Revolution of 1917, Sorokin served as secretary to Prime Minister Kerensky. Both Kerensky and Sorokin fell from favor, however, and Sorokin began his second career—as an American sociologist.

Whereas Comte read history as a progression from religion to science, Sorokin (1937–1940) suggested that societies alternate cyclically between two points of view, which he called "ideational" and "sensate." Sorokin's sensate point of view defines reality in terms of sense experiences. The ideational, by contrast, places a greater emphasis on spiritual and religious factors. Sorokin's reading of the historical record further indicated that the passage between the ideational and sensate was through a third point of view, which he called the "idealistic." This latter combined elements of the sensate and ideational in an integrated, rational view of the world.

These examples indicate some of the topics historical/comparative researchers have examined. To get a better sense of what historical/comparative research entails, let's look at a few examples in somewhat more detail.

Weber and the Role of Ideas In his analysis of economic history, Karl Marx put forward a view of economic determinism. That

is, he felt that economic factors determined the nature of all other aspects of society. For example, Marx's analysis showed that a function of European churches was to justify and support the capitalist status quo— religion was a tool of the powerful in maintaining their dominance over the powerless. "Religion is the sigh of the oppressed creature," Marx wrote in a famous passage, "the sentiment of a heartless world, and the soul of soulless conditions. It is the opium of the people" (Bottomore and Rubel 1956:27).

Max Weber, a German sociologist, disagreed. Without denying that economic factors could and did affect other aspects of society, Weber argued that economic determinism did not explain everything. Indeed, Weber said, economic forms could come from noneconomic ideas. In his research in the sociology of religion, Weber examined the extent to which religious institutions were the source of social behavior rather than mere reflections of economic conditions. His most noted statement of this side of the issue is found in *The Protestant Ethic and the Spirit of Capitalism* (1905). Here's a brief overview of Weber's thesis.

John Calvin (1509–1564), a French theologian, was an important figure in the Protestant reformation of Christianity. Calvin taught that the ultimate salvation or damnation of every individual had already been decided by God; this idea is called predestination. Calvin also suggested that God communicated his decisions to people by making them either successful or unsuccessful during their earthly existence. God gave each person an earthly "calling"—an occupation or profession—and manifested their success or failure through that medium. Ironically, this point of view led Calvin's followers to *seek* proof of their coming salvation by working hard, saving their money, and generally striving for economic success.

In Weber's analysis, Calvinism provided an important stimulus for the development of capitalism. Rather than "wasting" their money on worldly comforts, the Calvinists reinvested it in their economic enterprises, thus providing the *capital* necessary for the development of capitalism. In arriving at this interpretation of the origins of capitalism, Weber researched the official doctrines of the early Protestant churches, studied the preachings of Calvin and other church leaders, and examined other relevant historical documents.

In three other studies—originally published in 1934—Weber conducted detailed historical analyses of Judaism (1952) and the religions of China (1951) and India (1958). Among other things, Weber wanted to know why capitalism had not developed in the ancient societies of China, India, and Israel. In none of the three religions did he find any teaching that would have supported the accumulation and reinvestment of capitalism—strengthening his conclusion about the role of Protestantism in that regard.

Japanese Religion and Capitalism. Weber's thesis regarding Protestantism and capitalism has become a classic in the social sciences. Not surprisingly, other scholars have attempted to test it in other historical situations. No analysis has been more interesting, however, than Robert Bellah's examination of the growth of capitalism in Japan during the late nineteenth and early twentieth centuries, entitled *Tokugawa Religion* (1957).

Both as an undergraduate and as a graduate student, Bellah had developed interests in Weber and in Japanese society. Given these two interests, it was perhaps inevitable that he would, in 1951, first conceive his Ph.D. thesis topic as "nothing less than an 'Essay on the Economic Ethic of Japan' to be a companion to Weber's studies of China, India, and Judaism: *The Economic Ethic of the World Religions*" (recalled in Bellah 1967:168). Originally, Bellah sketched his research design as follows:

Problems would have to be specific and limited—no general history would be attempted—since time span is several centuries. Field work in Japan on the actual economic ethic practiced by persons in various situations, with, if possible, controlled matched samples from the U. S. (questionnaires, interviews, etc.).

(1967:168)

Bellah's original plan, then, called for surveys of contemporary Japanese and Americans. However, he did not receive the financial support necessary for the study as originally envisioned. So instead, he immersed himself in the historical records of Japanese religion, seeking the roots of the rise of capitalism in Japan.

Over the course of several years' research, Bellah uncovered numerous leads. In a 1952 term paper on the subject, Bellah felt he had found the answer in the samurai code of *Bushido* and in the Confucianism practiced by the samurai class:

Here I think we find a real development of this-worldly asceticism, at least equaling anything found in Europe. Further, in this class the idea of duty in occupation involved achievement without traditionalistic limits, but to the limits of one's capacities, whether in the role of bureaucrat, doctor, teacher, scholar, or other role open to the Samurai.

(quoted in Bellah 1967:171)

The samurai, however, only made up a portion of Japanese society. So Bellah kept looking at the religions among Japanese generally. His understanding of the Japanese language was not yet very good, but he wanted to read religious texts in the original. Under these constraints and experiencing increased time-pressure, Bellah decided to concentrate his attention on a single group: *Shingaku*, a religious movement among merchants in the eighteenth and nineteenth centuries. He found that Shingaku had two influences on the development of capitalism. It offered an attitude toward work similar to the Calvinist notion of a "calling," and it had the effect of making business a more acceptable calling for Japanese. Previously, commerce had had a very low standing in Japan.

In other aspects of his analysis, Bellah examined the religious and political roles of the Emperor and the economic impact of periodically appearing emperor cults. Ultimately, Bellah's researches pointed to the variety of religious and philosophical factors that laid the groundwork for the development of capitalism in Japan. It seems unlikely that he would have achieved anything approaching that depth of understanding if he had been able to pursue his original plan to interview matched samples of Americans and Japanese.

These examples of historical/comparative research should have given you some sense of the potential power in the method. Let's turn now to an examination of the sources and techniques used in this method.

Sources of Historical/Comparative Data

As we saw in the case of existing statistics, there is no end of data available for analysis in historical research. To begin, historians may have already reported on whatever it is you want to examine, and their analyses can give you an initial grounding in the subject, a jumping-off point for more in-depth research.

Ultimately, you will usually want to go beyond others' conclusions and examine some "raw data" and draw your own conclusions. These vary, of course, according to the topic under study. In Bellah's study of Tokugawa religion, raw data included the sermons of Shingaku teachers. When W. I. Thomas and Florian Znaniecki (1918) studied the adjustment process for Polish peasants coming to the United States early in this century, they examined letters written by the immigrants to their families in Poland. (They obtained the letters through newspaper advertisements.) Other researchers have analyzed old diaries. Such personal documents only scratch the surface, however.

In discussing procedures for studying the history of family life, Ellen Rothman points to the following sources:

In addition to personal sources, there are public records which are also revealing of family history. Newspapers are especially rich in evidence on the educational, legal, and recreational aspects of family life in the past as seen from a local point of view. Magazines reflect more general patterns of family life; students often find them interesting to explore for data on perceptions and expectations of mainstream family values. Magazines offer several different kinds of sources at once: visual materials (illustrations and advertisements), commentary (editorial and advice columns), and fiction. Popular periodicals are particularly rich in the last two. Advice on many questions of concern to families—from the proper way to discipline children to the economics of wallpaper—fills magazine columns from the early nineteenth century to the present. Stories that suggest common experiences or perceptions of family life appear with the same continuity.

(1981:53)

Organizations generally document themselves, so if you are studying the development of some organization—as Bellah studied Shingaku, for example—you should examine its official documents: charters, policy statements, speeches by leaders, etc. Once when I was studying the rise of a contemporary Japanese religious group—*Sokagakkai*—I discovered not only weekly newspapers and magazines published by the group, but also a published collection of all the speeches given by the original leaders. It was possible, then, for me to trace changes in recruitment patterns over time. At the outset, followers were enjoined to enroll all the world. Later, the emphasis shifted specifically to Japan. Once a sizable Japanese membership had been established, an emphasis on enrolling all the world returned (Babbie 1966).

Often, official government documents provide the data needed for analysis. To better appreciate the history of race relations in America, A. Leon Higginbotham, Jr. (1978), examined some 200 years of laws and court cases involving race. Himself the first black American appointed a federal judge, Higginbotham found that the law, rather than protecting blacks, was the embodiment of bigotry and oppression. In the earliest court cases, there was considerable ambiguity over whether blacks were indentured servants or, in fact, slaves. Later court cases and laws clarified the matter—holding blacks to be something less than human.

The sources of data for historical analysis are too extensive to cover even in outline here, though I trust the few examples I've given you so far will enable you to find whatever resources you need. I want to conclude this section with a couple of cautions.

As we saw in the case of existing statistics, you cannot trust the accuracy of records—official or unofficial, primary or secondary. Your protection lies in replication: in the case of historical research, in *corroboration*. If several sources point to the same set of "facts," your confidence in them might reasonably increase.

At the same time, you need always be wary of bias in your data sources. If all your data on the development of a political movement are taken from the movement itself, you are unlikely to gain a well-rounded view of it. The diaries of well-to-do gentry of the Middle Ages may not give you an accurate view of life in general during those times. Where possible, obtain data from a variety of sources, representing different points of view. Here's what Bellah said regarding his analysis of Shingaku:

One could argue that there would be a bias in what was selected for notice by Western scholars. However, the fact that there was material from Western scholars with varied interests from a number of countries and over a period of nearly a century reduced the probability of bias.

(Bellah 1967:179)

Analytical Techniques

I want to conclude this section of the chapter with some comments regarding the analysis of historical/comparative data. Since historical/comparative research is a qualitative method, there are no easily listed steps to follow in the analysis of historical data.

Max Weber used the German term *verstehen*—"understanding"—in reference to an essential quality of social research. He meant that the researcher must be able to take on, mentally, the circumstances, views, and feelings of those being studied so as to interpret their actions appropriately. More recently, social scientists have adopted the term *hermeneutics* for this aspect of social research. Originally a Christian theological term referring to the interpretation of spiritual truth in the Bible, the term has been secularized to mean the art, science, or skill of interpretation.

Whereas the conclusions drawn from quantitative research methods can rest, in part, on numerical calculations—x is either greater than y or it isn't—hermeneutic conclusions are harder to pin down and more subject to debate. But hermeneutics involves more than mere opinions. Albert Einstein described the foundation of science this way:

Science is the attempt to make the chaotic diversity of our sense-experience correspond to a logically uniform system of thought. In this system single experiences must be correlated with the theoretic structure in such a way that the resulting coordination is unique and convincing.

(1940:487)

The historical/comparative researcher must find patterns among the voluminous details describing the subject matter of study. Often the "theoretic structure" Einstein mentioned takes the form of what Weber called *ideal types*: conceptual models comprised of the essential characteristics of social phenomena. Thus, for example, Weber himself did considerable research on bureaucracy. Having observed numerous actual bureaucracies, Weber (1925) detailed those qualities essential to bureaucracies in general: jurisdictional areas, hierarchically structured authority, written files, etc. Weber did not merely list those characteristics common to all the actual bureaucracies he observed. Rather, he needed to fully understand the essentials of bureaucratic operation so as to create a theoretical model of the "perfect" (ideal type) bureaucracy.

Often historical/comparative research is informed by a particular theoretical paradigm. Thus Marxist scholars may undertake historical analyses of particular situations—such as the history of Hispanic minorities in the United States—to determine whether they can be understood in terms of the Marxist version of conflict theory. Sometimes, historical/comparative researchers attempt to replicate prior studies in new situations—for example, Bellah's study of Tokugawa religion in the context of Weber's studies of religion and economics.

This concludes our discussion of unobtrusive research methods. As you can see, social scientists have a variety of ways to study social life without having any impact on what they study.

MAIN POINTS

- Unobtrusive measures are ways of studying social behavior without affecting it in the process.

- Content analysis is a social research method appropriate for studying human communications. Besides being used to study communication processes, it may be used to study other aspects of social behavior.

- Units of communication, such as words, paragraphs, and books, are the usual units of analysis in content analysis.

- Standard probability sampling techniques are appropriate in content analysis.

- Manifest content refers to the directly visible, objectively identifiable characteristics of a communication, such as the specific words in a book, the specific colors used in a painting, and so forth. That is one focus for content analysis.

- Latent content refers to the meanings contained within communications. The determination of latent content requires judgments on the part of the researcher.

- Coding is the process of transforming raw data—either manifest or latent content—into standardized, quantitative form.

- A variety of government and nongovernment agencies provide aggregate data for studying aspects of social life.

- The ecological fallacy refers to the possibility that patterns found at a group level differ from those that would be found on an individual level; thus we can be misled when we analyze aggregated data for the purpose of understanding individual behavior.

- The problem of validity in connection with the analysis of existing statistics can usually be handled through logical reasoning and replication.

- Existing statistics often have problems of reliability, and it is necessary to use them with caution.

- Social scientists also use historical/comparative methods to discover patterns in the histories of different cultures.

■ Hermeneutics refers to interpreting social life by mentally taking on the circumstances, views, and feelings of the participants.

■ An ideal type is a conceptual model comprised of the essential qualities of a social phenomenon.

REVIEW QUESTIONS AND EXERCISES

1. In two or three paragraphs, outline a content analysis design to determine whether the Republican or the Democratic party is the more supportive of free speech. Be sure to specify units of analysis, sampling methods, and the relevant measurements.

2. Social scientists often contrast the sense of "community" in villages, small towns, and neighborhoods from life in large, urban societies. Try your hand at constructing an ideal type of community: listing its essential qualities.

ADDITIONAL READINGS

Andreski, Stanislav, *The Uses of Comparative Sociology* (Berkeley, Calif.: University of California Press, 1969). An excellent introduction and overview of the theory and methods of historical/comparative research. Andreski provides numerous examples to illustrate the method.

Holsti, Ole, *Content Analysis for the Social Sciences and Humanities* (Reading, Mass.: Addison-Wesley, 1969). A more recent comprehensive overview of content analysis as a method. This excellent book examines the place of content analysis within the context of studying communication processes, discusses and illustrates specific techniques, and cites numerous reports utilizing this method. This book concludes with a substantial discussion of the use of computers in both the coding and analysis of content.

Stouffer, Samuel, *Social Research to Test Ideas* (New York: Free Press of Glencoe, 1962), Chapter 6: "Effects of the Depression on the Family." A minor, little-known study by a master that illustrates what can be done with existing statistics when specially collected data are not available. Wishing to learn whether the depression of the 1930s had substantially altered traditional marriage and family patterns, Stouffer asks how such an alteration would show up in regularly compiled government statistics and then looks to see. Also instructive is Chapter 7, which examines the effects of radio on newspaper circulation.

The U.S. Fact Book: The American Almanac (New York: Grosset & Dunlap, 1979). A commercial reprinting of *Statistical Abstract of the United States,* compiled and published by the United States Department of Commerce, Bureau of the Census. This is absolutely the best book bargain available (present company excluded). Although the hundreds of pages of tables of statistics are not exciting bedtime reading—the plot is a little thin—it is an absolutely essential resource volume for every social scientist.

Webb, Eugene T.; Campbell, Donald T., Schwartz, Richard D.; Sechrest, Lee; and Grove, Janet Belew, *Nonreactive Measures in the Social Sciences* (Boston: Houghton Mifflin, 1981). A compendium of unobtrusive measures. Includes physical traces, a variety of achival sources, and observation. Good discussion of the ethics involved and the limitations of such measures.

12

Evaluation Research

What You'll Learn in This Chapter

Now you're going to see one of the most rapidly growing uses of social research: the evaluation of social interventions. You'll come away from this chapter able to judge whether social programs have succeeded or failed.

INTRODUCTION

TOPICS COMMONLY SUBJECTED TO EVALUATION RESEARCH

FORMULATING THE PROBLEM
    Measurement
    Experimental Designs
    Quasi-experimental Designs
    Operationalizing Success/Failure

THE SOCIAL CONTEXT
    Logistical Problems
    Some Ethical Issues
    Use of Research Results

SOCIAL INDICATORS RESEARCH
    The Death Penalty and Deterrence
    Computer Simulation

MAIN POINTS

REVIEW QUESTIONS AND EXERCISES

ADDITIONAL READINGS

INTRODUCTION

Evaluation research—sometimes called *program evaluation*—refers to a research purpose rather than a specific research method. Its special purpose is to evaluate the impact of social interventions such as new teaching methods, innovations in parole, and a wide variety of such programs. Many methods—surveys, experiments, etc.—can be used in evaluation research.

Evaluation research is probably as old as social science research generally. Whenever people have instituted a social reform for a specific purpose, they have paid attention to its actual consequences, even if they have not always done so in a conscious, deliberate, or sophisticated fashion. In recent years, however, the field of evaluation research has become an increasingly popular and active research specialty, which has been reflected in textbooks, courses, and projects. The growth of evaluation research also indicates a more general trend in the social sciences. As a consequence, you are likely to read increasing numbers of evaluation reports, and as a researcher you are likely to be asked to conduct evaluations.

In part, the growth of evaluation research no doubt reflects social scientists' increasing desire to actually make a difference in the world. At the same time, we cannot discount the influence of (1) increased federal requirements for program evaluations to accompany the implementation of new programs and (2) the availability of research funds to fulfill that requirement. Whatever the mixture of these influences, it seems clear that social scientists will be bringing their skills into the real world more in the future than ever before.

In this chapter, we're going to look at some of the key elements in this form of social research. We'll start by considering the kinds of topics commonly subjected to evaluation, and then we'll move through some of the main operational aspects of it: measurement, study design, and execution. As we'll see, formulating questions is as important as answering them. Evaluation research, since it occurs within real life, has special problems, and we're going to look at some of those. There are particular logistical problems, and we'll see that there are special ethical issues involved in evaluation research generally and its specific, technical procedures. As you review reports of program evaluations, you should be especially sensitive to these logistical problems.

Evaluation is a form of *applied* research—it is intended to have some real-world effect. It will be useful, therefore, to consider whether and how it is actually applied. As will become evident, the clear and obvious implications of an evaluation research project do not necessarily have any impact on real life. They may become the focus of ideological, rather than scientific, debates. They may simply be denied out of hand, as occurred when former President Nixon summarily dismissed the conclusions drawn by his commission on pornography. Or, perhaps most typically, they are simply ignored and forgotten, left to warp shelves and collect dust in bookcases across the land.

To conclude the chapter, I'm going to focus on a particular resource for large-scale evaluation—*social indicators research*. This type of research is also a rapidly growing specialty. Essentially it involves the creation of aggregated indicators of the "health" of society, similar to the economic indicators that give diagnoses and prognoses of economies.

TOPICS COMMONLY SUBJECTED TO EVALUATION RESEARCH

Most fundamentally, evaluation research is appropriate whenever some *social interven-*

tion occurs or is planned. A social intervention is an action taken within a social context for the purpose of producing some intended result. In its simplest sense, evaluation research is a process of determining whether the intended result was produced.

Suppose, for example, that we have the good idea that conjugal visits would improve morale among prison inmates. (In such programs, prisoners are permitted to have sex periodically with their spouses.) If we were to institute such a program, it would be nice to know if morale actually improved. Conceivably, the program might have no overall effect on morale, and it could even make matters worse than before. An evaluation research project could be designed to test the impact of the program. Essentially, it would involve devising some measure of morale, creating experimental and control groups of prisoners, letting the experimental group have conjugal visits for a while, then measuring the levels of morale in the two groups. If morale was significantly higher in the experimental group, we might conclude that conjugal visits did the trick. As we'll see, there's much more to evaluation research than this simple illustration suggests, but you should get the general idea of what's involved.

To take another example, you might believe, as some educational reformers do, that grading in schools is counterproductive to the process of real learning. If you were in a position to do something about it, you might be tempted to put a halt to grading. Again, however, it would be nice to know if the innovation produced the intended result, did nothing, or even produced some unintended result that you'd prefer not to have.

The substantive topics appropriate to evaluation research are limitless. When the federal government abolished the selective service system, military researchers began paying special attention to the impact on enlistments. As individual states have liberalized their marijuana laws, researchers have sought to learn the consequences, both for marijuana use and for other forms of social behavior. Do no-fault divorce reforms increase the number of divorces, and are related social problems lessened or increased? Has no-fault automobile insurance really brought down insurance policy premiums?

A project evaluating the nation's driver education programs, conducted by the National Highway and Transportation Safety Administration (NHTSA), stirred up a controversy. Philip Hilts reports the findings:

> For years the auto insurance industry has given large insurance discounts for children who take drivers' education courses, because statistics show that they have fewer accidents.
>
> The preliminary results of a new major study, however, indicate that drivers' education does not prevent or reduce the incidence of traffic accidents at all.
>
> (Hilts 1981:4)

Based on an analysis of 17,500 young people in DeKalb County, Georgia (including Atlanta), the preliminary findings indicate that students who take driver training have just as many accidents and traffic violations as those who don't. While the matter has not been fully resolved, the study has already revealed some subtle aspects of driver training.

First, it is suggested that the apparent impact of driver education is largely a matter of self-selection. The kind of students who take driver education are less likely to have accidents and traffic violations—with or without driver training. Students with high grades, for example, are more likely to sign up for driver training, and they are also less likely to have accidents.

More startling, however, is the suggestion that driver training courses may actually *increase* traffic accidents! The existence of driver education may encourage some students to get their licenses earlier than if there were no such courses. In a study of 10 Connecticut towns that discontinued driver training, it was found that about three-fourths of those who probably would have been licensed through their classes delayed getting licenses until they were 18 and older (Hilts 1981:4).

As you might imagine, the preliminary results have not been well received by those most closely associated with driver training. This matter was complicated, moreover, by the fact that the NHTSA study was also evaluating a new, more intensive, training program—and the preliminary results showed the new program was effective.

As you can see, the questions appropriate to evaluation research are of great practical significance: jobs, programs, and investments as well as beliefs and values are at stake. Let's now examine how these questions are answered—how evaluations are conducted.

FORMULATING THE PROBLEM

Several years ago, I headed an institutional research office that conducted research of direct relevance to the operation of the university. Often, we were asked to evaluate new programs in the curriculum. The following description is fairly typical of the problem that arose in that context, and it points to one of the key barriers to good evaluation research.

Faculty members would appear at my office to say they had been told by the university administration to arrange for an evaluation of the new program they had been given permission to try. The way I've put that points to a very common problem: often the people whose programs are being evaluated aren't thrilled at the prospect. For them, an independent evaluation threatens the survival of the program and perhaps even their jobs.

The main problem I want to introduce, however, has to do with the purpose of the intervention to be evaluated. The question "What is the intended result of the new program?" often produced a rather vague response; for example, "Students will get an in-depth and genuine understanding of mathematics, instead of simply memorizing methods of calculations." Fabulous! And how could we measure that "in-depth and genuine understanding?" Often, I was told that the program aimed at producing something that could not be measured by conventional aptitude and achievement tests. No problem there; that's to be expected when we're innovating and being unconventional. What would be an unconventional measure of the intended result? Sometimes this discussion came down to an assertion that the effects of the program would be "unmeasurable."

There's the common rub in evaluation research: measuring the "unmeasurable." Evaluation research is a matter of finding out whether something is there or not there, whether something happened or didn't happen. In order to conduct evaluation research, we must be able to operationalize, observe, and recognize the presence or absence of what is under study.

Often outcomes can be derived from published program documents. Thus, when Edward Howard and Darlene Norman (1981) evaluated the performance of the Vigo County Public Library in Indiana, they began with the statement of purpose previously adopted by the library's Board of Trustees.

To acquire by purchase or gift, and by recording and production, relevant and potentially useful information that is produced by, about, or for the citizens of the community;

To organize this information for efficient delivery and convenient access, furnish the equipment necessary for its use, and provide assistance in its utilization; and

To effect maximum use of this information toward making the community a better place in which to live through aiding the search for understanding by its citizens.

(1981:306)

As the researchers say, "Everything that VCPL does can be tested against the Statement of Purpose." They then set about creating operational measures appropriate to each of the purposes.

In setting up an evaluation, then, you must be sure you have constructed a research design that clearly specifies the outcome of the program. Let's see some of the elements in such a design.

Measurement

Earlier chapters in this book have already discussed the key issues involved in measurement, and those earlier discussions apply to evaluation research. In the present case, it will be more useful to focus our attention on *what* should be measured.

Specifying Outcomes   Clearly, a key variable for evaluation researchers to measure is the *outcome* or *response* variable. If a social program is intended to accomplish something, you must be able to measure that something. If you want to reduce prejudice, you need to be able to measure prejudice. If you want to increase marital harmony, you need to be able to measure that. As Riecken and Boruch (1974) point out, however, any program has many possible outcomes, some of which contradict its purpose.

For example, when Meyer and Borgatta (1959) set out to evaluate the effects of a mental rehabilitation program, they created a list of behaviors and conditions to specify the general goal of "patient recovery." Their list included the following dimensions and aspects of recovery (cited by Riecken and Boruch 1974:119):

- Not being recommitted to an institution
- Being independent of rehabilitation agencies
- Being effective in social relations
- Being economically independent
- Being oriented toward reality
- Enjoying a general well-being

Notice the value of specifying several different aspects of the desired outcome. If the rehabilitation program achieved one of these goals at the expense of the others, it might be considered unsuccessful. If patients, for example, were saved from being recommitted to mental health institutions by making them dependent on welfare agencies, that would probably be regarded as simply trading one problem for another. It is essential, therefore, that evaluation researchers recognize and take account of all possible aspects of the program's outcomes.

Intended outcomes such as those listed above, of course, are not specified sufficiently for measurement. How much *well-being* is enough? And what does *well-being* look like in real life? How can we tell if it occurred or not? Even something like not being recommitted to an institution is subject to varied interpretations. Suppose a patient stayed overnight for follow-up observation? That probably wouldn't be considered recommitment. But suppose it was three days of observation, or seven days? And suppose the observation was ordered by authorities because of the patient's behavior on the outside? You can see how the line between recommitment and non-recommitment can become fuzzy. Even where medical or legal definitions of commitment exist, they might not be appropriate to the evaluation of the program.

Measuring Experimental Contexts Measuring the dependent variables directly involved in the experimental program is only a beginning. As Riecken and Boruch (1974:120–21) point out, it is often appropriate and important to measure aspects of the context within which the experiment is conducted. These variables are external to the experiment itself, yet they affect it. Consider, for example, an evaluation of a program aimed at training unskilled people for employment. The primary outcome measure would be their success at gaining employment after completing the program. While you would, of course, observe and calculate the subjects' employment rate, you should also determine what has happened to the employment/unemployment rates of the society at large during the evaluation. A general slump in the job market should be taken into account in assessing what might otherwise seem a pretty low employment rate for subjects. Or, if all of the experimental subjects get jobs following the program, that might result more from a general increase in available jobs than from the value of the program itself. Combining complementary measures with proper control group designs should allow you to pinpoint the effects of the program you are evaluating.

Specifying Interventions Besides making measurements relevant to the outcomes of a program, it is also necessary to measure the program intervention—the experimental stimulus. In part, this measurement will be handled by the assignment of subjects to experimental and control groups, if that's the research design. Assigning a person to the experimental group is the same as scoring that person yes on the stimulus, and assignment to the control group represents a score of no. In practice, however, it's seldom that simple and straightforward.

Let's stick with the job-training example above. Some people will participate in the program; others will not. But imagine for a moment what job-training programs are probably like. Some subjects will participate fully, others will miss a lot of sessions or fool around when they are present. So we may need measures of the extent or quality of participation in the program. And if the program is effective, we should find that those participating fully have higher employment rates than those who participated less.

Other factors may further confound the administration of the experimental stimulus. Suppose you and I were evaluating a new form of psychotherapy that's designed to cure sexual impotence. Several therapists administer it to subjects composing an experimental group. We'll compare the recovery rate of the experimental group with that of a control group (a group receiving some other therapy or none at all). It might be useful to include the names of the therapists treating specific subjects in the experimental group, since some may be more effective than others. If that turns out to be the case, we must find out why the treatment worked better for some therapists than for others. What we learn will further elaborate our understanding of the therapy itself.

Specifying Other Variables It is usually necessary to measure the population of subjects involved in the program being evaluated. In particular, it is important to define those for whom the program is appropriate. If we are evaluating a new form of psychotherapy, it's probably appropriate for people with mental problems, but how should we define and measure mental problems more specifically? The job-training program mentioned above is probably intended for people who are having trouble finding work, but a more specific definition would be needed.

This process of definition and measurement has two aspects. First, the population of possible subjects for the evaluation must be defined. Then, ideally, all or a sample of appropriate subjects would be assigned to experimental and control groups as warranted by the study design. Beyond defining the relevant population, however, you should make fairly precise measurements on the variables considered in your definition for the specific subjects in the study. Even though the randomization of subjects in the psychotherapy study would ensure an equal distribution of those with mild and severe mental problems in the experimental and control groups, it's important for us to keep track of the relative severity of different subjects' problems in case the therapy turns out to be effective only for those with mild disorders. Similarly, we should measure such demographic variables as sex, age, race, and so forth in case the therapy works only for women, the elderly, or whatever.

Second, in providing for the measurement of these different kinds of variables, there is a continuing choice: to create new measures or use ones that have already been devised by other researchers. If your study addresses something that's never been measured before, the choice is an easy one. If not, you will have to evaluate the relative worth of various existing measurement devices in the context of your specific research situations and purpose. And you'll recall, this is a general issue in social research—applying well beyond evaluation research. Let me review briefly the advantages of the two options.

Creating measurements specifically for a study has the advantage of greater possible relevance and validity. If the psychotherapy we are evaluating is aimed at a specific aspect of recovery, we can create measures that pinpoint that aspect. We might not be able to find any standardized psychological measures that hit that aspect right on the head. However, creating our own measure will cost us the advantages to be gained from using preexisting measures. Creating good measures takes time and energy, both of which could be saved by adopting an existing technique. Of greater scientific significance, measures that have been used frequently by other researchers carry a body of possible comparisons that might be important to our evaluation. If the experimental therapy raises scores by an average of 10 points on a standardized test, we will be in a position to compare that therapy with others that had been evaluated using the same standardized measure. Finally, measures with a long history of use usually have known degrees of validity and reliability, while newly created measures will require pretesting or will be used with considerable uncertainty.

As you can see, measurement must be taken very seriously in evaluation research. You must carefully determine all the variables to be measured and get appropriate measures for each. However, you need to realize that such decisions are typically not purely scientific ones. Evaluation researchers often must work out their measurement strategy with the people responsible for the program that is being evaluated. It usually doesn't make sense to determine whether a program achieves Outcome X when its purpose is to achieve Outcome Y. (Realize, however, that evaluation designs sometimes have the purpose of testing for unintended consequences.)

There is a political aspect in these choices, also. Since evaluation research often affects other people's professional interests—their pet program may be halted, or they may be fired or lose professional standing—the results of evaluation research are often argued about.

Let's turn now to some of the evaluation designs commonly employed by researchers.

Experimental Designs

Chapter 8 has already given you a good introduction to a variety of experimental designs that researchers use in studying social life. Many of those same designs are appropriate to evaluation research. By way of illustration, let's see how the classical experimental model might be applied to our evaluation of the new psychotherapy mentioned above.

Since the therapy is designed to cure sexual impotence, we should begin by identifying a population of patients relevant to the therapy. This identification might be made by the group experimenting with the new therapy. Let's say we are dealing with a clinic that already has 100 patients being treated for sexual impotence. We might take that existing identification-definition as a starting point, and we should maintain any existing assessments of the severity of the problem for each specific patient.

For purposes of the evaluation research, however, we'll need to develop a more specific measure of impotence. Maybe it will involve whether patients have sexual intercourse at all (within a specified time), how often they have intercourse, or whether and how often they reach orgasm. Alternatively, the outcome measure might be based on the assessments of independent therapists who are not involved in the therapy but who interview the patients later. In any event, we will need to agree on the measures to be used.

In the simplest design, we would assign the 100 patients randomly to experimental and control groups; the former would receive the new therapy and the latter would be taken out of therapy altogether for the course of the experiment. Since ethical practice would probably prevent withdrawing therapy altogether from the control group, however, it's more likely that the control group would continue to receive their conventional therapy.

Having assigned subjects to the experimental and control groups, we need to agree on the length of the experiment. Perhaps the designers of the new therapy feel it ought to be effective within two months, and an agreement could be reached. The duration of the study doesn't need to be rigid, however. One purpose of the experiment and evaluation might be to determine how long it actually takes for the new therapy to be effective. Conceivably, then, an agreement could be struck to measure recovery rates weekly, say, and let the ultimate length of the experiment rest on a continual review of the results.

Let's suppose that the new therapy involves showing pornographic movies to patients. We'd need to specify that stimulus. How often would patients see the movies and how long would each session be? Would they see the movies in private or in groups? Should therapists be present? Perhaps we should observe the patients while the movies are being shown and include our observations among the measurements of the experimental stimulus. Do some patients watch the movies eagerly and others keep looking away from the screen? These are the kinds of questions that would need to be asked, and specific measurements would have to be created.

Having thus designed the study, all we have to do is "roll 'em." The study is set in motion, the observations are made and recorded, and the mass of data is accumulated for analysis. Once the study has run its course, we will be able to determine whether the new therapy had its intended— or perhaps some unintended—consequences. We can tell whether the movies were most effective for patients with mild problems or severe ones, whether they worked for men but not women, and so forth.

This simple illustration should show you how the standard experimental designs presented in Chapter 8 can be used in evaluation research. Many—perhaps most—of the evaluations you'll read about in the research literature, however, won't look exactly like the illustration. Being nested in real life, evaluation research often calls for *quasi-experimental* designs. Let's see what that means.

Quasi-Experimental Designs

Quasi-experiments, you'll recall, are distinguished from "true" experiments primarily by the lack of random assignment of subjects to an experimental and a control group. In evaluation research, it is often impossible to achieve such an assignment of subjects. Rather than forego evaluation altogether in such instances, it is sometimes possible to create and execute research designs that give some evaluation of the program in question. In this section, I'll describe some of the designs used.

Time-Series Designs   To illustrate the time-series design—studies of processes occurring over time—I will begin by asking you to assess the meaning of some hypothetical data. Suppose I come to you with what I say is an effective technique for getting students to *participate* in classroom sessions of a course I am teaching. To prove my assertion, I tell you that on Monday, only four students asked questions or made a comment in class; on Wednesday I devoted the class time to an open discussion of a controversial issue raging on campus; and on Friday, when we returned to the subject matter of the course, eight students asked questions or made comments. In other words, I contend, the discussion of a controversial issue on Wednesday has doubled classroom participation. This simple set of data is presented graphically in Figure 12-1.

Have I persuaded you that the open discussion on Wednesday has had the consequence I say it has? Probably you'd object that my data don't prove the case. Two observations (Monday and Friday) aren't

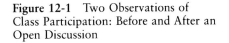

Figure 12-1   Two Observations of Class Participation: Before and After an Open Discussion

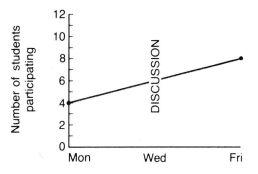

really enough to prove anything. Ideally I should have had two classes, with students assigned randomly to each, held an open discussion in only one, and then compared the two on Friday. But I don't have two classes with random assignment of students. Instead, I've been keeping a record of class participation throughout the semester for the one class. This record would allow you to conduct a time-series evaluation.

Figure 12-2 presents three possible patterns of class participation over time—both before and after the open discussion on Wednesday. Which of these patterns would give you some confidence that the discussion had the impact I contend it had?

If the time-series results looked like Pattern 1 in Figure 12-2, you'd probably conclude that the process of greater class participation had begun on the Wednesday before the discussion and had continued, unaffected, after the day devoted to the discussion. The long-term data seem to suggest that the trend would have occurred even without the discussion on Wednesday. Pattern 1, then, contradicts my assertion that the special discussion increased class participation.

Pattern 2 contradicts my assertion also. It indicates that class participation has been bouncing up and down in a regular pattern

Figure 12-2   Three Patterns of Class Participation in a Longer Historical Perspective

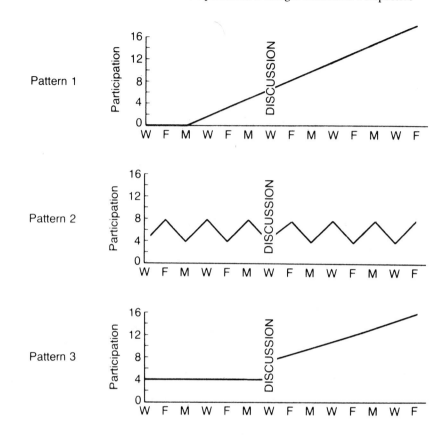

throughout the semester. Sometimes it increases from one class to the next, and sometimes it decreases; the open discussion on that Wednesday simply came at a time when the level of participation was due to increase. More to the point, we note that class participation decreased again at the class following the alleged postdiscussion increase.

Only Pattern 3 in Figure 12-2 supports my contention that the open discussion mattered. As we see, the level of discussion before that Wednesday had been a steady four students per class. Not only did the level of participation double following the day of discussion, but it continued to increase further afterward. Although these data do

not protect us against the possible influence of some extraneous factor (I might also have mentioned that participation would figure into students' grades), they do exclude the possibility that the increase results from a process of maturation (indicated in Pattern 1) or from regular fluctuations (indicated in Pattern 2).

Nonequivalent Control Groups   The time-series design just described involves only an "experimental" group, and you'll recall the value to be gained from having a control group. Sometimes, when it's not possible to create experimental and control groups by random asignment from a common pool, it is possible to find an existing "control" group that appears similar to the experimental group. If an innovative foreign language program is being tried in one class in a large high school, for example, you may be able to find another foreign language class in the same school that has a very similar student population: one that has about the same composition in terms of grade in school, sex, ethnicity, IQ, and so forth. The second class, then, could provide a point of comparison. At the end of the semester, both classes could be given the same foreign language test, and you could compare performances. Here's how two junior high schools were selected for purposes of evaluating a program aimed at discouraging tobacco, alcohol, and drug use.

The pairing of the two schools and their assignment to "experimental" and "control" conditions was not random. The local Lung Association had identified the school where we delivered the program as one in which administrators were seeking a solution to admitted problems of smoking, alcohol, and drug abuse. The "control" school was chosen as a convenient and nearby demographic match where administrators were willing to allow our surveying and breath-testing procedures. The principal of that school considered the existing program of health education to be effective and believed that the onset of smoking was relatively uncommon among his students. The communities served by the two schools were very similar. The rate of parental smoking reported by the students was just above 40 percent in both schools.

(McAlister et al. 1980:720)

Lacking random assignment of subjects into experimental and control groups, you do well to see if the two groups are comparable. Moreover, in the initial set of observations, the experimental and control groups reported virtually the same (low) frequency of smoking. Over the 21 months of the study, smoking increased in both groups, but it increased less in the experimental group than in the control group,

suggesting that the program had an impact on students' behavior.

Multiple Time-Series Designs Sometimes the evaluation of processes occurring outside of "pure" experimental controls can be made easier by the use of more than one time-series analysis. This design is an improved version of the nonequivalent control group design just described. Carol Weiss (1972) has presented a useful example of this design:

An interesting example of multiple time series was the evaluation of the Connecticut crackdown on highway speeding. Evaluators collected reports of traffic fatalities for several periods before and after the new program went into effect. They found that fatalities went down after the crackdown, but since the series had had an unstable up-and-down pattern for many years, it was not certain that the drop was due to the program. They then compared the statistics with time-series data from four neighboring states where there had been no changes in traffic enforcement. Those states registered no equivalent drop in fatalities. The comparison lent credence to the conclusion that the crackdown had had some effect.

(1972:69)

Although this study design is not as good as one in which subjects are assigned randomly, it is nonetheless an improvement over assessing the experimental group's performance without any comparison. That's what makes these designs *quasi-experiments* instead of just fooling around. The key in assessing this aspect of evaluation studies is *comparability,* as the following example illustrates.

Rural development is a growing concern in the poor countries of the world and one that has captured the attention and support of many rich countries. Through national foreign assistance programs and through international agencies such as the World Bank, the developed countries are in the process of sharing their technological knowledge and skills with the developing countries. Such programs have had mixed results, however. Often, modern techniques do not produce the intended results when applied in traditional societies.

Rajesh Tandon and L. Dave Brown (1981) undertook an experiment in which technological training would be accompanied by instruction in village organization. They felt it was important for poor farmers to learn how to organize and exert collective influence within their villages—getting needed action from government officials, for example. Only then would their new technological skills bear fruit.

Both intervention and evaluation were attached to an ongoing program in which 25 villages had been selected for technological training. Two poor farmers from each village had been trained in new agricultural technologies. Then they had been sent home to share their new knowledge with their fellow villagers and to organize other farmers into "peer groups" who would assist in spreading that knowledge. Two years later, the authors randomly selected two of the 25 villages (subsequently called Group A and Group B) for special training and 11 others as controls. A careful comparison of demographic characteristics showed the experimental and control groups to be strikingly similar to each other, suggesting they were sufficiently comparable for the study.

The peer groups from the two experimental villages were brought together for special training in organization-building. The participants were given some information about organizing and making demands on the government, and they were also given opportunities to act out dramas similar to the situations they faced at home. The training took three days.

The outcome variables considered by the evaluation all had to do with the extent to which members of the peer groups initiated group activities designed to improve their situation. Six types were studied. "Active initiative," for example, was defined as "active effort to influence persons or events affecting group members versus passive response or withdrawal" (Tandon and Brown 1981:180). The data for evaluation came from the journals that the peer group leaders had been keeping since their initial technological training. The researchers read through the journals and counted the number of initiatives taken by members of the peer groups. Two researchers coded the journals independently and compared their work to test the reliability of the coding process.

Figure 12-3 compares the number of active initiatives by members of the two experimental groups with those coming from the control groups. Similar results were found for the other outcome measures.

Notice two things about the graph. First, there is a dramatic difference in the number of initiatives by the two experimental groups as compared with the eleven controls. This would seem to confirm the effectiveness of the special training program. Second, notice that the number of initiatives also increased among the control groups. The researchers explain this latter pattern as a result of contagion. Since all the villages were near each other, the lessons learned by peer group members in the experimental groups were communicated in part to members of the control villages.

This example illustrates the strengths of multiple time-series designs where true experiments are inappropriate to the program being evaluated.

Operationalizing Success/Failure

Potentially, one of the most taxing aspects of evaluation research is determining whether the program under review succeeded or failed. The purpose of the foreign language program mentioned earlier may

Figure 12-3 Active Initiatives over Time

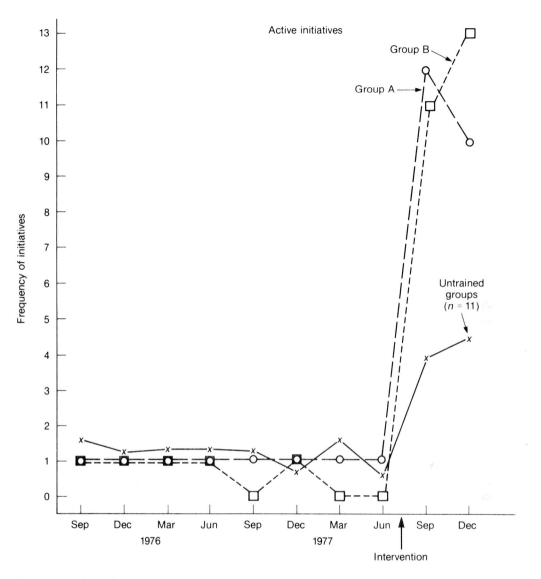

Source: Rajesh Tandon and L. Dave Brown, "Organization-Building for Rural Development: An Experiment in India," *The Journal of Applied Behavioral Science* (April-June 1981):182.

be to help students do better in learning the language, but how much better is *better enough*? The purpose of the conjugal visit program at a prison may be to raise morale, but *how high* does morale need to be raised to justify the program?

As you may anticipate, there are almost never clear-cut answers to questions like these. This dilemma has surely been the source of what is generally called *cost/benefit analysis*. How much does the program cost in relation to what it returns in benefits? If the benefits outweigh the cost, keep the program going. If the reverse, junk it.

That's simple enough, and it seems to apply in straightforward economic situations: if it cost you $20 to produce something and you can only sell it for $18, there's no way you can make up the difference in volume.

Unfortunately, the situations usually faced by evaluation researchers are seldom amenable to straightforward economic accounting. The foreign language program may cost the school district $100 per student, and it may raise students' performances on tests by an average of 15 points. Since the test scores can't be converted into dollars, there's no obvious grounds for weighing the costs and benefits.

Sometimes, as a practical matter, the criteria of success and failure can be handled through competition among programs. If a different foreign language program only costs $50 per student and produces an increase of 20 points in test scores, it would undoubtedly be considered more successful than the first program—assuming that test scores were seen as an appropriate measure of the purpose of both programs, and the less expensive program had no negative, unintended consequences.

Ultimately, the criteria of success and failure are often a matter of agreement. The people responsible for the program may commit themselves in advance to a particular outcome that will be regarded as an indication of success. If that's the case, all you need to do is make absolutely certain that the research design will measure the specified outcome. I mention something as obvious as this requirement simply because researchers sometimes fail to meet it, and there's little or nothing more embarrassing than that.

THE SOCIAL CONTEXT

Many of the comments in previous sections have hinted at the possibility of problems in the actual execution of evaluation research projects. Of course, all forms of research can run into problems, but evaluation research has a special propensity for it, and I want to draw your attention to some of these difficult aspects so you can recognize them in the reports you read. We're going to look at some of the logistical problems that can hinder evaluation research, and some of the special ethical issues evaluation touches. Finally, I will make a few comments about using evaluation research results.

Logistical Problems

In a military context, *logistics* refers to moving supplies around—making sure people have food, guns, and tent pegs when they need them. Here, I use it to refer to getting subjects to do what they're supposed to do, getting research instruments distributed and returned, and other seemingly unchallenging tasks. These tasks are more challenging than you would guess!

Motivating Sailors   When Kent Crawford and his colleagues (1980) set out to find a way to motivate "low performers" in the U.S. Navy, they found out just how many problems can occur. The purpose of the research was to test a three-pronged program for motivating sailors who were chronically poor performers and often in trouble aboard ship. First, a workshop was to be held for supervisory personnel, training them in effective leadership of low performers. Second, a few supervisors would be selected and trained as special counselors and role models—people the low performers could turn to for advice or just as sounding boards. Finally, the low performers themselves would participate in workshops aimed at training them to be more motivated and effective in their work and in their lives. The project was to be conducted aboard a particular ship, with a control group selected from sailors on four other ships.

To begin, the researchers report that the supervisory personnel were not exactly thrilled with the program.

Not surprisingly, there was considerable resistance on the part of some supervisors toward dealing with these issues. In fact, their reluctance to assume ownership of the problem was reflected by "blaming" any of several factors that can contribute to their personnel problem. The recruiting system, recruit training, parents, and society at large were named as influencing low performance—factors that were well beyond the control of the supervisors.

(Crawford et al. 1980:488)

Eventually, the reluctant supervisors came around and "this initial reluctance gave way to guarded optimism and later to enthusiasm" (1980:489). The low performers themselves were even more of a problem, however. The research design called for pre- and posttesting of attitudes and personalities, so that changes brought about by the program could be measured and evaluated.

Unfortunately, all of the LPs (Low Performers) were strongly opposed to taking these so-called personality tests and it was therefore concluded that the data collected under these circumstances would be of questionable validity. Ethical concerns also dictated that we not force "testing" on the LPs.

(Crawford et al. 1980:490)

As a consequence, the researchers had to rely on interviews with the low performers and on the judgments of supervisors for their measures of attitude change. The subjects continued to present problems, however.

Initially, the ship's command ordered fifteen low performers to participate in the experiment. Of the fifteen, however, one went into the hospital, another was assigned

duties that prevented participation, and a third went over the hill (absent without leave). Thus, the experiment began with twelve subjects. But before it was completed three more subjects completed their enlistments and left the Navy, and another was thrown out for disciplinary reasons. The experiment concluded, then, with eight subjects. While the evaluation pointed to positive results, the very small number of subjects warrants caution in any generalizations from the experiment.

The special, logistical problems of evaluation research grow out of the fact that it occurs within the context of real life. Although evaluation research is modeled after the experiment—which suggests that the researchers have control over what happens—it takes place within frequently uncontrollable daily life. Of course, the participant observer in field research doesn't have control over what is observed either, but that method does not strive for control. If you realize the importance of this lack of control, I think you'll start to understand the dilemma facing the evaluation researcher.

Administrative Control   As suggested in the example above, the logistical details of an evaluation project are often under the control of program administrators. Let's suppose you're evaluating the conjugal visit program I've referred to earlier. On the fourth day of the program, a male prisoner knocks out his wife, dresses up in her clothes, and escapes. Although you might be tempted to assume that his morale was greatly improved by escaping, that turn of events would complicate your study design in many ways. Perhaps the warden will terminate the program altogether, and where's your evaluation then? Or, if the warden is braver, he or she may review the files of all those prisoners you selected randomly for the experimental group and veto the "bad risks." There goes the comparability of your experimental and control groups. As an alternative, stricter security measures may be introduced to prevent further escapes, and the security measures may have a dampening effect on morale. So the experimental stimulus has changed in the middle of your research project. Some of the data will reflect the original stimulus, other data will reflect the modification. Although you'll probably be able to sort it all out, your carefully designed study has become a logical snakepit.

Maybe you've been engaged to evaluate the effect of race relations lectures on prejudice in the army. You've carefully studied the soldiers available to you for study, and you've randomly assigned some to attend the lectures and others to stay away. The rosters have been circulated weeks in advance, and at the appointed day and hour, the lectures begin. Everything seems to be going smoothly until you begin processing the files: the names don't match. Checking around you discover that military field exercises, KP duty, and a variety of emergencies required some of the experimental subjects to be elsewhere at the time of the lectures. That's bad enough, but then you learn that helpful commanding officers sent others to fill in for the missing soldiers. And whom do you suppose they picked to fill in? Soldiers who didn't have anything else to do or who couldn't be trusted to do anything important. You might learn this bit of information a week or so before the deadline for submitting your final report on the impact of the race relations lectures.

These are some of the logistical problems confronting evaluation researchers. It is important that you be familiar with them to understand why some research procedures may not measure up to the design of the classical experiment. As you read reports of evaluation research, however, you'll find that—all my earlier comments notwithstanding—it is possible to carry out controlled social research in conjuction with real-life experiments.

Just as evaluation research has special logistical problems, so it also can have special ethical problems. Since those problems can affect the scientific quality of the research, we should look at them briefly.

Some Ethical Issues

Ethics and evaluation are intertwined in many ways. Sometimes the social interventions being evaluated raise ethical issues. Evaluating the impact of busing school children to achieve educational integration will throw the researchers directly into the political, ideological, and ethical issues of busing itself. It's not possible to evaluate a sex education program in elementary schools without becoming involved in the heated issues surrounding sex education itself, and the researcher will find it difficult to remain impartial. The evaluation study design will *require* that some children be exposed to sex education—in fact, you may very well be the one who decides which children are exposed. (From a scientific standpoint, you *should* be in charge of selection.) That means that when parents become outraged that *their* child is being taught about sex, you will be directly responsible.

Now let's look on the "bright" side. Maybe the experimental program is of great value to those participating in it. Let's say that the new industrial safety program being evaluated reduces injuries dramatically. What about the control group members who were deprived of the program by the research design? The evaluators' actions could be an important part of the reason that a control group subject suffered an injury.

My purpose in these comments has not been to cast a shadow on evaluation research. Rather, I want to bring home the real-life consequences of the evaluation researcher's actions. Ultimately, all social research has ethical components, and we'll return to this topic in Chapter 19.

Use of Research Results

There's one more facts-of-life aspect of evaluation research that you should be aware of. Since the purpose of evaluation research is to determine the success or failure of social interventions, you might think it reasonable that a program would automatically be continued or terminated based on the results of the research.

Reality isn't that simple and reasonable, however. Other factors intrude on the assessment of evaluation research results, sometimes blatantly and sometimes subtly. As president, Richard Nixon appointed a blue-ribbon national commission to study the consequences of pornography. After a diligent, multifaceted evaluation, the commission reported that pornography didn't appear to have any of the negative social consequences often attributed to it. Exposure to pornographic materials, for example, didn't increase the likelihood of sex crimes. You might have expected liberalized legislation to follow from the research. Instead, the president said the commission was wrong.

Less dramatic examples of the failure to follow the implications of evaluation research could be listed endlessly. Undoubtedly every evaluation researcher can point to studies he or she conducted—studies providing clear research results and obvious policy implications—that were ignored. I want to discuss this issue a bit, since your own evaluation of research reports may depend in part on whether others make use of the findings.

There are three important reasons why the implications of the evaluation research results are not always put into practice. First, the implications may not always be presented in a way that the nonresearchers can understand. Second, evaluation results sometimes contradict deeply held beliefs. That was certainly the case with the pornography commission mentioned above. If everybody *knows* that pornography is bad, that it causes all manner of sexual deviance, then it is likely that research results to the contrary will have little immediate impact. By the same token, people thought Copernicus was crazy when he said the earth revolved around the sun. Anybody could tell the earth was standing still. The third barrier to the use of evaluation results is *vested interests*. If I have devised a new rehabilitation program that I'm convinced will keep ex-convicts from returning to prison, and if people have taken to calling it "the Babbie Plan," how do you think I'm going to feel when your evaluation suggests that the program doesn't work? I might apologize for misleading people, fold up my tent, and go into another line of work. But more likely, I'd call your research worthless and begin intense lobbying with the appropriate authorities to have the program continue.

In our earlier example of the evaluation of driver education training, Philip Hilts reported some of the reactions to the researchers' preliminary results:

Ray Burneson, traffic safety specialist with the National Safety Council, criticized the study, saying that it was a product of a group (NHTSA) run by people who believe "that you can't do anything to train drivers. You can only improve medical facilities and build stronger cars for when the accidents happen. . . . . This knocks the whole philosophy of education."

(1981:4)

By its nature, evaluation research takes place in the midst of real life: affecting it and being affected by it. Here's a final example, well known to social researchers.

Evaluating Criminal Justice Programs

by R. John Kinkel
Department of Sociology, University of Michigan at Flint

In 1979, millions of Americans had the opportunity to watch the Oscar-winning film *Scared Straight* on national television. Developed at Rahway State Prison, New Jersey, the film dramatized the sordid side of prison life to young toughs in hopes of "scaring" the juvenile offenders out of future criminal behavior. The film's narrator, Peter Falk, claimed the program was 90 percent successful; 9 out of 10 juveniles who took part in the program went "straight." A recent evaluation of the program came up with some different figures.

Professor James Finckenauer, Rutgers University School of Criminal Justice, was hired by the New Jersey Department of Corrections to undertake a rigorous evaluation of the *Scared Straight* program (officially known as the Juvenile Awareness Project). *Scared Straight* was a curious combination of juveniles, criminal justice operatives, and prison inmates working on a joint endeavor. For about three years juveniles (some delinquent and others, volunteers) were sent for grueling two-hour sessions inside the Rahway maximum security prison. Once inside, the youths were ushered into a room with a group of convicts who were serving sentences

of 25 years or more. The convicts went through their well-practiced routine for berating the juveniles' tough-guy postures. The convicts impressed the kids with the sordid side of prison life: the loss of privacy, individuality, and the constant threat of assault and homosexual slavery. The *Scared Straight* program became so popular that it was adopted in one form or another by a large number of states as well as some provinces in Canada.

Finckenauer's study[1] began in December 1977. He used a small but representative sample of juveniles from nine different agencies that refer kids to the project. The first part of the evaluation focused on nine different measures of attitudes concerning crime, law, justice, police, punishment, and obeying the law. The results of the testing showed no appreciable difference between the experimental and control groups in terms of attitude change—not a good sign if one were anticipating dramatic behavioral change. But the big question still remained: Did *Scared Straight* deter future delinquent behavior?

[1] James Finckenauer, *Evaluation of Juvenile Awareness Project: Reports 1 and 2* (Newark, N.J.: Rutgers School of Criminal Justice, 1979).

Manhattan Bail Bond Project The Manhattan Bail Bond Project is a frequently cited example of evaluation research in action (Botein 1965). It's a reasonably neat illustration, and it has the added appeal that

the program under evaluation proved an effective alternative to what many regard as a social problem. The problem, in this case, is the system of bail bonds, a traditional element in our legal system. People

The results of Finckenauer's six-month follow-up study of juvenile offenders showed that the experimental group (supposedly scared straight!) had a success rate lower than the control group.

Two Reports of the *Scared Straight* Program

	Two Views of Reality	
	Falk's Facts	Finckenauer's Figures
Program	*Scared Straight*	*Scared Straight*
Time Frame of Analysis	3 months	6 months
Type of Sample	Not Representative	Representative
Sample Size	17	81
Control Group	no	yes*
Success Rate	90%	Experimental 59% Control 89%

*Random assignment plus subjects were comparable on key demographic variables: age, sex, race, criminal history.

Each juvenile's court record was tracked: any further recorded offense was counted as evidence of failure. A significantly higher proportion of the juveniles who *did not attend* the *Scared Straight* program did better at avoiding crime than their juvenile delinquent counterparts. The success rate of the control group was 89 percent whereas the outcome of the experimental group was only 59 percent effective. Furthermore, the juveniles in the experimental group committed more serious crimes than the control group. Finckenauer speculates that a "delinquent-fulfilling prophecy" was at work. By demeaning and belittling the young "tough guys," the convicts may have compelled them to go out and prove they were not impressed.

Evaluation research can provide some sobering facts for policy makers and citizens alike after the initial rave reviews of a program have worn off—endorsements of movie stars notwithstanding.

awaiting trial are often allowed to spend the waiting time outside of jail if they can post a substantial amount of money to ensure that they will not skip town. The profession of bail bondsman has grown up and flour-ished around that system. Those who cannot afford, say, a $10,000 bond may be able to pay a bondsman 10 percent of that sum, $1,000. The bondsman then puts up the other $9,000. Once the accused appears for trial, the bond—all $10,000 of it—is returned to the bondsman, and the accused gets nothing.

Many people have criticized the bail system. Some people object to the economic discrimination it fosters. Others have complained that judges sometimes use it inappropriately: they may set extremely high bail in notorious cases, even though the crime alleged is relatively minor.

Other people have contended that the bail system is not really necessary, or at least that it need not be used as widely as it is. The Manhattan Bail Bond Project, initiated by the Vera Institute in New York, was designed as a test of that contention. The purpose of the project was to determine whether certain kinds of defendants—those with close ties to the community—could be released without bail and still be counted on to appear for their trials.

To undertake the study, the Vera Institute staff interviewed thousands of defendants and examined their files. They rated each defendant's integration into the community so as to identify those expected to stick around even if they were released without bail. Those scored as "good risks" were randomly divided into two groups, an experimental and a control group. The staff recommended release without bail for all those in the experimental group and made no recommendations for those in the control group.

Ideally all those recommended for release without bail would have gotten it, and all those not recommended wouldn't have. Naturally, it didn't turn out exactly that way. In the first year of study, the judges granted release without bail to 59 percent of those recommended by the researchers and to 16 percent of the control group. In spite of this variation, it was still possible to determine the impact of releasing defendants without bail. More than 99 percent appeared in court for trial at the appropriate time! This level of appearance was easily

as high as the normal level under the bail system.

Given the powerful and obvious success of the experiment, the program of release without bail has expanded in a number of ways. First, with increased experience, the Vera staff has gotten better at evaluating defendants and has improved the validity and reliability of its scoring systems. Second, the staff has found it feasible to lower the threshold of "good risk," thus recommending more defendants for release without bail. The judges, for their part, have steadily increased their reliance on Vera staff recommendations, going along with a larger proportion of them. Finally, the program has spread to many other jurisdictions, and the bail system in America has been significantly changed by the project.

By now, you have seen the various scientific and nonscientific aspects of evaluation research that affect the scientific quality of the results. You should now be prepared to design evaluation studies and to evaluate the evaluations you will be reading in the research literature. I want to conclude this chapter with a type of research that combines what you have learned about evaluation research and also the analysis of existing data.

SOCIAL INDICATORS RESEARCH

Now let's consider a special form of evaluation research hinted at in the earlier discussion of existing statistics. Another rapidly growing field in social research involves the development and monitoring of *social indicators,* aggregated statistics that reflect the social condition of a society or social subgroup. Just as economists use indexes such as gross national product (GNP) per capita as an indicator of a nation's economic development, we can monitor aspects of society in a similar fashion.

If we wanted to compare the relative health conditions in different societies, we could compare their death rates (number of deaths per 1,000 population). Or, more specifically, we could look at infant mortality: the number of infants who die during their first year of life among every 1,000 births. Depending on the particular aspect of health conditions we were interested in, we could devise any number of other measures: physicians per capita, hospital beds per capita, days of hospitalization per capita, and so forth. Notice that intersocietal comparisons are facilitated by calculating per capita rates (dividing by the size of the population or by some fixed unit such as 1,000s of population).

Before we go further with social indicators, recall from Chapter 11 the problems involved in existing statistics. In a word, they are often unreliable, reflecting their modes of collection, storage, and calculation. Bearing that caution in mind, we'll look at some of the ways in which social indicators can be used for the purposes of evaluation research on a large scale.

The Death Penalty and Deterrence

Does the death penalty deter capital crimes such as murder? That question is hotly debated every time a state considers elimi-nating or reinstating capital punishment. Those supporting capital punishment often argue that the threat of execution will keep potential murderers from killing people. Opponents of capital punishment often argue that it has no effect in that regard. Social indicators can be used to shed some light on the question.

If capital punishment actually deters people from committing murder, then we should expect to find murder rates lower in those states that have the death penalty than in those that do not. The relevant comparisons in this instance are not only possible, they have been compiled and published. Table 12-1 presents data compiled by William Bailey (1975) that directly contradict the view that the death penalty deters murderers. In both 1967 and 1968, those states with capital punishment had dramatically *higher* murder rates than those without capital punishment. Some people criticized the interpretation of Bailey's data, saying that most states have not used the death penalty in recent years, even when they had it on the books. That could explain why it hasn't seemed to work as a deterrent. Further analysis, however, contradicts that explanation. When Bailey compared those states that hadn't used the death penalty with those that *had*, he found no real difference in murder rates.

Another counterexplanation is possible, however. It could be the case that the inter-

Table 12-1 Average Rate per 100,000 Population of First- and Second-Degree Murders for Capital-Punishment and Non-Capital-Punishment States, 1967 and 1968

	Non-Capital-Punishment States		Capital-Punishment States	
	1967	1968	1967	1968
First-degree murder	.18	.21	.47	.58
Second-degree murder	.30	.43	.92	1.03
Total murders	.48	.64	1.38	1.59

Source: Adapted from William C. Bailey, "Murder and Capital Punishment," in William J. Chambliss (ed.), *Criminal Law in Action.* Copyright © 1975 by John Wiley & Sons, Inc. Used by permission.

pretation given Bailey's data was *backwards*. Maybe the existence of the death penalty as an option was a consequence of high murder rates: those states with high rates instituted it, those with low rates didn't institute it or repealed it if they had it on the books. It could be the case, then, that instituting the death penalty would bring murder rates down, while repealing it would increase murders and still produce—in a broad aggregate—the data presented in Table 12-1. Not so, however. Analyses over time do not show an increase in murder rates when a state repeals the death penalty nor a decrease in murders when one is instituted.

Notice from the discussion above that it's possible to use social indicators data either for comparison across groups at one time or across some period of time. And often doing both sheds the most light on the subject.

At present, work on the use of social indicators is proceeding on two fronts. On the one hand, researchers are developing ever more refined indicators—finding which indicators of a general variable are the most useful in monitoring social life. At the same time, research is being devoted to discovering the relationships among variables within whole societies.

Computer Simulation

One of the more exciting prospects for social indicators research is in the area of *computer simulation*. As we begin compiling mathematical equations describing the relationships that link social variables to one another (for example, what is the relationship between population growth and increases in the number of automobiles?), those equations can be stored and linked to one another in a computer. With a sufficient number of sufficiently accurate equations on tap, it will one day be possible

to test the implications of specific social changes by computer rather than in real life.

Suppose a state contemplated doubling the size of its tourism industry, for example. It would be possible to enter that proposal into a computer simulation model and receive in seconds or minutes a description of all the direct and indirect consequences of the increase in tourism. It would be possible to know what new public facilities would be required, which public agencies such as police and fire departments would have to be increased and by how much, what the labor force would look like, what kind of training would be required to provide it, how much new income and tax revenue would be produced, and so forth through all the intended and unintended consequences of the action. Depending on the results, the public planners might say, "Suppose we only increased the industry by half," and have a new printout of consequences immediately.

An excellent illustration of computer simulation linking social and physical variables is to be found in the research of Donella and Dennis Meadows (1972, 1973) and their colleagues at Dartmouth and Massachusetts Institute of Technology. They have taken as input data, known and estimated reserves of various nonreplaceable natural resources (for example, oil, coal, iron), past patterns of population and economic growth, and the relationships between growth and use of resources. Using a complex computer simulation model, they have been able to project, among other things, the probable number of years various resources will last in the face of alternative usage patterns in the future. Going beyond the initially gloomy projections, such models also make it possible to chart out less gloomy futures, specifying the actions required to achieve them. Clearly, the value of computer simulation is not limited to evaluation research, though it can serve an important function in that regard.

This potentiality points to the special value of evaluation research in general. Throughout human history, we have been tinkering with our social arrangements, seeking better results. Evaluation research provide a means for us to learn right away whether a particular tinkering really makes things better. Social indicators allow us to make that determination on a broad scale; coupling them with computer simulation opens up the possibility of knowing how much we would like a particular intervention without having to suffer through it for real.

MAIN POINTS

■ Evaluation research is a good example of applied research in social science.

■ Evaluation research is especially appropriate whenever a *social intervention* is undertaken.

■ A careful formulation of the problem, including relevant measurements and criteria of success or failure, is essential in evaluation research.

■ Evaluation researchers typically use experimental or quasi-experimental designs.

■ A time-series design involves the observation of an experimental group over time. It is a weak design in that something other than the experimental stimulus may explain any observed change.

■ Evaluation research entails special logistical and ethical problems because it is embedded in the day-to-day events of real life.

■ It cannot be assumed that the implications of evaluation research will necessarily be put into practice, especially if they conflict with official points of view.

■ Social indicators are aggregated descriptions of populations. They can provide an understanding of broad social processes.

■ Sometimes, computer simulation models can be constructed so as to point to the possible results of social intervention without having to experience those results in real life.

REVIEW QUESTIONS AND EXERCISES

1. Review the evaluation of the Navy Low Performer program that was discussed in the chapter. Redesign the program and the evaluation so as to handle the problems that appeared in the actual study.

2. Take a minute to think of the many ways your society has changed during your own lifetime. Specify those changes as social indicators that could be used in monitoring the quality of life in your society.

ADDITIONAL READINGS

Bennet, Carl A., and Lumsdaine, Arthur A. (eds.), *Evaluation and Experiment* (New York: Academic Press, 1975). Packed with illustrative examples, this reader digs into a number of special aspects of evaluation research. About every problem you are likely to hit is discussed in the book.

Riecken, Henry W., and Boruch, Robert F. (eds.), *Social Experimentation: A Method of Planning and Evaluating Social Intervention* (New York: Academic Press, 1974). As my several references to this book throughout the chapter suggest, it is an excellent basic text for the serious evaluation researcher. It is an especially appropriate companion piece for the Bennet-Lumsdaine book listed above. If you were to master both, you'd be ready to set about some serious (or fun) evaluations.

Weiss, Carol, *Evaluation Research* (Englewood Cliffs, N.J.: Prentice-Hall,

1972). Here's a quicker and easier introduction to evaluation research. In a short paperback, the author gives a good overview of the method and points you toward aspects you might want to learn more about. It is an especially good beginning if you don't have any prior experience in social research in general. This introduction may let you discover that you'd like to get some experience.

Wilcox, Leslie D., et al., *Social Indicators and Societal Monitoring* (New York: Elsevier, 1972). This is not a textbook on social indicators or even an example of their use. Rather, it is a seemingly exhaustive, annotated *bibliography* on the subject. Although it is now a few years old, it provides an excellent entry into further study. Whatever your particular substantive interest, this book will direct you to those studies that have addressed that interest through social indicators research.

PART 4

Analysis of Data

In this part of the book, we'll be discussing several aspects of what is the most exciting portion of the research process: the analysis of data and the development of generalized understanding about social phenomena. In the chapters composing Part 4, we'll examine the steps that separate observation from the final reporting of findings.

Chapter 13 is addressed to the quantification of the data collected through the modes of observation discussed in Part 3. Today, much social science data is analyzed by machine: computers and other data-processing devices. Chapter 13 provides a brief overview of some of the equipment involved and describes the processes required to convert observations into forms suitable for machine processing.

The first of several discussions on the logic of data analysis is presented in

Chapter 14. We'll begin with an examination of methods of analyzing and presenting the data related to a single variable. Then we'll turn to the relationship between two variables and learn how to construct and read simple percentage tables. The chapter ends with a preview of multivariate analysis.

Chapter 15 is addressed to measurement, a matter that has been discussed several times earlier in the book. This chapter specifically examines techniques of constructing indexes and scales—composite measures of variables.

Chapter 16 describes the elaboration model of data analysis developed by Paul Lazarsfeld at Columbia University. The concluding theme in Chapter 14 will be picked up again and developed further. This chapter will present the logic of causal analysis through the use of percentage tables. The same logic will then be

applied in the use of other statistical techniques in subsequent chapters.

Chapter 17 provides an introduction to some of the more commonly used statistical methods in social science research. Rather than merely showing how to compute statistics by these methods (computers can do that), I have attempted to place them in the context of earlier theoretical and logical discussions. Thus, you should come away from this chapter knowing when to use various statistical measures as well as how to compute them.

Chapter 18 completes Part 4 with an overview of some of the more advanced methods of multivariate analysis. Again, the emphasis is on understanding the logic of their use rather than on how to compute them.

13

Quantifying Data

What You'll Learn in This Chapter

Having amassed a volume of observations, you are now about to learn how to transform them into a form appropriate to computer analysis. Here you'll see the social scientist's answer to microscopes, lasers, and cyclotrons.

INTRODUCTION

What the microscope was to biology, what the telescope was to astronomy—that's what the *computer* has been to modern social research. Moreover, you are taking this course at a time when the computer's contribution to social science is still being discovered. This chapter will introduce you to that contribution.

The purpose of this chapter is to describe methods of converting social science data into a *machine-readable* form—a form that can be read and manipulated by computers and similar machines used in **quantitative data analysis.** If you were conducting a research project more or less parallel to reading the chapters of this book, your data, at this point, would be in the form of completed questionnaires, content analysis code sheets, or the like. At the completion of the stage covered in this chapter, those data would have been recorded on microcomputer floppy disks, cassettes, punch-cards, or some other device that can be read by a machine.

Given the pace of computer development and dissemination today, I can't anticipate the kind of equipment you may have available to you for your use. As a result, I'm going to provide you with an overview of several stages in the evolution of computers in social research. That way, I should say something about whatever you have to work with. Moreover, it's useful for you to know about the earlier equipment and techniques, since they sometimes reveal the logic of data analysis more clearly than today's advanced equipment and techniques—in the same sense that you can learn the fundamentals of how an automobile works more easily from a VW Bug than from the latest, fanciest Maserati.

COMPUTERS IN SOCIAL RESEARCH

For our purposes, the history of computing in social research can begin in 1801, about half a century prior to the birth of modern sociology. That's the year a Frenchman, Joseph-Marie Jacquard, created a revolution in the textile industry that was to have an impact in the most unlikely corners of life.

To facilitate the weaving of intricate patterns, Jacquard invented an automatic loom that took its instructions from punched cards. As a series of cards passed through the loom's "reader," wooden pegs poked through the holes punched in the cards, and the loom translated that information into weaving patterns. To create new designs, Jacquard needed merely to punch the appropriate holes in new cards, and the loom responded accordingly.

The point to be recognized here is that *information* (e.g., a desired weaving pattern) could be *coded* and *stored* in the form of holes punched in a card and subsequently *retrieved* by a machine that read the holes and took action based on the meaning assigned to those holes. This is the fundamental logic that we'll see repeated in different forms in the following discussions.

The next step in our selective computer history takes place in the United States, during the 1890 census. As you know, the U.S. Constitution mandates a complete census of the nation's population every 10 years, beginning with the 1790 enumeration of just under 4 million Americans. As the new nation's population grew, however, so did the task of measuring it. The 1880 census enumerated over 62 million population—but it took the Census Bureau 9 *years* to finish its tabulations. Clearly, a technological breakthrough was required before the

1890 census was conducted. The bureau sought suggestions.

A former Census Bureau employee, Herman Hollerith, had an idea. Hollerith had worked on the 1880 census. As a young engineering instructor at MIT, he proposed to adapt the Jacquard card to the task of counting the nation's population. As local tallies were compiled, they would be punched into cards. Then a tabulating machine of Hollerith's creation would read the cards and determine the population counts for the entire nation.

Hollerith's system was tested in competition with other proposals and found to be the fastest. As a result, the Census Bureau rented $750,000 worth of equipment from Hollerith's new Tabulating Machine Company, and the 1890 population total was reported within six weeks, in contrast to the nine years required for the 1880 census. Hollerith's Tabulating Machine Company, incidentally, continued to develop new equipment, merged with other pioneering firms, and was eventually renamed the International Business Machines Corporation: IBM.

Storing Data on Cards

By the 1950s, punched cards—commonly called *IBM cards*—were being adapted for the storage and retrieval of social research data, and they are still commonly used for that purpose. Let's see how the kinds of data we've been discussing throughout the book might be stored on punched cards.

A punch card like the one shown in Figure 13-1 is divided into 80 vertical columns, which are usually numbered from left to right. Each vertical column is further divided into 10 spaces, numbered 0, 1, 2, 3, 4, 5, 6, 7, 8, 9, from top to bottom. Data are stored on the cards by punching holes within the columns. Later, computers and other data processing equipment can be used to retrieve data from the card by locating and reading specified columns.

A keypunch machine punches holes in the spaces in columns of punch cards. Using a keyboard similar to that of a typewriter, the keypunch operator can punch specified holes (0, 1, 2, . . .) into specified columns of a given card.

Data are put in machine-readable form

Figure 13-1   Standard Punch Card for Recording Data

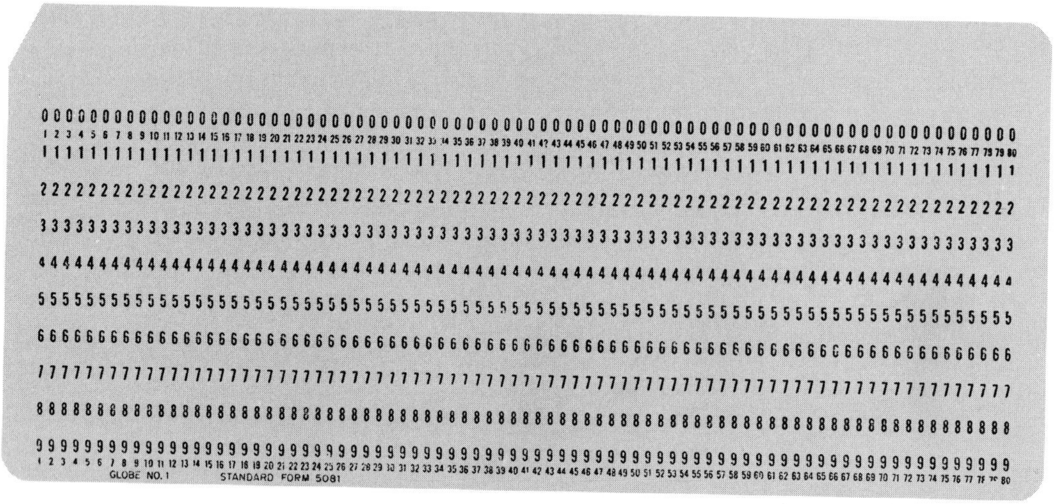

by assigning one or more specific columns of a data card (a *field*) to a variable, and assigning punches within that column to the various attributes composing that variable. For example, an experimental subject's sex might be recorded in column 5 of the card. If the subject were male, a 1 might be punched in that column; if female, a 2. Recalling our earlier terminology, notice that columns correspond to *variables*, and the different punches within a column correspond to the *attributes* constituting that variable. A subject's age might be assigned to columns 6 and 7 (a two-column code); if the subject were 35 years of age, 3 and 5, respectively, would be punched in those columns. Or ages could be recorded in categories and stored in a single column: for example, 1-punch for under 20, 2-punch for 20 to 29, and so forth.

A given card, then, represents the data about a given subject—the unit of analysis. If the units of analysis were newspaper editorials being examined in a content analysis, each data card would represent an editorial. The columns of each card would be assigned to specific variables describing that editorial. For example, two columns might be assigned to storing the last two digits of the year in which the editorial appeared.

The *precoding* of questionnaires and other data collection documents, which was mentioned in Chapter 9, is nothing more than the assignment of cards and columns for specific data items. If you turn back to the first page of Figure 9-7, you'll see what I mean. For example, the notation "(6–15)" in question A-1 means that the answers to items a through j in question 1 will be stored in columns 6 through 15. The numbers 1, 2, 3, 4, and 5 printed under the answer categories indicate the answer "SA" (strongly agree) and will be stored as 1-punch, the answer "A" (agree) will be stored as a 2-punch, and so forth. The notation "(1–4, 5/1)," which identifies case and deck, will be explained later in this chapter.

In survey research, a data card may stand for a questionnaire, with columns assigned to the various items in the questionnaire. Column 34 might store answers to the question "Have you ever smoked marijuana?" A 1-punch could represent "yes," and a 2-punch "no." The main ideas for you to grasp are that each card represents a single research unit of analysis, and that each column (or set of columns) stores the same variable on each card. For example, each survey respondent may have his or her answer to the marijuana question stored in column 34.

Retrieving Data from Cards

Several pieces of equipment are capable of reading punch cards. The simplest machine among these is the counter-sorter. While it's unlikely that you'll ever have a chance to use a counter-sorter, it's useful for you to understand the logic of how the machine works, since it will clarify what more complex machines do. The counter-sorter may be set to read a given column. Then, when the cards are fed into it, they are sorted into pockets corresponding to the punches found in the column you've specified, and a counter indicates the number of cards in each pocket. If sex is recorded in column 5 and the sorter is set for that column, men and women would be sorted into the 1 and 2 pockets, respectively, and the sorter would keep a running total of the cards in each pocket.

The counter-sorter can also be used to examine the relationships between variables. Suppose you want to determine whether men or women were more likely to have smoked marijuana, for example. Having separated the respondents by sex, you would set the counter-sorter to read the column containing responses to the question about smoking marijuana: column 35, for example. All the "men" cards would then be rerun through the counter-sorter to determine whether they had ever smoked marijuana, as indicated by the punches in column 35. The same procedure could be repeated for the women, and the distributions of responses would then be compared.

For years, the counter-sorter was the primary machine used for the analysis of social research data, but it had three basic limitations. First, it was limited to counting and sorting cards. Although you might use these capabilities for extremely sophisticated analyses, the machine itself couldn't perform sophisticated manipulations of data. Second, the counter-sorter was rather slow in comparison with machines invented later. Third, it was limited to the examination of one card per unit of analysis when looking at the relationships among variables. In effect, you were limited to 80 columns of data per unit of analysis.

Enter Computers

Most data analyses today are conducted with computers. I know that I don't need to tell you that computers are revolutionizing most areas of modern social life. I also know that some people worry that computers are "taking over." I hope the following discussion will make it clear that computers are merely *tools*, as are typewriters and pocket calculators. But what powerful tools!

The computer—through manipulation programs—can avoid the limitations of the counter-sorter. First, it can go beyond simple counting and sorting to perform intricate computations and provide sophisticated presentations of the results. The computer can be programmed to examine several variables simultaneously and to compute a variety of statistics. Second, if the data are stored on magnetic tape or magnetic disk rather than on cards, those data can be passed through the machine

much faster than is possible using cards and the counter-sorter. Moreover, the capability for simultaneous, extensive manipulations and computations further speeds the overall analysis. Finally, the computer is not limited to the 80 columns of a punch card.

Today, most quantitative social scientific data analyses use computer programs that cause the computer to simulate the counter-sorter process described above—and much more.

There are a number of computer programs available today for the analysis of social science data. Appendix H of this book gives some information and instructions about the use of one of the more popular of these: SPSS^x. If you can get a sense of how SPSS^x works, you will understand the general logic of using computer programs to carry out data analyses.

Up until the late 1970s, all computer analyses were performed on large, expensive computers—sometimes called "mainframe" computers—maintained by centralized computer centers, and most analyses still are. To make use of such facilities, you need to supply the data for analysis and the instructions for the analysis you want. Your instructions might take the form of an SPSS^x set-up, as mentioned above and described more fully in Appendix H. And you might take your data to the computer center in the form of cards or a magnetic tape, or you might simply reference a data set maintained in the center's data library. (Your instructor will tell you how to do this if you are to do computer analyses in the course.)

Once at the computer center, you will typically submit your data and analysis instructions to a machine operator who enters the job into the computer, though some centers are set up so that researchers can run their own jobs. Once your job has been submitted, your next job is to *wait*. Sometime later—minutes (rarely), hours, or days, depending on the center's workload—the machine operators will return your completed job, usually in the form of a *printout* of the results of your analysis.

In recent years, two developments have improved the process described above. *Remote job entry* systems place card readers and printers near the researchers and allow them to submit jobs and receive their results at locations some distance from the computer center. Your departmental office may have such equipment, with requests and results sent to and from the computer center over co-axial cables.

Time sharing is a further advance. In a sense, computers have always operated on a time-sharing basis—several users sharing the same computer. Initially, however, computer facilities were shared in a serial fashion: the computer would run your job, then mine, then someone else's. The current, more sophisticated computers, however, can perform several different tasks simultaneously. It can read my request, analyze yours, and print out someone else's all at the same time. In fact, the tremendous speed of computers makes it possible to sandwich small operations (which may take only thousandths of a second) in the middle of larger jobs. This capacity has made it possible for computers to handle requests from hundreds of users simultaneously, often giving the impression that each has the computer's complete attention. Such interactions with the computer typically use *computer terminals*—typewriter devices that either print on paper or display their operations on CRT (cathode ray tube) video monitors that look like television screens.

Time sharing through the use of computer terminals supports a variety of uses. Text-editing programs allow users to write, edit, and print out reports. Or, if your computer center supports a time-sharing system, you'll probably find a variety of video games stored somewhere in the system.

For our present purposes, I want to discuss the use of time sharing for social science data analysis. Here's a common pattern. Your data are maintained by the computer center, either on tape or disk. Instead of punching cards requesting a particular analysis, you type those instructions on a terminal. Once you have prepared the entire set of instructions, you type a final instruction (which will vary from computer to computer) requesting that the job be run. The computer then takes over, eventually producing your results, either for pick-up at the center or printed out on your terminal.

Making this process even more convenient, there are now a variety of portable computer terminals no larger than small, portable typewriters. Such terminals communicate with the computer over standard telephone lines. Thus, you can take a portable terminal home or on a trip around the world. To use it, you dial a special number on your regular phone. The computer answers—usually with a shrill tone. Then you fit the telephone receiver into two rubber cups—called an *acoustical coupler*—on the terminal. (Some have communications equipment built in so that you can plug your terminal directly into a standard telephone jack.) Now anything you type on the terminal is transmitted over telephone lines to the computer. It does what you ask and sends the results back to your terminal.

Time-sharing systems can also connect you with nationwide computer *networks*. The possible uses of such networks are mind-boggling, and presently available services only scratch the surface of their potential. You can, for example, dial a special number and connect with a computer that will allow you to search rapidly through past editions of the *New York Times* and locate articles on some topic of interest to you. If you wish, you can have the articles printed out on your terminal. (Appendix A on library use describes other variations on this facility.) Or, you can leave messages in the network, to be picked up by other users.

More relevant to our current discussion, computer networks make it possible for a researcher sitting at home in California to get a copy of a data set maintained on a computer in Massachusetts and to analyze those data using a program maintained on a computer in Texas. The results of the analysis would be returned to the user in California, and the results could also be stored for examination by a colleague in Michigan. I don't mean to suggest that the procedure described above is commonplace today, but it is likely to become commonplace early in your research career. And before the end of your career, you'll look back on all that as primitive.

Microcomputers

A newer, and in some ways more exciting, development has been the *microcomputer*. You're probably familiar with microcomputers and may have even used one. These machines are small, complete computers not much larger than a typewriter (or even smaller). Operations are displayed on a CRT (usually you can use a standard television set). The early systems used standard tape cassettes to store data between uses, though these have now been generally replaced by "floppy disks"—round sheets of magnetic tape either 5.25 or 3.5 inches in diameter. A small printer for producing permanent copies of results completes the basic system.

Microcomputers have already proven effective in a variety of tasks. This book, for example, was written on a microcomputer. In addition, I use the same machine for all my correspondence; it schedules my time and prints daily appointments and to-do lists, maintains my checkbook, handles my personal telephone directory, and performs other tasks too numerous to list. When I am traveling, I can check into a hotel, unplug the regular telephone in my room, plug in my computer, and be in touch with people and computers around the country. When

I want a break from writing, I can play chess with the computer or save the world from alien invaders.

Microcomputers are just starting to blossom in the arena of social science research. The main drawback has been their small *memory* size, but modern micros are overcoming that problem impressively. Here's an example.

When I was a graduate student 20 years ago, Berkeley's Survey Research Center had an IBM 1620 computer, which occupied approximately the same space as six or seven refrigerators. Its memory capacity was 24K, or approximately 24,000 characters worth of information. Yesterday, I purchased a microcomputer about half the size of a 19-inch television; its memory is 512K. I have another computer, about the size of a metropolitan telephone directory, which has a memory of 32K: a third larger than the old 1620.

As the memory capacity of microcomputers has mushroomed, data analysis programs have been developed to bring the examination of social science data within the capability of micros. Nor is the technological evolution complete. Introducing a special issue of *Sociological Methods & Research* on "Microcomputers and Social Research," David R. Heise says:

Microcomputers are cheap, reliable, portable, computationally powerful, and easy to use. This profile makes them significantly different from mainframe computers and guarantees wide diffusion. By the end of the decade, microcomputers will have changed the way social scientists do research, the way they teach courses, and the way they work in applied settings. Microcomputers also will create new topics for social analysis as the microcomputer revolution reaches diverse sectors of society.

(1981:395)

Now you have an overview of the role played by computers in social research. The remainder of this chapter will discuss the steps (and options) involved in converting data into forms amenable to computer analysis. We'll discuss the coding process and enumerate the several methods of transforming data into a machine-readable form.

CODING

For computers to work their magic, they must be able to read the data you've collected in your research. Moreover, computers are at their best with numbers. If a survey respondent tells you that he or she thinks the biggest problem facing Stowe, Vermont, today is "the threat of thermonuclear war," the computer can't understand that response. You must translate: a process called **coding**. The discussion of content analysis in Chapter 11 dealt with the coding process in a manner very close to our present concern. Recall that the content analysis must develop methods of assigning individual paragraphs, editorials, books, songs, and so forth with specific classifications or attributes. In content analysis, the coding process is inherent in data collection or observation.

When other research methods are employed, it is often necessary to engage in a coding process after the data have been collected. For example, open-ended questionnaire items result in nonnumerical responses, which must be coded before analysis. Or a field researcher might wish to undertake a quantitative analysis based on qualitative field notes. You might wish, for example, to quantify the open-ended interviews you conducted with participants in some social event under study.

As with content analysis, the task here is one of reducing a wide variety of idiosyncratic items of information to a more limited set of attributes composing a variable. Suppose, for example, that a survey researcher has asked respondents, "What is

your occupation?" The responses to such a question would vary considerably. Although it would be possible to assign each separate occupation reported a separate numerical code, this procedure would not facilitate analysis, which typically depends on several subjects having the same attribute.

The occupation variable has a number of preestablished coding schemes (none of them very good, however). One such scheme distinguishes professional and managerial occupations, clerical occupations, semiskilled occupations, and so forth. Another scheme distinguishes among different sectors of the economy: manufacturing, health, education, commerce, and so forth. Still others combine both.

The occupational coding scheme chosen should be appropriate to the theoretical concepts being examined in the study. For some studies, coding all occupations as either white-collar or blue-collar might be sufficient. For others, self-employed and not self-employed might be sufficient. Or a peace researcher might wish to know only whether the occupation was dependent on the defense establishment or not.

Although the coding scheme ought to be tailored to meet particular requirements of the analysis, one general rule of thumb should be kept in mind. If the data are coded so as to maintain a great deal of detail, code categories can always be combined during analysis that does not require such detail. (Appendix H describes how to do this in SPSS^x.) If the data are coded into relatively few, gross categories, however, there is no way during analysis to recreate the original detail. Thus, you would be well advised to code your data in somewhat more detail than you plan to use in the analysis.

Developing Code Categories

There are two basic approaches to the coding process. First, you may begin with a relatively well-developed coding scheme, derived from your research purpose. Thus, as suggested above, the peace researcher might code occupations in terms of their relationship to the defense establishment. Or let's suppose that you have been engaging in participant observation of an emerging new religion. You have been keeping very careful notes of the reasons new members have given for joining. Perhaps you have developed the impression that new members seem to regard the religion as a substitute for a family. You might, then, review your notes carefully—coding each new member's comments in terms of whether this aspect of the religion was mentioned. You might also code their comments in terms of their own family status: whether they have a family or not.

If you are fortunate enough to have assistance in the coding process, your task would be to refine your definitions of code categories and train your coders so that they will be able to assign given responses to the proper categories. You should explain the meaning of the code categories you have developed and give several examples of each. To ensure that your coders fully understand what you have in mind, it would be useful for you to code several cases. Then your coders should be asked to code the same cases, without knowing how you coded them, and your coders' work should be compared with your own. Any discrepancies will indicate an imperfect communication of your coding scheme to your coders. Even if there is perfect agreement between you and your coders, however, you should still *check-code* at least a portion of the cases throughout the coding process.

If you are not fortunate enough to have assistance in coding, it is still important to obtain some verification of your own reliability as a coder. Nobody is perfect, especially a researcher hot on the trail of a finding. In your study of an emerging religion,

let's suppose you have the impression that people who do not have a regular family will be more likely to regard the new religion as a family substitute. The danger is that whenever you discover a subject who reports no family, you will unconsciously try to find some evidence in the subject's comments that the religion is a family substitute. If at all possible, then, you should try to get someone else to code some of your cases to see if that person would make the same assignments you made. (Note how this relates to the characteristic of *intersubjectivity* in science.)

The second approach to coding is appropriate whenever you are not sure initially how your data should be coded—you do not know what variables they represent among your subjects of study. Suppose, for example, that you have asked, "What do you think about the Moral Majority?" Although you might anticipate coding responses as being positive, negative, or neutral, it is unlikely that you could anticipate the full range of variation in responses. In such a situation, it would be useful to prepare a list of perhaps 50 or 100 actual responses to this open-ended question. You could then review that list, noting the different dimensions that those responses reflect. Perhaps you would find that several of the positive responses contained references to the fight against domestic communism; perhaps a number of the negative responses referred to racial prejudice.

Once you have developed a coding scheme based on the list of 50 or 100 responses, you should ensure that each of the listed responses fits into one of the code categories. Then you would be ready to begin coding the remaining responses. If you have coding assistance, the previous comments regarding the training and checking of coders would apply here; if you do not, the comments on having your own work checked apply.

Like the set of attributes composing a variable, and like the response categories in a closed-ended questionnaire item, code categories should be both exhaustive and mutually exclusive. Every piece of information being coded should fit into *one and only one* category. Problems arise whenever a given response appears to fit equally into more than one code category, or when it fits into none.

CODEBOOK CONSTRUCTION

The end product of the coding process is the conversion of data items into numerical codes. These codes represent attributes composing variables, which, in turn, are assigned card and column locations within a data file. A **codebook** is a document that describes the locations of variables and lists the code asignments to the attributes composing those variables. A codebook serves two essential functions. First, it is the primary guide used in the coding process. Second, it is your guide for locating variables and interpreting punches in your data file during analysis. If you decide to correlate two variables as a part of your analysis of your data, the codebook tells you where to find the variables and what the punches represent.

Figure 13-2 illustrates portions of the codebook used with the survey questionnaire illustrated in Chapter 9, a questionnaire requiring more than one card per case for data storage. (It would be useful for you to refer back to the questionnaire—paying special attention to the precoding notations.)

If we wanted to know if students had attended a peace rally, we'd know that information was stored in column 44. The political party they identified with, if any, would be found in column 76. Either a counter-sorter or a computer could be used to discover how many students gave each of the answers shown.

CODING AND DATA ENTRY OPTIONS

There are a number of ways in which the coding process may be integrated with the data entry process (keypunching or entry directly to tape or disk) so as to provide the desired end product: a set of numerically coded data. I'll begin with some comments on data entry options and then discuss several options for linking coding and data entry.

Data Entry Options

As I've already indicated, until recently, nearly all data entry took the form of manual key-punching, and it is still very common. Once the data have been punched into cards, as described above, they are *verified*, using a machine that looks very much like the keypunch machine, but with two differences. First, the machine operator loads an already punched set of cards into the verifier. Second, when the operator proceeds to enter the data, the verifier reads the punches that already exist, rather than punching new ones. Whenever the data entered on the verifier differ from the punches already in the cards, the machine signals that there is an error. It can then be corrected.

Recent years have brought useful advances in data entry. As one option, some equipment allows you to key data onto tape cassettes rather than into punched cards. There are several advantages to this. For example, a small cassette can contain the equivalent of many punch cards. Also, errors can be

Figure 13-2   Partial Example of a Codebook

Column	Description
1-4	Respondent identification number
5	A-1a. "It would be a good thing if the United Nations were someday converted into a world government."
	1. Strongly agree
	2. Agree
	3. Disagree
	4. Strongly disagree
	5. Don't know
	0. No answer
6	A-1b. "People who defile the American flag should be put in prison."
	1. Strongly agree
	2. Agree
	3. Disagree
	4. Strongly disagree
	5. Don't know
	0. No answer

....

A-9.   "Have you personally supported the current peace movement in any of the following ways?"

corrected more easily on a cassette file than in the case of punch cards.

As a more advanced alternative, computer time-sharing has made it possible to create data entry programs, so that data are keyed into computer terminals and stored directly in the computer, for subsequent analysis.

Until fairly recently, microcomputers have not been very effective for the analysis of the (typically) large data sets analyzed by social scientists. Greatly expanded memories, however, have opened up powerful new possibilities for data entry. Now data can be keyed into microcomputers for storage on disks. Then they can either be analyzed by the same micro or transferred electronically to a mainframe computer for analysis. Earlier in the chapter, we saw how to code data for processing, and we've just seen some of the options for data entry. Now let's look at some ways of bridging those two processes.

44 A-9a. "Attended a peace rally."
      1. Yes
      2. No
      0. No answer

45 A-9b. "Participated in a peace march."
      1. Yes
      2. No
      0. No answer

46 A-9c. "Written a letter to a public official."
      1. Yes
      2. No
      0. No answer

. . . .

76 A-14. "Do you normally identify yourself with any particular political party? (Please indicate which party, if any, you identify with.)"
      1. Democratic party
      2. Republican party
      3. American Independent party
      4. Peace and Freedom party
      5. Other
      6. No party identification, independent
      0. No answer

Transfer Sheets

The traditional method of data processing involves the coding of data and the transfer of code assignments to a *transfer sheet* or *code sheet*. Such sheets are ruled off in 80 columns, corresponding to the data card columns or other data configurations appropriate to the data entry method. (Figure 13-3 provides an illustration.) Coders write numbers corresponding to the desired punches in the appropriate columns of the sheets. The code sheets are then used for data entry—key-punching, for example.

Edge-Coding

Edge-Coding does away with the need for code sheets. The outside margin of each page of a questionnaire or other data source-doc-

Figure 13-3   A Partial Coding Transfer Sheet

01	02	03	04	05	06	07	08	09	10		71	72	73	74	75	76	77	78	79	80
0	0	1	3	7	8	9	3	1	1		4	5	2	1	1	7	8	7	1	2
0	0	2	4	2	4	2	4	1	2		2	2	5	1	1	2	8	2	2	2
0	0	3	6	6	1	2	3	1	1		1	3	6	2	1	3	9	2	2	3
0	0	4	5	3	4	4	2	2	1		1	4	1	0	3	6	0	4	2	1

ument is left blank or is marked with spaces corresponding to data card columns. Rather than transferring code assignments to a separate sheet, the codes are written in the appropriate spaces in the margins. The edge-coded source-documents are then used for data entry.

Punching Directly

The earlier discussion of precoding was presented in anticipation of direct punching. This method is especially useful with lengthy questionnaires and other data-collection documents that would present a formidable coding task. If the questionnaires have been adequately designed and precoded, you can *punch directly* from them without using separate code sheets or even edge-coding. The precoded questionnaire would contain indications of the columns and the punches to be assigned to questions and responses, and data can be entered directly.

When a *punch-direct* method is to be used, it is essential that documents be *edited* before data entry. An editor should read through each to ensure that every question has been answered (enter a 0 or some other standard code when no answer is given), to ensure that there are no multiple answers (change to a single code according to a uniform procedure), and to clarify any unclear responses.

If most of the document is amenable to direct punching (for example, closed-ended questions presented in a clear format), it is also possible to code a few open-ended items and still punch directly. In such a situation, you should enter the code for a given question in a specified location near the question to ease the data entry job.

The layout of the document is extremely important for effective direct punching. If most of the question and response categories are presented on the right side of the page but one set is presented on the left side, those entering the data frequently miss the deviant set. (*Note:* Many respondents will make the same mistake, so a questionnaire carefully designed for data entry will be more effective for data collection as well.)

For content analysis and similar situations in which coding takes place during data collection, it makes sense to record the data in a form amenable to direct punching. Perhaps a precoded form would be appropriate, or, in some cases, the data might be recorded directly on transfer sheets.

Coding to Optical Scan Sheets

Manual data entry can be avoided through the use of an *optical scanner*. This machine reads black pencil marks on a special code sheet and creates data files to correspond with those marks. (These sheets are frequently called *op-sense* or *mark-sense* sheets.)

It is possible for coders to transfer coded data to such special sheets by blacking in the appropriate spaces. The sheets are then fed into an optical scanner and data files are created automatically.

Although an optical scanner provides greater accuracy and speed to manual data entry, it has disadvantages as well. Some coders find it very difficult to transfer data to the special sheets. It can be difficult to locate the appropriate column, and once the appropriate column is found, the coder must search for the appropriate space to blacken.

Second, the optical scanner has relatively rigid tolerances. Unless the black marks are sufficiently black, the scanner may make mistakes. (You will have no way of knowing when this has happened until you begin your analysis.) Moreover, if the op-sense sheets are folded or mutilated, the scanner may refuse to read them at all.

Direct Use of Optical Scan Sheets

It is sometimes possible to use optical scan sheets a little differently and possibly avoid the difficulties they may offer coders. Persons asked to complete questionnaires may be asked to record their responses directly on such sheets. Either standard sheets can be provided with instructions on their use, or special sheets can be prepared for the particular study. Questions can be presented with the several answer categories, and the respondents can be asked to blacken the spaces provided beside the answers they choose. If such sheets are properly laid out, the optical scanner can read and punch the answers directly. This method may be even more feasible in recording experimental observation or in compiling data in a content analysis.

Direct-Data-Entry

A more advanced data-processing system is *direct-data-entry*, now being used at major research institutes such as the Institute for Social Research at the University of Michigan. The process used is similar to Computer-Assisted Telephone Interviewing, discussed in Chapter 9.

Each coder sits before a computer video terminal. A coding form is displayed on the video screen, with an indicator specifying an item of information to be entered. The coder examines a completed questionnaire, determines the appropriate code category, and types that code on the terminal keyboard. The video screen then specifies the next item of information needed. The computer's prompting ensures that the coder enters the correct items in the correct order.

As soon as a questionnaire is coded in this fashion, the data are transferred automatically into a growing data file for the study. Notice that this process avoids the need for any manual data entry.

DATA CLEANING

Whichever data-processing method you have used, you will now have a set of machine-readable data that purport to represent the information collected in your study. The next important step is the elimination of errors: "cleaning" the data.

No matter how, or how carefully, the data have been entered, some errors are inevitable. Depending on the data-processing method, these errors may result from incorrect coding, incorrect reading of written codes, incorrect sensing of blackened marks, and so forth.

Two types of cleaning should be done: *possible-punch* cleaning and *contingency* cleaning.

Possible-Punch Cleaning

For any given variable, there is a specified set of legitimate attributes, translated into a set of possible punches. In the variable *sex*, there will be perhaps three possible punches: 1 for male, 2 for female, and 0 for no answer. If a case is found to contain, say, a 7-punch in the column assigned to sex, it is clear that an error has been made.

Possible-punch cleaning can be accomplished in two different ways. First, you may have access to computer programs designed for this purpose. You may be able to specify the possible punches associated with each card column, and the computer will then read all the data cards and indicate those cards that have one or more errors. Alternatively, you can examine the distribution of punches in each column (using either the computer or the sorter) and determine whether there are any inappropriate punches. If the column assigned to sex has a 7-punch reported, you might use the sorter to locate the card having this punch. Then you could locate the source-document corresponding to that card (using the ID number), determine what the punch should have been, and make the necessary correction.

In direct-data-entry, the program that asks for, accepts, and transfers data also checks for errors. If there are only two code categories—male and female coded 1 and 2, for example—and the coder erroneously enters a 3, the program catches the error immediately and asks for the correct code.

Contingency Cleaning

Contingency cleaning is more complicated. The logical structure of the data may place special limits on the responses of certain respondents. For example, a questionnaire may ask for the number of children women have had. All female respondents, then, should have a response punched (or a special code for failure to answer), while no male respondent should have a punch (or should have a special punch indicating the question is inappropriate). If a given male respondent is punched as having borne three children, an error has been made and should be corrected.

Contingency cleaning may be accomplished through computer programs, if available, or through the use of the counter-sorter. In either event, however, the process is more complicated than that for possible-punch cleaning. Computer programs will require a rather complicated set of if-then statements. Manual cleaning will require two or more passes through the counter-sorter to clean each set of items. The programs that support direct-data-entry automatically check for proper contingencies.

Although data cleaning is an essential step in data processing, it may be safely avoided in certain cases. Perhaps you will feel you can safely exclude the very few erroneous punches that appear in a given column—if the exclusion of those cases will not significantly affect your results. Or, some inappropriate contingency responses may be safely ignored. If some men have been given motherhood status, you can limit your analysis of this variable to women. However, you should not use these comments as rationalizations for sloppy research. "Dirty" data will almost always produce misleading research findings.

MAIN POINTS

- The quantification of data is necessary in order to permit subsequent statistical manipulations and analyses.

- The observations describing each unit of analysis must be transformed into standardized, numerical codes for retrieval and manipulation by machine.

- A given variable is assigned a specific location in the data storage medium: in terms of punch card columns, for example. That variable is assigned the same location in all the data files containing the data describing the different cases about which observations were made.

- The attributes of a given variable are represented by different punches in the columns assigned to that variable. (If cards are not being used, other terms apply, but the general idea is the same.)

- A codebook is the document that describes the locations assigned to different variables and the punches assigned to represent different attributes.

- Data entry can be accomplished by keypunching cards, writing the data onto tape cassettes, or entering data directly into a computer. A transfer sheet is a special coding sheet upon which numerical codes are recorded. These transfer sheets are then used for data entry (e.g., keypunching).

- Edge-coding is an alternative to the use of transfer sheets. The numerical coding is done in the margins of the original documents—such as questionnaires—instead of on transfer sheets.

- Precoding refers to the assignment of variable locations and appropriate punches for attributes printed on a questionnaire or similar document, simplifying the data entry process.

- Optical scan sheets or mark-sense sheets may be used in some research projects to save time and money in data processing. These are the familiar sheets used in examinations, on which answers are indicated by black marks in the appropriate spaces. Optical scanners are machines that read the black marks and transfer the same information to data cards or other storage formats.

- In direct-data-entry, coders type coded data into computer terminals where it is transferred directly into computer data files.

- Possible-punch cleaning refers to the process of checking punches to see that only those punches assigned to particular attributes—possible punches—appear in given card columns. This process guards against one class of data-processing error.

- Contingency cleaning is the process of checking to see that only those cases that *should* have data on a particular variable do in fact have such data. This process guards against another class of data-processing error.

REVIEW QUESTIONS AND EXERCISES

1. Find out the data-processing facilities available to social researchers on your campus and describe how survey questionnaires might be processed using those facilities.

2. Create a codebook—with column and code assignments—for the following questions in a questionnaire:

   a. Did you vote in the 1980 general election?

     ☐ Yes → If yes, who did you vote for in the mayor's race?

     ☐ No   ☐ Smith ☐ Brown

   b. Do you generally consider yourself a Republican, a Democrat, an Independent, or something else?

     ☐ Republican
     ☐ Democrat
     ☐ Independent
     ☐ Other: _____

   c. What do you feel is the most important problem facing this community today?

d. In the spaces provided below, please indicate the three community problems that most concern you by putting a 1 beside the one that most concerns you, a 2 beside your second choice, and a 3 beside your third choice.

_____ Crime
_____ Traffic
_____ Drug Abuse
_____ Pollution
_____ Prejudice and discrimination
_____ Inflation
_____ Unemployment
_____ Housing shortage

ADDITIONAL READINGS

Cozby, Paul C., *Using Computers in the Behavioral Sciences* (Palo Alto: Mayfield, 1984). A brief introduction to computing and common statistical packages. Contains a review of computer applications as well as an appendix on computer programming.

Edwards, Perry, and Broadwell, Bruce, *Data Processing,* 2nd Edition (Belmont, Calif.: Wadsworth, 1982). If you want to learn more about computers and the logic of programming, here's a good introduction.

Heise, David (ed.), *Microcomputers in Social Research* (Beverly Hills, Calif.: Sage, 1981). This special issue of *Sociological Methods and Research* examines the role of the microcomputer in several areas of social research, including anthropology, urban planning, social-psychophysiology, and simulations of social systems. Contains some how-to discussions also.

14

Elementary Analyses

What You'll Learn in This Chapter

You'll come away from this chapter able to perform a number of simple though powerful ways to manipulate data for the purpose of reaching research conclusions.

INTRODUCTION

Most social science analysis falls within the general rubric of **multivariate analysis,** and the bulk of Part 4 of this book is devoted to a variety of multivariate analyses. This term refers simply to the examination of several variables simultaneously. The analysis of the simultaneous association among age, education, and prejudice would be an example of multivariate analysis.

You should realize that multivariate analysis is a general term and is not a specific form of analysis. Specific techniques for conducting a multivariate analysis include factor analysis, smallest-space analysis, multiple correlation, multiple regression, and path analysis, among others. The basic logic of multivariate analysis can best be seen through the use of simple tables, called **contingency tables** or *cross-tabulations.* Thus the present chapter is devoted to the construction and understanding of such tables.

Multivariate analysis cannot be fully understood without a firm understanding of even more fundamental analytic modes: univariate and bivariate analyses. The chapter, therefore, will begin with these.

UNIVARIATE ANALYSIS

Univariate analysis is the examination of the distribution of cases on only one variable at a time. We'll begin with the logic and formats for the analysis of univariate data.

Distributions

The most basic format for presenting univariate data is to report all individual cases: that is, to list the attribute for each case

under study in terms of the variable in question. Suppose you are interested in the ages of corporate executives. (Your data might have come from *Who's Who in America.*) The most direct manner of reporting the ages of corporate executives would be to list them: 63, 57, 49, 62, 80, 72, 55, and so forth. Such a report would provide your reader with the fullest details of the data, but it would be too cumbersome for most purposes. You could arrange your data in a somewhat more manageable form without losing any of the detail by reporting that 5 executives were 38 years old, 7 were 39, 18 were 40, and so forth. Such a format would avoid duplicating data on this variable.

For an even more manageable format—with a certain loss of detail—you could report executives' ages as *marginals,* which are **frequency distributions** of *grouped data:* 246 executives under 45 years of age, 517 between 45 and 50 years of age, and so forth. In this case, your reader would have fewer data to examine and interpret, but he or she would not be able to reproduce fully the original ages of all the executives. Thus, for example, the reader would have no way of knowing how many executives were 41 years of age.

The above example presented marginals in the form of raw numbers. An alternative form would be the use of *percentages.* Thus, for example, you could report that x percent of your corporate executives were under 45, y percent were between 45 and 50, and so forth. (See Table 14-1.) In computing percentages, you frequently must make a decision about the *base* from which to compute: the number that represents 100 percent. In the most straightforward examples, the base is the total number of cases under study. A problem arises, however, whenever some cases have missing data. Let's assume, for example, that you have conducted a survey in which respondents were asked to report their ages. If some respondents failed to answer that question, you have two alternatives. First, you might still base your percentages on the total number of respondents, reporting those who failed to give their ages as a percentage of the total. Second, you could use the number of persons giving an answer as the base from which to compute the percentages. You should still report the number who did not answer, but they would not figure in the percentages.

The choice of a base depends wholly on the purposes of the analysis. If you wish to compare the age distribution of your survey sample with comparable data describing the population from which the sample was drawn, you will probably want to omit the "no answers" from the computation. Your best estimate of the age distribution of all respondents is the distribution for those answering the question. Since "no answer" is not a meaningful age category, its presence among the base categories would confuse the comparison of sample and population figures. (See Table 14-1 for an example.)

Central Tendency

Beyond simply reporting marginals, you may choose to present your data in the form of

Table 14-1   An Illustration of a Univariate Analysis

Ages of Corporate Executives (hypothetical)	
Under 35	9%
36–45	21
46–55	45
56–65	19
66 and older	6
	100% = (433)
No data =	(18)

summary **averages** or measures of *central tendency.* Your options in this regard are the **mode** (the most frequent attribute, either grouped or ungrouped), the arithmetic **mean**, or the **median** (the *middle* attribute in the ranked distribution of observed attributes). Here's how the three averages would be calculated from a set of data.

Suppose that you are conducting an experiment that involves teenagers as subjects. They range in age from 13 to 19, as indicated below:

Age	Number
13	3
14	4
15	6
16	8
17	4
18	3
19	3

Now that you've seen the actual ages of the 31 subjects, how old would you say they are in general, or on the average? Let's look at three different ways you might answer that question.

The easiest average to calculate is the *mode,* the most frequent value. As you can see, there were more 16-year-olds (8 of them) than any other age, so the modal age is 16, as indicated in Figure 14-1.

Figure 14-1 also demonstrates the calculation of the mean. There are three steps: (1) multiply each age by the number of subjects who have that age, (2) total the results of all those multiplications, and (3) divide that total by the number of subjects. As indicated in Figure 14-1, the mean age in this illustration is 15.87.

The *median* represents the "middle" value: half are above it, half below. If we had the *precise* ages of each subject (e.g., 17

Figure 14-1   Three "Averages"

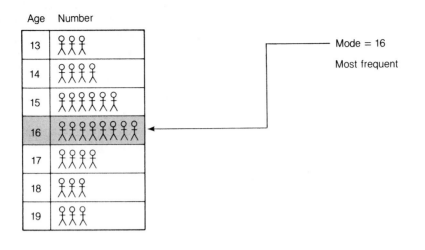

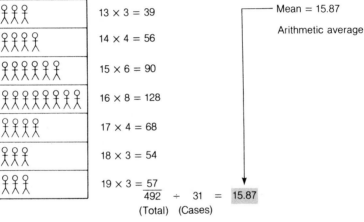

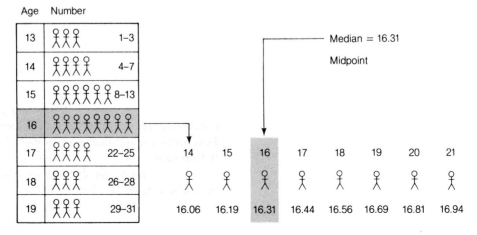

years and 124 days), we'd be able to arrange all 31 subjects in order by age and the median for the whole group would be the age of the middle subject.

As you can see, however, we do not know precise ages; our data constitute "grouped data" in this regard: three people who are not precisely the same age have been grouped in the category "13 years old," for example.

Figure 14-1 illustrates the logic of calculating a median for grouped data. Since there are 31 subjects altogether, the "middle" subject would be number 16, if they were arranged by age—15 would be younger and 17 would be older. Look at the bottom portion of Figure 14-1, and you'll see that the middle person is one of the eight 16-year-olds. In the enlarged view of that group, we see that number 16 is the third from the left.

Since we do not know the precise ages of the subjects in this group, the statistical convention here is to assume they are evenly spread along the width of the group. In this instance, the *possible* ages of the subjects go from 16 years and no days to 16 years and 364 days. Strictly speaking, the range, then, is 364/365 years. As a practical matter, it's sufficient to call it 1 year.

If the eight subjects in this group were evenly spread from one limit to the other, they would be one-eighth of a year apart from each other—a 0.125-year interval. Look at the illustration and you'll see that if we place the first subject half the interval from the lower limit and add a full interval to the age of each successive subject, the final one is half an interval from the upper limit.

What we have done, therefore, is calculate, hypothetically, the precise ages of the eight subjects—assuming their ages were spread out evenly. Having done that, we merely note the age of the middle subject—16.31—and that is the median age for the group.

Whenever the total number of subjects is an even number, of course, there is no mid-

dle case. In that case, you merely calculate the mean of the two values it falls between. Suppose there were one more 19-year-old, for example. The midpoint in that case would fall between number 16 and number 17. The mean, in that case, would be calculated as $(16.31 + 16.44) / 2 = 16.38$.

In the research literature, you will find both means and medians presented. Whenever means are presented, you should be aware that they are susceptible to extreme values: a few very large or very small numbers. For example, the 1980 mean per capita gross national product (GNP) for the United States was $9,700, contrasted, for example, with $190 for Sri Lanka, $3,470 for Ireland, and $7,920 for Australia. The tiny oil sheikdom of Kuwait, however, had a mean per capita GNP of $14,890, yet most residents of that country are impoverished, as may be inferred from the fact that their infant mortality rate was three times that of the United States in 1980, and their life expectancy at birth was 18 years less. The high mean per capita GNP in Kuwait reflects the enormous petro-wealth of a few (Population Reference Bureau 1980).

Dispersion

Averages have the special advantage to the reader of reducing the raw data to the most manageable form: a single number (or attribute) can represent all the detailed data collected in regard to the variable. This advantage comes at a cost, of course, since the reader cannot reconstruct the original data from an average. This disadvantage of averages can be somewhat alleviated through the reporting of summaries of the dispersion of responses. The simplest measure of dispersion is the *range:* the distance separating the highest from the lowest value. Thus, besides reporting that our subjects have a mean age of 15.87, we might also indicate that their ages ranged from 13 to 19. A somewhat more sophisticated measure of dispersion is the *standard deviation*. The logic of this measure was discussed in Chapter 5 as the standard error of a sampling distribution.

There are many other measures of dispersion. In reporting intelligence test scores, for example, you might determine the *interquartile range*, the range of scores for the middle 50% of subjects, the second fourth, and so forth. If the highest one-fourth had scores ranging from 120 to 150, and if the lowest one-fourth had scores ranging from 60 to 90, you could report that the interquartile range was 120 to 90, or 30, with a mean score of, let's say, 102.

Continuous and Discrete Variables

The calculations described above are not appropriate for all variables. To understand this, we must examine two types of variables: *continuous* and *discrete*. Age is a continuous, ratio variable; it increases steadily in tiny fractions instead of jumping from category to category as does a discrete variable such as sex or military rank. If discrete variables were being analyzed—a nominal or ordinal variable, for example—then some of the techniques discussed above would not be applicable. Strictly speaking, medians and means should be calculated only for interval and ratio data, respectively. If the variable in question were sex, for example, raw number or percentage marginals would be appropriate and useful analyses. Calculating the mode would be a legitimate, though not very revealing, analysis, but reports of mean, median, or dispersion summaries would be inappropriate. While researchers can sometimes learn something of value by violating rules like these, you should only do so with caution.

Measuring Nursing Faculty Interactions

As you read the research literature, you'll find numerous "gray-area" situations regarding the calculation of averages. For example, to find out how nursing faculty members viewed their interactions with colleagues, Judith Beyer (1981) first established a set of eight general questions (e.g., "Is there confidence and trust among faculty colleagues?") and then created three statements to reflect each of the questions. The eight general dimensions were grouped under the global heading "Collegial Communication."

Subjects were asked to respond to each of the three statements included under each question on the basis of a 5-point extent scale: 1 = to a very little extent; 2 = to a little extent; 3 = to some extent; 4 = to a great extent; and 5 = to a very great extent. . . .

The overall mean score . . . was 2.897 (standard deviation = .697). The collective responses of participants indicated that actual interpersonal interactions among colleagues fell slightly below the midpoint of the original 5-point extent scale, or were supportive "to some extent."

(Beyer 1981:113–14)

In reviewing this presentation, you should note that the base data constitute an ordinal level measurement: the various extents to which respondents found statements reflected their collegial experiences. Although the numbers 1 through 5 were assigned to those answers, there is no reason to believe that the distance from response 1 to response 2 is the same as the distance from response 4 to response 5, for example. By calculating means and standard deviations, however, Beyer has treated the numerical scores as though they were real values.

While unjustified on technical, statistical terms, this procedure is a common and useful one. A mean score of 2.897 on collegial communication is meaningless in itself, but it could be useful in comparing the views held by different kinds of nurses. Since Beyer also asked nurses to evaluate the statements in terms of how they would like things to be, the mean scores provided a useful device for comparing discrepancies between actual and desired states of affairs on the eight dimensions. Beyer also reports that the questionnaire items used in her study have been used extensively by previous researchers. While this does not guarantee their validity, it adds some weight to that conclusion.

The key here is *utility*. If you find that a researcher's statistical calculations are useful in revealing the nature of social affairs, then you should be somewhat lenient in the application of statistical techniques to data that do not warrant them. The other edge of this sword, however, is the danger of being lulled into thinking that the results represent something truly precise. In this case, for example, you might question the utility and appropriateness of carrying the means and standard deviations out to three decimal points.

Detail versus Manageability

In presenting univariate—and other—data, you will be constrained by two often conflicting goals. On the one hand, you should attempt to provide your reader with the fullest degree of detail regarding those data. On the other hand, the data should be presented in a manageable form. As these two goals often go directly counter to each other, you will find yourself continually seeking the best compromise between them. One useful solution is to report a given set of data in more than one form. In the case of age, for example, you might report the marginals on ungrouped ages *plus* the mean age and standard deviation.

As you can see from this introductory discussion of univariate analysis, this seemingly simple matter can be rather complex. The lessons of this section, in any event, will be important as we move now to a consideration of subgroup comparisons and bivariate analyses.

SUBGROUP COMPARISONS

Univariate analyses *describe* the units of analysis of a study and, if they are a sample drawn from some larger population, allow us to make descriptive inferences about the larger population. Bivariate and multivariate analyses are aimed primarily at *explanation*. Before turning to explanation, however, we should consider the case of subgroup description.

Often it's appropriate to describe subsets of cases, subjects, or respondents. Table 14-2, for example, presents income data for men and women separately. In addition, the table presents the ratio of women's median income to that of men, showing that women in the labor force earn a little over half what men earn.

In some situations, the researcher presents subgroup comparisons purely for descriptive purposes. More often, the purpose of subgroup descriptions is comparative: women earn less than men. In the present case, it is assumed that there is something about being a woman that results in their lower incomes. When we compare incomes of blacks and whites, a similar assumption is made. In such cases, the analysis is based on an assumption of *causality:* one variable causing another, as in sex causing income. At this point, it is appropriate to turn to a discussion of bivariate analysis.

Table 14-2   Median Earnings of
Year-Round, Full-Time Civilian Workers
with Earnings by Sex: 1967 to 1977

Year	Women	Men	Ratio of women's to men's earnings
1977	$8,618	$14,626	.59
1976	8,622	14,323	.60
1975	8,449	14,175	.60
1974	8,565	14,578	.59
1973	8,639	15,254	.57
1972	8,551	14,778	.58
1971	8,369	14,064	.61
1970	8,307	13,993	.59
1969	8,227	13,976	.59
1968	7,763	13,349	.58
1967	7,503	13,021	.58

Source: Adapted from the U. S. Bureau of the Census,
"A Statistical Portrait of Women in the United States:
1978," Series P-23, No. 100, p. 73.

BIVARIATE ANALYSIS

In contrast to univariate analysis, subgroup comparisons constitute a kind of **bivariate analysis** in that two variables are involved. As we noted earlier, the purpose of univariate analysis is purely descriptive. The purpose of subgroup comparisons is also largely descriptive—independently describing the subgroups—but the element of comparison is added. Most bivariate analysis in social research adds another element: relationships among the variables themselves. Thus, while univariate analysis and subgroup comparisons focus on describing the *people* (or other units of analysis) under study, bivariate analysis focuses on the *variables*.

Notice, then, that Table 14-3 could be regarded as an instance of subgroup comparison: it independently describes the atti-

Table 14-3   "Do you approve or disapprove of the proposition that men and women should be treated equally in all regards?"

	Men	Women
Approve	63%	75%
Disapprove	37	25
	100%	100%
	(400)	(400)
No answer =	(12)	(5)

tudes of men and women toward sexual equality. It shows—comparatively and descriptively—that the women under study are more supportive of equality than the men.

The same table, seen as an *explanatory* bivariate analysis, tells a somewhat different story. It suggests that the variable *sex* has an effect on the variable *attitude toward sexual equality*. The attitude is seen as a *dependent variable* that is partially determined by the *independent variable,* sex. Explanatory bivariate analyses, then, involve the "variable language" introduced in Chapter 1. In a subtle shift of focus, we are no longer talking about men and women as different subgroups but of sex as a variable: a variable that has an influence on other variables. The logic of interpreting Table 14-3 is as follows:

1. Women generally are accorded an inferior status in American society; thus they should be more supportive of the proposed equality of the sexes.

2. A respondent's sex should therefore affect (cause) his or her response to the questionnaire item: women should be more likely to approve than men.

3. If the male and female respondents in the survey are described separately in terms

of their responses, a higher percentage of the women should approve.

The data presented in Table 14-3 confirm this reasoning. Of the women, 75 percent approve of sexual equality as compared to 63 percent of the men.

Adding the logic of causal relationships among variables has an important implication for the construction and reading of percentage tables. One of the chief bugaboos for new data analysts is deciding on the appropriate "direction of percentaging" for any given table. In Table 14-3, for example, I have divided the group of subjects into two subgroups—men and women—and then described the attitudes of each subgroup. That is the correct method for constructing this table.

Notice, however, that it would have been possible—though inappropriate—to construct the table differently. We could have first divided the subjects into those approving of sexual equality and those disapproving of it, and then we could have described each of those subgroups in terms of the percentage of men and women in each. This method would make no sense in terms of explanation, however.

Table 14-3 suggests that your sex will affect how you feel about sexual equality. Had we used the other method of construction, the table would suggest that your attitude toward sexual equality affects whether you are a man or a woman—which makes no sense. Your attitude cannot determine your sex.

There is another, related problem that complicates the lives of new data analysts. How do you *read* a percentage table? There is a temptation to read Table 14-3 as follows: "Of the women, 75 percent approved and only 25 percent disapproved; therefore being a woman makes you more likely to approve." That is *not* the correct way to read the table, however. The conclusion that sex—as a variable—has an effect on atti-

tudes must hinge on a comparison between men and women. Specifically, we note that *women are more likely than men* to approve of sexual equality: comparing the 75 percent with the 63 percent. Suppose, for example, that 100 percent of the men approved. Regardless of the fact that women approved 3 to 1, it wouldn't make sense to say that being a woman increased the likelihood of approval. In fact, the opposite would be true in such a case. The comparison of subgroups, then, is essential in reading an explanatory bivariate table.

In constructing and presenting Table 14-3, I have used a convention called *percentage down*. This term means that you can add the percentages down each column to total 100 percent. You read this form of table *across* a row. For the row labeled "approve," what percentage of the men approve? What percentage of the women approve?

The direction of percentaging in tables is arbitrary, and some researchers prefer to percentage across. They would organize Table 14-3 so that "men" and "women" were shown on the left side of the table, identifying the two rows, and "approve" and "disapprove" would appear at the top to identify the columns. The actual numbers in the table would be moved around accordingly, and each *row* of percentages would total 100 percent. In that case, you would read the table down a column, still asking what percentage of men and women approved. The logic and the conclusion would be the same in either case; only the form would be different.

In reading a table that someone else has constructed, therefore, you need to find out in which direction it has been percentaged. Usually that will be apparent in the labeling of the table or in the logic of the variables being analyzed. As a last resort, however, you should add the percentages in each column and each row. If each of the columns totals 100 percent, the table has been percentaged down. If the rows total 100 percent each, it has been percentaged across. The rule of thumb, then, is as follows:

1. If the table is percentaged down, read across.

2. If the table is percentaged across, read down.

Table 14-4   Hypothetical Data Regarding Newspaper Editorials on the Legalization of Marijuana

Editorial Policy toward Legalizing Marijuana	Community Size	
	Under 100,000	Over 100,000
Favorable	11%	32%
Neutral	29	40
Unfavorable	60	28
100% =	(127)	(438)

Percentaging a Table

Figure 14-2 reviews the logic by which we create percentage tables from two variables. I've used the same variables as in the previous example—gender and attitudes toward equality for men and women—but I have reduced the numbers to make the illustration more manageable. See pp. 352–353.

Here's another example. Suppose we are interested in learning something about newspaper editorial policies regarding the legalization of marijuana. We undertake a content analysis of editorials on this subject that have appeared during a given year in a sample of daily newspapers across the nation. Each editorial has been classified as favorable, neutral, or unfavorable toward the legalization of marijuana. Perhaps we wish to examine the relationship between editorial policies and the types of communities in which the newspapers are published, thinking that rural newspapers might be more conservative in this regard than urban ones. Thus, each newspaper (hence, each editorial) has been classified in terms of the population of the community in which it is published.

Table 14-4 presents some hypothetical data describing the editorial policies of rural and urban newspapers. Note that the unit of analysis in this example is the individual editorial. Table 14-4 tells us that there were 127 editorials about marijuana in our sam-

ple of newspapers published in communities with populations under 100,000. (*Note:* This cutting point is chosen for simplicity of illustration and does not mean that *rural* refers to a community of less than 100,000 in any absolute sense.) Of these, 11 percent (14 editorials) were favorable toward legalization of marijuana, 29 percent were neutral, and 60 percent were unfavorable. Of the 438 editorials that appeared in our sample of newspapers published in communities of more than 100,000 residents, 32 percent (140 editorials) were favorable toward legalizing marijuana, 40 percent were neutral, and 28 percent were unfavorable.

When we compare the editorial policies of rural and urban newspapers in our imaginary study, we find—as expected—that rural newspapers are less favorable toward the legalization of marijuana than are urban ones. That is determined by noting that a larger percentage (32 percent) of the urban editorials were favorable than of the rural ones (11 percent). We might note, as well, that more rural than urban editorials were unfavorable (60 percent compared to 28 percent). Note that this table assumes that the size of a community might affect its newspapers' editorial policies on this issue, rather than that editorial policy might affect the size of communities.

Constructing and Reading Tables

Before introducing multivariate analysis, let's review the steps involved in the construction of explanatory bivariate tables:

1. The cases are divided into groups according to their attributes of the independent variable.

2. Each of these subgroups is then described in terms of attributes of the dependent variable.

3. Finally, the table is read by comparing the independent variable subgroups with one another in terms of a given attribute of the dependent variable.

Let's repeat the analysis of sex and attitude on sexual equality following these steps. For the reasons outlined above, sex is the independent variable; attitude toward sexual equality constitutes the dependent variable. Thus, we proceed as follows:

1. The cases are divided into men and women.

2. Each sex subgrouping is described in terms of approval or disapproval of sexual equality.

3. Men and women are compared in terms of the percentages approving of sexual equality.

In the example of editorial policies regarding the legalization of marijuana, size of community is the independent variable and a newspaper's editorial policy the dependent variable. The table would be constructed as follows:

1. Divide the editorials into subgroups according to the sizes of the communities in which the newspapers are published.

2. Describe each subgroup of editorials in terms of the percentages favorable, neutral, or unfavorable toward the legalization of marijuana.

3. Compare the two subgroups in terms of the percentages favorable toward the legalization of marijuana.

Bivariate analyses typically have an explanatory causal purpose. These two hypothetical examples have hinted at the nature of causation as it is used by social scientists. I hope the rather simplified approach to causation employed in these examples will have a commonsense acceptability for you at this point. This rather superficial, commonsense view of causation will assist you in understanding this chapter and the next. Chapter 16 will take a much closer look at causation. A fundamental understanding of the subjects covered in this chapter and the next one should help you understand more fully the complex nature of causation.

Bivariate Table Formats

Tables such as those we've been examining are commonly called *contingency tables:* values of the dependent variable are contingent upon values of the independent variable. While contingency tables are very common in social science, their format has never been standardized. As a result, a variety of formats will be found in research literature. As long as a table is easy to read and interpret, there is probably no reason to strive for standardization. However, there are a number of guidelines that should be followed in the presentation of most tabular data.

1. A table should have a heading or a title that succinctly describes what is contained in the table.

2. The original content of the variables should be clearly presented—in the table

Figure 14-2   Percentaging a Table

A. Some men and women who either favor (=) sexual equality or don't (≠) favor it.

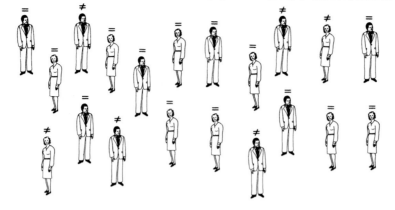

B. Separate the men and the women (the independent variable).

Women   Men

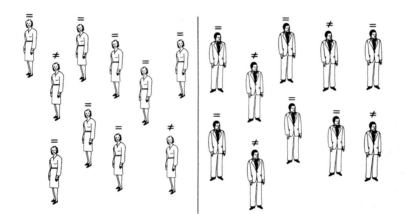

C. Within each gender group, separate those who favor equality from those who do not (the dependent variable).

Women   Men

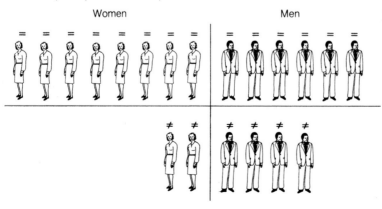

Figure 14-2 *(Continued)*

D. Count the numbers in each cell of the table.

Women   Men

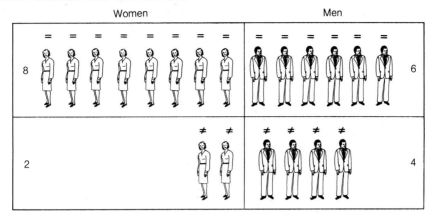

E. What percentage of the women favor equality?

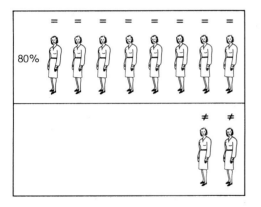

F. What percentage of the men favor equality?

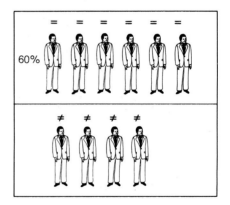

G. Conclusions

While a majority of both men and women favored sexual equality, women were more likely than men to do so.

Thus, gender appears to be one of the causes of attitudes toward sexual equality.

	Women	Men
Favor equality	80%	60%
Don't favor equality	20%	40%
Total	100%	100%

itself if at all possible, or in the text with a paraphrase in the table. This information is especially critical when a variable is derived from responses to an attitudinal question, since the meaning of the responses will depend largely on the wording of the question.

3. The attributes of each variable should be clearly indicated. Complex categories will have to be abbreviated, but the meaning should be clear in the table and, of course, the full description should be reported in the text.

4. When percentages are reported in the table, the base upon which they are computed should be indicated. It is redundant to present all of the raw numbers for each category, since these could be reconstructed from the percentages and the bases. Moreover, the presentation of both numbers and percentages often confuses a table and makes it more difficult to read.

5. If any cases are omitted from the table because of missing data ("no answer," for example), their numbers should be indicated in the table.

INTRODUCTION TO MULTIVARIATE ANALYSIS

The logic of **multivariate analysis** is the topic of later chapters in this book—especially Chapters 16 and 17. At this point, however, it will be useful to discuss briefly the construction of multivariate tables: those constructed from several variables.

Multivariate tables may be constructed on the basis of a more complicated subgroup description by following essentially the same steps outlined above for bivariate tables. Instead of one independent variable and one dependent variable, however, we will have more than one independent variable. Instead

of explaining the dependent variable on the basis of a single independent variable, we'll seek an explanation through the use of more than one independent variable.

Let's return to the example of attitudes toward sexual equality. Suppose we believed age would also affect such attitudes, that young people would approve of sexual equality more than older people. As the first step in table construction, we would divide the total sample into subgroups based on the various attributes of *both* independent variables simultaneously: young men, old men, young women, and old women. Then the several subgroups would be described in terms of the dependent variable, and comparisons would be made. Table 14-5 is a hypothetical table that might result.

Following the convention presented here, this table has also been percentaged down, and therefore should be read across. The interpretation of this table warrants several conclusions.

1. Among both men and women, younger people are more supportive of sexual equality than older people. Among women, 90 percent of those under 30 and 60 percent of those 30 and older approve.

2. Within each age group, women are more supportive than men. Among those respondents under 30, 90 percent of the women approve, compared with 78 percent of the men. Among those 30 and over, 60 percent of the women and 48 percent of the men approve.

3. As measured in the table, age appears to have a stronger effect on attitudes than sex. For both men and women, the effect of age may be summarized as a 30 percentage point difference. Within each age group, the percentage point difference between men and women is 12.

4. Age and sex have independent effects on attitudes. Within a given attribute of one

Table 14-5 Multivariate Relationship: Attitude, Sex, and Age
"Do you approve or disapprove of the proposition that men and women should be treated equally in all regards?"

	Under 30		30 and Over	
	Women	Men	Women	Men
Approve	90%	78%	60%	48%
Disapprove	10	22	40	52
	100%	100%	100%	100%
	(200)	(200)	(200)	(200)
No Answer =	(2)	(10)	(3)	(2)

independent variable, different attributes of the second still affect attitudes.

5. Similarly, the two independent variables have a cumulative effect on attitudes. Young women are most supportive, and older men are the least supportive.

Chapter 16 on the *elaboration model* will examine the logic of multivariate analysis in much greater detail. Before we conclude this section, however, it will be useful to note an alternative format for presenting such data.

Several of the tables presented in this chapter are somewhat inefficient. When the dependent variable—attitude toward sexual equality—is dichotomous (two attributes), knowing one attribute permits the reader to easily reconstruct the other. Thus, if we know that 90 percent of the women under 30 approve of sexual equality, then we know automatically that 10 percent disapprove. So reporting the percentages who disapprove is unnecessary. On the basis of this recognition, Table 14-5 could be presented in the alternative format of Table 14-6.

In Table 14-6, the percentages approving of sexual equality are reported in the cells representing the intersections of the two independent variables. The numbers pre-

sented in parentheses below each percentage represent the number of cases upon which the percentages are based. Thus, for example, the reader knows that there are 200 women under 30 years of age in the sample, and 90 percent of those approved of sexual equality. This shows, moreover, that 180 of those 200 women approved, and that the other 20 (or 10 percent) disapproved. This new table is easier to read than the former one, and it does not sacrifice any detail.

I want to conclude this discussion with a somewhat more complicated multivariate table, drawn from the social science literature on self-perception. This example represents an attempt by sociologist Morris

Table 14-6 A Simplication of Table 14-5
"Do you approve or disapprove of the proposition that men and women should be treated equally in all regards?"

	Percentage Who Approve	
	Women	Men
Under 30	90 (200)	78 (200)
30 and over	60 (200)	48 (200)

Rosenberg (1965) to shed some light on *self-esteem* among adolescent boys. As we see in Table 14-7, Rosenberg examined the simultaneous impact of three variables on self-esteem:

1. *Sex distribution of siblings:* Do the subjects live in families where girls outnumber boys or where boys either equal or outnumber girls?

2. *Ordinal position:* Are the subjects older or younger than others within their families?

3. *Grades:* What kinds of grades do the subjects get in school?

Let's see what Table 14-7 tells us about self-esteem. To simplify matters, let's focus on the percentages of adolescent boys who are high in self-esteem. To determine the impact of the sex distribution of siblings, we compare the top rows of percentages in the two halves of the table: 56 to 51 percent, 45 to 40 percent, 41 to 29 percent, 46 to 42 percent, 60 to 44 percent, and 64 to 30 percent. What pattern do you notice in all those comparisons? In each case, the boys living in families with a sister majority (top half of table) are more likely to have high self-esteem than boys similar to them in every other regard except sibling sex distribution. Consistently, living in a sister majority family seems to promote higher self-esteem. Although consistent, the differences are not uniform, however. Overall, the sex distribution of siblings seems to matter most for

Table 14-7 Self-Esteem of Adolescent Boys in Relation to Sex Distribution of Siblings, Ordinal Position, and Grades

Self-Esteem	Respondent in First Half or Middle of Family			Respondent in Last Half of Family (Younger Minority)		
	Grades			Grades		
	A–B	C	D–F	A–B	C	D–F
No Brothers or Brothers in the Minority						
High	56%	45%	41%	46%	60%	64%
Medium	20	27	27	19	18	18
Low	24	28	32	35	22	18
Total percent	100%	100%	100%	100%	100%	100%
Number	(79)	(104)	(41)	(26)	(65)	(22)
Brothers in the Majority or Equal						
High	51%	40%	29%	42%	44%	30%
Medium	26	27	18	32	33	20
Low	23	32	53	26	23	50
Total percent	100%	99%	100%	100%	100%	100%
Number	(168)	(240)	(102)	(78)	(86)	(56)

Source: Adapted from Morris Rosenberg, *The Logic of Survey Analysis* (New York: Basic Books, 1968), p. 214. Used by permission.

Note: Study is of families with three or more children.

those boys who get bad grades in school. There are only small differences among those with good grades.

How about ordinal position? Is self-esteem affected by whether boys are older or younger within their set of brothers and sisters? To find out, we make a different set of comparisons, comparing the right and left halves of the table: 56 to 46 percent, 45 to 60 percent, 41 to 64 percent (in the top half of the table), 51 to 42 percent, 40 to 44 percent, and 29 to 30 percent (in the bottom half). Once again, we are comparing groups of boys who are similar to each other except for their ordinal position. There doesn't seem to be much of a pattern in this latest set of comparisons. Although the various comparisons reveal differences in self-esteem, we cannot conclude that there is a consistent relationship between ordinal position and high self-esteem. Sometimes the older boys have higher self-esteem; sometimes the younger ones do.

Finally, what effect do grades have on self-esteem? We would probably suspect that good grades would result in high self-esteem and bad grades in low self-esteem. Let's see if that's true. Here the relevant comparisons are among the three grade groupings in each of the four parts of the table: 56 to 45 to 41 percent, 46 to 60 to 64 percent, 51 to 40 to 29 percent, and 42 to 44 to 30 percent. Is our suspicion confirmed by the data?

Grades seem to have the expected effect on self-esteem among those boys who are older than their brothers and sisters, but we find a very different pattern among the younger minority brothers. For Rosenberg, the latter set of data pointed to

. . . the possibility that the younger-minority boy might be characterized by a particular *type* of self-esteem, namely, *unconditional self-acceptance*. While the self-esteem of others appeared to be influenced by their level of academic performance, the self-esteem of the younger-minor-

ity boy appeared to be relatively impervious to it. It might thus be that the self-esteem of the younger-minority boy was so firmly established in the family by the interest and affection of his father, mother, and older sisters that it was relatively independent of later extra-familial experiences.

(1968:214)

This latest illustration should give you a fuller view of multivariate analysis through the use of percentage tables. At a superficial level, you have now been exposed to the entire process of data analysis.

In this sense, the remaining chapters of this book are a review—at a much deeper level— of materials already covered. Chapter 15 presents the topic of measurement at a more sophisticated level than our earlier discussion as we take up the construction of composite scales and indexes. And although we have looked fleetingly at the topic of causation, Chapter 16 examines it more seriously. Chapters 17 through 19 review and expand on the basic topic of this chapter—the logic of data analysis.

MAIN POINTS

■ Univariate analysis is the analysis of a single variable.

■ The full original data collected with regard to a single variable are, in that form, usually impossible to interpret. *Data reduction* is the process of summarizing the original data so as to make them more manageable, all the while maintaining as much of the original detail as possible.

■ A frequency distribution shows the number of cases having each of the attributes of a given variable.

■ Grouped data are created through the combination of attributes of a variable.

■ *Averages* (the mean, median, and mode) reduce data to an easily manageable form, but they do not convey the detail of the original data.

■ Measures of dispersion give a summary indication of the distribution of cases around an average value.

■ To undertake a subgroup comparison: (a) divide cases into the appropriate subgroups, (b) describe each subgroup in terms of a given variable, and (c) compare those descriptions across the subgroups.

■ Bivariate analysis is nothing more than a different interpretation of subgroup comparisons: (a) divide cases into subgroups in terms of their attributes on some *independent variable,* (b) describe each subgroup in terms of some *dependent variable,* (c) compare the dependent variable descriptions of the subgroups, and (d) interpret any observed differences as a statistical association between the independent and dependent variables.

■ As a rule of thumb in interpreting bivariate percentage tables: (a) "percentage down" and "read across" in making the subgroup comparisons, *or* (b) "percentage across" and "read down" in making subgroup comparisons.

■ Multivariate analysis is a method of analyzing the simultaneous relationships among several variables and may be used in more fully understanding the relationship between two variables.

REVIEW QUESTIONS AND EXERCISES

1. Construct and interpret a contingency table from the following information: 100 Democrats favor increased military spending, and 300 oppose it; 150 Republicans favor increased military spending, and 50 oppose it.

2. Using the data in the table below, construct and interpret tables showing
   a. The bivariate relationship between age and attitude toward abortion.
   b. The bivariate relationship between political orientation and attitude toward abortion.
   c. The multivariate relationship linking age, political orientation, and attitude toward abortion.

ADDITIONAL READINGS

Cole, Stephen, *The Sociological Method* (Chicago: Markham, 1972). A readable introduction to analysis. Cole begins with the general question of what social scientific inquiry is, and then illustrates with easily understood examples. He goes on to an introduction of the elaboration model, and that material is useful also.

Davis, James, *Elementary Survey Analysis* (Englewood Cliffs, N.J.: Prentice-

Age	Political Orientation	Attitude toward Abortion	Frequency
Young	Liberal	Favor	90
Young	Liberal	Oppose	10
Young	Conservative	Favor	60
Young	Conservative	Oppose	40
Old	Liberal	Favor	60
Old	Liberal	Oppose	40
Old	Conservative	Favor	20
Old	Conservative	Oppose	80

Hall, 1971). An extremely well-written and well-reasoned introduction to analysis. In addition to covering the materials of the present book's Chapter 14, Davis's book is well worth reading in terms of measurement, statistics, and the elaboration model.

Labovitz, Sanford, and Hagedorn, Robert, *Introduction to Social Research* (New York: McGraw-Hill, 1971). Another useful introduction to analysis. Against the background of more general concerns for social scientific inquiry, the authors provide a very readable and useful introduction to elementary analyses in their Chapter 6. Like Cole and Davis, they then go on to a consideration of multivariate analysis and the elaboration model.

Ziesel, Hans, *Say It with Figures* (New York: Harper & Row, 1957). An excellent discussion of table construction and other elementary analyses. Though several years old, this is still perhaps the best available presentation of that specific topic. It is eminently readable and understandable and has many concrete examples.

15

Indexes, Scales, and Typologies

What You'll Learn in This Chapter

Now we return to the issue of measurement, discussed at length in Chapters 5 and 6. You'll learn the logic and skills of constructing composite measures from among several indicators of variables.

INTRODUCTION

Chapter 15 is a logical continuation of our earlier discussion of conceptualization (Chapter 5) and operationalization (Chapter 6). These earlier discussions examined some of the ways in which social researchers deal with measurement in the design of a study; the present chapter describes the continuation of that concern during the analysis of data.

This chapter discusses the construction of indexes and scales as composite measures of variables. A short section at the end of the chapter considers typologies. Each of these types of composite or cumulative measures combines several empirical indicators of a variable into a single measure.

Composite measures are very frequently used in social science research, for several reasons. First, despite the care taken in designing studies so as to provide valid and reliable measurements of variables, the researcher seldom is able to develop in advance single indicators of complex concepts. That is especially true with regard to attitudes and orientations. The survey researcher, for example, is seldom able to devise single questionnaire items that adequately tap respondents' degrees of prejudice, religiosity, political orientations, alienation, and the like. More likely, you will devise several items, each of which provides *some* indication of the variables. Each of these, however, is likely to prove invalid or unreliable for many respondents.

You should realize that *some* variables are rather easily measured through single indicators. We may determine a survey respondent's sex by asking: Sex: [ ] Male [ ] Female. We may determine a newspaper's circulation by merely looking at the figure the newspaper reports. The number of times an experimental stimulus is administered to an experimental group is clearly defined in the design of the experiment. Nonetheless,

social scientists, using a variety of research methods, frequently wish to study variables that have no clear and unambiguous single indicators.

Second, you may wish to employ a rather refined ordinal measure of your variable, arranging cases in several ordinal categories from—for example—very low to very high on a variable such as alienation. A single data item might not have enough categories to provide the desired range of variation, but an index or scale formed from several items would.

Finally, indexes and scales are *efficient* devices for data analysis. If considering a single data item gives us only a rough indication of a given variable, considering several data items may give us a more comprehensive and more accurate indication. For example, a single newspaper editorial may give us some indication of the political orientations of that newspaper. Examining several editorials would probably give us a better assessment, but the manipulation of several data items simultaneously could be very complicated. Indexes and scales (especially scales) are efficient *data-reduction devices:* several indicators may be summarized in a single numerical score, while sometimes very nearly maintaining the specific details of all the individual indicators.

INDEXES VERSUS SCALES

The terms **index** and **scale** are typically used imprecisely and interchangeably in social research literature. Before considering the distinctions that this book will make between indexes and scales, let's first see what they have in common.

Both scales and indexes are typical *ordinal* measures of variables. Both rank-order people (or other units of analysis) in terms of specific variables such as religiosity, alienation, socioeconomic status, prejudice, or intellectual sophistication. A person's score on a scale or index of religiosity, for example, gives an indication of his or her relative religiosity vis-à-vis other people.

As the terms will be used in this book, both scales and indexes are *composite measures of variables:* measurements based on more than one data item. Thus, a survey respondent's score on an index or scale of religiosity would be determined by the specific responses given to several questionnaire items, each of which would provide some indication of his or her religiosity. Similarly, a person's IQ score is based on answers to a large number of test questions. The political orientation of a newspaper might be represented by an index or scale score reflecting the newspaper's editorial policy on a number of political issues.

In this book, we shall distinguish indexes and scales through the manner in which scores are assigned. An *index* is constructed through the simple accumulation of scores assigned to *individual* attributes. A *scale* is constructed through the assignment of scores to *patterns* of attributes. Thus, a scale takes advantage of any *intensity structure* that may exist among attributes. A simple example should clarify this distinction.

Figure 15-1 provides a graphic illustration of the difference between indexes and scales. Let's assume we want to develop a measure of political activism, distinguishing those people who are very active in political affairs, those who don't participate much at all, and those who are somewhere in between.

The first part of Figure 15-1 illustrates the logic of indexes. I've represented six different political actions. While you and I might disagree on some specifics, I think we could agree that the six actions represent roughly the same degree of political activism. While some people might give money more easily than write letters to the editor—or vice versa—the six actions are probably more or less equal if we consider the population as a whole.

We could construct an index of political activism, using the six items, by giving each person 1 point for each of the actions he or she has taken. So if you wrote to a public official and signed a petition, you'd get a total of 2 points. If I gave money to a candidate and persuaded someone to change their vote, I'd get the same score as you. Using this approach, we'd conclude that you and I had the same degree of political activism, even though we had taken different actions.

The second part of Figure 15-1 describes the logic of scale construction. In this case, the actions clearly represent *different* degrees of political activism—ranging from simply voting to running for office. Moreover, it seems safe to assume a *pattern* of actions in this case. For example, all those who contributed money probably also voted. Those who worked on a campaign probably also gave some money and voted. This suggests that most people will only fall into one of five "ideal" action patterns, represented by the small illustrations at the bottom of the figure. The discussion of scales, later in this chapter, describes ways of identifying people with the type they most closely represent.

It should be apparent that scales are generally superior to indexes, if for no other reason than that scale scores convey more information than index scores do. Still you should be wary of the common misuse of the term *scale;* clearly, calling a given measure a scale rather than an index does not make it better. You should be cautioned against two other misconceptions about scaling. First, whether the combination of several data items results in a scale almost always depends on the particular sample of observations under study. Certain items may form a scale among one sample but not among another, and you should not assume that a given set of items *are* a scale because they have formed a scale among a given

Figure 15-1   Indexes versus Scales

Index-Construction Logic

Here are several types of political
actions people may have taken. By and
large, the different actions seem to
represent similar *degrees* of political
activism. To create an *index* of
overall political activism, we might give
people 1 point for each of the actions
they've taken.

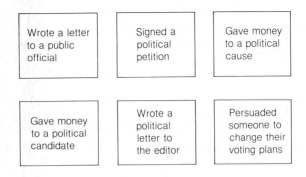

Scale-Construction Logic

Here are some political actions that represent very different degrees of
activism: e.g., running for office represents a higher degree of activism than
simply voting. It seems likely, moreover, that anyone who has taken one of
the more demanding actions would have taken all the easier ones as well.
To construct a *scale* of political activism, we might score people on
the basis of which of the following "ideal" patterns comes closest to
describing them.

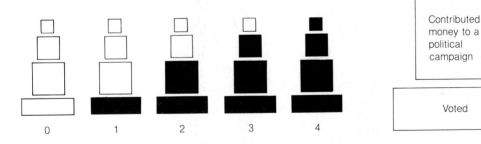

sample. Second, the use of certain *scaling
techniques* to be discussed does not assure
the creation of a scale any more than the
use of items that have previously formed
scales can offer such assurance.

An examination of the substantive literature based on social science data will show
that indexes are used much more frequently
than scales. Ironically, however, the methodological literature contains little if any
discussion of index construction, while discussions of scale construction abound. There

appear to be two reasons for this disparity.
First, indexes are more frequently used
because scales are often difficult or impossible to construct from the data at hand.
Second, methods of index construction are
not discussed because they seem obvious and
straightforward.

Index construction is not a simple undertaking, though the general failure to develop
index construction techniques has resulted
in the creation of many bad indexes in social
research. With this in mind, I have devoted

most of this chapter to the methods of index construction. Once you fully understand the logic of this activity, you will be better equipped to attempt the construction of scales. Indeed, the carefully constructed index may turn out to be a scale anyway.

INDEX CONSTRUCTION

Let's look now at the several steps involved in the creation of an index: selecting possible items, examining their empirical relationships, combining some items into an index, and validating it. I have presented these steps in some detail, since they are not all obvious. You should come away from this section able to create a composite measure that will fully support your subsequent analyses.

Item Selection

A composite index is created to measure some variable. The first criterion for selecting items to be included in the index is *face validity* (or logical validity). If you want to measure political conservatism, for example, each of your items should appear *on its face* to indicate conservatism (or its opposite: liberalism). Political party affiliation would be one such item. If people were asked to approve or disapprove of the views of a well-known conservative public figure, their responses might logically provide another indication of their conservatism. In constructing an index of religiosity, you might consider items such as church attendance, acceptance of certain religious beliefs, and frequency of prayer; each of these appears to offer some indication of religiosity.

The methodological literature on conceptualization and measurement stresses the need for *unidimensionality* in scale and index construction: a composite measure should represent only one dimension. Thus, items reflecting religiosity should not be included in a measure of political conservatism, even though the two variables might be empirically related to one another.

At the same time, you should be aware of subtle nuances that may exist within the general dimension you are attempting to measure. Thus in the example of religiosity, the indicators mentioned above represent different *types* of religiosity—ritual participation, belief, etc. If you wished to focus on ritual participation in religion, you should choose items specificlly indicating this type of religiosity: church attendance, communion, confession, and the like. If you wished to measure religiosity in a more general way, you would include a balanced set of items, representing each of the different types of religiosity. Ultimately, the nature of the items included will determine how specifically or generally the variable is measured.

In selecting items for an index, you must also be concerned with the amount of *variance* provided by those items. If an item is intended to indicate political conservatism, for example, you should note what proportion of respondents were identified as conservatives by the item. If a given item identified no one as a conservative or everyone as a conservative—for example, if nobody indicated approval of a radical right political figure—that item would not be very useful in the construction of an index.

To guarantee variance, you have two options. First, you may select several items on which responses divide people about equally in terms of the variable; for example, about half conservative and half liberal. Although no single response would justify characterization of a person as very conservative, a person who responded as a conservative on all of them might be so characterized.

The second option is to select items differing in variance. One item might identify about half the subjects as conservative, while another might identify few of the respondents as conservative. (*Note:* This latter option is necessary for scaling, but it is reasonable for index construction as well.)

Bivariate Relationships among Items

The second step in index construction is to examine the bivariate relationships among the items being considered for inclusion. Assuming that each of the items is indeed valid on its face, then the several items should be related to one another empirically. For example, if several items all reflect conservatism or liberalism, then respondents who appear conservative in terms of one item should appear conservative in terms of others. Recognize, however, that such items will seldom if ever be perfectly related to one another; persons who appear conservative on one item will appear liberal on another. (This disparity creates the need for constructing composite measures in the first place.) Nevertheless, persons who appear conservative on Item A should be more likely to appear conservative on Item B than are persons who appear liberal on Item A.

You should examine all the possible bivariate relationships among the several items being considered for inclusion in the index to determine the relative strengths of relationships among the several pairs of items. Either percentage tables or correlation coefficients (see Chapter 18), or both, may be used for this purpose. The primary criterion for evaluating these several relationships is the strength of the relationships. The use of this criterion, however, is rather subtle. (The box entitled "'Cause' and 'Effect' Indicators" examines some of those subtleties.)

Clearly, you should be wary of items that are not related to one another empirically. It is unlikely that they measure the same variable if they are unrelated. A given item that is not related to several other items probably should be dropped from consideration.

At the same time a *very* strong relationship between two items presents a different problem. If two items are perfectly related to one another, then only one is necessary for inclusion in the index, since it completely conveys the indications provided by the other. (This problem will become even clearer in the next section.)

To illustrate the testing of bivariate relationships in index construction, an example from the substantive literature may be useful. A few years ago, I conducted a survey of medical school faculty members to find out about the consequences of a "scientific perspective" on the quality of patient care provided by physicians. The primary intent was to determine whether more scientifically inclined doctors treated patients more impersonally than other doctors.

The survey questionnaire offered several possible indicators of respondents' scientific perspectives. Of those, three items appeared to provide especially clear indications of whether the doctors were scientifically oriented:

1. As a medical school faculty member, in what capacity do you feel you can make your greatest *teaching* contribution: as a practicing physician or as a medical researcher?

2. As you continue to advance your own medical knowledge, would you say your ultimate medical interests lie primarily in the direction of total patient management or the understanding of basic mechanisms?

3. In the field of therapeutic research, are you generally more interested in articles reporting evaluations of the effectiveness of various treatments or articles exploring the basic rationale underlying the treatments?

(Babbie 1970:27–31)

"Cause" and "Effect" Indicators

by Kenneth Bollen
Department of Sociology, Dartmouth College

While it often makes sense to expect indicators of the same variable to be positively related to one another, as discussed in the text, this is not always the case.

Indicators should be related to one another if they are essentially "effects" of a variable. For example, to measure self-esteem, we might ask a person to indicate whether they agree or disagree with the statements (1) "I am a good person" and (2) "I am happy with myself." A person with high self-esteem should agree with both statements while one with low self-esteem would probably disagree with both. Since each indicator depends on or "reflects" self-esteem, we expect them to be positively correlated. More generally, indicators that depend on the same variable should be associated with one another if they are valid measures.

But, this is not the case when the indicators are the "cause" rather than the "effect" of a variable. In this situation the indicators may correlate positively, negatively, or not at all. For example, we could use sex and race as indicators of the variable *exposure to discrimination*. Being nonwhite or female increases the likelihood of experiencing discrimination, so both are good indicators of the variable. But we would not expect the race and sex of individuals to be strongly associated.

Or, we may measure *social interaction* with three indicators: time spent with friends, time spent with family, and time spent with coworkers. Though each indicator is valid, they need not be positively correlated. Time spent with friends, for instance, may be *inversely* related to time spent with family. Here, the three indicators "cause" the degree of social interaction.

As a final example, *exposure to stress* may be measured by whether a person recently experienced divorce, death of a spouse, or loss of a job. Though any of these events may indicate stress, they need not correlate with one another.

In short, we expect an association between indicators that depend on or "reflect" a variable, that is, if they are the "effects" of the variable. But if the variable depends on the indicators—if the indicators are the "causes"—those indicators may be either positively or negatively correlated, or even unrelated. Therefore, we should decide whether indicators are causes or effects of a variable before using their intercorrelations to assess their validity.

For each of these items, we might conclude that those respondents who chose the second answer are more scientifically oriented than respondents who chose the first answer. This *comparative* conclusion is a reasonable one, but we should not be misled into thinking that respondents who chose the second answer to a given item are scientists in any absolute sense. They are simply *more scientific* than those who chose the first answer to the item. To see this point more clearly, let's examine the distribution of responses to each item. From the first item—best teaching role—only about one-third of the respondents appeared scientifically oriented. (Approximately one-third said they could make their greatest teaching contribution as medical researchers.) In response to the second item—ultimate medical interests—approximately two-thirds chose the scientific answer, saying they were more interested in learning about basic mechanisms than learning about total patient management. In response to the third item— reading preferences—about 80 percent chose the scientific answer.

So these three questionnaire items cannot tell us how many "scientists" there are in the sample, for none of them is related to a set of criteria for what constitutes being a scientist in any absolute sense. Using the items for this purpose would present us with the problem of three quite different estimates of how many scientists there were in the sample.

However, these items do provide us with three independent indicators of respondents' *relative* inclinations toward science in medicine. Each item separates respondents into the *more* scientific and the *less* scientific. But each grouping of more or less scientific respondents will have a somewhat different membership from the others. Respondents who seem scientific in terms of one item will not seem scientific in terms of another. Nevertheless, to the extent that each item measures the same general dimension, we should find some correspondence among the several groupings. Respondents who appear scientific in terms of one item should be more likely to appear scientific in their response to another item than would those who appeared nonscientific in their response to the first. We should find an association or correlation between the responses given to two items.

Figure 15-2 shows the associations among the responses to the three items. Three bivariate tables are presented, showing the conjoint distribution of responses for each pair of items. Although each single item produces a different grouping of "scientific" and "nonscientific" respondents, we see in Figure 15-2 that the responses given to each of the items correspond, to a degree, to the responses given to each of the other items.

An examination of the three bivariate relationships presented in Figure 15-2 supports the suggestion that the three items all measure the same variable: scientific orientations. To see why this is so, let's begin by looking at the first bivariate relationship in the table. The table shows that faculty who responded that "researcher" was their best teaching role were more likely to identify their ultimate medical interests as "basic mechanisms" than were those who answered "physician." The data show that 87 percent of the "researchers" also chose the scientific response to the second item, as opposed to 51 percent of the "physicians." (*Note:* The fact that the "physicians" are about evenly split in their ultimate medical interests is irrelevant. It is only relevant that they are *less* scientific in their medical interests than are the "researchers.") The strength of this relationship may be summarized as a 36 percentage point difference.

The same general conclusion applies to the other bivariate relationships. The strength of the relationship between reading preferences and ultimate medical interests may be summarized as a 38 percentage point difference; the strength of the relationship between reading preferences and the two teaching roles may be summarized as a 21 percentage point difference.

Initially, the three items were selected on the basis of face validity—each appeared to give some indication of faculty members' orientations to science. By examining the bivariate relationship between the pairs of items, we have found support for the expectation that they all measure basically the same thing. However, that support is not

Figure 15-2 Bivariate Relationships among Scientific Orientation Items

A.

Ultimate Medical Interest	Best Teaching Role: Physician	Best Teaching Role: Researcher
Total patient management	49%	13%
Basic mechanisms	51%	87%
	100%	100%
	(285)	(196)

B.

Ultimate Medical Interest	Reading Preferences: Effectiveness	Reading Preferences: Rationale
Total patient management	68%	30%
Basic mechanisms	32%	70%
	100%	100%
	(132)	(349)

C.

Best Teaching Role	Reading Preferences: Effectiveness	Reading Preferences: Rationale
Physician	85%	64%
Researcher	15%	36%
	100%	100%
	(132)	(349)

sufficient justification to include the items in a composite index.

Multivariate Relationships among Items

Before combining them in a single index, we need to examine the multivariate relationships among the several variables. Recall that the primary purpose of index construction is to develop a method of classifying subjects in terms of some variable such as political conservatism, religiosity, scientific orientation, or whatever. An index of political conservatism should identify those who are very conservative, moderately conservative, not very conservative, and not at all conservative (or moderately liberal and very liberal, respectively, in place of the last two categories). The several gradations of the variable are provided by the combination

Figure 15-3 Trivariate Relationships among Scientific Orientation Items

Percentage Interested in Basic Mechanisms

		Best Teaching Role	
		Physician	Researcher
Reading Preferences	Effectiveness	27% (66)	58% (12)
	Rationale	58% (219)	89% (130)

of responses given to the several items included in the index. Thus, the respondent who appeared conservative on all the items would be considered very conservative overall.

For an index to provide meaningful gradations in this sense, each item must add something to the evaluation of each respondent. Recall that in the preceding section it was suggested that two items perfectly related to one another should not be included in the same index. If one item were included, the other would add nothing to our evaluation of respondents. The examination of multivariate relationships among the items is another way of eliminating deadwood. It also determines the overall power of the particular collection of items in measuring the variable under consideration.

The purposes of this multivariate examination will become clearer if we return to the earlier example of measuring scientific orientations among medical school faculty members. Figure 15-3 presents the trivariate relationships among the three items.

Figure 15-3 has been presented somewhat differently from Figure 15-2. In this instance, the sample respondents have been categorized in four groups according to (1) their best teaching roles and (2) their reading preferences. The numbers in parentheses indicate the number of respondents in each group. (Thus 66 of the faculty mem-

bers who said they could best teach as physicians also said they preferred articles dealing with the effectiveness of treatments.) For each of the four groups, the percentage that say they are ultimately more interested in basic mechanisms has been presented. (Of the 66 faculty mentioned above, 27 percent are primarily interested in basic mechanisms.)

The arrangement of the four groups is based on a previously drawn conclusion regarding scientific orientations. The group in the upper left corner of the table is presumably the least scientifically oriented, based on best teaching role and reading preference. The group in the lower right corner is presumably the most scientifically oriented in terms of those items.

Recall that expressing a primary interest in basic mechanisms was also taken as an indication of scientific orientations. As we should expect, then, those in the lower right corner are the most likely to give this response (89 percent) and those in the upper left corner are the least likely (27 percent). The respondents who gave mixed responses in terms of teaching roles and reading preferences have an intermediate rank in their concern for basic mechanisms (58 percent in both cases).

This table tells us many things. First, we may note that the original relationships between pairs of items are not significantly affected by the presence of a third item.

Recall, for example, that the relationship between teaching role and ultimate medical interest was summarized as a 36 percentage point difference. Looking at Figure 15-3, we see that among only those respondents who are most interested in articles dealing with the effectiveness of treatments, the relationship between teaching role and ultimate medical interest is 31 percentage points (58 percent minus 27 percent: first row), and the same is true among those most interested in articles dealing with the rationale for treatments (89 percent minus 58 percent: second row). The original relationship between teaching role and ultimate medical interest is essentially the same as in Figure 15-2, even among those respondents judged as scientific or nonscientific in terms of reading preferences.

The same conclusion may be drawn from the columns in Figure 15-3. Recall that the original relationship between reading preferences and ultimate medical interests was summarized as a 38 percentage point difference. Looking only at the "physicians" in Figure 15-3, we see that the relationship between the other two items is now 31 percentage points. The same relationship is found among the "researchers" in the second column.

The importance of these observations becomes clearer when we consider what might have happened. Figure 15-4 presents hypothetical data to illustrate that. These data tell a much different story than did the actual data reported in Figure 15-3. In this instance, it is evident that the original relationship between teaching role and ultimate medical interest persists, even when reading preferences are introduced into the picture. In each row of the table the "researchers" are more likely to express an interest in basic mechanisms than are the "physicians." Looking down the columns, however, we note that there is no relationship between reading preferences and ultimate medical interest. If we know whether a respondent feels he or she can best teach as a physician or as a researcher, knowing the respondent's reading preference adds nothing to our evaluation of his or her scientific orientation. If something like Figure 15-4 resulted from the actual data, we would conclude that reading preference should not be included in the same index as teaching role, since it contributes nothing to the composite index.

This example used only three questionnaire items. If more were being considered, then more complex multivariate tables would be in order: constructed of four, five, or more variables. The purpose of this step in index construction, again, is to discover the simultaneous interaction of the items to determine whether they are all appropriate for inclusion in the same index.

Figure 15-4 Hypothetical Trivariate Relationship among Scientific Orientation Items

Percentage Interested in Basic Mechanisms

		Best Teaching Role	
		Physician	Researcher
Reading Preferences	Effectiveness	51% (66)	87% (12)
	Rationale	51% (219)	87% (130)

Index Scoring

When you have chosen the best items for the index, you next assign scores for particular responses, thereby creating a single composite index out of the several items. There are two basic decisions to be made in this step.

First, you must decide the desirable range of the index scores. Certainly a primary advantage of an index over a single item is the range of gradations it offers in the measurement of a variable. As noted earlier, political conservatism might be measured from "very conservative" to "not at all conservative" (or "very liberal"). How far to the extremes, then, should the index extend?

In this decision, the question of variance enters once more. Almost always, as the possible extremes of an index are extended, fewer cases are to be found at each end. The researcher who wishes to measure political conservatism to its greatest extreme may find there is almost no one in that category.

The first decision, then, concerns the conflicting desire for (1) a range of measurement in the index and (2) an adequate number of cases at each point in the index. You will be forced to reach some kind of compromise between these conflicting desires.

The second decision concerns the actual assignment of scores for each particular response. Basically you must decide whether to give each item an equal weight in the index or to give them different weights. Although there are no firm rules, I suggest—and practice tends to support this method—that items be weighted equally unless there are compelling reasons for differential weighting. That is, the burden of proof should be on differential weighting; equal weighting should be the norm.

Of course, this decision must be related to the earlier issue regarding the balance of items chosen. If the index is to represent the composite of slightly different aspects of a given variable, then you should give each aspect the same weight. In some instances, however, you may feel that, say, two items reflect essentially the same aspect, while the third reflects a different aspect. If you wished to have both aspects equally represented by the index, you might decide to give the different item a weight equal to the combination of the two similar ones. In such a situation, you might want to assign a maximum score of 2 to the different item and a maximum score of 1 to each of the similar ones.

Although the rationale for scoring responses should take such concerns as these into account, you will typically experiment with different scoring methods, examining the relative weights given to different aspects but at the same time worrying about the range and distribution of cases provided. Ultimately, the scoring method chosen will represent a compromise among these several demands. (*Note:* In this activity, as in most research activities, the decision is open to revision on the basis of later examinations. Validation of the index, to be discussed shortly, may lead you to recycle your efforts and to construct a completely different index.)

In the example taken from the medical school faculty survey, I decided to weight the items equally, since they had been chosen, in part, on the basis of their representing slightly different aspects of the overall variable—scientific orientation. On each of the items, the respondents were given a score of 1 for choosing the "scientific" response to the item and a score of 0 for choosing the "nonscientific" response. Each respondent, then, had a chance of receiving a score of 0, 1, 2, or 3, depending on the number of "scientific" responses he or she chose. This scoring method provided what was considered a useful range of variation—four index categories—and also provided enough cases in each category for analysis.

Handling Missing Data

Regardless of your data collection method, you will frequently face the problem of missing data. In a content analysis of the political orientations of newspapers, for example, you may discover that a particular newspaper has never taken an editorial position on one of the issues being studied—it may never have taken a stand on the United Nations, for example. In an experimental design involving several retests of subjects over time, some subjects may be unable to participate in some of the sessions. In virtually every survey, some respondents fail to answer some questions (or choose a "don't know" response). Although missing data present problems at all stages of analysis, it is especially troublesome in index construction. There are, however, several methods of dealing with the problem of missing data.

First, if there are relatively few cases with missing data, you may decide to exclude them from the construction of the index and the analysis. (In the medical school faculty example discussed above, this was the decision I made regarding missing data.) The primary concerns in this instance are whether the numbers available for analysis will still be sufficient, and whether the exclusion will result in a biased sample whenever the index is used in the analysis. The latter possibility can be examined through a comparison— on other relevant variables—of those who would be included and excluded from the index.

Second, you may sometimes have grounds for treating missing data as one of the available responses. For example, if a questionnaire has asked respondents to indicate their participation in a number of activities by checking "yes" or "no" for each, many respondents may have checked some of the activities "yes" and left the remainder blank. In such a case, you might decide that a failure to answer meant "no," and score missing data in this case as though the respondents had checked the "no" space.

Third, a careful analysis of missing data may yield an interpretation of their meaning. In constructing a measure of political conservatism, for example, you may discover that respondents who failed to answer a given question were generally as conservative on other items as those who gave the conservative answer. As another example, a recent study measuring religious beliefs found that people who answered "don't know" about a given belief were almost identical to the "disbelievers" in their answers about other beliefs. (*Note:* You should not take these examples as empirical guides in your own studies, but only as suggestive of ways to analyze your own data.) Whenever the analysis of missing data yields such interpretations, then, you may decide to score such cases accordingly.

There are a number of other ways for handling this problem. If an item has several possible values, you might assign the middle value to cases with missing data; for example, you could assign a 2 if the values are 0, 1, 2, 3, and 4. For a continuous variable such as age, you could similarly assign the mean to cases with missing data. Or, missing data can be supplied by assigning values at random. All of these are conservative solutions in that they work against any relationships you may expect to find.

If you're creating an index out of several items, it sometimes works to handle missing data by using proportions based on what is observed. Suppose your index is composed of six indicators, and you only have four observations for a particular subject. If the subject has earned 4 points out of a possible 4, you might assign an index score of 6; if the subject has 2 points (half the possible score on four items), you could assign a score of 3 (half the possible score on six observations).

The choice of a particular method to be used depends so much on the research situation as to preclude the suggestion of a single "best" method or a ranking of the several I have described. Excluding all cases with missing data can bias the representativeness of the findings, but including such cases by assigning scores to missing data can influence the nature of the findings. The safest and best method would be to construct the index using alternative methods and see whether the same findings follow from each. Understanding your data is the final goal of analysis anyway.

Index Validation

Up to this point, we have discussed all the steps in the selection and scoring of items that result in a composite index purporting to measure some variable. If each of the above steps is carried out carefully, the likelihood of the index actually measuring the variable is enhanced. To demonstrate success, however, there must be *validation* of the index. In the basic logic of validation, we assume that the composite index provides a measure of some variable; that is, the successive scores on the index arrange cases in a rank order in terms of that variable. An index of political conservatism rank-orders people in terms of their relative conservatism. If the index does that successfully, then persons scored as relatively conservative on the index should appear relatively conservative in all *other indications* of political orientation, such as questionnaire items. There are several methods for validating a composite index.

Item Analysis   The first step in index validation is an internal validation called *item analysis*. In item analysis, you examine the extent to which the composite index is related to (or predicts responses to) the items in the index itself. Simply create tables in which

the index is the independent variable and one of the items is the dependent variable. If the index has been carefully constructed through the examination of bivariate and multivariate relationships among several items, this step should confirm the validity of that index, with each individual item correlating with index scores.

In a complex index containing many items, this step provides a convenient test of the independent contribution of each item to the index. If a given item is found to be poorly related to the index, it may be assumed that other items in the index cancel out the contribution of that item. If the item in question contributes nothing to the index's power, it should be excluded.

Although item analysis is an important first test of the index's validity, it is scarcely a sufficient test. If the index adequately measures a given variable, it should successfully predict other indications of that variable. To test that, we must turn to items not included in the index.

External Validation   Persons scored as politically conservative on an index should appear conservative in their responses to other items in the questionnaire. Of course, we are talking about *relative* conservatism, as we are unable to make a final absolute definition of what constitutes conservatism. However, those respondents scored as the most conservative on the index should be the most conservative in answering other questions. Those scored as the least conservative on the index should be the least conservative on other items. Indeed, the ranking of groups of respondents on the index should predict the ranking of those groups in answering other questions dealing with political orientations.

In our example of the scientific orientation index, several questions in the questionnaire offered the possibility of further validation. Table 15-1 presents some of those items.

Table 15-1   Validation of Scientific Orientation Index

	Index of Scientific Orientation			
	Low 0	1	2	High 3
Percentage interested in attending scientific lectures at the medical school	34	42	46	65
Percentage who say faculty members should have experience as medical researchers	43	60	65	89
Percentage who would prefer faculty duties involving research activities only	0	8	32	66
Percentage who engaged in research during preceding academic year	61	76	94	99

These items provide several lessons regarding index validation. First, we note that the index strongly predicts the responses to the validating items in the sense that the rank order of scientific responses among the four groups is the same as the rank order provided by the index itself. At the same time, each item gives a different *description* of scientific orientations overall. For example, the last validating item indicates that the great majority of *all* faculty were engaged in research during the preceding year. If this were the only indicator of scientific orientation, we would conclude that nearly all faculty were scientific. Nevertheless, those scored as more scientific on the index are more likely to have engaged in research than those who were scored as relatively less scientific. The third validating item provides a different descriptive picture: only a minority of the faculty overall say they would prefer duties limited exclusively to research. Nevertheless, the percentages giving this answer correspond to the scores assigned on the index.

Bad Index versus Bad Validators   Nearly every index constructor at some time must face the apparent failure of external items to validate the index. If the internal item

analysis shows inconsistent relationships between the items included in the index and the index itself, something is wrong with the index. But if the index fails to predict strongly the external validation items, the conclusion to be drawn is more ambiguous. You must choose between two possibilities: (1) the index does not adequately measure the variable in question, or (2) the validation items do not adequately measure the variable and thereby do not provide a sufficient test of the index.

The researcher who has worked long and conscientiously on the construction of an index will find the second conclusion very compelling. Typically, you will feel you have included the best indicators of the variable in the index; the validating items are, therefore, second-rate indicators. Nevertheless, you should recognize that the index is purportedly a very powerful measure of the variable; thus, it should be somewhat related to any item that taps the variable even poorly.

When external validation fails, you should reexamine the index before deciding that the validating items are insufficient. One method of doing that is to examine the relationships between the validating items and the individual items included in the index. If you discover that some of the index items relate to the validators while others do not, that will improve your understanding of the index as it was initially constituted.

There is no cookbook solution to this dilemma; it is an agony serious researchers must learn to survive. Ultimately, the wisdom of your decision to accept an index will be determined by the usefulness of that index in your later analyses. Perhaps you will initially decide that the index is a good one and that the validators are defective, and later find that the variable in question (as measured by the index) is not related to other variables in the ways you expected. Then you may have to compose a new index.

Likert Scaling

Earlier in this chapter, I defined a scale as a composite measure based on *intensity structure* among the items composing the measure. In scale construction, response patterns across several items are scored, whereas in index construction, individual responses are scored and those independent scores are summed. By this definition, the measurement method developed by Rensis Likert, called Likert scaling, represents a systematic and refined means for constructing indexes from questionnaire data. I'll discuss this method here, therefore, rather than in the sections on scaling to follow.

The term **Likert scale** is associated with a question format that is very frequently used in contemporary survey questionnaires. Basically, the respondent is presented with a *statement* in the questionnaire and is asked to indicate whether he "strongly agrees," "agrees," "disagrees," "strongly disagrees," or is "undecided." Modifications of the wording of the response categories (for example, "approve") may be used, of course.

The particular value of this format is the unambiguous *ordinality* of response cate-

gories. If respondents were permitted to volunteer or select such answers as "sort of agree," "pretty much agree," "really agree," and so forth, the researcher would find it impossible to judge the relative strength of agreement intended by the various respondents. The Likert format resolves this dilemma.

The Likert format also lends itself to a rather straightforward method of index construction. Since identical response categories are used for several items intended to measure a given variable, each such item can be scored in a uniform manner. With five response categories, scores of 0 to 4 or 1 to 5 might be assigned, taking the direction of the items into account (for example, assign a score of 5 to "strongly agree" for positive items and to "strongly disagree" for negative items). Each respondent would then be assigned an overall score representing the summation of the scores he or she received for responses to the individual items.

The Likert method is based on the assumption that an overall score based on responses to the many items reflecting a particular variable under consideration provides a reasonably good measure of the variable. These overall scores are not the final product of index construction; rather, they are used in an *item analysis* to select the *best* items. Essentially, each item is correlated with the large, composite measure. Items that correlate highest with the composite measure are assumed to provide the best indicators of the variable, and only those items would be included in the index ultimately used for analyses of the variable.

It should be noted that the uniform scoring of Likert-item response categories assumes that each item has about the *same intensity* as the rest. That is the key respect in which the Likert method differs from scaling as the term is used in this book.

You should also realize that Likert-type items can be used in a variety of ways: you are by no means bound to the method described above. Such items can be combined with other types of items in the construction of simple indexes; similarly, they can be used in the construction of scales. However, if all the items being considered for inclusion in a composite measure are in the Likert format, then the method described above should be considered.

Semantic Differential

As we've seen, Likert-type items ask respondents to agree or disagree with a particular position. The *semantic differential* format asks them to choose between two opposite positions. Here's how it works.

Suppose that you are conducting an experiment to evaluate the effectiveness of a new music appreciation lecture on subjects' appreciation of music. Let's say that you have created experimental and control groups as described in Chapter 8. Now you want to play some musical selections and have the subjects report their feelings about them. A good way to tap those feelings would be to use a semantic differential format.

To begin, you must determine the *dimensions* along which each selection should be judged by subjects. Then you need to find two *opposite* terms, representing the polar extremes along each dimension. Let's

suppose one dimension that interests you is simply whether subjects enjoyed the piece or not. Two opposite terms in this case could be "enjoyable" and "unenjoyable." Similarly, you might want to know whether they regarded the individual selections as "complex" or "simple," "harmonic" or "discordant," and so forth.

Once you have determined the relevant dimensions and have found terms to represent the extremes of each, you might prepare a rating sheet to be completed by each subject for each piece of music. Figure 15-5 shows an example of what it might look like.

On each line of the rating sheet, the subject would indicate how he or she felt about the piece of music: whether it was enjoyable or unenjoyable, for example, and whether it was "somewhat" that way or "very much" so. To avoid creating a biased pattern of responses to such items, it's a good idea to vary the placement of terms that are likely to be related to each other. Notice, for example, that "discordant" and "traditional" are on the left side of the sheet, with "harmonic" and "modern" on the right side. Very likely, those selections scored as "discordant" would also be scored as "modern" as opposed to "traditional."

Both the Likert and semantic differential formats have a greater rigor and structure than other question formats. Despite common references to Likert scales and semantic differential scales, these formats produce

Figure 15-5   Semantic Differential

	Very Much	Some-what	Neither	Some-what	Very Much	
Enjoyable	☐	☐	☐	☐	☐	Unenjoyable
Simple	☐	☐	☐	☐	☐	Complex
Discordant	☐	☐	☐	☐	☐	Harmonic
Traditional	☐	☐	☐	☐	☐	Modern
			etc.			

data suitable to both indexing and scaling, as the latter terms are distinguished from one another in this chapter.

Now we'll turn our attention from the creation of cumulative indexes to an examination of scaling techniques. Although many methods of scaling are available, I'm going to limit our discussion to three: the Bogardus, Thurstone, and Guttman scales.

SCALE CONSTRUCTION

Good indexes provide an ordinal ranking of cases on a given variable. All indexes are based on this kind of assumption: a senator who voted for seven conservative bills is considered to be more conservative than one who only voted for four of them. What an index may fail to take into account, however, is that not all indicators of a variable are equally important or equally strong. The first senator might have voted in favor of seven mildly conservative bills, whereas the second senator might have voted in favor of four extremely conservative bills. (The second senator might have considered the other seven bills too liberal and voted against them.)

Scales offer more assurance of ordinality by tapping *structures* among the indicators. The several items going into a composite measure may have different *intensities* in terms of the variable. The three scaling procedures described below will illustrate the variety of techniques available.

Bogardus Social Distance Scale

Let's suppose that you are interested in the extent to which Americans are willing to associate with, say, Albanians. You might ask the following questions:

1. Are you willing to permit Albanians to live in your country?

2. Are you willing to permit Albanians to live in your community?

3. Are you willing to permit Albanians to live in your neighborhood?

4. Would you be willing to let an Albanian live next door to you?

5. Would you let your child marry an Albanian?

Note that the several questions increase in the closeness of contact the respondents may or may not want with Albanians. Beginning with the original concern to measure willingness to associate with Albanians, we have developed several questions indicating differing degrees of intensity on this variable. The kinds of items presented above constitute a **Bogardus social distance scale.**

The clear differences of intensity suggest a structure among the items. Presumably if a person is willing to accept a given kind of association, he or she would be willing to accept all those preceding it in the list—those with lesser intensities. For example, the person who is willing to permit Albanians to live in the neighborhood will surely accept them in the community and the nation but may or may not be willing to accept them as next-door neighbors or relatives. This, then, is the logical structure of intensity inherent among the items.

Empirically, one would expect to find the largest number of people accepting co-citizenship and the fewest accepting intermarriage. In this sense, we speak of "easy items" (e.g., residence in the United States) and "hard items" (e.g., intermarriage). More people agree to the easy items than to the hard ones. With some inevitable exceptions, logic demands that once a person has refused a relationship presented in the scale, he or she will also refuse all those harder ones that follow it.

The Bogardus social distance scale illustrates the important economy of scaling as a data-reduction device. By knowing *how many* relationships with Albanians a given respondent will accept, we know *which* relationships were accepted. Thus, a single number can accurately summarize five or six data items without a loss of information.

Thurstone Scales

Often the inherent structure of the Bogardus social distance scale is not appropriate to the variable being measured. Indeed, such a logical structure among several indicators is seldom apparent. **Thurstone scaling** is an attempt to develop a format for generating groups of indicators of a variable that have at least an *empirical* structure among them. One of the basic formats is that of "equal-appearing intervals."

A group of judges is given perhaps a hundred items felt to be indicators of a given variable. Each judge is then asked to estimate how strong an indicator of a variable each item is—by assigning scores of perhaps 1 to 13. If the variable were prejudice, for example, the judges would be asked to assign the score of 1 to the very weakest indicators of prejudice, the score of 13 to the strongest indicators, and intermediate scores to those felt to be somewhere in-between.

Once the judges have completed this task, the researcher examines the scores assigned to each item by all the judges to determine which items produced the greatest agreement among the judges. Those items on which the judges disagreed broadly would be rejected as ambiguous. Among those items producing general agreement in scoring, one or more would be selected to represent each scale score from 1 to 13.

The items selected in this manner might then be included in a survey questionnaire. Respondents who appeared prejudiced on those items representing a strength of 5 would then be expected to appear prejudiced on those having lesser strengths, and if some of those respondents did not appear prejudiced on the items with a strength of 6, it would be expected that they would also not appear prejudiced on those with greater strengths.

If the Thurstone scale items were adequately developed and scored, the economy and effectiveness of data reduction inherent in the Bogardus social distance scale will appear. A single score might be assigned to each respondent (the strength of the hardest item accepted), and that score would adequately represent the responses to several questionnaire items. And as is true of the Bogardus scale, a respondent scored 6 might be regarded as more prejudiced than one scored 5 or less.

Thurstone scaling is not often used in research today, primarily because of the tremendous expenditure of energy required for the judging of items. Ten to 15 judges would have to spend a considerable amount of time to score the many initial items. Since the quality of their judgments would depend on their experience with and knowledge of the variable under consideration, the task might require professional researchers. Moreover, the meanings conveyed by the several items indicating a given variable tend to change over time. Thus an item having a given weight at one time might have quite a different weight later on. For a Thurstone scale to be effective, it would have to be periodically updated.

Guttman Scaling

A very popular scaling technique used by researchers today is the one developed by Louis Guttman. Like both Bogardus and Thurstone scaling, **Guttman scaling** is based on the fact that some items under consideration may prove to be harder indicators of the variable than others. One example should suffice to illustrate this pattern.

In the earlier example of measuring scientific orientations among medical school faculty members, you'll recall that a simple index was constructed. As it happens, however, the three items included in the index essentially form a Guttman scale. This possibility first appears when we look for relatively hard and easy indicators of scientific orientation.

The item asking respondents whether they could best serve as practicing physicians or as medical researchers is the hardest of the three: only about one-third would be judged scientific if this were the single indicator of the variable. If the item concerning ultimate medical interests (total patient management versus basic mechanisms) were used as the only indicator, almost two-thirds would be judged scientific. Reading preferences (effectiveness of treatments versus the underlying rationales) is the easiest of the three items: about 80 percent of the respondents would be judged as scientific in terms of this item.

To determine whether a scale structure exists among the responses to all three items, we must examine the several possible response patterns given to all three items

simultaneously. In Table 15-2, all the possible patterns have been presented in a schematic form. For each of the three items, pluses and minuses have been used to indicate the scientific and nonscientific responses, respectively. (A plus indicates a scientific response, and a minus indicates a nonscientific response.)

The first four response patterns in the table compose what we would call the *scale types:* those patterns that form a scalar structure. Following those respondents who selected all three scientific responses (line 1), we see (line 2) that those with only two scientific responses have chosen the two easier ones; those with only one such response (line 3) chose the easiest of the three. And finally, there are some respondents who selected none of the scientific responses (line 4).

The second part of the table presents those response patterns that violate the scalar structure of the items. The most radical departures from the scalar structure are the last two response patterns: those who accepted only the hardest item, and those who rejected only the easiest one.

The final column in the table indicates the number of survey respondents who gave each of the response patterns. It is imme-

Table 15-2 Scaling Scientific Orientations

	Reading Preference	Ultimate Interests	Teaching Role	Number of Cases
	+	+	+	116
Scale Types:	+	+	−	127
Total = 383	+	−	−	92
	−	−	−	48
	−	+	−	18
Mixed Types:	+	−	+	14
Total = 44	−	−	+	5
	−	+	+	7

diately apparent that the great majority (90 percent) of the respondents fit into one of the scale types. The presence of mixed types, however, indicates that the items do not form a perfect Guttman scale.

We should recall at this point that one of the chief functions of scaling is efficient data reduction. Scales provide a technique for presenting data in a summary form while maintaining as much of the original information as possible.

When the scientific orientation items were formed into an index in our earlier discussion, respondents were given one point for each scientific response they gave. If these same three items were scored as a Guttman scale, some respondents would be assigned those scale scores that would permit the most accurate reproduction of their original responses to all three items.

Respondents fitting into the scale types would receive the same scores as were assigned in the index construction. Persons selecting all three scientific responses would still be scored 3, persons who selected scientific responses to the two easier items and a nonscientific response to the hardest would be scored 2, and so on. For each of the four scale types we could predict accurately all the actual responses given by all the respondents based on their scores.

The mixed types in the table present a problem, however. The first mixed type (− + −) was scored 1 on the index to indicate only one scientific response. But, if 1 were assigned as a scale score, we would predict that all respondents in this group had chosen only the easiest item (+ − −), and we would be making two errors for each such respondent. Scale scores are assigned, therefore, with the aim of minimizing the errors that would be made in reconstructing the original responses. Table 15-3 illustrates the index and scale scores that would be assigned to each of the response patterns in our example. Note that one error is made for

each respondent in the mixed types. This is the minimum we can hope for in a mixed type pattern. In the first mixed type, for example, we would erroneously predict a scientific response to the easiest item for each of the 18 respondents in this group, making a total of 18 errors.

The extent to which a set of empirical responses form a Guttman scale is determined by the accuracy with which the original responses can be reconstructed from the scale scores. For each of he 427 respondents in this example, we will predict three questionnaire responses, for a total of 1,281 predictions. Table 15-3 indicates that we will make 44 errors using the scale scores assigned. The percentage of *correct* predictions is called the **coefficient of reproducibility**: the percentage of reproducible responses. In the present example, the coefficient of reproducibility is 1,237/1,281 or 96.6 percent.

Except for the case of perfect (100 percent) reproducibility, there is no way of saying that a set of items does or does not form a Guttman scale in any absolute sense. Virtually all sets of such items *approximate* a scale. As a rule of thumb, however, coefficients of 90 or 95 percent are the commonly used standards in this regard. If the observed reproducibility exceeds the level you've set, you will probably decide to score and use the items as a scale.

The decision as to criteria in this regard is, of course, arbitrary. Moreover, a high degree of reproducibility does not ensure that the scale constructed in fact measures the concept under consideration, although it increases confidence that all the component items measure the same thing. Also, you should realize that a high coefficient of reproducibility is more likely when few items are involved.

One concluding remark should be made with regard to Guttman scaling: it is based on the structure observed among the *actual*

Table 15-3 Index and Scale Scores

	Response Patterns	Number of Cases	Index Scores	Scale Scores*	Total Scale Errors
	+ + +	116	3	3	0
Scale Types:	+ + −	127	2	2	0
	+ − −	92	1	1	0
	− − −	48	0	0	0
	− + −	18	1	2	18
Mixed Types:	+ − +	14	2	3	14
	− − +	5	1	0	5
	− + +	7	2	3	7

$$\text{Coefficient of reproducibility} = 1 - \frac{\text{number of errors}}{\text{number of cases} \times \text{number of items each} = \text{number of guesses}}$$

$$= 1 - \frac{44}{427 \times 3 = 1{,}281}$$
$$= .966$$
$$= 96.6\%$$

*This table presents one common method for scoring mixed types, but you should be advised that other methods are also used.

data under examination. This is an important point that is often misunderstood. It does not make sense to say that a set of questionnaire items (perhaps developed and used by a previous researcher) constitutes a Guttman scale. Rather, we can say only that they form a scale within a given body of data being analyzed. Scalability, then, is a sample-dependent, empirical question. Although a set of items may form a Guttman scale among one sample of survey respondents, for example, there is no guarantee that they will form such a scale among another sample. In this sense, then, a set of questionnaire items in and of themselves never form a scale, but a set of empirical observations may.

TYPOLOGIES

We shall conclude this chapter with a short discussion of typology construction and analysis. Recall that indexes and scales are constructed to provide ordinal measures of given variables. We attempt to assign index or scale scores to cases in such a way as to indicate a rising degree of prejudice, religiosity, conservatism, and so forth. In such cases, we are dealing with single dimensions.

Often, however, the researcher wishes to summarize the intersection of two or more variables. You may, for example, wish to examine the political orientations of newspapers separately in terms of domestic issues

Table 15-4 A Political Typology of Newspapers

	Foreign Policy	
Domestic Policy	Conservative	Liberal
Conservative	A	B
Liberal	C	D

and foreign policy. The fourfold presentation in Table 15-4 describes such a typology.

Newspapers in cell A of the table are conservative on both foreign policy and domestic policy; those in cell D are liberal in both. Those in cells B and C are conservative on one and liberal on the other. (For purposes of analysis, each cell type might be presented by a data card punch [A = 1, B = 2, C = 3, D = 4] and could be easily manipulated in examining the typology's relationship to other variables.)

Frequently, you arrive at a typology in the course of an attempt to construct an index or scale. The items that you felt represented a single variable appear to represent two. We might have been attempting to construct a single index of political orientations for newspapers but discovered—empirically—that foreign and domestic politics had to be kept separate.

In any event, you should be warned against a difficulty inherent in typological analysis. Whenever the typology is used as the *independent variable*, there will probably be no problem. In the example above, you might compute the percentages of newspapers in each cell that normally endorse Democratic candidates; you could then easily examine the effects of both foreign and domestic policies on political endorsements.

It is extremely difficult, however, to analyze a typology as a *dependent variable*. If

you want to discover why newspapers fall into the different cells of typology, you're in trouble. That becomes apparent when we consider the ways in which you might construct and read your tables. Assume, for example, that you want to examine the effects of community size on political policies. With a single dimension, you could easily determine the percentages of rural and urban newspapers that were scored conservative and liberal on your index or scale. With a typology, however, you would have to present the distribution of the urban newspapers in your sample among types A, B, C, and D. Then you would repeat the procedure for the rural ones in the sample and compare the two distributions. Let us suppose that 80 percent of the rural newspapers are scored as type A (conservative on both dimensions) as compared with 30 percent of the urban ones. Moreover, suppose that only 5 percent of the rural newspapers are scored as type B (conservative only on domestic issues) compared with 40 percent of the urban ones. It would be incorrect to conclude from an examination of type B that urban newspapers are more conservative on domestic issues than rural ones, since 85 percent of the rural newspapers, compared with 70 percent of the urban ones, have this characteristic. The relative sparsity of rural newspapers in type B is due to their concentration in type A. It should be apparent that an interpretation of such data would be very difficult in anything other than description.

In reality, you would probably examine two such dimensions separately, especially if the dependent variable has more categories of responses than the example given.

Don't think that typologies should always be avoided in social research; often they provide the most appropriate device for understanding the data. You should be warned, however, against the special difficulties involved in using typologies as dependent variables.

MAIN POINTS

- Single indicators of variables seldom have sufficiently clear validity to warrant their use.

- Composite measures, such as scales and indexes, solve this problem by including several indicators of a variable in one summary measure.

- Both scales and indexes are intended as ordinal measures of variables, though scales typically satisfy this goal better than indexes.

- Indexes are based on the simple cumulation of indicators of a variable.

- Scales take advantage of any logical or empirical intensity structures that exist among the different indicators of a variable.

- Face validity is the first criterion for the selection of indicators to be included in a composite measure; the term means that an indicator seems, on face value, to provide some measure of the variable.

- If different items are indeed indicators of the same variable, then they should be related empirically to one another. If, for example, frequency of church attendance and frequency of prayer are both indicators of religiosity, then those people who attend church frequently should be found to pray more than those who attend church less frequently.

- Once an index or a scale has been constructed, it is essential that it be validated. Internal validation refers to the relationship between individual items included in the composite measure and the measure itself. External validation refers to the relationships between the composite measure and other indicators of the variable—indicators *not* included in the measure.

- Likert scaling is a measurement technique based on the use of standardized response categories (for example, strongly agree, agree, disagree, strongly disagree) for several questionnaire items. Although Likert scaling is not often used in social research today, the Likert format for questionnaire items is very popular and extremely useful. Likert-format items may be used appropriately in the construction of either indexes or scales.

- The Bogardus social distance scale is a device for measuring the varying degrees to which a person would be willing to associate with a given class of people, such as an ethnic minority. Subjects are asked to indicate whether or not they would be willing to accept different kinds of association. The several responses produced by these questions can be adequately summarized by a single score, representing the closest association that is acceptable, since those willing to accept a given association also would be willing to accept more distant ones.

- Thurstone scaling is a technique for creating indicators of variables that have a clear intensity structure among them. Judges determine the intensities of different indicators.

- Guttman scaling is probably the most popular scaling technique in social research today. It is a method of discovering and utilizing the empirical intensity structure among several indicators of a given variable.

- A coefficient of reproducibility is a measure of the extent to which all the particular responses given to the individual items included in a scale can be reproduced from the scale score alone.

- A typology is a nominal composite measure often used in social research. Typologies may be used effectively as independent variables, but interpretation is difficult when they are used as dependent variables.

REVIEW QUESTIONS AND EXERCISES

1. In your own words, describe the difference between an index and a scale.

2. Make up three questionnaire items—measuring attitudes toward nuclear power—that would probably form a Guttman scale.

ADDITIONAL READINGS

Glock, Charles; Ringer, Benjamin; and Babbie, Earl, *To Comfort and to Challenge: A Dilemma of the Contemporary Church* (Berkeley: University of California Press, 1967). An empirical study illustrating composite measures. Since the construction of scales and indexes can be most fully grasped through concrete examples, this might be a useful study to examine. The authors use a variety of composite measures, and they are relatively clear about the methods used in constructing them.

Lazarsfeld, Paul; Pasanella, Ann; and Rosenberg, Morris (eds.), *Continuities in the Language of Social Research* (New York: Free Press, 1972), especially Section 1. An excellent collection of conceptual discussions and concrete illustrations. The construction of composite measures is presented within the more general area of conceptualization and measurement.

Miller, Delbert, *Handbook of Research Design and Social Measurement* (New York: Longman, 1983). An excellent compilation of frequently used and semistandardized scales. The many illustrations reported in Part 4 of the Miller book may be directly adaptable to studies or at least suggestive of modified measures. Studying the several different illustrations, moreover, may also give a better understanding of the logic of composite measures in general.

Oppenheim, A. N., *Questionnaire Design and Attitude Measurement* (New York: Basic Books, 1966). An excellent presentation on composite measures, with special reference to questionnaires. Although Oppenheim says little about index construction, he gives an excellent presentation of the logic and the skills of scale construction—the kinds of scales discussed in Chapter 15 of the present book and many not discussed here.

16

The
Elaboration Model

What You'll Learn in This Chapter

This chapter will take you through the fundamental logic of multivariate analysis. Having seen that logic in action in the form of simple percentage tables, you'll then be prepared to see the sense in more complex analytical methods.

INTRODUCTION

Chapter 16 is devoted to a perspective on social scientific analysis that is referred to variously as the elaboration model, the interpretation method, the Columbia school, or the Lazarsfeld method. This varied nomenclature derives from the fact that the method we'll be discussing aims at the *elaboration* on an empirical relationship among variables in order to *interpret* that relationship in the manner developed by Paul Lazarsfeld while he was at Columbia University.

The *elaboration model* is used to understand the relationship between two variables through the simultaneous introduction of additional variables. It was developed primarily through the medium of contingency tables, but later chapters of this book will show how it may be used with other statistical techniques.

It is my firm belief that the elaboration model offers the clearest available picture of the logic of analysis. Especially through the use of contingency tables, this method portrays the logical process of scientific analysis. Moreover, if you are able to comprehend fully the use of the elaboration model using contingency tables, you should be in a far better position to use and understand more sophisticated statistical techniques. The box "Why Do Elaboration?" by one of the elaboration model's creators, Patricia Kendall, provides another powerful justification.

HISTORY OF THE ELABORATION MODEL

The historical origins of the elaboration model are especially instructive for a realistic appreciation of scientific research in

practice. During World War II, Samuel Stouffer organized and headed a special social research branch within the U.S. Army, already discussed in Chapter 1. Throughout the war, this group conducted a large number and variety of surveys among American servicemen. Although the objectives of these studies varied somewhat, they generally focused on the factors affecting soldiers' combat effectiveness.

Several of the studies examined the issue of morale in the military. Since morale seemed to affect combat effectiveness, improving morale would make the war effort more effective. Stouffer and his research staff sought to uncover some of the variables that affected morale. In part, the group sought to confirm, empirically, some commonly accepted propositions. Among them were the following:

1. Promotions surely affect soldiers' morale, so soldiers serving in units with low promotion rates should have relatively low morale.

2. Given racial segregation and discrimination in the South, black soldiers being trained in northern training camps should have higher morale than those being trained in the South.

3. Soldiers with more education should be more likely to resent being drafted into the army as enlisted men than those with less education.

Each of these propositions made sense logically, and common wisdom held each to be true. Stouffer decided to test each empirically. To his surprise, none of the propositions was confirmed.

First, soldiers serving in the Military Police—where promotions were the slowest in the army—had fewer complaints about the promotion system than those serving in the Army Air Corps—where promotions were the fastest in the army. Second, black

Why Do Elaboration?

by Patricia L. Kendall
Department of Sociology, Queens College, CUNY

There are several aspects of a true controlled experiment. The most crucial are: (a) creating experimental and control groups that are *identical* within limits of chance (this is done by assigning individuals to the two groups through processes of randomization: using tables of random numbers, flipping coins, etc.); (b) making sure that it is the *experimenter* who introduces the stimulus, not external events; and (c) waiting to see whether the stimulus has had its presumed effect.

We may have the hypothesis, for example, that attending Ivy League colleges leads to greater success professionally than attending other kinds of colleges and universities. How would we study this through a true experiment? Suppose you said, "Take a group of people in their 40s, find out which ones went to Ivy League colleges, and see whether they are more successful than those who went to other kinds of colleges." If that is your answer, you are wrong.

A true experiment would require the investigator to select several classes of high school seniors, divide each class at random into experimental and control groups, send the experimental groups to Ivy League colleges (regardless of their financial circumstances or academic qualifications and regardless of the desire of the colleges to accept them)

and the control group to other colleges and universities, wait 20 years or so until the two groups have reached professional maturity, and then measure the relative success of the two groups. Certainly a bizarre process.

Sociologists also investigate the hypothesis that coming from a broken home leads to juvenile delinquency. How would we go about studying this experimentally? If you followed the example above, you would see that studying this hypothesis through a true experiment would be totally impossible. Just think of what the experimenter would have to do!

The requirements of true experiments are so unrealistic in sociological research that we are forced to use other, and less ideal, methods in all but the most trivial situations. We *can* study experimentally whether students learn more from one type of lecture than another, or whether a film changes viewers' attitudes. But these are not always the sorts of questions in which we are truly interested.

We therefore resort to approximations—generally surveys—that have their own shortcomings, as we have seen in Chapter 9. However, the elaboration model allows us to examine survey data, take account of their possible shortcomings, and draw rather sophisticated conclusions about important issues.

soldiers serving in northern training camps and those serving in southern training camps seemed to differ little if at all in their general morale. Third, less educated soldiers were more likely to resent being drafted into the army than were those with more education.

As we saw in Chapter 1, rather than trying to hide the findings, or just running tests of statistical significance and publishing the results, Stouffer, instead, asked *why?* He found the answer to this question within the concepts of *reference group* and *relative deprivation*. Put simply, Stouffer suggested that soldiers did not evaluate their positions in life in accord with absolute, objective standards, but on the basis of their relative position vis-à-vis others around them. The people they compared themselves with were in their reference group, and they felt relative deprivation if they did not compare favorably in that regard.

Within the concepts of reference group and relative deprivation, Stouffer found an answer to each of the anomalies in his empirical data. Regarding promotion, he suggested that soldiers judged the fairness of the promotion system based on their own experiences relative to others around them. In the Military Police, where promotions were few and slow, few soldiers knew of a less qualified buddy who had been promoted faster than they had. In the Army Air Corps, however, the rapid promotion rate meant that many soldiers knew of less qualified buddies who had been promoted faster than seemed appropriate. Thus, ironically, the MPs said the promotion system was generally fair while the air corpsmen said it was not.

A similar analysis seemed to explain the case of the black soldiers. Rather than comparing conditions in the North with those in the South, black soldiers compared their own status with the status of the black civilians around them. In the South, where discrimination was at its worst, they found that being a soldier insulated them somewhat from adverse cultural norms in the surrounding community. Whereas southern black civilians were grossly discriminated against and denied self-esteem, good jobs, and so forth, black soldiers had a slightly better status. In the North, however, many of the black civilians they encountered held well-paying defense jobs. And with discrimination less severe, being a soldier did not help one's status in the community.

Finally, the concepts of reference group and relative deprivation seemed to explain the anomaly of highly educated draftees accepting their induction more willingly than those with less education. Stouffer reasoned as follows:

1. A person's friends, on the whole, have about the same educational status as that person does.

2. Draft-age men with less education are more likely to engage in semi-skilled production-line occupations and farming than more educated men.

3. During wartime, many production-line industries and farming are vital to the national interest; workers in those industries and farmers are exempted from the draft.

4. A man with little education is more likely to have friends in draft-exempt occupations than a man with more education.

5. When each compares himself with his friends, a less educated draftee is more likely to feel discriminated against than a draftee with more education.

(1949:122–27)

Stouffer's explanations unlocked the mystery of the three anomalous findings. Because they were not part of a preplanned study design, he lacked empirical data for testing them, however. Nevertheless, Stouffer's logical exposition provided the basis for the later development of the elaboration model: understanding the relationship between two variables through the controlled introduction of other variables.

The formal development of the elaboration model was the work of Paul Lazarsfeld and his associates at Columbia University in 1946. In a methodological review of Stouffer's army studies, Lazarsfeld and Patricia Kendall used the logic of the elaboration model to present hypothetical tables that would have proved Stouffer's contention regarding education and acceptance of induction had the empirical data been available (Kendall and Lazarsfeld 1950).

Kendall and Lazarsfeld began with Stouffer's data showing the positive association between education and acceptance of induction (see Table 16-1). Following Stouffer's explanation, they created a hypothetical table, compatible with the empirical data, to show that education was related to whether one had friends who were deferred. In Table 16-2, we note that 19 percent of those with high education reported having friends who were deferred, as compared with 79 percent among those with less education.

Stouffer's explanation next assumed that soldiers with friends who had been deferred would be more likely to resent their own induction than would those who had no

Table 16-1 Summary of Stouffer's Data on Education and Acceptance of Induction

	High Ed.	Low Ed.
Should not have been deferred	88%	70%
Should have been deferred	12	30
	100%	100%
	(1,761)	(1,896)

Source: Tables 16-1, 16-2, 16-3, and 16-4 are modified with permission of Macmillan Publishing Co., Inc., from *Continuities in Social Research: Studies in the Scope and Method of "The American Soldier"* by Robert K. Merton and Paul F. Lazarsfeld (eds.). Copyright 1950 by The Free Press, a Corporation, renewed 1978 by Robert K. Merton.

Table 16-2 Hypothetical Relationship between Education and Deferment of Friends

Friends deferred?	High Ed.	Low Ed.
Yes	19%	79%
No	81	21
	100%	100%
	(1,761)	(1,876)

deferred friends. Table 16-3 presents the hypothetical data that would have supported that assumption.

The hypothetical data in Tables 16-2 and 16-3 confirm linkages that Stouffer had specified in his explanation. First, soldiers with low education were more likely to have friends who were deferred than soldiers with more education. And, second, having friends who were deferred made a soldier more likely to think he should have been deferred. Stouffer had suggested that these two relationships would clarify the original relationship between education and acceptance of induction. Kendall and Lazarsfeld created a hypothetical table that would confirm Stouffer's explanation (see Table 16-4).

Recall that the original finding was that draftees with high education were more likely to accept their induction into the army as

Table 16-3 Hypothetical Relationship between Deferment of Friends and Acceptance of One's Own Induction

	Friends Deferred?	
	Yes	No
Should not have been deferred	63%	94%
Should have been deferred	37	6
	100%	100%
	(1,819)	(1,818)

Table 16-4   Hypothetical Data Relating Education to Acceptance
of Induction through the Factor of Having Friends Who Were Deferred

	Friends Deferred		No Friends Deferred	
	High Ed.	Low Ed.	High Ed.	Low Ed.
Should not have been deferred	63%	63%	94%	95%
Should have been deferred	37	37	6	5
	100%	100%	100%	100%
	(335)	(1,484)	(1,426)	(392)

fair than those with less education. In Table 16-4, however, we note that level of education has no effect on the acceptance of induction among those who report having friends deferred: 63 percent among *both* educational groups say they should not have been deferred. Similarly, educational level has no significant effect on acceptance of induction among those who reported having no friends deferred: 94 and 95 percent say they should not have been deferred.

On the other hand, among those with high education the acceptance of induction is strongly related to whether or not one's friends were deferred: 63 percent versus 94 percent. And the same is true among those with less education. The hypothetical data in Table 16-4, then, support Stouffer's contention that education affected acceptance of induction only through the medium of having friends deferred. Highly educated draftees were less likely to have friends deferred and, by virtue of that fact, were more likely to accept their own induction as fair. Those with less education were more likely to have friends deferred and, by virtue of that fact, were less likely to accept their own induction.

It is important to recognize that neither Stouffer's explanation nor the hypothetical data denied the reality of the original relationship. As educational level increased, acceptance of one's own induction also increased. The nature of this empirical relationship, however, was interpreted through the introduction of a third variable. The variable, deferment of friends, did not deny the original relationship; it merely clarified the mechanism through which the original relationship occurred. This, then, is the heart of the elaboration model and of multivariate analysis.

Having observed an empirical relationship between two variables, we seek to understand the nature of that relationship through the effects produced by introducing other variables. Mechanically, we accomplish this by first dividing our sample into subsets on the basis of the **control** or **test variable**. For example, having friends deferred or not is the control variable in our present example, and the sample is divided into those who have deferred friends and those who do not. The relationship between the original two variables is then recomputed separately for each of the subsamples. The tables produced in this manner are called the *partial tables*, and the relationships found in the partial tables are called the *partial relationships*. The partial relationships are then compared with the initial relationship discovered in the total sample.

THE ELABORATION PARADIGM

This section presents guidelines for the reader to follow in the understanding of an elab-

Figure 16-1   Intervening Test Variable

oration analysis. To begin, we must know whether the test variable is *antecedent* (prior in time) to the other two variables or whether it is *intervening* between them, because these positions suggest different logical relationships in the multivariate model. If the test variable is intervening, as in the case of education, deferment of friends, and acceptance of induction, then the analysis is based on the model shown in Figure 16-1. The logic of this multivariate relationship is that the independent variable (educational level) affects the intervening test variable (having friends deferred or not), which in turn affects the dependent variable (accepting induction).

If the test variable is antecedent to both the independent and dependent variables, a very different model must be used (see Figure 16-2). Here the test variable affects both the "independent" and "dependent" variables. Realize, of course, that the terms *independent variable* and *dependent variable* are, strictly speaking, used incorrectly in the diagram. In fact, we have one independent variable (the test variable) and two dependent variables. The incorrect terminology has been used only to provide continuity with the preceding example. Because of their individual relationships to the test variable, the "independent" and "dependent" variables are empirically related to

Figure 16-2   Antecedent Test Variable

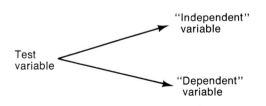

each other, but there is no causal link between them. Their empirical relationship is merely a product of their coincidental relationships to the test variable. (Subsequent examples will further clarify this relationship.)

Table 16-5 is a guide to the understanding of an elaboration analysis. The two columns in the table indicate whether the test variable is antecedent or intervening in the sense described above. The left side of the table shows the nature of the partial relationships as compared with the original relationship between the independent and dependent variables. The body of the table gives the technical notations—replication, explanation, interpretation, and specification—assigned to each case. We will discuss each in turn.

Replication

Whenever the partial relationships are essentially the same as the original relationship, the term *replication* is assigned to the result, regardless of whether the test variable is antecedent or intervening. This means that the original relationship has been replicated under test conditions. If, in our previous example, education still affected acceptance of induction both among those who had friends deferred and those who did not, then we would say the original relationship had been replicated. Note, however, that this finding would not confirm Stouffer's explanation of the original relationship. Having friends deferred or not would not be the mechanism through which education affected the acceptance of induction.

To see what a replication looks like, turn back to Tables 16-3 and 16-4 for a minute. Imagine that our initial discovery was that having friends deferred strongly influenced how soldiers felt about being drafted, as

Table 16-5   The Elaboration Paradigm

	Test Variable	
Partial Relationships Compared with Original	Antecedent	Intervening
Same relationship	Replication	
Less or none	Explanation	Interpretation
Split*	Specification	

*One partial the same or greater, while the other is less or none.

shown in Table 16-3. Had we first discovered this relationship, we might have wanted to see whether it was equally true for soldiers of different educational backgrounds. To find out, we would have made education our control or test variable.

Table 16-4 contains the results of such an examination, though it is constructed somewhat differently from what we would have done had we used education as the control variable. Nevertheless, we see in the table that having friends deferred or not still influences attitudes toward being drafted among those soldiers with high education and those with low education. (Compare columns 1 and 3, then 2 and 4.) This result represents a replication of the relationship between having friends deferred and attitude toward being drafted.

Researchers frequently use the elaboration model rather routinely in the hope of replicating their findings among subsets of the sample. If we discovered a relationship between education and prejudice, for example, we might introduce such test variables as age, region of the country, race, religion, and so forth, to test the stability of the original relationship. If the relationship were replicated among young and old, among persons from different parts of the country, and so forth, that would be grounds for concluding that the original relationship was a genuine and general one.

In the box "Attending an Ivy League College and Success in Later Professional Life," Patricia Kendall recalls a study in which the researcher suspected an explanation but found a replication.

Explanation

Explanation is the term used to describe a *spurious relationship;* an original relationship that is explained away through the introduction of a test variable. Two conditions are required for that to occur. The test variable must be antecedent to both the independent and dependent variables, and the partial relationships must be zero or significantly less than those found in the original. Three examples will illustrate this situation.

There is an empirical relationship between the number of storks in different areas and the birthrates for those areas. The more storks in an area, the higher the birthrate. This empirical relationship might lead one to assume that the number of storks affects the birthrate. An antecedent test explains away this relationship, however. Rural areas have both more storks and higher birthrates than urban areas. Within rural areas, there is no relationship between the number of storks and the birthrate; nor is there a relationship within urban areas.

Figure 16-3 illustrates how the rural/urban variable causes the apparent relationship between storks and birthrates. Part I of the

Figure 16-3   The Facts of Life about Storks and Babies

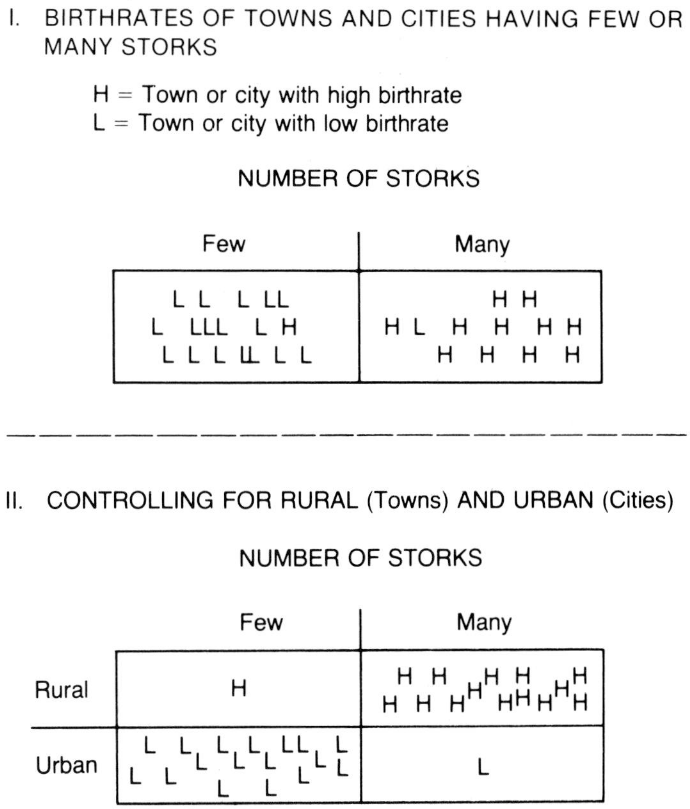

I.   BIRTHRATES OF TOWNS AND CITIES HAVING FEW OR MANY STORKS

    H = Town or city with high birthrate
    L = Town or city with low birthrate

NUMBER OF STORKS

Few	Many
L L L LL L LLL L H L L L LL L L	H H H L H H H H H H H H

II.   CONTROLLING FOR RURAL (Towns) AND URBAN (Cities)

NUMBER OF STORKS

	Few	Many
Rural	H	H H H H H H H H^H HH H^HH
Urban	L L L L LL L L L L L L L L L L	L

figure shows the original relationship. Notice how all but one of the entries in the box for towns and cities with few storks have high birthrates; with one exception, all those in the box for towns and cities with few storks have low birthrates. In percentage form, we say that 93 percent of the towns and cities with many storks also had high birthrates, as contrasted with 7 percent of those with few storks. That's a very large percentage point difference and represents a strong association between the two variables.

Part II of the figure separates the towns from the cities, the rural from urban areas, and examines storks and babies in each type of place separately. Now we can see that all

the rural places have high birthrates, and all the urban places have low birthrates. Also notice that only one rural place had few storks and only one urban place had lots of storks.

Here's a similar example. There is a positive relationship between the number of fire trucks responding to a fire and the amount of damage done. If more trucks respond, more damage is done. One might assume from this fact that the fire trucks themselves cause the damage. However, an antecedent test variable, the size of the fire, explains away the original relationship. Large fires do more damage than small ones, and more fire trucks respond to large fires than to small ones. Looking only at large fires,

Attending an Ivy League College and Success in Later Professional Life

by Patricia L. Kendall
Department of Sociology, Queens College, CUNY

Probably the main danger for survey analysts is that a relationship they hope is causal will turn out to be spurious. That is, the original relationship between X and Y is explained by an antecedent test factor. More specifically, the partial relationships between X and Y reduce to 0 when that antecedent test factor is held constant.

This was a distinct possibility in a major finding from a study carried out nearly 35 years ago. One of my fellow graduate students at Columbia University, Patricia Salter West, based her dissertation on questionnaires obtained by *Time Magazine* from 10,000 of its male subscribers. Among many of the hypotheses developed by West was that male graduates of Ivy League schools (Columbia, Cornell, Dartmouth, Harvard, University of Pennsylvania, Princeton, and Yale) were more successful in their later professional careers, as defined by their annual earnings, than those who graduated from other colleges and universities.

The initial four-fold table supported West's expectation.

Although I made up the figures, they conform closely to what West actually found in her study. Having attended an Ivy League school seems to lead to considerably greater professional success than being a graduate of some other kind of college or university.

But wait a minute. Isn't this a relationship that typically could be spurious? Who can afford to send their sons to Ivy League schools? Wealthy families, of course.† And who can provide

†Since she had no direct data on family socio-economic status, West defined as wealthy or having high socioeconomic status those who supported their sons completely during all four years of college. She defined as less wealthy or having low socioeconomic status those whose sons worked their way through college, in part or totally.

Table 1*

Later Profes-sional Success (Y)	College Attended (X)	
	Ivy League College	Other College or University
Successful	1,300 (65%)	2,000 (25%)
Unsuccessful	700 (35%)	6,000 (75%)
Total	2,000 (100%)	8,000 (100%)

*I have had to invent relevant figures because the only published version of West's study contained no totals. See Ernest Havemann and Patricia Salter West, *They Went to College* (New York: Harcourt, Brace), 1952.

the business and professional connections that could help sons become successful in their careers? Again, wealthy or well-to-do families.

In other words, the socioeconomic status of the student's family may explain away the apparent causal relationship. In fact, some of West's findings suggest that this might indeed be the case.

A third of those coming from families defined as wealthy, compared with 1 in 11 coming from less well-to-do backgrounds, attended Ivy League colleges. Thus there is a very high correlation between the two variables, X and T. (There is a similarly high correlation between family socioeconomic status [T] and later professional success [Y].)

The magnitude of these so-called marginal correlations suggest that West's hypothesis regarding the causal nature of having attended an Ivy League college might be incorrect; it suggests instead that the socioeconomic status of the students' families accounted for the original relationship she observed.

We are not done yet, however. The crucial question is what happens to the *partial relationships* once the test factor is controlled. These are shown in Table 3.

These partial relationships show that, even when family socioeconomic status is held constant, there is still a marked relationship between having attended an Ivy League college and success in later professional life. As a result, West's initial hypothesis receives support from the analysis she carried out.

Despite this, West has in no way *proved* her hypothesis. There are almost always additional antecedent factors that might explain the original relationship. Consider, for example, the *intelligence* of the students (as measured by IQ tests or SAT scores). Ivy League colleges pride themselves on the excellence of their student bodies. They may therefore be willing to award merit scholarships to students with exceptional qualifications but not enough money to pay tuition and board. Once admitted to these prestigious colleges, bright students may develop the skills—and connections—that will lead to later professional suc-

Table 2 Attendance at Ivy League Colleges According to Family Socioeconomic Status (SES)

College Attended (X)	Family SES (T)	
	High SES	Low SES
Ivy League colleges	1,500 (33%)	500 (9%)
Other colleges and universities	3,000 (67%)	5,000 (91%)
Total	4,500 (100%)	5,500 (100%)

Table 3 Partial Relationships between X and Y with T Held Constant

| Later success (Y) | High Family SES (T) | | Low Family SES (T) | |
	Ivy League College (X)	Other College (X)	Ivy League College (X)	Other College (X)
Successful	1,000 (67%)	1,000 (33%)	300 (60%)	1,000 (20%)
Not successful	500 (33%)	2,000 (67%)	200 (40%)	4,000 (80%)
Total	1,500 (100%)	3,000 (100%)	500 (100%)	5,000 (100%)

cess. Since West had no data on the intelligence of the men she studied, she was unable to study whether the partial relationships disappeared once this test factor was introduced.

In sum, the elaboration paradigm permits the investigator to rule out certain possibilities and to gain support for others. It does *not* permit us to *prove* anything.

we would see that the original relationship vanishes (or perhaps reverses itself); and the same would be true looking only at small fires.

Finally, let's take a real research example. There is an empirical relationship between the region of the country in which medical school faculty members attended medical school and their attitudes toward Medicare (Babbie 1970). To simplify matters, only the East and the South will be examined. Of faculty members attending eastern medical schools, 78 percent said they approved of Medicare, compared with 59 percent of those attending southern medical schools. This finding makes sense in view of the fact that the South seems generally more resistent to such programs than the East, and medical school training should presumably affect a doctor's medical attitudes. However, this relationship is explained away when we introduce an antecedent test variable: the region of the country in which the faculty member was raised. Of faculty members raised in the East, 89 percent

attended medical school in the East, and 11 percent in the South. Of those raised in the South, 53 percent attended medical school in the East and 47 percent in the South. Moreover, the areas in which faculty members were raised related to attitudes toward Medicare. Of those raised in the East, 84 percent approved of Medicare, as compared with 49 percent of those raised in the South.

Table 16-6 presents the three-variable relationship among region in which raised, region of medical school training, and attitude toward Medicare. Faculty members raised in the East are quite likely to approve of Medicare, regardless of where they attended medical school. Those raised in the South are relatively less likely to approve of Medicare, but, again, the region of their medical school training has little or no effect. These data indicate, therefore, that the original relationship between region of medical training and attitude toward Medicare was spurious; it was due only to the coincidental effect of region of origin on both region of medical training and on attitude toward Medicare. When region of origin is *held constant,* as we have done in Table 16-6, the original relationship disappears in the partials.

Interpretation

Interpretation is similar to explanation, except for the time placement of the test variable and the implications that follow from that difference. The earlier example of education, friends deferred, and acceptance of induction is an excellent illustration of interpretation. In terms of the elaboration model, the effect of education on acceptance of induction is not explained away; it is still a genuine relationship. In a real sense, educational differences *cause* differential acceptance of induction. The intervening variable, deferment of friends, merely helps to interpret the mechanism through which the relationship occurs.

Here's another example of interpretation. Researchers have observed that children from homes with working mothers are more likely to become delinquent than those whose mothers do not work. This relationship may be interpreted, however, through the introduction of supervision as a test variable. Among children who are supervised, delinquency rates are not affected by whether or not their mothers work. The same is true among those who are not supervised. It is the relationship between working mothers and the lack of supervision that produced the original relationship.

Specification

Sometimes the elaboration model produces partial relationships that differ significantly from each other. For example, one partial relationship is the same as/or stronger than the original two-variable relationship, while the second partial relationship is less than the original and may be reduced to zero. This situation is referred to as **specification** in the elaboration paradigm. We have specified the conditions under which the original relationship occurs.

In a study of the sources of religious involvement, Glock and his associates (1967:92) discovered that among Episcopal church members, involvement decreased as social class increased. This finding is reported in Table 16-7, which examines mean levels of church involvement among women parishioners at different levels of social class.

Table 16-6 Region of Origin, Region of Schooling, and Attitude toward Medicare

		Percentage Who Approve of Medicare	
		Region in Which Raised	
		East	South
Region of Medical School Training	East	84	50
	South	80	47

Source: Earl R. Babbie, *Science and Morality in Medicine* (Berkeley: University of California Press, 1970) p. 181.

Table 16-7 Social Class and Mean Church Involvement among Episcopal Women

	Social Class Levels				
	Low 0	1	2	3	High 4
Mean Involvement	.63	.58	.49	.48	.45

Source: Tables 16-7, 16-8, and 16-9 are from Charles Y. Glock, Benjamin B. Ringer, and Earl R. Babbie, *To Comfort and to Challenge* (Berkeley: University of California Press, 1967). Used with permission of The Regents of the University of California.

Note: *Mean* scores rather than percentages have been used here.

Glock interpreted this finding in the context of others in the analysis and concluded that church involvement provides an alternative form of gratification for people who are denied gratification in the secular society. This conclusion explained why women were more religious than men, why old people were more religious than young people, and so forth. Glock reasoned that people of lower social class (measured by income and education) had fewer chances to gain self-esteem from the secular society than did people of higher social class. To illustrate this idea, he noted that social class was strongly related to the likelihood that a woman had ever held an office in a secular organization (see Table 16-8).

Glock then reasoned that if social class were related to church involvement only by virtue of the fact that lower-class women would be denied opportunities for gratification in the secular society, the original relationship should *not* hold among women who were getting gratification. As a rough indicator of the receipt of gratification from the secular society, he used as a variable the holding of secular office. In this test, social class should be unrelated to church involvement among those who had held such office.

Table 16-8 Social Class and the Holding of Office in Secular Organizations

	Social Class Levels				
	Low 0	1	2	3	High 4
Percentage who have held office in a secular organization	46	47	54	60	83

Note: *Percentages* are used in this table.

Table 16-9 presents an example of a specification. Among women who have held office in secular organizations, there is essentially no relationship between social class and church involvement. In effect, the table specifies the conditions under which the original relationship holds: among those women lacking gratification in the secular society.

The term *specification* is used in the elaboration paradigm regardless of whether the test variable is antecedent or intervening. In either case, the meaning is the same. We have specified the particular conditions under which the original relationship holds.

Refinements to the Paradigm

The preceding sections have presented the primary logic of the elaboration model as

Table 16-9 Church Involvement by Social Class and Holding Secular Office

	Mean Church Involvement for Social Class Levels				
	Low 0	1	2	3	High 4
Have held office	.46	.53	.46	.46	.46
Have not held office	.62	.55	.47	.46	.40

developed by Lazarsfeld and his colleagues. Morris Rosenberg (1968) has offered an excellent presentation of the paradigm described above, and he goes beyond it to suggest additional variations.

Rather than reviewing Rosenberg's comments, let's consider the logically possible variations. Some of these points are found in Rosenberg's book; others were suggested by it.

First, the basic paradigm assumes an initial relationship between two variables. It might be useful, however, in a more comprehensive model to differentiate between positive and negative relationships. Moreover, Rosenberg suggests using the elaboration model even with an original relationship of *zero*. He cites as an example a study of union membership and attitudes toward having Jews on the union staff (see Table 16-10). The initial analysis indicated that length of union membership did not relate to the attitude: those who had belonged to the union less than four years were just as willing to accept Jews on the staff as were those who had belonged for more than four years. The *age* of union members, however, was found to *suppress* the relationship between length of union membership and attitude toward Jews. Overall, younger members were more favorable to Jews than were older members. At the same time, of course, younger members were not likely to have been in the union as long as the old members. Within specific age groups, however, those in the union longest were the most supportive of having Jews on the staff. Age, in this case, was a *suppressor variable*, concealing the relationship between length of membership and attitude toward Jews.

Second, the basic paradigm focuses on partials being the same or weaker than the original relationship, but does not provide guidelines for specifying what constitutes a significant difference between the original

Table 16-10 Example of a Suppressor Variable

I: No Apparent Relationship between Attitudes toward Jews and Length of Time in the Union

Jews on Union Staff	In Union Less than 4 Years	In Union 4 Years or Longer
Don't care either way	49.2% (126)	50.4% (256)

II. In Each Age Group, Length of Time in Union Increases Willingness to Have Jews on Union Staff

	Distribution of Answers by Percentage, According to Age and Longevity					
	29 Years and Under		30–49 Years		50 Years and Older	
	Years in Union					
Jews on Union Staff	Less than 4	4 or More	Less than 4	4 or More	Less than 4	4 or More
Don't care either way	56.4 (78)	62.7 (51)	37.1 (35)	48.3 (116)	38.4 (13)	56.1 (89)

Source: Morris Rosenberg, *The Logic of Survey Analysis* (New York: Basic Books, 1968), pp. 88–89. Used by permission.

and the partials. When you use the elaboration model, you will frequently find yourself making an arbitrary decision as to whether a given partial is significantly weaker than the original. This, then, suggests another dimension that could be added to the paradigm.

Third, the limitation of the basic paradigm to partials that are the same as or weaker than the original neglects two other possibilities. A partial relationship might be *stronger* than the original. Or, on the other hand, a partial relationship might be the reverse of the original—negative where the original was positive.

Rosenberg provides a hypothetical example of that by first suggesting that a researcher might find working-class respondents in his study more supportive of the civil rights movement than middle-class respondents (see Table 16-11). He further suggests that *race* might be a *distorter variable* in this instance, distorting the true relationship between class and attitudes. Presumably, black respondents would be more supportive of the movement than whites, but blacks would also be overrepresented among working-class respondents and underrepresented among the middle class. Middle-class black respondents might be more supportive of the movement than working-class blacks, however; and the same relationship might be found among whites. *Holding race constant*, then, the researcher would conclude that support for the civil rights movement was greater among the middle class than among the working class.

All these new dimensions further complicate the notion of specification. If one

Table 16-11 Example of a Distorter Variable (Hypothetical)

I: Working-Class Subjects Appear More Liberal on Civil Rights than Middle-Class Subjects

Civil Rights Score	Middle Class	Working Class
High	37%	45%
Low	63	55
	100%	100%
	(120)	(120)

II: Controlling for Race Shows the Middle Class to Be More Liberal than the Working Class

	Social Class			
	Blacks		Whites	
Civil Rights Score	Middle Class	Working Class	Middle Class	Working
High	70%	50%	30%	20%
Low	30	50	70	80
	100%	100%	100%	100%
	(20)	(100)	(100)	(20)

Source: Morris Rosenberg, *The Logic of Survey Analysis* (New York: Basic Books, 1968), pp. 94–95. Used by permission.

partial is the same as the original, while the other partial is even stronger, how should you react to that situation? You have specified one condition under which the original relationship holds up, but you have also specified another condition under which it holds even more clearly.

Finally, the basic paradigm focuses primarily on dichotomous test variables. In fact, the elaboration model is not so limited—either in theory or in use—but the basic paradigm becomes more complicated when the test variable divides the sample into three or more subsamples. And the paradigm becomes more complicated yet when more than one test variable is used simultaneously.

These comments are not made with the intention of faulting the basic elaboration paradigm. To the contrary, my intention is to impress upon you that the elaboration model is not a simple algorithm—a set of procedures through which to analyze research. Rather, it is primarily a logical device for assisting the researcher in understanding his or her data. A firm understanding of the elaboration model will make a sophisticated analysis easier. It does not suggest which variables should be introduced as controls, however, nor does it suggest definitive conclusions about the nature of elaboration results. For all these things, you must look to your own ingenuity. Such ingenuity, moreover, will come only through extensive experience. By pointing to oversimplifications in the basic elaboration paradigm, I have sought to bring home the point that the model provides only a logical framework. Sophisticated analysis will be far more complicated than the examples used to illustrate the basic paradigm.

At the same time, the elaboration paradigm is a very powerful logical framework. If you fully understand the basic model, you will be in a far better position for understanding other techniques such as correlations, regressions, factor analyses, and so

forth. The next chapter will attempt to place such techniques as partial correlations and partial regressions in the context of the elaboration model.

ELABORATION AND EX POST FACTO HYPOTHESIZING

Before we leave the discussion of the elaboration model, one further word is in order regarding its power in connection with *ex post facto hypothesizing*, a form of fallacious reasoning. The reader of methodological literature will find countless references warning against it. But although the intentions of such injunctions are correct, inexperienced researchers can sometimes be confused about its implications.

When you observe an empirical relationship between two variables and then simply suggest a reason for that relationship, that is sometimes called ex post facto hypothesizing. You have generated a hypothesis linking two variables after their relationship is already known. You will recall, from an early discussion in this book, that all hypotheses must be subject to disconfirmation. Unless you can specify empirical findings that would disprove your hypothesis, the hypothesis is essentially useless. You might reason, therefore, that once you have *observed* a relationship between two variables, any hypothesis regarding that relationship cannot be disproved.

That is a fair assessment if you are doing nothing more than dressing up your empirical observations with deceptive hypotheses after the fact. Having observed that women are more religious than men, you should not simply assert that women will be more religious than men because of some general dynamic of social behavior and then rest your case on the initial observation.

The unfortunate spin-off of the injunction against ex post facto hypothesizing is in its inhibition of good, honest hypothesizing after the fact. Inexperienced researchers are often led to believe that they must make all their hypotheses before examining their data—even if that process means making a lot of poorly reasoned ones. Furthermore, they are led to ignore any empirically observed relationships that do not confirm some prior hypothesis.

Surely, few researchers would now wish that Sam Stouffer had hushed up his anomalous findings regarding morale among soldiers in the army. Stouffer noted peculiar empirical observations and set about hypothesizing the reasons for those findings. And his reasoning has proved invaluable to researchers ever since.

There is a another, more sophisticated, point to be made here, however. Anyone can generate hypotheses to explain observed empirical relationships in a body of data, but the elaboration model provides the logical tools for *testing* those hypotheses within the same body of data. A good example of this testing may be found in the earlier discussion of social class and church involvement. Glock explained the original relationship in terms of social deprivation theory. If he had stopped at that point, his comments would have been interesting but hardly persuasive. He went beyond that point, however. He noted that if the hypothesis was correct, then the relationship between social class and church involvement should disappear among those women who were receiving gratification from the secular society—those who had held office in a secular organization. This hypothesis was then subjected to an empirical test. Had the new hypothesis not been confirmed by the data, he would have been forced to reconsider.

These additional comments should further illustrate the point that data analysis is a continuing process, demanding all the ingenuity and perseverance you can muster.

The image of a researcher carefully laying out hypotheses and then testing them in a ritualistic fashion results only in ritualistic research.

In case you are concerned that the strength of ex post facto proofs seems to be less than that of the traditional kinds, let me repeat the earlier assertion that "scientific proof" is a contradiction in terms. Nothing is ever *proved* scientifically. Hypotheses, explanations, theories, or hunches can all escape a stream of attempts at disproof, but none can be proved in any absolute sense. The acceptance of a hypothesis, then, is really a function of the extent to which it has been tested and not disconfirmed. No hypothesis, therefore, should be considered sound on the basis of one test—whether the hypothesis was generated before or after the observation of empirical data. With that in mind, you should not deny yourself some of the most fruitful avenues available to you in data analysis. You should always try to reach an honest understanding of your data, develop meaningful theories for more general understanding, and not worry about the manner of reaching that understanding.

MAIN POINTS

■ The elaboration model is a method of multivariate analysis appropriate to social research.

■ The elaboration model is primarily a logical model that can illustrate the basic logic of other multivariate methods.

■ The basic steps in elaboration are as follows: (a) a relationship is observed to exist between two variables; (b) a third variable is held constant in the sense that the cases under study are subdivided according to the attributes of that third variable; (c) the original two-variable relationship is recomputed within each of the subgroups; and

(d) the comparison of the original relationship with the relationships found within each subgroup provides a fuller understanding of the original relationship itself.

■ An intervening control variable is one that occurs in time between the occurrence of the independent variable and the occurrence of the dependent variable.

■ An antecedent control variable is one that occurs earlier in time than either the independent or the dependent variable.

■ A zero-order relationship is the observed relationship between two variables *without* a third variable being held constant or controlled.

■ A partial relationship is the observed relationship between two variables—within a subgroup of cases based on some attribute of the control variable. Thus, the relationship between age and prejudice among men only (that is, controlling for sex) would be a partial relationship.

■ If a set of partial relationships is essentially the same as the corresponding zero-order relationship, this outcome is called a replication, regardless of whether the control variable is intervening or antecedent. This means, simply, that the originally observed relationship has been replicated within smaller subgroups, and that the control variable has no influence on that original relationship.

■ If a set of partial relationships is reduced essentially to zero when an antecedent variable is held constant, this outcome is called an explanation, meaning that the originally observed "relationship" was a spurious or ungenuine one. This outcome suggests that the control variable has a causal effect on each of the variables examined in the zero-order relationship, thus resulting in a statistical relationship between those two that does not represent a causal relationship in itself.

■ If a set of partial relationships is reduced essentially to zero when an intervening variable is held constant, this outcome is called an interpretation, meaning that we have interpreted the manner in which the independent variable has its influence on the dependent variable: the independent variable influences the intervening variable, which, in turn, influences the dependent variable. In this instance, we conclude that the original relationship was a genuine causal relationship; we have shed further light on how that causal process operates.

■ If one partial relationship is reduced (ideally to zero) while the other remains about the same as the original relationship (or is stronger), this outcome is called a specification, regardless of whether the control variable was intervening or antecedent. This means, simply, that we have specified the conditions under which the originally observed relationship occurs.

■ A suppressor variable is one that conceals the relationship between two other variables.

■ A distorter variable is one that causes an apparent reversal in the relationship between two other variables: from negative to positive or positive to negative.

■ Ex post facto hypothesizing refers to the development of hypotheses "predicting" relationships that have already been observed. This is invalid in science, since it is impossible to disconfirm such hypotheses. Of course, nothing prevents us from suggesting reasons that observed relationships may be the way they are; we simply should not frame those reasons in the form of "hypotheses." More important, one observed relationship and possible reasons for it may suggest hypotheses about other relationships that have not been examined. The elaboration model is an excellent logical device for this kind of unfolding analysis of data.

REVIEW QUESTIONS AND EXERCISES

1. In your own words describe the elaboration logic of
    a. Replication
    b. Interpretation
    c. Explanation
    d. Specification

2. Review the Stouffer-Lazarsfeld example of education, friends deferred, and attitudes toward being drafted. Suppose they had begun with an association between friends deferred and attitudes toward being drafted, and then they controlled for education. What conclusion would they have reached?

ADDITIONAL READINGS

Glock, Charles (ed.), *Survey Research in the Social Sciences* (New York: Russell Sage Foundation, 1967), Chapter 1. An excellent discussion of the logic of elaboration. Glock's own chapter in this book presents the elaboration model, providing concrete illustrations.

Hirschi, Travis, and Selvin, Hanan, *Delinquency Research: An Appraisal of Analytic Methods* (New York: Free Press, 1967). Excellent logical discussions and concrete examples. This book examines the empirical research in the field of delinquency from a rigorously logical perspective. Critiques of specific research examples often set the stage for important and insightful general discussions of elaboration and other aspects of the logic of scientific inquiry.

Hyman, Herbert, *Survey Design and Analysis* (New York: Free Press, 1955). A somewhat dated but milestone statement of the elaboration model. The fundamental paradigm is discussed and illustrated through a number of real surveys. Lazarsfeld's foreword is the most available classic statement of the logic of elaboration. This was and still is an important book. Later sections of the book illustrate the relationship between the logical model and the nitty-gritty details of analyzing data by counter-sorter, an excellent method of developing hand-brain coordination in social research.

Lazarsfeld, Paul; Pasanella, Ann; and Rosenberg, Morris (eds.), *Continuities in the Language of Social Research* (New York: Free Press, 1972). An excellent and classic collection of conceptual discussions and empirical illustrations. Section II is especially relevant, though the logic of elaboration runs throughout most of the volume.

Rosenberg, Morris, *The Logic of Survey Analysis* (New York: Basic Books, 1968). The most comprehensive statement of elaboration available. Rosenberg presents the basic paradigm and goes on to suggest logical extensions of it. It is difficult to decide what is most important, this aspect of the book or the voluminous illustrations. Both are simply excellent, and this book serves an important instructional purpose.

17

Social Statistics

What You'll Learn in This Chapter

Here you'll learn about a few simple statistics frequently used in social research. If you have an aversion to statistics, you may be pleasantly surprised.

INTRODUCTION

Many people are intimidated by empirical research because they feel uncomfortable with mathematics and statistics. And indeed, many research reports are filled with unspecified computations. The role of statistics in social research is very important, but it is equally important for that role to be seen in its proper perspective.

Empirical research is first and foremost a logical rather than a mathematical operation. Mathematics is merely a convenient and efficient language for accomplishing the logical operations inherent in good data analysis. Statistics is the applied branch of mathematics especially appropriate to a variety of research analyses.

I want to start this chapter with an informal look at one of the concerns I find people have when they approach statistics. I suspect this exercise will make it easier for you to understand and feel comfortable with the relatively simple statistics that are introduced in the remainder of the chapter. We'll be looking at two types of statistics: *descriptive* and *inferential*. **Descriptive statistics** is a medium for describing data in manageable forms. **Inferential statistics,** on the other hand, assists you in drawing conclusions from your observations; typically, that involves drawing conclusions about a population from the study of a sample drawn from it.

THE DANGER OF SUCCESS IN MATH

Since I began teaching research methods that include at least a small amount of statistics, I've been struck by the large number of students who report that they are "simply no good at math." Just as some people are reported to be inherently tone-deaf and others unable to learn foreign languages, about 90 percent of my college students seemed to suffer from *congenital math deficiency syndrome* (CMDS). Some of its common symptoms are frustration, boredom, and drowsiness. I'm delighted to report that I have finally uncovered a major cause of the disease and have brewed up a cure. In the event that you may be a sufferer, I'd like to share it with you before we delve into the statistics of social research.

You may be familiar with the story of Typhoid Mary, whose real name was Mary Mallon. Mary was a typhoid carrier who died in 1938 in New York. Before her death, she worked as a household cook, moving from household to household, and causing ten outbreaks of typhoid fever. Over fifty people caught the disease from her, and three of them died.

The congenital math deficiency syndrome has a similar cause. After an exhaustive search, I've discovered the culprit, whom I'll call Mathematical Marvin, though he has used countless aliases. If you suffer from CMDS, I suspect you've met him. Take a minute to recall your years in high school. Remember the person that your teachers and your classmates regarded as a "mathematical genius." Getting A's in all the math classes was only part of it; often the math genius seemed to know math better than the teachers.

Now that you have that math genius in mind, let me ask you a few questions. First, what was the person's sex? I'd guess he was probably male. Most of the students I've asked in class report that. But let's consider some other characteristics:

1. How athletic was he?

2. Did he wear glasses?

3. How many parties did he get invited to during high school?

4. If he was invited to parties, did anyone ever talk to him?

5. How often did you find yourself envying the math genius, wishing you could trade places with him?

I've been asking students (including some adult classes) these questions for several years, and the answers I've gotten are amazing. Marvin is usually unathletic, often either very skinny or overweight. He usually wears glasses, and he seems otherwise rather delicate. During his high school years, he was invited to an average (mean) of 1.2 parties, and nobody talked to him. His complexion was terrible. Almost nobody ever wanted to change places with him; he was a social misfit, more to be pitied than envied.

Here's the point of my report on Mathematical Marvin. As I've discussed Marvin with my students, it has become increasingly clear that most of them have formed a subconscious association between mathematical proficiency and Marvin's unenviable characteristics. Most have concluded that doing well in math and statistics would turn them into social misfits, and they have regarded that as too high a price to pay.

So if you are one of those people who is "just no good at math," it's possible you are carrying around a hidden fear that your face will break out in pimples if you do well in statistics in this course. If so, you're going to be reading the rest of this chapter in a terrible state: wanting to understand it at least until the next exam and, at the same time, worrying that you may understand it too well and lose all your friends.

Before exposing you to any numbers, then, I want to assure you that the level of statistics contained in the rest of this chapter has been proven safe for humans. There has not been a single documented case of pimples connected to understanding *lambda, gamma, chi square,* or any of the other statistics discussed in the pages to follow. In fact, this level of exposure has been found to be *beneficial* to young social researchers.

By the way, uncovering Marvin can clear up a lot of mysteries. It did for me. (In my high school class, he didn't wear glasses, but he squinted a lot.) In the first research methods book I wrote, I presented three statistical computations and got one of them wrong. In the first edition of this book, I got a different one wrong. Most embarrassing of all, however, the first printing of the earlier book had a unique feature. I thought it would be fun to write a computer program to generate my own table of random numbers rather than reprinting one that someone else had created. In doing that, I had the dubious honor of publishing the world's first table of random numbers that *didn't have any nines!* It was not until I tracked Marvin down that I discovered the source of my problems, and statistics has been much more fun (and trouble-free) ever since. So enjoy.

DESCRIPTIVE STATISTICS

As I've already suggested, descriptive statistics is a method for presenting quantitative descriptions in a manageable form. Sometimes we want to describe single variables, and sometimes we want to describe the associations that connect one variable with another. Let's look at some of the ways that is done.

Data Reduction

Scientific research often involves the collection of large masses of data. Suppose we had surveyed 2,000 people, asking each of them 100 questions—not an unusually large study. We would now have a staggering 200,000 answers! No one could possibly read all those 200,000 answers and reach any meaningful conclusion about them. Thus, much scientific analysis involves the *reduction* of data from unmanageable details to manageable summaries.

To begin our discussion, let's look briefly at the raw data matrix created by a quantitative research project. Table 17-1 presents a partial data matrix. Notice that each of the rows in the matrix represents a person (or other unit of analysis), each column represents a variable, and each cell in the matrix represents the coded attribute or value a given person has on a given variable. The first column in Table 17-1 represents a person's sex. Let's say a "1" represents male and "2" represents female. That means that persons 1 and 2 are male, person 3 is female, and so forth.

In the case of age, person 1's "3" might mean 30–39 years old, person 2's "4" might mean 40–49. However age had been coded (see Chapter 13), the code numbers shown in Table 17-1 would describe each of the people represented there.

Notice that the data have already been reduced somewhat by the time a data matrix like this one has been created. If age had been coded as suggested above, the specific answer "33 years old" has already been reduced to the category "30–39." The people responding to our survey may have given us 60 or 70 different ages, but we have now reduced them to 6 or 7 categories.

Chapter 14 has already discussed some of the ways of further summarizing univariate data: averages such as the mode, median, and mean; and measures of dispersion such as the range, the standard deviation, and so forth. It's also possible to summarize the association between variables.

Measures of Association

The association between any two variables can also be represented by a data matrix, this time produced by the joint frequency distributions of the two variables. Table 17-2 presents such a matrix. It provides all the information needed to determine the nature and extent of the relationship between education and prejudice.

Notice, for example, that 23 people (a) have no education and (b) scored high on prejudice; 77 people (a) had graduate degrees and (b) scored low on prejudice.

Like the raw-data matrix in Table 17-1, this matrix gives you more information than you can easily comprehend. If you study the table carefully, however, you will note that as education increases from "None" to "Graduate degree," there is a general tendency for prejudice to decrease, but no more than a general impression is possible. A

Table 17-1 Partial Raw Data Matrix

	Sex	Age	Education	Income	Occupation	Political Affiliation	Political Orientation	Religious Affiliation	Importance of Religion
Person 1	1	3	2	4	1	2	3	0	4
Person 2	1	4	2	4	4	1	1	1	2
Person 3	2	2	5	5	2	2	4	2	3
Person 4	1	5	4	4	3	2	2	2	4
Person 5	2	3	7	8	6	1	1	5	1
Person 6	2	1	3	3	5	3	5	1	1

Table 17-2   Hypothetical Raw Data on Education and Prejudice

			Education Level		
Prejudice	None	Grade School	High School	College	Graduate Degree
High	23	34	156	67	16
Medium	11	21	123	102	23
Low	6	12	95	164	77

variety of descriptive statistics permit the summarization of this data matrix, however. Selecting the appropriate measure depends initially on the nature of the two variables.

We'll turn now to some of the options available for summarizing the association between two variables. This discussion and those to follow are taken largely from an excellent statistics textbook by Linton C. Freeman (1968). Each measure of association we'll discuss is based on the same model—*proportionate reduction of error* (PRE). To see how this model works, let's assume that I asked you to guess respondents' attributes on a given variable; for example, whether they answered yes or no to a given questionnaire item.

To assist you, let's first assume that you know the overall distribution of responses in the total sample—say, 60 percent said yes and 40 percent said no. You would make the fewest errors in this process if you always guessed the *modal* (most frequent) response: yes.

Second, let's assume that you also know the empirical relationship between the first variable and some other variable: say, sex. Now, each time I ask you to guess whether a respondent said yes or no, I'll tell you whether the respondent is a man or a woman. If the two variables are related, you should make fewer errors the second time. It is possible, therefore, to compute the PRE by knowing the relationship between the two

variables: the greater the relationship, the greater the reduction of error.

This basic PRE model is modified slightly to take account of different levels of measurement—nominal, ordinal, or interval. The following sections will consider each level of measurement and present one measure of association appropriate to each. You should realize that the three measures discussed are only an arbitrary selection from among many appropriate measures.

Nominal Variables   If the two variables consist of nominal data (for example, sex, religious affiliation, race), lambda (λ) would be one appropriate measure. Lambda is based on your ability to guess values on one of the variables: the PRE achieved through knowledge of values on the other variable. A simple hypothetical example will illustrate the logic and method of lambda. Table 17-3 presents hypothetical data relating sex to employment status. Overall, we note that 1,100 people are employed, and 900 are unemployed. If you were to predict whether people were employed, knowing only the overall distribution on that variable, you would always predict "employed," since that would result in fewer errors than always predicting "unemployed." Nevertheless, this strategy would result in 900 errors out of 2,000 predictions.

Let's suppose that you had access to the data in Table 17-3 and that you were told each person's sex before making your pre-

Table 17-3 Hypothetical Data Relating Sex to Employment Status

	Mean	Women	Total
Employed	900	200	1,100
Unemployed	100	800	900
Total	1,000	1,000	2,000

diction of employment status. Your strategy would change in that case. For every man, you would predict "employed," and for every woman, you would predict "unemployed." In this instance, you would make 300 errors—the 100 employed men and the 200 employed women—or 600 fewer errors than you would make without knowing the person's sex.

Lambda, then, represents the reduction in errors as a proportion of the errors that would have been made on the basis of the overall distribution. In this hypothetical example, lambda would equal .67: that is, 600 fewer errors divided by the 900 total errors based on employment status alone. In this fashion, lambda measures the statistical association between sex and employment status.

If sex and employment status were statistically independent, we would find the same distribution of employment status for men and women. In this case, knowing sex would not affect the number of errors made in predicting employment status, and the resulting lambda would be zero. If, on the other hand, all men were employed and all women were unemployed, by knowing sex you would avoid errors in predicting employment status. You would make 900 fewer errors (out of 900), so lambda would be 1.0—representing a perfect statistical association.

Lambda is only one of several measures of association appropriate to the analysis of two nominal variables. You might want to

look at Freeman (1968) for a discussion of other appropriate measures.

Ordinal Variables If the variables being related are ordinal (for example, social class, religiosity, alienation), gamma (γ) is one appropriate measure of association. Like lambda, gamma is based on your ability to guess values on one variable by knowing values on another. Instead of guessing exact values, however, gamma is based on the ordinal arrangement of values. For any given *pair* of cases, you guess that their ordinal ranking on one variable will correspond (positively or negatively) to their ordinal ranking on the other. For example, if you suspect that religiosity is positively related to political conservatism, and if Person A is more religious than Person B, you guess that A is also more conservative than B. Gamma is the proportion of paired comparisons that fit this pattern.

Table 17-4 presents hypothetical data relating social class to prejudice. The general nature of the relationship between these two variables is that as social class increases, prejudice decreases. There is a negative association between social class and prejudice.

Gamma is computed from two quantities: (1) the number of pairs having the same ranking on the two variables and (2) the number of pairs having the opposite ranking on the two variables. The pairs having the same ranking are computed as fol-

Table 17-4 Hypothetical Data Relating Social Class to Prejudice

Prejudice	Lower Class	Middle Class	Upper Class
Low	200	400	700
Medium	500	900	400
High	800	300	100

lows. The frequency of each cell in the table is multiplied by the sum of all cells appearing below and to the right of it—with all these products being summed. In Table 17-4, the number of pairs with the same ranking would be 200(900 + 300 + 400 + 100) + 500(300 + 100) + 400(400 + 100) + 900(100) or 340,000 + 200,000 + 200,000 + 90,000 = 830,000.

The pairs having the opposite ranking on the two variables are computed as follows: the frequency of each cell in the table is multiplied by the sum of all cells appearing below and to the left of it—with all these products being summed. In Table 17-4, the numbers of pairs with opposite rankings would be 700(500 + 800 + 900 + 300) + 400(800 + 300) + 400(500 + 800) + 900(800) or 1,750,000 + 440,000 + 520,000 + 720,000 = 3,430,000.

Gamma is computed from the numbers of same-ranked pairs and opposite-ranked pairs as follows:

$$gamma = \frac{same - opposite}{same + opposite}$$

In our example, gamma equals: (830,000 − 3,430,000) divided by (830,000 + 3,430,000) or −.61. The negative sign in this answer indicates the negative association suggested by the initial inspection of the table. Social class and prejudice, in this hypothetical example, are negatively associated with one another. The numerical figure for gamma indicates that 61 percent more of the pairs examined had the opposite ranking than had the same ranking.

Note that while values of lambda vary from 0 to 1, values of gamma vary from −1 to +1, representing the *direction* as well as the magnitude of the association. Since nominal variables have no ordinal structure, it makes no sense to speak of the direction of the relationship. (A negative lambda would indicate that you made more errors in predicting values on one variable while

knowing values on the second than you made in ignorance of the second, and that's not logically possible.)

Here's an example of the use of gamma in contemporary social research. To study the extent to which widows sanctified their deceased husbands, Helena Znaniecki Lopata (1981) administered a questionnaire to a probability sample of 301 Chicago area widows. In part, the questionnaire asked the respondents to characterize their deceased husbands in terms of the *semantic differentiation scale* shown below:

	Characteristic							
Positive Extreme								Negative Extreme
Good	1	2	3	4	5	6	7	Bad
Useful	1	2	3	4	5	6	7	Useless
Honest	1	2	3	4	5	6	7	Dishonest
Superior	1	2	3	4	5	6	7	Inferior
Kind	1	2	3	4	5	6	7	Cruel
Friendly	1	2	3	4	5	6	7	Unfriendly
Warm	1	2	3	4	5	6	7	Cold

Respondents were asked to describe their deceased spouses by circling a number for each pair of opposing characteristics. Notice that the series of numbers connecting each pair of characteristics is an ordinal measure.

Next, Lopata wanted to discover the extent to which the several measures were related to each other. Appropriately, she chose gamma as the measure of association. Table 17-5 shows how she presented the results of her investigation.

The format presented in Table 17-5 is called a *correlation matrix*. For each pair of measures, Lopata has calculated the gamma. Good and Useful, for example, are related to each other by a gamma equal to .79. The matrix is a convenient way of pre-

Table 17-5 Gamma Associations among the
Semantic Differentiation Items of the Sanctification Scale

	Useful	Honest	Superior	Kind	Friendly	Warm
Good	.79	.88	.80	.90	.79	.83
Useful	—	.84	.71	.77	.68	.72
Honest		—	.83	.89	.79	.82
Superior			—	.78	.60	.73
Kind				—	.88	.90
Friendly					—	.90

Source: Helena Znaniecki Lopata, "Widowhood and Husband Sanctification,"
Journal of Marriage and the Family (May 1981):439–50.

senting the intercorrelations among several variables, and you'll find it frequently in the research literature. In this case, we see that all the variables are quite strongly related to each other, though some pairs are more strongly related than others.

Gamma is only one of several measures of association appropriate to ordinal variables. Again, Freeman (1968) gives a more comprehensive treatment of this subject.

Interval or Ratio Variables If interval or ratio variables (for example, age, income, grade point average, and so forth) are being associated, one appropriate measure of association is *Pearson's product-moment correlation (r)*. The derivation and computation of this measure of association is complex enough to lie outside the scope of this book, so only a few general comments will be made.

Like both gamma and lambda, *r* is based on guessing the value of one variable by knowing the other. For continuous interval or ratio variables, however, it is unlikely that you would be able to predict the *precise* value of the variable. But on the other hand, predicting only the ordinal arrangement of values on the two variables would not take advantage of the greater amount of information conveyed by an interval or ratio var-

iable. In a sense, *r* reflects *how closely* you can guess the value of one variable through your knowledge of the value of the other.

To understand the logic of *r*, consider the manner in which you might hypothetically guess values that particular cases have on a given variable. With nominal variables, we have seen that you might always guess the modal value. But for interval or ratio data you would minimize your errors by always guessing the mean value of the variable. Although this practice produces few if any perfect guesses, the extent of your errors will be minimized.

In the computation of lambda, we noted the number of errors produced by always guessing the modal value. In the case of *r*, errors are measured in terms of the sum of the squared differences between the actual value and the mean. This sum is called the *total variation*.

To improve your guessing, you construct a *regression line* (see Chapter 18), stated in the form of a regression equation that permits the estimation of values on one variable from values on the other. The general format for this equation is $Y' = a + b(X)$, where a and b are computed values, X is a given value on one variable, and Y' is the estimated value on the other. The values of a and b are computed so as to minimize the differences between actual values of Y and the corresponding estimates (Y') based on the known value of X. The sum of squared differences between actual and estimated values of Y is called the *unexplained variation* because it represents errors that still exist even when estimates are based on known values of X.

The *explained variation* is the difference between the total variation and the unexplained variation. Dividing the explained variation by the total variation produces a measure of the *proportionate reduction of error* corresponding to the similar quantity in the computation of lambda. In the present case, this quantity is the correlation *squared: r^2*. Thus, if $r = .7$, then $r^2 = .49$: meaning that about *half* the variation has been explained. In practice, we compute r rather than r^2, since the product-moment correlation can take either a positive or negative sign, depending on the direction of the relationship between the two variables. (Computing r^2 and taking a square root would always produce a positive quantity.) See Freeman (1968) or any other standard statistics textbook for the method of computing r, although I anticipate that most readers using this measure will have access to computer programs designed for this function.

Mixed Types of Variables Often, you will find that your interest lies in the association between two variables that differ in type: one ordinal variable and one nominal variable. A variety of special statistics are appropriate to these different possibilities, and you are encouraged to examine Freeman (1968) for the appropriate statistics for a particular situation. The box "Selecting Appropriate Statistical Techniques" by Patricia Fisher offers some additional guidelines to follow in the selection of the appropriate statistical technique.

This is an opportune point for a general comment regarding types of variables and

the appropriateness of statistical measures. A quick review of social scientific research literature will yield countless examples of statistical measures applied to data that do not meet the logical requirements of the measures. The computation of Pearson's r for ordinal data is perhaps the most typical example. The person who argues against such computations is correct on statistical grounds: correlation coefficients assume interval data, and ordinal data do not meet that criterion. On the other hand, it is my personal orientation to accept, and even to encourage, the use of whatever statistical techniques help the researcher (and the reader) to understand the body of data under analysis. If the computation of r from ordinal data serves this purpose, then it should be encouraged. However, I strongly object to (and discuss in the next section) the practice of making statistical inferences from such computations. We are justified in bending the rules if it helps us understand our data, but we must be aware of the implications of bending those rules.

INFERENTIAL STATISTICS

Many, if not most, social scientific research projects involve the examination of data collected from a sample drawn from a larger population. A sample of people may be interviewed in a survey; a sample of divorce records may be coded and analyzed; a sample of newspapers may be examined through content analysis. Researchers seldom if ever study samples just to describe the samples per se; in most instances, their ultimate purpose is to make assertions about the larger population from which the sample has been selected. Frequently, then, you will wish to interpret your univariate and multivariate sample findings as the basis for *inferences* about some population.

Selecting Appropriate
Statistical Techniques

by Patricia Fisher
Graduate School of Planning,
University of Tennessee

The fact that there are so many different statistical techniques available can be both a help and a hindrance to the conscientious researcher. The choice of a statistical test to use for a given data analysis problem can be quite a difficult one. Even statisticians often find themselves in a quandary over this decision, so it is no surprise that researchers without a strong statistical background frequently throw up their hands in despair. However, the good news is that a few fairly simple guidelines can serve to at least reduce the menu of appropriate techniques to consider, making the decision a little less of a chore.

There are several different ways in which statistical techniques can be categorized. For example, we have all heard of univariate and multivariate techniques. Some statisticians refer to any technique that accommodates more than one independent variable (such as linear regression analysis) as multivariate, whereas others reserve the term for those techniques that also allow for more than one *dependent* variable (such as multivariate analysis of variance—MANOVA).

We also have a choice between nonparametric and parametric (or classical) techniques. Nonparametric techniques are usually considered those that apply to nominal or ordinal levels of measurement, do not necessarily depend on the assumption of a normal distribution, or deal with hypotheses about something *other* than population parameters.

Another important factor to consider is the number of groups of subjects represented by the data. There are techniques for drawing inferences about a single population, for comparing one population with another, and for contrasting three or more populations or

---

This section will examine the statistical measures used for making such inferences and their logical bases. We'll begin with univariate data and move to multivariate.

Univariate Inferences

The opening sections of Chapter 14 dealt with methods of presenting univariate data.

Each summary measure was intended as a method of describing the sample studied. Now we will use those measures to make broader assertions about the population. This section is addressed to two univariate measures: percentages and means.

If 50 percent of a sample of people say they have had colds during the past year, 50 percent is also our best estimate of the proportion of colds in the total population from which the sample was drawn. (This

subgroups simultaneously. In addition, it is important to consider the nature of the questions being asked of the data. There are statistical techniques available to explore population parameters, relationships between variables, shapes of distributions, and many other types of inquiries that a researcher might wish to make.

Finally, it is important to realize that even very simple statistical techniques may have unique underlying assumptions upon which they are based. Sometimes the techniques perform adequately even when some of these assumptions are violated, but this is not always the case. It is wise to be alert to ways in which your research environment might not match the requirements of the statistical technique.

Since there is such an abundant menu of statistical techniques at our disposal, our task is to make an intelligent choice among them. One helpful approach is to describe our statistical problem in such a way so as to eliminate some techniques that clearly do not fulfill our needs. Those remaining can then be further evaluated for suitability based on the nature of their individual underlying assumptions. Eventually, one or a few techniques will usually emerge as being the most *technically* appropriate for the problem. The researcher may then have to make some rather subjective judgments in order to select one to use, or may decide to use several different techniques in the analysis.

Most statistics books will provide you with the details for computing a wide range of statistics and will discuss the major requirements and assumptions of each. In selecting the most appropriate technique for your data, you will need to pay special attention to the following:

1. The required minimal level of measurement: nominal, ordinal, interval, ration. This means, for example, that techniques requiring at least ordinal data may be used with interval data but not the other way around.

2. The number of groups or samples being examined (and compared).

3. The number of variables to be analyzed simultaneously.

estimate assumes a simple random sample, of course.) It is rather unlikely, however, that *precisely* 50 percent of the population have had colds during the year. If a rigorous sampling design for random selection has been followed, however, we will be able to estimate the expected range of error when the sample finding is applied to the population.

Chapter 7 on sampling theory covered the procedures for making such estimates, so they will only be reviewed here. In the case of a percentage, the quantity

$$\sqrt{\frac{p \times q}{n}}$$

where p is a percentage, q equals $1 - p$, and n is the sample size, is called the *standard error*. As noted in Chapter 7, this quantity is very important in the estimation of sampling error. We may be 68 percent confident that the population figure falls within plus or minus one standard error of the sample figure, we may be 95 percent confident that it falls within plus or minus two standard errors, and 99.9 percent confident that it falls within plus or minus three standard errors.

Any statement of sampling error, then, must contain two essential components: the *confidence level* (for example, 95 percent) and the *confidence interval* (for example ± 2.5 percent). If 50 percent of a sample of 1,600 people say they have had colds during the year, we might say we are 95 percent confident that the population figure is between 47.5 percent and 52.5 percent.

Recognize in this example that we have moved beyond simply describing the sample into the realm of making estimates (inferences) about the larger population. In doing that, we must be wary of several assumptions.

First, the sample must be drawn from the population about which inferences are being made. A sample taken from a telephone directory cannot legitimately be the basis for statistical inferences about the population of a city.

Second, the inferential statistics assume simple random sampling, which is virtually never the case in sample surveys. The statistics assume sampling with replacement, which is almost never done; but that is probably not a serious problem. Although systematic sampling is used more frequently than random sampling, that, too, probably presents no serious problem if done correctly. Stratified sampling, since it improves representativeness, clearly presents no problem. Cluster sampling does present a problem, however, as the estimates of sampling error may be too small. Quite clearly, street corner sampling does not warrant the use of inferential statistics. This standard error sampling technique also assumes a 100 percent completion rate. This

problem increases in seriousness as the completion rate decreases.

Third, inferential statistics are addressed to sampling error only; they do not take account of **nonsampling errors**. Thus, although it might be correct to state that between 47.5 and 52.5 percent of the population (95 percent confidence) would *report* having colds during the previous year, we could not so confidently guess the percentage who had actually had them. Since nonsampling errors are probably larger than sampling errors in a respectable sample design, we need to be especially cautious in generalizing from our sample findings to the population.

Tests of Statistical Significance

There is no scientific answer to the question of whether a given association between two variables is significant, strong, important, interesting, or worth reporting. Perhaps the ultimate test of significance rests with your ability to persuade your audience (present and future) of the association's significance. At the same time, there is a body of inferential statistics to assist you in this regard, called *parametric tests of significance*. As the name suggests, parametric statistics are those that make certain assumptions about the parameters describing the population from which the sample is selected.

Although tests of **statistical significance** are widely reported in social scientific literature, the logic underlying them is rather subtle and is often misunderstood. Tests of significance are based on the same sampling logic that has been discussed elsewhere in this book. To understand that logic, let's return for a moment to the concept of sampling error in regard to univariate data.

Recall that a sample statistic normally provides the best single estimate of the corresponding population parameter, but the statistic and the parameter seldom correspond precisely. Thus, we report the probability that the parameter falls within a certain range (confidence interval). The degree of uncertainty within that range is due to normal sampling error. The corollary of such a statement is, of course, that it is *improbable* that the parameter would fall outside the specified range only as a result of sampling error. Thus, if we estimate that a parameter (99.9 percent confidence) lies between 45 percent and 55 percent, we say by implication that it is *extremely improbable* that the parameter is actually, say, 90 percent if our only error of estimation is due to normal sampling. That is the basic logic behind tests of significance.

I think I can illustrate this logic of statistical significance best in a series of diagrams representing the selection of samples from a population. The elements in the logic I'll illustrate are

1. Assumptions regarding the *independence* of two variables in the population study.

2. Assumptions regarding the *representativeness* of samples selected through conventional probability sampling procedures.

3. The observed *joint distribution* of sample elements in terms of the two variables.

Figure 17-1 represents a hypothetical population of 256 people, half women and half men. The diagram also indicates how each person feels about women enjoying equality to men. In the diagram, those favoring equality have open circles, those opposing it have their circles shaded in.

The question we'll be investigating is whether there is any relationship between gender and feelings about equality for men and women. More specifically, we'll see if women are more likely to favor equality than men, since they would presumably

benefit more from it. Take a moment to look at Figure 17-1 and see what the answer to that question is.

The illustration in the figure indicates there is no relationship between gender and attitudes about equality. Exactly half of each group favors equality and half opposes it. Recall the earlier discussion of proportionate reduction of error. In this instance, knowing a person's gender would not reduce the "errors" we'd make in guessing his or her attitude toward equality. The table at the bottom of Figure 17-1 provides a tabular view of what you can observe in the graphic diagram.

Figure 17-2 represents the selection of a one-fourth sample from the hypothetical population. In terms of the graphic illustration, a "square" selection from the center of the population provides a representative sample. Notice that our sample contains 16 of each type of person: half are men and half women, and half of each gender group favors equality while the other half opposes it.

The sample selected in Figure 17-2 would allow us to draw accurate conclusions about the relationship between gender and equality in the larger population. Following the sampling logic you learned in Chapter 7, we would note there was no relationship between gender and equality in the sample; thus, we'd conclude there was similarly no relationship in the larger population—since we've presumably selected a sample in accord with the conventional rules of sampling.

Of course, real-life samples are seldom such perfect reflections of the populations from which they are drawn. It would not be unusual for us to have selected, say, one of two extra men who opposed equality and a couple of extra women who favored it— even if there was no relationship between the two variables in the population. Such minor variations are part and parcel of probability sampling, as you learned in Chapter 7.

Figure 17-1 A Hypothetical Population of Men and Women Who Either Favor or Oppose Sexual Equality

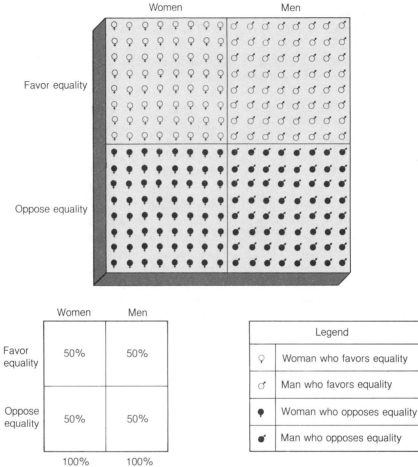

	Women	Men
Favor equality	50%	50%
Oppose equality	50%	50%
	100%	100%

Legend	
♀	Woman who favors equality
♂	Man who favors equality
♀	Woman who opposes equality
♂	Man who opposes equality

Figure 17-3, however, represents a sample that falls far short of the mark in reflecting the larger population. Notice it has selected far too many supportive women and too many opposing men. As the table shows, three-fourths of the women in the sample support equality, while only one-fourth of the men do so. If we had selected this sample from a population in which the two variables were unrelated to each other, we'd be sorely misled by the analysis of our sample.

As you'll recall, it's unlikely that a properly drawn probability sample would ever be as inaccurate as the one shown in Figure 17-3. In fact, if we actually selected a sample that gave us the results this one does, we'd look for a different explanation. Figure 17-4 illustrates that other explanation.

Notice that the sample selected in Figure 17-4 also shows a strong relationship between gender and equality. The reason is quite different this time. We've selected a perfectly representative sample, but we see that there is actually a strong relationship between the two variables in the population at large. In this latest figure, women are more likely to support equality than men: that's the case in the population, and the sample reflects it.

Figure 17-2 A Representative Sample

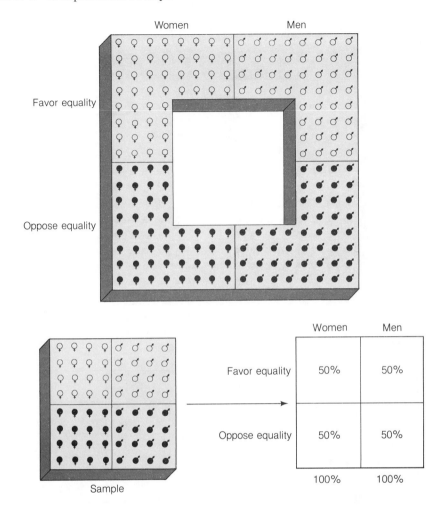

Sample

In practice, of course, we never know what's so for the total population; that's why we select samples. So if we selected a sample and found the strong relationship presented in Figures 17-3 and 17-4, we would need to decide whether that finding accurately reflected the population or was simply a product of sampling error.

The fundamental logic of tests of statistical significance, then, is this: faced with *any* discrepancy between the assumed independence of variables in a population and the observed distribution of sample elements, we may explain that discrepancy in either of two ways: (1) we may attribute it to an unrepresentative sample; or (2) we may reject the assumption of independence. The logic and statistics associated with probability sampling methods offer guidance about the varying probabilities of varying degrees of unrepresentativeness (expressed as sampling error). Most simply put, there is a *high* probability of a *small* degree of unrepresentativeness and a *low* probability of a *large* degree of unrepresentativeness.

The *statistical significance* of a relationship that is observed in a set of sample data

Figure 17-3   An Unrepresentative Sample

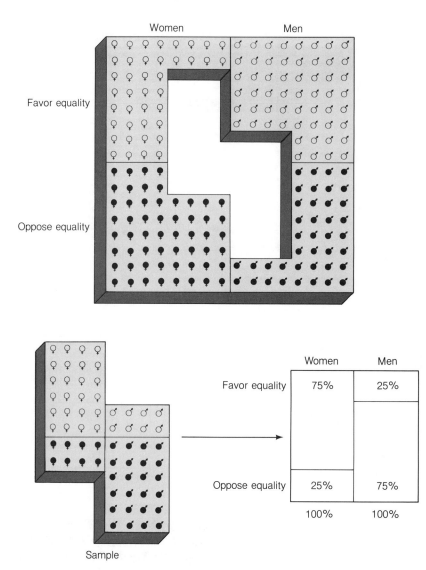

Sample

then, is always expressed in terms of probabilities. Significant at the .05 level ($p \leq$ .05) simply means that the probability of a relationship as strong as the observed one being attributable to sampling error alone is no more than 5 in 100. Put somewhat differently, *if* two variables are independent of one another in the population, and if 100 probability samples were selected from that population, no more than 5 of those samples should provide a relationship as strong as the one that has been observed.

There is, then, a corollary to confidence intervals in tests of significance, which represent the probability of the measured associations being due *only* to *sampling* error. This is called the **level of significance.** Like confidence intervals, levels of significance

Figure 17-4 A Representative Sample from a Population in Which the Variables Are Related

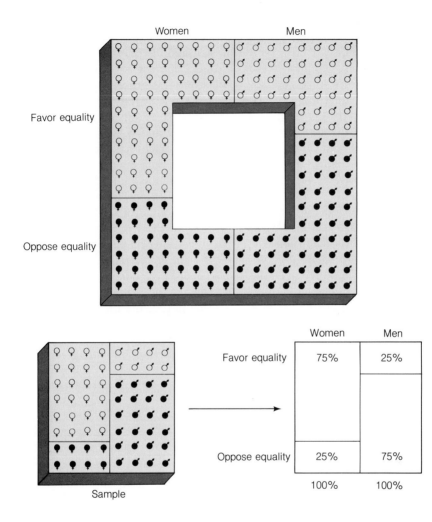

are derived from a logical model in which several samples are drawn from a given population. In the present case, we assume that there is no association between the variables in the population, and then ask what proportion of the samples drawn from that population would produce associations at least as great as those measured in the empirical data. Three levels of significance

are frequently used in research reports: .05, .01, and .001. These mean, respectively, that the chances of obtaining the measured association as a result of sampling error are 5/100, 1/100, and 1/1,000.

Researchers who use tests of significance normally follow one of two patterns. Some specify in advance the level of significance they will regard as sufficient. If any measured association is statistically significant at that level, they will regard it as representing a genuine association between the two variables. In other words, they are willing to discount the possibility of its resulting from sampling error only.

Other researchers prefer to report the specific level of significance for each association, disregarding the conventions of .05, .01, and .001. Rather than reporting that a given association is significant at the .05 level, they might report significance at the .023 level, indicating the chances of its having resulted from sampling error as 23 out of 1,000.

Chi square (χ^2) is a frequently used test of significance in social science. It is based on the **null hypothesis**: the assumption that there is no relationship between the two variables in the total population. Given the observed distribution of values on the two separate variables, we compute the conjoint distribution that would be expected if there were no relationship between the two variables. The result of this operation is a set

of *expected frequencies* for all the cells in the contingency table. We then compare this expected distribution with the distribution of cases actually found in the sample data, and we determine the probability that the discovered discrepancy could have resulted from sampling error alone. An example will illustrate this procedure.

Let's assume that we are interested in the possible relationship between church attendance and gender of the members of a particular church. To test this relationship, we select a sample of 100 church members at random. We find our sample is made up of 40 men and 60 women, and that 70 percent of our sample report having attended church during the preceding week, while the remaining 30 percent say they did not.

If there is no relationship between sex and church attendance, then 70 percent of the men in the sample should have attended church during the preceding week and 30 percent should have stayed away. Moreover, women should have attended in the same proportion. Table 17-6 (Part I) shows

Table 17-6   A Hypothetical Illustration of Chi Square

I.	Expected cell frequencies	Men	Women	Total
	Attended church	28	42	70
	Did not attend church	12	18	30
	Total	40	60	100

II.	Observed cell frequencies	Men	Women	Total
	Attended church	20	50	70
	Did not attend church	20	10	30
	Total	40	60	100

III.	(Observed − expected)^2 ÷ expected	Men	Women	
	Attended church	2.29	1.52	$x^2 = 12.70$
	Did not attend church	5.33	3.56	$p < .001$

that, based on this model, 28 men and 42 women would have attended church, with 12 men and 18 women not attending.

Part II of Table 17-6 presents the observed attendance for the hypothetical sample of 100 church members. Note that 20 of the men report having attended church during the preceding week, while the remaining 20 say they did not. Among the women in the sample, 50 attended church and 10 did not. Comparing the expected and observed frequencies (Parts I and II), we note that somewhat fewer men attended church than expected, while somewhat more women than expected attended.

Chi square is computed as follows. For each cell in the tables, the researcher (1) subtracts the expected frequency for that cell from the observed frequency, (2) squares this quantity, and (3) divides the squared difference by the expected frequency. This procedure is carried out for each cell in the tables, and the several results are added together. (Part III of Table 17-6 presents the cell-by-cell computations.) The final sum is the value of chi square: 12.70 in the example.

This value is the overall discrepancy between the observed conjoint distribution in the sample and the distribution that we should have expected if the two variables were unrelated to one another. Of course, the mere discovery of a discrepancy does not prove that the two variables are related, since normal sampling error might produce discrepancies even when there was no relationship in the total population. The magnitude of the value of chi square, however, permits us to estimate the probability of that having happened.

To determine the statistical significance of the observed relationship, we must use a standard set of chi square values. That will require the computation of the *degrees of freedom*. For chi square, the degrees of freedom are computed as follows: the number of rows in the table of observed frequencies, minus one, is multiplied by the number of columns, minus one. This may be written as $(r - 1)(c - 1)$. In the present example, we have two rows and two columns (discounting the *totals,* so there is one degree of freedom.

Turning to a table of chi square values (see Appendix E), we find that for one degree of freedom and random sampling from a population in which there is no relationship between two variables, 10 percent of the time we should expect a chi square of at least 2.7. Thus, if we selected 100 samples from such a population, we should expect about 10 of those samples to produce chi squares equal to or greater than 2.7. Moreover, we should expect chi square values of at least 6.6 in only 1 percent of the samples, and chi square values of 7.9 in only .5 percent of the samples. The higher the chi square value, the less probable it is that the value could be attributed to sampling error alone.

In our example, the computed value of chi square is 12.70. If there were no relationship between sex and church attendance in the church member population, and a large number of samples had been selected and studied, then we would expect a chi square of this magnitude in fewer than .1 percent of those samples. Thus, the probability of obtaining a chi square of this magnitude is less than .001, if random sampling has been used and there is no relationship in the population. We report this finding by saying the relationship is statistically significant at the .001 level. Since it is so improbable that the observed relationship could have resulted from sampling error alone, we are likely to reject the null hypothesis and assume that there is a relationship between the two variables in the population of church members.

Most measures of association can be tested for statistical significance in a similar manner. Standard tables of values permit us to determine whether a given association is statistically significant and at what level. Any standard statistics textbook provides instructions on the use of such tables, and we shall not pursue the matter further here.

Tests of significance provide an objective yardstick against which to estimate the significance of associations between variables. They assist us in ruling out associations that may not represent genuine relationships in the population under study. The researcher who uses or reads reports of significance tests should remain wary of several dangers in their interpretation, however.

First, we have been discussing tests of *statistical* significance; there are no objective tests of substantive significance. Thus, we may be legitimately convinced that a given association is not due to sampling error, but we may be in the position of asserting without fear of contradiction that two variables are only slightly related to one another. Recall that sampling error is an inverse function of sample size; the larger the sample, the smaller the expected error. Thus, a correlation of, say, .1 might very well be significant (at a given level) if discovered in a large sample, whereas the same correlation between the same two variables would not be significant if found in a smaller sample. Of course that makes perfectly good sense if one understands the basic logic of tests of significance: in the larger sample, there is less chance that the correlation could be simply the product of sampling error. In both samples, however, it might represent a very weak and essentially zero correlation.

Second, tests of significance are based on the same sampling assumptions we used in the computation of confidence intervals. To the extent that these assumptions are not met by the actual sampling design, the tests of significance are not strictly legitimate.

Third, you should be wary of applying tests of significance to data that represent a total population rather than a sample. If, for example, you study *all* the newspapers in the country and discover a correlation of .3 between two variables, you should not report that the association is significant at the .001 level. Since you did not sample, there is *no* chance that the association could be due to sampling error. The association between the two variables as measured in the population is *precisely* a correlation of .3. Whether that degree of association is a *substantively significant* one, whether it is important, cannot be answered through any objective test. Some researchers feel a test of significance in such a case can indicate the probability that the relationship is a general one over time—that it describes newspapers over time and not just at the time of the study.

As is the case for most matters covered in this book, I have a personal prejudice. In this instance, it is against tests of significance. My objection is not the statistical logic of those tests, since the logic is sound. Rather, I am concerned that such tests seem to mislead more than they enlighten. My principal reservations are the following:

1. Tests of significance make sampling assumptions that are virtually never satisfied by actual sampling designs.

2. They depend on the absence of nonsampling errors, a questionable assumption in most actual empirical measurements.

3. In practice, they are too often applied to measures of association that have been computed in violation of the assumptions made by those measures (for example, product-moment correlations computed from ordinal data).

4. Statistical significance is too easily misinterpreted as "strength of association," or substantive significance.

At the same time—perhaps paradoxically—I feel that tests of significance can be a valuable asset to the researcher—useful tools for the understanding of data. Although the above comments suggest an extremely conservative approach to tests of significance—that you should use them only when all assumptions are met—my general perspective is just the reverse. I encourage you to use any statistical technique—any measure of association or any test of significance—on any set of data if it will help you understand your data. If the computation of product-moment correlations among nominal variables and the testing of statistical significance in the context of uncontrolled sampling will meet this criterion, then I would encourage such activities. I say this in the spirit of what Hanan Selvin has referred to as data-dredging techniques. Anything goes, if it leads ultimately to the understanding of data and of the social world under study.

The price of this radical freedom, however, is the giving up of strict, statistical interpretations. You will not be able to base the ultimate importance of your finding solely on a significant correlation at the .05 level. Whatever the avenue of discovery, empirical data must ultimately be presented in a legitimate manner, and their importance must be argued logically.

MAIN POINTS

■ Descriptive statistics are used to summarize data under study. Some descriptive statistics summarize the distribution of attributes on a single variable; others summarize the associations between variables.

■ Inferential statistics are used to estimate the generalizability of findings arrived at the analysis of a sample to the larger population from which the sample has been selected. Some inferential statistics estimate the single-variable characteristics of the population; others—tests of statistical significance—estimate the relationships between variables in the population.

■ Descriptive statistics summarizing the relationships between variables are called measures of association.

■ Many measures of association are based on a proportionate reduction of error (PRE) model. This model is based on a comparison of (a) the number of errors we would make in attempting to guess the attributes of a given variable for each of the cases under study—if we knew nothing but the distribution of attributes on that variable—and (b) the number of errors we would make if we knew the joint distribution overall and were told for each case the attribute of one variable each time we were asked to guess the attribute of the other.

■ Lambda (λ) is an appropriate measure of association to be used in the analysis of two nominal variables. It also provides a clear illustration of the PRE model.

■ Gamma (γ) is an appropriate measure of association to be used in the analysis of two *ordinal* variables.

■ Pearson's product-moment correlation (r) is an appropriate measure of association to be used in the analysis of two *interval* or *ratio* variables.

■ Inferences about some characteristic of a population—such as the percentage of voters favoring Candidate A—must contain an indication of a *confidence interval* (the range within which the value is expected to be: for example, between 45 and 55 percent favor Candidate A) and an indication of the *confidence level* (the likelihood the value does fall within that range: for example, 95 percent confidence). Computations of confidence levels and intervals are based on probability theory and assume that conventional probability sampling techniques have been employed in the study.

■ Inferences about the generalizability to a population of the associations discovered between variables in a sample involve tests of statistical significance. Most simply put, these tests estimate the likelihood that an association as large as the observed one could result from normal sampling error if no such association exists between the variables in the larger population. Tests of statistical significance, then, are also based on probability theory and assume that conventional probability sampling techniques have been employed in the study.

■ Statistical significance must not be confused with *substantive* significance, the latter meaning that an observed association is strong, important, meaningful, or worth writing home to your mother about.

■ The level of significance of an observed association is reported in the form of the probability that that association could have been produced merely by sampling error. To say that an association is significant at the .05 level is to say that an association as large as the observed one could not be expected to result from sampling error more than 5 times out of 100.

■ Social researchers tend to utilize a particular set of levels of significance in connection with tests of statistical significance: .05, .01, and .001. That is merely a convention, however.

■ Tests of statistical significance, strictly speaking, make assumptions about data and methods that are almost never satisfied completely by real social research. Despite this, the tests can serve a very useful function in the analysis and interpretation of data. You should be wary of interpreting the "significance" of the test results too precisely, however.

REVIEW QUESTIONS AND EXERCISES

1. In your own words, explain the logic of *proportionate reduction of error* (PRE) measures of associations.

2. In your own words, distinguish between measures of association and tests of statistical significance.

ADDITIONAL READINGS

Freeman, Linton, *Elementary Applied Statistics* (New York: John Wiley, 1968). An excellent introductory statistics textbook. Everyone has a favorite statistics text, and this is mine. It is clear, well organized, and understandable. In addition to describing the most frequently used statistical methods in detail, Freeman provides briefer descriptions of many more that might be appropriate in special situations.

Jendrek, Margaret Platt, *Through the Maze: Statistics with Computer Applications* (Belmont, Calif.: Wadsworth). An innovative, practical introduction to social statistics. Jendrek explains the logic of various statistical techniques and then illustrates how the reader can calculate them with simple computer programs or through the use of systems such as SPSS[x].

Kish, Leslie, *Survey Sampling* (New York: John Wiley, 1965). The definitive reference for sampling statistics. In addition to discussing the logic of statistical inference, Kish provides formulas to cover just about any aspect of sampling that is likely to be encountered.

Morrison, Denton, and Henkel, Ramon (eds.), *The Significance Test Controversy: A Reader* (Chicago: Aldine-Atherton, 1970). A compilation of perspectives—pro and con—on tests of statistical significance. The question of the validity, utility, or significance of tests of statistical significance is one that reappears periodically in social science journals. Each reappearance is marked by an extended exchange between different points of view. This collection of such articles offers an excellent picture of the persistent debate.

18

Overview of Advanced Analyses

What You'll Learn in This Chapter

You are now going to get a Cook's tour of some of the many advanced analytical techniques used by social scientists. Your job is not one of learning to do such analyses but to familiarize yourself with their names, their logic, and some of their strengths and weaknesses.

INTRODUCTION

For the most part, this book has focused on rather rudimentary forms of data manipulation, such as the use of contingency tables and percentages. The elaboration model of analysis was presented in this form, as were the statistical techniques presented in the preceding chapter.

Now we move one step further and consider briefly a few more complex methods of data analysis and presentation. Each technique examined in this chapter will be presented from the logical perspective of the elaboration model. Seven methods of analysis will be discussed: regression analysis, time-series analysis, path analysis, factor analysis, smallest-space analysis, analysis of variance, and log-linear models. These seven techniques are only an arbitrary selection from among the many available to the analyst.

My intention is to *introduce* you to these techniques. You won't come away from this chapter proficient in the use of the techniques, just familiar with them when you see them in research reports. At the same time, you may find you want to learn more about how to use one or more of these advanced techniques, so I've given you some references for further study.

REGRESSION ANALYSIS

At several points in this text, I have referred to the general formula for describing the association between two variables: $Y = f(X)$. This formula is read "Y is a function of X," meaning that values of Y can be explained in terms of variations in the values of X. Stated more strongly, we might say that X causes Y, so the value of X determines the value of Y. **Regression analysis** is a method of determining the specific function relating Y to X. There are several forms of

regression analysis, depending on the complexity of the relationships being studied. Let's begin with the simplest.

Linear Regression

The regression model can be seen most clearly in the case of a perfect linear association between two variables. Figure 18-1 is a scattergram presenting in graphic form the conjoint values of X and Y as produced by a hypothetical study. It shows that for the four cases in our study, the values of X and Y are identical in each instance. The case with a value of 1 on X also has a value of 1 on Y, and so forth. The relationship between the two variables in this instance is described by the equation $Y = X$; this is called the *regression equation*. Since all four points lie on a straight line, we could superimpose that line over the points; this is the *regression line*.

The linear regression model has important descriptive uses. The regression line offers a graphic picture of the association between X and Y, and the regression equation is an efficient form for summarizing that association. The regression model has inferential value as well. To the extent that the regression equation correctly describes the *general* association between the two variables, it may be used to predict other sets of values. If, for example, we know that a new case has a value of 3.5 on X, we can predict the value of 3.5 on Y as well.

In practice, of course, studies are seldom limited to four cases, and the associations between variables are seldom as clear as the one presented in Figure 18-1.

A somewhat more realistic example is presented in Figure 18-2, representing a hypothetical relationship between population and crime rate in small- to medium-sized cities. Each dot in the scattergram is a city, and its placement reflects that city's

Figure 18-1 Simple Scattergram of Values of X and Y

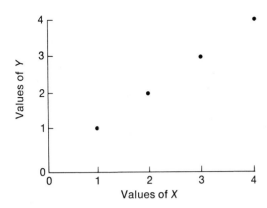

the regression equation allows us to infer values of Y when we have values of X. Recalling Figure 18-2, we could estimate crime rates of cities if we knew their populations.

Unfortunately, social life is so complex that the simple linear regression model is not sufficient to represent the state of affairs. As we saw in Chapter 15, it is possible, using percentage tables, to analyze more than two variables. As the number of variables increases, such tables become increasingly complicated and hard to read. But the regression model offers a useful alternative in such cases.

population and its crime rate. As was the case in our previous example, the values of Y (crime rates) generally correspond to those of X (populations); and as values of X increase, so do values of Y. However, the association is not nearly as clear as it was for the case in Figure 18-1.

It is not possible in Figure 18-2 to superimpose a straight line that will pass through all the points in the scattergram. But we can draw an approximate line showing the best possible linear representation of the several points. I've drawn that line on the graph.

If you've ever studied geometry, you'll know that any straight line on a graph can be represented by an equation of the form $Y = a + bX$, where X and Y are values of the two variables. In this equation, a equals the value of Y when X is 0, and b represents the slope of the line. If we know the values of a and b, we can calculate an estimate of Y for every value of X.

Regression analysis is a technique for establishing the regression equation representing the geometric line that comes closest to the distribution of points. This equation is valuable both descriptively and inferentially. First, the regression equation provides a mathematical description of the relationship between the variables. Second,

Multiple Regression

Very often, social researchers find that a given dependent variable is affected simultaneously by several independent variables. *Multiple regression* analysis provides a means to analyzing such situations. That was the case when Beverly Yerg (1981) set about studying teacher effectiveness in physical education. She stated her expectations in the form of a multiple regression equation:

$$F = b_0 + b_1I + b_2X_1 + b_3X_2 \\ + b_4X_3 + b_5X_4 + e$$

where,

F = Final pupil performance score
I = Initial pupil performance score
X_1 = Composite of guiding and supporting practice
X_2 = Composite of teacher mastery of content
X_3 = Composite of providing specific, task-related feedback
X_4 = Composite of clear, concise task presentation
b = Regression weight
e = Residual

(Adapted from Yerg 1981:42)

Figure 18-2 A Scattergram of the Values of Two Variables with Regression Line Added (Hypothetical)

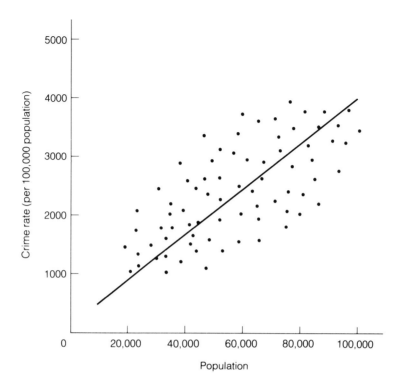

Notice that in place of the single X variable in a linear regression, there are several Xs and there are also several bs instead of just one. Also, Yerg has chosen to represent a as b_0 in this equation but with the same meaning as discussed above. Finally, the equation ends with a residual factor (e), which represents the variance in Y that is not accounted for by the X variables analyzed.

Beginning with this equation, then, Yerg calculated the values of the several bs so as to show the relative contributions of the several independent variables in determining final student performance scores. She also calculated the multiple-correlation coefficient as an indicator of the extent to which all six variables predict the final scores. This follows the same logic as the simple

bivariate correlation discussed earlier, and it is traditionally reported as a capital R. In this case, $R = .877$, meaning that 77 percent of the variance in final scores is explained by the six variables acting in concert.

Partial Regression

In explaining the elaboration model, we paid special attention to the relationship between two variables when a third test variable was held constant. Thus, we might examine the effect of education on prejudice with age held constant, testing the independent effect of education. To do so, we would compute the tabular relationship between education and prejudice separately for each age group.

Partial regressions are based on this same logical model. The equation summarizing the relationship between variables is computed on the basis of the test variables remaining constant. As in the case of the elaboration model, the result may then be compared with the uncontrolled relationship between the two variables to further clarify the overall relationship.

Curvilinear Regression

Up to now, we have been discussing the association among variables as represented by a straight line—though in more than two dimensions. The regression model is even more general than our discussion thus far implies.

If you have a knowledge of geometry, you will already know that curvilinear functions also can be represented by equations. For example, the equation $X^2 + Y^2 = 25$ describes a circle with a radius of 5. Raising variables to powers greater than 1 has the effect of producing curves rather than straight lines. And in empirical research, there is no reason to assume that the relationship among every set of variables will be linear. In some cases, then, curvilinear regression analysis can provide a better understanding of empirical relationships than can any linear model.

Recall, however, that a regression line serves two functions. It describes a set of empirical observations, and it provides a *general* model for making inferences about the relationship between two variables in the general population that the observations represent. A very complex equation might produce an erratic line that would indeed pass through every individual point. In this sense, it would perfectly describe the empirical observations. There would be no guarantee, however, that such a line could adequately predict new observations, or that

it in any meaningful way represented the relationship between the two variables in general. Thus, it would have little or no inferential value.

Earlier in this book, we discussed the need for balancing detail and utility in data reduction. Ultimately, researchers attempt to provide the most faithful, yet also the simplest, representation of their data. This practice also applies to regression analysis. Data should be presented in the simplest fashion (thus, linear regressions are most frequently used) that best describes the actual data. Curvilinear regression analysis adds a new option to the researcher in this regard, but it does not solve the problems altogether. Nothing does that.

Cautions in Regression Analysis

The use of regression analysis for statistical inferences is based on the same assumptions made for correlational analysis: simple random sampling, the absence of nonsampling errors, and continuous interval data. Since social scientific research seldom completely satisfies these assumptions, you should use caution in assessing the results in regression analyses.

Also, regression lines—linear or curvilinear—can be useful for *interpolation* (estimating cases lying between those observed) but they are less trustworthy when used for *extrapolation* (estimating cases that lie beyond the range of observations). This limitation on extrapolations is important in two ways. First, you are likely to come across regression equations that seem to make illogical predictions. An equation linking population and crimes, for example, might seem to suggest that small towns with, say, a population of 1,000 should produce -123 crimes a year. This failure in predictive ability does not disqualify the equation but dramatizes that its applicability is limited to a particular range of population sizes. Second, researchers sometimes overstep this limitation, drawing inferences that lie outside their range of observation, and you are right in criticizing them for that.

TIME-SERIES ANALYSIS

The various forms of regression analysis are often used to examine *time-series* data, representing changes in one or more variables over time. As I'm sure you know, American crime rates have generally increased over the years. A time-series analysis of crime rates could express the long-term trend in a regression format and provide a way of testing explanations for the trend—such as population growth or economic fluctuations—and could permit forecasting of future crime rates.

In a simple illustration, Figure 18-3 graphs the larceny rates of a hypothetical city over time. Each dot on the graph represents the number of larcenies reported to police during the year indicated.

Suppose we feel that larceny is largely a function of economic conditions—specifically, unemployment rates. When people are out of work, we reason, they will be more likely to steal. Recalling the discussion of regression analysis, we could create a regression equation representing the relationship between larceny and unemployment rates—using the actual figures for each variable with years being the units of analysis. Having created the best-fitting regression equation, we could then calculate a larceny rate for each year, based on that year's unemployment rate. These regression estimates are represented by the dashed regression line in Figure 18-3.

Time-series relationships are often more complex than this simple illustration suggests. Pursuing our example of larceny and unemployment, we might reason that people do not begin stealing as soon as they lose

Figure 18-3   The Larceny Rates over Time in a Hypothetical City

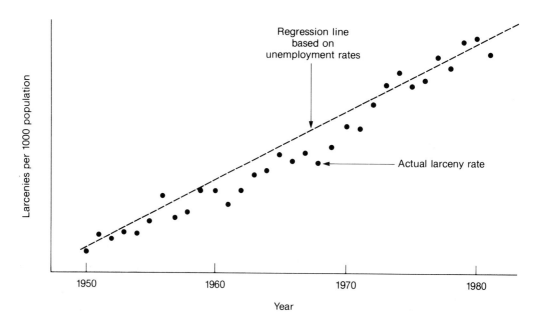

their jobs. Typically, they might first exhaust their savings, borrow from friends, and keep hoping for work. Larceny would be a last resort.

Time-lagged regression analysis could be used to address this more complex case. Thus, we might create a regression equation that predicted a given year's larceny rate based on the *previous* year's unemployment rate or perhaps on an average of the two years' unemployment rates. The possibilities are endless.

If you think about it, a great many causal relationships are likely to involve a time lag. Many of the world's poor countries survive by matching high death rates with equally high birth rates. It has been observed repeatedly, moreover, that when a society's death rate is drastically reduced—through improved medical care, public sanitation, and improved agriculture, for example— that society's birth rate drops sometime later on, but with an intervening period of rapid population growth. Or, to take a very different example, a crackdown on speeding on a state's highways is likely to reduce the average speed of cars. Again, however, the causal relationship would undoubtedly involve a time lag—days, weeks, or months, perhaps—as motorists began realizing the seriousness of the crackdown.

In all such cases, the regression equations generated might take many forms. In any event, the criterion for judging success or failure is the extent to which the researcher is able to account for the actual values observed in the dependent variable.

PATH ANALYSIS

Path analysis is a *causal* model for understanding relationships between variables. It is based on regression analysis, but it can provide a more useful graphic picture of relationships among several variables than

is possible through other means. Path analysis assumes that the values on one variable are caused by the values on another, so it is essential that independent and dependent variables be distinguished. This requirement is not unique to path analysis, of course, but path analysis provides a unique way of displaying explanatory results for interpretation.

Recall for a moment one of the ways I represented the elaboration model in Chapter 16. Here's how we might diagram the logic of interpretation:

Independent→ Intervening → Dependent
Variable   Variable   Variable

The logic of this presentation was that an independent variable had an impact on an intervening variable which, in turn, had an impact on a dependent variable. The path analyst constructs similar patterns of relationships among variables, but the typical path diagram contains many more variables than shown above.

Besides diagramming a network of relationships among variables, path analysis also shows the strengths of those several relationships. The strengths of relationships are calculated from a regression analysis that produces numbers analogous to the partial relationships in the elaboration model. These *path coefficients*, as they are called, represent the strengths of the relationships between pairs of variables with the effects of all other variables in the model held constant.

The analysis in Figure 18-4, for example, focuses on the religious causes of anti-Semitism among Christian church members. The variables in the diagram are, from left to right, (1) orthodoxy, or the extent to which the subjects accept conventional beliefs about God, Jesus, the biblical miracles, and so forth; (2) particularism, the belief that one's religion is the "only true faith"; (3) acceptance of the view that the Jews crucified

Figure 18-4   Diagramming the Religious Sources of Anti-Semitism

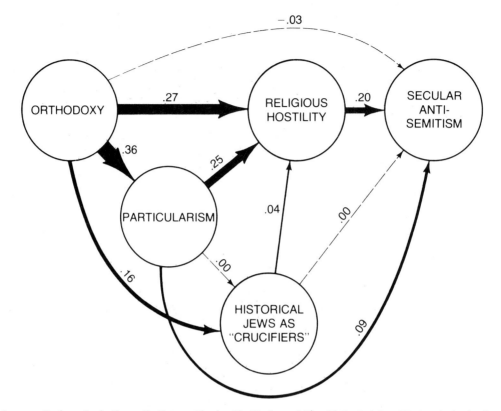

Source: Rodney Stark, Bruce D. Foster, Charles Y. Glock, and Harold E. Quinley, *Wayward Shepherds—Prejudice & the Protestant Clergy.* Copyright © 1971 by Anti-Defamation League of B'nai Brith. Reprinted by permission of Harper & Row, Publishers, Inc.

Jesus; (4) religious hostility toward contemporary Jews, such as believing that God is punishing them or that they will suffer damnation unless they convert to Christianity; and (5) secular anti-Semitism, such as believing that Jews cheat in business, are disloyal to their country, and so forth.

To start with, the researchers who conducted this analysis proposed that secular anti-Semitism was produced by moving through the five variables: orthodoxy caused particularism, which caused the view of the historical Jews as crucifiers, which caused religious hostility toward contemporary

Jews, which resulted, finally, in secular anti-Semitism.

The path diagram tells a different story. The researchers found, for example, that belief in the historical role of Jews as the crucifiers of Jesus doesn't seem to matter in the process. And, although particularism is a part of one process resulting in secular anti-Semitism, the diagram also shows that anti-Semitism is created more directly by orthodoxy and religious hostility. Orthodoxy produces religious hostility even without particularism, and religious hostility generates secular hostility in any event.

One last comment on path analysis is in order. Although it is an excellent way of handling complex causal chains and networks of variables, you must realize that path analysis itself does not tell the causal order of the variables. Nor was the path diagram generated by computer. The researcher decided the structure of relationships among the variables, and used computer analysis merely to calculate the path coefficients that apply to such a structure.

FACTOR ANALYSIS

Factor analysis is a different approach to multivariate analysis than regression analysis. Its statistical basis is complex enough and different enough from the foregoing discussions to suggest a very general discussion here.

Factor analysis is used to discover patterns among the variations in values of several variables. This is done essentially through the generation of artificial dimensions (factors) that correlate highly with several of the real variables and that are independent of one another. A computer must be used to perform this complex operation.

Let's suppose for the moment that a data file contains several indicators of subjects' prejudice. Each item should provide some indication of prejudice, but none of them will give a perfect indication. All of these items, moreover, should be highly intercorrelated empirically. In a factor analysis of the data, the researcher would create an artificial dimension that would be highly correlated with each of the items measuring prejudice. Each subject would essentially receive a value on that artificial dimension, and the value assigned would be a good predictor of the observed attributes on each item.

Suppose now that the same study provided several indicators of subjects' mathematical ability. It is likely that the factor analysis would also generate an artificial dimension highly correlated with each of those items.

The output of a factor analysis program consists of columns representing the several factors (artificial dimensions) generated from the observed relations among variables plus the correlations between each variable and each factor—called the *factor loadings*.

In the above example, it is likely that one factor would more or less represent prejudice, and another would more or less represent mathematical ability. Data items measuring prejudice would have high loadings on (correlations with) the prejudice factor and low loadings on the mathematical ability factor. Data items measuring mathematical ability would have just the opposite pattern.

In practice, however, factor analysis does not proceed in this fashion. Rather, the variables are input to the program, and a series of factors with appropriate factor loadings are the output. You must then determine the meaning of a given factor on the basis of those variables that load highly on it. The generation of factors, however, has no reference to the meaning of variables, only to their empirical associations. Two criteria are taken into account: (1) a factor must explain a relatively large portion of the variance found in the study variables; and (2) every factor must be more or less independent of every other factor. Here's an example of the use of factor analysis.

Many social researchers have studied the problem of delinquency. When you look deeply into the problem, however, you discover that there are many different types of delinquents. In a survey of high school students in a small Wyoming town, Morris

Forslund (1980) set out to create a typology of delinquency. His questionnaire asked students to report whether they had committed a variety of delinquent acts. He then submitted their responses to factor analysis. The results are shown in Table 18-1.

As you can see in Table 18-1, the various delinquent acts are listed on the left. The numbers shown in the body of the table are the factor loadings on the four factors constructed in the analysis. You'll notice that Forslund has labeled the dimensions. I've bracketed the items on each factor that led to his choice of labels. Forslund summarizes the results as follows:

> For the total sample four fairly distinct patterns of delinquent acts are apparent. In order of variance explained, they have been labeled: 1) Property Offenses, including both vandalism and theft; 2) Incorrigibility; 3) Drugs/Truancy; and 4) Fighting. It is interesting, and perhaps surprising, to find both vandalism and theft appear together in the same factor. It would seem that those high school students who engage in property offenses tend to be involved in both vandalism and theft. It is also interesting to note that drugs, alcohol and truancy fall in the same factor.
>
> (1980:4)

Having determined this overall pattern, Forslund reran the factor analysis separately for boys and for girls. Essentially the same patterns emerged in both cases.

I think this example shows that factor analysis is an efficient method of discovering predominant patterns among a large number of variables. Instead of you and the researcher being forced to compare countless correlations—simple, partial, and multiple—to discover those patterns, factor analysis can be used for this task. Incidentally, this is a good example of a helpful use of computers.

Factor analysis also presents data in a form that can be interpreted by the reader or researcher. For a given factor, the reader can easily discover the variables loading highly on it, thus noting clusters of variables. Or, the reader can easily discover which factors a given variable is or is not loaded highly on.

But factor analysis also has disadvantages. First, as noted above, factors are generated without any regard to substantive meaning. Often researchers will find factors producing very high loadings for a group of substantively disparate variables. They might find, for example, that prejudice and religiosity have high positive loadings on a given factor with education having an equally high negative loading. Surely the three variables are highly correlated, but what does the factor represent? All too often, inexperienced researchers will be led into naming such factors as "religio-prejudicial lack of education" or something similarly nonsensical.

Second, factor analysis is often criticized on basic philosophical grounds. Recall an earlier statement that to be legitimate, a hypothesis must be disconfirmable. If the researcher is unable to specify the conditions under which the hypothesis would be disproved, the hypothesis is in reality either a tautology or useless. In a sense, factor analysis suffers this defect. No matter what data are input, factor analysis produces a solution in the form of factors. Thus if the researcher were asking, "Are there any patterns among these variables?" the answer always would be yes. This fact must also be taken into account in evaluating the results of factor analysis. The generation of factors by no means ensures meaning.

My personal view of factor analysis is the same as that of other complex modes of analysis. It can be an extremely useful tool for the social science researcher. Its use should be encouraged whenever such activity may assist researchers in understanding a body of data. As in all cases, however, you must remain aware that such tools are only tools and never magical solutions.

Table 18-1 Factor Analysis: Delinquent Acts, Whites

Delinquent Act	Property Offenses Factor I	Incorrigibility Factor II	Drugs/ Truancy Factor III	Fighting Factor IV
Broke street light, etc.	.669	.126	.119	.167
Broke windows	.637	.093	.077	.215
Broke down fences, clothes lines, etc.	.621	.186	.186	.186
Taken things worth $2 to $50	.616	.187	.233	.068
Let air out of tires	.587	.243	.054	.156
Taken things worth over $50	.548	−.017	.276	.034
Thrown eggs, garbage, etc.	.526	.339	−.023	.266
Taken things worth under $2	.486	.393	.143	.077
Taken things from desks, etc., at school	.464	.232	−.002	.027
Taken car without owner's permission	.461	.172	.080	.040
Put paint on something	.451	.237	.071	.250
Disobeyed parents	.054	.642	.209	.039
Marked on desk, wall, etc.	.236	.550	−.061	.021
Said mean things to get even	.134	.537	.045	.100
Disobeyed teacher, school official	.240	.497	.223	.195
Defied parents to their face	.232	.458	.305	.058
Made anonymous telephone calls	.373	.446	.029	.135
Smoked marijuana	.054	.064	.755	−.028
Used other drugs for kicks	.137	.016	.669	.004
Signed name to school excuse	.246	.249	.395	.189
Drank alcohol, parents absent	.049	.247	.358	.175
Skipped school	.101	.252	.319	.181
Beat up someone in a fight	.309	.088	.181	.843
Fought—hit or wrestled	.242	.266	.070	.602
Percent of variance	67.2	13.4	10.9	8.4

Source: Morris A. Forslund, "Patterns of Delinquency Involvement: An Empirical Typology." Paper presented to the Annual Meeting of the Western Association of Sociologists and Anthropologists, Lethbridge, Alberta, February 8, 1980. The table above is adapted from page 10.

SMALLEST-SPACE ANALYSIS

Smallest-space analysis (SSA) is rather different from the previously discussed methods of multivariate analysis, and although it is still relatively new, it appears to hold considerable potential for the understanding of data.

Smallest-space analysis is based on the correlations among variables. Any measure of association may be used for this purpose, although we shall use Pearson's *r* in the examples to follow. Let's begin with a sim-

Table 18-2   Simple Correlation Matrix

	A	B	C
A	x	.8	.2
B		x	.5
C			x

ple correlation matrix describing the associations among the variables *A, B,* and *C* (Table 18-2).

Now let's plot these three variables as points on a plane, letting distance between two points represent the *inverse* of the correlation between the two variables. That is, if two variables are highly correlated, they will be close together; if they are weakly correlated, they will be farther apart. The following diagram would satisfy this design.

A   B   C

Since *A* and *B* are the most highly correlated variables, they have been placed relatively close together. The next highest correlation is between *B* and *C,* and the distance between these two points is the next shortest. Finally, the correlation between *A* and *C* is the weakest of the three correlations, and the distance between *A* and *C* is the longest distance in the diagram.

Now let's enlarge our correlation matrix by adding variable *D* (Table 18-3). It is still possible to plot these four points so that the distance between two points corresponds to the inverse of the correlation between the two variables. It should be noted, however, that the distances do not *equal* the inverse of the correlations. The metric distances are irrelevant; thus SSA is referred to as a *nonmetric* technique. However, the *rank order* of distances between points should be the inverse of the rank order of correlations. The diagram in Figure 18-5 satisfies the correlation matrix in Table 18-3.

To clarify the new diagram, the points have been connected by lines labeled with the correlations between the pairs of variables. In the diagram, the longest distance (*AD*) corresponds to the weakest correlation, and the shortest distance (*CD*) to the strongest correlation. The same is true for all other distances and correlations. (An understanding of plane geometry will help to explain how the diagram was constructed.)

You have probably already realized that some correlation matrices could not be represented in accordance with the rules laid down. That is especially true as more and more variables are added. Given such a situation, SSA permits you to move in two different directions.

First, SSA is not limited to two dimensions (although this textbook essentially is). Like multiple regression, SSA can employ an unlimited number of geometric dimensions. As a general guideline, *n* variables can be plotted perfectly in SSA format within *n* − 1 dimensions. Thus, any two variables can be plotted on a line, any three can be plotted on a plane, any four can be plotted in three dimensions, and so forth. As we have seen in other contexts, however, such liberties can lead into uninterpretable situations.

The second solution to this problem lies in the familiar area of compromise. Perhaps you cannot plot six variables perfectly within two dimensions (a graphic presentation that would be easily read), but you may be able

Table 18-3   Correlation Matrix with Four Variables

	A	B	C	D
A	x	.8	.2	.1
B		x	.5	.3
C			x	.9
D				x

Figure 18-5 Smallest-Space Analysis: Four Variables

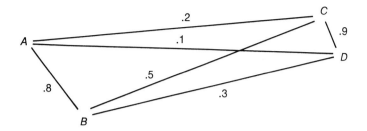

to come close. Thus, it may be possible to plot the points to *more or less* satisfy the correspondence of rankings between correlations and distances.

At this point, and with the addition of many variables generally, hand tabulations and hand-drawn diagrams become too difficult. But the computer handles this sort of task easily. Computer programs now exist to generate SSA diagrams from an input in the form of a correlation matrix. You must specify the number of dimensions desired in your solution, and the computer works on that basis. In addition to the diagram, moreover, the computer provides a summary statistic called the **coefficient of alienation**. Although the statistic has no common-sensible interpretation, it represents the extent to which the SSA diagram violates the rules of correspondence between distances and correlations. The lower the coefficient, the better the fit of the diagram to the rules.

The computer output from an SSA program will look something like the configuration in Figure 18-6. Since each letter in this diagram represents a study variable, the diagram would be interpreted in terms of the observed clustering of variables. For example, we note that variables *J, K, L,* and *M* are closely clustered, and *A-B-C-D* forms another cluster, with both of these clusters being rather distant from the cluster *N-O-P-Q.*

SSA is quite similar to factor analysis, and it is sometimes referred to as *nonmetric factor analysis.*

ANALYSIS OF VARIANCE

Analysis of variance, abbreviated ANOVA, applies the logic of statistical significance discussed in Chapter 17. Fundamentally, the cases under study are combined into groups representing an independent variable, and we analyze the extent to which the groups differ from one another in terms of some dependent variable. The extent to which the groups do differ is compared with the standard of random distribution: could we expect to obtain such differences if we had assigned cases to the various groups through random selection?

Noting that ANOVA was first developed for use in agriculture and biology, E. M. Uslaner suggests the following uses among social scientists:

Political analysts, who can postulate a fixed set of groups, such as political parties, and determine the degree to which members differ in their behavior. . . .

Communications researchers, who can experimentally assess the impact of communication within a research setting optimally exploiting

Figure 18-6   Sample Smallest-Space Analysis Results (Hypothetical)

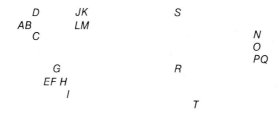

the potential of analysis of variance for causal inference.

Economists who can contrast rates of economic growth by classifying countries into general systems and employing data sets on growth rates.

Public policy analysts, who can evaluate programs by employing analysis of variance to assess the effect of a particular program by comparing it either to alternative programs or to the "policy" of no program at all.

Researchers in psychology or education, who might be concerned with the effects of education and race on standard intelligence or achievement tests. In such cases, test scores would serve as the variable to be predicted, grouping race and level of education to test for differences within and between the subgroups of the sample. . . .
(1976:6)

Let's look briefly now at two common forms of ANOVA: *one-way* and *two-way* analysis of variance.

One-Way Analysis of Variance

Let's suppose we want to compare income levels of Republicans and Democrats to see if Republicans are really richer. So we select a sample of individuals for our study. Then, using a questionnaire, we ask them which political party they feel most aligned with, and we also ask them to tell us their total income for last year. We calculate the mean

or median incomes for each group, finding that the Republicans in our sample have a mean income of $21,000, compared to $19,000 for the Democrats. Clearly, our Republicans are richer than our Democrats, but is the difference "significant?" Would we have been likely to get a $2,000 difference if we had created two groups by way of random selection?

ANOVA answers this question through the use of *variance*. Most simply put, the variance of a distribution—of incomes, for example—is a measurement of the extent to which the set of values are clustered close to the mean or range very high and low away from it.

Figure 18-7 illustrates these two possibilities. Notice that in both distributions Republicans have a mean income of $21,000 and Democrats $19,000. In Part A, most of the actual incomes of Republicans are relatively close to the mean of $21,000, and most Democrats have incomes close to their party's mean of $19,000. Part B, however, presents quite a different picture. Although the group means are the same as in Part A, both Republicans and Democrats have incomes ranging from very high to very low with considerable overlap in the parties' distributions. In technical terms, there is a higher degree of variance in Part B than in Part A.

Impressionistically, we would conclude that Part A of Figure 18-7 indicates a genuine difference in the incomes of Republicans and Democrats. With data like those

Figure 18-7 Two Distribution Patterns of the Incomes of Republicans and Democrats

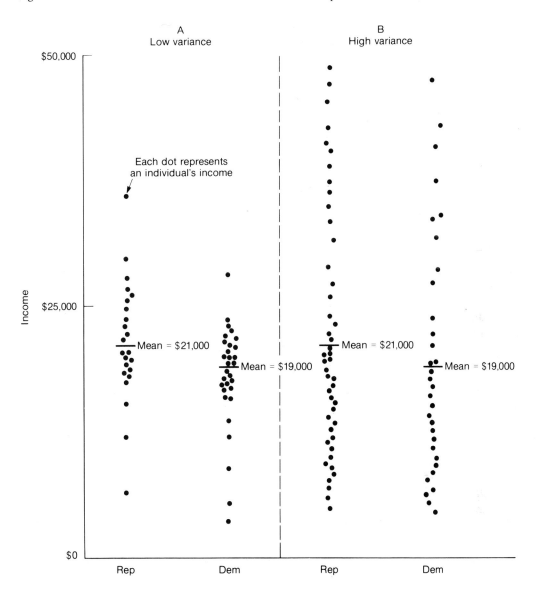

presented in Part B, we wouldn't be so sure. There seems more likelihood that the normal variations produced by random sampling error could have produced means of $21,000 and $19,000.

In an actual ANOVA, statistical calculations rather than impressions are used to make this decision. The observed difference

in means is expressed as standardized multiples and fractions of the observed variance. Since the variance in Part A of Figure 18-7 is smaller than in Part B, $2,000 would represent a larger difference in Part A than in Part B. The resulting difference of means—standardized by the variance—would then be checked against a standard statistical table showing the theoretical distribution of such values, as in the earlier discussion of statistical significance. Ultimately, we would conclude the difference was significant at some level of significance. We might discover, for example, that sampling error would produce a difference as large as the one we observed only one time in a thousand. Thus, we'd say the difference was "significant at the 99.9 percent level."

In the above example, I have glossed over the actual calculations in favor of the basic logic of the procedure. In practice, such calculations are now typically done by computer programs such as SPSS.

This simplest case is often referred to as a "*t*-test" for the difference between two means. With more than two groups, the calculations become more complex, since there are more comparisons to be made. Basically, it's necessary to compare the group means with one another and examine the variation among the values in each group. The end result of the analysis, as discussed in the simplest case, is expressed in terms of statistical significance—the likelihood of the observed differences resulting from sampling error in random selection.

Two-Way Analysis of Variance

One-way ANOVA represents a form of bivariate analysis: political party and income in the example. As we've seen earlier, however, social scientists often engage in multivariate analysis. Two-way ANOVA permits the simultaneous examination of more than two variables. Suppose, for example, that we suspect that the income differences between Republicans and Democrats are a function of education: Republicans are better educated than Democrats, and educated people—regardless of party—earn more, on the average, than those with less education. A two-way ANOVA would sort out the

effects of the two explanatory variables, in a manner similar to that of elaboration and of partial correlations and regressions, discussed earlier.

LOG-LINEAR MODELS

Suppose we want to know whether political orientation is related to party affiliation: are liberals, for example, more likely than conservatives to be Democrats? By dividing our sample into two groups—liberal and conservative—we can calculate the percentage of Democrats in each group. If we find a higher percentage among the liberals, we conclude that political orientation and party affiliation are indeed related.

In this example, and in the tabular analyses of Chapters 14 and 16, all the dependent variables analyzed were dichotomous: comprised of two attributes. When the dependent variable is not dichotomous, however, matters become more complex. Let's suppose that besides some Democrats and some Republicans, our sample includes Independents, Socialists, and Libertarians. It no longer makes sense to examine the percentage of liberals and conservatives who are Democrats, any more than it does to look only at the percentages affiliated with any one of the other groups. Looking at each group independently would result in more tables than you could easily interpret.

The complexity of this situation is increased if the explanatory variable is not dichotomous. Suppose we add "moderates" to the liberals and conservatives. Or suppose we examine the interactive effects of other explanatory variables such as race and religion on the political equation. As you can imagine, the resulting percentage tables would become impossibly complicated.

Log-linear models present a potential solution to this complexity. Involving rather elaborate logarithmic calculations, this technique is based on specifying models that describe the interrelations among variables and then comparing expected and observed table-cell frequencies. (The logic here is similar to that for *chi square*, described in Chapter 17.) H. T. Reynolds describes the process:

At the outset of log-linear analysis, as in most statistical procedures, the investigator proposes a model that he feels might fit the data. The model is a tentative statement about how a set of variables are interrelated. After choosing the model, he next estimates the frequencies expected in a sample of the given size *if the model were true*. He then compares these estimates, F̂, with the observed values.

(1977: 76–77)

In specifying the models to be tested in a log-linear analysis, the researcher will consider direct relationships between the dependent variable and each of the independent variables, relationships between pairs of independent variables, and three-variable (and more, depending on the total number of variables) relationships similar to those already discussed in the elaboration model (Chapter 16). Let's consider a three-variable case taken from the above example.

We might suspect that a person's political party affiliation ("party") is a function of political orientation ("philosophy") and race. The components of this model, then, include (1) the direct effect of philosophy on party, (2) the direct effect of race on party, (3) the effect of race on philosophy, (4) the effect of race on the relationship between philosophy and party (as in the elaboration model), and (5) the effect of philosophy on the relationship between race and party. While each of these components will have *some* explanatory power, log-linear analysis provides a means of identifying which are the most important and which can, as a practical matter, be ignored.

Although the calculations involved in log-linear analysis are many and complex, computer programs can perform them all handily.

Log-linear analysis seems to be growing in popularity in the social sciences, though it is still not used as much as some of the other methods discussed in this chapter. It is a relatively new technique and not many social scientists have been trained in its use.

There are two main shortcomings in this technique. First, its logic makes certain mathematical assumptions that may not be satisfied by a particular set of data, though this issue is far too complex to be pursued here. Second, as with other summary techniques we've discussed, the results of log-linear analysis do not permit the immediate, intuitive grasp possible in simple comparisons of percentages or means. So log-linear methods would not be appropriate—even if statistically justified—in cases where the analysis can be managed through simple percentage tables. It is best reserved for complex situations in which tabular analyses are not powerful enough.

This, then, completes our discussion of some of the analytical techniques commonly used by social scientists. I have only brushed the surface of each, and there are many other techniques I haven't touched on at all. My purpose has been to give you a preview of some of the techniques you may want to study in more depth later on and to familiarize you with them in the event you run across them in reading the research reports of others.

MAIN POINTS

■ Regression analysis represents the relationships between variables in the form of equations, which can be used to predict the values of a dependent variable on the basis of values of one or more independent variables.

- The basic regression equation—for a simple linear regression—is of the form $Y = a + bX$. Y in this case is the value (estimated) of the dependent variable; a is some constant value; b is another numerical value, which is multiplied by X, the value of the independent variable.

- Regression equations are computed on the basis of a *regression line:* that geometric line that represents, with the least amount of discrepancy, the actual location of points in a scattergram.

- A multiple regression analysis results in a regression equation, which estimates the values of a dependent variable from the values of several independent variables.

- A partial regression analysis examines the effects of several independent variables, but with each independent variable's effect expressed separately while the effects of all others are held constant.

- A curvilinear regression analysis permits the "best-fitting" regression line to be something other than a straight line. The curvature of the regression line is achieved by permitting the values of the independent variables to be raised to powers greater than 1; for example, squared, cubed, and so forth.

- Time-series analysis involves the study of processes occurring over time, such as population growth, crime rates, etc.

- Path analysis is a method of presenting graphically the networks of causal relationships among several variables. It illustrates graphically the primary "paths" of variables through which independent variables cause dependent ones.

- Path coefficients are standardized regression coefficients representing the partial relationships between variables.

- Factor analysis, feasible only by computer, is an analytical method of discovering the general dimensions represented by a collection of actual variables. These gen-

eral dimensions, or *factors*, are calculated hypothetical dimensions that are not perfectly represented by any of the empirical variables under study, but that are highly associated with groups of empirical variables.

- A factor loading indicates the degree of association between a given empirical variable and a given factor.

- Smallest-space analysis (SSA) is a nonmetric method of graphically displaying the associations between a large number of variables.

- Variables in SSA are presented by points, and the associations between variables are represented by the distances between points, with short distances representing high associations and long distances representing low associations.

- The primary rule in SSA is that the rank order of the distances between points should be the inverse of the rank order of the associations between the variables those points represent.

- The coefficient of alienation is a measure of the extent to which an actual SSA display fails to follow the rank-order rule exactly.

- The "best" analysis of data would be one that employed several different analytical modes and resulted in the same set of conclusions from each mode.

- Analysis of variance (ANOVA) is based on comparing variations between and within groups.

- Log-linear models offer a method for analyzing complex relationships among several nominal variables having more than two attributes each.

REVIEW QUESTIONS AND EXERCISES

1. In your own words, explain partial regression analysis in terms of the logic of elaboration analysis.

2. Pick any one of the analytical techniques discussed in this chapter and describe a research situation for which that technique would be particularly appropriate.

ADDITIONAL READINGS

Borgatta, Edgar (ed.), *Sociological Methodology* (San Francisco: Jossey-Bass, 1969), especially Chapters 1 and 2. Good discussions of the logic and techniques of path analysis. The chapters by Kenneth Land and David Heise examine a variety of aspects of path analysis and its potential contribution to social research, especially in regard to the discovery of causal relationships. These are both more advanced than would be desired in an introductory presentation, but good introductions to path analysis are hard to find.

Ezekiel, Mordecai, and Fox, Karl, *Methods of Correlation and Regression Analysis: Linear and Curvilinear* (New York: John Wiley, 1959). A rather comprehensive presentation of correlation and regression methods. This book begins with a very simple introduction to the subject and then moves progressively to more complex aspects. In addition to describing a wide variety of statistical computations, the authors are sensitive to the practical con-

siderations that apply to the use of correlation and regression in social research.

Harmon, Harry, *Modern Factor Analysis* (Chicago: University of Chicago Press, 1967). A rather comprehensive presentation of factor analytic methods. Harmon discusses both the logic and the specific computational techniques associated with this method of social scientific analysis.

Iversen, Gudmund, and Norpoth, Helmut, *Analysis of Variance* (Beverly Hills: Sage Publications, 1976). An excellent introduction to ANOVA. The authors begin with the simplest comparison of means and proceed to illustrate increasingly complex cases.

Katz, Elihu; Gurevitch, Michael; and Haas, Hadassah, "On the Use of the Mass Media for Important Things," *American Sociological Review,* Vol. 38 (April 1973), pp. 164–81. A more complex illustration of SSA. In addition to evaluating the relative roles played by the different mass media in Israel, the authors present their data in several analytical formats, further clarifying the interpretation of SSA.

Ostrom, Charles W., Jr., *Time-Series Analysis: Regression Techniques* (Beverly Hills: Sage Publications, 1978). An excellent introduction to regression-based time-series analyses. Ostrom discusses both lagged and nonlagged analyses.

PART 5

The Social Context of Research

19 The Ethics and Politics of Social Research

I have concluded this book with an examination of a rather different aspect of social research, yet one that is vital to your successful and worthwhile inquiries.

In the preceding chapters, we have seen that there are certain scientific goals and principles to be satisfied in research design and execution and certain practical, administrative constraints that require well-thought-out compromises. In Chapter 19, we'll see that ethical and political considerations also require compromises on what might otherwise seem perfect "scientific" practices.

19

The Ethics and Politics of Social Research

What You'll Learn in This Chapter

In this final chapter, you'll see something of the social context within which social research is conducted. As you'll see, ethical and political considerations must be taken into account alongside scientific ones in the design and execution of research.

INTRODUCTION

We have now just about completed our exploration of social scientific research methods. My purpose in this book has been to give you a realistic and useful introduction to doing social research. For the introduction to be fully realistic, we need to recognize that there are four main constraints on research projects: scientific, administrative, ethical, and political.

The preceding eighteen chapters have focused on scientific and administrative constraints. We've seen that the logic of science suggests certain research procedures, but we've also seen that some scientifically appropriate designs wouldn't be administratively feasible: some "perfect" study designs would be too expensive or take too long to execute. Throughout the book, therefore, we've dealt with workable compromises.

But what of the two other important considerations in doing research in the real world: *ethics* and *politics*? Since they are somewhat subtler and less obvious, I want to devote this chapter to them. Just as you wouldn't use certain procedures because they are impractical, so there are procedures you couldn't use, either because of ethical considerations or because they are politically difficult or impossible. Here's a story to show you what I mean.

Several years ago, I was invited to sit in on a planning session to design a study of legal education in California. The joint project was to be conducted by a university research center and the state bar association. The purpose of the project was to improve legal education by learning which aspects of the law school experience were related to success on the bar exam. Essentially, the plan was to prepare a questionnaire that would get detailed information about the law school experiences of individuals. People would be required to answer the questionnaire when they took the bar

exam. By analyzing how people with different kinds of law school experiences did on the bar exam, it would be possible to find out what sorts of things worked and what didn't. The findings of the research could be made available to law schools, and ultimately legal education could be improved.

The exciting thing about collaborating with the bar association was that all the normally aggravating logistical hassles would be handled. There would be no problem getting permission to administer questionnaires in conjunction with the exam, for example, and the problem of *nonresponse* could be eliminated altogether.

I left the meeting excited about the prospects for the study. When I told a colleague about it, I glowed about the absolute handling of the nonresponse problem. Her immediate comment turned everything around completely. "That's unethical. There's no law requiring the questionnaire, and participation in research has to be voluntary." The study wasn't done.

In retelling this story, it is obvious to me that requiring participation would have been inappropriate. You may have seen that before I told you about my colleague's comment. I still feel a little embarrassed over the matter. Yet, I have a specific purpose in telling this story about myself.

All of us consider ourselves ethical; not perfect perhaps, but more ethical than most of humanity. The problem in social research—and probably in life—is that ethical considerations are not always apparent to us. As a result, we often plunge into things without seeing ethical issues that may be apparent to others and may even be obvious for us when they are pointed out. When I reported back to the others in the planning group, for example, no one disagreed with the inappropriateness of requiring participation. Everyone was a bit embarrassed about not having seen it.

Any of us can immediately see that a study that requires the torturing of small children is unethical. I know you'd speak out immediately if I suggested we interview people about their sex lives and then publish what they said in the local newspaper. But, as ethical as you are, you'd totally miss the ethical issue in some other situations—not because you're bad, but because we all do that.

The first half of this chapter, then, deals with the ethics of social research. In part, I'll present some of the broadly agreed-on norms describing what's ethical and what's not. More importantly, however, my purpose is to *sensitize* you to the ethical component in research so that you'll look for it whenever you plan a study. Even when the ethical aspects of a situation are arguable, you should know there's something to argue about.

Political considerations in research are also subtle, ambiguous, and arguable. Notice that the law school example involves politics as well as ethics. Although social scientists have an ethical norm that participation in research should be voluntary, that norm clearly grows out of our political norms protecting civil liberties. In other nations, the proposed study would not have been considered unethical at all.

In the second half of this chapter, we'll look at some cases of social research projects that were crushed or nearly crushed by political considerations. As with ethical concerns, there is often no "correct" answer to the situation. People of goodwill disagree. Again, however, my purpose is to assist you in becoming more sensitive to the political considerations involved without giving you a party line of what's politically acceptable or unacceptable.

ETHICAL ISSUES IN SOCIAL RESEARCH

In most dictionaries and in common usage, ethics is typically associated with morality,

and both deal with matters of right and wrong. But what *is* right and what wrong? What is the source of the distinction? For individuals the sources vary. They may be religions, political ideologies, or the pragmatic observation of what seems to work and what doesn't.

Webster's New World Dictionary is typical among dictionaries in defining ethical as "conforming to the standards of conduct of a given profession or group." Although the idea may frustrate those in search of moral absolutes, what we regard as morality and ethics in day-to-day life is a matter of agreement among members of a group. And, not surprisingly, different groups have agreed on different codes of conduct. If you are going to live in a particular society, then, it is extremely useful for you to know what that society considers ethical and unethical. The same holds true for the social research "community."

If you are going to do social scientific research, you should be aware of the general agreements shared by researchers as to what's proper and improper in the conduct of scientific inquiry. The section that follows summarizes some of the more important ethical agreements that prevail in social research.

Voluntary Participation

Social research often, though not always, represents an intrusion into people's lives. The interviewer's knock on the door or the arrival of a questionnaire in the mail signals the beginning of an activity that the respondent has not requested and one that may require a significant portion of his or her time and energy. Participation in a social experiment disrupts the subject's regular activities.

Social research, moreover, often requires that people reveal personal information about themselves—information that may be unknown to their friends and associates. And social research often requires that such information be revealed to strangers. Other professionals, such as physicians and lawyers, also require such information. Their requests may be justified, however, because the information is required for them to serve the personal interests of the respondent. The social researcher can seldom make this claim. Like medical scientists, we can only argue that the research effort may ultimately help all humanity.

A major tenet of medical research ethics is that experimental participation must be *voluntary*. (Interestingly, the indictment of Nazi medical experimentation was based not so much on its cruelty—such research is often unavoidably cruel—but on the fact that prisoners were forced to participate.) The same norm applies to social research. No one should be forced to participate. This norm is far easier to accept in theory than to apply in practice, however.

Again, medical research provides a useful parallel. Many experimental drugs are tested on prisoners. In the most rigorously ethical cases, the prisoners are told the nature—and the possible dangers—of the experiment, they are told that participation is completely voluntary, and they are further instructed that they can expect no special rewards—such as early parole—for participation. Even under these conditions, it is often clear that volunteers are motivated by the belief that they will personally benefit from their cooperation.

When the instructor in an introductory sociology class asks students to fill out a questionnaire that he or she hopes to analyze and publish, students should always be told that their participation in the survey is completely voluntary. Even so, most students will fear that nonparticipation will somehow affect their grade. So the instructor should be especially sensitive to the implied sanctions and make special provisions to obviate them. For example, the instructor could leave the room while the questionnaires are being completed. Or, students could be asked to return the questionnaires by mail or to drop them in a box near the door just before the next course meeting.

You should be clear that this norm of voluntary participation goes directly against a number of scientific concerns. In the most general terms, the scientific goal of *generalizability* is threatened if experimental subjects or survey respondents are all the kinds of people who willingly participate in such things. This orientation probably reflects more general personality traits; possibly, then, the results of the research will not be generalizable to all kinds of people. Most clearly, in the case of a descriptive survey, a researcher cannot generalize the sample survey findings to an entire population unless a substantial majority of the scientifically selected sample actually participates—the willing respondents and the somewhat unwilling.

As you may recall from Chapter 10, field research has its own ethical dilemmas in this regard. Very often, the researcher cannot even reveal that a study is being done, for fear that that revelation might significantly affect the social processes being studied. Clearly, the subjects of study in such cases are not given the opportunity to volunteer or refuse to participate.

You should realize that the norm of voluntary participation is an important one, and you should also know that it is often impossible to follow it. In cases where you feel ultimately justified in violating it, it is all the more important that you observe the other ethical norms of scientific research, such as bringing no harm to the people under study.

No Harm to the Participants

Social research should never injure the people being studied, regardless of whether they volunteer for the study. Perhaps the clearest instance of this norm in practice concerns the revealing of information that would embarrass them or endanger their home life, friendships, jobs, and so forth. This norm is discussed more fully in the next section.

It is possible for subjects to be harmed psychologically in the course of a study, however, and the researcher must be aware of the often subtle dangers and guard against them. Very often, research subjects are asked to reveal deviant behavior, attitudes they feel are unpopular, or demeaning personal characteristics such as low income, the receipt of welfare payments, and the like. Revealing such information is very likely to make them feel at least uncomfortable.

Social research projects may also force participants to face aspects of themselves that they do not normally consider. That can happen even when the information is not revealed directly to the researcher. In retrospect, a certain past behavior may appear unjust or immoral. The project, then, can be the source of a continuing, personal agony for the subject. If the study concerns codes of ethical conduct, for example, the subject may begin questioning his or her own morality, and that personal concern may last long after the research has been completed and reported.

By now, you should have realized that just about any research you might conduct runs the risk of injuring other people somehow. There is no way for the researcher to insure against all these possible injuries. Yet, some study designs make such injuries more likely than others. If a particular research procedure seems likely to produce unpleasant effects for subjects—asking survey respondents to report deviant behavior, for example—the researcher should have the firmest of scientific grounds for doing it. If the research design is essential and also likely to be unpleasant for subjects, you will find yourself in an ethical netherworld and may find yourself forced to do some personal

agonizing. Although agonizing has little value in itself, it may be a healthy sign that you have become sensitive to the problem.

Although the fact often goes unrecognized, subjects can be harmed by the analysis and reporting of data. Every now and then, research subjects read the books published about the studies they participated in. Reasonably sophisticated subjects will be able to locate themselves in the various indexes and tables. Having done so, they may find themselves characterized—though not identified by name—as bigoted, unpatriotic, irreligious, and so forth. At the very least, such characterizations are likely to trouble them and threaten their self-images. Yet the whole purpose of the research project may be to explain why some people are prejudiced while others are not.

I conducted a survey of church women some years back (Babbie 1967). Ministers in a sample of churches were asked to distribute questionnaires to a specified sample of members, collect them, and return them to the research office. One of these ministers read through the questionnaires from his sample before returning them, and then delivered a hell-fire and brimstone sermon to his congregation, saying that many of them were atheists and were going to hell. Even though he could not identify the respondents who gave particular responses, it seems certain that many respondents were personally harmed by the action.

Like voluntary participation, not harming people is an easy norm to accept in theory, but it is often difficult to ensure in practice. Sensitivity to the issue and experience with its applications, however, should improve the researcher's tact in delicate areas of research.

Increasingly, in recent years, social researchers have been getting support for abiding by this norm. Federal and other funding agencies typically require an independent evaluation of the treatment of human subjects for research proposals, and most universities now have human subject committees to serve that evaluative function. Although sometimes troublesome and inappropriately applied, such requirements not only guard against unethical research but can also reveal ethical issues overlooked by the most scrupulous of researchers.

Anonymity and Confidentiality

The clearest concern in the protection of the subjects' interests and well-being is the protection of their identity, especially in survey research. If revealing their survey responses would injure them in any way, adherence to this norm becomes all the more important. Two techniques—*anonymity* and *confidentiality*—assist you in this regard, although the two are often confused.

Anonymity   A respondent may be considered *anonymous* when the researcher cannot identify a given response with a given respondent. This means that an interview survey respondent can never be considered anonymous, since an interviewer collects the information from an identifiable respondent. (I assume here that standard sampling methods are followed.) An example of anonymity would be the mail survey in which no identification numbers are put on the questionnaires before their return to the research office.

As we saw in Chapter 9 on survey research, assuring anonymity makes it difficult to keep track of who has or hasn't returned the questionnaires. Despite this problem, there are some situations in which you may be advised to pay the necessary price. In one study of drug use among university students during the 1960s, I decided that I specifically did not want to know the identity of respondents. I felt that honestly assuring anonymity would increase the likelihood and accuracy of responses. Also,

I did not want to be in the position of being asked by authorities for the names of drug offenders. In the few instances in which respondents volunteered their names, such information was immediately obliterated on the questionnaires.

Confidentiality   In a *confidential* survey, the researcher is able to identify a given person's responses but essentially promises not to do so publicly. In an interview survey, for example, the researcher would be in a position to make public the income reported by a given respondent, but the respondent is assured that this will not be done.

You can use a number of techniques to ensure better performance on this guarantee. To begin, interviewers and others with access to respondent identifications should be trained in their ethical responsibilities. As soon as possible, all names and addresses should be removed from questionnaires and replaced by identification numbers. A master identification file should be created linking numbers to names to permit the later correction of missing or contradictory information, but this file should not be available except for legitimate purposes. Whenever a survey is confidential rather than anonymous, it is the researcher's responsibility to make that fact clear to the respondent. Never use the term *anonymous* to mean *confidential*.

The Researcher's Identity

We've seen that the handling of subjects' identities is an important ethical consideration. Handling your own identity as a researcher can be tricky also. Sometimes it's useful and even necessary to identify yourself as a researcher to those you want to study. You'd have to be a master con artist to get people to participate in a laboratory experiment or complete a lengthy questionnaire without letting on that you were conducting research.

Even when it's possible and important to conceal your research identity, as Randy Alfred did while studying the Church of Satan (Chapter 10), there is an important ethical dimension to be considered. Deceiving people is unethical, and within social research, deception needs to be justified by compelling scientific or administrative concerns. Even then, the justification will be arguable.

Sometimes researchers admit that they are doing research but fudge about why they are doing it or for whom. Suppose you've been asked by a public welfare agency to conduct a study of living standards among aid recipients. Even if the agency is looking for ways of improving conditions, the recipient-subjects are likely to fear a witch-hunt for "cheaters." They might be tempted, therefore, to give answers making them seem more destitute than they really are. Unless they provide truthful answers, however, the study will not produce accurate data that will contribute to an effective improvement of living conditions. What do you do? One solution would be to tell subjects that you are conducting the study as part of a university research program—concealing your affiliation with the welfare agency. Doing that improves the scientific quality of the study, but it raises a serious ethical issue in the process.

Analysis and Reporting

As a social researcher, then, you have a number of ethical obligations to your subjects of study. At the same time, you have ethical obligations to your colleagues in the scientific community, and a few comments on those are in order.

In any rigorous study, the researcher should be more familiar than anyone else with the technical shortcomings and failures of the study. You have an obligation to make those shortcomings known to your readers. Even though you may feel foolish admitting mistakes, you should do it anyway.

Negative findings should be reported if they are at all related to your analysis. There is an unfortunate myth in scientific reporting that only positive discoveries are worth reporting (and journal editors are sometimes guilty of believing that as well). In science, however, it is often as important to know that two variables are *not* related as to know that they are. Recall the earlier discussion of Stouffer's examination of attitudes toward the promotion system in the army. It was a mark of his caliber as a researcher that he insisted on finding out *why* the MPs thought the system was fair while the air corpsmen didn't. Had he simply set the puzzling findings aside for later analysis, our understanding of reference groups and relative deprivation would have been held back.

Similarly, it is important to avoid the temptation to save face by describing your findings as the product of a carefully preplanned analytical strategy when that is not the case. Many findings arrive unexpectedly—even though they may seem obvious in retrospect. So you uncovered an interesting relationship by accident—so what? Embroidering such situations with descriptions of fictitious hypotheses is dishonest and tends to mislead inexperienced researchers into thinking that all scientific inquiry is rigorously preplanned and organized.

In general, science progresses through honesty and openness, and it is retarded by ego-defenses and deception. You can serve your fellow researchers—and scientific discovery as a whole—by telling the truth about all the pitfalls and problems you have experienced in a particular line of inquiry. Perhaps you'll save them from the same problems. The box entitled "Ethical Issues in Research on Human Sexuality" examines some of the ethical issues involved in a specific research arena.

A Professional Code of Ethics

Because ethical issues in social research are both important and ambiguous, most of the professional associations have created and published formal codes of conduct describing what is considered acceptable and unacceptable professional behavior. As an illustration, I have presented the code of conduct of the American Association for Public Opinion Research, since AAPOR is an interdisciplinary research association in the social sciences (see Figure 19-1).

TWO ETHICAL CONTROVERSIES

As you may already have guessed, the adoption and publication of professional codes of conduct have not totally resolved the issue of research ethics. Social scientists still disagree on some general principles, and those who seem to agree in principle debate specifics.

In this section, I am going to describe briefly two research projects that have provoked ethical controversy and discussion in recent years. These are not the only two controversial projects that have been done; they simply illustrate ethical issues in the real world, and I thought you'd find them interesting and perhaps provocative. The first project studied homosexual behavior in public restrooms, and the second examined obedience in a laboratory setting.

Trouble in the Tearoom

As a graduate student, Laud Humphreys became interested in the study of homosexuality. He developed a special interest in the casual and fleeting homosexual acts engaged in by some nonhomosexuals. In particular, his research interest focused on homosexual acts between strangers meeting in the public restrooms in parks, called "tearooms" among homosexuals. The result was the publication in 1970 of *Tearoom Trade*.

What particularly interested Humphreys about the tearoom activity was that the participants seemed to live "normal" lives otherwise, as family men and as accepted members of the community. They did nothing else that might qualify them as homosexuals. Thus, it was important to them that they remain anonymous in their tearoom visits. How would you study something like that?

Humphreys decided to take advantage of the social structure of the situation. Typically, the tearoom encounter involved three people: the two men actually engaged in the homosexual act and a lookout, called the "watchqueen." Thus, Humphreys began showing up at public restrooms, offering to serve as watchqueen whenever it seemed appropriate. Since the watchqueen's payoff was the chance to watch the action, Humphreys was able to conduct field observations as he would in a study of political rallies or jaywalking behavior at intersections.

To round out his understanding of the tearoom trade, Humphreys needed to know something more about the people who participated. Since the men probably would not have been thrilled about being interviewed, Humphreys developed a different solution. Whenever possible, he noted down the license numbers of participants' cars and tracked down their names and addresses

Ethical Issues in Research on Human Sexuality

by Kathleen McKinney
Department of Sociology, Oklahoma State University

When studying any form of human behavior, ethical concerns are paramount. This statement may be even more true for studies of human sexuality because of the topic's highly personal, salient, and perhaps threatening nature. Concern has been expressed by the public and by legislators about human sexuality research. Three commonly discussed ethical criteria have been related specifically to research in the area of human sexuality.

Informed Consent This criterion emphasizes the importance of both accurately informing your subject or respondent as to the nature of the research and obtaining his or her verbal or written consent to participate. Coercion is not to be used to force participation and subjects may terminate their involvement in the research at any time. There are many possible violations of this standard. Misrepresentation or deception may be used when describing an embarrassing or personal topic of study because the researchers fear high rates of refusal or false data. Covert research, such as some observational studies, also violate the informed consent standard since subjects are unaware that they are being studied. Informed consent may create special problems with certain populations. For example, studies of the sexuality of children are limited by the concern that children may be cognitively and emotionally unable to give informed consent. Although there can be problems such as those discussed, most research is clearly voluntary, with informed consent from those participating.

Right to Privacy Given the highly personal nature of sexuality and society's tremendous concern with social control of sexuality, the right to privacy is a very important ethical concern for

through the police. Humphreys then visited the men at their homes, disguising himself enough to avoid recognition, and announced that he was conducting a survey. In that fashion, he collected the personal information he was unable to get in the restrooms.

Humphreys's research provoked considerable controversy both within and outside the social scientific community. Some critics charged Humphreys with a gross invasion of privacy in the name of science. What men did in public restrooms was their own business and not Humphreys's. Others were mostly concerned about the deceit involved—Humphreys had lied to the participants by leading them to believe he was only a voyeur-participant. People who felt that the tearoom participants, because they were doing their stuff in a public facility, were fair game for observation nonetheless protested the follow-up survey. They felt it was unethical for Humphreys to trace the participants to their homes and to interview them under false pretenses. Still others jus-

research in this area. Individuals may risk losing their jobs, having family difficulties, or being ostracized by peers if certain facets of their sexual lives are revealed. This is especially true for individuals involved in sexual behavior categorized as deviant (e.g., homosexuality, transvestism). Violations of right to privacy occur when researchers identify members of certain groups they have studied, release or share an individual's data or responses, or covertly observe sexual behavior. In most cases, right to privacy is easily maintained by the researcher. In survey research, self-administered questionnaires can be anonymous and interviews can be kept confidential. In case and observational studies, the identity of the person or group studied can be disguised in any publications. In most research methods, analysis and reporting of data should be at the group or aggregate level.

Protection from Harm Harm may include emotional or psychological distress, as well as physical harm. Potential for harm varies by research method; it is more likely in experimental studies where the researcher manipulates or does something to the subject than in observational or survey research. Emotional distress, however, is a possibility in all studies of human sexuality. Respondents may be asked questions that elicit anxiety, dredge up unpleasant memories, or cause them to evaluate themselves critically. Researchers can reduce the potential for such distress during a study by using anonymous, self-administered questionnaires or well-trained interviewers, and by wording sensitive questions carefully.

All three of these ethical criteria are quite subjective. Violations are sometimes justified by arguing that the risk to the subject or respondent is outweighed by the benefit to them or to society. The issue here, of course, is *who* makes that critical decision. Usually, such decisions are made by the researcher and often a screening committee that deals with ethical concerns. Most creative researchers have been able to follow all three ethical guidelines and still do important research.

tified Humphreys's research. The topic, they said, was worth study. It couldn't be studied any other way, and they regarded the deceit to be essentially harmless, noting that Humphreys was careful not to harm his subjects by disclosing their tearoom activities.

The tearoom trade controversy, as you might imagine, has never been resolved. It is still debated, and it probably always will be, since it stirs emotions and contains ethical issues people disagree about. What do you think? Was Humphreys ethical in doing what he did? Are there parts of the research you feel were acceptable and other parts that were not? Whatever you feel in the matter, you are sure to find others who disagree with you.

Observing Human Obedience

The second illustration differs from the first in many ways. Whereas Humphreys's study

Figure 19-1   Code of Conduct of the American Association for Public Opinion Research

---

CODE OF PROFESSIONAL ETHICS AND PRACTICES

We, the members of the American Association for Public Opinion Research, subscribe to the principles expressed in the following code.

Our goal is to support sound practice in the profession of public opinion research. (By public opinion research we mean studies in which the principal source of information about individual beliefs, preferences, and behavior is a report given by the individual himself or herself.)

We pledge ourselves to maintain high standards of scientific competence and integrity in our work, and in our relations both with our clients and with the general public. We further pledge ourselves to reject all tasks or assignments which would be inconsistent with the principles of this code.

THE CODE

I.   *Principles of Professional Practice in the Conduct of Our Work*

A. We shall exercise due care in gathering and processing data, taking all reasonable steps to assume the accuracy of results.

B. We shall exercise due care in the development of research designs and in the analysis of data.

1. We shall employ only research tools and methods of analysis which, in our professional judgment, are well suited to the research problem at hand.
2. We shall not select research tools and methods of analysis because of their special capacity to yield a desired conclusion.
3. We shall not knowingly make interpretations of research results, nor shall we tacitly permit interpretations, which are inconsistent with the data available.
4. We shall not knowingly imply that interpretations should be accorded greater confidence than the data actually warrant.

C. We shall describe our findings and methods accurately and in appropriate detail in all research reports.

---

involved participant observation, this study setting was in the laboratory. The first study was sociological, this one psychological. And where the first examined a form of human deviance, the study we're going to look at now examined conformity.

One of the more unsettling clichés to come out of World War II was the German soldier's common excuse for atrocities: "I was only following orders." From the point of view that gave rise to this comment, any behavior—no matter how reprehensible—could be justified if someone else could be assigned responsibility for it. If a superior officer ordered a soldier to kill a baby, the fact of the *order* was said to exempt the soldier from personal responsibility for the action.

Although the military tribunals that tried the war crime cases did not accept the excuse, social scientists and others have recognized the extent to which this point of view pervades social life. Very often people seem willing to do things they know would be considered wrong by others, *if* they can cite some higher authority as ordering them to

II. *Principles of Professional Responsibility in Our Dealings with People*

A. The Public:

1. We shall cooperate with legally authorized representatives of the public by describing the methods used in our studies.
2. We shall maintain the right to approve the release of our findings, whether or not ascribed to us. When misinterpretation appears, we shall publicly disclose what is required to correct it, notwithstanding our obligation for client confidentiality in all other respects.

B. Clients or Sponsors:

1. We shall hold confidential all information obtained about the client's general business affairs and about the findings of research conducted for the client, except when the dissemination of such information is expressly authorized.
2. We shall be mindful of the limitations of our techniques and facilities and shall accept only those research assignments which can be accomplished within these limitations.

C. The Profession:

1. We shall not cite our membership in the Association as evidence of professional competence, since the Association does not so certify any persons or organizations.
2. We recognize our responsibility to contribute to the science of public opinion research and to disseminate as freely as possible the ideas and findings which emerge from our research.

D. The Respondent:

1. We shall not lie to survey respondents or use practices and methods which abuse, coerce, or humiliate them.
2. We shall protect the anonymity of every respondent, unless the respondent waives such anonymity for specified uses. In addition, we shall hold as privileged and confidential all information which tends to identify the respondent.

Source: American Association for Public Opinion Research, *By-Laws* (May 1977). Used by permission.

do it. Such was the pattern of justification in the My Lai tragedy of Vietnam, and it appears less dramatically in day-to-day civilian life. Few would disagree that this reliance on authority exists, yet Stanley Milgram's study (1963, 1965) of the topic provoked considerable controversy.

To observe people's willingness to harm others when following orders, Milgram brought 40 adult men—from many different walks of life—into a laboratory setting designed to create the phenomenon under study. If you had been a subject in the

experiment, you would have had something like the following experience.

You would have been informed that you and another subject were about to participate in a learning experiment. Through a draw of lots, you would have been assigned the job of "teacher" and your fellow subject the job of "pupil." He would have then been led into another room, strapped into a chair, and had an electrode attached to his wrist. As the teacher, you would have been seated in front of an impressive electrical control panel covered with dials, gauges, and switches. You would have noticed that each switch had a label giving a different number of volts, ranging from 15 to 315. The switches would have had other labels, too, some with the ominous phrases "Extreme-Intensity Shock," "Danger—Severe Shock," and "XXX."

The experiment would run like this. You would read a list of word pairs to the learner and then test his ability to match them up. Since you couldn't see him, a light on your control panel would indicate his answer. Whenever the learner made a mistake, you would be instructed by the experimenter to throw one of the switches—beginning with the mildest—and administer a shock to your pupil. Through an open door between the two rooms, you'd hear your pupil's response to the shock. Then you'd read another list of word pairs and test him again.

As the experiment progressed, you'd be administering ever more intense shocks, until your pupil was screaming for mercy and begging for the experiment to end. You'd be instructed to administer the next shock anyway. After a while, your pupil would begin kicking the wall between the two rooms and screaming. You'd be told to give the next shock. Finally, you'd read a list and ask for the pupil's answer—and there would be no reply whatever, only silence from the other room. The experimenter would inform you that no answer was considered an error and instruct you to administer the next higher shock. This would continue up to the "XXX" shock at the end of the series.

What do you suppose you would have done when the pupil first began screaming? When he began kicking on the wall? Or when he became totally silent and gave no indication of life? You'd refuse to continue giving shocks, right? Of the first 40 adult men Milgram tested, nobody refused to administer the shocks until the pupil began kicking the wall between the two rooms. Of the 40, 5 did so then. Two-thirds of the

subjects, 26 of the 40, continued doing as they were told through the entire series—up to and including the administration of the highest shock.

As you've probably guessed, the shocks were phony, and the "pupil" was another experimenter. Only the "teacher" was a real subject in the experiment. You wouldn't have been hurting another person, even though you would have been led to think you were. The experiment was designed to test your *willingness* to follow orders, to the point of presumably killing someone.

Milgram's experiments have been criticized both methodologically and ethically. On the ethical side, critics particularly cited the effects of the experiment on the subjects. Many seem to have personally experienced about as much pain as they thought they were administering to someone else. They pleaded with the experimenter to let them stop giving the shocks. They became extremely upset and nervous. Some had uncontrollable seizures.

How do *you* feel about this research? Do you think the topic was important enough to justify such measures? Can you think of other ways in which the researcher might have examined obedience?

DISCUSSION EXAMPLES

Research ethics, then, is an important though very ambiguous topic. The difficulty of resolving ethical issues should not be an excuse for ignoring them. To further sensitize yourself to the ethical component in social research, I've prepared a list of real and hypothetical research situations. See if you can see the ethical component in each. How do you feel about it? Do you feel the procedures described are ultimately acceptable or unacceptable? It would be useful to discuss some of these with others in your methods course.

1. A psychology instructor asks students in an introductory psychology class to complete questionnaires that the instructor will analyze and use in preparing a journal article for publication.

2. After a field study of deviant behavior during a riot, law enforcement officials demand that the researcher identify those people who were observed looting. Rather than risk arrest as an accomplice after the fact, the researcher complies.

3. After completing the final draft of a book reporting a research project, the researcher-author discovers that 25 of the 2,000 survey interviews were falsified by interviewers—but chooses to ignore that fact and publish the book anyway.

4. Researchers obtain a list of right-wing radicals they wish to study. They contact the radicals with the explanation that each has been selected "at random" from among the general population to take a sampling of "public opinion."

5. A college instructor who wants to test the effect of unfair berating administers an hour exam to both sections of a specific course. The overall performance of the two sections is essentially the same. The grades of one section are artificially lowered, however, and the instructor berates them for performing so badly. The instructor then administers the same final exam to both sections and discovers that the performance of the unfairly berated section is worse. The hypothesis is confirmed, and the research report is published.

6. In a study of sexual behavior, the investigator wants to overcome subjects' reluctance to report what they might regard as deviant behavior. To get past their reluctance, subjects are asked: "Everyone masturbates now and then; about how much do you masturbate?"

7. A researcher discovers that 85 percent of the university student body smoke mar-

ijuana regularly. Publication of this finding will probably create a furor in the community. Since no extensive analysis of drug use is planned, the researcher decides to ignore the finding and keep it quiet.

8. To test the extent to which people may try to save face by expressing attitudes on matters they are wholly uninformed about, the researcher asks for their attitudes regarding a fictitious issue.

9. A research questionnaire is circulated among students as part of their university registration packet. Although students are not told they must complete the questionnaire, the hope is that they will believe they must—thus ensuring a higher completion rate.

10. A participant-observer pretends to join a radical, political group in order to study it and is successfully accepted as a member of the inner planning circle. What should the researcher do if the group makes plans for:
   a. a peaceful, though illegal, demonstration?
   b. the bombing of a public building during a time it is sure to be unoccupied?
   c. the assassination of a public official?

THE POLITICS OF SOCIAL RESEARCH

As I've indicated earlier, both ethics and politics hinge on ideological points of view. What is unacceptable from one point of view will be acceptable from another. Thus, we are going to see that people disagree on political aspects of research just as they disagree on ethical ones. As we change topics now, I want to distinguish ethical from political issues in two ways.

First, although ethics and politics are often closely intertwined, the ethics of social research deals more with the methods employed, while political issues are more concerned with the substance and use of research. Thus, for example, some critics raise ethical objections to the Milgram experiments, saying that the methods used harmed the experimental subjects. A political objection would be that obedience is not a worthy topic for study: either that (1) we should not tinker with people's willingness to follow orders from higher authority or, from the opposite political point of view, that (2) the results of the research could be used to make people *more* blindly obedient.

The second thing that distinguishes ethical from political aspects of social research is that there are no formal codes of accepted political conduct comparable to the codes of ethical conduct that we've discussed earlier. Although some ethical norms have political aspects—for example, not harming subjects clearly relates to our protection of civil liberties—no one has developed a set of political norms that could be agreed on by social researchers.

The only partial exception to the lack of political norms is in the generally accepted view that a researcher's personal political orientation should not interfere with or unduly influence his or her scientific research. It would be considered improper for you to employ shoddy techniques or lie about your research as a way of furthering your political views. Although you are permitted to *have* political views, you are expected to hold them aside when you enter the realm of science. It is in this context that science is idealized as apolitical, amoral, and objective.

Objectivity and Ideology

In Chapter 1, I suggested that social research can never be totally objective, since researchers are humanly subjective. Science, as a collective enterprise, achieves the equivalent of objectivity through intersubjectivity. That is, different scientists, having different subjective views, can and should arrive at the same results when they employ accepted research techniques. Essentially, that will happen to the extent that each is able to set personal values and views aside for the duration of the research.

The classic statement on objectivity and neutrality in social science is Max Weber's 1918 lecture on "Science as a Vocation." In his talk, Weber coined the phrase "value-free sociology," urging that sociology, like other sciences, needed to be unencumbered by personal values if it was to make a special contribution to society. Liberals and conservatives alike could recognize the "facts" of social science, regardless of how those facts accorded with their personal politics.

Most, but not all, social scientists have agreed with this abstract ideal. Increasingly in recent years, Marxist and neo-Marxist scholars have argued that social science and social action cannot and should not be separated. Explanations of the status quo in society, they contend, shade subtly into defenses of that same status quo. Simple explanations of the social functions of, say, discrimination can easily become justifications for its continuance. By the same token, merely studying society and its ills without a commitment to making society more humane has been called irresponsible.

Quite aside from abstract disagreements about whether social science can or should be value-free, there have been numerous disagreements about whether particular research undertakings *are* value-free or whether they represent an intrusion of the researcher's own political values. Typically, researchers have denied the intrusion, and the denial has been challenged. Let's look at some examples of the controversies that have raged and continue to rage over this issue.

Social Research and Race   Nowhere have social research and politics been more controversially intertwined than in the area of race relations. Social scientists studied the topic for a very long time, and often the products of the social research have found their way into practical politics. A few brief references should illustrate the point.

When the U.S. Supreme Court, in 1896, established the principle of "separate but equal" as a means of reconciling the Fourteenth Amendment's guarantee of equality to blacks with the norms of segregation, it neither asked for nor cited social science research. Nonetheless, it is widely believed that the Court was influenced by the writings of William Graham Sumner, a leading social scientist of his era. Sumner was noted for his view that the mores and folkways of a society were relatively impervious to legislation and social planning. His view has often been paraphrased as "stateways do not make folkways." Thus the Court ruled that it could not accept the assumption that "social prejudices may be overcome by legislation" and denied the wisdom of "laws which conflict with the general sentiment of the community" (Blaunstein and Zangrando 1970:308).

There is no doubt that Gunnar Myrdal's classic two-volume study of race relations in America entitled *An American Dilemma* (1944) had a significant impact on the topic of his research. Myrdal amassed a great deal of data to show that the position of black Americans directly contradicted American values of social and political equality. And, Myrdal did not attempt to hide his own point of view in the matter.

When the doctrine of "separate but equal" was overturned in 1954 (*Brown* v. *Board of Education of Topeka*), the new Supreme Court decision was based in part on the conclusion that segregation had a detrimental effect on black children. In drawing that conclusion, the Court cited a number of sociological and psychological research reports (Blaunstein and Zangrando 1970).

For the most part, social scientists in this century have supported the cause of black equality in America. Many have been actively involved in the civil rights movement, some more radically than others. Thus, social scientists have been able to draw research conclusions supporting the cause of equality without fear of criticism from colleagues. To recognize the solidity of the general social science position in the matter of equality, we need only examine a few research projects that have produced conclusions disagreeing with the predominant ideological position.

Most social scientists have—overtly, at least—supported the end of even de facto school segregation. Thus, an immediate and heated controversy was provoked in 1966 when James Coleman, a respected sociologist, published the results of a major national study of race and education. Contrary to general agreement, Coleman found little difference in academic performance between black students attending integrated schools and those attending segregated ones. Indeed, such obvious things as libraries, laboratory facilities, and high expenditures per student made little difference. Instead, Coleman reported that family and neighborhood factors had the most influence on academic achievement.

Coleman's findings were not well received by many of the social scientists who had been active in the civil rights movement. Some scholars criticized Coleman's work on methodological grounds, but many others objected hotly on the grounds that the findings would have segregationist political consequences. The controversy that raged around the Coleman report was reminiscent of that provoked earlier by Daniel Moynihan (1965) in his critical analysis of the black family in America.

Another example of political controversy surrounding social research in connection with race concerns the issue of IQ scores of black and white people. In 1969, Arthur Jensen, a Harvard psychologist, was asked to prepare an article for the *Harvard Educational Review* examining the data on racial differences in IQ test results (Jensen 1969). In the article, Jensen concluded that genetic differences between blacks and whites accounted for the lower average IQ scores of blacks. Jensen became so identified with that position that he appeared on college campuses across the country discussing it.

Jensen's position has been attacked on numerous methodological bases. It was charged that much of the data upon which Jensen's conclusion was based were inadequate and sloppy—there are many IQ tests, some worse than others. Similarly, it was argued that Jensen had not taken social-environmental factors sufficiently into account. Other social scientists raised other appropriate methodological objections.

Beyond the scientific critique, however, Jensen was condemned by many as a racist. He was booed and his public presentations drowned out by hostile crowds. Jensen's reception by several university audiences was not significantly different from the reception received by abolitionists a century before.

Many social scientists limited their objections to the Moynihan, Coleman, and Jensen research to scientific, methodological grounds. The purpose of my account, however, is to point out that political ideology often gets involved in matters of social research. Although the abstract model of science is divorced from ideology, the practice of science is not.

Project Camelot Among social scientists *Camelot* is a household term in discussions of research and politics. Today, it is frequently referenced with no further description, it is so well known. Irving Louis Horowitz (1967), a man who has criticized government agencies on occasion, said that Project Camelot "has had perhaps the worst public relations record of any agency or subagency of the U.S. government." What provoked such a stir?

On 4 December 1964, the Special Operations Research Office of American University sent an announcement to a number of social scientists about a project being organized around the topic of internal war. The announcement contained, in part, the following description:

Project *Camelot* is a study whose objective is to determine the feasibility of developing a general social systems model which would make it possible to predict and influence politically significant aspects of social change in the developing nations of the world. Somewhat more specifically, its objectives are:

First, to devise procedures for assessing the potential for internal war within national societies;

Second, to identify with increased degrees of confidence those actions which a government might take to relieve conditions which are assessed as giving rise to a potential for internal war.

(Horowitz 1967:47)

Of course, few people are openly in favor of war, and most would support research aimed at ending or preventing war. By the summer of 1965, however, with the national debate on Vietnam gaining momentum, Camelot was being hotly argued in social science circles as a Department of Defense attempt to co-opt scientists into a *counter-insurgency* effort in Chile. Some claimed that the Defense Department intended to sponsor social scientific research aimed at putting down political and potentially revolutionary dissatisfaction in that volatile Latin American nation. Whatever the motivations of the social scientists, it was feared that their research would be used to strengthen established regimes and thwart popular reformist and revolutionary movements in foreign countries.

Many social scientists who had agreed in principle to participate in the project soon felt they were learning a lesson learned decades before them by Robert Oppenheimer and some of the atomic scientists—that scientific findings can be used for purposes that the scientists themselves oppose. Charges and countercharges were hurled around professional circles. Names were called, motives questioned. Old friendships ended. The Defense Department was roundly damned by all for attempting to subvert social research. Foreign relations with Latin America simultaneously chilled and got hot. Finally, under the cloud of growing criticism, Camelot was canceled and dismantled.

It is interesting to imagine what might have happened to Project Camelot had it been proposed to a steadfastly conservative and anticommunist social research community. I think there is no doubt but that it would have been supported, executed, and completed without serious challenge or controversy. Certainly war per se was not the issue. There was no serious criticism when Sam Stouffer organized the research branch in the army during World War II to conduct research aimed at *supporting* the war effort, making our soldiers more effective fighters. Ultimately science is neutral on the topics of war and peace, but scientists are not.

Politics in Perspective

The role of politics and related ideologies is not unique to social research. The natural sciences have experienced and continue to experience similar situations. The preceding discussion has three main purposes in a textbook on the *practice* of social research.

First, it seems important to me that you realize that science is not untouched by politics. Social science, in particular, is a part of social life. We study things that matter to people, things they have firm, personal feelings about, and things that affect their lives. Scientists are human beings, and their human feelings often show through in

their professional lives. To think otherwise would be naive.

Second, I'd like you to see that science does proceed even under political controversy and hostility. Even when researchers get angry and call each other names, or when the research community comes under attack from the outside, the job of science gets done anyway. Scientific inquiry persists, studies are done, reports are published, and new things are learned. In short, ideological disputes do not bring science to a halt but simply make it more exciting.

Finally, I want you to make ideological considerations a part of the backdrop you create—a backdrop that will increase your awareness as you learn the various techniques of social science methods. Many of the established techniques of science function to cancel out or hold in check our human shortcomings, especially those we are unaware of. Otherwise, we might look into the world and never see anything but ourselves—our personal biases and beliefs.

MAIN POINTS

■ In addition to technical, scientific considerations, social research projects are likely to be shaped by administrative, ethical, and political considerations.

■ What's ethically "right" and "wrong" in research is ultimately a matter of what people *agree* is right and wrong.

■ Scientists agree that participation in research should, as a general norm, be voluntary. This norm, however, can conflict with the scientific need for generalizability.

■ Probably all scientists agree that research should not harm those that participate in it, unless they willingly and knowingly accept the risks of harm.

■ *Anonymity* refers to the situation in which even the researcher cannot identify specific information with the individuals it describes.

■ *Confidentiality* refers to the situation in which the researcher—although knowing which data describe which subjects—agrees to keep that information confidential.

■ Although science is neutral on political matters, scientists are not.

■ Even though the norms of science cannot force individual scientists to give up their personal values, the intersubjective character of science provides a guard against "scientific" findings being the product of bias only.

REVIEW QUESTIONS AND EXERCISES

1. Review the discussion of the Milgram experiment on obedience. See if you can design a study that would have accomplished the same purpose but would have avoided the ethical criticisms leveled at Milgram.

2. Suppose a researcher who is personally in favor of small families—as a response to the problem of overpopulation—wants to conduct a survey to determine why some people want many children and others don't. Discuss the personal-involvement problems he or she would face and how those might be avoided.

ADDITIONAL READINGS

Golden, M. Patricia (ed.), *The Research Experience* (Itasca, Ill.: Peacock, 1976). An excellent collection of pieces about *doing* research in a social context. The book presents an excerpt from a published report and follows it with a more informal account by the researcher. In several of the informal accounts, you will get an inside view of the way political and ethical issues are involved in social research.

MacRae, Duncan, Jr., *The Social Function of Social Science* (New Haven, Conn.: Yale University Press, 1976). A historical analysis of the interplay of social science and social reform in America. Both the values of the general community and the values of the social scientists themselves are examined.

Richter, Maurice, Jr., *Science as a Cultural Process* (Cambridge, Mass.: Schenkman, 1972). A sociological analysis of science as a human process, occurring within a sociocultural context. Richter provides both a historical and contemporary picture of the interplay between science and society.

Ritzer, George (ed.), *Social Realities: Dynamic Perspectives* (Boston: Allyn & Bacon, 1974). A lively collection of views regarding political and ethical issues in social science. Ritzer has done an excellent job of presenting widely divergent views regarding the same issue. This book not only portrays "social realities," it will also give you an opportunity to make up your own mind in these matters.

Appendices

A

Using the Library

INTRODUCTION

Throughout this book we have been assuming that you will be reading reports of social science research. In this appendix, I want to talk a little about how you'll find reports to read.

As I've indicated repeatedly, you live in a world that is filled with social science research reports. Your daily newspaper, magazines, professional journals, alumni bulletins, club newsletters—virtually everything you pick up to read may carry reports dealing with a particular topic. Usually, you'll pursue that interest through your library. Although I'll give you just a brief overview here, you can get more information in an excellent little book—Alden Todd's *Finding Facts Fast* (Berkeley, Calif.: Ten Speed Press, 1979).

GETTING HELP

When you want to find something in the library, your best friend is the reference librarian, who is specially trained to find things in the library. Sometimes it's hard to ask people for help, but you'll do yourself a real service to make an exception in this case.

Some libraries have specialized reference librarians—for the social sciences, humanities, government documents, and so forth. Find the one you need and tell him or her what you're interested in. The reference librarian will probably put you in touch with some of the many available reference sources.

REFERENCE SOURCES

You have probably heard the expression *information explosion*. Your library is one of the main battlefields. Fortunately, a large number of reference volumes offer a guide to the information that's available.

Books in Print This volume lists all the books currently in print in the United States—listed separately by author and by title. Out-of-print books can often be found in older editions of *Books in Print*.

Readers' Guide to Periodical Literature This annual volume with monthly updates lists articles published in many journals and magazines. Since the entries are organized by subject matter, this is an excellent source for organizing your reading on a particular topic. Figure A-1 presents a sample page from the *Readers' Guide*.

Figure A-1 A Page from the
Readers' Guide to Periodical Literature

CONSTRUCTION industry
Gentler squeeze in homebuilding. il Fortune 103:12 Ap 20 '81
CONSTRUCTION workers

Salaries, pensions, etc.
Toppling a pillar of U.S. labor law [Davis-Bacon Act] il Bus W p38 Je 1 '81
CONSUMER and Corporate Affairs Department (Canada) See Canada—Consumer and Corporate Affairs, Department of
CONSUMERS
See also
Old age market
CONTACT lenses
Long wear lenses OK'd [Hydrocurve II, by Soft Lenses, Inc.] FDA Consumer 15:2 Ap '81
CONTAMINATED milk. See Milk contamination
CONTINENTAL drift
Mobile telescope for measuring continental drift [Transportable Laser Ranging Station and Laser Geodynamics Earth Orbiting Satellite] E. C. Silverberg and D. L. Byrd. il map Sky & Tel 61:405-8 My '81
CONTRACEPTIVES
Cervical caps—the perfect, untested contraceptive. J. Willis. il FDA Consumer 15:20-1 Ap '81
Contraceptive foams and birth defects. Sci News 119:229 Ap 11 '81
Male "pill" blocks sperm enzyme [gossypol inhibition of lactate dehydrogenase X] T. H. Maugh, 2d. Science 212:314 Ap 17 '81
More birth control blues [study by H. Jick linking use of spermicidal contraceptives to birth defects and miscarriages] P. DeVries. il Macleans 94:47-8 My 11 '81
CONTRACTS, Government
See also
Municipal contracts
United States—Labor, Department of—Federal Contract Compliance Programs, Office of
CONTROL Laser Corporation
We prefer to follow. S. N. Chakravarty. il pors Forbes 127:83+ Ap 13 '81
CONVERSATION
"What's the matter, dear?" or, How to get him to talk to you. K. Fury. il Redbook 157:27+ My '81
CONVICT labor
Prisoners who work [rehabilitative value of income in Canada] M. Dewey. il World Press R 28:55 Ap '81
COOKBOOKS
Great recipes from our new cookbook [excerpt from The Good housekeeping illustrated cookbook; ed by Z. Coulson] il Good H 192:156-71+ My '81
COOKE, Cynthia W. and Dworkin, Susan
Good health. il Ms 9:68-9 Ja; 92+ F; 89-91 Mr; 15-16 Ap '81
COOKE, Janet
Ben's world. Winston. Nat R 33:530-2 My 15 '81 •
COOKING
See also
Barbecue cooking
Menus
Meringue

Couples who share the cooking. A. C. Scotton. il Redbook 157:124-5+ My '81
Food journal. il Ladies Home J 98:118+ Mr; 62 Ap; 122 My '81
Food notes: off-the-shelf substitutes. Bet Hom & Gard 59:122 My '81
Off-the-shelf cooking: new main dishes to make from what's on hand. J. Johnson. il Bet Hom & Gard 59:116-21 My '81

Cereals
See Cooking—Grain

Grain
Try triticale. il Bet Hom & Gard 59:154 My '81

Meat
Summer-easy meals: cold meat platters. il Good H 192:304 My '81

Organic food
Sprouts [Rodale Press' natural foods luncheon at the Four Seasons] New Yorker 57:38-40 Je 1 '81

Poultry
Drumstick beat around the world. il Ladies Home J 98:100-1+ My '81

Rice
Spanish accents. C. Claiborne and P. Franey. il N Y Times Mag p 130 My 17 '81

Vegetables
Stir-fried vegetables. il Good H 192:48 My '81
Super-quick stuffed peppers. il Good H 192:92 My '81

Wine
Flavor made easy: fabulous wine cookery. V. Newborn. il Essence 12:129-31+ My '81
COOKING, Bahamian
Friends & food: Island gourmets. il Essence 11:108, 119+ Ap '81
COOKING, Caribbean
See also
Cooking, Bahamian

Caribbean. V. Newborn. Essence 11:121-2 Ap '81
COOKING, Indian (American)
Indian cooking's gifts. J. Wongrey. il Outdoor Life 167:138 My '81
COOKING, Mexican
Enchilada stack. il Seventeen 40:49-50+ My '81
COOKING, Spanish
Spanish accents. C. Claiborne and P. Franey. il N Y Times Mag p 130 My 17 '81
COOKS
Masters [meeting of American and French chapters of Maîtres Cuisiniers] N. Hazelton. Nat R 33:568-9 My 15 '81
COONEY, Gerry
Great white question mark. V. Ziegel. il pors N Y 14:88-9 My 25 '81 •
There were no doubts about it. il pors Sports Illus 54:30-1 My 25 '81 •
COOPER, James C.
(ed) Business outlook. Bus W p23-4 Je 1 '81
COOPERATION
See also
Educational cooperation
COOPERATION, Inter-American. See Inter-American relations
COPEPODS
Encystment discovered in a marine copepod [heteropsyllus nunni] B. C. Coull and J. Grant. bibl f il Science 212:342-4 Ap 17 '81
COPYRIGHT
Court sets first guidelines for manufacturing clause [ruling by Judge E. Weinfeld in Stonehill Publishing Company suit against U.S. Customs Service] M. Reuter. il Pub W 219:152 My 8 '81

Picture writing
Battle over a manner of speaking [copyright suit by inventor C. Bliss against Blissymbolics Communication Institute of Toronto] I. Allaby. il por Macleans 94:45-6 My 11 '81
CORALS

Larvae
See Larvae
CORN, Ira George, 1921-
Changing role of corporations in political affairs: corporate free speech, February 17, 1981] Vital Speeches 47:463-8 My 15 '81
CORN
Wild in the fields [primitive relative of modern corn, zea diploperennis] il SciQuest 54:4-5 Mr '81
CORN futures. See Commodity futures
CORN roots. See Roots
CORPORATE couples. See Married couples
CORPORATE names. See Corporations—names
CORPORATION lawyers. See Lawyers
CORPORATIONS

Accounting
See also
Air freight service—Accounting

Acquisitions and mergers
See also
Hospitals—Acquisitions and mergers
Motion picture industry—Acquisitions and mergers

Exxon scraps motor device [link between alternating current synthesizer and 1979 acquisition of Reliance Electric Company] R. J. Smith. Science 212:311 Ap 17 '81
Take-over fever in the boardrooms [views of J. Srodes] W. Lowther. il Macleans 94:30-1 My 18 '81
Tuning in [Jack Eckerd Corp-American Home Video Corp. merger] T. Jaffe. il por Forbes 127:96+ Ap 13 '81

Laws and regulations
See also
Canada—Consumer and Corporate Affairs, Department of

New ploy to foil the big grab [Canadian law] I. Anderson. il Macleans 94:35 My 18 '81

Canada
New ploy to foil the big grab. I. Anderson. il Macleans 94:35 My 18 '81

Sweden
For Volvo, a shift away from autos [merger with Beijerinvest] Bus W p75 My 25 '81

In addition to these general reference volumes, you'll find a great variety of specialized references. A few are listed below as examples.

- Popular Guide to Government Publications
- New York Times Index
- Facts on File
- Editorial Research Reports
- Business Periodicals Index
- Monthly Catalog of Government Publications
- Public Affairs Information Service Bulletin
- Education Index
- Applied Science and Technology Index
- A Guide to Geographic Periodicals
- General Science Index
- Biological and Agricultural Index
- Nursing and Applied Health Index
- Index of Dental Literature
- Nursing Studies Index
- Index to Periodical Articles by and about Negroes
- Index to Little Magazines
- Popular Periodical Index
- Biography Index
- Congressional Quarterly Weekly Report
- Library Literature
- Bibliographic Index

USING THE STACKS

For serious research, you should learn to use the stacks, where most of the library's books are stored. In this section, I'll give you some information about finding books in the stacks.

The Card Catalog

Your library's card catalog is the main reference system for finding out where books are stored. Each book is described on three separate 3×5 cards. The cards are then filed in three alphabetic sets. One set is arranged by author, another by title, and the third by subject matter.

If you want to find a particular book, you can look it up in either the author or the title file. If you only have a general subject area of interest, you should thumb through the subject catalog. Figure A-2 presents a sample card in the card catalog.

1. Subject heading (always in capital letters)

2. Author's name (last name, first name)

3. Title of the book

4. Publisher

5. Date of publication

6. Number of pages in the book plus other information (Here we are told that the book contains illustrations.)

7. Call number (This is needed to find a nonfiction book on the library shelves. A book of fiction generally carries no number and is found in alphabetical order by the author's name.)

Library of Congress Classification

Here's a useful strategy to use when you're researching a topic. Once you've identified the call number for a particular book in your subject area, go to the stacks, find that book, *and* look over the other books on the shelves near it. Since the books are arranged by subject matter, this method will help you locate relevant books you didn't know about.

Alternatively, you may want to go directly to the stacks and look at books in your subject area. In most libraries, books are

Figure A-2 Sample Subject Catalog Card

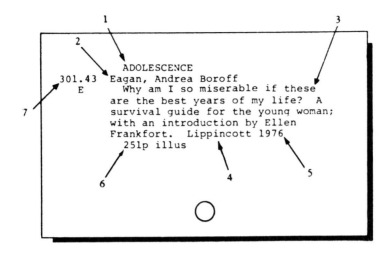

```
                              1                              3
              2
                         ADOLESCENCE
             301.43   Eagan, Andrea Boroff
                 E        Why am I so miserable if these
                        are the best years of my life?  A
         7              survival guide for the young woman;
                        with an introduction by Ellen
                        Frankfort.  Lippincott 1976
                           251p illus

                6                         4        5
```

Source: Lilian L. Shapiro, *Teaching Yourself in Libraries* (New York: H. W. Wilson, 1978) pp. 3-4. Used by permission.

arranged and numbered according to a subject matter classification developed by the Library of Congress. Below is a selected list of Library of Congress categories.

Library of Congress Classifications (partial)

A   GENERAL WORKS

B   PHILOSOPHY, PSYCHOLOGY, RELIGION

B-BD	Philosophy
BF	Psychology
BL-BX	Religion

C   HISTORY-AUXILIARY SCIENCES

D   HISTORY (except America)

DA-DR	Europe
DS	Asia
DT	Africa

E-F HISTORY (America)

E	United States
E51-99	Indians of North America
E185	Negroes in the United States
F101-1140	Canada
F1201-3799	Latin America

G   GEOGRAPHY-ANTHROPOLOGY

G-GF	Geography
GC	Oceanology and oceanography
GN	Anthropology
GV	Sports, amusements, games

H   SOCIAL SCIENCES

HB-HJ	Economics and business
HM-HX	Sociology

J   POLITICAL SCIENCE

JK	United States
JN	Europe
JQ	Asia, Africa
JX	International relations

K   LAW

L   EDUCATION

M   MUSIC

N   FINE ARTS

NA	Architecture
NB	Sculpture
NC	Graphic arts
ND	Painting
NE	Engraving
NK	Ceramics, textiles

P   LANGUAGE AND LITERATURE

RE	English language
PG	Slavic language
PJ-PM	Oriental language
PN	Drama, oratory, journalism
PQ	Romance literature
PR	English literature
PS	American literature
PT	Germanic literature

Q   SCIENCE

QA	Mathematics
QB	Astronomy
QC	Physics
QD	Chemistry
QE	Geology
QH-QR	Biology

R   MEDICINE

RK	Dentistry
RT	Nursing

S   AGRICULTURE-PLANT AND ANIMAL INDUSTRY

T   TECHNOLOGY

TA-TL	Engineering
TR	Photography

U   MILITARY SCIENCE

V   NAVAL SCIENCE

Z   BIBLIOGRAPHY AND LIBRARY SCIENCE

COMPUTERIZED LIBRARY FILES

It seems certain that, in the years to come, you'll be finding library materials increasingly by computer. For example, you'll sit at a computer terminal, type the title of a book, and in seconds see a video display of a catalog card. If you wanted to explore the book further, you could type an instruction at the terminal and see an abstract of the book, or perhaps the whole book. Alternatively, you might type a subject name and see a listing of all the books and articles written on that topic. You could skim through the list and indicate which ones you wanted to see.

While this may seem pretty futuristic, it's closer at hand than you may think. Computer network systems such as The Source already allow microcomputer owners to locate and retrieve articles from the *New York Times,* United Press International, and many other similar information sources by connecting their microcomputers over telephone lines to a central computer perhaps thousands of miles away.

Many college libraries now have access to the Educational Resources Information Center (ERIC). This computer-based system allows you to search through some 780 major educational journals to find articles published in the subject area of your interest (within the field of education). Once you identify the articles you are interested in, the computer will print out abstracts of those articles. Outside the field of education, the Lockheed Dialogue system offers about 120 different files like ERIC, including psychological abstracts, sociological abstracts, social science citation index, public affairs informational service, and many others. Check with your librarian to find out what's available to you.

Taking the long view, it would be a good idea for you to begin familiarizing yourself with such computer-based systems now, since you are likely to be using them a great deal in the future. Ultimately, you may do all your library searching from your own home, using your own computer.

ADDITIONAL READINGS

Bart, Pauline, and Frankel, Linda, *The Student Sociologist's Handbook,* 3rd edition (Glenview, IL: Scott, Foresman, 1981).

A survival kit for doing sociological research. Contains a step-by-step guide for writing research papers; chapters on periodicals, abstract and indexing services, bibliographies, bibliographic aids, and other secondary sources; and a complete guide to governmental and nongovernmental sources of data. Special section on sex roles and women's studies.

Becker, Leonard, and Gustafson, Clair, *Encounter with Sociology: The Term Paper* (San Francisco: Boyd and Fraser, 1976). An excellent guide for writing term and research papers in the social sciences. Contains some good discussion of methodological issues to consider as well.

Gruber, James; Pryor, Judith, and Berge, Patricia, *Materials and Methods for Sociology Research* (New York: Neal-Schuman, 1980). This workbook offers a "hands-on," problem-oriented approach to the use of a wide variety of reference and research tools through individual chapters and assignments. Also available for political science, history, and other fields.

Li, Tze-chung, *Social Science Reference Sources: A Practical Guide* (Westport, CT: Greenwood Press, 1980). Lists and describes all types of reference materials, including data bases and archives as well as published sources. Organized into two parts: social sciences in general and by discipline.

Mark, Charles, *Sociology of America: A Guide to Information* (Detroit: Gale, 1976). An annotated bibliography covering all aspects of American society: population, regional studies, ethnic groups, religion, work, stratification, the family, etc. Includes sections on reference materials.

B

The Research Report

INTRODUCTION

This book has considered the variety of activities that compose the *doing* of social research. In this appendix, we'll turn to an often neglected subject: reporting the research to others. Unless the research is properly communicated, all the efforts devoted to previously discussed procedures will go for naught.

Before proceeding further on this topic, I should suggest one absolutely basic guideline. Good social scientific reporting requires good English (unless you are writing in a foreign language). Whenever we ask the "figures to speak for themselves," they tend to remain mute. Whenever we use unduly complex terminology or construction, communication is reduced. Every researcher should read and reread (at approximately three-month intervals) an excellent small book by William Strunk, Jr., and E. B. White, *The Elements of Style.* * If you do this faithfully, and if even 10 percent of the contents rub off, you stand a rather good chance of making yourself understood and your findings perhaps appreciated.

*William Strunk, Jr., and E. B. White, 3rd ed. (New York: Macmillan, 1979). The following are other useful references on writing: H. W. Fowler, *A Dictionary of Modern English Usage* (New York: Oxford University Press, 1965).

Scientific reporting has several functions, and it is a good idea to keep these in mind. First, the report communicates to an audience a body of specific data and ideas. The report should provide those specifics clearly and with sufficient detail to permit an informed evaluation. Second, the scientific report should be viewed as a contribution to the general body of scientific knowledge. While remaining appropriately humble, you should always regard your research report as an addition to what we know about social behavior. Finally, the report should serve the function of stimulating and directing further inquiry.

SOME BASIC CONSIDERATIONS

Despite these general guidelines, different reports serve different purposes. A report appropriate for one purpose might be wholly inappropriate for another. This section of this appendix deals with some of the basic considerations in this regard.

Audience

Before drafting your report, you must ask yourself who you hope will read it. Normally, you should make a distinction between fellow scientists and general readers. If written for the former, you may make certain assumptions as to their existing knowledge and may perhaps summarize certain points rather than explaining them in detail. Similarly, you may appropriately use more technical language than would be appropriate for a general audience.

At the same time, you should remain always aware that any science is composed of factions or cults. Terms and assumptions acceptable to your immediate colleagues may only confuse other scientists. That applies with regard to substance as well as techniques. The sociologist of religion who is writing for a general sociology audience, for example, should explain previous findings in more detail than would be necessary if he or she were addressing an audience of other sociologists of religion.

Form and Length of Report

I should begin this subsection by saying that my comments apply to both written and oral reports. These two forms, however, will affect the nature of the report.

It is useful to think about the variety of reports that might result from a research project. To begin, you may wish to prepare a short *research note* for publication in an academic or technical journal. Such reports should be approximately one to five pages in length (typed, double-spaced) and should be concise and direct. In a short amount of space, you will not be able to present the state of the field in any detail, and your methodological notes must be somewhat abbreviated as well. Basically, you should tell the reader why you feel a brief note is justified by your findings, then tell what those findings are.

Often, researchers must prepare reports for the sponsors of their research. These may vary greatly in length, of course. In preparing such a report, however, you should bear in mind the audience for the report—scientific or lay—and their reasons for sponsoring the project in the first place. It is both bad politics and bad manners to bore the sponsors with research findings that have no interest or value to them. At the same time, it may be useful to summarize the ways in which the research has advanced basic scientific knowledge (if it has).

Working papers or monographs are another form of research reporting. Especially in a large and complex project, it will be useful to obtain comments on your analysis and the interpretation of your data. A working paper constitutes a tentative presentation with an implicit request for comments. Working papers can also vary in length, and they may present all of the research findings of the project or only a portion of them. Since your professional reputation is not at stake in a working paper, you should feel free to present tentative interpretations that you cannot altogether justify—identifying them as such and asking for evaluations.

Many research projects result in papers delivered at professional meetings. Often, these serve the same purpose as working papers. You are able to present findings and ideas of possible interest to your colleagues and ask for their comments. Although the length of professional papers may vary depending on the organization of the meetings, I'd encourage you to say too little rather than too much. Although a working paper may ramble somewhat through a variety of tentative conclusions, conference participants should not be forced to sit through an oral unveiling of the same. Interested listeners can always ask for more details later, and uninterested ones can gratefully escape.

Probably the most popular research report is the article published in an academic journal. Again, lengths vary and you should examine the lengths of articles previously published by the journal in question. As a rough guide, however, 25 typed pages is as good as any. A subsequent section on the organization of the report is primarily based on the structure of a journal article, so I shall say no more at this point, except to indicate that student term papers should be written on this model. As a general rule, a term paper that would make a good journal article would also make a good term paper.

A book, of course, represents the most prestigious form of research report. It has all the advantages of the working paper—length, detail—but it should be a more polished document. Since the publication of research findings as a book gives those findings an appearance of greater substance and worth, you have a special obligation to your audience. Although you will still hope to receive comments from colleagues, possibly leading you to revise your ideas, you must realize that other readers may be led to accept your findings uncritically.

Aim of the Report

Earlier in this book, we considered the different *purposes* of social research projects. In preparing your report, you should keep these different purposes in mind.

Some reports may focus primarily on the *exploration* of a topic of interest. Inherent in this aim is the tentativeness and incompleteness of the conclusions. You should clearly indicate to your audience the exploratory aim of the study and point to the shortcomings of the particular project. An important aspect of an exploratory report is to point the way to more refined research on the topic.

Most studies have a *descriptive* purpose, and the research reports from such studies will have a descriptive element. You should carefully distinguish for the reader those descriptions that apply only to the sample and those that are inferred to the population. Whenever inferential descriptions are

to be made, you should give your audience some indication of the probable range of error in those descriptions.

Many reports have an *explanatory* aim; you wish to point to causal relationships among variables. Depending on the probable audience for your report, you should carefully delineate the rules of explanation that lie behind your computations and conclusions, and as in the case of description, you must give your readers some guide to the relative certainty of your conclusions.

Finally, some research reports may have the aim of *proposing action*. For example, the researcher of prejudice may wish to suggest ways in which prejudice may be reduced, on the basis of the research findings. This aim often presents knotty problems, however, because your own values and orientations may interfere with your proposals. Although it is perfectly legitimate for your proposals to be motivated by personal values, you must ensure that the specific actions you propose are warranted by your data. Thus, you should be especially careful to spell out the logic by which you move from empirical data to proposed action.

ORGANIZATION OF THE REPORT

Although the organization of reports differs somewhat on the basis of form and purpose, it is possible to suggest a general format for presenting research data. The following comments apply most directly to a journal article, but with some modification they apply to most forms of research reports.

Purpose and Overview

It is always helpful to the reader if you begin with a brief statement of the purpose of the study and the main findings of the analysis. In a journal article, this overview may sometimes be given in the form of an *abstract* or *synopsis*.

Some researchers find this difficult to do. For example, your analysis may have involved considerable detective work, with important findings revealing themselves only as a result of imaginative deduction and data manipulation. You may wish, therefore, to lead the reader through the same exciting process, chronicling the discovery process with a degree of suspense and surprise. To the extent that this form of reporting gives an accurate picture of the research process, I feel it has considerable instructional value. Nevertheless, many readers may not be interested in following your entire research account, and not knowing the purpose and general conclusions in advance may make it difficult for them to understand the significance of the study.

An old forensic dictum says: "Tell them what you're going to tell them; tell them; and tell them what you told them." You would do well to follow this dictum in the preparation of research reports.

Review of the Literature

Since every research report should be placed in the context of the general body of scientific knowledge, it is important to indicate where your report fits in that picture. Having presented the general purpose of your study, you should then bring the reader up to date on the previous research in the area, pointing to general agreements and disagreements among the previous researchers.

In some cases, you may wish to challenge previously accepted ideas. You should carefully review the studies that had led to the acceptance of those ideas, then indicate the factors that have not been previously con-

sidered or the logical fallacies present in the previous research.

When you are concerned with resolving a disagreement among previous researchers, you should organize your review of the literature around the opposing points of view. You should summarize the research supporting one view, then summarize the research supporting the other, and finally suggest the reasons for the disagreement.

To an extent, your review of the literature serves a bibliographic function for readers, indexing the previous research on a given topic. This can be overdone, however, and you should avoid an opening paragraph that runs three pages, mentioning every previous study in the field. The comprehensive bibliographic function can best be served by a bibliography at the end of the report, and the review of the literature should focus only on those studies that have direct relevance to the present study.

Study Design and Execution

A research report containing interesting findings and conclusions can be very frustrating when the reader is unable to determine the methodological design and execution of the study. The worth of all scientific findings depends heavily on the manner in which the data were collected and analyzed.

In reporting the design and execution of a survey, for example, you should always include the following: the population, the sampling frame, the sampling method, the sample size, the data collection method, the completion rate, and the methods of data processing and analysis. Comparable details should be given if other methods are used. The experienced researcher is able to report these details in a rather short space, without omitting anything required for the reader's evaluation of the study.

Analysis and Interpretation

Having set the study in the perspective of previous research and having described the design and execution of it, you should then present your data. The following major section will provide further guidelines in this regard. For now, a few general comments are in order.

The presentation of data, the manipulations of those data, and your interpretations should be integrated into a logical whole. It is frustrating to the reader to discover a collection of seemingly unrelated analyses and findings with a promise that all the loose ends will be tied together later on in the report. Every step in the analysis should make sense—at the time it is taken. You should present your rationale for a particular analysis, present the data relevant to it, interpret the results, then indicate where that result leads next.

Summary and Conclusions

Following the forensic dictum mentioned earlier, I believe it is essential to summarize the research report. You should avoid reviewing every specific finding but you should review all of the significant ones, pointing once more to their general significance.

The report should conclude with a statement of what you have discovered about your subject matter and where future research might be directed. A quick review of recent journal articles will probably indicate a very high frequency of the concluding statement "It is clear that much more research is needed." This is probably always a true conclusion, but it is of little value unless you can offer pertinent suggestions as to the nature of that future research. You should review the particular shortcomings of your own study and suggest ways in which those shortcomings might be avoided by future researchers.

GUIDELINES FOR REPORTING ANALYSES

The presentation of data analyses should be such as to provide a maximum of detail without being cluttered. You can accomplish that best by continually examining your report to see whether it achieves the following aims.

Quantitative data should be presented in such a way as to permit recomputations by the reader. In the case of percentage tables, for example, the reader should be able to collapse categories and recompute the percentages. Readers should be given sufficient information as to permit them to compute percentages in the table in the opposite direction from your own presentation.

All aspects of the analysis should be described in sufficient detail to permit a secondary analyst to replicate the analysis from the same body of data. This means that he or she should be able to create the same indexes and scales, produce the same tables, arrive at the same regression equations, obtain the same factors and factor loadings, and so forth. That will seldom be done, of course, but if the report is presented in such a manner as to make it possible, the reader will be far better equipped to evaluate the report.

A final guide to the reporting of methodological details is that the reader should be in a position to completely replicate the entire study independently. It should be recalled from an earlier discussion that replicability is an essential norm of science generally. A single study does not prove a point; only a series of studies can begin to do so.

Unless studies can be replicated, there can be no meaningful series of studies.

I have previously mentioned the importance of integrating data, analysis, and interpretations in the report. A more specific guideline can be offered in this regard. Tables, charts, and figures, if any, should be integrated into the text of the report—appearing near that portion of the text discussing them. Sometimes students describe their analyses in the body of the report, and place all the tables in an appendix at the end. This procedure greatly impedes the reader. As a general rule, it is best to (1) describe the purpose for presenting the table, (2) present it, and (3) review and interpret it.

Be explicit in drawing conclusions. Although research is typically conducted for the purpose of drawing general conclusions, you should carefully note the specific basis for such conclusions. Otherwise you may lead your reader into accepting unwarranted conclusions.

Point to any qualifications or conditions warranted in the evaluation of conclusions. Typically, you are in the best position to know the shortcomings and tentativeness of your conclusions, and you should give the reader the advantage of that knowledge. Failure to do so can misdirect future research and result in a waste of research funds.

I will conclude with a point made at the outset of this appendix, since it is extremely important. Research reports should be written in the best possible literary style. Writing lucidly is easier for some people than for others, and it is always harder than writing poorly. You are again referred to the Strunk and White volume. Every researcher would do well to follow this procedure: Write. Read Strunk and White. Revise. Reread Strunk and White. Revise again. That will be a difficult and time-consuming endeavor, but so is science.

A perfectly designed, carefully executed, and brilliantly analyzed study will be altogether worthless unless you are able to communicate your findings to others. This appendix has attempted to provide some general and specific guidelines toward that end. The best guides are logic, clarity, and honesty. Ultimately, there is probably no substitute for practice.

C

Commission on Aging Survey

RESPONDENT'S IDENTIFYING INFORMATION

Name:

Address:

Census Tract Number:

Telephone:

Social Security Number:

Birthdate:

Marital Status:
[ ] Single
[ ] Married
[ ] Divorced
[ ] Separated
[ ] Widowed

Interviewer's Name:

Date of Interview:

Respondent # _____

COMMISSION ON AGING SURVEY

Respondent's Name: _____

Respondent's Address:
Street _____
City/Town _____

Name of Interviewer: _____

Number of Visits

	1	2	3	4	5
Date					
Time Started					
Time Ended					
Time Spent					
Result*					
Appointment Date and Time					

*Codes:
1. Interview completed.
2. Interview partly completed - Appointment made.
3. Appointment made for interview later,
4. Refusal - No interview obtained.
5. No one at home.
6. Eligible respondent not home.
7. Other (SPECIFY) _____

Field Supervisor: _____ Date: _____

Editor: _____ Date: _____

Coder: _____ Date: _____

Keypuncher: _____ Date: _____

Serial Number

481

482

I. SATISFACTORY HOME AND COMMUNITY ENVIRONMENT

(1) To begin the interview, we would like to learn something about your current living arrangements. First, do you live alone or do you share your quarters with other people?

[ ] Live alone
[ ] Share quarters ———→   21/ _____

1a. Who do you live with?

[ ] Spouse
[ ] Children: Number _____
[ ] Grandchildren: Number _____
[ ] Other relatives: Number _____
[ ] Unrelated persons: Number _____   22-26/ _____
                                                 _____
                                                 _____
                                                 _____
                                                 _____

1b. How many people is that altogether?   27/ _____

(2) Do you own or rent these living quarters?

[ ] Own
[ ] Rent ———→   28/ _____

2a. Do you own it fee-simple, leasehold, or do you have other arrangements?

[ ] Fee-simple
[ ] Leasehold
[ ] Other (specify): _____   29/ _____

(3) How long have you been living in these quarters?

_____ (enter number of years)   30-31/ _____

(4) If you had your choice, do you think you (and your husband/wife) would prefer living alone or living with other people (other than your husband/wife)?

[ ] Prefer living alone
[ ] Prefer living with others   32/ _____

(5) How many rooms do you have in these quarters, other than bathrooms, halls, lanais, and so forth?   33/ _____

34/b

I. SATISFACTORY HOME AND COMMUNITY ENVIRONMENT

(6) Do you have a private bathroom or do you share it with other people (other than your husband/wife)?

[ ] Private bathroom
[ ] Shared bathroom   35/ _____

(7) Is there a telephone readily available for your use?

[ ] Yes
[ ] No   36/ _____

(8) Do you have hot and cold running water?

[ ] Yes
[ ] Cold only
[ ] Neither   37/ _____

(9) Do you find the temperature in your home:

[ ] Usually comfortable
[ ] Usually uncomfortable
[ ] About half and half   38/ _____

(10) Do you have enough windows for adequate light on most days?

[ ] Yes
[ ] No   39/ _____

(11) Do you have enough electric lighting in all rooms, in some rooms only, or not enough in any room?

[ ] Enough in all rooms
[ ] Enough in some only
[ ] Not enough in any
[ ] No electrical lighting   40/ _____

(12) Generally speaking, how would you rate the physical condition of your living quarters—such things as plumbing, the roof, the floor, windows, and so forth? Would you describe it as:

[ ] Excellent
[ ] Good
[ ] Fair
[ ] Poor   41/ _____

42/b

I. SATISFACTORY HOME AND COMMUNITY ENVIRONMENT

(13) Would you say that the size of your living quarters is:

[ ] Too large
[ ] Too small
[ ] Just about right

43/

(14) How well do you think your present home satisfies your current needs for comfort, convenience, and safety?

[ ] Very well
[ ] Fairly well
[ ] Not too well
[ ] Not at all

44/

(15) Would you say that you find such things as home maintenance, keeping up repairs, and general housework:

[ ] Difficult
[ ] Sometimes difficult
[ ] Never a problem

45/

(16) Do you have a room where you can usually go and shut the door to be alone if you want to?

[ ] Yes
[ ] No

46/

(17) Does noise from either outside or other parts of the building in which you live bother you? (IF YES: Would you say *often* or only *sometimes*?)

[ ] No
[ ] Sometimes
[ ] Often

47/

(18) For each of the following, please tell me if it represents a big problem for you, a slight problem, or no problem.

	Big Prob.	Slight Prob.	No. Prob.
a. Pests such as mice, rats, and so forth.	[ ]	[ ]	[ ]
b. Insects	[ ]	[ ]	[ ]
c. Refuse collection	[ ]	[ ]	[ ]
d. Overcrowding in stores, restaurants, and so forth	[ ]	[ ]	[ ]
e. Air pollution	[ ]	[ ]	[ ]

48-52/

53/b

I. SATISFACTORY HOME AND COMMUNITY ENVIRONMENT

(19) All things considered, how do you feel about staying in these quarters to moving somewhere else? Would you say you:

[ ] Would definitely prefer to stay here
[ ] Would probably prefer to stay here
[ ] Would probably prefer to move elsewhere
[ ] Would definitely prefer to move elsewhere
[ ] Don't know

54/

(20) Since you have lived here, would you say that the neighborhood has changed for the better, for the worse, or stayed about the same?

[ ] For the better
[ ] Stayed about the same
[ ] For the worse

55/

(21) How attached are you to your neighborhood? Would you say you:

[ ] Are very attached
[ ] Are fairly attached
[ ] Have no real feeling
[ ] Do not like it and would like to move

56/

(22) How good do you think your neighborhood is for the older people to live?

[ ] A good place
[ ] A fair place
[ ] A poor place

57/

(23) Generally speaking, are the following places or people a convenient distance from where you live? (If the respondent is not in need of or does not care about being near these things such as a bank, park, etc., then mark "N.A.") (Let the respondent decide convenience.)

	Yes	No	N.A.
a. Friends	[ ]	[ ]	[ ]
b. Relatives	[ ]	[ ]	[ ]
c. Church	[ ]	[ ]	[ ]
d. Stores	[ ]	[ ]	[ ]
e. Medical facilities	[ ]	[ ]	[ ]
f. Bank	[ ]	[ ]	[ ]
g. Park	[ ]	[ ]	[ ]
h. Other recreational facilities	[ ]	[ ]	[ ]
i. Restaurant	[ ]	[ ]	[ ]

58 66/

67-80/b

ID No.: 1-5/

II. PERSONAL HEALTH, SAFETY, AND PHYSICAL WELL-BEING

(1) Here is a list of health problems that people often have. I'll read them and you tell me if you have any of them. First, a list of conditions which usually continue to require care or treatment or restrict activities:
(Interviewer: check "Yes" or "No" for each item.)

	Yes	No
a. Diabetes	[ ]	[ ]
b. High blood pressure	[ ]	[ ]
c. Heart trouble	[ ]	[ ]
d. Stroke	[ ]	[ ]
e. Arthritis	[ ]	[ ]
f. Cancer	[ ]	[ ]
g. Paralysis or Parkinson's disease	[ ]	[ ]
h. Glaucoma (cataracts) or other eye trouble not relieved by glasses	[ ]	[ ]

7-14/

(2) How many days have you been sick to the point of being unable to carry on your regular activities during the *last four weeks*?

[ ] No days (Interviewer: check "Not sick" on Question 3 and go on to Question 4.)
[ ] 1 to 7 days
[ ] 8 to 14 days
[ ] 15 to 21 days
[ ] 22 days or more

15/

(3) While you were sick during this time, were you mostly:
[ ] (Not sick)
[ ] Just at home
[ ] In bed at home
[ ] In the hospital

16/

(4) For doing each of the following activities: please tell me if you have no difficulty, can do it with some difficulty, or if you cannot do it.

	No Difficulty	Some Difficulty	Cannot Do It
a. Going up and down stairs	[ ]	[ ]	[ ]
b. Getting about the house	[ ]	[ ]	[ ]
c. Washing and bathing	[ ]	[ ]	[ ]

17-19/

20/6

II. PERSONAL HEALTH, SAFETY, AND PHYSICAL WELL-BEING

(4) (cont.)

	No Difficulty	Some Difficulty	Cannot Do It
d. Dressing and putting on shoes	[ ]	[ ]	[ ]
e. Getting out of the house	[ ]	[ ]	[ ]
f. Watching television	[ ]	[ ]	[ ]
g. Feeding yourself	[ ]	[ ]	[ ]

21-24/

(5) Please tell me whether you currently need each of the following health aids, and if so, whether you currently have it?

	Need?		If YES: do you have it?	
	Yes	No	Yes	No
a. Eyeglasses	[ ]	[ ]	[ ]	[ ]
b. Hearing aid	[ ]	[ ]	[ ]	[ ]
c. False teeth	[ ]	[ ]	[ ]	[ ]
d. Cane or crutch	[ ]	[ ]	[ ]	[ ]
e. Leg brace	[ ]	[ ]	[ ]	[ ]
f. Special shoes	[ ]	[ ]	[ ]	[ ]
g. Truss or abdominal brace	[ ]	[ ]	[ ]	[ ]
h. Wheelchair	[ ]	[ ]	[ ]	[ ]
i. Other health aids	[ ]	[ ]	[ ]	[ ]

25-33/

34-42/6

48-51/

52/

53/

54/

55/

56/

57/b

II. PERSONAL HEALTH, SAFETY, AND PHYSICAL WELL-BEING

(8) During the past year have you been injured in any of the following kinds of accidents?

	Yes	No
a. An automobile accident	[ ]	[ ]
b. Falling in the home	[ ]	[ ]
c. An injury on the job	[ ]	[ ]
d. Other	[ ]	[ ]

(9) Are you currently registered for Medicare?

[ ] Yes
[ ] No

(10) Are you a member of any health care program such as Kaiser, HMSA, Blue Cross, or some program like that?

[ ] Yes
[ ] No

IF YES: Which program do you belong to?

[ ] Kaiser
[ ] HMSA
[ ] Blue Cross
[ ] Other _____

(11) Now I will list to you some groups of food. Would you please tell me how often you eat something from each of the groups. That is, do you eat something from the group almost every day, sometimes, or almost never?

a. Milk, cheese, ice cream, or anything else made out of milk.

[ ] Almost every day
[ ] Sometimes
[ ] Almost never

b. Any kind of meat, including beef, veal, pork, lamb, poultry, or fish, eggs, dry beans, peas, tofu, or nuts.

[ ] Almost every day
[ ] Sometimes
[ ] Almost never

II. PERSONAL HEALTH, SAFETY, AND PHYSICAL WELL-BEING

(6) Have you had a medical checkup in the last year?

[ ] Yes
[ ] No

Was there any special reason why you didn't get a checkup?

(7) Have you had all the immunizations and inoculations you think you should have?

[ ] Yes
[ ] No
[ ] Don't know

Which additional ones do you think you should have?

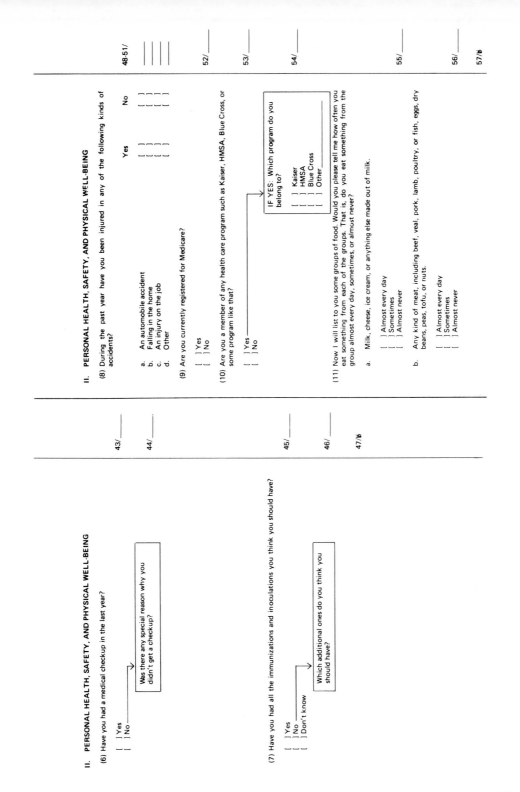

485

6/3

II. PERSONAL HEALTH, SAFETY, AND PHYSICAL WELL-BEING

(11) (cont.)

c. Any fruit or vegetable or juice.

  [ ] Almost every day
  [ ] Sometimes
  [ ] Almost never

d. Any kind of food made of bread or cereal, or rice.

  [ ] Almost every day
  [ ] Sometimes
  [ ] Almost never

(12) Do you take vitamin pills every day or almost every day?

  [ ] Yes
  [ ] No

(13) In general, would you say your appetite is poor, fair, or good?

  [ ] Poor
  [ ] Fair
  [ ] Good

(14) Has your appetite been like this only recently, during the past year, or most of your life?

  [ ] Recently
  [ ] Past year
  [ ] Most of life

(15) Would you say you have been gaining weight, staying the same, or losing weight over the past two years?

  [ ] Gaining
  [ ] Losing
  [ ] Staying the same

(16) Do you have trouble buying foods that you like?

  [ ] Yes
  [ ] No
  [ ] Sometimes

58/
59/
60/
61/
62/
63/
64/
6J-80/b

III. ECONOMIC SATISFACTION

Now we would like to learn just a little about your financial situation.

(1) To begin, could you tell me whether you (and your husband/wife) are responsible for managing your day-to-day finances such as buying food and clothing, paying the rent or mortgage payments, and so forth, or are your finances handled by someone else?

  [ ] Handled by respondent
  [ ] Handled by someone else

(1a) Who is responsible for handling your finances?

(1b) Do you receive any financial support from your children or other relatives?

  [ ] Yes
  [ ] No

7/

8/

(2) During the past year did you (or the person handling your finances) receive any income from the following sources?

	Yes	No
Wages	[ ]	[ ]
Income from a business or professional practice	[ ]	[ ]
Income from farming	[ ]	[ ]
Social Security	[ ]	[ ]
Retirement payments or pensions	[ ]	[ ]
Interest on savings or dividends	[ ]	[ ]
Others	[ ]	[ ]

9/

10-16/

(3) Could you tell me approximately how much income you (and the person responsible for your finances) had from all sources during the past year?

$ _____

17-21/

(4) How many people were supported by that income?

_____

22-23/

24/b

486

III. ECONOMIC SATISFACTION

(5) Do you currently have a job?   [ ] Yes   [ ] No →

IF YES

(5a) Do you work full-time or part-time?

[ ] Full-time
[ ] Part-time

                           25/ _____

IF NO

(5b) Would you like a job if you could find work you liked and could do?

[ ] Yes
[ ] No

                           26/ _____

(6) How well do you think your income and assets satisfy your needs:

[ ] Very well
[ ] Well
[ ] Adequately
[ ] Barely
[ ] Poorly

                           27/ _____

IF ANSWER IS "POORLY" OR "BARELY" TO 6 ABOVE:

(6a) How much more money do you and your family need each month to live comfortably?

[ ] Less than $50
[ ] $50 to $99
[ ] $100 to $149
[ ] $150 or more

                           28/ _____

                           29/ _____

                           30/b

IV. INTELLECTUAL AND SOCIAL SATISFACTION

(1) How often did you visit in person with a member of your family last week?

[ ] Every day
[ ] A few times
[ ] Once
[ ] Not at all
[ ] No family nearby

                           31/ _____

(2) How often did you visit in person with friends or neighbors last week?

[ ] Every day
[ ] A few times
[ ] Once
[ ] Not at all

                           32/ _____

(3) About how often last week did you talk to friends, relatives, business contacts, or others on the telephone?

[ ] Every day
[ ] Several times
[ ] Once
[ ] Not at all

                           33/ _____

(4) Of all your neighbors, about how many do you know well enough to visit with?

[ ] 5 or more
[ ] 3 or 4
[ ] 1 or 2
[ ] None

                           34/ _____

(5) Do you have as much contact as you would like with a person you feel close to—somebody that you can trust and confide in?

[ ] Yes
[ ] No

                           35/ _____

(6) Do you think that you see enough of your friends, relatives, and neighbors?

[ ] Yes
[ ] No

                           36/ _____

                           37/b

IV. INTELLECTUAL AND SOCIAL SATISFACTION

(7) How often do you find yourself feeling lonely?

[ ] Never or hardly
[ ] Sometimes
[ ] Fairly often
[ ] Very often or always

38/ ____

(8) How often do you get out of doors beyond just outside the door to the mailbox?

[ ] Every day
[ ] Several times a week
[ ] Once a week
[ ] Less than weekly

39/ ____

(9) About how many hours a day on the average do you watch television?

[ ] 5 or more hours
[ ] 3 or 4
[ ] 1 or 2
[ ] Less than 1

40/ ____

(10) About how many hours a day would you say you spend reading newspapers, magazines, or books?

[ ] 5 or more hours
[ ] 3 or 4
[ ] 1 or 2
[ ] Less than 1

41/ ____

(11) How active would you say you are in the following kinds of activities: would you say very active, fairly active, or not very active?

	Very Active	Fairly Active	Not Very Active
a. Religious activities	[ ]	[ ]	[ ]
b. Politics	[ ]	[ ]	[ ]
c. Social clubs	[ ]	[ ]	[ ]
d. Sports as a participant	[ ]	[ ]	[ ]
e. Sports as a spectator	[ ]	[ ]	[ ]

42-46/ ____

(12) In general, do you usually have enough to do?

[ ] Yes
[ ] No

47/ ____

48/b

IV. INTELLECTUAL AND SOCIAL SATISFACTION

(13) How would you describe your general satisfaction with life at the present?

[ ] Excellent
[ ] Good
[ ] Fair
[ ] Poor

49/ ____

(14) Do you feel that the following services and facilities are generally adequate to your needs and desires or are they generally inadequate? (Note: if respondent indicates no need or desire, check "Not appl.")

	Adeq.	Inadeq.	Not Appl.
a. Libraries	[ ]	[ ]	[ ]
b. Museums	[ ]	[ ]	[ ]
c. Cultural events	[ ]	[ ]	[ ]
d. Adult education courses	[ ]	[ ]	[ ]
e. Training programs in skills you might want to learn	[ ]	[ ]	[ ]

50-54/ ____

(15) Do you usually expect that things will turn out well for you?

[ ] Yes
[ ] No

55/ ____

(16) How much would you say you worry about things?

[ ] Not at all
[ ] Not much
[ ] Fairly often
[ ] A great deal

56/ ____

57/b

V. PROTECTION OF CIVIL RIGHTS AND PROPERTY

(1) During the past year, have you been the victim of any of the following crimes? (IF YES: was it reported to the police?)

	Victim?		Reported to police?	
	Yes	No	Yes	No
a. Arson	[ ]	[ ]	[ ]	[ ]
b. Assault	[ ]	[ ]	[ ]	[ ]
c. Burglary	[ ]	[ ]	[ ]	[ ]
d. Fraud	[ ]	[ ]	[ ]	[ ]
e. Malicious damage to property	[ ]	[ ]	[ ]	[ ]
f. Hold up	[ ]	[ ]	[ ]	[ ]

58-63/

IF ANY CRIME WAS NOT REPORTED TO POLICE:

What was the main reason for not reporting that crime (those crimes) to the police?

64/

65-71/b

V. PROTECTION OF CIVIL RIGHTS AND PROPERTY

(2) During the past year, have you needed legal services of any kind?

[ ] Yes
[ ] No

72/

IF YES: what kind of legal services did you need?

73/

Were you able to get the services you needed?

[ ] Yes, all
[ ] Some of them
[ ] No

74/

(3) During the past year, have you needed family counseling services?

[ ] Yes
[ ] No

75/

IF YES: were you able to get the services needed?

[ ] Yes
[ ] No

76/

77-80/b

489

ID No.: 1-5/

V. PROTECTION OF CIVIL RIGHTS AND PROPERTY

(4) During the past year, have you needed financial counseling?   6/4

[ ] Yes
[ ] No

→ IF YES: were you able to get the counseling needed?   7/

[ ] Yes
[ ] No

(5) Some older people report that they are often taken advantage of because of their age. Do you feel this has happened to you during the past year?   8/

[ ] Yes
[ ] No

→ IF YES: please describe what happened.   9/

(6) Now would you tell me if you think you need or would like to have counseling services available to you on the following matters?   10/

	Yes	No	Not appl.
a. Planning retirement	[ ]	[ ]	[ ]
b. Health protection and care	[ ]	[ ]	[ ]
c. Consumer protection	[ ]	[ ]	[ ]
d. Leisure time activities	[ ]	[ ]	[ ]

11-14/

15/b

PERSONAL CHARACTERISTICS

Finally, we would like to know just a little about you, so that we will be able to understand the answers different kinds of people give in this survey.

(1) INTERVIEWER: CHECK SEX   [ ] Male   [ ] Female   16/

(2) What is your age please?   17-18/

(3) Where were you born?   19-20/

[ ] Oahu
[ ] Neighbor Island (Which: _____)
[ ] Mainland U. S. (State: _____)
[ ] Foreign Country (Country: _____)

(4) Which of the following best describes your racial or ethnic group?   21-22/

01. [ ] Caucasian, haole.
02. [ ] Chinese
03. [ ] Filipino
04. [ ] Hawaiian or part-Hawaiian
05. [ ] Japanese
06. [ ] Korean
07. [ ] Negro, Black
08. [ ] Samoan
09. [ ] Cosmopolitan (without Hawaiian)
10. [ ] Other: _____

23-80/b

D

Random Numbers

```
10480  15011  01536  02011  81647  91646  69179  14194  62590  36207  20969  99570  91291  90700
22368  46573  25595  85393  30995  89198  27982  53402  93965  34095  52666  19174  39615  99505
24130  48360  22527  97265  76393  64809  15179  24830  49340  32081  30680  19655  63348  58629
42167  93093  06243  61680  07856  16376  39440  53537  71341  57004  00849  74917  97758  16379
37570  39975  81837  16656  06121  91782  60468  81305  49684  60672  14110  06927  01263  54613

77921  06907  11008  42751  27756  53498  18602  70659  90655  15053  21916  81825  44394  42880
99562  72905  56420  69994  98872  31016  71194  18738  56869  44013  48840  63213  21069  10634  12952
96301  91977  05463  07972  18876  20922  94595  56869  69014  25331  18425  84903  42508  32307
89579  14342  63661  10281  17453  18103  57740  84378  25331  12566  58678  44947  05585  56941
85475  36857  53342  53988  53060  59533  38867  62300  08158  17983  16439  11458  18593  64952

28918  69578  88231  33276  70997  79936  56865  05859  90106  31595  01547  85590  91610  78188
63553  40961  48235  03427  49626  69445  18663  72695  52180  20847  12234  90511  33703  90322
09429  93969  52636  92737  88974  33488  36320  17617  30015  08272  84115  27156  30613  74952
10365  61129  87529  85689  48237  52267  67689  93394  01511  26358  85104  20285  29975  89868
07119  97336  71048  08178  77233  13916  47564  81056  97735  85977  29372  74461  28551  90707

51085  12765  51821  51259  77452  16308  60756  92144  49442  53900  70960  63990  75601  40719
02368  21382  52404  60268  89368  19885  55322  44819  01188  65255  64835  44919  05944  55157
01011  54092  33362  94904  31273  04146  18594  29852  71585  85030  51132  01915  92747  64951
52162  53916  46369  58586  23216  14513  83149  98736  23495  64350  94738  17752  35156  35749
07056  97628  33787  09998  42698  06691  76988  13602  51851  46104  88916  19509  25625  58104

48663  91245  85828  14346  09172  30168  90229  04734  59193  22178  30421  61666  99904  32812
54164  58492  22421  74103  47070  25306  76468  26384  58151  06646  21524  15227  96909  44592
32639  32363  05597  24200  13363  38005  94342  28728  35806  06912  17012  64161  18296  22851
29334  27001  87637  87308  58731  00256  45834  15398  46557  41135  10367  07684  36188  18510
02488  33062  28834  07351  19731  92420  60952  61280  50001  67658  32586  86679  50720  94953

81525  72295  04839  96423  24878  82651  66566  14778  76797  14780  13300  87074  79666  95725
29676  20591  68086  26432  46901  20849  89768  81536  86645  12659  92259  57102  80428  25280
00742  57392  39064  66432  84673  40027  32832  61362  98947  96067  64760  64584  96096  98253
05366  04213  25669  26422  44407  44048  37937  63904  45766  66134  75470  66520  34693  90449
91921  26418  64117  94305  26766  25940  39972  22209  71500  64568  91402  42416  07844  69618

00582  04711  87917  77341  42206  35126  74087  99547  81817  42607  43808  76655  62028  76630
00725  69884  62797  56170  86324  88072  76222  36086  84637  93161  76038  65855  77919  88006
69011  65795  95876  55293  18988  27354  26575  08625  40801  59920  29841  80150  12777  48501
25976  57948  29888  88604  67917  48708  18912  82271  65424  69774  33611  54262  85963  03547
09763  83473  73577  12908  30883  18317  28290  35797  05998  41688  34952  37888  38917  88050

91567  42595  27958  30134  04024  86385  29880  99730  55536  84855  29080  09250  79656  73211
17955  56349  90999  49127  20044  59931  06115  20542  18059  02008  73708  83517  36103  42791
46503  18584  18845  49618  02304  51038  20655  58727  28168  15475  56942  53389  20562  87338
92157  89634  94824  78171  84610  82834  09922  25417  44137  48413  25555  21246  35509  20468
14577  62765  35605  81263  39667  47358  56873  56307  61607  49518  89656  20103  77490  18062

98427  07523  33362  64270  01638  92477  66969  98420  04880  45585  46565  04102  46880  45709
34914  63976  88720  82765  34476  17032  87589  40836  32427  70002  70663  88863  77775  69348
70060  28277  39475  46473  23219  53416  94970  25832  69975  94884  19661  72828  00102  66794
53976  54914  06990  67245  68350  82948  11398  42878  80287  88267  47363  46634  06541  97809
76072  29515  40980  07391  58745  25774  22987  80059  39911  96189  41151  14222  60697  59583

90725  52210  83974  29992  65831  38857  50490  83765  55657  14361  31720  57375  56228  41546
64364  67412  33339  31926  14883  24413  59744  92351  97473  89286  35931  04110  23726  51900
08962  00358  31662  25388  61642  34072  81249  35648  56891  69352  48373  45578  78547  81788
95012  68379  93526  70765  10592  04542  76463  54328  02349  17247  28865  14777  62730  92277
15664  10493  20492  38391  91132  21999  59516  81652  27195  48223  46751  22923  32261  85653
```

16408	81899	04153	53381	79401	21438	83035	92350	36693	31238	59649	91754	72772	02338
18629	81953	05520	91962	04739	13092	97662	24822	94730	06496	35090	04822	86774	98289
73115	35101	47498	87637	99016	71060	88824	71013	18735	20286	23153	72924	35165	43040
57491	16703	23167	49323	45021	33132	12544	41035	80780	45393	44812	12515	98931	91202
30405	83946	23792	14422	15059	45799	22716	19792	09983	74353	68668	30429	70735	25499
16631	35006	85900	98275	32388	52390	16815	69298	82732	38480	73817	32523	41961	44437
96773	20206	42559	78985	05300	22164	24369	54224	35083	19687	11052	91491	60383	19746
38935	64202	14349	82674	66523	44133	00697	35552	35970	19124	63318	29686	03387	59846
31624	76384	17403	53363	44167	64486	64758	75366	76554	31601	12614	33072	60332	92325
78919	19474	23632	27889	47914	02584	37680	20801	72152	39339	34806	08930	85001	87820
03931	33309	57047	74211	63445	17361	62825	39908	05607	91284	68833	25570	38818	46920
74426	33278	43972	10119	89917	15665	52872	73823	73144	88662	88970	74492	51805	99378
09066	00903	20795	95452	92648	45454	09552	88815	16553	51125	79375	97596	16296	66092
42238	12426	87025	14267	20979	04508	64535	31355	86064	29472	47689	05974	52468	16834
16153	08002	26504	41744	81959	65642	74240	56302	00033	67107	77510	70625	28725	34191
21457	40742	29820	96783	29400	21840	15035	34537	33310	06116	95240	15957	16572	06004
21581	57802	02050	89728	17937	37621	47075	42080	97403	48626	68995	43805	33386	21597
55612	78095	83197	33732	05810	24813	86902	60397	16489	03264	88525	42786	05269	92532
44657	66999	99324	51281	84463	60563	79312	93454	68876	25471	93911	25650	12682	73572
91340	84979	46949	81973	37949	61023	43997	15263	80644	43942	89203	71795	99533	50501
91227	21199	31935	27022	84067	05462	35216	14486	29891	68607	41867	14951	91696	85065
50001	38140	66321	19924	72163	09538	12151	06878	91903	18749	34405	56087	82790	70925
65390	05224	72958	28609	81406	39147	25549	42627	45233	57202	94617	23772	07896	
27504	96131	83944	41575	10573	08619	64482	73923	36152	05184	94142	25299	84387	34925
37169	94851	39117	89632	00959	16487	65536	49071	39782	17095	02330	74301	00275	48280
11508	70225	51111	38351	19444	66499	71945	05422	13442	78675	84081	66938	93654	59894
37449	30362	06694	54690	04052	53115	62757	95348	78662	11163	81651	50245	34971	52924
46515	70331	85922	38329	57015	15765	97161	17869	45349	61796	66345	81073	49106	79860
30986	81223	42416	58353	21532	30502	32305	86482	05174	07901	54339	58861	74818	46942
63798	64995	46583	09785	44160	78128	83991	42865	92520	83531	80377	35909	81250	54238
82486	84846	99254	67632	43218	50076	21361	64816	51202	88124	41870	52689	51275	83556
21885	32906	92431	09060	64297	51674	64126	62570	26123	05155	59194	52799	28225	85762
60336	98782	07408	53458	13564	59089	26445	29789	85205	41001	12535	12133	14645	23541
43937	46891	24010	25560	86355	33941	25786	54990	71899	15475	95434	98227	21824	19585
97656	63175	89303	16275	07100	92063	21942	18611	47348	20203	18534	03862	78095	50136
03299	01221	05418	38982	55758	92237	26759	86367	21216	98442	08303	56613	91511	75928
79626	06486	03574	17668	07785	76020	79924	25651	83325	88428	85076	72811	22717	50585
85636	68335	47539	03129	65651	11977	02510	26113	99447	68645	34327	15152	55230	93448
18039	14367	61337	06177	12143	46609	32989	74014	64708	00533	35398	58408	13261	47908
08362	15656	60627	36478	65648	16764	53412	09013	07832	41574	17639	82163	60859	75567
79556	29068	04142	16268	15387	12856	66227	38358	22478	73373	88732	09443	82558	05250
92608	82674	27072	32534	17075	27698	98204	63863	11951	34648	88022	56148	34925	57031
23982	25835	40055	67006	12293	02753	14827	23235	35071	99704	37543	11601	35503	85171
09915	96306	05908	97901	28395	14186	00821	80703	70426	75647	76310	88717	37890	40129
59037	33300	26695	62247	69927	76123	50842	43834	86654	70959	79725	93872	28117	19233
42488	78077	69882	61657	34136	79180	97526	43092	04098	73571	80799	76536	71255	64239
46764	86273	63003	93017	31204	36692	40202	35275	57306	55543	53203	18098	47625	88684
03237	45430	55417	63282	90816	17349	88298	90183	36600	78406	06216	95787	42579	90730
86591	81482	52667	61582	14972	90053	89534	76036	49199	43716	97548	04379	46370	28672
38534	01715	94964	87288	65680	43772	39560	12918	86537	62738	19636	51132	25739	56947

Abridged from *Handbook of Tables for Probability and Statistics,* Second Edition, edited by William H. Beyer (Clevelend: The Chemical Rubber Company, 1968). Used by permission of The Chemical Rubber Company.

Critical Values of Chi Square

d.f.	$\chi^2 0.995$	$\chi^2 0.990$	$\chi^2 0.975$	$\chi^2 0.950$	$\chi^2 0.900$
1	0.0000393	0.0001571	0.0009821	0.0039321	0.0157908
2	0.0100251	0.0201007	0.0506356	0.102587	0.210720
3	0.0717212	0.114832	0.215795	0.351846	0.584375
4	0.206990	0.297110	0.484419	0.710721	1.063623
5	0.411740	0.554300	0.831211	1.145476	1.61031
6	0.675727	0.872085	1.237347	1.63539	2.20413
7	0.989265	1.239043	1.68987	2.16735	2.83311
8	1.344419	1.646482	2.17973	2.73264	3.48954
9	1.734926	2.087912	2.70039	3.32511	4.16816
10	2.15585	2.55821	3.24697	3.94030	4.86518
11	2.60321	3.05347	3.81575	4.57481	5.57779
12	3.07382	3.57056	4.40379	5.22603	6.30380
13	3.56503	4.10691	5.00874	5.89186	7.04150
14	4.07468	4.66043	5.62872	6.57063	7.78953
15	4.60094	5.22935	6.26214	7.26094	8.54675
16	5.14224	5.81221	6.90766	7.96164	9.31223
17	5.69724	6.40776	7.56418	8.67176	10.0852
18	6.26481	7.01491	8.23075	9.39046	10.8649
19	6.84398	7.63273	8.90655	10.1170	11.6509
20	7.43386	8.26040	9.59083	10.8508	12.4426
21	8.03366	8.89720	10.28293	11.5913	13.2396
22	8.64272	9.54249	10.9823	12.3380	14.0415
23	9.26042	10.19567	11.6885	13.0905	14.8479
24	9.88623	10.8564	12.4011	13.8484	15.6587
25	10.5197	11.5240	13.1197	14.6114	16.4734
26	11.1603	12.1981	13.8439	15.3791	17.2919
27	11.8076	12.8786	14.5733	16.1513	18.1138
28	12.4613	13.5648	15.3079	16.9279	18.9392
29	13.1211	14.2565	16.0471	17.7083	19.7677
30	13.7867	14.9535	16.7908	18.4926	20.5992
40	20.7065	22.1643	24.4331	26.5093	29.0505
50	27.9907	29.7067	32.3574	34.7642	37.6886
60	35.5346	37.4848	40.4817	43.1879	46.4589
70	43.2752	45.4418	48.7576	51.7393	55.3290
80	51.1720	53.5400	57.1532	60.3915	64.2778
90	59.1963	61.7541	65.6466	69.1260	73.2912
100	67.3276	70.0648	74.2219	77.9295	82.3581

$\chi^2 0.100$	$\chi^2 0.050$	$\chi^2 0.025$	$\chi^2 0.010$	$\chi^2 0.005$	d.f.
2.70554	3.84146	5.02389	6.63490	7.87944	1
4.60517	5.99147	7.37776	9.21034	10.5966	2
6.25139	7.81473	9.34840	11.3449	12.8381	3
7.77944	9.48773	11.1433	13.2767	14.8602	4
9.23635	11.0705	12.8325	15.0863	16.7496	5
10.6446	12.5916	14.4494	16.8119	18.5476	6
12.0170	14.0671	16.0128	18.4753	20.2777	7
13.3616	15.5073	17.5346	20.0902	21.9550	8
14.6837	16.9190	19.0228	21.6660	23.5893	9
15.9871	18.3070	20.4831	23.2093	25.1882	10
17.2750	19.6751	21.9200	24.7250	26.7569	11
18.5494	21.0261	23.3367	26.2170	28.2995	12
19.8119	22.3621	24.7356	27.6883	29.8194	13
21.0642	23.6848	26.1190	29.1413	31.3193	14
22.3072	24.9958	27.4884	30.5779	32.8013	15
23.5418	26.2962	28.8454	31.9999	34.2672	16
24.7690	27.5871	30.1910	33.4087	35.7185	17
25.9894	28.8693	31.5264	34.8053	37.1564	18
27.2036	30.1435	32.8523	36.1908	38.5822	19
28.4120	31.4104	34.1696	37.5662	39.9968	20
29.6151	32.6705	35.4789	38.9321	41.4010	21
30.8133	33.9244	36.7807	40.2894	42.7956	22
32.0069	35.1725	38.0757	41.6384	44.1813	23
33.1963	36.4151	39.3641	42.9798	45.5585	24
34.3816	37.6525	40.6465	44.3141	46.9278	25
35.5631	38.8852	41.9232	45.6417	48.2899	26
36.7412	40.1133	43.1944	46.9630	49.6449	27
37.9159	41.3372	44.4607	48.2782	50.9933	28
39.0875	42.5569	45.7222	49.5879	52.3356	29
40.2560	43.7729	46.9792	50.8922	53.6720	30
51.8050	55.7585	59.3417	63.6907	66.7659	40
63.1671	67.5048	71.4202	76.1539	79.4900	50
74.3970	79.0819	83.2976	88.3794	91.9517	60
85.5271	90.5312	95.0231	100.425	104.215	70
96.5782	101.879	106.629	112.329	116.321	80
107.565	113.145	118.136	124.116	128.299	90
118.498	124.342	129.561	135.807	140.169	100

From "Tables of the Percentage Points of the χ^2-Distribution." *Biometrika*, Vol. 32 (1941), pp. 188–189, by Catherine M. Thompson. Used by permission of Professor E.S. Pearson.

F

Normal Curve Areas

z	.00	.01	.02	.03	.04	.05	.06	.07	.08	.09
0.0	.0000	.0040	.0080	.0120	.0160	.0199	.0239	.0279	.0319	.0359
0.1	.0398	.0438	.0478	.0517	.0557	.0596	.0636	.0675	.0714	.0753
0.2	.0793	.0832	.0871	.0910	.0948	.0987	.1026	.1064	.1103	.1141
0.3	.1179	.1217	.1255	.1293	.1331	.1368	.1406	.1443	.1480	.1517
0.4	.1554	.1591	.1628	.1664	.1700	.1736	.1772	.1808	.1844	.1879
0.5	.1915	.1950	.1985	.2019	.2054	.2088	.2123	.2157	.2190	.2224
0.6	.2257	.2291	.2324	.2357	.2389	.2422	.2454	.2486	.2517	.2549
0.7	.2580	.2611	.2642	.2673	.2704	.2734	.2764	.2794	.2823	.2852
0.8	.2881	.2910	.2939	.2967	.2995	.3023	.3051	.3078	.3106	.3133
0.9	.3159	.3186	.3212	.3238	.3264	.3289	.3315	.3340	.3365	.3389
1.0	.3413	.3438	.3461	.3485	.3508	.3531	.3554	.3577	.3599	.3621
1.1	.3643	.3665	.3686	.3708	.3729	.3749	.3770	.3790	.3810	.3830
1.2	.3849	.3869	.3888	.3907	.3925	.3944	.3962	.3980	.3997	.4015
1.3	.4032	.4049	.4066	.4082	.4099	.4115	.4131	.4147	.4162	.4177
1.4	.4192	.4207	.4222	.4236	.4251	.4265	.4279	.4292	.4306	.4319
1.5	.4332	.4345	.4357	.4370	.4382	.4394	.4406	.4418	.4429	.4441
1.6	.4452	.4463	.4474	.4484	.4495	.4505	.4515	.4525	.4535	.4545
1.7	.4554	.4564	.4573	.4582	.4591	.4599	.4608	.4616	.4625	.4633
1.8	.4641	.4649	.4656	.4664	.4671	.4678	.4686	.4693	.4699	.4706
1.9	.4713	.4719	.4726	.4732	.4738	.4744	.4750	.4756	.4761	.4767
2.0	.4772	.4778	.4783	.4788	.4793	.4798	.4803	.4808	.4812	.4817
2.1	.4821	.4826	.4830	.4834	.4838	.4842	.4846	.4850	.4854	.4857
2.2	.4861	.4864	.4868	.4871	.4875	.4878	.4881	.4884	.4887	.4890
2.3	.4893	.4896	.4898	.4901	.4904	.4906	.4909	.4911	.4913	.4916
2.4	.4918	.4920	.4922	.4925	.4927	.4929	.4931	.4932	.4934	.4936
2.5	.4938	.4940	.4941	.4943	.4945	.4946	.4948	.4949	.4951	.4952
2.6	.4953	.4955	.4956	.4957	.4959	.4960	.4961	.4962	.4963	.4964
2.7	.4965	.4966	.4967	.4968	.4969	.4970	.4971	.4972	.4973	.4974
2.8	.4974	.4975	.4976	.4977	.4977	.4978	.4979	.4979	.4980	.4981
2.9	.4981	.4982	.4982	.4983	.4984	.4984	.4985	.4985	.4986	.4986
3.0	.4987	.4987	.4987	.4988	.4988	.4989	.4989	.4989	.4990	.4990

Abridged from Table I of *Statistical Tables and Formulas*, by A. Hald (New York: John Wiley & Sons, Inc., 1952). Used by permission of John Wiley & Sons, Inc.

G

Estimated Sampling Error

How to use this table: Find the intersection between the sample size and the approximate percentage distribution of the binomial in the sample. The number appearing at this intersection represents the estimated sampling error, at the 95 percent confidence level, expressed in percentage points (plus or minus).

Example: in a sample of 400 respondents, 60 percent answer yes and 40 percent answer no. The sampling error is estimated at plus or minus 4.9 percentage points. The confidence interval, then, is between 55.1 percent and 64.9 percent. We would estimate (95 percent confidence) that the proportion of the total population who would say yes is somewhere within that interval.

Sample Size	Binomial Percentage Distribution				
	50/50	60/40	70/30	80/20	90/10
100	10	9.8	9.2	8	6
200	7.1	6.9	6.5	5.7	4.2
300	5.8	5.7	5.3	4.6	3.5
400	5	4.9	4.6	4	3
500	4.5	4.4	4.1	3.6	2.7
600	4.1	4	3.7	3.3	2.4
700	3.8	3.7	3.5	3	2.3
800	3.5	3.5	3.2	2.8	2.1
900	3.3	3.3	3.1	2.7	2
1000	3.2	3.1	2.9	2.5	1.9
1100	3	3	2.8	2.4	1.8
1200	2.9	2.8	2.6	2.3	1.7
1300	2.8	2.7	2.5	2.2	1.7
1400	2.7	2.6	2.4	2.1	1.6
1500	2.6	2.5	2.4	2.1	1.5
1600	2.5	2.4	2.3	2	1.5
1700	2.4	2.4	2.2	1.9	1.5
1800	2.4	2.3	2.2	1.9	1.4
1900	2.3	2.2	2.1	1.8	1.4
2000	2.2	2.2	2	1.8	1.3

H

A Learner's Guide to SPSS^x

Prepared by Jeffrey M. Jacques
Florida A&M University

By the time you complete this appendix and do all the suggested exercises, you will know

1. *When to use SPSS^x*
2. *How to build a basic SPSS^x command file*
3. *How to build an enhanced SPSS^x command file*
4. *Which basic SPSS^x commands to use when performing statistical analyses such as*
   a) *univariate analysis*
   b) *bivariate analysis*
   c) *scaling*

INTRODUCTION

By now you have probably mastered the fundamentals of how to structure a
research project, how to develop an instrument, and how to select your sample.
Indeed, you have probably collected more data than you know what to do with.
Of course, your instructor may have collected the data for you, or you may be
working with a group of other students who have collected a substantial amount
of data. In any case, the reality of doing social research includes not only the
design and implementation of good research methods and data collection, but also
the management and analysis of the collected data.

As you know, the purpose of research includes the exploration, description,
and/or explanation of social phenomena. The analysis of data, therefore, is the
intermediary step that will enable you, the researcher, to explore and describe
social patterns and explain why such patterns exist. With the help of SPSS^x, *The
Statistical Package for the Social Sciences,* you should be able to accomplish these
goals in a fast, efficient, and cost-effective manner.

All you need to do is to determine what you wish to find out, master a series of
Englishlike SPSS^x commands, and learn a little about how to create and manage
files at your computer site.

Strange as it may seem, the best place to begin a discussion of when to use the
computer is not at the computer. Nor is a discussion of the software the best
approach. The best place to start is with a clear conception of what you wish to
find out. The computer and the SPSS^x package are simply tools to help you 1)
summarize your data, 2) create appropriate tables and graphs, 3) examine
relationships among your variables, and 4) perform tests of statistical significance
on your hypotheses. Indeed, because the computer and the SPSS^x package are
extremely fast, you will be able to examine data and variables in a variety of ways
heretofore unimaginable. The basic point is that if you understand your research
question(s) thoroughly, SPSS^x can be very helpful when it comes to manipulating
large amounts of data, finding patterns, and testing hypotheses.

There are a couple of things that this appendix will not do. It will not make
you an expert at using SPSS^x. Nor will it specify which commands are unique to
your computer site. Rather, the purpose of this appendix is to teach you the basic
commands of SPSS^x and to show you step-by-step how to use the computer and
SPSS^x to facilitate the analysis of data.

To illustrate each step, we will use a recent study of race relations in a small
Southern city. Data were collected by students like yourself. These students started
with the basic question, Do racial attitudes differ between black and white city
residents? The questionnaire they used is reproduced in Figure 1. Take a minute to
review the questionnaire before you go any further.

The students hypothesized that in this city there were diverse racial attitudes
and that these diverse racial attitudes could be explained, at least in part, by
respondents' race/ethnicity, income, political behavior, and age. Therefore, in
addition to summarizing the overall patterns and racial attitudes of city residents,
the students investigated the following questions:

1. Are there significant differences between racial groups on the variables used to
measure racial attitudes?

FIGURE 1 SURVEY QUESTIONNAIRE

Hello. My name is ------------------------------------.
I am a student at the University. We are conducting a survey
on race relations in the local area and I would like to ask some
questions. It should take a couple of minutes. Your answer to
these questions will be treated confidentially. Your name was
chosen through a random sampling from the local telephone
directory. Your responses will be added to a group of other
responses and no one will be able to trace them back to you.

DIRECTIONS: I will read a few statements of opinion about race
relations. You may find that you agree with some of the
statements and disagree with others. Please indicate your
agreement or disagreement by stating STRONGLY AGREE, AGREE,
DISAGREE or STRONGLY DISAGREE to each statement.

ID#   (1-3)
----

1. I feel that children of   4   3   2   1   (4)
    different races should   SA A   D   SD
    attend the same schools.

2. I feel that members of different   4   3   2   1   (5)
    races should live in my   SA A   D   SD
    neighborhood.

3. I feel that members of different   4   3   2   1   (6)
    races should attend my church.   SA A   D   SD

4. I am willing to have a qualified   4   3   2   1   (7)
    member of a different race be my   SA A   D   SD
    supervisor.

5. I am willing to have a member of   4   3   2   1   (8)
    a different race live next door   SA A   D   SD
    to me.

6. I am willing to allow a member of 4   3   2   1   (9)
    a different race to date my child. SA A   D   SD

7. I am willing to allow a member of 4   3   2   1   (10)
    a different race to marry my child. SA A   D   SD

8. What do you perceive to be
    the appropriate mixture of   0% 20% 40% 60% 80% 100%   (11-13)
    minorities in your public
    school?

I have just a few background questions.

9. Are you a registered voter?   0   1   (14)
                                             No   Yes

10. Did you vote in the last senatorial   0   1   (15)
    elections?   No   Yes

11. To which political party do you   0   1   (16)
    belong?   Democrat Republican

12. What is your ethnic/racial affiliation?
                                                      (17)
                        White (4)   -------
                        Black (3)
                     Hispanic (2)
                        Other (1)

13. What is your approximate annual income?
                                                      (18)
              $7,000 or less (1)   -------
              $7,001 - 14,000 (2)
              $14,001 - 20,000 (3)
              $20,001 - 28,000 (4)
              $28,001 & above (5)

14. Are you married?
                                                      (19)
                        No   (0)   -------
                        Yes (1)

15. What is your sex?
                                                      (20)
                        Male   (0)   -------
                        Female (1)

16. What year were you born?   19   (21-22)
                                             ----

2. Are there significant differences between men and women on the variables used
to measure racial attitudes?

3. Are there significant correlations between the variables of racial attitudes and
income or between racial attitudes and when a person was born?

4. What variable(s) or combinations of variables are the best predictors of racial
attitudes in this city?

These questions will guide our use of the computer and SPSS^x.

Getting the Data to the Computer

Here we will assume that you have mastered the basics of what a computer is, what data files are, and how to create a codebook. If not, you may need to reread the chapter on quantifying data. In any case, in Table 1 you will find a copy of the codebook created from our questionnaire.

Once we know where to enter the data, it's easy to build a data file. Take a look at Table 2. Here you will find the data for each of the respondents from our race relations study. Look back to Table 1, the codebook, and note that for all sixty respondents, the data for the statement "children and schools" were entered in column 4, the data for "race and neighborhood" were entered in column 5, etc.

Note that the data on question 8, "perceived appropriate minority mixture in public schools," could have required us to enter a three-digit number, so columns 11 through 13 were reserved for these responses. Because each record (line) of Table 2 contains the data for each variable in the same column format, we call this structure a fixed formatted rectangular file. With this kind of file, we can tell SPSS^x how to read the fields, which variables are single-digit numbers, and which require more than a single digit or column.

Exercise 1

Before we go any further, you need to develop a codebook for your research project. Use the codebook format of Table 1. When you're finished, code your data set. Take a sheet of paper and divide it into several rows, one for each respondent, and columns—as many columns as you need according to your codebook. Now label each column or column set or field according to your variable names and enter your test data.

Finding Out About Your Computer Site

Now that you have a data set, it's time to find out about your college's computer site. If you don't know about it, ask a friend. You should be able to get the help you need by telling the computer personnel what you plan to do—that is, that you plan to enter data and use SPSS^x to perform the analysis. They will probably set up an account for you and give you some documentation on how to use the system and its text editor—how to create a file, enter data into a file, and correct any data entry errors.

Unfortunately, there is no single standard for text editors. You will have to get help from colleagues and university personnel. Just remember that your goal is to create a data file in which every card, record, or line of data represents one respondent and every response for the same variable is entered in the same fields or columns across all the respondents' records.

TABLE 1. RACE RELATIONS CODEBOOK

==

VARIABLE NAME	VARIABLE LABEL	COLUMN NO. Begin	COLUMN NO. End	VALUES Min	VALUES Max	VALUE LABELS	MISSING VALUES
IDNUM	Instrument number	1	3	101	610	N/A	N/A
RR1	Race & School	4	4	1	4	1- Strongly Disagree 2- Disagree 3- Agree 4- Strongly Agree	9
RR2	Race & Neighborhood	5	5	1	4	same	9
RR3	Race & Church	6	6	1	4	same	9
RR4	Race & Work-Supervisor	7	7	1	4	same	9
RR5	Race & Next Door	8	8	1	4	same	9
RR6	Race & Dating	9	9	1	4	same	9
RR7	Race & Marriage	10	10	1	4	same	9
MINMIX	Appropriate Minority Mix	11	13	0	100	variable	999
REGVTE	Registered Voter	14	14	0	1	0 = No 1 = Yes	9
VOTE	Vote in Last Senatorial Elections	15	15	0	1	0 = No 1 = Yes	9
POLPTY	Political Party Membership	16	16	0	1	0 = Democrat 1 = Republican	9
RACE	Race of Respondent	17	17	1	4	4 = White 3 = Black 2 = Hispanic 1 = Other	9
INCOME	Approximate Annual Income	18	18	1	6	1 = $7,000 or less 2 = $7,001 - 14,000 3 = $14,001 - 20,000 4 = $20,001 - 28,000 5 = $28,0001 & above	9
MARST	Marital Status	19	19	0	1	0 = No 1 = Yes	9
SEX	Sex of Respondent	20	20	0	1	0 = Male 1 = Female	9
YRBRTH	Year of Birth	21	22	00	65	variable	99

TABLE 2. SURVEY DATA ON RACE RELATIONS

COLUMN IDENTIFIER #	COLUMN IDENTIFIER #
1 2	1 2
123456789012345678 9012	123456789012345678 9012
1013333333 20111130145	4014444332 20110230150
1023444444 0110121151	4024444421 40110311158
1034443391 40110430032	4031111111 0110430021
1043443339 40110440133	4043333111 20110490120
1053333322 40101440122	4054444422 40110311057
1063333333 60110340135	4064333322 20110431053
1072221221 0111420030	4073333221 20110420120
1083929921 20110420029	4083333321 20110421150
1093333333 40100310157	4094442322 40110340015
1103323321 40110311057	4103333333 20110491157
2013323221 40111420149	5013332333 40001411163
2023333221 60110320044	5024444444 40110111161
2033333333 60110391159	5033333322 40010430041
2044323332 40110420047	5043333311 40110330054
2053223224 20111430133	5054443333 60110330143
2063332222 20100321153	5063333333 40110320046
2073333321 40110311057	5073322211 40110420032
2083333321 40110330152	5083333333 60110420025
2092242111 20111490120	5093333333 40111430140
2102222111 20111450015	5103333322 40110420138
3013333333 40111430035	6014444433 40110421153
3023333333 40110420048	6021213211 20001430142
3033333333 40110420150	6034434433 20111310146
3043333322 40110320030	6044333333 40110421155
3053333322 40111430040	6053344422 40110421121
3063333333 20111420050	6064444422 40110420156
3073333333 40111421052	6074333333 40111421157
3083333322 60110420053	6084323311 60110321056
3093323322 60110320038	6094343322 40110351158
3103313322 60110320148	6104333333 40110311149

This will probably take some time and considerable care. But it will save you hours when you reach the data analysis step. Take the time to do it right, and don't be afraid to talk to the necessary people.

MINIMAL SPSS[x] OR JUST THE FACTS, MA'AM

Now that we have entered the data into a file, we need to tell the computer how to read and manipulate the data. This is where we will use SPSS[x], that is, Englishlike commands that tell the computer what to do with the data we have entered.

Just as a data file is composed of individual data records, SPSS[x] files are composed of individual records. Each record instructs the computer about the data file or tells it what kind of analysis to perform. Each complete SPSS[x] record has two component parts. The first part of the record has an SPSS[x] procedure or

command name, such as DATA LIST, FREQUENCIES, VALUE LABELS, etc.
These are unique SPSS^x command names. You must enter these names exactly as
SPSS^x spells them, or you will get an error message.

The second part of any record is called the specification field. After you key in
the command name, hit the spacebar. Now you are ready to tell SPSS^x about
your data or the variables with which you wish to work. This is where you will
be able to specify variable names and what action is to be taken on which
variables. For example, if we wished SPSS^x to list the recorded values we entered
on the variables of RACE and SEX for the first ten respondents (cases) in our
data file, we would simply enter the following command:

```
LIST  VARIABLES=SEX, RACE / CASES=10
```

We'll have more to say about this later. For now, it is important to remember
that command names (e.g., LIST) begin in column 1 and specifications (e.g.,
VARIABLES = SEX,RACE/CASES = 10), that which is specific about your study,
begin after a space.

Reading the Data with SPSS^x Commands

Now that you know the two parts of an SPSS^x command record, let's get started
with telling the computer how to read your data. Indeed, until you have given
SPSS^x the essential information on how to read your data, you will not be able to
manipulate your variables or produce even the simplest reports.

The information on how to read your data is processed through the DATA
LIST command. This command enables you to specify the names for each
variable in your study and the columns in which SPSS^x will find the values.
Continuing to work with our race relations study, our DATA LIST record might
look like this:

```
DATA LIST /1
  IDNUM 1-3, RR1 4, RR2 5, RR3 6, RR4 7, RR5 8, RR6 9, RR7 10,
  MINMIX 11-13, REGVTE 14, VOTE 15, POLPTY 16,
  RACE 17, INCOME 18, MARST 19, SEX 20, YRBRTH 21-22
```

The words DATA LIST are a procedure name and are, therefore, required. They
tell SPSS^x that we wish to define how to read a data file. The /1 tells SPSS^x to
read the first record.

Just as we did in our codebook, we have assigned a unique variable name to
each of the questions in our questionnaire. Note that at no time do I repeat
exactly any of the variable names. For example, I distinguish between voting
behavior and whether or not the person is a registered voter with the variable

names VOTE and REGVTE, respectively. Similarly, each question about race relations has a different variable name. That is, RR1 is the first question about race relations, RR2 is the second question about race relations, and so on.

The numbers that follow the variable names identify the column(s) where SPSS^x can find each variable. For example, answers to RR1 may be found in column 4, answers to RR2 may be found in column 5, etc. Note that I left a single space between the variable name (e.g., RR1) and the column where the data for that variable may be found (e.g., 4). Without a blank between the variable name and the variable column identifier, SPSS^x would not know that I had finished typing the variable name.

If the variable requires more than a single column, I followed the variable name and the space with the beginning column number, a dash, and then the ending column number. For example, the variable of YRBRTH was entered as a two-digit field in columns 21 and 22 with the expression YRBRTH 21-22. Similarly, IDNUM uses columns 1 through 3, expressed as IDNUM 1-3.

Variable names must be assigned carefully. In addition to being unique, every variable name must meet several restrictions. First, every variable name must start with an alphabetic character. Although you may use numbers as part of the variable name, the first character in the name must be a letter. RR1 is a valid variable name but 1RR is not.

Another restriction applies to the number of characters in each variable name. A maximum of eight contiguous characters may be used for each variable name. That is why you see year of birth entered into the DATA LIST command as YRBRTH. By the way, note that these characters are contiguous—that is, I left no blanks between YR and BRTH. If I had, SPSS^x would interpret these as two separate variable names, YR and BRTH, rather than one variable, YRBRTH.

While we are on the subject of variable names, it should be pointed out that SPSS^x reserves certain words that cannot be used as variable names. These include

```
ALL   EQ   LE   NOT   TO
AND   GE   LT   OR    WITH
BY    GT   NE   THRU
```

Nor should you use special symbols such as -, &, !, /, or '. Many of these symbols have a particular meaning which we will encounter shortly.

In sum, when constructing your DATA LIST command keep the following things in mind:

1. Variable names must be unique.

2. Variable names must start with an alphabetic character.

3. Variable names may have a maximum of eight characters.

4. Variable names must not use a reserved word or use reserved special characters as part of their name.

5. Choose variable names that help you identify the nature of the data to be stored in that variable. (Since future references to each variable will use the variable names you declare in your DATA LIST command, it's helpful to use names such as RACE or SEX whenever you can.)

6. If you need more than one record to complete your DATA LIST command— that is, to list all your variables, make sure you indent (leave at least the first column blank) the next variable name on the next record. Any time you indent, SPSS^x continues working on the same procedure command.

7. Sometimes you may wish to work with data that are not whole numbers. For example, the variable MINMIX, "appropriate minority mixture in public schools," might be expressed as a proportion rather than a percent. We can tell SPSS^x to store these data as a proportion by modifying our third DATA LIST command record to read:

```
MINMIX 11-13 (2), REGVTE 14, VOTE 15, POLPTY 16,
```

The (2) tells SPSS^x to place a decimal point two columns to the left of the far righthand value. A response of 40% will now be stored as .40.

Similarly, there are ways to handle alphabetic data in a file. You simply place an A in parentheses following the column identifiers for that variable. You will find, however, that declaring and using alphabetic values will limit your ability to manipulate the data. So try to use only numeric values when creating your data file.

Exercise 2

Whether you are working on your own project or analyzing someone else's data, try to create your DATA LIST command. Take a few moments, get a copy of a codebook, and develop an appropriate DATA LIST.

Short Cuts and Other Points

Here is another way to create the DATA LIST command for our race relations study. These records are equivalent to our earlier DATA LIST command.

```
DATA LIST RECORDS=1/1
  IDNUM 1-3, RR1 TO RR7 4-10,
  MINMIX 11-13, REGVTE 14, VOTE 15, POLPTY 16,
  RACE INCOME MARST SEX 17-20, YRBRTH 21-22
```

Sometimes you may have more than one record, or line of data, for each respondent. If this occurs, then the RECORDS = n command, where n is replaced with the number of records for each respondent, is used.

Note the use of the reserved keyword TO in the second record. Since it occurs between the variable names RR1 and RR7, SPSS^x is smart enough to figure out that it needs to generate all the missing variables, (i.e., RR2, RR3, RR4, etc.). Once all the variables are generated by the program, SPSS^x will assign each of the variables an equal column width. In this case, SPSS^x will assign the data stored in column 4 to RR1, the data stored in column 5 to RR2, the data stored in column 6 to RR3, etc. When you have a large number of variables, all of which cover the same type(s) of information and each variable has the same column width, the use of the TO convention can be very helpful.

Error Checking and Data Cleaning

No matter how careful you were in entering the data from your study, it's likely you made some mistakes. Even the most meticulous data entry person makes a few errors.

Errors in SPSS^x command records will be caught by SPSS^x. It will give you an error message, telling you which error you made and where it occurred. Don't worry. If you get an error message, SPSS^x will also tell you what is wrong with what you said. Just make the necessary changes and run the program again.

Error checking the data is only a little more difficult. There are several ways to find data entry errors. One way is to have SPSS^x produce a listing of all values assigned to each variable for every respondent. The LIST command will accomplish this goal very nicely. For example, if you wanted a listing of all the variables and the values for each person in the race relations study, you would type the command

LIST VARIABLES=ALL

You could be more specific:

LIST VARIABLES=ALL/CASES=FROM 1 TO EOF BY 1

That is, starting with (FROM) the first case (1), go to the end of the file (EOF) one case at a time (BY 1) and list ALL the VARIABLES and their associated values. You could LIST just the first ten cases (/CASES = 10) or every tenth case starting with person 5 (/CASES = FROM 5 TO EOF BY 10). In any case, this command can be used to accomplish two goals. First, when you examine the values for each variable, you will be able to tell easily if your DATA LIST command was created correctly. All values for MINMIX, should be 0, 20, 40, 60, 80, or 100. A value of 2, 400, or 600 would indicate that you did not define the DATA LIST command correctly or that you entered some of the data incorrectly.

Second, if you make a complete LIST of all the cases and variables, you will have a complete record of each person's responses in a simple table format. This may help identify incorrect entries for certain respondents. Table 3 is a subset of what this table would look like if you were using the race relations example.

A supplemental method for checking data entry errors involves running the procedure FREQUENCIES. This procedure will produce a table of values for each variable. Since you know from your codebook the valid maximum and minimum values for each variable, any reported value(s) outside this range would indicate a data entry error. For example, you know that the minimum value for the variable SEX is 0 (male) and the maximum value is 1 (female). You also know that nonresponses to this variable were coded with a 9. Therefore, any value other than 0, 1, or 9 would indicate a data entry error for this variable.

The FREQUENCIES command is easy to enter:

```
FREQUENCIES VARIABLES=ALL
```

This command will produce a frequency table for all variables. A comparison of the values reported in the value column of the table and the values listed in your codebook will enable you to locate invalid entries. Your output should look like that found in Table 4.

```
                  TABLE 3. PARTIAL LISTING FROM LIST PROCEDURE
========================================================================================

Produced using the LIST command:


    LIST VARIABLES=IDNUM RR1 MINMIX VOTE RACE INCOME/CASES=10


        IDNUM    RR1    MINMIX    VOTE    RACE    INCOME

         101      3       20       1       1        3
         102      3        0       1       1        2
         103      4       40       1       4        3
         104      3       40       1       4        4
         105      3       40       0       4        4
         106      3       60       1       3        4
         107      2        0       1       4        2
         108      3       20       1       4        2
         109      3       40       0       3        1
         110      3       40       1       3        1

     NUMBER OF CASES READ =    10      NUMBER OF CASES LISTED =    10

-----------------------------------------------------------------------------
```

```
                        TABLE 4. FREQUENCIES COMMAND OUTPUT
=================================================================================

Produced using the FREQUENCIES command:

              FREQUENCIES VARIABLES=RACE INCOME SEX


        RACE
                                                     VALID    CUM
            VALUE LABEL          VALUE  FREQUENCY  PERCENT  PERCENT  PERCENT
                                  1        3        5.0      5.0     5.0
                                  2        1        1.7      1.7     6.7
                                  3       21       35.0     35.0    41.7
                                  4       35       58.3     58.3   100.0
                                        ------   ------   ------
                                 TOTAL    60      100.0    100.0

    VALID CASES     60    MISSING CASES     0

        INCOME
                                                     VALID    CUM
            VALUE LABEL          VALUE  FREQUENCY  PERCENT  PERCENT  PERCENT
                                  1        9       15.0     15.0    15.0
                                  2       27       45.0     45.0    60.0
                                  3       14       23.3     23.3    83.3
                                  4        4        6.7      6.7    90.0
                                  5        2        3.3      3.3    93.3
                                  9        4        6.7      6.7   100.0
                                        ------   ------   ------
                                 TOTAL    60      100.0    100.0

    VALID CASES     60    MISSING CASES     0


        SEX
                                                     VALID    CUM
            VALUE LABEL          VALUE  FREQUENCY  PERCENT  PERCENT  PERCENT
                                  0       26       43.3     43.3    43.3
                                  1       34       56.7     56.7   100.0
                                        ------   ------   ------
                                 TOTAL    60      100.0    100.0

    VALID CASES     60    MISSING CASES     0

---------------------------------------------------------------------------------
```

Running the First Procedure

We are now ready to execute our first SPSS^x run. This run will allow us to check our data entries as well as the specifications (i.e., variable names and column locations) we used in creating the DATA LIST command. Examine Table 5. It will show you the structure and commands used to make this run.

Note that we are asking SPSS^x to read the data in the format described in our DATA LIST command and produce a listing of the first ten cases and a simple FREQUENCIES distribution for several variables in our study. You will see that there are two additional records in this file. They define where the data begin

TABLE 5. FIRST RUN OF SPSS^x ‡

```
=================================================================================
      COLUMN IDENTIFIER ‡                      COLUMN IDENTIFIER ‡
    ---------------------                    ---------------------
         1         2                              1         2
    123456789012345678901 2                  123456789012345678901 2
---------------------------------------------------------------------------------
    DATA LIST RECORDS=1/1                     2053223224 20111430133
      IDNUM 1-3, RR1 TO RR7 4-10,             2063332222 20100321153
      MINMIX 11-13, REGVTE 14, VOTE 15, POLPTY 16,    2073333321 40110311057
      RACE INCOME  MARST  SEX 17-20, YRBRTH 21-22     2083333321 40110330152
    LIST VARIABLES=IDNUM RR1 MINMIX VOTE RACE         2092242111 20111490120
      INCOME/CASES=10                         2102222111 20111450015
    BEGIN DATA                                 !  !   !   !   !   !
    1013333333 20111130145                     !  !   !   !   !   !
    1023444444  0110121151                    6014444433 40110421153
    1034443391 40110430032                    6021213211 20001430142
    1043443339 40110440133                    6034434433 20111310146
    1053333322 40101440122                    6044333333 40110421155
    1063333333 60110340135                    6053344422 40110421121
    1072221221  0111420030                    6064444422 40110420156
    1083929921 20110420029                    6074333333 40111421157
    1093333333 40100310157                    6084323311 60110321056
    1103323321 40110311057                    6094343322 40110351158
    2013323221 40111420149                    6104333333 40110311149
    2023333221 60110320044                    END DATA
    2033333333 60110391159                    FREQUENCIES VARIABLES=RACE INCOME SEX
    2044323332 40110420047                    FINISH
---------------------------------------------------------------------------------
```

‡NOTE: Some computer sites will require systems records before any SPSS^x records can be processed. Check with your computer site and SPSS^x coordinator.

(BEGIN DATA) and where they end (END DATA). Without these records, SPSS^x would not be able to tell which records are commands and which are data.*

As the saying goes, these are "just the facts." They tell SPSS^x how to read your data and produce a basic tabular summary of each variable. Read on if you'd like to learn some more sophisticated techniques.

SPSS^x WITH A LITTLE CLASS

Social science research involves sharing your results with others. One large step you can take to facilitate the sharing of information is to provide complete and titled results. SPSS^x provides a large number of sophisticated options that will help you title your reports and label your variables. It allows you to label each value of every variable.

---

*Some people prefer to create two separate files. The first would contain only the data or responses from the people. The second would contain only SPSS^x commands. If you choose this option, simply modify your DATA LIST command to include the expression FILE = mydata, where mydata is the name of your data file name. For our purposes, however, we will combine the commands and the data into one file.

Let's start with the easiest command. If you want SPSS^x to produce a title on every page of output, enter the command

```
TITLE 'specification'
```

The procedure name, TITLE, begins in column 1, and whatever you want printed on every page is simply enclosed in single quotation marks in the specifications field. For example,

```
TITLE 'RACE RELATIONS IN A SOUTHERN CITY'
```

will produce the phrase RACE RELATIONS IN A SOUTHERN CITY on every page of output.

Within the body of each page of output, the results of each statistical procedure, (e.g., FREQUENCIES, ANOVA, etc.) will be displayed. To help clarify things for the reader it is useful to label the variables that may not be readily understood. While the reader may have no trouble figuring out that the variable name RACE stands for respondent's race, he or she may not be sure what the variable names RR1, MINMIX, MARST, or even YRBRTH stand for. SPSS^x will print out the label for each variable name when you use the command

```
VARIABLE LABELS varname 'label'
```

For example, the following statements may be used for our race relations study:

```
VARIABLE LABELS RR1, 'RACE AND SCHOOL'/
  RR2, 'RACE AND NEIGHBORHOOD'/
  RR3, 'RACE AND CHURCH'/
  RR4, 'RACE AND WORK-SUPERVISOR'/
  RR5, 'RACE AND NEXT DOOR'/
  RR6, 'RACE AND DATING'/
  RR7, 'RACE AND MARRIAGE'/
  MINMIX, 'MINORITY MIXTURE IN PUBLIC SCHOOLS'/
  MARST, 'MARITAL STATUS'/
  YRBRTH, 'YEAR OF BIRTH'/
```

Note that the command name, VARIABLE LABELS, is needed only once and that the specifications—variable names and labels—are indented properly. All the variable labels are identified by the variable name used in the DATA LIST command. A comma separates the variable labels from the label for each, which is enclosed in single quotation marks. A slash is placed at the end of each variable label so that SPSS[x] can keep them separate.

You can help the reader master the material more quickly by also labeling the values for certain variables. Although it is not necessary to label every value for every variable (variables such as YRBRTH require no value label since the numeric values are self-evident statements), such variables as RACE or SEX, which use coded values, should be labeled. Similarly, whenever you use codes for response categories—1 for "strongly disagree," 2 for "disagree," etc.—as we did for our first seven race relations questions, you should report what these value codes mean. This may be easily accomplished with the command

```
VALUE LABELS varname, value 'label' value 'label'
   ...value 'label'
```

For example, returning to our study, here are several ways to implement the VALUE LABEL command:

```
VALUE LABELS   SEX   0 'MALE'   1 'FEMALE'/
POLPTY   0 'DEMOCRAT'   1 'REPUBLICAN'/
RACE   4 'WHITE'   3 'BLACK'   2 'HISPANIC'   1 'OTHER'/
REGVTE VOTE MARST   0 'NO'   1 'YES'/
RR1 TO RR7   1 'STRONGLY DISAGREE'   2 'DISAGREE'
   3 'AGREE'   4 'STRONGLY AGREE'/
```

Note that the command name, VALUE LABELS, begins in column 1 and is followed by a space, the specification of a variable name, its value, and the label, inside single quotation marks. Additional values and labels for the variable follow the same format. Note also that when all the values and their labels for each variable have been indicated, a slash is entered. The next variable is entered after indenting at least one column on the next record.

When several variables use the same values and labels for each value, you can list all the variable names together (e.g., REGVTE VOTE MARST), followed by their values and labels (e.g., 0 'NO' 1 'YES'). The TO convention can be used when several variables are listed one after another (e.g., RR1 TO RR7 1 'STRONGLY DISAGREE' 2 'DISAGREE', etc.).

To see these commands, and others, in the context of the larger SPSS[x] program, examine Table 6.

To see the effects of using these procedure statements, examine Tables 4 and 7. Compare the information on RACE for both tables. Note the ease of figuring out what each value means in Table 7 as compared with Table 4.

```
                    TABLE 6. ENHANCED SPSS* PROGRAM LISTING
================================================================================
JCL
TITLE 'JACQUES/BABBIE RUN--RACE RELATIONS IN A SOUTHERN CITY'
DATA LIST RECORDS=1/1
 IDNUM 1-3
 RR1 TO RR7 4-10, MINMIX 11-13,
 REGVTE VOTE POLPTY 14-16,
 RACE INCOME MARST SEX 17-20, YRBRTH 21-22
VARIABLE LABELS RR1, 'RACE AND SCHOOL'/
 RR2, 'RACE AND NEIGHBORHOOD'/
 RR3, 'RACE AND CHURCH'/
 RR4, 'RACE AND WORK-SUPERVISOR'/
 RR5, 'RACE AND NEXT DOOR'/
 RR6, 'RACE AND DATING'/
 RR7, 'RACE AND MARRIAGE'/
 MINMIX, 'MINORITY MIXTURE IN PUBLIC SCHOOLS'/
 MARST, 'MARITAL STATUS'/
 YRBRTH, 'YEAR OF BIRTH'/
 RACE, 'RACE OF RESPONDENT'/
 INCOME, 'ANNUAL INCOME'/
 SEX, 'SEX OF RESPONDENT'/
VALUE LABELS SEX  0 'MALE' 1 'FEMALE'/
 POLPTY 0 'DEMOCRAT' 1 'REPUBLICAN'/
 RACE  4 'WHITE'  3 'BLACK' 2 'HISPANIC' 1 'OTHER'/
 RR1 TO RR7 1 'STRONGLY DISAGREE' 2 'DISAGREE'
      3 'AGREE'  4 'STRONGLY AGREE'/
 REGVTE VOTE MARST  0 'NO'  1 'YES'/
 INCOME  5000 ' LESS THAN $7,000'  10500 ' $7,001 - $14,000'
      17000 '$14,001 - $20,000'  24000 '$20,001 - $28,000'
      30000 '$28,000 AND ABOVE'/
MISSING VALUES RR1 TO RR7, REGVTE TO SEX (9)/ MINMIX (999)/
RECODE INCOME (1=5000)(2=10500)(3=17000)(4=24000)(5=30000)
RECODE RACE (1,2=9)(3=0)(4=1) INTO NRACE
VARIABLE LABELS NRACE 'BLACK AND WHITE RESPONDENTS ONLY'
VALUE LABELS NRACE 0 'BLACK' 1 'WHITE'
COMPUTE YRBRTH = YRBRTH + 1900
COMPUTE RR = RR1 + RR2 + RR3 + RR4 + RR5 + RR6 + RR7
COMPUTE RACSEX=9
IF (RACE EQ 3 AND SEX EQ 0)RACSEX=1
IF (RACE EQ 3 AND SEX EQ 1)RACSEX=2
IF (RACE EQ 4 AND SEX EQ 0)RACSEX=3
IF (RACE EQ 4 AND SEX EQ 1)RACSEX=4
MISSING VALUES NRACE RACSEX (9)/ YRBRTH (1999)/
VARIABLE LABELS RR, 'RACE RELATIONS SCALE'
               RACSEX, 'RACE AND SEX IDENTIFIER'
VALUE LABELS   RACSEX 1 'BL-MALE' 2 'BL-FEMALE' 3 'WH-MALE' 4 'WH-FEMALE'
LIST VARIABLES=IDNUM,RR1,MINMIX,VOTE,RACE,INCOME/CASES=10
BEGIN DATA
1013333333 20111130145
1023444444  0110121151
 :  :  :  :  :
6104333333 40110311149
END DATA
FREQUENCIES VARIABLES=RACE,INCOME,SEX
 /STATISTICS=ALL
FINISH
--------------------------------------------------------------------------
```

```
                    TABLE 7. FREQUENCIES COMMAND OUTPUT
================================================================================

Produced using the following FREQUENCIES command:

                FREQUENCIES VARIABLES=RACE INCOME SEX

and VARIABLE LABELS, VALUE LABELS commands.


       RACE     RACE OF RESPONDENT
                                                      VALID    CUM
           VALUE LABEL         VALUE  FREQUENCY PERCENT PERCENT PERCENT
           OTHER                 1        3       5.0    5.0    5.0
           HISPANIC              2        1       1.7    1.7    6.7
           BLACK                 3       21      35.0   35.0   41.7
           WHITE                 4       35      58.3   58.3  100.0
                                       ------  ------  ------
                            TOTAL      60     100.0   100.0

       VALID CASES    60    MISSING CASES    0


       INCOME   ANNUAL INCOME
                                                      VALID    CUM
           VALUE LABEL         VALUE  FREQUENCY PERCENT PERCENT PERCENT
           LESS THAN $7000     5000       9      15.0   16.1   16.1
           $7,001 - $14,000   10500      27      45.0   48.2   64.3
           $14,001 - $20,000  17000      14      23.3   25.0   89.3
           $20,001 - $28,000  24000       4       6.7    7.1   96.4
           $28,000 AND ABOVE  30000       2       3.3    3.6  100.0
                                 9        4       6.7  MISSING
                                       ------  ------  ------
                            TOTAL      60     100.0   100.0

       VALID CASES    54    MISSING CASES    4


       SEX      SEX OF RESPONDENT
                                                      VALID    CUM
           VALUE LABEL         VALUE  FREQUENCY PERCENT PERCENT PERCENT
           MALE                  0       26      43.3   43.3   43.3
           FEMALE                1       34      56.7   56.7  100.0
                                       ------  ------  ------
                            TOTAL      60     100.0   100.0

       VALID CASES    60    MISSING CASES    0
```

Exercise 3

Here's your chance to make your results more easy to read. (It will help you remember what each variable name and value means, too.) Take a few minutes and develop appropriate VARIABLE LABELS and VALUE LABEL procedures for your study.

What to Do When You Don't Know: MISSING VALUES

Let's face it. Not everyone will answer every question. Some people are reluctant to tell you how much money they make or when they were born. When this case occurs, or when you don't know what the valid value should be, you can tell the computer to ignore it. (Recall that in our codebook when we did not have a valid response we used a value of 9 to indicate missing information.) There is a way to tell SPSS[x] which variables will have which missing values. It follows the usual command format of the procedure name in column 1, followed by a space and variable name(s) and the values with which you wish to work. It looks like this:

```
MISSING VALUES varname (value)
```

Here's the command for our study on race relations:

```
MISSING VALUES RR1 TO RR7, REGVTE TO SEX (9)/ YRBRTH (99)/
  MINMIX (999)/
```

Note that when we have several contiguous variables, all of which have the same missing value, we can use the TO convention. Also note that when we change the value we choose as missing, a slash is placed between the value and the next variable name. As always, we use the exact variable name that we assigned in our DATA LIST statement.

Why use a MISSING VALUES command? Look again at Tables 4 and 7. Locate the variable INCOME. Now compare the columns labeled VALID PERCENT in both tables. In Table 4, the VALID PERCENT column reported the same information as the PERCENT column. That's because we did not declare any missing values in this first run. In Table 7, however, the values reported in the VALID PERCENT column are different from the values reported in the PERCENT column. Why? Because SPSS[x] omitted the four people who did not answer the question on income before it computed each of the percents reported in the VALID PERCENT column. Also, SPSS[x] knew that the CUM (cumulative) PERCENT column should contain only those values based on valid responses. You will, therefore, find the CUM PERCENT values different on Tables 4 and 7 for the variable INCOME.

Exercise 4

Create a MISSING VALUES command for the questions in your study that have missing answers. (If everyone answered all your questions, you do not need to use this procedure statement.)

Converting Coded Values to Real Values: RECODE

You have probably noticed other differences between Tables 4 and 7. If not, reexamine the variable of INCOME on both tables. Notice that the reported values in Table 4 go from 1 to 9, while the reported values in Table 7 start with 5000.

One of the nice features of SPSS^x is that you can easily reassign the entered values of a data file to some other, more appropriate data values. For example, we know that we entered coded values for the variable INCOME. That is, for people who reported that their income was equal to or less than $7,000, we entered a coded value of 1, for people who reported that their annual income was between $7,001 and $14,000, we entered a value of 2, etc.

Rather than continue to work with these coded values we can have SPSS^x store the "true" values. What are the "true" values? Well, if we take the average of each class interval

- $7,001 + $14,000 / 2 = $10,500
- $14,001 + $20,000 / 2 = $17,000
- $20,001 + $28,000 / 2 = $24,000

and choose reasonable beginning (say $5,000) and ending (say $30,000) values, then we can have SPSS^x store the "true" values rather than the entered coded values. This is accomplished with the RECODE command. The format of the RECODE command is

```
RECODE varname (old value = new value) (old value = new value)
    ... (old value = new value)
```

With our race relations study, the variable INCOME was recoded with the expression

```
RECODE INCOME (1=5000) (2=10500) (3=17000) (4=24000) (5=30000)
```

Note the standard form of the expression (i.e., use of blanks, parentheses, and equal signs). Note also that no commas are used.

While it may not be apparent from this example, you may recode several old values into a new value in the same statement. For example, if we wished to recode respondents who were neither black nor white into the general missing value (9), we could specify

```
RECODE RACE (1,2=9)
```

Several other options exist when working with old values. For example, you could recode a range of values (say, 1 THRU 5) in a single command rather than listing each of these values separately.

You can even use the RECODE facility to create new variables that retain some of the same values as the original variable while taking on some new values. This is not difficult to do, and it can save you many aggravating hours. For example, since we are particularly interested in the attitudes of black and white respondents we can create a new variable, which we will call NRACE, with the expression

```
RECODE RACE (1,2=9)(3=0)(4=1) INTO NRACE
```

Those who were neither black nor white were coded into this new variable, NRACE, as 9's, black respondents (current code of 3) were recoded to 0, and white respondents (current code of 4) were recoded as 1. (We could just as easily have recoded whites as 0 and blacks as 1.) We can keep track of what these codes mean by inserting our VARIABLE LABELS and VALUE LABELS commands for our new variable of NRACE:

```
VARIABLE LABELS NRACE 'BLACK AND WHITE RESPONDENTS ONLY'
VALUE LABELS NRACE   0 'BLACK'   1 'WHITE'
```

—immediately after our RECODE statement. (Note: we cannot use the VARIABLE LABELS or the VALUE LABELS statement until we have created the new variable. SPSS^x must have a variable name to attach any label. It is through the variable name that all work is accomplished. So make sure you create a variable name before you try to do anything with it.)

Working with Valid Values and Creating New Variables: COMPUTE and IF Commands

We have already noted the use of the RECODE procedure to transform a coded value into a "true" value and then store it. This can sometimes be done more efficiently with the COMPUTE procedure. When we are working with interval and ratio level data, the COMPUTE statement will enable us to manipulate the data in the variable with all the typical mathematical operators. We can add values ($+$), subtract values ($-$), multiply values ($*$), divide values ($/$), and even take values to a power ($**$). The format of the procedure is

```
COMPUTE targetvariable = oldvariable  operator  oldvariable
```

For example, to work with the true year of birth (stored in YRBRTH) of our respondents, we can add 1900 years to each coded value. We can use the expression

```
COMPUTE YRBRTH = YRBRTH + 1900
```

The value 45 entered in the data set will be reported as 1945. Pretty easy and pretty neat.

Once we know the true year, we can create a new variable and have SPSS^x report the age of each respondent with the expression

```
COMPUTE AGE = 1985 - YRBRTH
```

That is, for each respondent, create a new variable called AGE. Then we find the information about the respondent's year of birth (YRBRTH) and subtract this value from 1985. Voila. You can now work with the variable AGE. Not too shabby.

As you may have guessed, the COMPUTE statement is not limited to working with a single variable, operator, and value. Rather, complex statements may be made and assigned to the same or to new target variables. For example, in our study we can combine the responses of each interviewee across all the race relations questions—that is, we can create a summative index score for each respondent. We can then store this value in a new variable, which we will call RR (the race relations index score). We can find each respondent's RR score by instructing SPSS^x to add all the values of each response to each race relations question (RR1 through RR7). One way to write this command is

```
COMPUTE RR = RR1 + RR2 + RR3 + RR4 + RR5 + RR6 + RR7
```

This procedure tells SPSS^x to create a new variable, RR, and to store in this new variable the sum total of RR1, RR2, RR3, etc., for each respondent. This will produce an index or scale value for each person who responded to all the race relations statements. This will enable you to examine what relationships exist between this summary scale and other variables, such as RACE, INCOME, etc. Once again, we can keep track of what this variable name means with the VARIABLE LABELS command:

```
VARIABLE LABELS RR, 'RACE RELATIONS SCALE'
```

Since this is an interval level variable, there is no need to use the VALUE LABELS procedure.

You may be wondering what happens with the people who did not answer all the questions or did not state their year of birth. You will recall that we have declared missing values for all these variables. When SPSS^x encounters a value previously defined as missing for the old variable (e.g., YRBRTH, RR1, etc.) it assigns the target variable (e.g., AGE, RR) as missing, too. Therefore, those who did not respond to all the race relations statements will be treated as missing values. This makes logical sense since you could not know what a person's overall scale score would be unless you knew how he or she responded to all the items.

Before we conclude this section, it is interesting to note that you can combine the COMPUTE command with IF statements to create new variables and assign appropriate values. The IF command enables you to use a logical expression— that is, a test condition—before you assign a value to a target variable. It takes the form of

```
IF (logical expression) targetvariable = value
```

Logical expressions test to see if a condition is true. You may use, for example, a phrase such as RACE EQ 1. This logical expression contains a variable name, RACE, a logical operator, EQ, and a test value, 1. If the first part of the command is true, then the second part of the command (targetvariable = value) is performed. More on this later.

For now, it is important to note that you can work with several logical expressions and link them to each other as long as you include the appropriate logical operator(s) such as AND, OR, or NOT. Additionally, you have several alternate operators available. They include

- EQ or = Equal to   NE or <> Not equal to
- LT or < Less than   LE or <= Less than or equal to
- GT or > Greater than GE or >= Greater than or equal to

Here's an example. Let us assume that we wish to create a new variable that combines the variables RACE and SEX. That is, we wish to be able to work with a variable that identifies black males, black females, white males, and white females. We can combine our COMPUTE and IF statements to create this new variable (RACESEX) by using the following command set:

```
COMPUTE RACESEX=9
IF (RACE EQ 3 AND SEX EQ 0)RACESEX=1
IF (RACE EQ 3 AND SEX EQ 1)RACESEX=2
IF (RACE EQ 4 AND SEX EQ 0)RACESEX=3
IF (RACE EQ 4 AND SEX EQ 1)RACESEX=4
```

The COMPUTE statement first creates a new variable, RACESEX, and assigns everyone a value of 9. The IF statements then check the RACE and SEX value codes for each respondent. If a respondent was black (RACE EQ 3) and male (SEX EQ 0), then his RACESEX code would be reassigned from the value 9 to the value of 1. Similarly, if the respondent was white (RACE EQ 4) and female (SEX EQ 1), then she would have her RACESEX code reassigned to the value 4. Only where both conditions were true would SPSS^x change the assigned value of 9 to some other value.

To help keep track of this new variable and its values, we can use our labeling procedures:

```
VARIABLE LABELS RACESEX, 'RACE AND SEX IDENTIFIER'
VALUE LABELS RACESEX   1 'BL-MALE'    2 'BL-FEMALE'
                       3 'WH-MALE'    4 'WH-FEMALE'
```

Exercise 5

Now you can modify or create any additional variables with which you wish to work. Identify the variables you entered as coded values that should really be changed to "true" values. Then think back to your study goals. Ask yourself what combinations of variables, if any, are needed to more adequately examine your hypotheses. Use your RECODE, COMPUTE, and IF statements to make the necessary changes. Then label these, when necessary, with the VARIABLE LABELS and VALUE LABELS procedure statements.

MISSING VALUES Revisited

We have now changed several original values for the variable YRBRTH. Similarly, we have created new variables. We will want SPSS^x to know which values for each of these variables should be treated as missing values. To accomplish this we add an additional MISSING VALUES command after all our RECODE, COMPUTE, and IF statements:

```
MISSING VALUES NRACE RACESEX (9)/ YRBRTH (1999)/
```

Let's move on to our data analysis—where we'll describe our respondents, test our hypotheses, and find the best predictor(s) of the race relations index value.

SPSS^x STATISTICAL PROCEDURE COMMANDS

SPSS^x is an extremely powerful software package. All we have to do to produce a
great variety of sophisticated tables, graphs, and statistics is to change a few procedure commands.

I will assume here that you have either mastered Part 4 of this textbook,
Analysis of Data, or mastered basic statistical procedures from some other
source. In any case, I will not discuss how SPSS^x computes statistics or how such
statistics are normally computed. I will, however, point out some useful
information on when to use which statistical measure. Now for some substance.

Univariate Analysis

Any good research report begins with a descriptive summary of the
characteristics of the respondents as well as an overall statement of their
attitudes and/or behaviors. SPSS^x will compute tabular, graphic, and statistical
summaries of each variable with the FREQUENCIES command. The general
format of this command is

```
FREQUENCIES VARIABLES=(varlist, ALL)
 /FORMAT = option
 /STATISTICS list
```

Here's what I recommend for getting SPSS^x to produce a simple descriptive
summary of any variable set

```
FREQUENCIES VARIABLES=ALL
/FORMAT = ONEPAGE
/STATISTICS DEFAULT MEDIAN
```

You no doubt recognize it from our previous work. The FREQUENCIES
command will produce a simple frequency table for each identified variable. (The
use of the keyword ALL causes SPSS^x to produce a table for each variable.) The
format of these tables depends on the number of different values found in the
variable. That is, given the expression /FORMAT = ONEPAGE, SPSS^x will use
the standard page format for most variables. For variables with too many
different values to fit on one page, it uses a condensed style output. (You can
force condensed style printing by using the expression /FORMAT =
CONDENSE.) See Table 8.

TABLE 8. FREQUENCIES COMMAND OUTPUT
==

Produced using the following FREQUENCIES command:

```
FREQUENCIES VARIABLES=MINMIX RACESEX RR/
     FORMAT=ONEPAGE/
     STATISTICS=DEFAULTS MEDIAN
```

MINMIX MINORITY MIXTURE IN PUBLIC SCHOOLS

VALUE LABEL	VALUE	FREQUENCY	PERCENT	VALID PERCENT	CUM PERCENT
	0	3	5.0	5.0	5.0
	20	15	25.0	25.0	30.0
	40	33	55.0	55.0	85.0
	60	9	15.0	15.0	100.0
		------	------	------	
	TOTAL	60	100.0	100.0	

MEAN	36.000	MEDIAN	40.000	STD DEV	15.093
MINIMUM	0.000	MAXIMUM	60.000		

VALID CASES   60   MISSING CASES   0

RR   RACE RELATIONS SCALE

VALUE	FREQ	PCT	CUM PCT	VALUE	FREQ	PCT	CUM PCT	VALUE	FREQ	PCT	CUM PCT
7	1	2	2	17	7	12	26	24	4	7	93
11	2	4	5	18	5	9	35	25	1	2	95
12	1	2	7	19	6	11	46	26	1	2	96
13	1	2	9	20	3	5	51	27	1	2	98
14	1	2	11	21	15	26	77	28	1	2	100
15	1	2	12	22	4	7	84				
16	1	2	14	23	1	2	86				

MISSING DATA

VALUE	FREQ	VALUE	FREQ	VALUE	FREQ
	3				

MEAN	19.474	MEDIAN	20.000	STD DEV	3.947
MINIMUM	7.000	MAXIMUM	28.000		

VALID CASES   57   MISSING CASES   3

RACESEX RACE AND SEX IDENTIFIER

(Continued)

(Continued)

VALUE LABEL	VALUE	FREQUENCY	PERCENT	VALID PERCENT	CUM PERCENT
BL-MALE	1	10	16.7	17.9	17.9
BL-FEMALE	2	11	18.3	19.6	37.5
WH-MALE	3	16	26.7	28.6	66.1
WH-FEMALE	4	19	31.7	33.9	100.0
	9	4	6.7	MISSING	100.0
		------	------	------	
	TOTAL	60	100.0	100.0	

MEAN	2.786	MEDIAN	3.000	STD DEV	1.107
MINIMUM	1.000	MAXIMUM	4.000		

VALID CASES   56   MISSING CASES   4

In addition, the inclusion of the STATISTICS command tells SPSS^x to calculate the mean, the standard deviation, and minimum and maximum values for each listed variable. Look again at Table 8. In addition to these descriptive statistics, SPSS^x can, on command, calculate the values for the mode, median, skewness, kurtosis, standard error, etc. All you would need to do is include the appropriate keywords for the statistics you wish it to calculate. Of course, the keyword ALL causes SPSS^x to calculate all of them.

As you can tell from the output, SPSS^x will compute a variety of summary statistics for every variable. It is up to you to know which statistic(s) to report. Here's a rule of thumb based on the earlier discussion of levels of measurement.

IF THE VARIABLE IS MEASURED AT THE	THEN USE
NOMINAL LEVEL	MODE & reported percents
ORDINAL LEVEL	+ MEDIAN
INTERVAL & RATIO LEVEL	+ MEAN, STD DEV

For example, when reporting race/sex information in Table 8, SPSS^x computed summary descriptive statistics that had no useful meaning. It did not know that this was a nominal level variable. It assumed that you knew not to use these values. When reporting our summary scale measure (RR), however, we could use all our summary statistics.

Finally, the FREQUENCIES command may be used to produce simple bar charts and histograms. Not surprisingly, the format of the command would be

```
FREQUENCIES VARIABLES=varlist
/BARCHART HISTOGRAM
```

For variables such as RACE or SEX with relatively few categories, the BARCHART command will make the most sense. For continuous variables such as YRBRTH or our race relations index score (RR), HISTOGRAM would be most appropriate. See Table 9. In both cases, the output lists the value and graphically displays the frequency of occurrence for each found value. The BARCHART command also lists the value label and the number of occurrences in the body of the table.

The HISTOGRAM command reports the number of occurrences of each value at the left of the midpoint of the class interval. Asterisks are used to represent the number of occurrences in the body of the table. Note that the HISTOGRAM command includes information from the lowest through the highest possible value, even if the value was not found. Thus, several reported values in the histogram part of Table 9 have a count of zero.

Well, what does SPSS[x] tell us about our study? If you ran our race relations study data, then you know that most of the respondents were white (58.3%) and female (56.7%), with an average income of about $12,000. Additionally, most (95%) reported that they were registered to vote—most of them (73.3%) as Democrats—and did vote (91.7%) in the last election.

Attitudes toward other races varied by type of question. Although most respondents reported either "agree" or "strongly agree" to such statements as "children of different races should attend the same schools" (mean = 3.167, sd = .668) and "members of different races should live in my neighborhood" (mean = 3.085, sd = .596), respondents were less likely to "agree" to statements about their child dating someone of a different race (mean = 2.322, sd = .753) or marrying someone of a different race (mean = 2.119, sd = .930). If we consider all seven race relations items, the scale score indicated that most people agreed with some items and disagreed with other items (mean = 19.474, sd = 3.947).

Exercise 6

Now after reexamining the format of the FREQUENCIES command, modify your SPSS[x] commands to produce the appropriate tables, graphs, and summary statistics for your study.

Once you have described your respondents, you can begin to explore the relationships among the variables. One place to begin is to examine the bivariate relationships. But what relationships are of interest? You should probably begin with the hypotheses you stated at the onset of the study. Additionally, you will be interested in testing the hypotheses across several indexed or scaled items.

Scaling

We noted earlier that we are interested in testing our race relations index as a reliable measure of racial attitudes. By substituting the RELIABILITY command

```
                        TABLE 9. BAR CHARTS AND HISTORGRAMS
======================================================================
Produced using the following commands:


              FREQUENCIES VARIABLES=MINMIX RACESEX/BARCHART
              FREQUENCIES VARIABLES=RR YRBRTH/HISTOGRAM/


MINMIX  MINORITY MIXTURE IN PUBLIC SCHOOLS


          I
          ----+
    0. I 3 :
          ----+
          I
          -------------------+
   20. I              15 :
          -------------------+
          I
          ----------------------------------------+
   40. I                                     33 :
          ----------------------------------------+
          I
          -----------+
   60. I     9 :
          -----------+
          I
          I........I........I........I........I........I
          0        8       16       24       32       40
                        FREQUENCY


VALID CASES    60    MISSING CASES    0



RACESEX  RACE AND SEX IDENTIFIER


          I
    1.00  -------------------------+
 BL-MALE  I                 10 :
          -------------------------+
          I
    2.00  ----------------------------+
BL-FEMALE I                  11 :
          ----------------------------+
          I
    3.00  ---------------------------------------+
 WH-MALE  I                             16 :
          ---------------------------------------+
          I
    4.00  --------------------------------------------+
WH-FEMALE I                               19 :
          --------------------------------------------+
          I
          I........I........I........I........I........I
          0        4        8       12       16       20
                        FREQUENCY


VALID CASES    56    MISSING CASES    4
```

(Continued)

RR   RACE RELATIONS SCALE

```
COUNT   MIDPOINT   ONE SYMBOL EQUALS APPROXIMATELY   .40 OCCURRENCES
   0      2.5
   0      4.0
   0      5.5
   1      7.0     ***
   0      8.5
   0     10.0
   3     11.5     *********
   1     13.0     ***
   2     14.5     *****
   1     16.0     ***
  12     17.5     *********************************
   6     19.0     ****************
  18     20.5     *************************************************
   4     22.0     **********
   5     23.5     *************
   1     25.0     ***
   2     26.5     *****
   1     28.0     ***
   0     29.5
   0     31.0
   0     32.5
              I....+....I....+....I....+....I....+....I....+....I
              0        4        8        12       16       20
                          HISTOGRAM FREQUENCY
```

VALID CASES   57   MISSING CASES   3

YRBRTH   'YEAR OF BIRTH'

```
COUNT   MIDPOINT   ONE SYMBOL EQUALS APPROXIMATELY   .20 OCCURRENCES
   2     1914.0    **********
   0     1916.5
   3     1919.0    ***************
   3     1921.5    ***************
   1     1924.0    *****
   0     1926.5
   3     1929.0    ***************
   2     1931.5    **********
   4     1934.0    ********************
   0     1936.5
   4     1939.0    ********************
   2     1941.5    **********
   3     1944.0    ***************
   3     1946.5    ***************
   8     1949.0    ****************************************
   3     1951.5    ***************
   6     1954.0    ******************************
   8     1956.5    ****************************************
   3     1959.0    ***************
   1     1961.5    *****
   1     1964.0    *****
              I....+....I....+....I....+....I....+....I....+....I
              0        2        4        6        8        10
                          HISTOGRAM FREQUENCY
```

VALID CASES   60   MISSING CASES   0

----

for the FREQUENCIES command we can have SPSS[x] test the internal consistency among our seven race relations items. The general format is

```
RELIABILITY VARIABLES=varlist/
 SCALE(name)=varlist/
STATISTICS list
```

For our study, the command becomes

```
RELIABILITY VARIABLES=RR1 TO RR7/
 SCALE(RACEREL)=RR1 TO RR7/
STATISTICS 1,4,5,8,9
```

The format of this command follows the usual procedure of a SPSS[x] procedure name beginning in column 1 and the specifications beginning immediately after a space. Since RR1 through RR7 contain our race relations items, they are identified in this specification field. The SCALE subcommand tells SPSS[x] which items to include in the specific scale—in this case we use all seven items. (Alternately, we might have wished to use only the first four of these items [e.g., SCALE(RACEREL) = RR1 TO RR4] instead of all seven.) The STATISTICS command produces our measures of interest; means and standard deviations for each item (STATISTICS 1), summary scale statistics (STATISTICS 4,5,8), and most importantly, item-to-total statistics (STATISTICS 9). (We could have requested additional computations, but these statistics will be sufficient for our needs.)

As you will recall from previous chapters, a reliable index has at least three characteristics. First, each item is positively correlated with every other item. Second, each item is positively correlated with the overall scale score. Third, all possible split half index scores of these items are well correlated. Note that we are not testing the validity of the items. Rather, we are testing the reliability of our index by examining the degree of internal consistency.

The SPSS[x] output, as seen in Table 10, provides information on all three criteria. First, interitem summary statistics are reported in the row labeled INTER-ITEM CORRELATIONS—including the mean, minimum, maximum, etc. Second, item-to-total correlations are reported for each variable in the ITEM-TOTAL CORRELATION column. This is a simple Pearson r between the item (e.g., RR1, RR2, etc.) and the overall scale score (excluding the contribution of that score to the scale). In fact these item-to-total statistics also report the effect on the scale of each item or what would happen to the scale score if you deleted that item. Finally, overall internal consistency, Chronbach's alpha or Kuder-Richardson 20, is reported.

On the basis of this output, our race relations scale, RR, demonstrates good interitem correlations (mean = .54699), generally acceptable item-to-total correlations (mean about .69), and acceptable overall split half correlations

TABLE 10. RELIABILITY COMMAND OUTPUT

===

Produced using the following RELIABILITY command:

```
          RELIABILITY VARIABLES=RR1 TO RR7/
           SCALE(RACEREL)=RR1 TO RR7
           STATISTICS 1,4,5,8,9
```

* * * * * * * * * R E L I A B I L I T Y   A N A L Y S I S   F O R   S C A L E (R A C E R E L) * * * * * * * * *

1.	RR1	RACE AND SCHOOL
2.	RR2	RACE AND NEIGHBORHOOD
3.	RR3	RACE AND CHURCH
4.	RR4	RACE AND WORK-SUPERVISOR
5.	RR5	RACE AND NEXT DOOR
6.	RR6	RACE AND DATING
7.	RR7	RACE AND MARRIAGE

		MEANS	STD DEV	CASES
1.	RR1	3.15789	0.675 85	57.0
2.	RR2	3.05263	0.580 06	57.0
3.	RR3	2.94737	0.765 81	57.0
4.	RR4	2.98246	0.640 63	57.0
5.	RR5	2.85965	0.742 55	57.0
6.	RR6	2.31579	0.759 65	57.0
7.	RR7	2.15789	0.921 75	57.0

\# OF CASES =   57.0

STATISTICS FOR	MEAN	VARIANCE	STD DEV	\# VARIABLES
SCALE	19.47368	15.57519	3.94654	7

ITEM MEANS	MEAN	MINIMUM	MAXIMUM	RANGE	MAX/MIN	VARIANCE
	2.78195	2.15789	3.15789	1.00000	1.46341	.14916

INTER-ITEM CORRELATIONS	MEAN	MINIMUM	MAXIMUM	RANGE	MAX/MIN	VARIANCE
	.54699	.31555	.84561	.53006	2.67979	.02761

ITEM-TOTAL STATISTICS

	SCALE MEAN IF ITEM DELETED	SCALE VARIANCE IF ITEM DELETED	CORRECTED ITEM-TOTAL CORRELATION	SQUARED MULTIPLE CORRELATION	ALPHA IF ITEM DELETED
RR1	16.31579	11.89850	.69059	.64978	.86603
RR2	16.42105	12.03383	.79636	.82166	.85779
RR3	16.52632	11.78947	.60834	.48976	.87615
RR4	16.49123	12.11153	.68475	.61949	.86732
RR5	16.61404	11.09837	.79342	.71365	.85219
RR6	17.15789	11.42105	.69668	.77796	.86471
RR7	17.31579	11.29135	.55438	.74287	.88983

RELIABILITY COEFFICIENTS   7 ITEMS

ALPHA = 0.88441   STANDARDIZED ITEM ALPHA = 0.89420

(alpha = .884). Furthermore, omitting any item (even item RR7) will not substantially improve our internal consistency measure. We may, therefore, use all seven items in our scale.

Exercise 7

If you have several variables in your study that are logically related to one
another, you may wish to develop a scale or index, and then test it with the
RELIABILITY command.

Bivariate Analysis

Now that we have faith in the reliability of our scale, we can measure to what
degree blacks and whites are different from each other in terms of specific
questions and overall scale scores.

For example, we can replace our FREQUENCIES command with the
CROSSTABS command to perform our first bivariate analysis. The general
format of the CROSSTABS command is

```
CROSSTABS TABLES=  varlist, varlist BY varlist...varlist
OPTIONS  list
STATISTICS  list
```

If we wished to examine each race relations item and the overall scale score, we
could do so with the following command

```
RECODE RR(LO THRU 20=1)(21 THRU 28=2)
VALUE LABELS   RR   1 'LOW'   2 'HIGH'
CROSSTABS TABLES= RR1 TO RR7, RR BY NRACE
OPTIONS 4
STATISTICS 1,4,8,10,11
```

This CROSSTABS command will produce a total of eight tables. First, a table for
RR1 and NRACE will be produced. Then a table for RR2 and NRACE will be
produced. This will continue until a table for our scale score RR and NRACE is
produced.*

As you can see in Table 11, each table produced by the command
CROSSTABS is consistent. The variable declared immediately after the TABLES =
specification is treated as a dependent variable. Its values are listed down the
page, while the variable declared after the keyword BY is treated as an
explanatory variable and its values are listed across the page. Row and column

---

*The RECODE command tells SPSS^x to RECODE the values of anyone with a scale score of 20 or less
to a value of 1 and anyone with a scale score between 21 and 28 to a value of 2. By adding a new
VALUE LABELS command, the output will label 1 with LOW and 2 with HIGH. If we did not RECODE
these values, we would have too few cases in too many of the cells to determine if patterns exist in the
data when using the CROSSTABS command.

```
                    TABLE 11. CROSSTABS COMMAND OUTPUT
==========================================================================
Produced using the following CROSSTABS command and other related
commands:
                RECODE RR(LO THRU 20=1)(21 THRU 28=2)
                VALUE LABELS RR 1 'LOW'  2 'HIGH'
                CROSSTABS TABLES=RR1,RR6, RR BY NRACE RACESEX/
                OPTIONS 4
                STATISTICS 1,4,8,10,11


* * * * * * * * * * * * * * *  C R O S S T A B U L A T I O N  O F * * *
      RR1    RACE AND SCHOOL                    BY    NRACE
* * * * * * * * * * * * * * * * * * * * * * * * * * * * * * * * * * * *


                        NRACE
               COUNT  I
               COL PCT IBLACK   WHITE     ROW
                      I                  TOTAL
                      I    0.0 I   1.00I
      RR1      --------I--------I--------I
                    1  I        I    2  I    2
      STRONGLY DISAGRE I        I   5.7 I   3.6
                      -I--------I--------I
                    2  I        I    3  I    3
      DISAGREE         I        I   8.6 I   5.4
                      -I--------I--------I
                    3  I   13  I   23  I   36
      AGREE            I  61.9 I  65.7 I  64.3
                      -I--------I--------I
                    4  I    8  I    7  I   15
      STRONGLY AGREE   I  38.1 I  20.0 I  26.8
                      -I--------I--------I
               COLUMN      21      35      56
               TOTAL     37.5    62.5   100.0


CHI SQUARE   D.F.   SIGNIFICANCE   MIN E.F.   CELLS WITH E.F.< 5
----------   -----  ------------   --------   -------------------
 4.63407       3       0.2006        0.750     4 of   8 ( 50.0%)

                                     WITH RR1     WITH NRACE
         STATISTIC        SYMMETRIC   DEPENDENT    DEPENDENT
         ---------        ---------   ---------    ---------

LAMBDA                     0.02439     0.00000      0.04762
ETA                                    0.27682      0.28767



         STATISTIC          VALUE      SIGNIFICANCE
         ---------          -----      ------------
PEARSON'S R              -0.27682        0.0194
GAMMA                    -0.52105

NUMBER OF MISSING OBSERVATIONS =     4

* * * * * * * * * * * * * *  C R O S S T A B U L A T I O N  O F * *
      RR6    RACE AND DATING                  BY    NRACE
* * * * * * * * * * * * * * * * * * * * * * * * * * * * * * * * * * *
```

(Continued)

(Continued)

```
                          NRACE
                 COUNT  I
                 COL PCT IBLACK   WHITE    ROW
                        I               TOTAL
                        I   0.0 I   1.00I
      RR6        --------I--------I--------I
                      1 I    2 I    6 I    8
      STRONGLY DISAGRE I  9.5 I 17.6 I 14.5
                       -I--------I--------I
                      2 I   12 I   14 I   26
      DISAGREE         I 57.1 I 41.2 I 47.3
                       -I--------I--------I
                      3 I    7 I   14 I   21
      AGREE            I 33.3 I 41.2 I 38.2
                       -I--------I--------I
                 COLUMN     21      34      55
                 TOTAL    38.2    61.8   100.0
```

```
CHI SQUARE    D.F.   SIGNIFICANCE   MIN E.F.   CELLS WITH E.F.< 5
----------    ----   ------------   --------   ------------------
  1.49815      2        0.4728        3.055     2 OF  6 ( 33.3%)
```

STATISTIC	SYMMETRIC	WITH RR6 DEPENDENT	WITH NRACE DEPENDENT
LAMBDA	0.00000	0.00000	0.00000
ETA		0.00198	0.16504

STATISTIC	VALUE	SIGNIFICANCE
PEARSON'S R	-0.00198	0.4943
GAMMA	0.02752	

NUMBER OF MISSING OBSERVATIONS =   5

```
*************  C R O S S T A B U L A T I O N  O F *******
RR    RACE RELATIONS SCALE          BY    NRACE
*********************************************
```

```
                          NRACE
                 COUNT  I
                 COL PCT IBLACK   WHITE    ROW
                        I               TOTAL
                        I   0.0 I   1.00I
      RR         --------I--------I--------I
                   1.00 I   10 I   19 I   29
      LOW              I 47.6 I 59.4 I 54.7
                       -I--------I--------I
                   2.00 I   11 I   13 I   24
      HIGH             I 52.4 I 40.6 I 45.3
                       -I--------I--------I
                 COLUMN     21      32      53
                 TOTAL    39.6    60.4   100.0
```

(Continued)

```
CHI SQUARE   D.F.   SIGNIFICANCE   MIN E.F.   CELLS WITH E.F.< 5
----------   -----  ------------   --------   -------------------


 0.31233      1       0.5763         9.509          NONE
 0.70722      1       0.4004       ( BEFORE YATES CORRECTION )
```

```
                                          WITH RR       WITH NRACE
          STATISTIC          SYMMETRIC    DEPENDENT     DEPENDENT
          ---------          ---------    ------------  -------------


LAMBDA                        0.02222       0.04167      0.00000
ETA                                         0.11551      0.11551
```

```
          STATISTIC           VALUE        SIGNIFICANCE
          ---------           -----        ------------
PEARSON'S R                  -0.11551         0.2050
GAMMA                        -0.23304
```

```
NUMBER OF MISSING OBSERVATIONS =      7
```

```
* * * * * * * * * * * * * * *  C R O S S T A B U L A T I O N   O F * *
RR    RACE RELATIONS SCALE       BY   RACESEX RACE AND SEX IDENTIFIER
* * * * * * * * * * * * * * * * * * * * * * * * * * * * * * * * * * * *

                   RACESEX
             COUNT I
             COL PCT IBL-MALE BL-FEMAL WH-MALE  WH-FEMAL  ROW
                   I     E                 E            TOTAL
                   I  1.00I   2.00I   3.00I   4.00I
     RR      --------I--------I--------I--------I--------I
              1.00 I    7 I    3 I    9 I   10 I    29
     LOW           I 70.0 I 27.3 I 64.3 I 55.6 I  54.7
                   -I--------I--------I--------I--------I
              2.00 I    3 I    8 I    5 I    8 I    24
     HIGH          I 30.0 I 72.7 I 35.7 I 44.4 I  45.3
                   -I--------I--------I--------I--------I
             COLUMN    10      11      14      18      53
             TOTAL   18.9    20.8    26.4    34.0   100.0
```

```
CHI SQUARE   D.F.   SIGNIFICANCE   MIN E.F.   CELLS WITH E.F.< 5
----------   -----  ------------   --------   -------------------
 4.80891      3       0.1863        4.528      2 OF   8 (25.0%)
```

```
                                          WITH RR       WITH RACESEX
          STATISTIC          SYMMETRIC    DEPENDENT     DEPENDENT
          ---------          ---------    ------------  -------------


LAMBDA                        0.08475       0.20833      0.00000
ETA                                         0.30122      0.00385
```

(Continued)

(Continued)

```
                STATISTIC              VALUE        SIGNIFICANCE
                ---------              -----        ------------
                PEARSON'S R           -0.00385         0.4891
                GAMMA                 -0.01901


                NUMBER OF MISSING OBSERVATIONS =      7

------------------------------------------------------------------
```

totals (frequencies and percents) are reported in the marginals of each table. In the body of the table the number of people who had each value and their percentage are reported. For example, thirteen black respondents (61.9%) and twenty-three white respondents (65.7%) responded "agree" to our statement on race and schools.

Similar patterns appear for each of the other variables. Indeed, the differences between black and white respondents become more minimal with the more extreme items about dating and marriage. The overall scale scores, when dichotomized at the median value and categorized as low and high, showed that blacks and whites did not differ significantly from one another.

In addition to tabular output, summary statistics were requested with our STATISTICS command. By entering specific numbers in the specifications field, we chose the statistics chi square, lambda, gamma, eta, and Pearson r. The chi square measure enables you to test whether the observed differences in the sample are sufficiently large for you to have faith that such differences exist in the population. (For this study, the observed differences were not very great, and the chi square values were not statistically significant.)

The lambda, gamma, eta, and Pearson r values are all measures of association. Which one to use depends on the level of measurement of each variable. Use the following table to help you decide which measure(s) of association are most appropriate for your study.

Dependent Variable Level of Measurement	Independent Variable Level of Measurement		
	Nominal	Ordinal	Interval/Ratio
Nominal	lambda	lambda	lambda
Ordinal	lambda	gamma	gamma
Interval/Ratio	eta	eta/gamma	Pearson r

(Some people argue that you can treat ordinal level variables that are not very skewed and that have relatively few categories as interval level data and use Pearsonian r values.)

One of the nicer features of SPSSˣ is the power it gives you to examine relationships using dependent, independent, and control variables. For example, you may be interested in comparing race relations attitudes by race controlling for sex—that is, comparing black and white men with each other and black and white women with each other. This is easily accomplished by substituting the current CROSSTABS command with

```
CROSSTABS TABLES=RR BY RACE BY SEX
```

Note that the intervening or control variable, in this case SEX, must be listed after an additional BY keyword. (You may have up to four levels of control variables or a maximum of five BY keywords.) This command will produce a separate table for males and for females. You can then compare black and white respondents' racial attitude scores within the two tables.

Or, since we created a new variable, RACESEX, we could directly compare all four race/sex groups with each other. This could be accomplished by modifying the CROSSTABS command with

```
CROSSTABS TABLES= RR1 TO RR7, RR BY RACESEX
```

(See the last part of Table 11 for what this output would look like.) You have to decide if it is better to compare all four categories at once or to make comparisons between an independent and a dependent variable using one or more control variables.

Just as there are graphic forms and summary statistics for describing a single distribution, SPSSˣ provides procedures for producing scatterplots and summary correlation/regression statistics. The general form of this procedure statement is

```
SCATTERGRAM varlist, varlist WITH varlist...varlist
OPTIONS list
STATISTICS list
```

There are no surprises here. The format of the SCATTERGRAM command is consistent with procedures discussed earlier. Once the command name is given, you enter your variables of interest, the keyword WITH, and your explanatory variables. The variables listed first will be treated as dependent variables—they will be graphed down the Y-axis and summary regression statistics will be computed accordingly. Of course, SPSS[x] will assume you know which levels of measurement to use to ensure that the statistics computed are meaningful.

Table 12 provides an example of the output produced when you use the SCATTERGRAM command:

```
SCATTERGRAM RR WITH INCOME YRBRTH
STATISTICS ALL
```

The output is divided into two parts. The first part is a scatterplot, and the second part reports the summary statistics. In the scatterplot, the values listed across the bottom of the page correspond to the variable listed after the WITH keyword. The values listed down the page correspond to the variable of interest, or the dependent variable. The body of the chart includes asterisks and numbers. An asterisk indicates that one respondent had those coordinates (e.g., 28 on the race relations scale and $5,000). A number indicates how many people had those coordinates (e.g., 3 people had scores of 22 on our race relations index and incomes of $10,500).

The reported summary statistics include all you would expect to find when working with a simple linear equation. You will find your correlation values, both r and R^2, a test of significance, and the values for the equation—slope and intercept points.

By the way, if you are using SPSS[x] Version 2.1 or later, you may wish to use the PLOT command. You can get most of these SCATTERGRAM results using the REGRESSION option of the PLOT command. The general form of of the PLOT command is

```
PLOT  FORMAT=REGRESSION/

 PLOT = varlist WITH varlist
```

Using our variables:

```
PLOT  FORMAT=REGRESSION/
 PLOT = RR WITH INCOME YRBRTH
```

Returning to our study, overall race relations index scores were related to income ($r = -.267$, sig $< .03$) and year of birth ($r = .483$, sig $< .001$). The higher the income, the lower the race relations index. The later a person's date of birth—the younger he or she was—the higher the race relations index score. Interesting results.

TABLE 12. SCATTERGRAM COMMAND OUTPUT

===

Produced using the following SCATTERGRAM command:

```
          SCATTERGRAM RR WITH INCOME YRBRTH
          STATISTICS  ALL

SCATTERGRAM OF   (DOWN)   RR    RACE RELATIONS SCALE        (ACROSS)   INCOME
              6250.0   8750.0   11250.0  13750.0  16250.0  18750.0  21250.0  23750.0  26250.0  28750.0
        .+----+----+----+----+----+----+----+----+----+----+----+----+----+----+----+----+----+----+----+.
 28.000 +‡                     I                     I                                       +    28.000
        I                      I                     I                                       I
        I             ‡        I                     I                                       I
        I                      I                     I                                       I
        I                      I                     I                                       I
 25.900 +             ‡        I                     I                                       +    25.900
        I                      I                     I                                       I
        I‡                     I                     I                                       I
        I                      I                     I                                       I
        I                      I                     I                                       I
 23.800 +‡            ‡        I                   2 I                                       +    23.800
        I                      I                     I                                       I
        I‡                     I                     I                                       I
        I                      I                     I                                       I
        I‡            3        I                     I                                       I
 21.700 +                      I                     I                                       +    21.700
        I                      I                     I                                       I
        I‡---------------------6---------------------3---------------------2----------------‡I
        I                      I                     I                                       I
        I‡            ‡        I                   ‡ I                                       I
 19.600 +                      I                     I                                       +    19.600
        I             3        I                   2 I            ‡                          I
        I                      I                     I                                       I
        I                      I                     I                                       I
        I‡            2        I                   2 I                                       I
 17.500 +                      I                     I                                       +    17.500
        I‡            5        I                   ‡ I                                       I
        I                      I                     I                                       I
        I                      I                     I                                       I
        I             ‡        I                     I                                       I
 15.400 +                      I                     I                                       +    15.400
        I                      I                     I                                       I
        I                      I                     I                                       I
        I---------------------‡------------------------------------------------------------I
        I                      I                     I                                       I
 13.300 +                      I                     I                                       +    13.300
        I                      I                     I                                       I
        I                      I                     I                                       I
        I             ‡        I                     I                                       I
        I                      I                     I                                       I
 11.200 +                      I                   ‡ I                                     ‡+    11.200
        I                      I                     I                                       I
        I                      I                     I                                       I
        I                      I                     I                                       I
        I                      I                     I                                       I
  9.100 +                      I                     I                                       +     9.100
        I                      I                     I                                       I
        I                      I                     I                                       I
        I                      I                     I                                       I
        I                      I                   ‡ I                                       I
  7.000 +                      I                   ‡ I                                       +     7.000
        .+----+----+----+----+----+----+----+----+----+----+----+----+----+----+----+----+----+----+----+.
       5000.0   7500.0  10000.0  12500.0  15000.0  17500.0  20000.0  22500.0  25000.0  27500.0  30000.0
```

(Continued)

(Continued)

STATISTICS..

CORRELATION (R)-	-.26685	R SQUARED -	.07121	SIGNIFICANCE -	.02671
STD ERR OF EST -	3.82758	INTERCEPT (A) -	21.83181	SLOPE (B) -	-.00017
PLOTTED VALUES -	53	EXCLUDED VALUES-	0	MISSING VALUES -	7

'::::::::' IS PRINTED IF A COEFFICIENT CANNOT BE COMPUTED. *(Continued)*

Exercise 8

Now that you know how to modify an SPSS[x] file, try it on your own file. Run the appropriate CROSSTABS and SCATTERGRAM procedures. All you need to do is substitute the last statistical procedure with the current one. Then, take a few moments and think about what your outputs mean.

Since we are working with variables at the interval level of measurement, this is a good time to discuss two hypotheses-testing measures—the T-test and ANOVA, or analysis of variance. The T-test procedure statement is straightforward:

```
T-TEST GROUPS=varname (val1,val2)/
  VARIABLES=varlist
```

After the procedure name, the word GROUPS must appear if you wish to run a test of independent samples. (The keyword PAIRS is used when working with related samples.) Since T-tests can compare only two groups at a time, you are asked to specify which two values of an independent variable should be used by SPSS[x] when creating each group. The VARIABLES specification gives you an opportunity to list which dependent variables you wish to test. For example, in our study, the following T-TEST procedure works well:

```
T-TEST GROUPS=RACE(3,4)/VARIABLES=RR1 TO RR7,RR
```

This tells SPSS[x] to execute a T-test on each of our race relations questions as well as on our index score by comparing blacks (RACE(3)) with whites (RACE(4)). Note that no STATISTICS command is needed. See Table 13.

The output from the T-TEST procedure is segmented by variables and types of information. For each dependent variable, SPSS[x] reports descriptive statistics (number of cases, mean, etc.) for each grouping (in this case, GROUP 1 is black respondents, while GROUP 2 is white respondents). An F-value is then calculated.

(Continued)

```
SCATTERGRAM OF   (DOWN)   RR   RACE RELATIONS SCALE          (ACROSS)   YRBRTH YEAR OF BIRTH
              1917.4   1922.2   1927.0   1931.8   1936.6   1941.4   1946.2   1951.0   1955.8   1960.6
         .+----+----+----+----+----+----+----+----+----+----+----+----+----+----+----+----+----+----+----+.
 28.000 +                        I                       I                                      &    +  28.000
        I                        I                       I              &                       I
        I                        I                       I                                      I
        I                        I                       I                                      I
 25.900 +                        I                       I              &                       +  25.900
        I                        I                       I                                      I
        I                        I                     & I                                      I
        I                        I                       I                                      I
        I                        I                       I                                      I
 23.800 +                        I                     & I      &          & &                  +  23.800
        I                        I                       I                                      I
        I                        I                       I                        &             I
        I                        I                       I                                      I
        I           &            I                       I    &        &  &                     I
 21.700 +                        I                       I                                      +  21.700
        I&----------------+----------------2---------+-----+---&---2---+--------2--&-&--------I
        I                        I                       I                                      I
        I                        I                       I&         &                        &I
 19.600 +                        I                       I                                      +  19.600
        I              &         I   & I                 & & & I                 &              I
        I                        I                       I                                      I
        I                        I                       I                                      I
        I                        I                &      I   &   &        &                    I
 17.500 +                        I                       I                                      +  17.500
        I           &            I                     & I  &      & &    & &                   I
        I                        I                       I                                      I
        I                        I                       I     &                               I
 15.400 +                        I                       I                                      +  15.400
        I           &            I                       I                                      I
        I                        I                       I                                      I
        I----------------------------+--------------------------------------------------------I
        I                        I                       I                                      I
 13.300 +                        I                       I                                      +  13.300
        I           &            I                       I                                      I
        I                        I                       I                                      I
        I                     &  I                       I                                      I
        I                        I                       I                                      I
 11.200 +&                       I                     & I                                      +  11.200
        I                        I                       I                                      I
        I                        I                       I                                      I
        I                        I                       I                                      I
  9.100 +                        I                       I                                      +   9.100
        I                        I                       I                                      I
        I                        I                       I                                      I
        I                        I                       I                                      I
  7.000 +           &            I                       I                                      +   7.000
         .+----+----+----+----+----+----+----+----+----+----+----+----+----+----+----+----+----+----+----+.
```

(Continued)

It will help you determine which T-test value to use (if the F-value is not significant, then use the pooled-variance T-value). For our study, some

(Continued)

1915.0	1919.8	1924.6	1929.4	1934.2	1939.0	1943.8	1948.6	1953.4	1958.2	1963.0

STATISTICS..

CORRELATION (R)-	.48349	R SQUARED	-	.23376	SIGNIFICANCE	-	.00007
STD ERR OF EST -	3.48586	INTERCEPT (A)	-	-261.14246	SLOPE (B)	-	.14435
PLOTTED VALUES -	57	EXCLUDED VALUES-		0	MISSING VALUES -		3

'ıııııııı' IS PRINTED IF A COEFFICIENT CANNOT BE COMPUTED

----

differences exist between black and white respondents on specific questions, but no significant difference is found for the overall race relations index score.

If you wish to compare more than two groups at the same time, you will need to use an analysis of variance procedure. SPSS^x has several such procedures. The one that best fits our needs here is called ONEWAY. Not surprisingly, it is a one-way analysis of variance test. In addition to calculating appropriate sums of squares and F-values, it will report tests for homogeneity of variance and allow you to make contrast comparisons of any combination of groups and *a posteriori* comparisons. Here is the general format of this command:

```
ONEWAY varlist BY varname (min,max)/
 CONTRASTS wt  wt  wt  wt/
 RANGES  test
 OPTIONS list
STATISTICS list
```

For the sake of illustration, let us assume that we wish to compare the race-sex groups (black male, black female, white male, and white female) on our index variable. Additionally, we wish to test the hypothesis that black males' and white males' responses differ. Finally, we wish to find out if there are any other differences. Our procedure command would look like this:

```
ONEWAY RR BY RACESEX (1,4)/
 CONTRASTS -1 0 1 0/
 RANGES  DUNCAN(.05)/
STATISTICS ALL
```

Table 14 illustrates this output. First, SPSS^x produces the standard analysis of variance F-test table. Then, for each group, it produces summary descriptive

TABLE 13. T-TEST COMMAND OUTPUT

===

Produced using the following T-TEST command:

T-TEST GROUPS=RACE(3,4)/VARIABLES=RR1 TO RR7, RR

- T - T E S T -

GROUP 1 - RACE EQ   3.
GROUP 2 - RACE EQ   4.

VARIABLE	NUMBER OF CASES	MEAN	STANDARD DEVIATION	STANDARD ERROR	‡ POOLED VARIANCE ESTIMATE ‡			SEPARATE VARIANCE ESTIMATE		
					F VALUE / 2-TAIL PROB.	T VALUE	DEGREES OF FREEDOM	2-TAIL PROB.	T VALUE	DEGREES OF FREEDOM	2-TAIL PROB.
RR1 RACE AND SCHOOL											
GROUP 1	21	3.3810	0.498	0.109	2.14 0.076	2.12	54	0.039	2.32	52.96	0.024
GROUP 2	35	3.0000	0.728	0.123							
RR2 RACE AND NEIGHBORHOOD											
GROUP 1	21	3.2381	0.436	0.095	2.03 0.099	2.10	53	0.040	2.28	52.01	0.027
GROUP 2	34	2.9118	0.621	0.107							
RR3 RACE AND CHURCH											
GROUP 1	21	3.0000	0.775	0.169	1.01 0.961	0.67	54	0.506	0.67	42.16	0.507
GROUP 2	35	2.8571	0.772	0.131							
RR4 RACE AND WORK-SUPERVISOR											
GROUP 1	21	3.0476	0.498	0.109	1.75 0.192	1.16	53	0.249	1.24	50.68	0.219
GROUP 2	34	2.8529	0.657	0.113							
RR5 RACE AND NEXT DOOR											
GROUP 1	21	3.0476	0.498	0.109	2.62 0.026	1.89	53	0.064	2.11	53.00	0.039
GROUP 2	34	2.6765	0.806	0.138							
RR6 RACE AND DATING											
GROUP 1	21	2.2381	0.625	0.136	1.41 0.426	0.01	53	0.989	0.02	47.92	0.988
GROUP 2	34	2.2353	0.741	0.127							
RR7 RACE AND MARRIAGE											
GROUP 1	21	2.0000	0.837	0.183	1.21 0.669	-0.24	53	0.812	-0.24	45.58	0.808
GROUP 2	34	2.0588	0.919	0.158							
RR RACE RELATIONS SCALE											
GROUP 1	21	19.9524	2.674	0.583	2.44 0.041	1.44	51	0.155	1.58	50.99	0.121
GROUP 2	32	18.4688	4.174	0.738							

TABLE 14. ONEWAY COMMAND OUTPUT
==

Produced using the following ONEWAY command:

```
            ONEWAY RR BY RACESEX(1,4)/
            CONTRASTS = -1 0 1 0/
            RANGES=DUNCAN(.05)/
            STATISTICS ALL
```

- O N E W A Y -

```
        VARIABLE    RR        RACE RELATIONS SCALE
    BY  VARIABLE    RACESEX   RACE AND SEX IDENTIFIER
```

ANALYSIS OF VARIANCE

SOURCE	D.F.	SUM OF SQUARES	MEAN SQUARES	F RATIO	F PROB.
BETWEEN GROUPS	3	69.0925	23.0308	1.759	0.1674
WITHIN GROUPS	49	641.7377	13.0967		
TOTAL	52	710.8302			

GROUP	COUNT	MEAN	STANDARD DEVIATION	STANDARD ERROR	MINIMUM	MAXIMUM	95 PCT CONF INT FOR MEAN		
GRP 1	10	18.9000	2.3781	0.7520	17.0000	24.0000	17.1988	TO	20.6012
GRP 2	11	20.9091	2.6629	0.8029	17.0000	25.0000	19.1201	TO	22.6980
GRP 3	14	17.5714	4.6029	1.2302	7.0000	21.0000	14.9138	TO	20.2291
GRP 4	18	19.1667	3.7924	0.8939	11.0000	26.0000	17.2807	TO	21.0526
TOTAL	53	19.0566	3.6973	0.5079	7.0000	26.0000	18.0375	TO	20.0757
FIXED EFFECTS MODEL			3.6189	0.4971			18.0576	TO	20.0556
RANDOM EFFECTS MODEL				0.6698			16.9251	TO	21.1881

RANDOM EFFECTS MODEL - ESTIMATE OF BETWEEN COMPONENT VARIANCE   0.7638

TESTS FOR HOMOGENEITY OF VARIANCES

```
        COCHRANS C = MAX. VARIANCE/SUM(VARIANCES) = 0.4385, P = 0.097 (APPROX.)
        BARTLETT-BOX F =                          1.882, P = 0.130
        MAXIMUM VARIANCE / MINIMUM VARIANCE =      3.746
```

CONTRAST COEFFICIENT MATRIX

```
          GRP01      GRP03
                GRP02      GRP04
CONTRAST  1  -1.0   0.0   1.0   0.0
```
                                                                              (Continued)

information (e.g., counts, mean, standard deviation, etc.). To help you determine
how much confidence you can have in your F-value, tests for homogeneity of

(Continued)

	VALUE	S. ERROR	POOLED VARIANCE ESTIMATE T VALUE	D.F.	T PROB.	S. ERROR	SEPARATE VARIANCE ESTIMATE T VALUE	D.F.	T PROB.
CONTRAST 1	-1.3286	1.4984	-0.887	49.0	0.380	1.4418	-0.921	20.4	0.368

MULTIPLE RANGE TEST

DUNCAN PROCEDURE

RANGES FOR THE 0.050 LEVEL -

     2.84 2.99 3.09

THE RANGES ABOVE ARE TABLE RANGES.
THE VALUE ACTUALLY COMPARED WITH MEAN(J)-MEAN(I) IS..
    2.5590 * RANGE * DSQRT(1/N(I) + 1/N(J))

(*) DENOTES PAIRS OF GROUPS SIGNIFICANTLY DIFFERENT AT THE 0.050 LEVEL

```
                        G G G G
                        R R R R
                        P P P P

     MEAN    GROUP      3 1 4 2

    17.5714  GRP 3
    18.9000  GRP 1
    19.1667  GRP 4
    20.9091  GRP 2       *
```

variances are performed. (Generally, if these are significant, you cannot have a great deal of faith in your ANOVA output.)

The second page of the output reports the contrasts. These are basically T-tests. Several contrasts may be run at any one time. Here we were just interested in running black males versus white males. Note that no reliable difference was found.

The final section of the ONEWAY output contains the *a posteriori* comparisons. Our procedure indicated that we wished to run the DUNCAN test using the .05 criterion. The asterisk points out which groups are different. In this case, only group 3 and group 2 are significantly different. We cannot have much faith in this finding since our overall ANOVA F-value was not statistically significant.

Exercise 9

Take a few minutes to run appropriate T-TEST and ONEWAY procedures on your data. Remember to let your earlier work on your hypotheses guide you in selecting which variables to use as independent variables and which to use as dependent variables.

Multivariate Analysis

The best known and most widely used multivariate technique is multiple regression. It is the logical extension of the simple linear model that we encountered earlier in the SCATTERGRAM and PLOT procedures. While these procedures work well with one independent and one dependent variable, they are not the most powerful tools. The REGRESSION procedure is a powerful tool that works well with two, three, or more independent variables. It can be used to find the best linear fit among several independent or explanatory variables and a single dependent variable. The general form of the REGRESSION procedure for SPSS^x is

```
REGRESSION WIDTH=n/
 DESCRIPTIVES=DEFAULTS VARIANCE COV SIG N/
 VARIABLES = varlist/
 CRITERIA = DEFAULTS PIN(value) POUT(value)/
 STATISTICS = DEFAULTS CHA CI HISTORY/
 DEPENDENT = variable/
 method/     (single option of FORWARD, STEPWISE, etc.)
 RESIDUALS=DEFAULTS/
 SCATTERPLOT (select temporary variable names)/
```

As you can see, SPSS^x provides a great deal of options. It can be used to find the best predictors of any interval level variable as long as each independent variable can be treated as an interval level variable or as a dichotomy. Here's one way to run it with our data to find the best predictors of the index (RR) variable:

```
REGRESSION WIDTH=80/
 DESCRIPTIVES/
 VARIABLES = RR REGVTE TO YRBRTH/
 CRITERIA = PIN(.15) POUT(.20)/
 STATISTICS = DEFAULTS CHA HISTORY/
 DEPENDENT = RR/
 STEPWISE/
 RESIDUALS=DEFAULTS/
 SCATTERPLOT (*PRED,*RESID)/
```

This command sequence looks harder than it really is. First, the WIDTH command tells SPSS^x to print the report to fit on 8½ by 11 inch paper. If you omit the WIDTH command, SPSS^x will assume that you want the standard 132-column width.

The DESCRIPTIVES keyword will produce means and standard deviation values for each variable, as well as a zero-order correlation matrix of all the variables listed in the VARIABLES = statement. Of course, if you wish, you could request SPSS^x to compute and display the values for variance (use the option VARIANCE) and the covariance matrix (use the option COV), as well as other related statistics.

The VARIABLES= specification enables you to specify which variables are to be included in your run. There is nothing really new here. As always, all listed variables must be spelled as they appeared in the DATA LIST command. Additionally, you will note that we used the TO convention to identify all the variables from REGVTE through YRBRTH. This works fine as long as all the relevant variables are listed sequentially in the DATA LIST command. If you wished to include fewer variables, you would simply list each one by its variable name instead of using the TO convention.

The CRITERIA specifications are used to set variable entry/removal limits. The probability criteria used to enter a variable for our study was set at .15 and the criteria used to remove a variable was set at .20. (The default values for CRITERIA are .05 for entry [PIN] and .10 for removal [POUT] of each independent variable.) You could have converted these probability values to F-values and used FIN(value) and FOUT(value) instead of PIN or POUT. Most people will find it easier to use PIN and POUT, however.

The DEPENDENT= specification subcommand is the easiest of all REGRESSION subcommands. It simply enables you to identify which variable is to be treated as the dependent variable.

Optionally, we can request that the REGRESSION procedure be run as a FORWARD, BACKWARD, or STEPWISE procedure. That is, whether we want SPSS^x to enter all the independent variables one at a time and check the F-value and criterion (PIN) tests (FORWARD), enter all the variables at once and then begin removing the least powerful explanatory variables one at a time (BACKWARD), or enter each independent variable one at a time, starting with the most powerful predictor, and then find the second-best predictor, third-best predictor, etc. (STEPWISE). In the STEPWISE procedure, entry of an additional independent variable is based on the value of the partial correlation coefficient— those with the largest partial are entered first. Additional predictor variables are entered, or are removed if they are no longer useful, until all the variables are in the equation or until the limits set in the CRITERIA subcommand, or other subcommand, are reached. Each entry of a new independent variable is treated as a new step, and—assuming the STATISTICS subcommand is present—all equation summary statistics (e.g., Multiple R, R-squared, ANOVA, etc.), equation coefficients (e.g., slope, BETA values, significance, etc.), and summary data of those variables not in the equation (e.g., partial correlations, significance, etc.) are recalculated (see Table 15).

By the way, you can force a variable to be included in the equation—use the

```
ENTER variable list/
```

subcommand. To remove a variable from the equation use the

```
REMOVE variable list/
```

subcommand.

TABLE 15. MULTIPLE REGRESSION COMMAND OUTPUT
==

Produced using the following REGRESSION command and associated commands:

```
TEMPORARY
RECODE RACE(1,2=9)(3=0)(4=1)
REGRESSION WIDTH=80/
 CRITERIA=PIN(.15) POUT(.20)/
 DESCRIPTIVES/
 VARIABLES=RR REGVTE TO YRBRTH/
 STATISTICS=DEFAULTS CHA HISTORY/
 DEPENDENT=RR/
 STEPWISE/
 RESIDUALS=DEFAULTS/
 SCATTERPLOT (*PRED,*RESID)/
```

‡‡‡‡ M U L T I P L E   R E G R E S S I O N ‡‡‡‡

VARIABLE LIST NUMBER 1. LISTWISE DELETION OF MISSING DATA.

	MEAN	STD DEV	LABEL
RR	19.184	3.678	RACE RELATIONS SCALE
REGVTE	.939	.242	REGISTERED TO VOTE
VOTE	.898	.306	VOTE IN LAST ELECTION
POLPTY	.286	.456	POLITICAL PARTY
RACE	.592	.497	RACE OR RESPONDENT
INCOME	12683.673	6090.202	ANNUAL INCOME
MARST	.327	.474	MARITAL STATUS
SEX	.510	.505	SEX OF RESPONDENT
YRBRTH	1943.755	12.797	YEAR OF BIRTH

N OF CASES =   49

CORRELATION

	RR	REGVTE	VOTE	POLPTY	RACE	INCOME	MARST	SEX	YRBRTH
RR	1.00	.177	.147	-.144	-.163	-.254	.276	.285	.388
REGVTE	.177	1.000	476	-.215	-.212	-.013	-.004	-.080	-.099
VOTE	.147	.476	1.000	-.235	-.006	.021	-.053	-.330	-.097
POLPTY	-.144	-.215	-.235	1.000	.433	.179	-.151	.077	-.138
RACE	-.163	-.212	-.006	.433	1.000	.111	-.130	.017	-.255
INCOME	-.254	-.013	.021	.179	.111	1.000	-.303	-.021	-.475
MARST	.276	-.004	-.053	-.151	-.130	-.303	1.000	.160	.512
SEX	.285	-.080	-.330	.077	.017	-.021	.160	1.000	.174
YRBRTH	.388	-.099	-.097	-.138	-.255	-.475	.512	.174	1.000

‡‡‡‡ M U L T I P L E   R E G R E S S I O N ‡‡‡‡

EQUATION NUMBER 1.

DEPENDENT VARIABLE..   RR   RACE RELATIONS SCALE

(Continued)

```
BEGINNING BLOCK NUMBER  1.  METHOD:  STEPWISE

VARIABLE(S) ENTERED ON STEP NUMBER

     1..    YRBRTH    YEAR OF BIRTH



MULTIPLE R           .38826
R SQUARE            .15075        R SQUARE CHANGE    .15075
ADJUSTED R SQUARE   .13268        F CHANGE          8.34263
STANDARD ERROR      3.42538       SIGNIF F CHANGE    .0058

ANALYSIS OF VARIANCE
                    DF      SUM OF SQUARES    MEAN SQUARE
REGRESSION          1          97.88589        97.88589
RESIDUAL           47         551.46105        11.73321

F =     8.34263     SIGNIF F =  .0058


----------------- VARIABLES IN THE EQUATION -----------------

VARIABLE            B        SE B       BETA       T    SIG T

YRBRTH           .11159    .03863     .38826    2.888   .0058
(CONSTANT)   -197.71706   75.09632             -2.633   .0114



------------ VARIABLES NOT IN THE EQUATION ------------

VARIABLE    BETA IN  PARTIAL  MIN TOLER     T    SIG T

  REGVTE    .21715    .23448    .99019    1.636   .1087
  VOTE      .18607    .20095    .99059    1.391   .1708
  POLPTY   -.09192   -.09880    .98107    -.673   .5041
  RACE     -.06875   -.07213    .93479    -.490   .6261
  INCOME   -.08928   -.08525    .77430    -.580   .5645
  MARST     .10435    .09729    .73820     .663   .5106
  SEX       .22403    .23937    .96957    1.672   .1013
```

```
        ‡‡‡‡  M U L T I P L E   R E G R E S S I O N  ‡‡‡‡


DEPENDENT VARIABLE..   RR     RACE RELATIONS SCALE

VARIABLE(S) ENTERED ON STEP NUMBER

     2..    SEX      SEX OF RESPONDENT


MULTIPLE R           .44655
R SQUARE            .19941        R SQUARE CHANGE    .04866
ADJUSTED R SQUARE   .16460        F CHANGE          2.79600
STANDARD ERROR      3.36175       SIGNIF F CHANGE    .1013
```

(Continued)

(Continued)

```
ANALYSIS OF VARIANCE

                  DF    SUM OF SQUARES    MEAN SQUARE
REGRESSION         2        129.48451       64.74225
RESIDUAL          46        519.86243       11.30136

F =      5.72871     SIGNIF F = .0060


----------------- VARIABLES IN THE EQUATION -----------------


VARIABLE           B       SE B      BETA       T   SIG T

YRBRTH         .10036     .03851    .34918    2.606  .0123
SEX           1.63142     .97566    .22403    1.672  .1013
(CONSTANT) -176.71684   74.76375            -2.364  .0224


------------ VARIABLES NOT IN THE EQUATION ------------


VARIABLE   BETA IN  PARTIAL  MIN TOLER      T   SIG T

 REGVTE     .23228   .25779    .96228    1.790   .0802
 VOTE       .28620   .30164    .87044    2.122   .0394
 POLPTY    -.11635  -.12810    .94661    -.866   .3908
 RACE      -.08384  -.09040    .90282    -.609   .5456
 INCOME    -.10775  -.10569    .74723    -.713   .4795
 MARST      .08350   .07990    .72939     .538   .5934



      ‡ ‡ ‡ ‡   M U L T I P L E   R E G R E S S I O N   ‡ ‡ ‡ ‡

DEPENDENT VARIABLE..   RR      RACE RELATIONS SCALE

VARIABLE(S) ENTERED ON STEP NUMBER

    3..    VOTE    VOTE IN LAST ELECTION


MULTIPLE R          .52178
R SQUARE            .27225      R SQUARE CHANGE      .07284
ADJUSTED R SQUARE   .22373      F CHANGE            4.50416
STANDARD ERROR     3.24058      SIGNIF F CHANGE      .0393

ANALYSIS OF VARIANCE
                  DF    SUM OF SQUARES    MEAN SQUARE
REGRESSION         3        176.78448       58.92816
RESIDUAL          45        472.56246       10.50139

F =      5.61146     SIGNIF F = .0023
```

(Continued)

```
----------------- VARIABLES IN THE EQUATION -----------------


VARIABLE              B        SE B       BETA        T  SIG T

YRBRTH           .10370      .03715     .36081    2.791  .0077
SEX             2.30502      .99261     .31653    2.322  .0248
VOTE            3.44184     1.62175     .28620    2.122  .0394
(CONSTANT)   -186.64652    72.22082              -2.584  .0131


------------ VARIABLES NOT IN THE EQUATION ------------

VARIABLE    BETA IN  PARTIAL  MIN TOLER       T  SIG T

 REGVTE      .13291   .13600     .68715     .911  .3675
 POLPTY     -.05592  -.06282     .84164    -.418  .6783
 RACE       -.08062  -.09117     .86755    -.607  .5468
 INCOME     -.10604  -.10910     .74604    -.728  .4705
 MARST       .07587   .07612     .72765     .506  .6151


FOR BLOCK NUMBER  1   PIN = 0.150 LIMITS REACHED.



        ‡‡‡‡  M U L T I P L E   R E G R E S S I O N  ‡‡‡‡

DEPENDENT VARIABLE..   RR      RACE RELATIONS SCALE


                      SUMMARY TABLE
                      -------------

STEP  MULTR   RSQ   F(EQU)  SIGF      VARIABLE  BETAIN

  1   .3883  .1507  8.343   .006  IN:  YRBRTH   .3883
  2   .4466  .1994  5.729   .006  IN:  SEX      .2240
  3   .5218  .2722  5.611   .002  IN:  VOTE     .2862



        ‡‡‡‡‡‡‡‡‡‡‡‡‡‡‡‡‡‡‡‡‡‡‡‡‡‡‡‡‡‡‡‡‡‡



RESIDUALS STATISTICS:

            MIN      MAX      MEAN    STD DEV   N

‡PRED    14.9661  22.1410  19.1837   1.9191   49
‡ZPRED   -2.1977   1.5410    .0000   1.0000   49
‡SEPRED    .6617   1.7294    .8894    .2600   49
‡ADJPRED 13.3597  22.2274  19.1738   1.9954   49
‡RESID   -8.9992   5.6230    .0000   3.1377   49
‡ZRESID  -2.7770   1.7352    .0000    .9682   49
‡SRESID  -2.9222   1.8646    .0013   1.0212   49
‡DRESID  -9.9648   6.4928    .0099   3.4995   49
‡SDRESID -3.2102   1.9194   -.0056   1.0492   49
‡MAHAL    1.0220  12.6907   2.9388   2.6718   49
‡COOK D    .0000    .2793    .0302    .0600   49
```

(Continued)

(Continued)

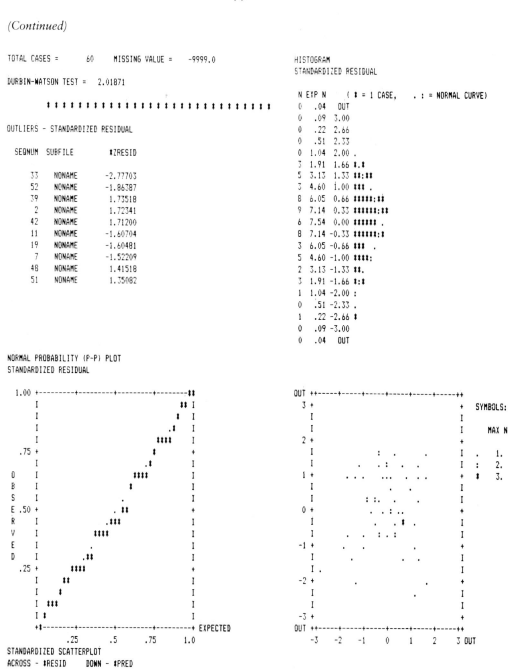

```
TOTAL CASES =      60    MISSING VALUE =    -9999.0        HISTOGRAM
                                                          STANDARDIZED RESIDUAL
DURBIN-WATSON TEST =   2.01871
                                                          N EXP N    ( * = 1 CASE,    . : = NORMAL CURVE)
                                                          0  .04   OUT
        ****************************************          0  .09   3.00
                                                          0  .22   2.66
OUTLIERS - STANDARDIZED RESIDUAL                          0  .51   2.33
                                                          0 1.04   2.00  .
   SEQNUM  SUBFILE        *ZRESID                         3 1.91   1.66  *.*
                                                          5 3.13   1.33  **:**
      33   NONAME        -2.77703                         3 4.60   1.00  ***  .
      52   NONAME        -1.86387                         8 6.05   0.66  ****:**
      39   NONAME         1.73518                         9 7.14   0.33  *****:**
       2   NONAME         1.72341                         6 7.54   0.00  ******  .
      42   NONAME         1.71200                         8 7.14  -0.33  ******:*
      11   NONAME        -1.60704                         3 6.05  -0.66  ***  .
      19   NONAME        -1.60481                         5 4.60  -1.00  ****:
       7   NONAME        -1.52209                         2 3.13  -1.33  **.
      48   NONAME         1.41518                         3 1.91  -1.66  *:*
      51   NONAME         1.35082                         1 1.04  -2.00  :
                                                          0  .51  -2.33  .
                                                          1  .22  -2.66  *
                                                          0  .09  -3.00
                                                          0  .04   OUT
```

The STATISTICS subcommand can be used to obtain more than just the statistics outlined above. By including the option CHA, a summary of R^2 changes is printed in addition to the F-value and significance level. The HISTORY option prints a final summary report at the end of all the steps.

Many researchers argue that it is essential to examine the residuals in order to make sure that they have not violated any of the basic statistical assumptions. SPSS^x is particularly strong in helping you to summarize and identify the residuals. This is accomplished with outputs that include histograms, normal probability plots, outliers, and the Durbin-Watson test.

You may be interested in having SPSS^x produce a scatterplot using the predicted values and the residual values as variables or, for that matter, a variety of other scatterplots. That's exactly what you get with the SCATTERPLOT subcommand (see Table 15). Another nice feature of SPSS^x is that you can select the size of the SCATTERPLOT output. Small outputs, like that in Table 15, are the default. Or, you can select LARGE size in the SCATTERPLOT subcommand—as long as the page width is sufficiently large.

As you can see, REGRESSION is an enormously powerful procedure that provides a substantial amount of information.

Back in the beginning of this appendix, we said that the students were interested in finding the best predictors of racial attitudes. We used, therefore, the STEPWISE method and liberal CRITERIA for independent variable entry and removal. While eight independent variables were identified on our VARIABLES = list, only three variables were found to be "good" predictors. Not surprisingly, given our bivariate analysis, the best predictor was year of birth. It was entered first and explained approximately 15% of the variation in the race relations index score. Next, the variable of sex was entered—since it had the largest partial correlation value. It accounted for another 5% of the variation in our index. Whether or not a person voted was the last variable to be entered. All the other variables, including the race (black or white) of the respondent, contributed too little to be of much use in this study. That is, for respondents in this small Southern city, race was not a good predictor of racial attitudes as measured by our racial attitude scale. Of course, another scale or another city might have produced different findings.

Exercise 10

If you are a hearty soul, try a multiple regression run. Follow your instincts and try the REGRESSION procedure using the minimum commands of

```
REGRESSION VARIABLES=varlist/
 DEPENDENT=variable
```

Then try some of the options listed earlier. Don't worry, you won't hurt the computer or damage the software.

CONCLUSION

Don't despair. It's not that hard. If you have been doing the exercises and working with your data, you have probably mastered most of the basics.

Now I will review the steps we took in working with our race relations data set. (These steps are applicable to just about any study.)

1. Know what your research questions are and specify your hypotheses in the light of the data you collected.

2. Specify the information and statistical procedures you need to use to efficiently answer your research questions.

3. Develop a codebook.

4. Build the data file.

5. Build a simple SPSS^x command file.

6. Clean the data.

7. Enhance your SPSS^x file.

8. Run your SPSS^x descriptive procedures.

9. Develop and test your scale.

10. Run your SPSS^x bivariate procedures.

11. Run your SPSS^x multivariate procedures.

Perhaps most importantly, stop after each step to consider what you did, how it relates back to your study, and what patterns there are among the variables.

Of course, all SPSS^x procedures can be run at once. Table 16 shows what the input would look like if all these commands reviewed thus far were incorporated into a single run.

I would be remiss if I didn't point out that we have only scratched the surface of SPSS^x. For those of you who would like to read more about this package, I recommend the SPSS^x manuals published by McGraw-Hill. If you expect to be using SPSS^x in the future, you will find them extremely useful.

Author's note:

There are several versions of SPSS^x on the market today. Just about all versions use the same command structure and sequence. But there are some differences between SPSS/PC for the IBM XT/AT and compatibles and the mini/mainframe versions. There are also some differences among some of the mini/mainframe versions. So find out from your SPSS^x site coordinator which version you will be using.

TABLE 16. FINAL COMPLETE PROGRAM LISTING

```
================================================================================
JCL
TITLE 'JACQUES/BABBIE RUN--RACE RELATIONS IN A SOUTHERN CITY'
DATA LIST RECORDS=1/1
 IDNUM 1-3
 RR1 TO RR7 4-10, MINMIX 11-13,
 REGVTE VOTE POLPTY 14-16,
 RACE INCOME MARST SEX 17-20, YRBRTH 21-22
VARIABLE LABELS RR1, 'RACE AND SCHOOL'/
 RR2, 'RACE AND NEIGHBORHOOD'/
 RR3, 'RACE AND CHURCH'/
 RR4, 'RACE AND WORK-SUPERVISOR'/
 RR5, 'RACE AND NEXT DOOR'/
 RR6, 'RACE AND DATING'/
 RR7, 'RACE AND MARRIAGE'/
 MINMIX, 'MINORITY MIXTURE IN PUBLIC SCHOOLS'/
 REGVTE, 'REGISTERED TO VOTE'/
 VOTE, 'VOTE IN LAST ELECTION'/
 POLPTY, 'POLITICAL PARTY'/
 RACE, 'RACE OF RESPONDENT'/
 INCOME, 'ANNUAL INCOME'/
 MARST, 'MARITAL STATUS'/
 SEX, 'SEX OF RESPONDENT'/
 YRBRTH, 'YEAR OF BIRTH'/
VALUE LABELS SEX  0 'MALE'   1 'FEMALE'/
 POLPTY  0 'DEMOCRAT'   1 'REPUBLICAN'/
 RACE  4 'WHITE'    3 'BLACK'   2 'HISPANIC'   1 'OTHER'/
 RR1 TO RR7  1 'STRONGLY DISAGREE'   2 'DISAGREE'
       3 'AGREE'    4 'STRONGLY AGREE'/
 REGVTE VOTE MARST  0 'NO'    1 'YES'/
 INCOME  5000 ' LESS THAN $7,000'  10500 ' $7,001 - $14,000'
      17000 '$14,001 - $20,000'  24000 '$20,001 - $28,000'
      30000 '$28,000 AND ABOVE'/
MISSING VALUES RR1 TO RR7, REGVTE TO SEX (9)/
 MINMIX (999)/
RECODE INCOME (1=5000)(2=10500)(3=17000)(4=24000)(5=30000)
RECODE RACE (1,2=9)(3=0)(4=1) INTO NRACE
VARIABLE LABELS NRACE 'BLACK AND WHITE RESPONDENTS ONLY'
VALUE LABELS NRACE 0 'BLACK' 1 'WHITE'
COMPUTE YRBRTH = YRBRTH + 1900
COMPUTE RR = RR1 + RR2 + RR3 + RR4 + RR5 + RR6 + RR7
COMPUTE RACESEX=9
IF (RACE EQ 3 AND SEX EQ 0)RACESEX=1
IF (RACE EQ 3 AND SEX EQ 1)RACESEX=2
IF (RACE EQ 4 AND SEX EQ 0)RACESEX=3
IF (RACE EQ 4 AND SEX EQ 1)RACESEX=4
MISSING VALUES NRACE RACESEX (9)/ YRBRTH (1999)/
VARIABLE LABELS RR, 'RACE RELATIONS SCALE'
          RACESEX, 'RACE AND SEX IDENTIFIER'
VALUE LABELS RACESEX 1 'BL-MALE' 2 'BL-FEMALE' 3 'WH-MALE' 4 'WH-FEMALE'
VALUE LABELS RR  1 'LOW'   2 'HIGH'
PRINT FORMATS YRBRTH (F4.0)/ INCOME (F5.0)/
LIST VARIABLES=IDNUM,RR1,MINMIX,VOTE,RACE,INCOME/CASES=10
BEGIN DATA
```

(Continued)

(Continued)

```
1013333333 20111130145        5083333333 60110420025
1023444444  0110121151        5093333333 40111430140
1034443391 40110430032        5103333322 40110420138
1043443339 40110440133        6014444433 40110421153
1053333322 40101440122        6021213211 20001430142
1063333333 60110340135        6034434433 20111310146
1072221221  0111420030        6044333333 40110421155
1083929921 20110420029        6053344422 40110421121
1093333333 40100310157        6064444422 40110420156
1103323321 40110311057        6074333333 40111421157
2013323221 40111420149        6084323311 60110321056
2023333221 60110320044        6094343322 40110351158
2033333333 60110391159        6104333333 40110311149
2044323332 40110420047        END DATA
2053223224 20111430133        FREQUENCIES VARIABLES=RACE,INCOME,SEX
2063332222 20100321153        FREQUENCIES VARIABLES=MINMIX RACESEX RR
2073333321 40110311057         /FORMAT=ONEPAGE INDEX
2083333321 40110330152         /STATISTICS=DEFAULT MEDIAN
2092242111 20111490120        FREQUENCIES VARIABLES=MINMIX, RACESEX/ BARCHART/
2102222111 20111450015        FREQUENCIES VARIABLES=RR YRBRTH/ HISTOGRAM/
3013333333 40111430035        RELIABILITY VARIABLES=RR1 TO RR7/
3023333333 40110420048         SCALE(RACREL)=RR1 TO RR7
3033333333 40110420150        STATISTICS 1, 4, 5, 8, 9
3043333322 40110320030        TEMPORARY
3053333322 40111430040        RECODE RR(LO THRU 20=1)(21 THRU 28=2)
3063333333 20111420050        CROSSTABS TABLES=RR1,RR6, RR BY NRACE, RACESEX
3073333333 40111421052        OPTIONS 4
3083333322 60110420053        STATISTICS ALL
3093323322 60110320038        SCATTERGRAM RR WITH INCOME YRBRTH
3103313322 60110320148        STATISTICS ALL
4014444332 20110230150        T-TEST GROUPS=RACE(3,4)/VARIABLES=RR1 TO RR7, RR
4024444421 40110311158        ONEWAY RR BY RACESEX(1,4)/
4031111111  0110430021         CONTRASTS = -1 0 1 0/
4043333111 20110490120         RANGES=DUNCAN(.05)/
4054444422 40110311057        STATISTICS ALL
4064333322 20110431053        TEMPORARY
4073333221 20110420120        RECODE RACE(1,2=9)(3=0)(4=1)
4083333321 20110421150        REGRESSION WIDTH=80/
4094442322 40110340015         CRITERIA=PIN(.15) POUT(.20)/
4103333333 20110491157         DESCRIPTIVES/
5013332333 40001411163         VARIABLES=RR, REGVTE TO YRBRTH/
5024444444 40110111161         STATISTICS=DEFAULTS CHA HISTORY/
5033333322 40010430041         DEPENDENT= RR/
5043333311 40110330054         STEPWISE/
5054443333 60110330143         RESIDUALS=DEFAULTS/
5063333333 40110320046         SCATTERPLOT(*PRED,*RESID)/
5073322211 40110420032        FINISH
```

Glossary

analysis of variance   A form of data analysis in which the variance of a dependent variable is examined for the whole sample and for separate subgroups created on the basis of some independent variable(s). See Chapter 18.

area probability sample   A form of multistage *cluster sample* in which geographical areas such as census blocks or tracts serve as the first-stage sampling unit. Units selected in the first stage of sampling are then listed—all the households on each selected block would be written down after a trip to the block—and such lists would be subsampled. See Chapter 7.

attributes   Characteristics of persons or things. See *variables* and Chapter 1.

average   An ambiguous term generally suggesting typical or normal. The *mean, median,* and *mode* are specific examples of mathematical *averages*. See Chapter 14.

bias   (1) That quality of a measurement device that tends to result in a misrepresentation of what is being measured in a particular direction. For example, the questionnaire item "Don't you agree that the president is doing a good job?" would be *biased* in that it would generally encourage more favorable responses. See Chapter 6 for more on this topic. (2) The thing inside you that makes other people or groups seem consistently better or worse than they really are. (3) What a nail looks like after you hit it crooked. (If you drink, don't drive.)

binomial variable   (1) A variable that has only two attributes is binomial. *Sex* would be an example, having the attributes *male* and *female*. (2) The advertising slogan used by the Nomial Widget Co.

bivariate analysis   The analysis of two variables simultaneously, for the purpose of determining the empirical relationship between them. The construction of a simple percentage table or the computation of a simple correlation coefficient would be examples of *bivariate analyses*. See Chapter 14 for more on this topic.

Bogardus social distance scale   A measurement technique for determining the willingness of people to participate in social relations—of varying degrees of closeness—with other kinds of people. It is an especially efficient technique in that several discrete answers may be summarized without losing any of the original details of the data. This technique is described in Chapter 15.

census   An enumeration of the characteristics of some population. A *census* is often similar to a survey, with the difference that the *census* collects data from *all* members of the population while the survey is limited to a sample.

cluster sample   (1) A multistage sample in which natural groups (*clusters*) are sampled initially, with the members of each selected group being subsampled afterward. For example, you might select a sample of U.S. colleges and universities from a directory, get lists of the students at all the selected schools, then draw samples of students from each. This procedure is discussed in Chapter 7. See also *area probability sample*. (2) Pawing around in a box of macadamia-nut clusters to take all the big ones for yourself.

codebook   (1) The document used in data processing and analysis that tells the location of different data items in a data file. Typically, the codebook identifies the card and column locations of data items and the meaning of the punches used to represent different attributes of variables. See Chapter 13 for more discussion and illustrations. (2) The document that cost you 38 boxtops just to learn that Captain Marvelous wanted you to brush your teeth and always tell the truth.

(3) The document that allows CIA agents to learn that Captain Marvelous wants them to brush their teeth.

coding   The process whereby raw data are transformed into standardized form suitable for machine processing and analysis. See Chapters 12 and 13.

coefficient of alienation   (1) A measurement of the extent to which a *smallest-space analysis (SSA)* solution satisfies the rule that the rank order of distances between points must be the inverse of the rank order of the correlations between the variables that the points represent. More accurately, the *coefficient of alienation* is a measure of the extent to which the solution *fails* to satisfy the rule: the smaller, the better. See Chapter 18. (2) The number of times you don't get invited to parties your friends get invited to.

coefficient of reproducibility   (1) A measure of the extent to which a *scale* score allows you to reconstruct accurately the specific data that went into the construction of the scale. See Chapter 15 for a fuller description and an illustration. (2) Fecundity.

cohort study   A study in which some specific group is studied over time although data may be collected from different members in each set of observations. A study of the occupational history of the class of 1970, in which questionnaires were sent every five years, for example, would be a cohort study. See Chapter 4 for more on this topic (if you want more).

conceptualization   The mental process whereby fuzzy and imprecise notions (*concepts*) are made more specific and precise. So you want to study *prejudice*. What do you *mean* by *prejudice*? Are there different kinds of prejudice? What are they? See Chapter 5, which is all about *conceptualization*, and Chapter 6 about its pal, *operationalization*.

confidence interval   (1) The range of values within which a population parameter is estimated to lie. A survey, for example, may show 40 percent of a sample favoring Candidate A (poor devil). Although the best estimate of the support existing among all voters would also be 40 percent, we would not expect it to be exactly that. We might, therefore, compute a *confidence interval* (e.g., from 35 to 45 percent) within which the actual percentage of the population probably lies. Note that it is necessary to specify a *confidence level* in connection with every *confidence interval*. See Chapters 7 and 17. (2) How close you dare to get to an alligator.

confidence level   The estimated probability that a population parameter lies within a given *confidence interval*. Thus, we might be 95 percent *confident* that between 35 and 45 percent of all voters favor Candidate A. See Chapters 7 and 17.

construct validity   The degree to which a measure relates to other variables as expected within a system of theoretical relationships. See Chapter 5.

content validity   The degree to which a measure covers the range of meanings included within the concept. See Chapter 5.

contingency question   A survey question that is to be asked only of *some* respondents, determined by their responses to some other question. For example, all respondents might be asked whether they belong to the Cosa Nostra, and only those who said yes would be asked how often they go to company meetings and picnics. The latter would be a *contingency question*. See Chapter 9 for illustrations of this topic.

contingency table   (1) A format for presenting the relationships among variables—in the form of percentage distributions. See Chapter 14 for several illustrations of it and for guides to doing it. (2) The card table you keep around in case your guests bring their seven kids with them to dinner.

control group   In experimentation, a group of subjects to whom *no* experimental stimulus is administered and who should resemble the experimental group in all other respects. The comparison of the *control group* and the experimental group at the end of the experiment points to the effect of the experimental stimulus. See Chapter 8.

control variable   A variable that is held constant in an attempt to further clarify the relationship between two other variables. Having discovered a relationship between education and prejudice, for example, we might hold sex constant by examining the relationship between education and prejudice among men only and then among women only. In this example, sex would be the *control variable*. See Chapter 16 to find out how important the proper use of control variables is in analysis.

criterion-related validity   The degree to which a measure relates with some external criterion. For example, the validity of the college board is shown in their ability to predict the college success of students. See Chapter 5.

cross-sectional study A study that is based on observations representing a single point in time. Contrasted with a *longitudinal study*.

deduction (1) The logical model in which specific expectations of *hypotheses* are developed on the basis of general principles. Starting from the general principle that all deans are meanies, you might anticipate that *this* one won't let you change courses. That anticipation would be the result of *deduction*. See also *induction* and Chapters 2 and 3. (2) What the Internal Revenue Service said your good-for-nothing moocher of a brother-in-law technically isn't. (3) Of a duck.

dependent variable (1) That variable that is assumed to *depend* on or be caused by another (called the *independent variable*). If you find that income is partly a function of amount of formal education, income is being treated as a *dependent variable*. (2) A wimpy variable.

descriptive statistics Statistical computations describing either the characteristics of a sample *or* the relationship among variables in a sample. *Descriptive statistics* merely summarize a set of sample observations, whereas *inferential statistics* move beyond the description of specific observations to make inferences about the larger population from which the sample observations were drawn.

dichotomy (1) A classification having only two categories. See also *binomial variable*. (2) The removal of a dike.

dispersion The distribution of values around some central value, such as an *average*. The *range* is a simple example of a measure of *dispersion*. Thus, we may report that the *mean* age of a group is 37.9, and the range is from 12 to 89.

ecological fallacy Erroneously drawing conclusions about individuals based solely on the observation of groups.

EPSEM *Equal probability of selection method*. A sample design in which each member of a population has the same chance of being selected into the sample. See Chapter 7.

external invalidity Refers to the possibility that conclusions drawn from experimental results may not be generalizable to the "real" world. See Chapter 8 and also *internal invalidity*.

external validation The process of testing the *validity* of a measure, such as an *index* or *scale*, by examining its relationship to other, presumed indicators of the same variable. If the index really measures *prejudice*, for example, it should correlate with other indicators of prejudice. See Chapter 15 for a fuller discussion of this topic and for illustrations.

face validity (1) That quality of an indicator that makes it seem a reasonable measure of some variable. That the frequency of church attendance is some indication of a person's religiosity seems to make sense without a lot of explanation. It has *face validity*. (2) When your face looks like your driver's license photo (rare).

factor analysis A complex algebraic method for determining the general dimensions or *factors* that exist within a set of concrete observations. See Chapter 18 for more details on this topic.

frequency distribution A description of the number of times the various attributes of a variable are observed in a sample. The report that 53 percent of a sample were men and 47 percent were women would be a simple example of a *frequency distribution*. Another example would be the report that 15 of the cities studied had populations under 10,000, 23 had populations between 10,000 and 25,000, and so forth.

generalizability (1) That quality of a research finding that justifies the inference that it represents something more than the specific observations upon which it was based. Sometimes this involves the *generalization* of findings from a sample to a population. Other times, it is a matter of concepts: if you are able to discover why people commit burglaries, can you *generalize* that discovery to other crimes as well? (2) The likelihood that you will ever be a general.

Guttman scale A type of composite measure used to summarize several discrete observations and to represent some more general variable. See Chapter 15.

Hawthorne effect A term coined in reference to a series of productivity studies at the Hawthorne plant of the Western Electric Company in Chicago, Illinois. The researchers discovered that their presence affected the behavior of the workers being studied. The term now refers to any impact of research on the subject of study. See Chapter 8.

hypothesis (1) An expectation about the nature of things derived from a theory. It is a statement of something that ought to be observed in the real world if the theory is correct. See *deduction* and also Chapters 2 and 4. (2) A graduate student paper explaining why hypopotamuses are the way they are.

hypothesis testing (1) The determination of whether the expectations that a hypothesis represents are, indeed, found to exist in the real world. See Chapters 2 and 4. (2) An oral examination centering around a graduate student paper explaining why hypopotamuses are the way they are.

independent variable A variable whose values are *not* problematical in an analysis but are taken as simply given. An *independent variable* is presumed to cause or determine a *dependent variable*. If we discover that religiosity is partly a function of sex—women are more religious than men—*sex* is the *independent variable* and *religiosity* is the dependent variable. Note that any given variable might be treated as *independent* in one part of an analysis and dependent in another part of an analysis. *Religiosity* might become an *independent variable* in the explanation of crime.

index A type of composite measure that summarizes several specific observations and represents some more general dimension. Contrasted with *scale*. See Chapter 15.

induction (1) The logical model in which general principles are developed from specific observations. Having noted that Jews and Catholics are more likely to vote Democratic than Protestants are, you might conclude that religious minorities in the United States are more affiliated with the Democratic Party and explain why. That would be an example of *induction*. See also *deduction* and Chapters 2 and 3. (2) The culinary art of stuffing ducks.

inferential statistics The body of statistical computations relevant to making inferences from findings based on sample observations to some larger population. See also *descriptive statistics* and Chapter 17. Not to be confused with infernal statistics, which have something to do with the population of Hell.

informant Someone well versed in the social phenomenon that you wish to study and who is willing to tell you what he or she knows. If you were planning participant observation among the members of a religious sect, you would do well to make friends with someone who already knows about them—possibly a member of the sect—who could give you some background information about them. Not to be confused with a *respondent*.

interchangeability of indexes A term coined by Paul Lazarsfeld referring to the logical proposition that if some general variable is related to another variable, then all indicators of the variable should have that relationship. See Chapter 3 for a fuller description of this topic and a graphic illustration.

internal invalidity Refers to the possibility that the conclusions drawn from experimental results may not accurately reflect what went on in the experiment itself. See Chapter 8 and also *external invalidity*.

internal validation The process whereby the individual items composing a composite measure are correlated with the measure itself. This provides one test of the wisdom of including all the items in the composite measure. See also *external validation* and Chapter 15.

interpretation A technical term used in connection with the elaboration model. It represents the research outcome in which a *control variable* is discovered to be the mediating factor through which an *independent variable* has its effect on a *dependent variable*. See Chapter 16.

intersubjectivity That quality of science (and other inquiries) whereby two different researchers, studying the same problem, arrive at the same conclusion. Ultimately, this is the practical criterion for what is called *objectivity*. We agree that something is "objectively true" if independent observers with different subjective orientations conclude that it is "true." See Chapter 2.

interval measure A level of measurement describing a variable whose attributes are rank-ordered and have equal distances between adjacent attributes. The Fahrenheit temperature scale is an example of this, since the distance between 17° and 18° is the same as that between 89° and 90°. See also *nominal measure, ordinal measure,* and *ratio measure*.

interview A data-collection encounter in which one person (an interviewer) asks questions of another (a *respondent*). *Interviews* may be conducted face-to-face or by telephone. See Chapter 9 for more information on interviewing as a method of survey research.

judgmental sample (1) A type of *nonprobability sample* in which you select the units to be observed on the basis of your own *judgment* about which ones will be the most useful or representative. Another name for this is *purposive sample*. See Chapter 7 for more details. (2) A sample of opinionated people.

latent content (1) As used in connection with content analysis, the underlying meaning of communications as distinguished from their *manifest content*. See Chapter 11. (2) What you need to make a latent.

level of significance In the context of *tests of statistical significance,* the degree of likelihood that an observed, empirical relationship could be attributable to sampling error. A relationship is *significant* at the .05 *level* if the likelihood of its being only a function of sampling error is no greater than 5 out of 100. See Chapter 17.

Likert scale A type of composite measure developed by Rensis Likert in an attempt to improve the levels of measurement in social research through the use of standardized response categories in survey *questionnaires*. *Likert*-items are those utilizing such response categories as strongly agree, agree, disagree, and strongly disagree. Such items may be used in the construction of true *Likert scales* and may also be used in the construction of other types of composite measures. See Chapter 15.

log-linear models A form of data analysis which uses logarithmic calculations to simplify the analysis of complex multivariate cross-tabulations. See Chapter 18.

longitudinal study A study design involving the collection of data at different points in time, as contrasted with a *cross-sectional study.* See also Chapter 4 and *trend study, cohort study,* and *panel study.*

manifest content (1) In connection with content analysis, the concrete terms contained in a communication, as distinguished from *latent content*. See Chapter 11. (2) What you have after a manifest bursts.

matching In connection with experiments, the procedure whereby pairs of subjects are *matched* on the basis of their similarities on one or more variables, and one member of the pair is assigned to the experimental group and the other to the *control group*. See Chapter 8.

mean (1) An *average,* computed by summing the values of several observations and dividing by the number of observations. If you now have a grade point average of 4.0 based on 10 courses, and you get an F in this course, your new grade point (mean) average will be 3.6. (2) The quality of the thoughts you might have if your instructor did that to you.

median (1) Another *average,* representing the value of the "middle" case in a rank-ordered set of observations. If the ages of five men are 16, 17, 20, 54, and 88, the *median* would be 20. (The *mean* would be 39.) (2) The dividing line between safe driving and *exciting* driving.

mode (1) Still another *average,* representing the most frequently observed value or attribute. If a sample contains 1000 Protestants, 275 Catholics, and 33 Jews, *Protestant* is the *modal* category. See Chapter 14 for more thrilling disclosures about averages. (2) Better than apple pie à la median.

multivariate analysis The analysis of the simultaneous relationships among several variables. Examining simultaneously the effects of age, sex, and social class on religiosity would be an example of *multivariate analysis*. See Chapters 14, 16, and 18.

nominal measure A level of measurement describing a variable whose different attributes are *only* different, as distinguished from *ordinal, interval,* or *ratio measures*. Sex would be an example of a nominal measure.

nonprobability sample A sample selected in some fashion other than those suggested by probability theory. Examples include *judgmental (purposive), quota,* and *snowball samples*. See Chapter 7.

nonsampling error (1) Those imperfections of data quality that are a result of factors other than sampling error. Examples include misunderstandings of questions by respondents, erroneous recordings by interviewers and coders, keypunch errors, and so forth. (2) The mistake you made in deciding to interview everyone rather than selecting a sample.

null hypothesis In connection with *hypothesis testing* and *tests of statistical significance,* that *hypothesis* that suggests there is *no* relationship between the variables under study. You may conclude that the two variables *are* related after having statistically rejected the *null hypothesis.*

objectivity Doesn't exist. See *intersubjectivity.*

operational definition The concrete and specific *definition* of something in terms of the *operations* by which observations are to be categorized. The *operational definition* of "earning an A in this course" might be: "correctly answering at least 90 percent of the final exam questions." See Chapter 6.

operationalization One step beyond *conceptualization. Operationalization* is the process of developing *operational definitions.*

ordinal measure A level of measurement describing a variable whose attributes may be *rank-ordered* along some dimension. An example would be *socioeconomic status* as composed of the attributes high, medium, low. See also *nominal measure, interval measure,* and *ratio measure.*

panel study A type of *longitudinal study,* in which data are collected from the same sample (the *panel*) at several points in time. See Chapter 4.

path analysis A form of *multivariate analysis* in which the causal relationships among variables are presented in graphic format. See Chapter 18.

PPS *Probability proportionate to size.* (This refers to a type of multistage *cluster sample* in which clusters are selected, not with equal probabilities (see *EPSEM*) but with *probabilities proportionate* to their *sizes*—as measured by the number of units to be subsampled. See Chapter 7.

probability sample The general term for a sample selected in accord with *probability* theory, typically involving some random-selection mechanism. Specific types of *probability samples* include *area probability sample, EPSEM, PPS, simple random sample,* and *systematic sample.* See Chapter 7.

probe A technique employed in interviewing to solicit a more complete answer to a question. It is a nondirective phrase or question used to encourage a respondent to elaborate on an answer. Examples include "Anything more?" and "How is that?" See Chapter 9 for a discussion of interviewing.

purposive sample See *judgmental sample* and Chapter 10.

qualitative analysis (1) The nonnumerical examination and interpretation of observations, for the purpose of discovering underlying meanings and patterns of relationships. This is most typical of field research and historical research. See Chapter 10. (2) A classy analysis.

quantitative analysis The numerical representation and manipulation of observations for the purpose of describing and explaining the phenomena that those observations reflect. See Chapter 13 especially, and also the remainder of Part 4.

questionnaire A document containing *questions* and other types of items designed to solicit information appropriate to analysis. *Questionnaires* are used primarily in survey research and also in experiments, field research, and other modes of observation. See Chapters 6 and 9.

quota sample A type of *nonprobability sample* in which units are selected into the sample on the basis of prespecified characteristics, so that the total sample will have the same distribution of characteristics as are assumed to exist in the population being studied. See Chapter 7.

randomization A technique for assigning experimental subjects to experimental and *control groups: randomly.* See Chapter 8.

range A measure of *dispersion,* composed of the highest and lowest values of a variable in some set of observations. In your class, for example, the *range* of ages might be from 17 to 37.

ratio measure A level of measurement describing a variable whose attributes have all the qualities of *nominal, ordinal,* and *interval measures* and in addition are based on a "true zero" point. Age would be an example of a *ratio measure.*

reductionism (1) A fault of some researchers: a strict limitation (reduction) of the kinds of concepts to be considered relevant to the phenomenon under study. (2) The cloning of ducks.

regression analysis (1) A method of data analysis in which the relationships among variables are represented in the form of an equation, called a *regression equation.* See Chapter 18 for a discussion of the different forms of *regression analysis.* (2) What seems to happen to your knowledge of social research methods just before an exam.

reification The process of regarding as real things that are not real.

reliability That quality of measurement method that suggests that the same data would have been collected each time in repeated observations of the same phenomenon. In the context of a survey, we would expect that the question "Did you attend church last week?" would have higher reliability than the question "About how many times have you attended church in your life?" This is not to be confused with *validity.*

replication Generally, the duplication of an experiment to expose or reduce error. It is also a technical term used in connection with the elaboration model, referring to the elaboration outcome in which the initially observed relationship between two variables persists when a *control variable* is held constant. See Chapter 16. See Chapter 1 and *intersubjectivity.*

representativeness (1) That quality of a sample of having the same distribution of characteristics as the population from which it was selected. By implication, descriptions and explanations derived from an analysis of the sample may be assumed to *represent* similar ones in the population. *Representativeness* is enhanced by *probability sampling* and provides for *generalizability* and the use of *inferential statistics*. See Chapter 7. (2) A noticeable quality in the presentation-of-self of some members of the U.S. Congress.

respondent A person who provides data for analysis by *responding* to a survey *questionnaire*.

response rate The number of persons participating in a survey divided by the number selected in the sample, in the form of a percentage. This is also called the completion rate or, in self-administered surveys, the return rate: the percentage of *questionnaires* sent out that are returned. See Chapter 9.

sampling frame That list or quasi list of units composing a population from which a sample is selected. If the sample is to be *representative* of the population, it is essential that the *sampling frame* include all (or nearly all) members of the population. See Chapter 7.

sampling interval The standard distance between elements selected from a population for a sample. See Chapter 7.

sampling ratio The proportion of elements in the population that are selected to be in a sample. See Chapter 7.

scale (1) A type of composite measure composed of several items that have a logical or empirical structure among them. Examples of *scales* include Bogardus social distance, Guttman, Likert, and Thurstone scales. Contrasted with *index*. See also Chapter 15. (2) One of the less appetizing parts of a fish.

secondary analysis (1) A form of research in which the data collected and processed by one researcher are reanalyzed—often for a different purpose—by another. This is especially appropriate in the case of survey data. Data archives are repositories or libraries for the storage and distribution of data for *secondary analysis*. (2) Estimating the weight and speed of an opposing team's linebackers.

simple random sample (1) A type of *probability sample* in which the units composing a population are assigned numbers, a set of *random* numbers is then generated, and the units having those numbers are included in the sample.

Although probability theory and the calculations it provides assume this basic sampling method, it is seldom used for practical reasons. An equivalent alternative is the *systematic sample* (with a random start). See Chapter 7. (2) A random sample with a low IQ.

smallest-space analysis (1) A method of *multivariate analysis* in which correlations among variables are represented graphically in the form of distances separating points. See Chapter 18. (2) The planning of college dorms.

snowball sample (1) A *nonprobability sampling* method often employed in field research. Each person interviewed may be asked to suggest additional people for interviewing. See Chapter 10. (2) Picking the icy ones to throw at your methods instructor.

specification Generally, the process through which concepts are made more specific. It is also a technical term used in connection with the elaboration model, representing the elaboration outcome in which an initially observed relationship between two variables is replicated among some subgroups created by the *control variable* and not among others. In such a situation, you will have *specified* the conditions under which the original relationship exists: e.g., among men but not among women. See Chapter 16.

statistical significance (1) A general term referring to the *un*likeliness that relationships observed in a sample could be attributed to sampling error alone. See *tests of statistical significance* and Chapter 17. (2) How important it would really be if you flunked your statistics exam. I mean, you could always be a poet.

stratification The grouping of the units composing a population into homogenous groups (or *strata*) before sampling. This procedure, which may be used in conjunction with *simple random, systematic,* or *cluster sampling,* improves the *representativeness* of a sample, at least in terms of the *stratification* variables. See Chapter 7.

systematic sample (1) A type of *probability sample* in which every *k*th unit in a list is selected for inclusion in the sample: e.g., every 25th student in the college directory of students. *k* is computed by dividing the size of the population by the desired sample size and is called the sampling interval. Within certain constraints, *systematic sampling* is a functional equivalent of *simple random sampling* and usually easier to do. Typically, the first unit is selected at random. See Chapter 7. (2) Picking every third one whether it's icy or not. See *snowball sample* (2).

tests of statistical significance (1) A class of statistical computations that indicate the likelihood that the relationship observed between variables in a sample can be attributed to sampling error only. See *inferential statistics* and Chapter 17. (2) A determination of how important statistics have been in improving humankind's lot in life. (3) An examination that can radically affect your grade in this course and your grade point average as well.

Thurstone scale A type of composite measure, constructed in accord with the weights assigned by "judges" to various indicators of some variables. See Chapter 15.

trend study A type of *longitudinal study* in which a given characteristic of some population is monitored over time. An example would be the series of Gallup Polls showing the political-candidate preferences of the electorate over the course of a campaign, even though different samples were interviewed at each point. See Chapter 4.

typology The classification (typically nominal) of observations in terms of their attributes on two or more variables. The classification of newspapers as liberal-urban, liberal-rural, conservative-urban, or conservative-rural would be an example. See Chapter 15.

units of analysis The *what* or *whom* being studied. In social science research, the most typical units of analysis are individual people. See Chapter 4.

univariate analysis The analysis of a single variable, for purposes of description. *Frequency distributions, averages,* and measures of *dispersion* would be examples of *univariate analysis,* as distinguished from *bivariate* and *multivariate analysis.* See Chapter 14.

validity A descriptive term used of a measure that accurately reflects the concept that it is intended to measure. For example, your IQ would seem a more *valid* measure of your intelligence than would the number of hours you spend in the library. It is important to realize that the ultimate *validity* of a measure can never be proven. Yet, we may agree to its relative *validity* on the basis of *face validity, criterion validity, content validity, construct validity, internal validation,* and *external validation.* This must not be confused with *reliability.* See Chapter 5.

variables Logical groupings of *attributes.* The variable *sex* is made of up of the attributes *male* and *female.*

weighting (1) A procedure employed in connection with sampling whereby units selected with unequal probabilities are assigned weights in such a manner as to make the sample *representative* of the population from which it was selected. See Chapter 7. (2) Olde English for hanging around for somebody who never gets there on time.

Bibliography

Alfred, Randall: 1976 "The Church of Satan," in Charles Glock and Robert Bellah (eds.), *The New Religious Consciousness*. Berkeley, Calif.: University of California Press, pp. 180–202.

Almond, Gabriel and Verba, Sidney: 1963 *The Civic Culture*. Princeton, N.J.: Princeton University Press.

Babbie, Earl R.:
1966 "The Third Civilization," *Review of Religious Research* (Winter): 101–21.
1967 "A Religious Profile of Episcopal Churchwomen," *Pacific Churchman* (January): 6–8, 12.
1970 *Science and Morality in Medicine*. Berkeley, Calif.: University of California Press.
1985 *You Can Make a Difference*. New York: St. Martin's Press.

Bailey, William C.: 1975 "Murder and Capital Punishment," in William J. Chambliss (ed.), *Criminal Law in Action*. New York: John Wiley & Sons.

Ball-Rokeach, Sandra J.; Grube, Joel W.; and Rokeach, Milton: 1981 "Roots: The Next Generation—Who Watched and with What Effect," *Public Opinion Quarterly*, 45:58–68.

Banfield, Edward: 1968 *The Unheavenly City: The Nature and Future of Our Urban Crisis*. Boston: Little, Brown.

Bellah, Robert N.: 1957 *Tokugawa Religion*. Glencoe, Ill.: Free Press.
1967 "Research Chronicle: Tokugawa Religion," in Phillip E. Hammond (ed.), *Sociologists at Work*. Garden City, N.Y.: Anchor Books, pp. 164–85.

Beveridge, W. I. B.: 1950 *The Art of Scientific Investigation*. New York: Vintage Books.

Beyer, Judith E.: 1981 "Interpersonal Communication as Perceived by Nurse Educators in Collegial Interactions," *Nursing Research* (March-April): 111–17.

Black, Donald: 1970 "Production of Crime Rates," *American Sociological Review*, Vol. 35 (August): 733–48.

Blaunstein, Albert and Zangrando, Robert (eds.): 1970 *Civil Rights and the Black American*. New York: Washington Square Press.

Botein, B.: 1965 "The Manhattan Bail Project: Its Impact in Criminology and the Criminal Law Process," *Texas Law Review*, Vol. 43: 319–31.

Bottomore, T. B. and Rubel, Maximilien (eds.): [1843] 1956 *Karl Marx: Selected Writings in Sociology and Social Philosophy*, T. B. Bottomore (trans.). New York: McGraw-Hill.

Brownlee, K. A.: 1975 "A Note on the Effects of Nonresponse on Surveys," *Journal of the American Statistical Association*, Vol. 52, No. 227:29–32.

Campbell, Donald and Stanley, Julian: 1963 *Experimental and Quasi-Experimental Designs for Research*. Chicago: Rand McNally.

Carmines, Edward G. and Zeller, Richard A.: 1979 *Reliability and Validity Assessment*. Beverly Hills, Calif.: Sage.

Census Bureau: *See* U.S. Bureau of the Census.

Chaffee, Steven and Sun Yuel Choe: 1980 "Time of Decision and Media Use during the Ford-Carter Campaign," *Public Opinion Quarterly* (Spring): 53–69.

Coleman, James: 1966 *Equality of Educational Opportunity*. Washington, D.C.: U.S. Government Printing Office.

Collins, G. C. and Blodgett, Timothy B.: 1981 "Sexual Harassment . . . Some See It . . . Some Won't," *Harvard Business Review* (March-April): 76–95.

Comstock, Donald: 1980 "Dimensions of Influence in Organizations," *Pacific Sociological Review* (January): 67–84.

Cook, Thomas D. and Campbell, Donald T.: 1979 *Quasi-Experimentation: Design and Analysis Issues for Field Settings*. Chicago: Rand McNally.

Cooper-Stephenson, Cynthia and Theologides, Athanasios: 1981 "Nutrition in Cancer: Physicians' Knowledge, Opinions, and Educational Needs," *Journal of the American Dietetic Association* (May): 472–76.

Crawford, Kent S.; Thomas, Edmund D.; and Fink, Jeffrey J.: 1980 "Pygmalion at Sea: Improving the Work Effectiveness of Low Performers," *The Journal of Applied Behavioral Science* (October-December): 482–505.

DeFleur, Lois: 1975 "Biasing Influences on Drug Arrest Records: Implications for Deviance Research," *American Sociological Review* (February): 88–103.

Dillman, Don A.: 1978 *Mail and Telephone Surveys: The Total Design Method*. New York: John Wiley & Sons.

Donald, Marjorie N.: 1960 "Implications of Nonresponse for the Interpretation of Mail Questionnaire Data," *Public Opinion Quarterly*, Vol. 24, No. 1: 99–114.

Durkheim, Emile: [1893] 1964 *The Division of Labor in Society*, George Simpson (trans.). New York: Free Press.
[1897] 1951 *Suicide*. Glencoe, Ill: Free Press.

Einstein, Albert: 1940 "The Fundamentals of Theoretical Physics," *Science* (May 24): 487.

Forslund, Morris A.: 1980 "Patterns of Delinquency Involvement: An Empirical Typology," paper presented to the Annual Meeting of the Western Association of Sociologists and Anthropologists, Lethbridge, Alberta, February 8.

Freeman, Linton C.: 1968 *Elementary Applied Statistics*. New York: John Wiley & Sons.

Funkhouser, G. Ray: 1973 "The Issues of the Sixties: An Exploratory Study," *Public Opinion Quarterly* 37: 62–75.

Gallup, George: "Where Parents Go Wrong," *San Francisco Chronicle*, December 13, 1984, p. 7.

Garant, Carol: 1980 "Stalls in the Therapeutic Process," *American Journal of Nursing* (December): 2166–67.

Glaser, Barney and Strauss, Anselm: 1967 *The Discovery of Grounded Theory*. Chicago: Aldine.

Glock, Charles Y.; Ringer, Benjamin B.; and Babbie, Earl R.: 1967 *To Comfort and to Challenge*. Berkeley, Calif.: University of California Press.

Glock, Charles Y. and Stark, Rodney: 1967 *Christian Beliefs and Anti-Semitism*. New York: Harper & Row.

Goffman, Erving: 1961 *Asylums: Essays on the Social Situation of Mental Patients and Other Inmates*. Chicago: Aldine.
1963 *Stigma: Notes on the Management of a Spoiled Identity*. Englewood Cliffs, N.J.: Prentice-Hall.
1974 *Frame Analysis*. Cambridge, Mass.: Harvard University Press.

Gold, Raymond L.: 1969 "Roles in Sociological Field Observation," in George J. McCall and J. L. Simmons (eds.), *Issues in Participant Observation*. Reading, Mass.: Addison-Wesley, pp. 30–39.

Heise, David R.: 1981 "Foreward: Special Issue on Microcomputers and Social Research," *Sociological Methods and Research*, Vol. 9, No. 4 (May): 395–96.

Hempel, Carl G.: 1952 "Fundamentals of Concept Formation in Empirical Science," *International Encyclopedia of United Science II*, No. 7.

Higginbotham, A. Leon, Jr.: 1978 *In The Matter of Color: Race and the American Legal Process*. New York: Oxford University Press.

Hilts, Philip J.: 1981 "Values of Driving Classes Disputed," *San Francisco Chronicle* (25 June): 4.

Hirschi, Travis and Selvin, Hanan: 1973 *Principles of Survey Analysis.* New York: Free Press.

Homans, George C.: 1981 "Reply to Blain," *Sociological Inquiry* 41 (Winter): 23.

Horowitz, Irving Louis: 1967 *The Rise and Fall of Project Camelot.* Cambridge, Mass.: MIT Press.

Howard, Edward N. and Norman, Darlene M.: 1981 "Measuring Public Library Performance," *Library Journal* (February): 305–8.

Howell, Joseph T.: 1973 *Hard Living on Clay Street.* Garden City, N.Y.: Doubleday Anchor.

Hughes, Michael: 1980 "The Fruits of Cultivation Analysis: A Reexamination of Some Effects of Television Watching," *Public Opinion Quarterly* (Fall): 287–302.

Humphreys, Land: 1970 *Tearoom Trade: Impersonal Sex in Public Places.* Chicago: Aldine.

Jackman, Mary R. and Scheuer Senter, Mary: 1980 "Images of Social Groups: Categorical or Qualified?" *Public Opinion Quarterly* 44: 340–61.

Jensen, Arthur: 1969 "How Much Can We Boost IQ and Scholastic Achievement?" *Harvard Educational Review* 39: 273–74.

Johnston, Hank: 1980 "The Marketed Social Movement: A Case Study of the Rapid Growth of TM," *Pacific Sociological Review* (July): 333–54.

Kahane, Howard: 1980 *Logic and Contemporary Rhetoric.* Belmont, Calif.: Wadsworth.

Kaplan, Abraham: 1964 *The Conduct of Inquiry.* San Francisco: Chandler.

Kasl, Stanislav V.; Chisolm, Rupert F.; and Eskenazi, Brenda: 1981 "The Impact of the Accident at Three Mile Island on the Behavior and Well-Being of Nuclear Workers," *American Journal of Public Health* (May): 472–95.

Kendall, Patricia L. and Lazarsfeld, Paul F.: 1950 "Problems of Survey Analysis," in Robert K. Merton and Paul F. Lazarsfeld (eds.), *Continuities in Social Research: Studies in the Scope and Method of "The American Soldier."* New York: Free Press.

Kish, Leslie: 1965 *Survey Sampling.* New York: John Wiley & Sons.

Kuhn, Thomas: 1970 *The Structure of Scientific Revolutions.* Chicago: University of Chicago Press.

Ladd, Everett C. and Ferree, G. Donald: 1981 "Were the Pollsters Really Wrong?" *Public Opinion* (December-January): 13–20.

Lazarsfeld, Paul: 1959 "Problems in Methodology," in Robert K. Merton (ed.), *Sociology Today.* New York: Basic Books.

Levin, Jack and Spates, James: 1970 "Hippie Values: An Analysis of the Underground Press," *Youth and Society* 2: 59–72. Reprinted in M. Patricia Golden (ed.), *The Research Experience.* Itasca, Ill.: Peacock, 1976.

Liebow, Elliot: 1967 *Tally's Corner.* Boston: Little, Brown.

Literary Digest: 1936a "Landon, 1,293,669: Roosevelt, 972,897," (31 October): 5–6. 1936b "What Went Wrong with the Polls?" (14 November): 7–8.

Lofland, John: 1984 *Analyzing Social Settings.* Belmont, Calif.: Wadsworth.

Lopata, Helena Znaniecki: 1981 "Widowhood and Husband Sanctification," *Journal of Marriage and the Family* (May): 439–450.

Marx, Karl: [1867] 1967 *Capital.* New York: International Publishers. 1880 *Revue Socialist,* 5 July. Reprinted in T. B. Bottomore and Maximilien Rubel (eds.), *Karl Marx: Selected Writings in Sociology and Social Philosophy,* New York: McGraw-Hill, 1956.

McAlister, Alfred; Perry, Cheryl; Killen, Joel; Slinkard, Lee Ann; and Maccoby, Nathan: 1980 "Pilot Study of Smoking, Alcohol, and Drug Abuse Prevention," *American Journal of Public Health* (July): 719–21.

McCall, George J. and Simmons, J. L. (eds.): 1969 *Issues in Participant Observation.* Reading, Mass.: Addison-Wesley.

McWirter, Norris: 1980 *The Guiness Book of Records.* New York: Bantam.

Meadows, Dennis, et al.: 1973 *The Dynamics of Growth in a Finite World.* Cambridge, Mass.: Wright-Allen.

Meadows, Donella, et al.: 1972 *The Limits to Growth*. New York: Universe Books.

Merton, Robert K.: 1938 "Social Structure and Anomie," *American Sociological Review*, Vol. 3: 672–82.

Meyer, H. J. and Borgatta, E. J.: 1959 *An Experiment in Mental Patient Rehabilitation*. New York: Russell Sage Foundation.

Milgram, Stanley: 1963 "Behavioral Study of Obedience," *Journal of Abnormal and Social Psychology*. 67: 371–78.
1965 "Some Conditions of Obedience and Disobedience to Authority," *Human Relations* 18: 57–76.

Morgan, Lewis H.: 1870 *Systems of Consanguinity and Affinity*. Washington, D.C.: Smithsonian Institute.

Moskowitz, Milt: 1981 "The Drugs That Doctors Order," *San Francisco Chronicle* (23 May): 33.

Moynihan, Daniel: 1965 *The Negro Family: The Case for National Action*. Washington, D.C.: U.S. Government Printing Office.

Myrdal, Gunnar: 1944 *An American Dilemma*. New York: Harper & Row.

New York Times: "Method of Polls in Two States," June 6, 1984, p. 12.

Nie, Norman, et al.: 1975 *Statistical Package for the Social Sciences*. New York: McGraw-Hill.

Parsons, Talcott and Shils, Edward A.: 1954 *Toward a General Theory of Action*. Cambridge, Mass.: Harvard University Press.

Perlman, David: 1982 "Fluoride, AIDS Experts Scoff at Nelder's Idea," *San Francisco Chronicle*, 6 September 1984, p. 1.

Petersen, Larry R. and Maynard, Judy L.: 1981 "Income, Equity, and Wives' Housekeeping Role Expectations," *Pacific Sociological Review* (January): 87–105.

Population Reference Bureau: 1980 "1980 World Population Data Sheet," (a poster) prepared by Carl Haub and Douglas W. Heisler. Washington, D.C.: Population Reference Bureau.

Powell, Elwin H.: 1958 "Occupation, Status, and Suicide: Toward a Redefinition of Anomie," *American Sociological Review*, Vol. 23: 131–39.

Public Opinion: 1984 "See How They Ran," (October-November): 38–40.

Ransford, H. Edward: 1968 "Isolation, Powerlessness, and Violence: A Study of Attitudes and Participants in the Watts Riots," *American Journal of Sociology* 73: 581–91.

Redfield, Robert: 1941 *The Folk Culture of Yucatan*. Chicago: University of Chicago Press.

Reynolds, H. T.: 1977 *Analysis of Nominal Data*. Beverly Hills, Calif.: Sage.

Riecken, Henry W. and Boruch, Robert F.: 1974 *Social Experimentation: A Method for Planning and Evaluating Social Intervention*. New York: Academic Press.

Roethlisberger, F. J. and Dickson, W. J.: 1939 *Management and the Worker*. Cambridge, Mass.: Harvard University Press.

Rosenberg, Morris: 1965 *Society and the Adolescent Self-Image*. Princeton, N.J.: Princeton University Press.
1968 *The Logic of Survey Analysis*. New York: Basic Books.

Rothman, Ellen K.: 1981 "The Written Record," *Journal of Family History* (Spring): 47–56.

Sacks, Jeffrey J.; Krushat, W. Mark; and Newman, Jeffrey: 1980 "Reliability of the Health Hazard Appraisal," *American Journal of Public Health* (July):730–32.

Sorokin, Pitirim A.: 1937–1940 *Social and Cultural Dynamics*, 4 vols. Englewood Cliffs, N.J.: Bedminster Press.

Srole, Leo: 1956 "Social Integration and Certain Corollaries: An Exploratory Study," *American Sociological Review*, Vol. 21: 709–16.

Stouffer, Samuel: [1937] 1962 "Effects of the Depression on the Family," reprinted in Samuel A. Stouffer, *Social Research to Test Ideas*. New York: Free Press.

Stouffer, Samuel, et al.: 1949, 1950 *The American Soldier*, 3 vols. Princeton, N.J.: Princeton University Press.

Takeuchi, David: 1974 "Grass in Hawaii: A Structural Constraints Approach," M.A. thesis, University of Hawaii.

Tan, Alexis S.: 1980 "Mass Media Use, Issue Knowledge and Political Involvement," *Public Opinion Quarterly* 44: 241–48.

Tandon, Rajesh and Brown, L. Dave: 1981 "Organization-Building for Rural Development: An Experiment in India," *The Journal of Applied Behavioral Science* (April-June): 172–89.

Thomas, W. I. and Znaniecki, Florian: 1918 *The Polish Peasant in Europe and America*. Chicago: University of Chicago Press.

Turk, Theresa Guminski: 1980 "Hospital Support: Urban Correlates of Allocation Based on Organizational Prestige," *Pacific Sociological Review* (July): 315–32.

Turner, Jonathan: 1974 *The Structure of Sociological Theory*. Homewood, Ill.: Dorsey.

U.S. Bureau of the Census: 1979 *Statistical Abstract of the United States*. Washington, D.C.: U.S. Government Printing Office.

U.S. Department of Labor (Bureau of Labor Statistics): 1978 "The Consumer Price Index: Concepts and Content Over the Years," Report 517.

Uslaner, E. M.: 1976 "Editor's Introduction," in Gudmund R. Iverson and Helmut Norpoth, *Analysis of Variance*. Beverly Hills, Calif.: Sage, pp. 5–6.

Votaw, Carmen Delgado: 1979 "Women's Rights in the United States," United States Commission of Civil Rights, Inter-American Commission on Women. Washington, D.C.: Clearinghouse Publications, p. 57.

Wallace, Walter: 1971 *The Logic of Science in Sociology*. Chicago: Aldine.

Walster, Elaine; Piliavian, Jane Allyn; and Walster, G. William: 1973 "The Hard-to-Get Woman," *Psychology Today* (September): 80–83.

Webb, Eugene, et al.: 1966 *Unobtrusive Measures: Nonreactive Research in the Social Sciences*. Chicago: Rand McNally.

Weber, Max: [1905] 1958 *The Protestant Ethic and the Spirit of Capitalism*, Talcott Parsons (trans.). New York: Scribners.

[1925] 1946 *From Max Weber: Essays in Sociology*, Hans Gerth and C. Wright Mills (trans., eds.). New York: Oxford University Press.

[1934] 1951 *The Religion of China*, Hans H. Gerth (trans.). New York: Free Press.

[1934] 1952 *Ancient Judaism*, Hans H. Gerth and Don Martindale (trans.). New York: Free Press.

[1934] 1958 *The Religion of India*, Hans H. Gerth and Don Martindale (trans.). New York: Free Press.

Weiss, Carol H.: 1972 *Evaluation Research*. Englewood Cliffs, N.J.: Prentice-Hall.

Wells, Richard H. and Picou, J. Steven.: 1981 *American Sociology: Theoretical and Methodological Structures*. Washington, D.C.: University Press of America.

White, Ralph: 1951 *Value-Analysis: The Nature and Use of the Method*. New York: Society for the Psychological Study of Social Issues.

Yankelovich, Daniel: 1981 "Stepchildren of the Moral Majority," *Psychology Today* (November): 5–10.

Yerg, Beverly J.: 1981 "Reflections on the Use of the RTE Model in Physical Education," *Research Quarterly for Exercise and Sport* (March): 38–47.

Yinger, J. Milton, et al.: 1977 *Middle Start: An Experiment in the Educational Enrichment of Young Adolescents*. London: Cambridge University Press.

York, James and Persigehl, Elmer: 1981 "Productivity Trends in the Ball and Roller Bearing Industry," *Monthly Labor Review* (January): 40–43.

Index

Note: Words in all caps represent computer printout.